Hemispheric Alliances

Hemispheric Alliances

Liberal Democrats and Cold War Latin America

ANDREW J. KIRKENDALL

The University of North Carolina Press
Chapel Hill

Set in Minion Pro by Westchester Publishing Services
Manufactured in the United States of America

The University of North Carolina Press has been a member of the
Green Press Initiative since 2003.

Library of Congress Cataloging-in-Publication Data
Names: Kirkendall, Andrew J., author.
Title: Hemispheric alliances : liberal Democrats and Cold War
    Latin America / Andrew J. Kirkendall.
Description: Chapel Hill : University of North Carolina Press, 2022. |
    Includes bibliographical references and index.
Identifiers: LCCN 2021046321 | ISBN 9781469668000 (cloth ; alk. paper) |
    ISBN 9781469668017 (paperback ; alk. paper) | ISBN 9781469668024 (ebook)
Subjects: LCSH: Democratic Party (U.S.)—History—20th century. | Cold War. |
    Liberalism—United States. | United States—Relations—Latin America—
    History—20th century. | Latin America—Relations—United States—History—
    20th century. | United States—Politics and government—20th century.
Classification: LCC F1418 .K53 2022 | DDC 973.922—dc23/eng/20211007
LC record available at https://lccn.loc.gov/2021046321

Cover illustrations: *Left to right*, Robert Kennedy, Edward "Ted" Kennedy, and
John F. Kennedy, August 28, 1963 (National Archives, Cecil Stoughton White House
Photographs, compiled 1/29/1961–12/31/1963, NAID 194238); *background*, American
continent blank map vector (Danzky/Shutterstock.com).

To Richard S. Kirkendall, one of the first liberal Democrats I ever met.

To Meg Reynard, my dear heart.

To Panalin, Book, and Eli: may they yet discover that
"another world is possible."

To Terry Anderson, Al Broussard, and Chester Dunning:
I have not forgotten.

Contents

Acknowledgments

When I was researching a book on Paulo Freire back in 2004, I had my first experience at the John F. Kennedy Presidential Library. I soon realized how rich it was in material on Latin America. That became clearer over the years as the consistent annual support of the Texas A&M University History Department for my research on this book enabled me to work my way through the presidential library system from Franklin Roosevelt to Ronald Reagan. Although people lambaste presidential libraries periodically, I rarely find historians among the naysayers. I am grateful that the system exists. Two of them, the Dwight David Eisenhower library and the Kennedy library, provided me with small research grants. In the case of the Kennedy library, I received a grant named after one of the main "characters" in this book, Arthur M. Schlesinger Jr. (That paid for my second trip to Boston.) My last and longest trip to the JFK library was paid for by A&M's much-lamented Program to Enhance Scholarly and Creative Activities. A Fasken grant helped me to do research in the Wayne Morse and Frank Church papers at the University of Oregon and Boise State University at a critical turning point in the project. The Princeton University library also supported my research in the Adlai Stevenson and George McGovern papers.

I have been presenting on this project at the Society for Historians of American Foreign Relations (SHAFR) since 2005. My debts to many foreign relations scholars are largely impersonal. I have read their books and articles with profit, and my notes reflect that. But there are a few people to whom my debt is rather more direct, particularly Tom Zeiler, B. J. C. McKercher, Mitch Lerner, Andy Johns, Matthew Masur, Dustin Walcher, Tom Maddux, and the incomparable Diane Labrosse. From the beginning, SHAFR's reputation for being among the friendliest academic organizations has been confirmed. Thanks as well to *Diplomacy and Statecraft* (published by Taylor and Francis), which gave permission for me to include material that originally appeared there as a 2007 article that developed out of that first paper I presented at SHAFR seventeen years ago.

There are far too many archivists and librarians whose names I cannot locate for me to feel comfortable citing only those whose names I can. I will bend this rule slightly to thank two people at the Sterling C. Evans Library in College Station, Joel Kitchens and Laura Sare. They were particularly helpful during the COVID-19 pandemic as I was finishing the book. I am also grateful to Congressman Donald Fraser for giving permission to do research in his papers at the Minnesota Historical Society.

I cannot pass up the opportunity to thank several friends. My favorite "reviews" of my books over the years have been those supplied by Manuel Serpa. He and his wonderful wife, Angela Colognesi, have long been dear friends. Manuel worked for many years as an engineer for a state-owned company in Brazil. In the evenings, he never talked about his work and spent much of his time reading novels in numerous languages. I always appreciated his thoughtful engagement with my books. I was thrilled one evening in Aracaju when he told his sons and some of their friends that they should read my first book if they wanted to understand Brazil. Harlan Gradin has been a constant friend since the 1980s. I much admire his work of many years at the North Carolina Humanities Council. In this age of social media, he remains the only nonfamily member with whom I speak regularly on the phone. My work at the Minnesota Historical Society made it possible for me to visit with my mom's best friend, Joan Watson. It is a testimony to my deep affection for this woman of tremendous warmth and endless curiosity that I can be grateful for experiencing kidney stones on the first trip, so that I had to return to finish my research a year later.

My colleagues in the Texas A&M University History Department have helped in various ways. Roger Reese inspires by his work ethic, and I am grateful that I have had an office right next door to him to share the daily professional grind, even during the pandemic. Brian Rouleau is a dear friend, whom I saw rarely during the pandemic, but who kept my spirits up even via e-mail. Toward the end, he read the whole manuscript, and had some valuable suggestions regarding final revisions. Dan Schwartz, a digital humanist, gave me more help with the computer than the people who are actually paid to do that sort of thing. Jason Parker and I always enjoyed long debriefing sessions following SHAFR meetings. Walter Kamphoefner has been supportive since the beginning. David Hudson has always been generous with his time. I miss model citizens Jim Bradford and John Lenihan. As my dedication shows, I have not forgotten how much I owe to Terry Anderson, Al Broussard, and Chester Dunning. Many thanks also to the front-office folks who kept things going over the years: Mary Johnson, Barbara Dawson, Rita Walker, Kelly Cook, Mary Speelman, and Erika Hernández, as well as department advisers Robyn Konrad and Phil Smith.

Richard S. Kirkendall will be happier than anyone to see this book in print. Although for many years I tried to avoid going into the "family business," I eventually succumbed and found that it was where I belonged all along. Dad was not surprised. He himself had an extraordinarily satisfying career in history in the Golden Age of academia. As I have said elsewhere, he showed me how to find my way around a library at an extremely young age. I believe we were looking up books about pirates! He was also a liberal Democrat committed to progress in civil rights. He served on a navy destroyer during the Korean War, and although he supported the Vietnam War initially, he came to see it as a misguided application of the containment policy following the congressional testimony of George Kennan in 1966. Dad served as cochair of the Robert Kennedy presidential campaign in Boone County, Missouri, alongside Betty Anne Ward McKaskill, mother of future Senator Claire McKaskill. Dad has often mentioned to me in recent years that if he had not left the University of Missouri in 1973 to head up the Organization of American Historians in Bloomington, Indiana, he might have run for Congress. I do not recall Dad ever talking about Latin America at any point growing up, which probably helped me as I "found myself" as a Brazilianist in the 1990s, getting my PhD at thirty-eight. I had already started publishing when I started presenting at SHAFR, and I remember a hilarious encounter with a fellow SHAFR-ite who kept insisting that he knew my work, and I kept responding, "No, my dad wrote that . . . no, my dad wrote that . . . no, my dad wrote that too." Fortunately, by this time, I was okay with the fact that I was always going to be "little Kirkendall" to many in the profession. Dad and his wife Kay enjoyed living in a retirement community in Seattle for many years; he gave roughly forty-six lectures to his friends there on Harry Truman. My dad has had some tough times since he turned ninety, not least of all the loss of his wife. I am grateful that he is still "around," if, sadly, not close. (I wish that my brothers were closer too.) Many thanks to Sherry Thompson and, especially, Merry Dale, Kay's daughters, for all that they have done for Dad over the years. (Above and beyond, Merry, always, above and beyond.)

My wife during these years suffered more personal losses, including the death of her only sibling, brother "Buv." During these years in which she was finally and completely "orphaned," she found tremendous personal satisfaction as an English as a second language teacher, which also employed her community development skills. She has loved meeting many students from foreign countries, from working-class people to professors. She continued the political work she had begun a decade earlier, and she and I attended a number of state Democratic conventions. She was a delegate many times. I often noted during those years that it said something about the state of the Texas Democratic Party that even I could be a delegate once. The party has been doing better of late, although certainly not as well as some pundits predicted.

I grew up heavily influenced by the New Left critique of liberalism, and then later was touched as well by both the libertarian critique thereof (think

Inquiry, not *Reason*) and the anti-interventionism of the 1980s ("No draft, no war, U.S. out of El Salvador"). As a historian of Latin America initially trained by Gil Joseph, and as a person who lived in Brazil for the first time during the last year of military rule, I identify strongly with Latin America and its democratizing currents.

I created the first history class on "Inter-American Relations" at Texas A&M, and for a long time, it was primarily a teaching field. A historically minded political scientist (and warm, generous, and gentle man), Lars Schoultz, to whom I owe much, told me during my Chapel Hill days that this was the most important subject I could teach my mostly U.S. citizen–students. I am grateful for so many undergraduates who have embraced the challenge of learning about topics they have often found emotionally fraught. Let me mention two former students who have kept in touch. A supporter of Ralph Nader when he took my class in 2000, Stephen Wright started dropping by for lunch on his way through town in the years following graduation. This has made me very happy. I have enjoyed his life's journey between teaching and union organizing and back again. I have enjoyed watching his delightful children grow up as well. I am very proud of a former undergraduate student who is now a Cuban historian. Kelly Urban has a tenure-track position at the University of South Alabama following her completion of a doctorate at the University of Pittsburgh. Two of my graduate students, David Tomlin and Sebastian Arandia, worked on topics that I discuss in this book, although I did not know at the time that I was going to write a book like this when they finished their master's degrees. Micah Wright was my first doctoral student, and I am grateful to have worked with him on his lovely dissertation on Puerto Rican military service in the age of intervention. I am looking forward to Laurence Nelson finishing his work on the U.S. Marine Corps and Augusto César Sandino. Jonathan Carroll and Ian Seavey, two graduate students who do not work with me, nevertheless were willing to try to help me with the mechanics of teaching a nightmarish "hybrid" course during the pandemic; I am pathetically grateful, even though, in the end, it didn't work.

Toward the end of my work on Paulo Freire, and for much of the next decade or so, I returned to an old love, community radio, which I had begun working in at fourteen, and continued once again from twenty-six to twenty-nine. Hosting *Listen Globally*, a "Brazilian and world music" show, for eleven and a half years kept me connected to Brazil. Community radio as I came to know it many years ago was in many ways a product of the counterculture, and I remain in my heart a community radio activist, inspired by the writings of Lorenzo Milam and the man who introduced me to them, Jeff Mintz. Over the years, I have been grateful for my radio ties to David Owens ("the anarchist at the wedding"), Susan Newstead, Butch Burrell, Paul and Win,

Bill Wax, Jay Brakefield, Stevo Schlemmer, Lance Paar, Donna Hanna-Calvert, and the wonderful Brazilian family choro band, Choro das 3, whom I got to know because of our dear friend Renata Myers, and who memorably not only appeared on my program many times but also played in our living room on Meg's fifty-eighth birthday in 2016.

It is a pleasure once again to be working with the University of North Carolina Press. I cannot begin to say how pleased I was when I ran into David Perry, who was by then already retired, at a jazz club on Frenchmen Street in New Orleans during an American Historical Association meeting; he mentioned how much it had meant to him that the press had published my book on Freire. Perry made the press a home for Latin American history; Elaine Maisner, with whom I worked last time, has continued to do so. Since this book is primarily, of course, about U.S. foreign relations, it was first "acquired" by Chuck Grench and was one of the last he worked on before his retirement. Chuck then passed the baton to Debbie Gershenowitz. Thanks to both of them, both consummate professionals with careers worth emulating, as well as Dylan White and Andrew Winters, who are following in their footsteps. Thanks also to the anonymous reviewers who helped make the book stronger. Any remaining errors are, of course, my own responsibility. What happens to a manuscript after one finishes writing is a bit of a mystery to many authors, and I am sure that I do not know how much I owe to many people in the production, design, and marketing end of the business. I know enough to thank Michelle Witkowski, Cate Hodorowicz, Wendy Muto, Iris Levesque, and Valerie Burton. May the rest of those who worked on the final product not think me ungrateful, just ignorant.

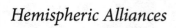

Hemispheric Alliances

Introduction

Liberal Democrats and U.S. Hemispheric and Global Leadership

In announcing his candidacy for the 1968 Democratic presidential nomination, New York Senator Robert Kennedy made it clear that the stakes were high. In his travels abroad in recent years in South America, Africa, and Europe, he had seen U.S. influence on the decline because of the war in Vietnam. "At stake is not simply the leadership of our party and even our country. It is our right to moral leadership of this planet."[1]

The New York senator struck a dramatically different tone than brother John in his inaugural address more than seven years earlier. President Kennedy had expressed a forceful confidence in U.S. global leadership. Fidel Castro's Cuba was challenging the legitimacy of that leadership, even on the regional level, but the young president from Massachusetts had affirmed a determination, in the now long-familiar words, "to pay any price, bear any burden, meet any hardship, support any friend, oppose any foe to assure the survival and the success of liberty." These words had a special meaning for Latin America.[2]

At key moments in the history of the global Cold War, liberal Democrats in opposition to existing Republican administration policies sought to create new models for U.S.-Latin American relations that went beyond containing communism. These policies were intended, as Samuel Moyn has written recently in another context, to embody "the notion that American power could be indistinguishable from the exercise of American virtue."[3] U.S. influence around the world was growing in the late 1950s, though it was increasingly contested by the Soviet Union under an adventurous leader, Nikita Khrushchev. During the Eisenhower administration, the United States began to take Great Britain's place as the foremost Western power in the Middle East. The dramatic acceleration of the process of decolonization also created new opportunities for the United States at the expense of its own allies.[4] Latin America, which had long been a region where the United States exercised power, needed to be a place in which the United States demonstrated its right to moral leadership in the world. In the age of decolonization and in response to the ideological challenge of the Cuban Revolution, the John Kennedy administration introduced the Alliance for Progress, which promised large-scale socioeconomic reform and democracy promotion in Latin America.[5] (The Peace Corps was a program for the Third World in general, which also was intended to demonstrate U.S. idealism.[6]) The Alliance for Progress offered more than containment, but it certainly assumed that the Alliance would aid containment. Immediate threats would be met, short-term opportunities with allies would be pursued, and ambitious long-term goals would be attempted. Over time, and particularly during the presidency of Lyndon Johnson, Alliance aid would be applied most where political need was greatest. As the United States faltered during the Vietnam War in the late 1960s and early 1970s, liberal Democrats, in particular, embraced human rights, which was presented as universal, but which would be applied particularly to Latin America. Human rights proponents did not abjure containment exactly; containment was, to some extent, assumed even in the age of détente. There was less of a threat to U.S. interests in the region generally. But the human costs of containment themselves had to be contained, and U.S. credibility in the world had to be restored, at home and abroad. Both the Alliance for Progress and human rights assumed a special U.S. responsibility for Latin America. Both the Alliance for Progress and human rights significantly complicated foreign policy making. Human rights, in particular, created problems for those who still prioritized containment within the Democratic Party. Human rights was an important factor in the breakdown of the Cold War consensus, and led to the departure of many from the party itself. But for those who made it a priority, it had the potential to reassert that moral leadership that many thought had been lost, as it promised to change the behavior of recalcitrant allies.[7]

This book pays particular attention to liberal Democratic Latin Americanists, those who thought Latin America was of particular or even primary importance, or who came to believe that this was so because of circumstances or experience. Within Latin America, some countries also mattered more than others, where threats seemed greater or when allies were available. Throughout the book I emphasize countries where liberal Democratic Latin Americanists were most engaged. Whether they chose wisely is up to the reader to decide. During both the Kennedy and Carter presidencies, the presidents were particularly attentive to Latin America, in the former case in large part but not only because the threats seemed so acute.

Fifty years before Robert Kennedy's announcement of his candidacy, Woodrow Wilson, father of liberal nationalism, was making his bid for world leadership. Although generations of U.S. leaders had believed that the world would eventually follow the U.S. example, the United States had not been ready to lead.[8] The United States had seen its power and influence expand in the Western Hemisphere, and the United States was a Pacific power to some degree as well. Wilson had benefited from a split in the Republican Party between incumbent William Howard Taft and his predecessor, Theodore Roosevelt, to become the first Democratic president since the 1890s. When the Great War broke out in 1914, Wilson had hoped that evenhanded neutrality would lead the Great Powers to look to the United States to mediate an end to the war. When the United States entered the war in 1917, the U.S. president announced a broad, sweeping justification for U.S. involvement in European affairs, which had been rejected in President James Monroe's message almost 100 years before.

Wilson supported open markets, multilateralism, U.S. leadership, and, in theory at least, democracy. But it was his call for "self-determination" that resonated particularly strongly in a world divided, to a great extent, into colonies controlled by a small number of European countries and Japan. From the fall of 1918 to the spring of 1919, during what historian Erez Manela has called "the Wilsonian Moment," many anti-colonial nationalists embraced U.S. leadership and looked to President Wilson for support at the peace table for their hopes for independence.[9]

This exaggerated faith in Wilson's intentions and the potential for U.S. world leadership might have been tempered if these nationalist leaders had known more about Wilson's leadership in Latin America. Despite a stirring rhetoric that has led generations of historians astray, U.S. policy in Central America and the Caribbean during Wilson's presidency was much as it had been since Theodore Roosevelt reinterpreted the Monroe Doctrine and turned the United States into a "policeman" for the Western Hemisphere. (Despite his broader claims, TR's policing was limited to the Caribbean Basin.) The occupation of Nicaragua continued, and Cuba and Panama remained U.S. protectorates. Under Wilson, U.S. troops invaded both Cuba and Panama. Wilson took advantage of heightened wartime perception of extra-hemispheric threats to send U.S. troops unilaterally into Haiti and the Dominican Republic to promote his vision of economic and political stabilization. The United States sent troops into Mexico twice during the Mexican Revolution. Even other members of his administration sought to temper Wilson's claims regarding U.S. commitment to small nations' autonomy. And democracy was not a primary goal in any of these countries. Regional leadership had made the United States a Great Power, but much of Latin America was still not part of the U.S. sphere of influence.[10]

A Republican Senate defeated Wilson's hopes for inclusion in a world body in which the United States could exercise world leadership and promote world peace. Republicans continued to support what they called a "protective tariff."

They promised not to "enter into political commitments which would involve the U.S. in the conflict of European politics." Republican leaders maintained U.S. leadership in Central America, the Caribbean, and the Philippines.[11]

Throughout the 1920s, Democrats praised Wilson, who, during the war, had "exhibited the very broadest conception of liberal Americanism." In the months and years following his death in 1924, the party would invoke his memory and his hope for cooperation between sovereign nations to prevent war and promote law and order. In the concluding paragraph of its 1924 platform, the party committed itself to "friendship" with Latin America: "God has made us neighbors—justice shall keep us friends." Democrats in opposition criticized U.S. interference in elections abroad, most notably in Nicaragua. They claimed that the Republicans had no foreign policy, and affirmed, "This great nation cannot afford to play a minor role in world politics."[12]

Public enthusiasm for U.S. occupations of Central American and Caribbean countries waned during the 1920s. Congressional criticism was strong at times, but only in the Dominican Republic were troops removed permanently. Herbert Hoover, perhaps the most influential U.S. secretary of commerce ever, thought that the presence of U.S. soldiers was hurting U.S. trade and investment opportunities. As president-elect, Hoover toured the region for seven weeks. As president, he affirmed that "In the large sense we do not wish to be represented abroad" by U.S. troops. Historians have a case for granting the Republican president paternity status for the Good Neighbor Policy, as he began a long-term process of removing U.S. troops. This was certainly a movement in a good neighborly direction. It is a stretch to call it a policy, however. While some Latin Americans may have been hopeful initially, relatively few seemed to have been aware of a dramatic change under President Hoover.[13]

Franklin Delano Roosevelt had been Wilson's assistant secretary of the navy. In that capacity, he had taken credit for Haiti's new constitution and had seen the occupation as uplifting "savage" people. As president, Roosevelt hoped that the United States would be a "good neighbor—the neighbor who resolutely respects himself and because he does so, respects the rights of others—the neighbor who respects his obligations and respects the sanctity of his agreements in and with a world of neighbors." FDR's hopes for a world leadership role were not accomplished as easily or as quickly as his vision of hemispheric leadership through the Good Neighbor Policy. In his first term in office, he began to make a dramatic change in U.S. policy, to abandon, as Sumner Welles put it, "the erroneous interpretations given to the Monroe Doctrine over many decades." He had many foreign policy aides with experience in Latin America; it had been easy to acquire that experience in recent decades. Some of them even spoke Spanish. More importantly, Roosevelt was responding to the hopes of generations of Latin Americans who had called for an end to foreign intervention. "Nonintervention" would remain an elusive concept; in Roosevelt's case, the emphasis was on removing the remaining U.S. troops (except those in the Panama Canal Zone and in Guantánamo) and renouncing any more invasions and occupations. But there was also a rejection of interference in internal affairs (more on this below). By 1936, the United States had abrogated the Platt Amendment, which had allowed the United States special rights to unilaterally intervene in Cuban affairs, and negotiated a new treaty with Panama that forsook such rights in Panama as well. For many in the United States, the most shocking application of the nonintervention pledge was President Roosevelt's steadfast refusal to send in troops following Mexico's nationalization of foreign oil companies. This would not be the only time the Roosevelt administration responded with a degree of sympathy to economic nationalism, which had begun to temper the long-standing Latin American embrace of free markets and foreign investment. In 1932, the Democratic platform blamed the Republicans for ruining foreign trade. Secretary of State Cordell Hull blamed Republican tariffs for "economic distress" in Latin America. (As historian Thomas Zeiler has argued, Roosevelt himself preferred "freer trade" to free trade.) Throughout the 1930s, Hull promoted free trade in the hemisphere, and following the passage of the Reciprocal Trade Agreements Act of 1934, the United States negotiated reductions in tariffs with Latin American countries one at a time. By 1938, the United States was the number one trading partner of every Latin American country except Argentina.[14]

Latin Americans responded positively to the new direction in U.S. policy. Roosevelt himself became personally popular and was greeted warmly during his travels in the region. Europe was rejecting Roosevelt's efforts at mediation in the 1930s, but U.S. leadership was expanding into much of South America, where U.S. influence previously had been limited. Democrats sought to employ the "good neighbor" analogy in reference to relations with other parts of the world, but it did not take.[15]

But nonintervention had its consequences, particularly in countries that had experienced long-term occupations in recent decades. The U.S. armed forces had trained constabularies to maintain order after U.S. troops eventually departed; they were ostensibly nonpartisan and apolitical. Rafael Trujillo, a former security guard who studied at the Haina Military Academy with U.S. forces during the occupation of the Dominican Republic, rose to power as the Hoover administration rejected pleas from the U.S. ambassador to send gunships to prevent him from doing so. Trujillo, one of the most notorious dictators in Latin American history, remained in power until 1961. In Nicaragua, control over the U.S.-trained National Guard enabled Anastasio Somoza

García to seize power in 1936; the Roosevelt administration refused to save the Nicaraguan political system that had evolved under his predecessor; Somoza and his sons ruled until 1979. In Cuba, U.S. officials also refused to send in troops during a period of unrest, but they cultivated a sergeant named Fulgencio Batista and used the power of nonrecognition to bring down a nationalist government. The Good Neighbor Policy did not promote democracy, and a pledge not to send in troops to occupy countries was adhered to more definitively than one not to interfere in internal affairs. These new allies would create as many problems during the Cold War as they solved.[16]

Nevertheless, the Roosevelt administration was successful in improving relations with its hemispheric neighbors. Progress was made toward mutual defense agreements. Republicans and Democrats in 1940 promised that the United States would avoid getting involved in foreign wars, but both parties promised to defend the Monroe Doctrine. When the Japanese attacked Pearl Harbor, Central American and Caribbean countries declared war. Other Latin American countries broke off diplomatic relations but did not declare war immediately. By the end of 1942, however, the hemisphere was, to a large degree, unified.[17]

An important figure in the Roosevelt administration during the 1940s was Nelson Rockefeller, heir to the family fortune and a man whose name came to define liberal internationalism in the Republican Party. Drawn to Latin American art and to the Latin American people ("They made him feel human"), Rockefeller had tried to promote what he considered a socially responsible capitalism based on his family's interests in Venezuela. As World War II began in Europe in 1939, Rockefeller sought to build on the Roosevelt administration's strengths in Latin America. In 1940, he became the coordinator of inter-American affairs, a position whose authority often overlapped with that of the more traditional State Department. He promoted efforts in public diplomacy to combat the influence of fascism in Latin America. He sponsored tours of Latin America by Hollywood stars and funded movies about the region by people like Walt Disney and others. He also initiated a wide variety of development projects that later were emulated by the Alliance for Progress.[18]

As most of the world divided between Allied and Axis sides, the advantage that the United States had in its geographical isolation would have meant little without the near hemispheric unity the United States achieved thanks to the Good Neighbor Policy. U.S. trade with Latin America continued to expand. Most Latin American countries allowed the United States to build or use air or naval bases in their territory, and the United States established military missions and achieved an unprecedented degree of cooperation between the United States and Latin American armed forces. The most important air base in South America was a relatively short plane ride away from Africa, in Natal on the northeast coast of Brazil, which provided what was called a "trampoline to victory." Although its government since 1937 had been borderline fascist, Brazil became the most important ally the United States had in Latin America following the $20 million U.S. loan to build a state-owned steel mill. Relations between the U.S. military and the Brazilian military grew strong, as a small Brazilian Expeditionary Force served alongside U.S. forces, primarily in the Italian campaign. Mexico also sent forces to fight in the Pacific war. While other countries did not participate so directly, the use of Latin American bases and the military missions expanded ties between U.S. and Latin American military men dramatically.[19]

The United States did not choose its allies based on their ideological orientation but on whether they cooperated with the war effort. Democracy in Latin America had always developed in response to internal dynamics, and tended to be stronger where U.S. influence was limited. Nevertheless, in many countries, the sense of a common struggle against fascism, encouraged by U.S. and Allied propaganda, enabled proponents of democracy in many Latin American countries to succeed, particularly as the war turned in the Allies' favor by 1944. This created opportunities for labor movements in many countries as well. Democratic governments were established unexpectedly in countries like Guatemala and Venezuela. This was more an inadvertent result of U.S. efforts to promote a clear ideological orientation for its own struggle rather than to promote democracy per se. Within the State Department, however, a vigorous debate developed over whether the United States actually should promote democracy in the region. This discussion was prompted by Spruille Braden, U.S. ambassador to Cuba, where communists were allied with Batista. In a new role as assistant secretary of state for inter-American affairs, Rockefeller supported Trujillo, who had benefited greatly from U.S. aid during the war. Other Foreign Service officers were sympathetic to Dominican prodemocracy exiles. U.S. Ambassador to the Dominican Republic Ellis Briggs argued that "Trujillo is primarily a Dominican problem, for solution by the Dominican people," but he presciently suggested that "Sooner or later American public opinion will interest itself in the kinds of governments existing in the other republics." Briggs also said that even while continuing to follow a nonintervention policy, the United States might have to take more "positive action" in cases like Trujillo's. Moreover, U.S. actions in "small Caribbean nations" were being "carefully examined by other—and more important nations with which we are dealing." Batista, at least, left power after completing a term as an elected leader in 1944. U.S. pressures played a small role in the ouster of valuable U.S. ally Getúlio Vargas in Brazil, but at a time when he was trying to remake himself as a prolabor leader. Bradenism,

such as it was, came to be discredited as Braden, who had succeeded Rockefeller as assistant secretary of state, became overly involved in trying to seek
to stop the election of Argentina's Juan Perón, a truly popular leader with an
authoritarian bent. His election in 1946 certainly was not hurt by U.S. opposition. This would not be the last time that elections in Latin America would
produce the wrong result as far as the United States was concerned.[20]

By the end of the war, U.S. influence in Latin America had never been
greater or more widespread. But the United States was not merely a hemispheric and a Pacific power anymore; it was a global power, and Latin America's relative importance had declined long before the war had ended. When
Rockefeller resigned as assistant secretary of state in 1945, U.S. Ambassador
to Brazil Adolf Berle Jr. noted in his diary that "men [in the administration]
who know the hemisphere and love it are few, and those who are known by
the hemisphere and loved by it are fewer still."[21]

The world was being divided up again. Enemies were becoming friends,
and allies enemies. Relations between the Soviet Union and the United States
broke down soon after the war. But even though the Soviet Union had experienced massive destruction during the war, its prestige was never greater.
Communist parties grew in many parts of Latin America, and they played a
part in political openings in some countries.[22] The Truman administration
saw the primary threats to U.S. global interests in Europe and, increasingly,
in Asia. In 1946, President Truman affirmed his commitment to a Western
Hemisphere free of "interference from outside" forces. There must continue
to be joint efforts to "work together as good neighbors in the solution of . . .
common problems." The United States consolidated its power in the hemisphere through a "reciprocal treaty of military assistance, the first in American history," signed in Rio de Janeiro in 1947, and through guarantees that
the United Nations' writ did not run there. The Organization of American
States, formed in 1948, would have primacy. But U.S. commitment to containing communism was global, particularly following the March 1947 announcement of the Truman Doctrine, with President Truman's assertion that
"it must be the policy of the United States to support free peoples who are
resisting attempted subjugation by armed minorities or by outside pressures."
The importance of Latin America was, inevitably, reduced. U.S. influence was
simply assumed in the hemisphere. Threats to U.S. influence—real, imaginary,
or exaggerated—would cause great concern in Washington periodically
throughout the Cold War.[23] Truman's rhetoric about the Free World was stirring, and suggested a global ideological struggle. But it was problematic. If
Latin American and other nations remained part of this world, even when
military dictatorships came to power, what was the ideological justification
for the Cold War struggle?[24]

The United States had high hopes for world trade after the war's end. Many U.S. politicians and officials feared that a return to the economic nationalism of the 1930s would curb economic recovery. Truman's rhetoric about free trade, though, obscured his willingness to support U.S. producers. He too preferred freer to free trade, as Roosevelt had done. But the United States strongly criticized the partial turn toward economic nationalism in Latin America, preferring Latin America to continue to stick to the support for free trade and foreign investment that had been axiomatic prior to the onset of the Great Depression.[25]

As the Cold War developed and the Truman administration made clear that it was going to maintain a global leadership role addressing threats in Europe and Asia, some (like a former U.S. ambassador to Great Britain named Joseph Kennedy) continued to argue for the primacy of the Western Hemisphere.[26] But in the short term, at least, the administration was able to enjoy a bipartisan consensus on the evolving containment policy and on foreign policy in general. This was good for Truman, since the 1946 elections had seen Republicans gain control of Congress for the first time since 1930.

In 1948, Truman was, unsurprisingly, his party's nominee, but his own party split. The States' Rights Party, or Dixiecrats, was focused on domestic issues and was trying to push back against movement on civil rights. Combative Minneapolis Mayor Hubert Humphrey had forced the party to take a stand on the issue at the party's convention. For the United States to play its role as a leader in the "Free World," Humphrey said, "we must be in a morally sound position." The Progressive Party, led by former Vice President and Secretary of Commerce Henry Wallace, hoped to reverse the Cold War direction of U.S. policy and rejected, among other things, the Marshall Plan. Wallace's party platform called for "a return to, and the strengthening of Franklin Roosevelt's good-neighbor policy," rejected the "inter-American military program," and called for "economic assistance without political conditions to further the independent economic development of the Latin American and Caribbean countries." The Republicans, for their part, sounded more like Truman than either the Dixiecrats or the Progressives and pledged support for "reciprocal trade," the "new spirit of cooperation" in the Americas, and a more truly bipartisan foreign policy than they believed Truman had allowed.[27]

Truman ran on a platform promising world leadership "toward a realization of the Four Freedoms," of speech and worship and from want and fear. The platform invoked FDR's military leadership and praised the creation of the United Nations. The Democrats backed "vital aid" for China, Greece, and Turkey. They promised the continuation of the Good Neighbor Policy and both economic and military cooperation. The United States would be the "principal protector of the free world."[28]

But what did that mean in the Latin American context? By 1948, a number of democracies established toward the end of the war had fallen. Historians have disagreed on whether the Truman administration could have done more to save the reformist Democratic Action government in Venezuela in 1948, for example. The professed commitment to nonintervention (increasingly used in a more general sense to include noninterference as well) let the United States off the hook when more creative thinking might have helped enable democracy to survive. Historians have also debated the degree to which U.S. influence led to the decline of pluralistic political systems in countries like Chile and Brazil, where Communist parties were outlawed and elected communists were removed from Congress. Labor movements, even those in which communists did not provide the primary energy, in general declined. This remained a problem for liberal anti-communists throughout the Cold War era who could not address how easily anti-communism was employed to weaken labor, which was assumed to be a natural and important political ally for liberals at home and abroad.[29]

Contending forces in the Western Hemisphere sought U.S. support. Costa Rica, which had democratized gradually over a long period of time, had suddenly fallen victim to a bloody but brief civil war in 1948. The leader of the victorious faction, José Figueres, defeated a party allied with the Communist Party and supported, ironically, by Nicaragua's Somoza. Over the next few years, Costa Rica would shelter exiles from nearby dictatorships and support efforts to bring down the dictators. Some Latin Americans hoped that the United States would support these efforts by what became known as the Caribbean Legion to promote democracy. Trujillo and Somoza, for their part, created an alliance to try and stop the spread of democracy. U.S. policy continued to favor stability and found both pro- and antidemocratic forces of this type to be disruptive.[30]

Historian Arthur M. Schlesinger Jr., who would later advise President John F. Kennedy on Latin American matters, wrote a polemical book-length essay in 1949, which offered a defense of "beleaguered liberal democracy." He saw Franklin Roosevelt as having rejected "plutocracy" (the domination of government by business and wealth) and affirmed the need for both capitalism and a "strong government." He supported the struggle against "totalitarian imperialism" abroad and communists at home, while affirming the need to support free speech, essential for the claim to "moral leadership." U.S. foreign policy should support the center and the anti-communist left (including, as we shall see, social democrats like Figueres) abroad. The United States was "in the great world to stay." The United States should avoid expressing "moral indignation," but focus on producing "real change in the real world." Despite the need to focus on Europe, Schlesinger argued for rather vaguely defined "special considerations and special solutions" to respond to the "social revolution" taking place in the former colonial world, as well as in Latin America.[31]

Following the 1948 election, President Truman announced an international technical assistance program known as Point Four. In the short term, its promised reach was to be as global as the Truman Doctrine. The Cold War meant not only "control," as Odd Arne Westad argues, but also "improvement." Not surprisingly, Nelson Rockefeller got involved. The president tried to reassure him he was "just as enthusiastic about Latin America as you, if not more so!" Unsurprisingly, perhaps, given global Cold War dynamics, Latin America was not really a focus. Rockefeller himself was more vocal in his support for the program than most Democrats. Foreign aid was not popular in Congress or with the U.S. public. Point Four did not proceed very far. The onset of the Korean War soon thereafter aided a shift toward a concentration on military aid in Latin America and elsewhere. But as President Truman noted in January 1952, "The areas most vulnerable to aggression are not in the Western Hemisphere." Latin Americans remained frustrated in their desire for development aid and, with the exception of Colombia, avoided participating in the Asian "police action," in part because they believed that they had not received what they deserved for aiding in World War II.[32]

Throughout the 1950s, there were a few liberal Democrats who sought to get the leaders of the party to focus more on the region. Frances Grant was among the most important, and her voice will be heard repeatedly in the course of this book. Like many people, Grant's interest in Latin America stemmed initially from a passion for the region's culture. That interest expanded through travel in the region and became increasingly more political as she became involved in the Pan-American Association of Women and then the International League for Human Rights. Grant had personal responsibility in the latter organization for Latin America. Despite the positive developments of previous years, by 1950 democracy in the region was, in her words, "being gradually devoured." She hoped to create a network of prodemocracy political leaders and activists that could influence the political development of the Western Hemisphere, including Rómulo Betancourt of Venezuela, Eduardo Frei and Salvador Allende of Chile, the aforementioned José Figueres of Costa Rica, and Juan Bosch of the Dominican Republic. All of them would be significant political figures over the next few decades. Figueres delivered a forceful critique of democratic nations that tolerated dictatorship and failed to promote democracy. Other "sponsors" of the 1950 meeting included leaders of the trade union movement in the United States. Hubert Humphrey, by now a senator from Minnesota, sent a statement expressing how "heartened" "American liberals" were by the "counter-offensive against the totalitarian ideology penetrating Latin America." The association's "many voices," Grant promised, would "be heard often when freedom is threatened and human rights violated in this hemisphere." The organization would "press against recognition of de facto governments" and support the "withholding of economic and technical aid" from what she called "totalitarian regimes." The Havana meeting laid the groundwork for the Inter-American Association for Democracy and Freedom, which Grant ran on a shoestring budget for the next three decades.[33]

Truman's last secretary of state, Dean Acheson, was no admirer of FDR, not least because he saw him as having been "interested only in Latin America." As biographer Robert Beisner has written, Acheson saw "no paramount national security issues there." He was a Europeanist and a free trader, who found his greatest challenges in Asia. But Acheson played a valuable role in Latin America nevertheless, blocking efforts to aid Somoza in removing Guatemala's elected leftist President Jacobo Árbenz. It was one of Roosevelt's most trusted Latin Americanists, Adolf Berle, who would later advise John Kennedy, who argued that nonintervention did not apply to those countries like Guatemala that were allegedly tied to extra-hemispheric powers. Historian Nick Cullather has argued that Acheson, for his part, "feared a blown operation would destroy the remnants of the Good Neighbor Policy carefully constructed by" Roosevelt.[34]

Frances Grant's conference in 1950 had been held in Havana. Cuba's democratic period was chaotic and brief. Batista had stepped down in 1944. But the elected governments of Ramón Grau San Martín and Carlos Prío Socarrás were marked by corruption. The former strongman hoped to be reelected in 1952, but Batista saw that the electoral route was blocked. He staged a coup and returned to power. The elections were canceled (blocking the congressional ambitions of a young lawyer named Fidel Castro). As historian Louis Pérez Jr. has written, "The apparent indifference with which the U.S. government reacted to the abrogation of civil liberties in Cuba shocked and appalled many on the island."[35]

In 1952, the Democratic Party had a new candidate, Illinois Governor Adlai Stevenson. The platform that year was filled with self-congratulations for the party's having put an end to "a tragic era of isolation," though it claimed it had done so in 1933. The Democrats promised "national security based on collective pacts," including the Rio pact. It promised "to continue the policy of the good neighbor," to "strengthen the bonds of friendship and cooperation with our Latin American allies," and to expand trade "among free nations," invoking Roosevelt's Secretary of State Cordell Hull.[36]

Truman's surprise victory in 1948, the communist victory in China in 1949, and the onset of the Korean War in 1950 all led to a decline in bipartisanship in foreign policy.[37] By 1952, the Republicans contended that the "good in our foreign policies" had been "accomplished with Republican cooperation." The Republicans had abandoned protectionism and supported "the expansion of mutually-advantageous world trade." But the Republicans charged that the Democrats had "shielded traitors to the nation in high place" and embraced the "negative, futile, and immoral policy of 'containment.'" The Republicans found it easy to blame the Truman administration for the "neglect" of Latin America, which was making people there "resentful."[38]

The Cold War consensus was forged around the perception of threats in Europe and Asia, and yet was applied globally. U.S. assumptions of dominance in Latin America were of even longer standing than actual U.S. interests in the region had been. If U.S. officials and politicians often seemed largely unaware during the Cold War years that U.S. influence had not been equally strong everywhere in the hemisphere (and was even fairly recent in some cases), they generally recognized that it was now stronger in more places in Latin America than it had ever been. The consensus regarding Latin America favored maintaining this influence. The most successful liberal Democratic Latin America policy was generally considered to have been Franklin Roosevelt's Good Neighbor Policy. It was never formally disavowed. Liberal Democrats in the 1950s and early 1960s frequently invoked both Roosevelt and his policy, particularly the nearly complete hemispheric solidarity on security issues forged in 1941 and 1942.[39]

Democrats promised to continue the Good Neighbor Policy in 1952 and to restore it in 1956, while Republicans claimed it as their own.[40] But in an age of covert action by the Central Intelligence Agency, it was not clear what a policy of nonintervention and noninterference really meant, and few Latin Americans still believed that the policy was in force.[41] Despite what was beginning to be recognized by some as a problematic "Free World" discourse, Cold War fears, even if they had been largely if intermittently exaggerated before the rise of Fidel Castro, had revived an emphasis on stability. The United States had been able to remain complacent about the region, confident that communism was being contained. But times were changing, and new policies were necessary.

In the opening chapter, we will see how in the late 1950s, not least because of the Cuban Revolution, the Cold War had really arrived in Latin America. Eisenhower, the first Republican president since Hoover, was an internationalist who promised to go beyond containment; promises of "rollback," however, proved largely hollow, with the exception, as he saw it, of Guatemala. In Latin America, the former general became associated with military leaders. But toward the middle point of his second term, a new "liberal hour" began when, as historian Robert David Johnson argues, congressional Democrats began to dominate the discussion of foreign policy. The "fears and opportunities" that defined the Cold War had not really been felt in the Western Hemisphere heretofore to a significant degree.[42] But now liberal Democrats in opposition to Eisenhower policies began to develop a new consensus regarding what they expected would be productive policies toward Latin America. Although they did not renounce the Good Neighbor Policy, they believed they had to embrace a new framework for relations with Latin America. Moreover, they wanted to move beyond mere containment. They supported aid for development rather than just free trade and foreign investment (which had been the policies of Harry Truman as well as Dwight Eisenhower).[43] And they wanted to promote democracy. Liberal Democrats like Wayne Morse and Frank Church thought that Eisenhower's policies were already inadequate even before Fidel Castro came to power. Liberal Democrats knowledgeable about Latin America were suspicious of military aid. John Kennedy would be more confident that he could increase military aid without encouraging military rule.

John Kennedy's commitment to liberalism was rather recent in the late 1950s, and even his aide Schlesinger argued that his definition of liberalism was quite vague. Whether Kennedy would revert to a default position of mere containment at times and not follow the new liberal Democratic commitment to democracy and development was a defining tension during his presidency. Frances Grant, founder of the Inter-American Association for Democracy and Freedom, as a non-state actor, and Wayne Morse from his position in the Senate, tried to push the Kennedy administration to be more consistent in its support for democracy and its degree of commitment to the region. (Within the administration, Schlesinger in particular did the same.) At the same time, the Latin Americanists within and outside of the administration had a narrow range of friends in Latin America whose prospects and policies they tried to promote, some of whom had felt "kicked . . . around" by the Eisenhower administration when they lived in exile.[44] More than many of the others, Grant's deep personal connection to the region also led her to often adopt attitudes of particular Latin American leaders, as can be seen later in her response to the military coup in Chile in 1973. She saw the coup through the perspective of Eduardo Frei, a strong opponent of Salvador Allende, rather than that of many of her presumed allies in the United States who were now embracing human rights.

Chapter 2 addresses the larger Kennedy vision, which was embodied in the Alliance for Progress. The United States was now committed to larger socioeconomic transformation to address long-standing issues. At the same time, it was forced to address pressing issues from the left, in Cuba, and from the right, in the Dominican Republic. The administration rejected Eisenhower administration critics' hopes of reducing military aid, but believed that it could control the impact of even dramatically enhanced military aid by attempting to discourage military coups and requiring timetables for the return to constitutional government. At the same time, the continuing reliance upon covert action by many of these leaders made a mockery of public promises of noninterference. The Kennedy administration hoped to make the Dominican Republic a showcase for democracy. There would always remain a tension between the larger long-term goals of the program and the more immediate needs of national security. Kennedy aides Schlesinger, Richard Goodwin, and Ralph Dungan fought repeatedly during the Kennedy years to keep the administration focused on these larger goals. John and Robert Kennedy too often focused on Cuba itself at the expense of the Alliance.

In chapter 3, I show how these goals began to come into conflict with the way threats were perceived in particular countries. Many countries did not have to address insurgencies inspired by or trained by the Cubans, for example. Nor were the stakes the same in every country. Therefore, U.S. policies in practice from one country to another necessarily would have to be different. Kennedy considered himself more of a pragmatist than many of his liberal advisers, and the way liberal "Latin Americanists" got sidelined (during the Cuban Missile Crisis, for example) is an important part of my analysis. Many in the Kennedy administration also began to suspect that Latin American and U.S. ideas about reform were not always compatible.

Finding allies the Kennedy administration could live with was a challenge, and the Kennedy administration was frequently impatient with even those they saw as allies. The administration wanted to keep its distance from military governments even as they expanded military aid and counterinsurgency training. The policy of encouraging military governments to establish a timetable for a return to constitutional government following a coup worked in Peru. But Kennedy's policy toward Brazil suggests an inconsistency. Kennedy did not trust Brazilian President João Goulart, and kept expecting that he would seize dictatorial powers and rule as a leftist. Kennedy worried that his policies toward Peru's recently established military government would work against him in Brazil. But while Kennedy was alive, a vigorous debate continued within the administration over what to do about Goulart, based largely on conflicts over the implementation of the Alliance for Progress. As it turned out, every coup that actually occurred while Kennedy was president happened without U.S. planning or permission. The administration was frustrated that military coups happened even when the United States did not want them to. The administration was not in control as much as it thought it was. When Kennedy was assassinated in November 1963, the president had made no final decisions to change Latin America policy. It is important to recognize that he did not know that he was going to die, and that he always wanted to believe that he had options.

Once Lyndon Johnson was president, as I demonstrate in chapters 5 and 6, many Kennedy liberals thought that they were, to a certain degree, in opposition again. They sought to be more consistent in their attitudes during the Lyndon Johnson years, and soon were claiming that LBJ had abandoned the Alliance for Progress. The period between 1963 and 1965, discussed in chapter 5, was a period in which developments that began during the Kennedy years led to full-blown crises, as in Brazil and the Dominican Republic.

Nevertheless, and particularly following the military coup in Brazil from 1964 on, liberal Democrats failed to live up to their democratic ideals in Latin America during the Johnson years. Johnson himself was somewhat ambivalent about military governments, but he had no doubts about the primacy of containment, and tended to favor free trade and foreign investment. In many ways, his policies were more in keeping with the early Cold War consensus. But his thinking about the coup in Brazil was not all that different from that of many other liberals, who by 1964 were ready to see Goulart go. The abandonment of their ideals in Brazil compromised their legacy for years to come. (As we shall see, only Senator Morse recognized the danger early on.) Johnson abandoned the early Kennedy-era goal of making the Dominican Republic a showcase for democracy, and was relieved when foreign aid helped stabilize the political situation under an old crony of Rafael Trujillo. But Johnson was still backing reform in Chile. Although the Democrats undermined democracy by covertly supporting one side in an election, that side in power was one of the most committed to reform in the Western Hemisphere in the 1960s. (This suggests that the Democrats might have had to be even more interventionist than they were if they were really going to promote reform in Latin America in the 1960s.)

As I examine in chapter 6, Schlesinger and Robert Kennedy, in particular, were trying to create a Kennedy legacy, I argue, that was far more idealistic than administration policy had been in practice. They were fairly successful with this, and the idealized Kennedy Alliance remained a potent political weapon to use to criticize U.S. policy in Latin America from that time forward. Meanwhile, the cost of containment generally was becoming evident in Southeast Asia. But Latin America was once again no longer a main focus of U.S. foreign policy, as fears about Castro's influence ebbed.

A full-throated discussion of the costs of containment erupted once the Democrats lost control of the White House. As I demonstrate in chapter 7, Richard Nixon was far more comfortable with military men as allies, and he was an easy target for those who wanted just to revive an idealized version of the Kennedy Alliance for Progress. But even his opponent in 1972, George

McGovern, found it difficult to focus on Latin America and to integrate it into a larger global strategy. Détente, the relaxation of tensions with the Soviet Union, and the onset of a new relationship with China, opened up the debate over U.S. foreign policy. Many liberals themselves were by now no longer convinced of the efficacy of foreign aid as a means of socioeconomic transformation, in part because of a growing distrust of the efficacy of government action of all sorts. Cold War institutions like the Central Intelligence Agency were increasingly distrusted. For many liberals, the costs of containment were most evident in the Western Hemisphere where military governments dominated and few allies were in power that the liberals wanted the United States to be associated with. Given a greater perception of the limitations of U.S. power, human rights became a minimalist way to influence the behavior of allies while seeking to regain moral leadership in the world. The salience of the human rights issue did not suggest the accuracy of the charge of a revival of isolationism. But what was seen as a lessening of the commitment to containment and a betrayal of traditional allies was one of the factors leading many "neoconservatives" to leave the Democratic Party.[45]

In chapters 8 and 9 we will see the challenges Democrats faced once they regained control of the White House. Latin America itself was no longer seen as one thing, and human rights were prioritized more in South America than in Central America and the Caribbean. What it meant to prioritize human rights and how it would be possible to change countries' behavior was not at all clear. In Central America and the Caribbean, for the most part, other issues would at times have to take precedence. Could the logic of an increasingly contested détente be applied to Cuba, as McGovern and others suggested? Could the Dominican Republic become a showcase for democracy in the Caribbean once again? Following an approach initiated by Secretary of State Henry Kissinger under President Gerald Ford, moreover, Carter was willing to embrace the logic of solving a problem that predated the Cold War by signing a treaty that would ultimately turn the canal over to Panama. This had political costs that he did not recognize, which were borne as much by his liberal Democratic allies in the Senate as by him personally. But President Carter took the political risk that his predecessor had not taken. And yet competing ideals of Good Neighbor noninterventionism and human rights within the Carter administration would complicate significantly the situation in Nicaragua. A victory for a left-wing insurgency there led to a small-scale Alliance for Progress in El Salvador.

The Reagan administration sought to return to Nixon's policies of unabashedly embracing military dictatorships in Latin America. Human rights had complicated containment, but even many Republicans were not willing to abandon such a popular policy. Rhetoric aside, Reagan had to demonstrate that there was more continuity between his policy and Carter's. This is certainly evident in El Salvador, where it took some time for the United States to find an ally it could live with. José Napoleón Duarte's memoir shows that the Salvadoran leader felt that the Reagan administration distrusted him in the beginning. The Reagan administration moved toward the liberal Democrats here, which worked dramatically to help them gain congressional support for their policies. (The Reagan administration moved toward the liberals on Augusto Pinochet's Chile in the second term as well.) But Reagan also sought to claim the Kennedy legacy, which he saw as misunderstood or misrepresented. Reagan faced a massive insurgency in El Salvador, larger than any Kennedy had experienced, in part because Reagan policies helped radicalize the situation still further. When the Cold War ended, it did so largely because of extra-hemispheric developments, of course, though Cuba never got the memo or earned a "peace dividend." By the end of the Cold War, a bipartisan consensus had been achieved around free trade even as democracy had arrived in much of Latin America, largely because of widespread economic crisis and not U.S. democracy promotion efforts. The Kennedy legacy was no longer relevant, but human rights continued to be for some time to come.

But in the 1950s, the Kennedy legacy was just in its embryonic stages, and that is where we must begin.

Chapter 1

Liberal Democrats and Latin America

Toward Engagement

In 1955, Adlai Stevenson "seemed surprised" when his sometime speechwriter, historian Arthur M. Schlesinger Jr., told him that, in planning for a Latin America trip, he should "by all means stay away from Venezuela," where "a rather squalid dictator" (Marcos Pérez Jiménez) was in power. Schlesinger, who had taken a strong interest in political trends in Latin America, particularly since he attended the 1950 meeting of the Inter-American Conference for Democracy and Freedom in Havana, had become friends with a number of liberal and social democratic leaders in the region. He was appalled when the Eisenhower administration expressed its admiration for the Venezuelan dictator, and he hoped that liberal Democrats, if elected, would promote democracy, unionism, and social reform in the Western Hemisphere. He was certainly more than disappointed that he had to explain to Stevenson, whom he greatly admired, why a trip to Venezuela was ill advised. "I do not see how the Governor could visit Venezuela without having some contact with the regime; and a picture of Stevenson shaking hands with Pérez Jiménez would profoundly disappoint and disillusion the people in the hemisphere who most admire Stevenson and are most like him, from [Puerto Rico Governor Luis] Muñoz Marín down. Pérez stands for exactly the kind of thing we have to get away from in this hemisphere."[1] But Latin America was no higher on Stevenson's list of priorities than it had been on those of so many U.S. leaders, Democrat or Republican, since the end of World War II.

The Eisenhower years seem more tumultuous in retrospect than they appeared to many at the time. The onset of the civil rights movement at home and the dramatic acceleration of the process of decolonization abroad certainly represented major changes. Eisenhower had criticized the Truman administration for a decline in U.S.-Latin American relations by 1952, but would do little to address many of the hemisphere's concerns. Good relations with the hemisphere were, to a large extent, assumed. By the end of the Eisenhower presidency, however, Latin America had become central to the Cold War in a way that it never had been before.[2] In opposition, Democrats did not take the lead on U.S. foreign policy in Eisenhower's first term, although, administration rhetoric notwithstanding, it continued largely to be defined by containment. But the 1950s saw some influential liberal Democrats, ultimately even Stevenson himself, searching for a new framework for U.S.-Latin American relations. The Good Neighbor Policy continued to have emotional appeal, and people continued to invoke it; it remained an important part of how many in the United States wanted to see the U.S. role in the Western Hemisphere. Its relevance to Cold War conditions was not altogether clear. Containment was considered essential. It was also insufficient, and many did not find it inspiring. In opposition, intellectuals, scholars, former government officials, and congressmen moved, haltingly, toward a new Latin America policy.

Arthur Schlesinger's interest in the region would be strong and long-lasting, and, like many of his colleagues, he would be focused on particular individuals he admired. He encouraged ties between Stevenson and Costa Rica's José Figueres, who, unlike Stevenson, became the president of his country in 1953. Throughout the 1950s, Figueres's government became a model for what many liberal Democrats thought could and should be achieved in the region. In 1954, Schlesinger visited Figueres at his coffee plantation home and shared Stevenson's "Call to Greatness," a collection of his Godkin Lectures at Harvard University.[3]

Stevenson had been involved in the early organizational phase of the United Nations and was governor of Illinois when he first ran as the Democratic presidential candidate in 1952. He was known for his eloquence and was seen as an intellectual. A critic of Joseph McCarthy, he was committed to a liberal Democratic struggle against global communism. He was no provincial. Following his defeat in 1952, he had embarked on a "world" tour, which did not include Latin America, but rather those areas of the world that concerned U.S. foreign policy makers most: Asia, the Middle East, and Europe. He developed a critical distance from European colonialism, which he recognized as being on the way out. Over the course of the 1950s, he and other liberal Democrats began to focus on issues of global socioeconomic development. As a lawyer, he visited African countries on behalf of clients interested in pursuing economic opportunity on the continent. Despite frequent plans to visit unfamiliar parts of the Western Hemisphere, however, he found various reasons to postpone a trip for many years. Over the years he expressed an occasional interest in the democratic forces in Latin America. But there was little public interest in Latin American democracy in the mid-1950s. Following a speech in which, following Schlesinger's advice, he praised Figueres, one newspaperman scoffed, "Well, what does the Governor think about the plight of the whooping crane!" For Stevenson, this reinforced his wariness about investing too much in the region.[4]

As the 1956 elections approached, people with an interest in Latin America sought to encourage the presumptive candidate to pay more attention. In early 1955, Rutgers University economist and rising Latin Americanist Robert Alexander encouraged him to visit the region and begin to speak out.

"Latin American democratic exiles" from Venezuela, Argentina, and the Dominican Republic who lived in the New York area had asked Alexander to arrange a meeting with Stevenson, and Alexander offered to introduce Stevenson to them. Nothing came of this, but the young professor was persistent. Following Stevenson's announcement at the end of the year that he would be running again, Alexander asked him to "devote at least one formal and fairly lengthy speech to the problems of hemispheric relations." Recent U.S. policies had let those who were friends of the United States become "sorely disillusioned." Their impression was, according to Alexander, that only economic interests in Latin America mattered as far as the United States was concerned. A speech on Latin America by Stevenson would make Latin Americans believe that a Democratic victory in the presidential election would result in "a more comprehending and helpful attitude." Alexander noted that the 1952 presidential candidate was widely admired "south of the border." While expressing some sympathy for Alexander's point, Stevenson noted his own lack of knowledge about Latin America and expressed "misgivings" regarding how interested people were. He still saw no "political value" in addressing such issues. Alexander wrote him again in late December, recognizing the public's lack of interest but focusing on the Latin American interest in Stevenson and the need for him to say something "concrete about their problems." The recipient of a Ford Foundation grant to study labor relations in South America, Alexander promised to send him reports on his findings. As the election year progressed, Stevenson expressed gratitude for receiving Alexander's "first-hand information," but he primarily mentioned Latin America when he was campaigning in the state of Florida. While he credited the Rutgers professor for influencing what he had to say there, he seems to have primarily relied upon former Franklin Roosevelt administration official and New York Liberal Party Chairman Adolf Berle for what were, in any case, largely generic remarks regarding hemispheric unity and a brief critique of "sterile military expenditures."[5]

Latin American leaders themselves, for their part, sought to engage Stevenson. Figueres wrote Schlesinger admiring letters regarding Stevenson, knowing that the historian would share them with the presidential candidate. Figueres lamented that the U.S. public was not "sufficiently aware of the role of the United States as a world leader." Stevenson would have to be "simultaneously the President of a contented country that wants little change, and the leader of a destitute world that badly needs a great deal of change." Those suffering from colonialism or dictatorship would put their hope in him. Figueres criticized what he called the neglect of the Cold War "philosophical front." Stevenson could be the philosopher-president offering an "international New Deal."[6]

In the late 1950s, there were indications that the United States was not going to be able to continue to pay little attention to Latin America. The Eisenhower administration, for its part, seemed to be unaware how it was viewed there. U.S. officials and the U.S. population at large were shocked at the displays of "anti-Americanism" during Vice President Richard Nixon's trip to South America in May 1958, when he was spat upon and attacked. Ironically, the Eisenhower administration's intent in sending Nixon had been "to help destroy the myth" that the United States supported dictatorships. (Rioters in Caracas had been angered that the United States had granted asylum to the recently deposed Pérez Jiménez.) Nixon and Secretary of State John Foster Dulles blamed international communism, but Central Intelligence Agency Director Allen Dulles assured his brother that there would be unrest in Latin America even "if there were no communists." Expressing regret for Nixon's treatment, Brazilian President Juscelino Kubitschek, committed to "fifty years' development in five" years in his own country, made a dramatic proposal called Operation Pan-America. The United States should commit itself to large-scale economic aid for countries in the Western Hemisphere in order "to fight the causes of unrest and discontent." The administration's response initially was rather tepid.[7]

But as his second term neared its end, President Eisenhower spent ten days in four Latin American countries, a trip that was vastly more successful than his vice president's almost two years before. (As president, he had only visited Mexico and Panama before.[8]) Although he was a lame duck president, as historian Stephen Rabe has suggested, U.S.-Latin America policy was undergoing another of its periodic shifts. Nixon's trip, combined with the rise to power of Fidel Castro and the beginnings of a radical transformation of Cuban society, led U.S. officials to pay attention to Latin America as they had not since the early stages of World War II. The faith in "trade, not aid" that had been the consensus under both President Truman and President Eisenhower, moreover, was diminishing. An Inter-American Development Bank was founded.[9] Eisenhower's seeming enthusiasm for military leaders was also now called into question. Even before Castro began to establish close relations with the Soviet Union and to inspire and train hemispheric insurgents, the United States had begun to recognize that its limited interest in Latin America had become problematic.

It is noteworthy that the countries Eisenhower visited in 1960 were all democracies, given the concern throughout the previous years that he and Secretary Dulles, by now deceased, had a predilection for military leaders. In Chile, President Jorge Alessandri was not only operating in a long-standing democratic political framework; he also shared Eisenhower's fondness for unalloyed free enterprise. Brazil, whose alliance with the United States during

World War II had been so critical, was now more democratic than it had ever been. Venezuela's democracy had only recently been established, following the overthrow of Dulles's favorite Latin American leader; its new leader, Rómulo Betancourt, had strong ties to Frances Grant, Adolf Berle, and other liberal Democrats. (Grant's "Second Inter-American Conference for Democracy and Freedom" was held in Venezuela in 1960.) Argentina was less democratic than it might have been since the former democratically elected leader Juan Perón himself was not allowed to be a candidate, and it was more than likely that he would have won a truly free and fair election. The countries were not directly defined as having been chosen because they were democracies. Indeed, President Eisenhower himself had to be convinced not to go to Paraguay because of its dictatorial regime. While recognizing that it might not be advisable, he privately commented that his recent Asian trip had left him with "the growing feeling that a benevolent form of dictatorship [was] not a bad form of government for newly-developing countries that were not prepared for full democracy." Nevertheless, in Latin America, "The present situation" warranted "a review of the policy and action of the U.S. government with respect to dictatorial governments," John C. Dreier, U.S. ambassador to the Organization of American States, wrote to Assistant Secretary of State for Inter-American Affairs Roy Rubottom.[10] As Castro turned left, some came to argue that it was U.S. support for Fulgencio Batista that had led to the radicalization of the Cuban political situation. Some longtime Latin Americanists in the State Department like John Moors Cabot suggested the need for a "positive constructive policy toward Latin America." Although Assistant Secretary of State Rubottom denied that one had been lacking, he did note that U.S. policies in the region were viewed as having been "the products of reaction more than of action." This was inevitable, he thought, inasmuch as they "related to and reflected the broader struggle in which we are engaged."[11]

Fear drove U.S. policy over the next few years, in ways that both spurred engagement and benefited the region, and distorted U.S. policy and hurt it. Fear and a sense of urgency were most pronounced among the Latin American reformers with the strongest ties to liberal Democrats and with those liberal Democrats who were already most engaged.

But the late 1950s was a time of hope and opportunity as well as fear. Oregon Senator Wayne Morse, chairman of the Subcommittee on Western Hemisphere Affairs, noted in late 1959 that few in the United States realized "the enormity of the social revolution through which Latin America is passing." Morse, a former law school dean who served on the National War Labor Board under Roosevelt and who was a proponent of what he called "constitutional liberalism," had left the Republican Party because of the unwillingness of its leaders, including President Eisenhower, to criticize Joseph McCarthy in the early 1950s. He had briefly been an independent before joining the Democratic Party in 1955. He was always a liberal who often was not convinced that anyone else besides himself deserved the label; he supported labor unions and civil liberties and opposed military aid. His new party affiliation made it possible for him to get a position on the Senate Foreign Relations Committee, which he had long coveted. Morse believed that "out of this turmoil" in Latin America, one could see "encouraging signs of progress, not only in economic development but in the growth of free and responsible political institutions." He stressed the notion that Latin America was living through what journalist Tad Szulc called the "twilight of the tyrants." The United States needed to offer "sympathetic help" to those seeking to change their countries, and it should return to what he saw as the tradition of supporting "the underdog." A failure to be ourselves by sacrificing "longer term principle for short-term expediency" had made the United States "bad actors in a role" that did not "come naturally."[12]

Morse blamed liberals themselves in part for "rigid and sterile" thinking about Latin America. They had "clung to policies of five or ten years ago simply because they were formulated by a liberal administration." "But a policy that was sound and wise five or ten years ago is not necessarily sound or wise today." "What American security objective," he had wondered, "is served by arming Batista?" U.S. interests, he insisted, could only be defended by U.S. arms or by NATO. He defended military aid for countries that had "the institutional and economic base to make it successful." What the rest of the world needed was economic, not military aid. (Even this, he contended, could be distributed by the United Nations in order to remove it from the "East-West struggle.") Military aid in Latin America meant that the United States was intervening "on the side of the status quo" in countries "so obnoxious and so oppressive of freedom that we have suffered from being associated with it." This allowed the communists "to pose as representing the hope for the future." Strategic bases and materials were of less importance in the Cold War struggle than "the allegiance and loyalty" of people "to democracy." President Eisenhower, Morse maintained, "seems to have no concept of the moral, ethical, and human values at stake in the world today." The "Eisenhower doctrine of military expediency" ignored the "world's masses" and their dreams of "rising above the depths of poverty in which they have lived for generations." This was the way the United States could "display its leadership."[13]

Like Morse, Idaho Senator Frank Church, who would succeed Morse as chairman of the Subcommittee on Western Hemisphere Affairs years later, had been critical of U.S. military aid for Latin American countries. Growing up, he had been an admirer of Senator William Borah, and discovered his life's ambition at the age of fourteen to be the chair of the Senate Foreign Relations

Committee. Throughout his political career, his internationalism was at war with the kind of reflexive isolationism associated with Idaho Republican Borah. (Church did become chairman of the Senate Foreign Relations Committee, but his time in that position, as we shall see, would be brief.) His experience in wartime Asia had made him distrustful of Nationalist Chinese leader Chiang Kai-Shek and a critic of colonialism. He believed that military aid led to an arms race and encouraged Latin American nations to limit their own spending to "economic development, public health, education, and improved living standards." He argued, furthermore, that U.S. military aid helped communists to spread a "new, ugly image" of the United States. The United States had supplied Batista with weapons "which he turned upon his own people," leading to the "hostility" visible in Cuba in 1959.[14] But in Rafael Trujillo's Dominican Republic and elsewhere, liberal Democrats like Frank Church found themselves (and their country) in a quandary. In a letter to an anti-Trujillo activist, Church noted "the somewhat difficult position the United States must take in supporting the widely shared ideal of democracy and freedom and the equally widely shared principle of nonintervention."[15]

The interest in Latin American economic development was growing in U.S. business and academic circles. Since the Great Depression, the Latin American enthusiasm for free trade and foreign investment had been tempered, to say the least, but even economic nationalists like Brazil's Kubitschek did not advocate a move toward economic autarky. A Harvard Business School professor who in the Kennedy and Johnson years would play a major role as U.S. ambassador to Brazil had already begun devoting his energies to promoting U.S. investment in the region. Lincoln Gordon was an economist who in his years had moved back and forth between academic employment and government service. He had worked on the Marshall Plan. Beginning in 1957 he organized a series of conferences at the business school. The Eisenhower administration at this time was committed to free trade and foreign investment and saw no need for the creation of any additional institutions that Latin Americans were calling for. A sense of urgency did not yet exist, but an awareness of opportunity did. Like congressional liberals, Gordon sought to shift the priorities of U.S. foreign aid policies, noting in a 1958 talk that "five-sixths" of all foreign aid went to "direct or indirect military purposes or for political crisis situations which are also generally a direct reflection of the Cold War." The remaining sixth was "for long-run constructive purposes," Gordon lamented in his call for a more "long-range approach to foreign aid." "If we consider economic betterment, social justice, and political freedom to be good things," he remarked further, "we are going to have to work for them rather than assuming that they are somehow built into the nature of things as a kind of wave of the future." Professor Gordon found himself increasingly drawn to Brazil and undertook a series of research trips there, including one supported by the Ford Foundation, in the Kubitschek years. He and his colleagues established ties with Brazilian politicians like Carlos Lacerda and technocrats like Roberto Campos, who became problematic interpreters of Brazilian political realities for the future ambassador.[16]

The turning point in Latin America's Cold War was certainly the triumph of Fidel Castro. The initial response to Castro's triumph over Batista was not uniform. Frances Grant believed that it represented a victory for the anti-dictatorial forces the Inter-American Association for Democracy and Freedom had been championing and expected that elections would be held soon to choose the successor to the interim government of Manuel Urrutia. For his part, Senator Morse, long a critic of Batista, was soon critical of Castro, following the speedy trials and executions of dozens of military men and Batista officials. Many liberal Democrats who had criticized Batista still did not support intervention against the Castro government. In February 1959, Senator Church wrote a constituent that "Time and patience are required." A year later, he was still puzzling over the extent of communist influence in the government. But he also was certain that U.S. support for Batista had given "rise to the hostility toward the United States which the Cuban people evidently feel and which Castro expresses at every opportunity." As a member of the Senate Foreign Relations Committee, Church sought to avoid repeating U.S. errors in Cuba by reducing military aid for military dictators elsewhere. In a "period of turmoil and modernization which will surely produce greater social, economic and political changes" in Latin America, "millions of people . . . view our behavior toward Cuba as a test of the sincerity of our expressions of sympathy and encouragement for their struggle for a better life." U.S. military intervention would lead the United States to forfeit "virtually all of our popularity in Latin America, as well as endangering the existence of many of the moderate governments which rule throughout most of that area." The next U.S. leader, Church confidently predicted, would have the "firmness, imagination, and determination" to address the Cuban problem.[17]

The new attention being paid to Latin America prompted the Democratic Party's twice-defeated standard-bearer, Adlai Stevenson, to finally take the long-delayed trip to Latin America. Schlesinger encouraged him to seek advice from Adolf Berle and José Figueres regarding the trip. While Schlesinger thought it unwise to make it look like his trip was "sponsored" by Figueres, Betancourt, and Muñoz Marín, "these people are our best friends in Latin America; and men of their type represent the best hope for the future of Latin America." Stevenson should "take their counsel into serious account." In fact, Figueres sent a long memorandum to Stevenson, calling on him to develop "a new relationship between the United States and the Latin America people."

Stevenson, Figueres asserted, was the right man to provide a modern version of the Good Neighbor Policy, which would promote "a new democratic Inter-Americanism, which would exclude every form of imperialism." Such a policy would promote "economic justice" and trade in the hemisphere while opposing dictatorship, and thereby eliminate "violent anti-American feelings." A statement in favor of such a policy could be delivered at a special celebration in Peru of the reformist APRA party (Alianza Popular Revolucionario Americana, American Popular Revolutionary Alliance) and of Stevenson himself, which Figueres and reformist leaders from Venezuela also planned to attend. This would contrast with the poor reception Vice President Nixon had received two years before. Fortunately for Stevenson, he was not able to make it to Peru by the time the rally was held, but he also made clear that he would not have attended such a meeting while abroad in any case.[18]

Prior to his departure for Latin America, Stevenson did issue a statement that included an affirmation that "By history and deep commitment we Americans, North and South, are on the side of the democratic forces we all hold dear." He said that he hoped to "return" from his trip of almost two months "a much better citizen of the hemisphere." Former assistant secretary of state for public and cultural relations, Connecticut Senator, and *Encyclopaedia Britannica* publisher William Benton accompanied Stevenson and paid their expenses. Ironically, Stevenson was traveling during the months Massachusetts Senator Kennedy was beginning to make his case as the Democratic presidential nominee. Stevenson himself was now as reluctant a noncandidate as he had been a candidate in 1952 and 1956. Despite Benton's concerns prior to departure about possible "anti-American" actions during their trip, none occurred. Indeed, Stevenson's visit to twelve North, Central, and South American countries over almost two months was rich and rewarding, and the response to his presence gratifying. When Stevenson traveled to a now democratic Venezuela in 1960, he visited Caracas slums with Betancourt's daughter; all those he encountered seemed to be "passionate Democrats and Stevenson fans." Benton believed that Stevenson represented Latin American hopes for what the United States could be. Liberal Democratic economist Kenneth Galbraith had promised Stevenson that he would be "impressed . . . at the depth of liberal and democratic passion in South America." (Galbraith insisted that "the hostility to Nixon reflected the feeling that he was an unreliable friend of democratic process.") Stevenson particularly enjoyed the hours he spent with Figueres and Betancourt. At his mountain home, Figueres spoke of the brutalities of U.S.-backed dictators like the Dominican Republic's Rafael Trujillo and the Somozas in Nicaragua and warned of the spread of communism in the hemisphere. Stevenson was struck by the appeal of Castro among Latin American students, but was less concerned about the spread of communism than others. He was impressed as well by the consolidated democracy in Chile and the economic dynamism in the parts of Brazil he visited, including the newly built capital of Brasília. Stevenson often spoke in vague generalities about changes in U.S. Latin America policy that would accompany a victory by a Democratic presidential candidate in the fall. He stated in a press conference in Chile that he did not like aid to dictators, and he encouraged Latin Americans to seek the transformations that had accompanied the New Deal in the United States. When he argued that there was no "particular point of view" that distinguished the Democratic Party from Americans generally, Benton suggested that the Democrats had liked "Batista a little less." Brazilian presidential aide Augusto Schmidt emphasized the need for the United States to support economic development, arguing that the Operation Pan-America proposal, intended as "an act of friendship" following Nixon's disastrous visit and intended to address "the anti-American feeling," was also "designed not to let the democratic experience die in Latin America." Benton, for his part, by the end of his trip, was convinced of the need for significant aid to Latin America in economic planning, land reform, and tax reform, as well as stabilizing commodity prices. He supported programs that would have visible impact. The United States should cooperate with Latin America as it had done under Roosevelt and show in some kind of "dramatic" way that "we don't like dictators." The U.S. press should pay more attention to Latin America, and universities should engage in more exchange programs.[19]

Senator Morse, for his part, traveled to six Latin American nations on behalf of the Senate Foreign Relations Committee. He "came away with the feeling that the United States has perhaps the best chance it has ever had to help bring into being in Latin America the kind of liberal social order on which firm and enduring hemispheric unity can be built." He found governments he saw as "progressively inclined," interested in being "friendly to the United States," who were "courageously grappling, each in its own way, with the problems of an abrupt social transition from an 18th-century economic order to the 20th century." He saw evidence of "political power . . . increasingly being exercised by the people instead of the tight little oligarchies which have traditionally ruled most of Latin America." Democratic governments needed to "reduce and improve the economic lot of the mass of people. The fight against communism is just as simple and difficult as that." Venezuela provided an opportunity for the United States to demonstrate its support for a "liberal revolution which give a country real democracy and genuine reform." (He called Rómulo Betancourt "one of the great liberals of our time.") He noted the enthusiasm in the region's governments for the Operation Pan-America proposal. He noted approvingly the "true democracy in Chile."

Brazil was singled out for its "growth at breakneck, devil-may-care speed and hang the consequences." He was confirmed in his conviction that "a substantial reduction in military aid to Latin America would strengthen U.S. prestige throughout the area."[20] Morse and Senator Bourke Hickenlooper (R-Iowa), also a member of the committee, attended the Bogotá conference on hemispheric social and economic development in September 1960, which they described as "perhaps one of those rare events which can be legitimately be described as a turning point in history." The nations gathered for this event promised to commit to "vigorous efforts and far-reaching institutional changes on the part of the Latin American people themselves."[21]

Church, for his part, was concerned that Eisenhower's July 1960 request for $500 million in aid for Latin America was a "promissory note." Private investment was declining in the region generally because of concerns about Cuba. If the United States was going to create a program designed to "improve living standards in Latin America," it would not only have to "have the continuity of a Marshall Plan," it could only be successful it was accompanied by tax and land reforms. "Otherwise, we shall be pouring our money into the sands, making the rich richer, and the poor will only breed new revolution and feed into the hands of the communists."[22]

The shape of the 1960 presidential campaign in the United States was slow to reveal itself. A new liberal era began with the 1958 election. But who the standard-bearer for the Democratic Party would be was not at all clear at the time; nor was it clear that such a man would be a liberal. Massachusetts Senator John F. Kennedy had not been embraced by liberal Democrats, not least of all because of his earlier failure to criticize Senator Joseph McCarthy. But following the Democratic success in 1958, Kennedy began to define himself as more of a liberal. In part, this was because he associated liberalism with forward motion and energy, in contrast to the inertia he perceived in the Eisenhower administration, including Vice President Nixon.

Morse was reluctant to support Kennedy. He did not think that Kennedy's voting record in the Senate had indicated a commitment to liberal causes. Morse saw Kennedy as no friend to the working man. Morse criticized the money spent by the Kennedy family on the election. He preferred Stevenson as the Democratic candidate for a third consecutive time. He even briefly ran a poorly organized and ineffective campaign himself. Following the Democratic convention, which he did not attend, Morse pledged to support the Kennedy-Johnson ticket. He did give speeches on behalf of Kennedy as the election approached.[23] Senator Church, for his part, was the keynote speaker at the Democratic convention and came to define himself as a "Kennedy man."[24] Schlesinger had met Kennedy at some point in 1946. The historian told his parents that Kennedy "seemed very sincere and not unintelligent, but kind of on the conservative side."[25] But after two failed presidential bids by Stevenson, Schlesinger had decided to support Kennedy and hoped to reinforce the more liberal turn that Kennedy was taking in the late 1950s. Prior to the nomination, Schlesinger wrote Stevenson that it was "most important for the sake of the election and for the sake of a future Democratic administration that [Kennedy's] vital backing come from the liberal Democrats and that his vital sense of obligation be to them."[26] As Galbraith wrote to Stevenson in August 1960, if a president "wants to act, it can only be along the lines of the liberal position. Conservatism has become identical with inaction."[27] "I believe him to be a liberal," Schlesinger wrote about Kennedy in his journal at the end of the convention, "but committed by a sense of history rather than consecrated by inner conviction."[28]

Although Kennedy would be known as a "foreign policy president," he had not paid particular attention to Latin America as a senator. He had supported the Truman Doctrine when it was announced during his first term in the House of Representatives. His reputation for independence of thought on matters relating to international affairs was based largely on his support for Algerian independence from France in the late 1950s, as well as, to a lesser extent, his rather skeptical attitude toward French efforts in Vietnam in the early 1950s. His most recent biographer argues that his trips abroad in 1951 made him understand the need for an approach to fighting the Cold War that relied upon more than military means. He had an early interest in nationalism in what was to become known as the Third World. He understood the dangers of supporting "corrupt and reactionary groups whose policies breed the discontent on which Soviet Communism feeds and fosters."[29] Kennedy was running in 1960 both as a liberal ("someone who looks ahead and not behind, someone who welcomes new ideas without rigid reactions") and as tougher than Nixon, who the campaign portrayed as part of an administration that had "lost" Cuba and which was allowing the United States to slip behind the Soviet Union.[30]

His major statement on Latin America came in December 1958 when he spoke at a Democratic Party dinner in San Juan, Puerto Rico. As had become mainstream thinking at that time, Kennedy stated that the island and U.S commonwealth demonstrated "the future glory of Latin America." Kennedy emphasized economics, the dependence on one export product, the need for investment, greater stability for commodity prices, new thinking on tariffs and what to do with agricultural surpluses, a capital development bank and loans, and opportunities for students. He called for a change in U.S. attitudes toward Latin America, to stop referring to it as the United States' "backyard," and to abandon paternalism. The United States should not "persist in believing that all Latin American agitation is communist-inspired [or] that every anti-American voice is the voice of Moscow." The United States could not "force out any duly constituted government." The United States "should not attempt to influence voters in their choice of governments." The United States also should not, Kennedy pointedly remarked, "give a dictator praise, or medals, or military assistance which will only be used to tighten his hold." Inter-American affairs could not be treated as a "step-child in the Department of State, the responsibility of lesser officials and too often the haven for ambassadors of less than top-flight quality." He quoted Brazilian President Kubitschek, who argued that Latin America "must be freed from the featureless rear guard position which it has held heretofore in the international scene." The United States could not simply return to "the good neighbor policy of a generation ago." Latin America was "certainly as essential to our security as Southeast Asia." Latin America received 3 to 5 percent of foreign aid, "and far too much of that has been in military assistance." The emphasis on military aid was "undesirable when it tightens the grip of dictatorial governments, makes friends with those in power today at the expense of those who may be in power tomorrow." Aid should not be used to "purchase allies—but to consolidate a free and democratic Western Hemisphere, alleviating those conditions which might foster opportunities for Communist infiltration, and uniting our peoples on the basis of mutual confidence, stability and constantly increasing living standards." Puerto Rico would be a model for Latin America in terms of "rising wages [and] productivity, a responsible labor movement, land ownership, [and] stable political parties."[31]

By early 1960, presidential candidate Kennedy suggested that "no area deserves more attention today than the vital area known as Latin America." At Stanford University in February, he made an overall critique of Eisenhower foreign policy. He called Asia policy inadequate, Middle Eastern policy deteriorating, European policy uncertain, and Africa policy impotent. As for Latin America, "No other area better symbolizes the deterioration since the days of Franklin Roosevelt and Harry Truman." He continued by saying that "In no other area has the work of anti-American agitators been made more easy by inconsistent, inconsiderate and inadequate economic and diplomatic policies." Latin America had to be the "first order of business." The United States had to adopt a "new attitude," a "new emphasis," and a "new policy for Latin America." "We do not have much time." He embraced the liberal critique of too little foreign aid and too much military aid. He promised that a Kennedy administration would work closely on separate policies for individual nations.[32]

Kennedy turned to Adolf Berle for advice. Berle had been assistant secretary of state for inter-American affairs under Franklin D. Roosevelt (1938–44) and U.S. ambassador to Brazil in 1945 and 1946. He became the bridge from the Good Neighbor Policy to the Alliance for Progress. Berle had maintained his interest in Latin America over the following decade and developed personal ties to some of the prodemocratic political figures in the region. Although frequently critical of President Eisenhower's administration, he did help the administration in its efforts to gain Latin American support against the government of Guatemalan President Jacobo Árbenz. But Berle was frustrated by what he considered the administration's mistreatment (and misjudgment) of Venezuela's Rómulo Betancourt, who had had dinner at his house in August 1957. Following the fall of Pérez Jiménez in January 1958, Berle recalled that the Venezuelan had predicted it, almost to the day. Soon thereafter they dined alone together, although the two men were joined by telephone by other Venezuelans as well as by President Figueres. (In a letter to Schlesinger, Berle referred to Figueres as "our mutual friend.") Berle remained in close contact with Figueres in 1958. He paid close attention to the rebellion against Fulgencio Batista in Cuba and hoped that liberals in Latin America and the United States (including Puerto Rican Governor Muñoz Marín) could influence the direction of events. As early as April 1958, however, Berle noted that he had a "fear" which he had not communicated, "that Fidel Castro may be more interested in power than in freedom. We cannot afford any more Trujillos." On the home front, Figueres suggested a hope that the State Department might be "beginning to be a little less afraid of liberals and their ideas." Berle tried not to get too hopeful, however, indicating in a letter to the president of Honduras, Ramón Villeda Morales, that government policy changed "only slowly under Republican Administrations." "We cannot expect any big ideas until 1961—which is a long time away."[33]

Even before Castro's victory, the Eisenhower administration had "come to the conclusion that the best thing [that] could happen [in Venezuela] was [Betancourt's] victory." "This is quite a change," Berle noted "from the days when under [Henry] Holland as Assistant Secretary State kicked him around."[34] "Anyhow, between Colombia, Venezuela, Costa Rica and Honduras, with friends elsewhere, we have a fairly good example of governments composed of exiles who at one time had few friends except Beatrice and me," Berle noted with no small satisfaction in December 1958.[35]

Berle had called the Democratic Party at the end of 1958 "a party without a man." He was concerned by late 1959 that Stevenson might run again, but stressed the limitations of all the candidates, including Kennedy, who had "gone about as far as he can." Berle thought that the best man would have been Chester Bowles, but he doubted this was possible. In 1960 he expressed private concerns about how "stupid" intellectuals looked joining bandwagons. By late June, however, he was convinced that Kennedy would be the nominee, and he intended to support him.[36]

Berle never thought much of Cuba's new leader Castro. "Liberals in this case have to restrain their instinctive desire to support any opposition merely because it is opposition, and stick to making certain demands in terms of principle."[37] Berle was always more skeptical of Castro than some of his Latin American friends, as well. His anti-Castro attitudes hardened not only because of the executions of political enemies, but more particularly because of the unpleasant experience of Figueres in March 1959 in Cuba. "The extremists—Communists or otherwise—want to take charge of the liberal revolution in Latin America and want to make it into a bloody Mexican-style social revolution instead." He considered social revolutions "wasteful," "unpredictable," and "necessary only in the last resort," and that they were "generally betrayed in the end."[38]

Over the course of 1959, Berle became more concerned about the possibility of Castro's influence increasing in Central America. If in early 1959 he thought that some kind of unspecified preemptive action could prevent this in Nicaragua, he grew increasingly concerned as he met with conspirators. "If Nicaragua gets into pro-Communist hands or for that matter stays in the hands of a rotting Somoza dynasty, the end can be somewhat terrible." He despaired as well of the Eisenhower administration, with "the brains of a clam and the capacity of a snail in these matters," finding a way to help. By May he was lamenting that the United States was failing to "behave as though it really were a great power."[39]

On the 23rd of June 1960, Berle and Kennedy attended a lunch with members of the New York Liberal Party. The two men sat close together. Kennedy broached the possibility of Berle advising him on Latin American affairs if Kennedy became the Democratic presidential nominee. Berle assured him that he would. Berle relayed how worried he was about Latin America; "the Cold War would be loosed on this continent if somebody did not move fast." He further suggested to Kennedy that there was an ongoing "attempt to paralyze the democratic movement, leaving only pro-Communist and pro-dictator forces in the field." Moreover, he declared, the doctrine of nonintervention did not apply "when any defense of the hemisphere is involved."[40]

In July 1960 Harvard Law School Professor Archibald Cox, who was working with the Kennedy campaign, met with Berle to encourage him to take part in a series of seminars, as well as possibly write speeches for Kennedy on Latin America. "This had not been a region to which Kennedy had given much thought." Berle remained somewhat skeptical of Kennedy, but he said he "would be glad to do that." Berle noted in his diary that he thought that Soviet Premier Nikita Khrushchev was "going to carry the Cold War as close to America as he can." (He later noted that he thought that hard-core communists were manipulating Cuba "either from Moscow or Peiping," and that Castro, like Alexander Kerensky, would "be eliminated if he becomes inconvenient.") Although Berle considered Kennedy "an untried young man," he certainly preferred him to Nixon, "not much older but a representative of policies which have failed."[41] Berle was convinced that Latin Americans needed plans for reform of their social structures and sympathetic leadership in the United States. He did not believe that Eisenhower administration policies of encouraging private investment were sufficient.[42]

Over the next few months, Berle's influence on the Kennedy campaign seems to have been more perceived than real. He was convinced that the Russians had "decided to make the world revolution" in Latin America. He suggested that the Eisenhower administration might finally be thinking of "measures in Latin America. I wish to God I thought it was not too late." Despite Kennedy campaign requests for help, Berle was not sure "that the Kennedy group thinks it needs any."[43] In early October, Berle gave a speech in which he suggested that a President Nixon would not be able to speak "in terms the rest of the world understands." This was particularly true in Latin America, which had during the Eisenhower years "looked vainly to the United States to lead these countries through transition into the twentieth century life through technical human progress." Later in the same month, he spoke on behalf of the New York Liberal Party, saying that Kennedy deserved support "on Cuba alone." Kennedy's vocal support of the Cuban opposition (to which I will turn my attention), Berle maintained, was not in violation of the principle of nonintervention as Nixon wrongly supposed.[44]

Although Democrats like Berle, Morse, Church, and Schlesinger were beginning to engage creatively with Latin America in ways that would influence Kennedy administration policy, the party as a whole did not demonstrate much originality regarding or interest in Latin America. The party platform merely promised a restoration of the Good Neighbor Policy, "based on far closer economic cooperation and increased respect and understanding." The United States would promote "orderly economic growth" while making "more effective use of aid." (The Republicans, for their part, promised "security, freedom and solidarity of the Western Hemisphere," with no external "intervention in our hemisphere" and no "government dominated by the foreign rule of communism.")[45]

No Democratic presidential candidate during the Cold War years, however, emphasized Latin America more than Senator Kennedy did in 1960. He accused the Eisenhower administration of having neglected the region. (As we saw, the Republicans had made the same accusation against the Truman administration in 1952.) Kennedy's people saw the Eisenhower administration as having been unsympathetic and unresponsive to a changing world. At times, Kennedy linked Latin America with Africa and Asia. In Africa and Latin America in particular, the Kennedy administration promised it would be paying attention. But in the region itself, Kennedy drew upon liberal Democratic legacies, however unexamined. "A new Democratic administration, as the legatee of Franklin Roosevelt, would have a great opportunity to rebuild close relations with Latin America." Many liberal Democrats had convinced themselves that the Good Neighbor Policy promoted democracy. This became one of the useful myths that many liberal Democrats embraced. JFK also glossed over Truman administration failures even as he criticized similar Eisenhower administration policies. He expressed regret that the new programs being developed late in Eisenhower's second term only reflected belated concerns following Castro's consolidation of power. He frequently linked Latin America with other parts of what was becoming known as the Third World; he saw them as "the great areas of the struggle" against communism. He expressed concern that the U.S. influence and prestige were in relative decline generally around the world, and that, increasingly, Third World leaders would look to improve their ties with communist leaders. As many African countries were gaining their independence, there was a belief that their loyalty was up for grabs. In Latin America, however, the need was to consolidate U.S. influence, which now seemed threatened with the rise of Castro.[46]

Privately, Kennedy, according to Schlesinger, "appeared fully to recognize the limitations on U.S. action against the Castro regime." In August he told Schlesinger that the United States could not do anything except through the Organization of American States, "and most of the members of the OAS don't want to do anything at all." "Our best hope," he continued, "is to stop the spread of Castro's influence by helping genuine democracy elsewhere in the continent."[47]

But, as a campaign issue, Cuba provided the Democratic candidate with a chance to criticize the Republicans for "losing" a country that had long had close ties to the United States (as the Republicans had previously criticized President Truman for "losing" China). Senator Kennedy remarked that when he had visited Cuba three years before he had been told that the U.S. ambassador "was the second most powerful man in Cuba. Probably he should not be, but he is not today." Kennedy criticized Vice President Nixon for having praised "the competence and stability of the Batista dictatorship" in 1955. He said that the Eisenhower administration lacked "the imagination and compassion to understand the needs of the Cuban people" (emphasizing providing weapons instead) and had failed to force the Cuban dictator to hold free elections. Kennedy promised that the age of the strongman in Latin America was over and that in three years there would not be any dictators— "Latin America will be free." He criticized the Eisenhower administration for backing Latin American dictators. Kennedy criticized Castro for having betrayed the ideas of the anti-Batista struggle and for having turned Cuba "into a hostile and militant Communist satellite—a base from which to carry Communist infiltration and subversion throughout the Americas." Kennedy's rhetoric regarding Cuba raised expectations and, to a certain degree, boxed himself in, policy-wise.[48] In the last weeks of the campaign, the IADF expressed concern regarding the way the Cuba issue had been handled during the campaign."[49]

Vice President and Republican presidential candidate Nixon found Kennedy's comments on Cuba an inviting target. Running on a promise of continued "peace and prosperity," Nixon criticized the Democratic candidate's comments regarding the vice president's failure to call for free elections in Cuba. Nixon criticized Kennedy's call for aid to anti-Castro forces within and outside of Cuba, which would be in violation of the United Nations and Organization of American States charters. Kennedy responded that Nixon had distorted his position, but Nixon clearly thought he had made a telling point and raised it repeatedly. (That the Eisenhower administration had been covertly supporting anti-Castro exiles since March was, of course, not something that he could comment on.)[50]

Nixon, for his part, had claimed that he himself was a liberal on foreign affairs in 1960. He noted that there were fewer dictators in Latin America at the end of the Eisenhower years than there had been at the beginning. (This was the reverse of the case in the Truman presidency.) Certainly, the vice president's support for foreign aid was strong in 1960. As a newly elected president in 1961, Nixon might not have created a program as ambitious as the Alliance for Progress, but he certainly would have built on the Eisenhower administration foreign aid policies of the end of the second term, such as the creation of the Inter-American Development Bank. Perhaps his policies would have defined a foreign policy ideal for the rest of the Cold War era, as President Kennedy's came to do. (By 1968, as we shall see, presidential candidate Nixon had returned to the policies of trade, not aid of the Truman and most of the Eisenhower years.)[51]

Following Kennedy's victory in November, Berle was formally asked by Kennedy aide Ted Sorensen to head up a task force on Latin America, which was to include Professor Gordon, Rutgers economist (and IADF member) Robert Alexander, and Puerto Rican politician, businessman, and economic development official Teodoro Moscoso. (Stevenson was in charge of the general task force report on foreign policy.) The priority was to be outlining immediate steps to take. Kennedy emphasized that "we are interested only in the most *urgent* and *significant* steps [emphasis in the original] on which you think the next Administration must decide in its first 60 days." If their proposals were "not of that priority and can be postponed, we trust you will be frank enough to say so." It was important that the administration could take advantage of already existing "funds, statutes, and agencies." Given Berle's own anxious state, it certainly could have been a report of import only for the moment. Nevertheless, and more significantly, it would also "indicate the lines of a dramatic revitalization of Latin American relations." Berle and his colleagues considered Venezuela to be "the hinge to the situation." They also encouraged the Puerto Rican governor to send President-Elect Kennedy a letter stating that his election "has fired the imagination and warmly encouraged the democratic forces in Latin America which feel the urgent need of setting in motion hemispheric policies to achieve technical, economic and social progress within our common heritage of freedom." The governor encouraged Kennedy to reaffirm "to our good neighbors your thinking on a great alliance for progress and freedom in this hemisphere . . . further impetus and confidence to Latin American democratic forces in their battle against want."[52]

Berle considered Latin America to be a "now major Cold War theatre [Berle's preferred spelling] with outcome in serious doubt." Besides suggesting a higher profile for a top position in U.S.-Latin American affairs in the State Department, he encouraged providing significant funds for Latin American through an Inter-American Development Fund. The United States should emphasize Venezuela and Colombia, whose leaders could become the "nucleus for hemispheric wide democratic progressive front for social development and ideological and political defense against communist and Castro attacks." He also suggested appointing a new ambassador to Nicaragua who could work toward negotiating the "peaceful organization of a transition government." He proposed ending the Dominican sugar quota.[53]

Prior to Kennedy's inauguration in January, Berle met with him and provided what Sorensen called "a liberal education in Latin American affairs." They spoke for an hour and a half, "more than I expected," Berle noted. JFK listened to what Berle had to say. "I think the field is new to him and he is studying it." At this point Berle rather fatalistically was convinced that eight governments might "go the way of Cuba in the next six months unless something was done." He made the famous remark (later attributed to President Kennedy), "Speaking personally, I said that while the great Cold War could not be decisively won in the Latin American theatre, it obviously could be lost there." By February, he had compared the situation to Europe in 1947. In May he lamented what he considered an inappropriate application of the Good Neighbor Policy of nonintervention, which had left Cuba a "Communist satellite" while seeing evidence of Soviet/Cuban interventions everywhere. By early June, he grumbled, "Obviously, if we are merely going to let Latin

America go with sweet phrases, I had best be somewhere else." By the end of the month, however, he had rallied and was calling for a major U.S. "psychological offensive" that would help bring focus to a "dynamic force of an inchoate movement for social change" throughout the hemisphere. This would prevent "a lapse into dictatorships whose only justification is meaningless order-keeping at the price of oppression and plunder and the wiping out of the most creative elements in the population." The task force report called for the United States to maintain "correct but very cool relations" with dictatorships, "taking care not to become identified with dictators" in places like Nicaragua, and generally to back democratic forces in the hemisphere. (He feared that many in the State Department would seek to block such a policy.) There were also suggestions that the new administration should provide "appropriate decorations" for people like Betancourt and Figueres, among others. Following the conclusion of his work with the task force, Berle would not play a major role in the Kennedy administration, however. Berle feared that Latin America would not be prioritized in the way he thought it should be. (He was not the only one who thought that this would entail creating a new position within the State Department structure.) He also regretted that there were no younger men with a reputation in Latin America.[54]

The Americans for Democratic Action convention called for a new policy toward Latin America. Members of the organization lamented the "failure to develop an intelligent policy." Their resolution called for support for democracy and an end to intervention on behalf of "tyrants." The United States also needed to help design an economic policy that would help stabilize prices for Latin American goods. An expanded aid and loan program would be developed based on "hemispheric cooperation instead of on mere bilateral aid."[55] In many ways, it would end up being ADA founding member Schlesinger himself as a member of the administration (with a few Democratic senators pressing from Capitol Hill) who would carry the torch for liberal democratic reform in Latin America in Berle's stead.

Kennedy's people saw the Eisenhower administration as having been unsympathetic and unresponsive to a changing world.[56] The Kennedy administration would be filled with people who believed that they knew better than their predecessors how to handle the challenges of that changing world.[57] Kennedy was more willing to accept neutralism in Africa and parts of Asia, but not to the same extent in Latin America.[58] One could argue that he was not willing to lose Latin America to the Third World. But he also believed that there was more at stake in the region. He was willing to offer more than containment. He was willing to embrace the region's dreams of development, as many Latin Americans believed that his predecessor had not done.[59]

In planning for Kennedy's foreign policy generally, Stevenson advised Kennedy aide Ted Sorensen that there should be a "recognition of a special U.S. responsibility for Latin America." Stevenson emphasized that the region had been "largely ignored," and that the feeling was widespread that the United States did not share Latin American "aspirations for basic social reform." He noted a significant enthusiasm for Castro's reforms in Cuba, and that whatever policy toward Cuba the Kennedy administration adopted should be acceptable to the other Latin American countries. He argued that "the solidarity of the hemisphere should be your primary concern, and unilateral action does not contribute to solidarity." He argued that an economic embargo was "self-defeating," and suggested the possibility of Castro becoming another Tito (in other words, an independent communist leader, like the Yugoslavian dictator). For Stevenson, the primary problems were political and not economic. He also passed on a recommendation from a Chilean friend, Hernán Santa Cruz, deputy director in Latin America for the UN's Food and Agriculture Organization, that the new administration needed to demonstrate that its primary concern was "the people of Latin America, not just the ruling classes and American business."[60] Along with Berle and Stevenson, Kennedy also relied upon Lincoln Gordon, who submitted material in December that he hoped would be included either in the inaugural address or in a special message to the Congress on Latin American development, "which should be among the early Administration actions." Besides mentioning "common goals of freedom, democracy, human rights, and social and economic progress," he also included values like "respect," "unity," and "non-intervention." He encouraged Kennedy to cite nineteenth-century Cuban independence leader José Martí, "or some other classical leader of Latin American democratic thought." (Martí was being claimed already by both Castro and his enemies in Miami.) Gordon argued that the region's "material and human resources . . . if properly organized could within a decade bring most of Latin America into economic step with the modern world and make a reality of the popular longing for new opportunities for human fulfillment." He noted that "energies" could be directed "toward a massive acceleration of economic progress" with the "widest possible participation." Gordon spoke of a "veritable alliance for progress." Gordon suggested that there would be perhaps "slight embarrassment" in building on the Act of Bogotá, which was associated with the outgoing administration; the Kennedy administration could demonstrate its resolve "to convert the aspirations into reality."[61]

Schlesinger had advised JFK during the presidential campaign, but his role in the administration, if there was going to be one, was uncertain. But as he became a presidential aide, Latin America was to be one of his major responsibilities, in part because of his long-standing interest in the region and because of what was understood to be a Latin American respect for intellectuals. Given "the disaffection of the Latin American intellectual community," it was presumed that Schlesinger could be useful.[62]

In the two years since Fidel Castro had come to power, no other governments, authoritarian or democratic, had fallen to forces interested in emulating the Cuban revolutionaries. That did not lessen the sense of urgency for the incoming administration or the president-elect. The United States no longer had an embassy in Havana following the Eisenhower administration's last-minute break in diplomatic relations with the island nation. Latin America was now high on the U.S. foreign policy agenda, and many signature Kennedy administration policies, not least of all the Alliance for Progress, were to be devoted to the region. Latin America, for better and worse, no longer was neglected. Liberal Democrats now in power had a chance to make up for what they saw as lost time. The Kennedy administration, Frances Grant affirmed, was "eagerly awaited" by "democratic forces abroad."[63] The new administration embraced many aspects of the liberal Democratic critique of Eisenhower administration policy, but it also rejected others, in ways that had significant consequences for the evolution of Latin America in the 1960s and 1970s.

Chapter 2

Let Us Begin

The Many Fronts of John F. Kennedy's
Latin American Cold War, Part I

In his inaugural address, President Kennedy spoke of "the power to abolish all forms of human poverty and all forms of human life." He addressed the Western Hemisphere in particular, promising "to assist free men and free governments in casting off the chains of poverty." (Stevenson had recommended that JFK mention the "special U.S. responsibility for Latin America.") Kennedy left unanswered the question of whether Kennedy's "free men" and Truman's "Free World" were one and the same. But he also warned that the United States would not let "this peaceful revolution of hope . . . become the prey of hostile powers." The United States would join with its neighbors "to oppose aggression or subversion anywhere in the Americas." Speaking for the hemisphere as a whole, Kennedy said that it "intends to remain the master of its own house."[1] In a news conference soon thereafter, Kennedy spoke of the need for governments to be established in Latin America that would "provide a better life for the people." But he quickly backtracked and suggested that "nearly all of them do, share the same view that we have to provide in this hemisphere a better life for the people involved." While invoking the "peaceful revolution of hope," he also "pledged to work with our sister republics to free the Americas of all such foreign domination and all tyranny."[2]

John Kennedy's Cold War in Latin America was going to be fought on many fronts with many different weapons (some rather blunt instruments, indeed). Not all of the means and ends were compatible with each other. Some came to undermine each other over the course of the 1960s. Short-term political and strategic concerns were, in the end, to be more easily addressed than those of long-term socioeconomic development. In this chapter I will examine both the larger goals of the administration for Latin America, and the more immediate steps that they thought had to be taken and threats that they thought had to be addressed.

In early February, President Kennedy asked his special assistant Schlesinger to accompany the Food for Peace mission to Latin America, "to underline," in Schlesinger's words, Kennedy's "concern about general Latin American problems."[3] The head of the mission was another historian, George McGovern, a South Dakota congressman who had recently lost a senatorial bid. McGovern was even then not a typical "Vital Center" liberal, having backed Henry Wallace in 1948 and never accepted many of the essential premises of the Cold War. Like Morse and Church, he opposed military aid for Latin American and other Third World countries. As the representative of an agricultural state, he had supported the use of surplus agricultural products to promote peace, noting that the Soviet Union could not afford to export food and arguing that hungry people were more likely to embrace communism. As its director, McGovern wanted Food for Peace to become a major instrument of U.S. foreign policy as well as Third World "development."[4] During their mission to Latin America, he and Schlesinger developed a bond that would last for the rest of McGovern's life.

The South American mission did not seem to have been clearly thought through. The first stop, Argentina, was a country that had been a leading exporter of food for generations. In early meetings with Argentine leaders, Schlesinger tried to assure them that the United States would be focusing on "human suffering" and not on promoting U.S. economic interests. President Arturo Frondizi wanted to make sure that the United States understood that food aid was no "substitute for basic economic development." McGovern and the others sought to assure him on this point as well. Moreover, Castro was "not the fundamental question," Frondizi insisted. There needed to be "a basic attack on the conditions which produce the Castros and facilitate their appeal." Schlesinger, however, found him "elusive on OAS measures," and thought he "was doing his best to avoid dealing with the central issue." Schlesinger generally was not impressed by his visit to Argentina, and dismissed the Frondizi administration as having "a banker's mentality." He was frustrated that the new approach of the Kennedy administration was not appreciated in Argentina.[5]

In Brazil, a country of vast socioeconomic and regional diversity, inequality, and social unrest, the McGovern team received a more positive response from the administration of Jânio Quadros. McGovern and Schlesinger had an opportunity to observe "areas of real despair," thanks to the insistence of U.S. Consul Ernest Guaderama. They went to the backlands of northeastern Brazil, an area of extreme poverty and recurring famine. There Schlesinger and his companions visited homes and saw children with distended bellies, suffering from extreme malnutrition. They met a naked baby, "covered with scabs and pockmarks." "We were afraid to touch him," Schlesinger wrote in his journal. "I had a moment of terrible guilt which compounded the general sense of discomfort one has in examining the squalor of these people's lives." They had brought cameramen along with them to document the conditions "for skeptical congressmen." They "kept flashing pictures of the desperate family while McGovern and I sat miserably around." "We came out vastly sobered and silent."[6]

At the same time, the response to a direct observation of Brazilian poverty was understood through the new, fraught Cold War framework that the Cuban Revolution produced. If the United States gave "democratic reformers effective backing, it might still be possible to save Northeast Brazil from being transformed into a Sierra Mestre [sic]." For some U.S. officials, Brazil's Castro was presumed to be a peasant league leader named Francisco Julião. The Alliance for Progress during the Kennedy years would focus not only on Brazil but, specifically, on the northeast region.[7]

Elsewhere in Latin America, however, Schlesinger was certain that Kennedy's election had "given rise to an enormous expectancy." Although Schlesinger recognized the danger of "future disenchantment," he thought that "any sort of reasonably developed interest and program" would be sufficient.[8] McGovern, for his part, focused on what these countries saw as their particular needs as he moved on to Bolivia, Chile, Colombia, and Peru. McGovern returned from South America impatient with bureaucratic obstacles and anxious to move forward. In the weeks afterward he arranged the largest shipment of powdered milk in the history of the Food for Peace program. Not surprisingly, it was sent to northeastern Brazil, where McGovern and Schlesinger had been so troubled by what they saw. Over the next year food grants to Latin America increased by 100 percent.[9]

The trip had many ramifications. U.S. interest was driven by a short-term perception of threat. As long as that fear remained acute, U.S. officials could remain focused on and engaged with Latin America. But the Kennedy administration claimed to be committing itself to addressing more long-term problems, which not only were deep-rooted but were also quite varied from one country to another and even (as in the case of Brazil) could be quite different from one part of a country to another.[10]

In his speech before congressmen and Latin American ambassadors formally announcing an Alliance for Progress, President Kennedy invoked the South American independence hero Simón Bolívar and his "dream of freedom and glory, . . . never . . . nearer to fulfillment, . . . never . . . in greater danger." Kennedy spoke both of U.S. failures in the past to comprehend the hemisphere's "common mission," as well as Latin American failures to "fully understand the urgency of the need to lift people from poverty and ignorance and despair." But Kennedy also spoke of "peril" well as "hope." He invoked the Monroe Doctrine and the threat posed by "alien forces which once again seek to impose the despotisms of the Old World on the people of the New." He sought to project an image of balance by expressing "our special friendship to the people of Cuba and the Dominican Republic, and the hope they will soon rejoin the society of free men, uniting with us in our common effort." The only living Latin American leader whom he quoted was Costa

Rica's Figueres, who said that "once dormant peoples are struggling toward the sun, toward the better life."[11] The United States promised a ten-year commitment, which certainly sounded good, although President Kennedy could not guarantee that he would be reelected or that his successor or successors would honor that commitment. For those congressmen and U.S. citizens skeptical of foreign aid, he did suggest that the program would lead to "self-sustaining growth" and ultimately end the "need for massive outside help."[12]

"Let us once again awaken our American revolution," Kennedy pledged. At times, as we shall see, Kennedy and his aides spoke too enthusiastically about reform, causing concern among Foreign Service officers.[13] Latin America, moreover, was expected to fund the vast majority of the reform programs on its own. If there was going to be progress, there were going to have to be many alliances. The administration looked to reformist leaders, but there were not enough of them, or not enough with whom liberal Democrats felt comfortable. For even those who wanted to see change did not necessarily envision change in exactly the same way that U.S. leaders did, and they did not always find the Kennedy administration or the State Department under Kennedy to be receptive to what they chose to do.

Lincoln Gordon agreed that the United States had taken "Latin America for granted" after World War II. He saw "no reason to apologize" for the Marshall Plan or U.S. efforts in Korea, but he noted that the United States had failed "to summon up the resources of energy and talent to pay corresponding attention to the urgent problems of our southern hemisphere." While Brazilian President Kubitschek's proposed Operation Pan-America may have had some problems (what Gordon referred to as "defects of detail"), the fundamental idea that there should be a large-scale joint effort in the hemisphere was sound. Having worked on the Marshall Plan and traveled in Latin America, he was more careful than others in distinguishing between the Alliance and the postwar efforts in Europe. The Marshall Plan had been designed to effect economic recovery in advanced societies with high levels of educational achievement and industrialization, while the Alliance was focused on "economic and social development." Furthermore, the United States needed to be "doctrinaire on liberty," the need for an independent judiciary, and "genuine elections."[14]

Kennedy's announcement was well received among democratic U.S. allies in the hemisphere. Costa Rica's Figueres helped prepare a joint declaration with Peru's Víctor Raúl Haya de la Torre, Venezuela's future presidents Raul Leoni and Rafael Caldera, the Dominican Republic's future president Juan Bosch, Uruguay's Luis Batlle Berres, and Colombia's future president Carlos Lleras Restrepo, among others. They welcomed the "new attitude of the United States toward Latin America, which is consistent with the historic North

American revolution, and with our own political and social aims." Figureres criticized "old dynastic dictatorship" and "new totalitarian tyranny." The democratic parties of Latin America had "fought alone until now."[15]

The very first goal listed in the Punta del Este agreement reached in Uruguay later in the year was "to improve and strengthen democratic institutions through application of the principle of self-determination by the people." In practice, this was carried out more often in those areas in which significant urbanization had already created the social basis for a democratic system.

The Alliance for Progress, in principle at least, was intended to support political democracy in the region. Other than Trujillo and Castro, however, the Kennedy administration did not intend to cut ties with nondemocratic governments. Schlesinger, however, suggested that the United States should "give every dictator a sense of impermanence" and make it clear that the Kennedy administration was opposed to "dictatorships in the long run."[16]

President Kennedy himself promised outgoing President Kubitschek of Brazil that "one of the cardinal objects of my administration will be the association of the United States with the peoples of Latin America in a common effort to improve the lives of people under the reign of liberty." As he remarked to a gathering of Latin American ambassadors in mid-March, "our unfulfilled task is to demonstrate to the entire world that man's unsatisfied aspiration for economic progress can best be achieved by free men working within a framework of democratic institutions."[17] The Latin dream of development was not necessarily the same thing as modernization, which many in the Kennedy administration thought they had found the key to. U.S. officials and economists saw a world evolving in stages toward what the United States had achieved for many of its citizens. The model was certainly mechanistic, a mirror image in some ways of rigid, dogmatic Soviet models of development in a time of rapid economic growth in the communist nation. U.S. officials believed they could provide the skills and some of the financial resources to promote economic "takeoff" and prevent revolution.[18]

Schlesinger argued that Latin America was on the verge of a "middle class revolution," which he believed was in U.S. interests to promote. He feared that the Latin American "oligarchy" would try to block it, thereby unintentionally bringing about a "proletarian revolution." In Brazil under Kubitschek, Schlesinger argued, "the bonds of the old agrarian society were burst by the sheer momentum of economic growth." The United States needed "to make it absolutely clear that we regard dictatorship as ultimately incompatible with the principles of the hemisphere." This did not mean an "anti-dictatorship crusade." Schlesinger recommended, in particular, "full backing for the Betancourt government," which might "be the best possible way of convincing aspiring Latin Americans that the democratic road to national fulfillment is both more reliable and more agreeable than the Castro road." Betancourt, he said, was a "tough, good-hearted man" who gave "an impression of strength, authority, and inextinguishable vitality." Meanwhile, he was concerned that "pro-Communist parties" were "making impressive gains in Chile."[19]

The Inter-American Association for Democracy and Freedom felt that its message was finally being heard. Domestic allies like the AFL-CIO expressed their hopes that the new administration would support "embattled democratic forces" and encourage the development of labor organizations.[20] At their meeting in May, the Americans for Democratic Action, which Schlesinger had cofounded, passed a resolution that stated the "ADA believes that, in the 'Alliance for Progress,' the Kennedy Administration has a great and perhaps final opportunity to assure the future of democracy in the Western Hemisphere." They further noted that they were opposed to "unilateral action" in Cuba.[21]

Schlesinger even spoke of creating a global "popular movement of pro-democratic forces." He hoped that the Democratic Party could lead the way. James Loeb, who had been national secretary of the ADA, noted that the party was not far enough to the left "to be useful in any direct relationship with pro-democratic forces in under-developed areas." He further noted that he could "hardly envisage [segregationist] Senator [James] Eastland sitting down" with the leaders like Peru's Haya de la Torre.[22]

Domestically, the Kennedy administration had to confront a U.S. public and a Congress often opposed to what were seen as "give-away" foreign aid programs. As had happened at the beginning of the Cold War more than a decade earlier, both the citizenry and their representatives would have to be convinced that the stakes were high in Latin America and that the region was deserving of U.S. effort and money. Liberal Democrats sympathetic to Latin America would have to convince others who had different priorities as well as conservatives who rejected their premises altogether. But Congress resisted. They only enacted legislation that allowed spending on obligations agreed to under the Act of Bogotá under Eisenhower in mid-April 1961. Congress was not going to support any kinds of reform it could not control. As the Alliance for Progress developed, it became clear that the U.S. officials primarily provided aid based not on need but on an assessment of where the political stakes were highest and the security threats perceived to be greatest.

And then there was the State Department itself. Schlesinger saw the Alliance as the best new idea that the administration had in foreign policy and "the only serious advance in our Latin American policy since" the Good Neighbor Policy. He was concerned with the tendency of Foreign Service officers and State Department officials to demonstrate a "built-in conventionality of thought and action which gets in the way of decision and effective policy." By June of 1961, he was already faced with what he considered opposition from the State Department (waged through leaks in the press) against "White House intervention in Latin America policy." "[A]ll we have been doing is filling the vacuum created by their own lack of energy." Furthermore, citing the opinions of the like-minded Puerto Rican social scientist Arturo Morales Carrión, those who worked in the Bureau of American Affairs were "predominantly out of sympathy" with the Alliance. The deputy assistant secretary for inter-American affairs thought that those who claimed to be Latin Americanists "have no realization of the forces at work in Latin America today." They did not realize that administration policy could "succeed only" if it enlisted "the support of the Latin America left." Morales Carrión noted the lack of "sympathy for the democratic left," as well as the lack of interest in "the intellectual community of Latin America or in the labor movement." Instead, those people in charge of operations exhibited "the same old attitudes and the same old clichés" and always found reasons not to take action.[23]

Contrary to the hopes of many liberal Democrats in the Eisenhower years, the Kennedy administration was going to provide much more aid for the Latin American military. President Kennedy was particularly concerned by the threat of Cuba-inspired and -trained insurgencies to internal security. Attorney General Robert Kennedy also was devoted to counterinsurgency as long as his brother was president.[24] The secretary of defense was instructed "to move to a new level of increased activity across the board" in counterinsurgency, with a particular emphasis on Latin America. Police training programs were also an important part of efforts to "counter Communist indirect aggression." (A review of previously existing programs in these areas focused first on Latin America.) Many were aware that care had to be taken not to upset "the political balance" in particular situations or there could be "hazardous political consequences." The U.S. ambassador in each country should decide whether these programs would serve U.S. interests and assess how they would affect internal dynamics. This was to be an essential check and balance.[25]

As a November 1961 memorandum from the Joint Chiefs of Staff made clear, military programs of all types were intended "for use in conjunction with and in support of existing U.S. political, economic and social measures and in implementation of the concept of the Alliance for Progress." So, in that sense, the United States in most cases presumed that the military would *support* rather than *lead* modernization. The hoped-for subordination of the military to civilian authority in Latin America was expected to be reinforced by the U.S. ambassadors' authority over what kind of military assistance programs would be adopted. Kennedy administration officials as well were hardly unaware of the potential that military aid had for enhancing pro-U.S.

attitudes among the Latin American military. The U.S. military seemed more concerned that the Latin American military would reject training because they would become "Americanized." Later critics of the program, however, were less convinced that the United States had carried through with its claim that it had stressed the "apolitical" role of the military and its subordination to civilian authority. U.S. officials recognized the dangers at the time.[26] "The reforms generated by the Alliance for Progress are likely to weaken, rather than strengthen, the fabric of society in most Latin American countries by increasing these tensions during the period before the long term programs of the Alliance become effective." The need to maintain stability by strengthening the forces of order could transform the political dynamics in the region. "In nearly every Latin American country the political balance is a delicate one, with the armed forces capable of tipping the scales." With "most governments . . . carefully nurturing the principle of civilian control," "[w]e cannot afford to be identified with any step backward either to repressive dictatorship or military intervention in political life."[27]

Within the administration, liberals like Chester Bowles raised another important issue. "We must make perfectly clear that this aid is not to be used to deter legitimate popular expressions of aspirations for greater social justice and political freedom." Bowles did not argue that the assistance could be used "to provide the capability to put down any major uprisings," but to control "spontaneous outbursts." But even here it was important that weapons provided by the United States would not be employed against nonviolent movements. If they were, "we would obviously be in grave danger of strengthening the popular appeal of forces unsympathetic to the United States." And the United States needed to guard against training armed forces that then would seize power.[28]

Schlesinger was concerned early on that the U.S. military was pursuing its own policies of opposing revolutions, supporting "our friends" (meaning the right), and rejecting democracy on the grounds that it would only open "the door to communism anyway."[29] From the beginning, the Kennedy administration was criticized for asking for increasing such aid for nondemocratic governments. In September 1962, Secretary of State Dean Rusk wrote Senator Morse, arguing that U.S. military assistance for Latin America represented only "five percent of our world-wide program" and "less than six percent of the military budgets of the Latin American nations themselves."[30] During his later European trip, Schlesinger noted a "particular concern" about the "reported Washington obsession with guerrilla warfare." He argued that successful counterinsurgency involved political solutions. Europeans thought that the struggles "against communism" were "still a matter for the long haul." Therefore, Schlesinger suggested, they were "much more impressed by the Alliance."[31]

Latin American leaders, for their part, were not shy about addressing their concerns regarding U.S. policy toward the military. Bringing "senior officers to Washington for nontechnical, political training would, in the Latin American climate, inevitably stimulate their interest in taking power," José Antonio Mayobre, Venezuela's ambassador to the United States, remarked on more than one occasion in meetings with U.S. officials. Mayobre also saw a danger in bringing Latin American military leaders together in an Inter-American Defense College. Assistant Secretary of State Edwin Martin insisted that "the curriculum could be so handled as to have the opposite effect," particularly with the people he knew would be involved in such a venture. President Kennedy made it clear that he wanted the ties between the Latin American militaries to be strengthened so that "they could work together better on the common hemisphere problems in the military field." President Kennedy sought to reassure the Venezuelan ambassador that the association with the U.S. military, who understood and accepted civilian authority, would prevent what the ambassador feared would take place. After leaving the president's office, Mayobre asked Martin to be certain that any announcement of the formation of such a program would "emphasize the democratic and civilian objectives of the training to be provided."[32]

Historian Thomas Field has argued that Bolivia was typical of Kennedy administration policy, though he does not compare it to other Latin American countries. The country had experienced a revolution in 1952 in which peasants had defeated the military. Eisenhower administration policy had been more subtle and had tamed the revolution, but when its primary figure, Victor Paz Estenssoro, returned to power in the early 1960s, he took a more uncertain path to the left, in part in order to get the attention of the Kennedy administration and encourage it to provide aid. Paz was more like many of the nonaligned leaders that Kennedy was trying to court in the Third World. Kennedy liberals, according to Field, saw the Bolivian left, particularly the militant tin miners, as blocking development. Although Paz told Schlesinger that Castro had to be "eliminated" somehow, Schlesinger, for his part, was concerned that Paz was not sufficiently anti-communist and hoped that Ambassador Ben Stephansky would be able to encourage the Bolivian leader to be more aggressive. Schlesinger's perception of the threat in Bolivia was high. "After Cuba we simply cannot let another Latin American nation go communist." Bolivia could become a base for subversion, and the Kennedy administration would hear "Who lost Bolivia?" While Schlesinger said that he usually opposed military aid, he was concerned with balancing the power of the miners, who had weapons. The administration, however, saw no alternative to Paz, particularly given the fact that his revolutionary credentials helped the administration look less opposed to revolution in principle. In meetings with him, Schlesinger emphasized the Kennedy administration's understanding of the need for "social change in Latin America." He talked about how important it was to protect the "integrity" of a vaguely defined "revolution" "from the oligarchy of the right," as well as from "the conspiracy and sabotage of the left." (He characterized the Cuban Revolution as having been "clearly seized by forces from outside the hemisphere.") Although the Kennedy administration strengthened the Bolivian military institutionally, it did not want to see it take power (and it did not do so during the Kennedy years).[33]

The Kennedy administration did not prefer authoritarian solutions. It rarely encouraged military coups. It preferred not to recognize governments that had come to power through the use of political violence. And it pressed countries in which military coups had taken place to establish timetables for a return to constitutional procedures.

In any case, the Kennedy administration in the short term had to address concrete threats and more diffuse ideological challenges. Cuba remained the single most important issue as the Kennedy administration came into office. The Joint Chiefs of Staff believed "that the primary objective of the United States in Cuba should be the speedy overthrow of the Castro government, followed by the establishment of a pro-U.S. government, which with U.S. support, will accomplish the desired objectives for the Cuban people."[34]

Schlesinger, for his part, believing that the most immediate goal was to convince Latin American intellectuals, set himself to the task of writing something to convince those who had initially been supportive of Castro that he had "betrayed the Cuban revolution." The United States Information Agency considered the mid-March "Cuban White Paper" "too racy and liberal a document" (and too critical of Batista).[35] The White Paper's most important point was "affirmation of our faith in social progress and our rejection of the Castro revolution, not as revolutionary, but as communist." "The hemisphere," he argued, "rejoiced at the overthrow of the Batista tyranny," and no one in Latin America would blame Kennedy for Eisenhower's support of Batista. What mattered was that the government was "subservient" (although there would long to be reason to doubt this) to the Soviet Union and that it intended to interfere "in the affairs of other Latin nations" (which was far more probable, and, indeed, which became the issue that drove a wedge between Cuba and its neighbors more than any other). Despite USIA concerns, the document was translated into Spanish and distributed by them (25,000 copies were sent to Mexico, with an additional 30,000 for the rest of Spanish-speaking Latin America and only 200 translated into Portuguese for Brazil).[36]

But Schlesinger's paper could hardly have the kind of immediate impact that many impatient Cold Warriors in the administration wanted. And the action they wanted had the opposite effect from that which had been intended.

Kennedy had inherited a plan to help Cuban exiles invade their home country, a covert action in which U.S. fingerprints were not to be visible, as President Eisenhower, fond of these kinds of operations, had insisted upon. If anything, President Kennedy was even more committed to "plausible deniability," aware of the stakes in Latin America and an expanding Third World, many of whose countries were in the process of gaining or consolidating their independence. Kennedy's people had not improved on the plan, to be sure, but they went ahead with the Bay of Pigs invasion anyway. Schlesinger worried about the ideological orientations of the exiles and told José Miró Cardona that "It is foolish if the Cuban Revolutionary Council turns out to be to the right of the New Frontier."[37] Only days before the invasion, President Kennedy had announced in a news conference that there would "not be, under any conditions, an intervention in Cuba by the United States Armed Forces." The arrival of the exiles was supposed to inspire an uprising on the island (in ways remarkably similar to the magical thinking embraced by Castro himself back in 1956). In the short term, Schlesinger had helped block the publication of a well-informed article on the invasion by a sympathetic journalist. He was talked out of making a final effort to reverse the decision by National Security Adviser McGeorge Bundy and his aide Walt Rostow. In any case, other than the U.S. public at large, few were unaware that the invasion was coming. Schlesinger thought that the "political risks" had not been thought through; even defining the public position of the administration remained unclear. Once it had failed, he noted, "Obviously, I must work now to minimize the political and diplomatic damage." (He complained that "political and diplomatic contingency planning" had been "much less advanced.")[38]

Those within and outside of the administration who most identified with the Alliance and had highest hopes for it were disappointed. Figueres regretted that he and Betancourt had not been "alerted" about the Bay of Pigs invasion. He worried publicly about U.S. public opinion, which he saw as ignorant of the stakes at play. "There is little realization," he said, "that a major battle of the Cold War (perhaps the decisive battle of the next 10 years) is being fought in the American Hemisphere as a whole." He spoke of "an immense power vacuum," which he compared to Europe at the end of World War II. In the United States, there was only a "prevailing hysteria" about one part (Cuba) and "a frivolous assumption that the mere overthrowal [sic] of the Cuban regime will finish the struggle." The U.S. government recognized the problem; "not so the majority of the people and the press." The United States had to focus on more than "spots of immediate crises," and address itself to the programs devoted to development that had been announced, so that "the prestige of the democratic system" could be recaptured." "Let us prove that the job can be done in freedom."[39]

Senator Morse had supported the kind of aid for socioeconomic reform exemplified by the Alliance for Progress. Yet he was soon caught in the contradictory ebb and flow of Kennedy administration policy. The Bay of Pigs invasion, in particular, put Senator Morse in an awkward position. Morse was an early critic of Castro and believed that Castro's government was unpopular inside Cuba. Morse had been misled by Central Intelligence Agency Director Allen Dulles about the training of Cuban exiles in Guatemala and had informed a constituent that these rumors were merely a ruse by Castro to "justify suspension of liberties and the establishment of a garrison state." The Kennedy administration continued to keep the chair of the Senate subcommittee most concerned with Latin American affairs in the dark. When the invasion occurred, he was enthusiastic and sent out a press release denying that there was a "scintilla of evidence" that the United States was involved. Moreover, he was confident that "the Cuban revolution conducted by Cubans against Castro will be successful." When U.S. participation became evident, he became frustrated with the Kennedy administration and criticized it for failing to consult with his subcommittee. In a telegram to Secretary of State Rusk, he noted that the subcommittee would have been able to provide information that would have led to a "reconsideration of the invasion plan." It would have been "constructive to at least touch base . . . before the fact."[40]

Adlai Stevenson also played a marginal role in the Bay of Pigs debacle. He had only reluctantly agreed to be the U.S. ambassador to the United Nations. (He had hoped to be secretary of state.) But Kennedy claimed that the UN's position would have an enhanced importance because of the creation of new nations through the ongoing large-scale decolonization process. "Stevenson assiduously courted the new nations, particularly the African ones," his biographer John Bartlow Martin wrote, "and the Latin Americans too."[41] Ambassador Stevenson had warned Secretary of State Rusk that "an overt strike" against Cuba "would have a disastrous effect at the UN."[42] If Morse had been uninformed regarding the U.S. involvement in the Bay of Pigs invasion, Stevenson had been inadequately informed regarding the extent of U.S. involvement, leading him to make false statements in the United Nations regarding planes that were said to be flown by defectors from Castro's air force. He also believed the promises that the United States was not intervening and would not do so. Stevenson somehow expected that the operation could be salvaged, making him, as political scientist Lars Schoultz has characterized him, "the final senior official to climb aboard a sinking ship."[43] In the end, the Bay of Pigs invasion, like the Cuban Missile Crisis the following year, demonstrated that Stevenson's role was to support Kennedy administration policy, not to define it. He sent a thoughtful essay that sought to encourage the administration to understand the developing world's understanding of how things worked. The United States needed to continue to be defined by an opposition to colonialism. The United States had "a vast and urgent task to undertake in hastening modernization in societies capable of it." "Brazil," he continued, "is worth many Cubas." The United States should help those countries that were committed to reform but not those that opposed it. The United States needed to talk "more about the cooperative, prosperous world we want to build." Stevenson assumed that in another ten years it would be clear that Castro's approach had failed. He noted that the United States had not gotten through "the agonies of the industrial revolution by relying wholly on the police force." While he did not reject the idea of military aid against guerrilla movements, he contended that other forms of aid were more important than what he called "premature and heavy-handed police work."[44]

The Inter-American Association for Democracy and Freedom criticized the invasion, particularly the role of the CIA. Its leaders worried about the impact of the move on the "highly promising new policy in Inter-American Relations." The administration had a "well-organized program to re-enforce social revolution and reform in the Latin American countries." The United States should not be seen as being opposed only to "dictatorships of the left."[45]

JFK publicly accepted the blame, but he also sought privately to criticize others. Kennedy sometimes suggested that Schlesinger himself would be sorry that the United States had not gone "full force into Cuba" during the Bay of Pigs invasion.[46] The experience left the president distrustful of advisers in the military and intelligence community and reluctant to let himself be backed into a corner.[47]

Schlesinger feared after the Bay of Pigs invasion that Kennedy had been "revealed as if no more than a continuation of the Eisenhower-Dulles past." While Kennedy had established "an impression of U.S. foreign policy as mature, controlled, and, above all, intelligent," it now seemed to look not only "like imperialists . . . [but] like stupid, ineffectual imperialists, which is worst of all." But he blamed the CIA's Allen Dulles and Richard Bissell for bringing "down in a day what Kennedy had been laboring patiently and successfully to build up in three months."[48]

Others like Senator Church believed that the invasion proved that the United States needed to "drastically change our whole policy toward the Latin American countries or run the risk of suffering similar defeats throughout the South American continent."[49] He continued to argue for a "policy of forbearance" and expressed a belief that an "imaginative implementation of the Alliance for Progress" would address the larger regional context. He even was bold enough to suggest that Castro had the support of the Cuban people.[50] Church would have agreed with Morse that the most important thing was the larger effort to "change Latin American attitudes" through "cooperation" and to "strengthen the political choice for freedom among the masses of the people of Latin America." "U.S. direct military action," he continued, "might be the way to win a battle but lose a peace." It could "lose most of the rest of Latin America for years to come." Moreover, Morse insisted that Cuba was "not a threat to the United States," but to Latin America.[51]

The Bay of Pigs helped Castro consolidate his hold internally while gaining a worldwide image as the David who had stood up to Goliath. In the United States the myths grew surrounding the magical "air cover" that would have somehow guaranteed the exiles' victory. This played well in Miami and in some Republican and military circles for years to come.

Attorney General Robert Kennedy's own obsessions with the defeat were not productive. He told General Maxwell Taylor in June, "We will take action against Castro. It might be tomorrow, it might be in five days or ten days, or not for months. But it will come." The younger brother sought through Operation Mongoose, created in November, to make up for the humiliation that accompanied the failed invasion. He developed an unfortunate attachment to Edward Lansdale, who promised that "firm action by the United States would solve 90 percent of our problems in Latin America." Even as they planned to increase internal turmoil in Cuba, through acts of sabotage among other forms of covert action, the guidelines assumed that this was not going to be enough: "final success" would "require US military intervention." In the short term, however, the United States was lacking "hard intelligence on the conditions inside Cuba." To an objective observer that might have suggested that those involved in the operation had barely begun to do what they themselves most thought needed to be done. The evidence available does not suggest that President Kennedy himself would have supported an invasion, since he had only authorized aid "to help the people of Cuba overthrow the Communist regime from within Cuba." Planning continued in the following months for a revolt by October 1962, but there was no indication that they were making progress in that direction. By July the number of intelligence agents had reportedly grown, but no guerrilla movement had been established. A far more skeptical State Department representative for Operation Mongoose in early August suggested that "short of the employment of U.S. military force the programs and actions of the U.S. aimed at the downfall of the Castro government will probably be only marginal." Despite deteriorating conditions on the island, he recommended that the United States "should avoid engaging U.S. prestige openly in operations, the success of which may be doubtful."[52]

These actions remained covert, in any case, not only because of the nature of the operations, but also because the Kennedy administration was not unaware of the larger costs of more overt approaches. Domestically, this hurt

Kennedy's image in some circles. Many wanted more aggressive action, and based on the letters many congressmen received, it seemed that some people in the United States would have approved an all-out invasion. But Kennedy had a bigger game in mind and a hemisphere to lose. A complete embargo on trade with Cuba was announced in early February 1962, and efforts to isolate the island nation continued. In the short term, covert actions continued as well, without any clear impact on internal Cuban political dynamics, and which, in part, led to the Cuban Missile Crisis the following year, which will be discussed in the next chapter.

Attorney General Robert Kennedy, for his part, developed and maintained strong personal ties to Cuban exiles that biographer Evan Thomas maintains were separate from the more formal and "elaborate structure created by Operation Mongoose." Rafael Quintero, in a private interview with the attorney general, made it clear that Cubans felt that they had been betrayed by his brother. One of those who had taken part in the Bay of Pigs invasion but had escaped, Roberto San Román, became almost like a member of his family. The attorney general, however, had no use for the Cuban Revolutionary Council, which was favored by the State Department and the CIA.[53]

For all his public criticism of Castro, President Kennedy in private demonstrated that he was not unaware of some of the reasons for the appeal of the Cuban model. He spoke "rather wistfully (as I have heard him speak before) of Castro's capacity to enlist Cubans in public efforts," noting approvingly the Cuban government's massive literacy campaign in the countryside. "There seem to be two main things" that explain the communist appeal. "One is the power of the police apparatus. The other is the Communist identification with economic and social well-being at the expense of political freedom, which is after all meaningless in so many of these countries." Schlesinger was encouraged to draft a "free world manifesto." "Each weekend 10,000 teachers go into the countryside to conduct a drive against illiteracy. An immense communal effort like this is attractive to people who wish to serve their country. And there seems to be no way of doing it in a country like Peru."[54]

The invasion, according to Schlesinger, had "dissipated the sense of wild and romantic expectation which greeted JFK everywhere in the world."[55] He feared a disinclination to act boldly after the Bay of Pigs invasion, but the administration would move forward with its larger Latin America programs.[56] Secretary of State Dean Rusk, however, hoped that the United States could now "transform the negative political atmosphere" stemming from the Bay of Pigs invasion and "regain a sense of positive initiative, redirecting Latin American attention toward our new affirmative programs." Schlesinger argued in a memo to the president that the Bay of Pigs experience meant that Richard Goodwin should gain more responsibility over Latin American affairs as assistant secretary for inter-American affairs. (This, however, was not to be.) Goodwin, who had clerked for Supreme Court Justice Felix Frankfurter and investigated the quiz show scandals of the late 1950s, was becoming one of the administration members most interested in Latin America.[57]

Following the failure of the invasion, Ambassador Stevenson was sent to Latin America on a three-week trip. Although he rejected the notion that this was a "good-will" trip, he could hardly have been surprised when that was what it turned out to be. Stevenson, to some degree like Schlesinger, was useful to the administration in Latin America. Unlike the year before, he was no longer a private citizen, but that visit had gained him some credibility to accompany his already significant prestige there. He visited the ten capitals of South America only, in the company of Ambassador Ellis Briggs and Harvard professor and future ambassador Lincoln Gordon. He was pleased with the results even if the experience was "as close to suicide as I have come, and as close to total success." He later portrayed himself as having been "a messenger of progress for the common man." More pragmatically, he said privately that he had "pulled some badly scorched chestnuts out of the fire and converted some thinking from negative to positive." He privately worried that it had been "fruitless of my good repute in those parts" and worried that there would be no follow-up. In his report to President Kennedy, he noted that the mostly democratic countries he visited (not including Paraguay) all were "under severe strain and attack," with the partial exceptions of Chile and Uruguay. Colombia was most in line with administration hopes and aspirations. Stevenson was concerned by now with what he considered Castro's popularity and influence, particularly among the young, the urban poor, union members, and the professoriate, which he considered misguided. Influential countries like Argentina and Brazil rejected the notion that Castro was a hemispheric problem and not simply an issue between the United States and Cuba. Nevertheless, Stevenson was pleased to see that despite the Bay of Pigs invasion, Kennedy's Alliance for Progress program stirred some enthusiasm. He assured *Baltimore Sun* editorialist Gerald W. Johnson, "I want to think that we are really on the point of new departures in our relations with Latin America—*really.*" He later promised the Inter-American Press Association that the Alliance for Progress would require "ten years of dedication" to "basic reform and self-help." "If political democracy is to prevail," he continued, "it must bring a better life." Rather than "destructive revolution," what was needed was "peaceful and creative evolution," but one "more rapid, and more comprehensive and touching the lives of more people, than any that our history has ever known."[58]

Stevenson was not alone in traveling to the region in the wake of the Bay of Pigs invasion. Other liberal Democrats who had embraced the Alliance for

Progress agenda included Senate Majority Whip Hubert Humphrey. He praised the Alliance as "probably the most important element of our foreign aid program." As a politician from an agricultural state, he observed and promoted the kinds of institutions (like agricultural cooperatives) in Latin America that he understood to have improved conditions in rural North America.[59]

Other liberals with an interest in Latin America were losing their influence in the administration. Berle, for example, was increasingly isolated, in part because of State Department opposition, in part because of his own feeling that his time had passed. Once the final report of the Latin American task force was delivered in early July, he was out of the picture.[60] Chester Bowles, a liberal who had resisted focusing on the region, also was being bypassed, although not before he had been offered a major opportunity. He was urged to take on "the biggest challenge and the most important job in the Americas— Brazil." But the suggestion for some unknown reason had a "shattering effect" on him, and he said that he "could not possibly consider the Brazilian embassy." Schlesinger was worried about the direction that the administration was taking and told Kennedy that "in his own ineffectual way," Bowles had "been the one champion of fresh ideas and of the New Frontier in the top echelons of State."[61]

In both the short and long term, the Dominican Republic was one of the more problematic Latin American countries for the new administration. Generations of Republican and Democratic leaders had supported Rafael Trujillo, who had received military training from U.S. occupation forces back in the 1920s and who had ruled over the country since 1930. Toward the end of the Eisenhower administration, many actions Trujillo had taken had led to his ostracism within the hemispheric community, the most extreme of which was the attempt to assassinate Venezuelan leader Betancourt. The Organization of American States imposed economic sanctions, which began to damage the Dominican economy. Betancourt and other democratic leaders were urging further action. For a while, Kennedy and others found it easier to seem more even-handed by pairing criticisms of Castro with denunciations of Trujillo. Since Castro had followed Batista, officials wondered, who would follow Trujillo? Although hardly known at the time, the Central Intelligence Agency had been in contact with Dominicans interested in removing Trujillo. The aging dictator was killed in May on a highway on his way to see a mistress. Following his death, a wave of terror swept over the island nation.[62]

In August Schlesinger praised a State Department paper on keeping the army, the Trujillo family, Joaquín Balaguer, and the moderate opposition together "to lay the foundations for democracy." He noted that the "anti-communist liberals" were not "strong enough." (JFK, for his part, had lost some of his "enthusiasm for democracy in Latin America after what has happened these last three days in Brazil," following the resignation of President Jânio Quadros, which will be discussed in the next chapter.) Arturo Morales Carrión, however, "was obviously distressed" over how the administration was addressing the issue. At a meeting with the president, Schlesinger said that Morales Carrión "finally spoke up with sober eloquence to deliver the best talk of the afternoon," deploring "the tendency to write down the opposition." They represented "the only possibility of democratic government in the D.R." He compared them to the "people who made democracy effective in Puerto Rico and Venezuela." If they were "not too well-disciplined at the moment," he reminded those present that they had "lived under tyranny for thirty years." Schlesinger noted that President Kennedy listened "with a mixture of sympathy and impatience." "Yes, yes, but the whole key in all these countries is the emergence of a leader—a liberal figure who can command popular support as against the military and who will carry out social and economic reform." Kennedy contended that "no such figure" had "emerged." An army takeover would "lead straight to Castro." President Kennedy wanted to avoid becoming "over-committed to either side."[63]

Over the next few months, one of the greatest dangers was that the Dominican situation would replicate what happened in Nicaragua, where the murdered Anastasio Somoza García was succeeded by his son Luis in 1956. The short-term alternative to another family dynasty in Latin America was Joaquín Balaguer. John Bartlow Martin, a veteran journalist and Stevenson and Kennedy speechwriter, had developed an interest in the Dominican Republic when he visited in the 1930s. The administration sent him to report on the situation. Martin considered Balaguer "an enigma posing as a poet, writer, [and] intellectual who favors liberty and democracy, dislikes authoritarianism, and for himself wants only to retire from public and end his days with his books," yet the man had been part of the Trujillo government for decades. The United States might need Balaguer, but he would always be viewed "with grave reservations." The Dominican people, Martin concluded, were "unarmed," and "they sometimes seem unmanned." After decades of dictatorship, the Dominican Republic was "a dishearteningly tragic shattered country." U.S. interests meant that the United States should work to create "a pro-Western and reasonably stable, and hopefully somewhat free government in this important area of the world." Martin argued that Balaguer and Trujillo's son Ramfis (as commander-in-chief) were necessary in the short term. Within two years, he thought, elections could be held.[64]

Richard Goodwin appreciated Martin's "excellent reportage," and told President Kennedy that previous understandings of the Dominican situation which Goodwin and others had shared were "unreal." "Unless we are prepared to use military force," Goodwin continued, "and we are not," Trujillo and his allies had the guns and were "prepared to use them to stay in power." The administration's "overriding objective" remained the "prevention of the establishment of a pro-communist or neutralist state." Goodwin noted the dangers of the opposition turning left or Ramfis Trujillo himself becoming a nationalist military leader like Egypt's Gamal Abdel Nasser. He suggested bargaining with the young Trujillo "to create an acceptable democratic facade." "We should negotiate with Ramfis under the shadow of the U.S. fleet. He does not realize how anti-interventionist we have become." The United States could at least make his uncles leave, end the use of terror by the state, and then lift the sanctions.[65]

As it turned out, however, more direct U.S. action was deemed necessary. U.S. ships off the coast of the Dominican Republic, a sight unseen in decades and awkwardly reminiscent of U.S. behavior in what was considered a bygone era, drove the Trujillo family from the island. A council was put in place. For the next year, the Kennedy administration sought to shore up the council's authority, to warn against any action against the interim government, and to prepare for presidential elections. The Dominican Republic was going to be seen as a test of the administration's commitment to democracy, but security concerns always emphasized the need to prevent "another Cuba." Popular anger soon drove Balaguer from the island, and the Kennedy administration would try to find a new leader, preferably one who could credibly be called a reformist democrat.[66]

The Cuban and Dominican situations had largely been inherited from the Eisenhower administration (though one could say in the case of the latter that the roots lay in the Hoover administration, and, in the case of the former, in the Roosevelt administration). Besides not being successful, the approaches the Kennedy administration had used to address them were hardly novel. The commitment to finding new leadership in the Dominican Republic was promising. But the administration and Kennedy himself were rarely patient. It was easy to spend more on the military. Achieving the larger goals of the Alliance for Progress was much more difficult, not least because it meant finding leaders that powerful forces in Latin American countries could live with and that the United States could live with as well. The challenges were only going to multiply.

Chapter 3

The Many Fronts of John F. Kennedy's Latin American Cold War, Part II

The Alliance for Progress ostensibly was a shared hemispheric project. The Kennedy administration needed to find willing allies. Unlike its predecessor, it wanted to be careful with the governments it associated with, or at least the ones it was seen as being associated with. The administration wanted to prevent military coups, not encourage them. The Kennedy administration had committed itself to a larger hemispheric transformation, and the Alliance for Progress became a complicated series of multiple alliances that were negotiated bilaterally. The administration often found it difficult to find leaders who would cooperate with them. The reformist leaders who were in power often did not see eye to eye with the United States. Furthermore, the administration was often baffled by internal Latin American dynamics that they could not control.

Central America in the Kennedy years was as it long had been. Countries with monocultures, low literacy rates, and limited experience with democratic forms of government predominated. It was assumed that these countries would be among the most vulnerable to a revolution along the lines of what was taking place in Cuba. Costa Rica was an exception to the rule, a country that had a consolidated democratic political system that had evolved over generations. For a time, it was hoped that prototypical banana republic Honduras might prove exceptional as well. A pro-American dictator named Somoza was in charge in Nicaragua, as had been true since Franklin Delano Roosevelt was president. But this was not necessarily seen as a good thing in the early Castro era, as many claimed that U.S. support for Batista had produced Castroism. Similar dynamics were thought to apply in Nicaragua. So what would the Kennedy administration and the Alliance for Progress mean for Central America?[1]

Central America had been a focus of U.S. interest for longer than many parts of Latin America, but it would be incorrect to think that U.S. interest in each country was uniform. The United States already had military assistance programs with Guatemala, Honduras, and Nicaragua, but not with Costa Rica, El Salvador, and Panama (always a distinct case, regardless, given the U.S. presence in the Canal Zone). These countries' vulnerability was due not only to their geographical location, socioeconomic inequalities, and slow economic growth, but also because of Castro's particular interest in the area. Although U.S. officials did not believe that the countries in the region could resist an actual invasion without U.S. help, they thought that they could benefit primarily from training in how to enhance internal security against "isolated, spontaneous attempts at internal subversion."[2]

Honduras had experienced frequent unconstitutional transfers of power. In 1956 the military had seized control of the government following an election marked by fraud and the exile of members of the Liberal Party. The military then promised new elections, which were won by Ramón Villeda Morales, a medical doctor who had become a prominent member of the Liberal Party in his forties. He had previously been elected by a slim margin in 1954 but had been prevented from taking power by another military coup. Villeda had ties with current and former U.S. officials affiliated with the Democratic Party, including, most prominently, Adolf Berle, who wrote Kennedy to encourage him to accept an invitation from the Honduran leader to meet even before Kennedy's inauguration. Villeda promised tax reform and social security legislation, and an agrarian reform law in compliance with the Alliance for Progress. The country continued to be plagued by one of the highest rates of illiteracy in the region, which President Kennedy included among the "internal enemies" Honduras had to face. In a meeting at the White House, President Villeda remarked that the two countries were joined in "indeed an alliance" whose "main objective is indeed progress."[3] In March of 1961, as a politically ambitious colonel threatened to topple Villeda, the State Department sent out a message to the U.S. ambassadors in Central America that the United States supported the Honduran president.[4]

Nicaraguan General Anastasio Somoza Debayle spoke with the press in September 1961 and promised that there would be free presidential elections in 1963, putting an end to the Somoza dynasty. (His brother Luis was president.) The Kennedy administration wanted to encourage this, but refused to employ overt pressure to accomplish it. The Inter-American Association for Democracy and Freedom expressed its concerns about the failure of the Kennedy administration to distance itself sufficiently from the Somozas. "We deplore the fraternal relations which seem to continue between our government and the Nicaraguan dictatorship." They also noted the fact that the younger brother continued to lead the National Guard. (The Frente Sandinista de Liberación Nacional [FSLN], a guerrilla movement inspired by native son Augusto César Sandino, who had fought the U.S. Marines in the late 1920s and early 1930s, as well as by Castro's Cuba, was not yet significant.) Following a conversation with an opposition politician in Nicaragua, a State Department official mused, "One always wonders after a conversation such as this whether the U.S. has fully faced the dilemma of weighing the evils of some pressure or intervention now as against the evils likely to arise in the future from a too-slow evolution in Nicaragua."[5]

In South America, the Kennedy administration faced a much more complex range of political situations and possibilities. U.S. Ambassador Allen Stewart considered Venezuela "the key country in Latin America today's fight against communism-Castroism." The recent timing of its transition to democracy, and the personal ties of people like Berle and Schlesinger to its leaders, made Venezuela of particular importance. Schlesinger considered Betancourt "in some respects our best friend and most influential supporter in Latin America." Betancourt struggled to develop popular support among the urban poor. But there were positive signs, as well. He had a strong following in the countryside, where he instituted land reform. His support was also strong among organized labor, which reached many new collective bargaining agreements under Betancourt, and in the middle class. Education improved significantly. The government weathered attempted coups, including one in late June 1961, and the threat from the right at least receded. The armed forces were "more solidly than ever under control of officers determined to support the constitutional civic government." President Kennedy's ties to President Betancourt grew dramatically during the time the two men were in power. Betancourt and Castro, in contrast, had quickly come to see each other as rivals. The threat of an insurgency (rare in a Latin American democracy) and the perception that the country had become "Castro's number one target for subversion" also tended to force the United States to pay more attention to Venezuela. Liberal Democrats gave Betancourt a pass regarding his frequent suspensions of constitutional guarantees because they thought that, as far as the Kennedy administration was concerned, the government must succeed. One might argue that if the friendship between Kennedy and Betancourt had not developed, it would have had to be invented. As Schlesinger told fellow presidential aide Ralph Dungan, letters from Kennedy to Betancourt "should have a). personal warmth and b). evidence of deep commitment to social progress." Over the course of his administration, President Kennedy frequently met and corresponded with the Venezuelan. President Kennedy told him, "Your leadership in the fight for free democracy is one of the great assets of our hemisphere."[6]

Venezuela's neighbor Colombia became one of the most important aid recipients under the Alliance for Progress. Alberto Lleras Camargo, president since 1958, had strongly supported Brazilian President Kubitschek's Operation Pan-America. Colombia had briefly emerged from a period of political violence known simply as *La Violencia* due to an agreement between the two long-standing Liberal and Conservative parties that, to a large degree, limited the country's democratic evolution while providing stability and support for reform. Like Venezuela, Colombia suffered from years of guerrilla warfare, but unlike Venezuela, there was not the same sense of strong ideological competition between Colombia and Cuba, and fears of a guerrilla victory were never pronounced. Also like Venezuela, civilians maintained control of the political system throughout the rest of the Cold War. (Unlike in Venezuela, guerrilla warfare outlasted the 1960s, and even the Cold War.) U.S. aid was consistent, but the consequences were not always those advertised. As historian Amy Offner has recently demonstrated, land reform in Colombia spared the large landowner but displaced those with small plots of land because they were seen as unproductive, leading to an accelerating process of mass movement to the cities.[7]

Schlesinger emphasized the need to make clear the administration's priorities by choosing the right leaders to meet with and host. It was clear to him that Betancourt in Venezuela and Lleras Camargo should be at the top of the list, and so he was pleased when the two countries became the first (and, as it turned out ultimately, only) South American countries Kennedy visited as president.[8] When the administration feared it could not visit both countries, the Colombian president make it clear that it would be okay if the North American president skipped Colombia, "since Betancourt needed visit more."[9]

Chile posed rather different challenges. President Alessandri had been an ideal Latin American president for Eisenhower. Had he been elected in the early 1950s, he might have been valued even more highly by that administration than Venezuela's Pérez Jiménez. But times were changing in Chile, and the challenge of the left there was unlike that virtually anywhere else in the hemisphere. Chile had a long tradition of political pluralism, and a number of left-wing political parties had grown accustomed to electoral politics. Even the Communist Party, which had been outlawed in the early Cold War era, had make a comeback, and, in coalition with Socialist Senator Salvador Allende, had come 40,000 votes shy of winning the presidency in 1958. Traditional parties were in decline, and U.S. goals could no longer be met by embracing the status quo. The Kennedy administration's identification "with the reform movements in Latin America" put it at odds with Alessandri, however, creating resentment on the Chilean leader's part as the administration believed that he was dragging his feet. Senate Majority Leader Mike Mansfield, D-Mont., warned that, based on conversations with a friend with "extensive personal and financial interests in Chile," the "Chilean man in the street" believed the "U.S. government" wanted "President Alessandri to fail."[10]

Many in the Kennedy administration considered the Alessandri government "inadequate," but knew they needed to continue to support him. The "political risk" of refusing any aid to the Alessandri government was too high. By the end of 1962 the administration already was focusing on the 1964 presidential election in Chile. It was assumed that if Alessandri remained intransigent and rejected reform, the appeal of the extreme left in the presidential election would only grow. The Kennedy administration focused on the future, working to press centrists and even rightists to work with reformist and progressive forces, as it sought to demonstrate the advantages of U.S.-backed reform in the short term.[11]

As frustration with Alessandri grew, Democratic congressmen and Kennedy aides developed ties with the reformist Christian Democratic Party, a fairly young political party that drew its inspiration from the social teachings of Catholic humanism and whose popularity in a pluralistic and divided political system was growing significantly. In April 1962, Eugene McCarthy, D-Minn., Humphrey, and William Fulbright, D-Ark., had lunch with Senators Radomiro Tomic and Eduardo Frei. The Christian Democrats sought to identify their goals with those of the United States.[12] The United States was becoming directly involved in the internal political life of Chile and would continue to be so for the next decade. President Kennedy, presidential aide Ralph Dungan, and others considered the party "the best hope for popular democracy in Latin America."[13]

It is important to understand the Kennedy administration's attitude toward and response to military coups in South America. Certainly, its early statements suggested a fairly categorical rejection of any new governments established through military action and a belief in maintaining a certain distance from those already in place. U.S. policy in the Kennedy years was not consistently prodemocratic, but it was certainly not pro-authoritarian. A country's particular circumstances, or at least perceptions of threats therein, did lead the administration to adopt particular approaches.[14] The Kennedy administration was more active in trying to prevent military coups than it was in fomenting them. That it failed on numerous occasions is important, but it does not, in any case, suggest a preference for military governments. In Venezuela, for example, the ambassador made it clear to U.S. military attachés that they could not "tolerate any activity and opposition to the established government."[15]

In other Latin American countries where constitutional processes were interrupted, the Kennedy administration also hoped for a gradual return to democracy. Argentina, for example, remained problematic because the military refused to accept a truly competitive political system, which inevitably would have meant the return to power of deposed populist leader Juan Perón. Secretary of State Rusk had told the embassy in Buenos Aires that "continued and extreme military pressure upon government would be contrary to U.S. interests." The U.S. ambassador had affirmed the U.S. position that the Kennedy administration "would deplore overthrow of constitutional government by military." Schlesinger deplored what he called the "slow-motion effort" by the Argentine military "to force out Frondizi." He was convinced that the Argentine leader himself was too committed to "economic orthodoxy." "For most Argentine workers," moreover, "the only time they can remember when government cared about them was the time of Perón." Fondizi was, nevertheless, "better than a right-wing military regime." When Frondizi allowed Peronists to participate in an election, the military moved. Schlesinger worried that the new government would not "attack the conditions which account for the resurgence of Peronism." Kennedy's aide worried that this would encourage conservative military groups to overthrow progressive civilian governments in Peru, Venezuela, the Dominican Republic, and Ecuador, "especially if there is no sign of disapproval from the United States." Schlesinger predicted that the continued refusal to allow Peronists to participate in the political process would drive them to the left (as, indeed, did happen for many young Peronists over the course of the 1960s).[16] Following the March 1962 overthrow of Frondizi, Assistant Secretary Edwin Martin, Dick Goodwin, Ralph Dungan, and Schlesinger urged "a public display of disapproval." The Kennedy administration did not rush to recognize the new government the military had put in place. But it did not feel that it could be as categorical as Venezuela's Betancourt, who vehemently denounced the Argentine coup. By the time the United States restored relations, dozens of countries, many of them democracies, had already done so. Although the Argentine government lacked a timetable for a return to civilian rule, the Kennedy administration did not believe that it had any means of influencing it to create one.[17]

Liberal Democrats like Minnesota Senator Hubert Humphrey lamented the fall of Frondizi. He had not expressed concern regarding the Argentine's failure to support U.S. policy regarding Cuba. Instead, he regretted his economic orthodoxy and his failure to address "the real needs of his people—low-cost housing, inflation, wages, and the cost of living." Humphrey worried that if the Alliance could not succeed in Argentina, where could it succeed? Although he maintained confidence in the Alliance, he worried that in the Argentine case, the democratic forces were too fragmented. As others noted, Frondizi had offered more austerity than reform. And, in any case, the coup in Argentina had more to do with Argentine history than the Cold War per se. The exile, Juan Perón, continued to be the main issue in that country. Liberal Democratic dreams were largely irrelevant in Argentina.[18]

Another event of critical importance in the early Kennedy presidency took place in Peru. Administration officials pinned their hopes on the Popular Revolutionary American Party (APRA), founded in 1924 by Víctor Raúl Haya de la Torre. Haya had never been elected president, but he remained, as far as U.S. officials were concerned, the leading anti-communist reformist leader. As Schlesinger noted in a letter to a mutual friend, "Haya should not doubt the fact that the Administration contains many people who look on the aspirations of APRA with sympathy and who regard Haya himself as one of the great democratic leaders in Latin America." U.S. Ambassador James Loeb, a former leader of the Americans for Democratic Action who had attended the 1950 IADF conference in Havana, warned Schlesinger that APRA was not the only democratic party in Peru. Nevertheless, the administration continued to focus on the party. But APRA (and the Kennedy administration) had a problem. APRA had staged a rebellion decades before, resulting in the death of members of the armed forces. These memories remained strong. As in the case of Argentina, one had to know more than the Cold War to understand the political situation. At least some in the State Department recognized that the armed forces might not accept an APRA victory. But Ambassador Loeb thought that a coup "against the strongest anti-Communist political force in the nation would be disastrous for Peru and for the United States."[19]

In the end, the weight of history hung heavily on Peru as well, and the military staged its coup following Haya's victory in the June 1962 election with only 33 percent of the vote. For the Kennedy administration, the use of U.S.-provided Sherman tanks to tear down "presidential palace's iron gates" gave the misleading impression that the United States supported the coup. The administration sought to make as forceful a statement as it could. The United States hoped that by refusing to recognize the government, it could force them to set up a timetable for new elections. Frances Grant praised the administration for providing "unequivocal evidence of our total repudiation of the military 'coup' in Latin America." While Kennedy was convinced that it was the right thing to do, as well, he soon regretted putting his own "presidential prestige" on the line. Both the coup and the U.S. response to it created difficulties for the administration. Averell Harriman insisted that the recalled Ambassador Loeb should return to Lima; otherwise, "it would look as if we were abandoning our policy of opposition to military dictatorships." Schlesinger found "force in this argument." JFK later insisted that he did not regret his vocal opposition to the military coup in Peru. But by 1 August he feared that the administration had "staked our prestige on reversing a situation which could not be reversed." Instead, the administration needed to demonstrate that its policies were leading to changed military policies. Schlesinger hoped that the United States would not "retreat too quickly," thereby nullifying "the gains made." In August a timetable for elections was set.[20] By October, President Kennedy was willing to restore military assistance to Peru. And elections were held the following year, in keeping with administration policy. Oddly enough, historians have tended to ignore the fact that the Peruvian case ended up being the most effective example of Kennedy administration policy in response to a military takeover.[21]

Following the coup in Peru, the administration aimed for a coordinated policy in which U.S. military missions reinforced the Kennedy administration's support for constitutional democracy. U.S. civilian and military officials were particularly active in this regard in Venezuela. In his meetings with Venezuelan military men, Ambassador Stewart found confirmation that contact with U.S. officers, both personally and in training programs, was "promoting more modern, professional, and pro-democratic attitude among local military." Venezuelan military leaders sought to assure President Kennedy that the military realized that "a dictatorship was not the best solution to the problems of the armed forces." Ambassador Stewart remained staunch in his support for military assistance programs, not only because of the benefits he mentioned, but also because of the pragmatic concerns that the military stay tied to the United States, given the role the military could be expected to continue playing in the region.[22]

Brazil became a focus of U.S. security concerns during the Kennedy years. Brazil had been the most important Latin American ally the United States had during World War II under dictator Getúlio Vargas. In the postwar period, Brazil was urbanizing and industrializing rapidly, but it suffered from vast socioeconomic inequality that hindered the development of the democracy that was established at the end of the war. Brazil was more democratic than it had ever been; its electorate was expanding rapidly as the cities grew. But this was viewed by many more traditional Brazilian politicians as unfortunate, and a sense that things were getting out of control unnerved the military and the elite, and, to some degree, the middle class as well.

Brazil was considered essential. "Just as the future of democracy of Asia depends considerably on the example of India," Schlesinger wrote President Kennedy, "so the future of democracy in Latin America depends considerably on the example of Brazil. The competition for the future of Latin America is between the Brazilian way and the Castro way."[23] NSC staffer Samuel Belk suggested to McGeorge Bundy that Brazil could serve "as a counter to Cuba in Latin America." It was "the only LA country possessing the potentialities of a great power." It "must be the example for LA." He suggested that if the newly elected leader Jânio Quadros chose a neutralist path, he did not think "we should try to persuade him." "In truth some of our best friends are neutralists."[24] But Quadros proved to be far too unpredictable even for his ostensible allies. He was a maverick politician who had risen rapidly to prominence in the second half of the 1950s. He had a record as an effective administrator as São Paulo mayor and governor, and he projected an image as being above party. Quadros impressed future U.S. Ambassador to Brazil

Lincoln Gordon by spending three hours with him and Stevenson instead of the one hour allotted to him during the June 1961 visit. Over the next few months, however, he tried his countrymen's and the Kennedy administration's patience. After some initial enthusiasm for Quadros, President Kennedy himself was soon disillusioned. "We've done everything for that son of a bitch, yet he kicks us in the shins every time he has a chance," President Kennedy complained privately. A combative attitude toward his opponents in the Brazilian Congress made it difficult for Quadros to accomplish anything, while the foreign policy actions he took to establish his independence, like awarding Castro's right-hand man, Ernesto "Che" Guevara, the highest medal the Brazilian government could bestow, the Order of the Southern Cross, alienated many Brazilian politicians who recently had been his supporters. In an attempt to demonstrate his popular support, he resigned the presidency in August, issuing a statement that farcically echoed the suicide note of Getúlio Vargas seven years before. Historians have long assumed that Quadros thought that popular pressures would enable him to be brought back with enhanced executive powers to push through favored policies. But his resignation failed to stir the Brazilian masses.[25]

Quadros presumably thought his fellow politicians would support him, considering that his successor was Vice President João Goulart, whom Schlesinger dismissed as "a left-wing demagogue . . . who has all of Jânio's drawbacks and none of his abilities." (Schlesinger feared the other option was a right-wing government, which would be "splendid on foreign policy but wholly uninterested in tackling Brazil's social and economic problems.") Goulart, a member of a prominent ranching family from Vargas's home state, was a Vargas protégé who had made his name in the labor party Vargas had created. Goulart had inevitably worked at times with communists who played a role in organized labor. Goulart served as Vargas's labor minister during Vargas's time as an elected leader before being forced to resign over his support for a dramatic increase in the minimum wage. He was no radical; nevertheless, he has often been portrayed as more ideologically consistent than he was. Goulart was consistently distrusted in military and mainstream political circles. U.S. officials had shared this distrust since the 1950s.[26] The Central Intelligence Agency predicted, however, that the Brazilian army "would be unlikely to allow him to exert real control of Brazilian policy."[27] The United States was reluctant to even make a statement in support of constitutional processes for fear of offending "our friends" who were anti-Goulart because of his "known communist sympathies." It seemed prudent to adhere to the principle of noninterference.[28]

Once it became clear that Goulart would become president, albeit with reduced and unclear authority, shared with a prime minister whose responsibilities were also not well defined, the United States sought to act "on assumption there has been no break in continuity [in the] traditionally close and cordial relations between our two countries." The Kennedy administration adopted a wait-and-see attitude toward the Goulart government as it defined itself, even though the "political antecedents of Goulart himself could scarcely be less promising from U.S. point of view." It was feared that those who hoped that his new responsibilities would have a "moderating and sobering effect" on Goulart were guilty of wishful thinking. The U.S. embassy was waiting to see whether he would "live down his fellow-traveling past."[29] It was suggested that Kennedy might send a message to Goulart, paying "particular tribute to strength and resiliency Brazilian national character and democratic institutions which have enabled nation surmount bloodshed and without sacrifice traditional democratic principles."[30] Although the military had supported an "unpopular cause," "ostensibly acting in contravention of constitution," they "were beyond doubt sincerely motivated by desire preserve ultimate democratic values."[31] By the end of 1961, U.S. intelligence estimates suggested that while communist influence was bound to grow under Goulart, it would still be quite limited. Goulart was not likely to do anything to upset conservative politicians or military leaders. He was seen as a survivor and a "shrewd" politician. Unfortunately, conservative politicians never warmed to him. Goulart's reduced powers made the already difficult Brazilian political system all but completely unworkable.[32]

Lincoln Gordon became U.S. ambassador. His role in the creation of the Alliance for Progress is sometimes understated, although not by Teodoro Moscoso, who referred to it as "your baby." He turned down an opportunity to be the assistant secretary for inter-American affairs, in part because he recognized the limits of his knowledge of other parts of Latin America beyond Brazil, and because he would have more independence in Rio de Janeiro. Gordon got to know Kennedy after becoming ambassador because of the president's interest in what was going on in the South American country. Gordon spent a good deal of time over the next few years keeping Kennedy informed about what was going on in Brazil. In the long run, although he would spend five years there, he found the experience somewhat disappointing. Gordon had hoped that being ambassador to Brazil would involve "working serenely at the implementation of the Alliance for Progress with an efficient administration led by Mr. Quadros." But by the time he arrived, there was a quite different political scenario in Brazil, with a conservative Congress, an ideologically inconsistent president with reduced powers who was perceived as a dangerous leftist, an unusual amount of social ferment in a country unaccustomed to pluralistic democracy, and inflation spiraling out of control. Gordon spent the Kennedy years looking for people he considered to be reliable allies.[33]

Former Brazilian President Kubitschek spoke with Kennedy and told him that he knew Goulart "extremely well" and "could say that Dr. Goulart was [a] careful man and not a communist." Given Goulart's background as "a wealthy landowner, he would lean toward conservative policies." Brazil "would remain a truly democratic nation." Brazilian communists were "at worst an active minority." Kubitschek noted that he hoped to return to the presidency in 1965, and that he was "confident that President Kennedy would still be in the White House." They "would still do great things together."[34]

Goulart was not himself "anti-American," although he was not as enthusiastic about the Alliance for Progress as the United States would have liked. Many of his supporters were strong nationalists, while many of his opponents were pro-U.S. (if not necessarily pro-Alliance).[35] Kubitschek's more positive opinion of Goulart, in the long run, never seemed to matter to many U.S. officials as much as did that of Guanabara Governor Carlos Lacerda. Lacerda, a former communist turned right-winger, was considered by some to be a "good friend of the United States [and] firmly anti-communist." Considering the fact that he had conspired against every elected government since 1950, it seems strange to characterize him as "publicly committed to democratic policies." Many people in the U.S. embassy in Brazil, as well as in the State Department, considered his "appraisal of the Brazilian scene for the most part accurate," even though they were aware of what was called his "blind personal ambition." But many U.S. officials were suspicious of Lacerda and remained so. In the fall of 1961, for example, L. D. Battle was not certain that there should be a meeting between President Kennedy and Governor Lacerda because of his singular responsibility "for the political tensions which preceded Quadros's resignation." He was, however, "the most dedicated and outspoken anti-Communist in Brazilian public life today."[36]

Naturally enough, Goulart himself tried to shape the U.S opinion of him. He told Ambassador Gordon that he and his government represented "forces of moderation" trying to avoid a revolution, "which would be disastrous for Brazil." Gordon suggested that Goulart would "not knowingly pave way for Communist infiltration, although number of his appointments continue[d to] give grounds for concern." Goulart thought that "by claiming loyalty of the masses who would otherwise seek more extreme solutions," he was limiting the influence of the Communist Party. U.S. officials may have wanted to be reassured, but they remained largely unconvinced. "Through him," Bond wrote, "they may ultimately reach power." Nevertheless, the United States thought that the new government was "the best" they could expect given "present circumstances in Brazil."[37]

In the early months following Goulart's rise to the presidency with reduced powers, the embassy in Brazil was cautiously optimistic. Gordon admired some members of Goulart's cabinet and mentioned, in a phrase that later became infamous, that there were "a considerable number of islands of administrative sanity with which we can work constructively." But he certainly had not yet soured on the Brazilian president himself. In March of 1962, Gordon wrote that Goulart had "succeeded gradually in convincing Brazilians that he seeks moderate, though slightly left of center government." Goulart's main concern was that the presidency regain its former authority as the hybrid government remained unwieldy, making the government ineffective in a time of rising inflation.[38] U.S. officials were correct in seeing Goulart as having no head for planning. They tended, however, to exaggerate his demagogic and radical tendencies.[39]

Some have argued that the peak of U.S.-Brazilian relations during the Goulart years occurred during the Brazilian president's Washington visit.[40] Schlesinger sought to ensure that Kennedy understood the importance of Brazil and that the president would address what he saw as Brazil's (and Goulart's) somewhat simplistic nationalist understandings of U.S.-Latin American relations, "considerably confused by the New Frontier and the Alliance for Progress." Goulart needed to be convinced that the United States under Kennedy backed progressive governments. Brazil was going to play an essential role in the success of the Alliance. Nevertheless, Schlesinger warned, Brazil was in a volatile situation, with potentially "disastrous consequences, least objectionable likely to be a military dictatorship." The potential threat to U.S. hemispheric interests in a country as large and important as Brazil were always so strong that many across the U.S. political spectrum consistently overestimated them. But U.S. officials were hopeful that the interaction between Goulart and Kennedy would have a moderating influence on the Brazilian leader and that he would leave the United States much more committed to the Alliance for Progress than he had ever been.[41] Goulart urged Kennedy aide Pierre Salinger to convince the president to visit the Brazilian northeast and meet with members of the peasant leagues, who could tell him that they were not communists.[42] Dungan, planning a trip to Brazil for the president, also suggested to him that he go to the northeastern city of João Pessoa and meet with members of the peasant leagues, "who were not communist and would hope for U.S. aid once land [was] divided into small farms."[43]

Many have emphasized the bond between Goulart and President Kennedy that supposedly developed at this time, but the relationship was, to say the least, one-sided. Having set aside significant time to speak privately with Goulart, Kennedy only spent an hour with him before cutting short the conversation and joining his other aides. He also preferred to meet Goulart with others on the following day, when he had initially intended to spend time alone with him. Schlesinger thought that President Kennedy found the Brazilian "boring." Schlesinger himself dismissed him as an "empty figure."[44]

Kennedy was worried that his opposition to the Peruvian coup might be misconstrued by other Brazilians. Kennedy's perception (encouraged increasingly by Ambassador Gordon) was that Brazilian president João Goulart would himself subvert the constitution and would have to be prevented from doing so by military defenders of the constitutional order. In comparing the two situations, Kennedy aide Richard Goodwin suggested that "A military action to save constitutionality" would be "fine."[45] While dining at Goodwin's with Schlesinger and Bundy, Gordon noted that he did not want the administration "to take a rigorously anti-military position because he feels that in Brazil the military might become the only salvation." Though "pessimistic about Brazilian prospects," Gordon insisted that one point of hope was Goulart's "great admiration for JFK and his desire to stay on good terms with him."[46] There were conspiracies in support of deposing Goulart as early as July 1962. Certainly, it is noteworthy how comfortable people felt talking about them early on with the U.S. ambassador. But it must be emphasized that Kennedy administration policy was based on expectations of what Goulart himself would do in a country where the stakes were high.

Rumors of Gordon's resignation in July led him to inform Afonso Arinos, the new foreign minister, that Gordon's "principal purpose in coming to Brazil" had been to make a "success" of the Alliance for Progress. He would stay as long as there "was some hope of doing this." Cooperation, however, "could not be unilateral" nor "limited to the Foreign Office." U.S. officials were increasingly frustrated with what they saw as the Brazilian president's lack of "understanding of economic or of broader policy problems." Foreign Service officer Niles Bond saw little hope of him putting significant reforms in place. On the other hand, the embassy thought it unlikely that the armed forces would allow Goulart to adopt any unconstitutional measures.[47] But the administration itself, as we shall see in the next chapter, remained torn over what to do with Goulart.

More generally, Schlesinger worried that Kennedy was "getting impatient about his liberal advisers."[48] Richard Goodwin, for example, whose interest in Latin America was growing, remained a somewhat marginal figure in the Kennedy administration. He was perceived as having "free-wheeling administrative habits," and as unwilling to use the proper channels. President Kennedy recognized that his appointment beyond certain levels was "politically impossible." By convincing the president to appoint Edwin Martin as assistant secretary of state, George Ball hoped to "clip Goodwin's wings," according to Schlesinger, "at a time when, as the President later said to me, he was not particularly thinking about Latin American affairs." Martin, however, proved to be "less cautious on political matters than Dick and I feared."[49] The situation remained volatile; by May of 1962, Goodwin told Schlesinger that he was leaving. What Martin was allowing "him to do" was "negligible." When he was in the White House, he had spent fourteen hours a day working on the Alliance for Progress. But he had not been able to work on it in the previous two months. "I have hardly been asked to a meeting dealing with Alliance problems or with the aid program."[50]

Schlesinger thought that the "main—and persisting—error of the Kennedy administration has been the appeasement of business."[51] "Wherever we have gone wrong—from Cuba to fiscal policy—it has been because we have not had sufficient confidence in the New Frontier approach to impose it on the government." He expressed concern regarding the "[p]ower of the permanent government and its ability to sabotage and dominate the political government."[52] By late summer 1962, Schlesinger was more convinced than ever that "the old continuities, the Eisenhower-Dulles continuities, are beginning to reassert themselves."[53]

Schlesinger continued to focus on Latin America, and begrudged the time, resources, and effort spent on Africa, where "Communism and democracy are equally irrelevant." "[I]f we could add the talent and resources presently invested in Africa to our effort in Latin America, we might stand a chance of succeeding with the Alliance for Progress. And both the ideas of communism and democracy are relevant to Latin America."[54]

As Goodwin left the White House for new responsibilities at the State Department, Ralph Dungan began to focus on Latin America as well. The presidential aide had worked with Kennedy in the Senate. After Kennedy's election, Dungan became Kennedy's "chief talent scout." If some thought that Dungan would keep an eye on "the crazy nuts on Latin America," he proved himself to be equally devoted to reform. His work on Latin America was a "natural extension of Ralph's Agency for International Development assignment," Schlesinger noted, "since obviously the Alliance for Progress represents the heart of our Latin American policy." National Security Adviser McGeorge Bundy preferred that only one person be in charge of the region. But their strengths (and weaknesses) were different. Schlesinger retained his focus on politics. Dungan focused on economic issues during the Kennedy years. Schlesinger's impatience with bureaucracy, and with the State Department in particular, remained an issue throughout the rest of the Kennedy administration. Dungan, for his part, was "much more of a believer in channels." (As Johnson's ambassador to Chile, as we shall see, Dungan took a dramatically different approach.)[55]

Schlesinger had begun to recognize the "larger and more disheartening fact—that is, there is no such thing as the New Frontier." The administration had "promised the American people a new beginning—not only new men but new ideas, new moods, new values, new policies." There had been few "bold new initiatives" since the Bay of Pigs invasion. Kennedy was "repeatedly constrained by an ever vivid sense of political reality." He needed to pay less attention to "Establishment" thinking and follow the logic of his campaign and "support his own instincts." Then things would be "in a much happier position."[56]

Schlesinger warned Dungan that the Alliance was "reverting to the Eisenhower policy of subordinating everything to the creation of a climate" for foreign investment.[57] He complained to Goodwin that "being right on Cuba 18 months ago" had "really benefitted me very little in the way of winning increased responsibility or respect." "I have the feeling that the President somewhat discounts my views, primarily because he regards me as a claimant agency for standardized liberalism, partly also because he considers me to be, after all, an intellectual and insufficiently practical and realistic." Dungan too felt that "he was being cut off of the main decisions in foreign policy—that often he would carry things up to a point and then not be present at the climax." Schlesinger and Dungan both lamented their lack of involvement in discussions on Cuba, "though both of us feel that we have things to contribute—both a knowledge of Latin America and a commitment to the President." The president, Schlesinger suggested, was being too "passive," accepting "whomever he finds at the meetings." Bundy is responsible for the "guest list," thinking "perhaps rightly—that, with the President and himself, the White House is sufficiently represented."[58]

The Cuban Missile Crisis was and was not a turning point in Kennedy administration relations with Latin America, as it was and was also not about Cuba itself. The Kennedy administration had continued with many attempts to undermine and even get rid of Castro, even as the Central Intelligence Agency warned against believing a popular uprising against Castro was likely. Secretary of Defense Robert McNamara said many years later that Cuba had good reason to fear an invasion in the fall of 1962. The Soviets, for their part, were expanding their commitment to Cuba, as they had promised following the Bay of Pigs invasion. Although the Kennedy administration never accepted the idea, to some degree the Soviet Union was correct in saying that it intended the missiles to be installed for defensive purposes, to defend an ally Soviet interest in enhancing its global reputation could not allow it to abandon. (The Soviet Union also wanted to make the nuclear balance less in favor of the United States, of course, and it wanted to make the United States understand the threat the USSR felt from Western missiles in Europe.) If the missiles remained in Cuba, however, it was feared that Castro would be able to pressure other Latin American governments to do his bidding. Attorney General Robert Kennedy, for his part, argued that the United States would not have a better chance to remove Castro than it did in October 1962. (Fortunately, efforts to give the United States a pretext during the crisis by attacking a Russian tanker, encouraged by the attorney general and to be executed by his close friend Roberto San Román, were stopped.) CIA Director John McCone, for his part, sought to find a way to get the Cubans to stop exporting revolution in Latin America. Secretary of State Rusk noted that the Soviet action violated the security agreement known as the Rio Pact. But he also suggested that a U.S. invasion of Cuba to remove the missiles could lead to the fall of a number of unspecified Latin American governments. The United States sought to communicate with Castro about the greater danger the missiles posed to his government's survival. But there was also a frequently expressed concern that what was at stake was not really Latin America, but the control of West Berlin. Kennedy himself frequently expressed concern that if the United States attacked Cuba, the Soviets would attack West Berlin. And he noted the Western European lack of interest in Cuba and lack of appreciation for U.S. concerns regarding Cuba among its European allies. President Kennedy ultimately worried that the risks were too great, and that the threat posed by the weapons did not justify nuclear war. His choice of a blockade, backed by the Organization of American States in keeping with the terms of the Rio Pact, as a grateful Secretary of State Rusk emphasized, was intended to avert that end, as was President Kennedy's public promise not to invade Cuba and his secret decision to remove missiles from Turkey. But even liberal Democrats and their allies like Venezuela's Betancourt worried that the no-invasion pledge might be construed as implying acceptance of the Castro government remaining in power for an indefinite period of time. In any case, few in the early 1960s imagined that the Castro government would survive.[59]

Liberals in the administration with an interest in Latin America were often sidelined during the crisis. Schlesinger's involvement was, in his own words, "peripheral." Dungan, just back from a trip to prepare for a presidential visit to Brazil, which had been months in preparation, had not even been informed that the trip had been postponed.[60] Stevenson was brought in late to discussions in the Cuban Missile Crisis, and he was not aware that some of his ideas had been discussed and dismissed. At the United Nations, he always had been more of a spokesman for U.S. policy than a policy maker; nevertheless, he had pushed for multilateral action involving the Organization of American States, since the United Nations would not act. Stevenson urged a political solution rather than a military one, suggesting "neutralization" and "demilitarization" as labels around which to gain international support. Stevenson had been willing to agree to changes in U.S. missile basing in Turkey and Italy, and even considered giving up Guantánamo if the Soviets would pull out all military forces from Cuba. Ultimately, his plan assumed that only Soviet support kept Castro in power and that his government would fall quickly without it. Stevenson is best remembered for stating at the UN itself that he would wait for the Soviet answer to his question regarding the missiles "until hell freezes over." This perceived dramatic and heroic moment notwithstanding, Stevenson felt dejected following the successful conclusion of the crisis when Kennedy administration officials undermined him by leaking information that sought to portray him as a would-be appeaser. The president ended up issuing a statement denying that this was a fair characterization, but the damage had been done.[61]

In the months following the Cuban Missile Crisis, ordinary Americans and others on the right lamented that Kennedy had not seized the opportunity to invade Cuba and remove Castro. Liberal Democrats, however, like Minnesota Representative Donald Fraser, a veteran of the late 1940s anti-communist struggle in his home state, thought the crisis had created more opportunities to "isolate Castro, reduce his influence, and strengthen the forces of freedom in Latin America." The Kennedy administration could not accept coexistence, but it would not invade the country either. Its policy largely emphasized increasing isolation in the region and containment of Castro's influence in the hemisphere, while expecting that, in the long run, the cost to the Soviet Union would prove too great.[62]

The war against Cuba continued on many fronts. Although Operation Mongoose itself was phased out by January and Lansdale removed, many covert operations continued, including various assassination attempts against Castro himself that never got very far. The CIA station in Miami was the largest in the world. The Kennedy administration had promised not to invade Cuba, but there was no formal agreement and there were frequent internal discussions regarding ways to get around the pledge.[63]

If at the time the Cuban Missile Crisis was largely seen as an administration success, it had a number of different unfortunate consequences. It certainly seemed to confirm Kennedy's characterization of the Cuban leader as a Soviet puppet. And it helped the administration further its efforts to isolate Cuba. But thinking of Castro as a Soviet puppet clouded strategic thinking and prevented the United States from taking advantage of the tensions between Cuba and the Soviet Union in the years following the missile crisis. And the appearance of "toughness" as the reason for success rather than the actual essential but covert diplomacy did not advance a thoughtful understanding of what U.S. options really were internationally.[64]

The Kennedy administration had needed Latin American support during the crisis, and, by and large, had received it. The isolation of those in the administration who most focused on Latin America was a bad sign for the future of the Alliance for Progress, as was the inability of many in the administration to understand a figure like João Goulart. But, for much of 1962 at least, the Kennedy administration's signals regarding new military governments were generally consistent. The broader picture of the future of Latin American reformism was uncertain.

Chapter 4

Kennedy's Unfinished Legacy and Intended and Unintended Consequences

In the last year of the Kennedy presidency, no liberal Democrat provided a more cutting critique of Kennedy administration policy in Latin America than JFK's former director of Food for Peace, George McGovern, elected to the Senate representing South Dakota in 1962. His maiden speech in the following year addressed what he called "Our Castro Fixation versus the Alliance for Progress." He contended that Castro's influence had declined since he had tied his fortunes so closely to those of the Soviet Union. Meanwhile, the United States had lost its focus on "the real dangers and challenges of Latin America," a region "beset by misery, sickness, injustice, illiteracy, malnutrition, and misrule." He rejected the notion that Khrushchev or Castro were responsible for the unrest in the region. He invoked his own encounter with poverty in the Brazilian northeast. As McGovern biographer Thomas Knock has written, "Latin America formed the pivot of McGovern's gravest concerns." The United States needed to address the deeper questions that "Castro's appeal" posed and engage in "the tough and sometimes painful tasks of making the Alliance for Progress work." He praised Kennedy for his "policy of wisdom and restraint since the Bay of Pigs fiasco," not least of all during the Cuban Missile Crisis. McGovern reaffirmed his faith in the Alliance, as well as in the Peace Corps and Food for Peace, but he thought that his former boss was as much to blame as his fellow politicians for the "Castro fixation."[1]

Ever a glass-half-full personality, Senator Hubert Humphrey in early 1963 reported on his trips to Latin America, arguing that while the Alliance had gotten off to a "slow, and often confused start," both U.S. and Latin American officials had recognized what had to be done and were beginning to see results. He emphasized the larger importance of Latin America to the Cold War struggle. He argued that communist influence on Latin American campuses was waning. He saw hope in Central American efforts at economic integration, greater availability of low-cost housing, a noncommunist labor movement, and a reformist Catholic Church. Given the predominance of the rural sector, he argued that most attention needed to be paid to it.[2]

In early 1963, President Kennedy continued to insist that Latin America occupied "a primary place in our policy considerations. Europe was relatively secure and prosperous while the situation in Latin America required our best efforts and attention."[3] Even within the administration, however, Schlesinger feared a certain complacency in response to Latin America's "passion for change." He emphasized his belief that Venezuela represented a "heartening example" of "social progress within a framework of political democracy." "Peaceful change by democratic means may not excite those who believe that apocalyptic transformations are required to usher in the millennium." He contrasted "the way of Cuba with the way of Venezuela."[4]

The Alliance for Progress certainly was running into difficulties at home and abroad. Senator Morse, who took pride in his early support for economic aid for the region in the late Eisenhower years, was "as disappointed as anyone by its seeming lack of achievement to date." He cited the "warning signal to Congress" from former Colombia President Alberto Lleras Camargo and former Brazilian President Kubitschek "that substantial changes" were needed. Morse was not interested "in preserving governments whose policies make the rich richer and the poor poorer despite American aid." A focus on internal security was misplaced, for that could only be achieved when "economic freedom and democratic procedures are granted to their masses." Morse faulted the lack of a "multi-lateral approach" and "clear-cut economic goals."[5]

The perception of threat in Latin America continued to vary greatly. In Chile, the stakes were high. The Kennedy administration continued to pressure the conservative president to embrace reforms that were hardly to his liking, although he was not averse to accepting U.S. aid. U.S. officials were arguing for a need for aid programs which would have an impact on the 1964 presidential elections. Otto Kerican, U.S. Agency for International Development economic adviser in Chile, wanted "*at once* [emphasis in the original], a New Deal for Chile's poor, underprivileged, rural and urban masses." They had to be shown that "their aspirations for a better life can become a reality under a non-Marxist government." U.S. officials were convinced that there was no possibility another conservative candidate would be elected. The United States did not want to be perceived as seeking to maintain the status quo in Chile. A non-Marxist and left-of-center candidate was the only option. Many liberal Democratic senators and congressmen, as well as many in the Kennedy administration, had already developed strong ties to members of the Christian Democratic Party and a strong admiration for what the party stood for. Senator Eduardo Frei had breakfasted with presidential aide Dungan; Frei praised Dungan outrageously, saying, "Believe me, it was most encouraging for us that there is someone in the White House and so close to the President, who is as well-informed, as objective, and with such a broad view of the problem as you." He continued, "To the extent that forces of democracy and progress, capable of making changes, even the most daring ones, can count on men such as you, the salvation of Latin America will be entirely possible."[6]

Many hoped that the Radical and the Christian Democratic parties could join together in a reformist coalition to challenge the presumed coalition of Marxist parties, but most recognized that this was unlikely. The United States also was not willing yet to back a Christian Democratic candidate on his own, despite the young party's impressive growth. Defeating Allende, most U.S. observers thought, was the United States' highest priority. U.S. Ambassador Charles Cole warned that a victory by the left-wing coalition FRAP would "very probably, end democratic government in Chile." To prevent such an occurrence, "U.S. aid of all sorts should be thought of as an important element in the political struggle in Chile."[7]

Political counselor in the Santiago embassy Norman M. Pearson was one of those who hoped to see a coalition formed between the traditional Liberal and Conservative parties and the middle-class reform parties, the Radical and the Christian Democratic parties. The Christian Democrats were convinced that only "a more dynamic program with a broader popular appeal" could defeat a left-wing coalition this time around. Pearson suggested "that we should respect the outcome of the democratic process in Chile would seem to be so obvious as not to need statement." Chile's "electoral system" was "sound," and its democratic institutions "well-respected." "If a cynical attitude is taken by the United States," he continued, "we will damage our moral position vis-à-vis the Soviet Union before the world." The United States should continue to "expand contacts with all opposition parties excepting only the Communists." The Socialists, he insisted, did not "want to be oriented toward the Soviet Union," and the United States should not push them "into the arms of the Soviet Union." Still, a victory by a left-wing coalition was not seen as being in the interest of the United States.[8] A military option was not rejected by all members of the State Department during the Kennedy years. "We must not overlook the possibility that a military coup, despite its many drawbacks for U.S. interests, might serve to be the only means of preventing a Communist-dominated government in 1964." In the short term, the United States needed to "cultivate an increased consciousness by Chilean military authorities of the responsibility of the armed forces for the protection of existing political institutions."[9] By the time of the April 1963 municipal elections, the Christian Democrats were the largest single party, but they still had only won 23 percent of the vote. No Latin American election in the 1960s was to be followed more closely than the 1964 presidential election in Chile.

There were hopeful signs in other parts of Latin America at the end of 1962, though there were contradictory signals regarding Kennedy administration support for democratic reformists. Elections that the Kennedy administration had been committed to were held in the Dominican Republic as planned. The United States had distanced itself from one-time Rafael Trujillo crony Joaquin Balaguer. Former journalist and Stevenson and Kennedy speechwriter John Bartlow Martin had become the U.S. ambassador to the Dominican Republic, as he had long hoped he would be. President Kennedy promised U.S. help in constructing "a democratic society on the ruins of tyranny." Martin argued that the Dominican Republic could provide "a showcase of democracy." The elections in late December took place without violent incidents. Kennedy administration engagement with Dominican affairs, furthermore, had an impact on internal developments. Years later Martin recalled that "Juan Bosch probably would not have been inaugurated had we not brought him to Washington and New York . . . almost immediately after his election." Bosch, an author and longtime opponent of Trujillo, assured U.S. leaders that he wanted "to be a key man in the fight against Fidel," and he congratulated President Kennedy on the Cuban blockade policy "that had unmasked Castro in the eyes of many Latin Americans." In meetings with President-Elect Bosch in early 1963, Schlesinger and Martin were sympathetic to his politics but uncertain about his personality. Schlesinger perceived "a certain inner vagueness about political plans and programs." Martin liked the man's allies in Latin America more than he liked the man himself, whom he considered "a bit difficult personally—vain, touchy, independent," even "manic-depressive." Since Bosch was an admirer of Stevenson, Martin encouraged the two to get together. Bosch had spent much of his life in the "conspiratorial world of Latin American exile politics," and Martin thought that Stevenson "could widen his horizons a bit." Some worried more about Bosch's ability to run a government, expressing reservations about the lack of "well-trained people" in his government, but they admired his commitment to reform. Both Schlesinger and Martin sought to avoid overly identifying "the White House with the new President."[10]

All too soon the Kennedy administration became concerned about and impatient with the Bosch government. Many U.S. officials had been bothered by the fact that the president had allowed communists to return to the country, despite his assurances to U.S. officials that his reforms would steal their thunder, and dismissed his belief that there was a greater threat to him from the right than the left. Unsurprisingly, Bosch resented being pressured by U.S. officials. Ambassador Martin is said to have actively discouraged Juan Bosch's land reform programs, which he thought the Kennedy administration would support. But, if anything, the evidence suggests that Martin was concerned that Bosch was too slow in getting his program off the ground. For months Ambassador Martin continued to express his own concerns regarding the survival of the government given the opposition of the military and the "propertied and professional classes." Martin did not expect the military to let him know if they were about to launch a coup. Nevertheless, the Kennedy administration was "heavily committed to democratic government in this country—perhaps more so than in any other country of Latin America." In August he supported loans to "help save" the government and warned that Bosch's overthrow "would be a setback in our policy and a blow to the Alliance for Progress." But only weeks later he worried that Bosch had failed "to satisfy the aspirations of the people who elected him"—failed "in a word to govern." Martin viewed him as an incompetent administrator who had proposed "no major legislation." Martin still insisted that the administration should support him, because he was a pro-Western and pro-American "noncommunist" who was "committed to the principles of the Alliance." He lamented the decline of U.S. influence, wistfully looking back to the employment of the navy in November 1961, which now seemed impossible (though how that would have helped with the issues he raised, so different from the problems of 1961, is hard to imagine). After seven months of rapid disaffection, author Eric Thomas Chester argues, the Kennedy administration refused to act to prevent a coup it would condemn publicly, though there is no evidence that the military was paying attention, by this point, to U.S. advice. Some liberals, for their part, regretted that Bosch had not been willing to allow U.S. intervention to prevent it. Once he was removed from power, the Kennedy administration did not seem to want him back, despite some congressional support for returning him to power. Even Frances Grant, who had been an observer of the elections and who had attended Bosch's inauguration at the invitation of the Dominican government, while hardly supporting the coup, argued that Bosch himself bore a good share of the blame for his removal.[11]

In Congress, Senator Humphrey spoke out, noting that "we are getting damn tired of voting American funds so that a machine-gun-happy colonel can knock down democratic governments." Alaska Senator Ernest Gruening argued that the Kennedy administration ought to work to return Bosch to power.[12] Seth Tillman, an aide to the Senate Foreign Relations Committee, warned Senator Morse about the possible consequences of the coup in the Dominican Republic. If it went unchallenged, "it could encourage a coup in Venezuela, with infinitely worse consequences." "A Venezuelan coup," he continued, "could presage the collapse of the Alliance for Progress and the disintegration of the Latin America policy of the United States."[13]

Following the coup in the Dominican Republic, there was a serious debate within the administration. Roving Ambassador Averell Harriman insisted that "the only thing that really counts for us in the world is our moral position. Every time we compromise our moral position we take a loss." Assistant Secretary Edwin Martin himself argued that the time had "come to blow the whistle on military coups" and that the Dominican Republic was "the place to do it." Kennedy expressed a concern that this would lessen U.S. ability to influence a government. Latin American leaders in Costa Rica and elsewhere were adamantly opposed to the Dominican coup, and within the administration people like Morales and Moscoso supported U.S. action to return Bosch to power. This was rejected by more powerful people in the administration. But there was also concern that this would "green light" a coup in Honduras, "perhaps even in Venezuela." Ambassador Martin was similarly opposed to the coup but was also simultaneously against bringing back Bosch. He still thought that it "might be possible to move toward a constitutional resolution of the situation."[14]

In the weeks following the coup, while it was clear that the Kennedy administration was not unhappy to see Bosch go, they were still hoping to avoid the creation of some kind of extra-constitutional government. But how they would define such a government in which Bosch was not a part was not easy to see. Ambassador Martin spent much of the remainder of the year in Washington trying to square the circle, but U.S. influence on events by this point was fairly limited. Schlesinger suggested either sending Martin back to prevent the impression of a "policy shift to the right" or sending "a cool, correct, and unenthusiastic" Foreign Service officer so that the United States could "to some extent disengage politically and have a fresh start."[15]

Latin American and Latino opinion among those who mattered to the administration was somewhat split between those who remained "skeptical of Bosch" and those who wanted the United States to actively return him to power.[16] By mid-November, Puerto Rican leader Muñoz Marín was reporting that Bosch was concerned that U.S. recognition of the Dominican government was "imminent." Dungan expressed a hope for "early elections . . . in a quiet atmosphere." Martin stuck to the Kennedy administration policy of using its influence "to bring about prompt proposals for elections and surrender power within specified time."[17] Unfortunately, the Dominican coup was not the last one during the Kennedy years.

As had been the case in South America in 1961, Kennedy wanted a trip abroad to demonstrate his administration's commitment to democracy and reform. In March of 1963 he went to Costa Rica. Never before had a U.S. president met with all of the region's leaders at the same time. Kennedy used the meeting as an opportunity to stress once again the threat from what he called "efforts to re-impose the despotisms of the Old World on the New." He referred to the Castro government as "a new imperialism more ruthless, more powerful, and more deadly in its pursuit of power than any that this hemisphere has ever known." He also made an interesting parallel while praising the efforts of Costa Rica in helping "to drive out William Walker" in the 1850s. He stressed the aid that Central Americans had already received under the Alliance for Progress. He emphasized the special ties between Costa Rica and the United States because of their democratic traditions. He visited an Alliance-funded housing project. He praised the current generation's "call for an end to social institutions which deny men and women the opportunity to live decent lives." He met with young members of the Christian Democratic Party and the labor movement, which he called "essential for a progressive democracy."[18]

Nicaraguan President Luis Somoza tried to use the visit to break out of the isolation his government had experienced. He held a dinner in Kennedy's honor and stressed the pro-American stance of his government, as well as the enthusiastic response Kennedy had received during his visit. The Central American presidents, he noted, found Kennedy "friendly and humane." Somoza affirmed that "we believe that all the problems put forward to him will be solved."[19]

Costa Rica's Figueres assured Ambassador Stevenson that President Kennedy's trip had been "a great success." Despite the serious economic problems that existed, the Alliance for Progress was "at least winning the *political* battle in Latin America."[20]

Following his trip to Central America, President Kennedy continued to argue that the way to prevent further Cuban Revolutions was "to bring about in all the countries of Latin America the conditions of hope, in which the peoples of this continent will know that they can shape a better future for themselves, not through obeying the inhuman commands of an alien and cynical ideology, but through personal self-expression, individual judgement, and the acts of responsible citizenship." He noted as well how "heartening" it was to observe "the increasing determination of the people of the region to build modern societies." And he noted that the United States would "concentrate our support on those countries adhering to the principles established in the Charter of Punta del Este."[21]

In no country in the Western Hemisphere did the Cold War impose more restrictions on its political evolution than in Guatemala. A CIA-backed coup in 1954 had ended an all-too-brief efflorescence of democracy. Liberal Democrats rarely held that against President Eisenhower. The Kennedy administration failed to uphold its commitment to Guatemalan democracy as well. Former President Juan José Arévalo, though far less committed to the transformation of his country than his successor Jacobo Árbenz had been, considered himself a supporter of the Alliance for Progress. Administration officials considered his books on U.S. Latin America policy anti-American and became concerned that he would win the presidential election in 1963. President

Kennedy found this unacceptable, despite assurances from Venezuela's Betancourt. When Arévalo returned from exile, the defense minister, Colonel Enrique Peralta Azurdia, staged a coup and canceled the elections, and the administration was relieved. Kennedy had failed Guatemala, as had his predecessor.[22]

Nicaragua under the Somozas had long supported U.S. policy and provided stability in the region. During the Kennedy years, however, there was hope that the United States could use its "considerable influence to encourage an atmosphere conducive to peaceful political evolution." There was an expectation that Luis Somoza, at least, was sincere in his commitment to a transition to democracy and that there would be no more presidents of Nicaragua named Somoza. If the opposition won the scheduled election and his brother Anastasio, commander of the National Guard, staged a coup, the United States, following the "Peruvian precedent of July 1962," would "suspend relations."

In 1963, Nicaragua held the elections that had been promised, although they left much to be desired. The Conservative opposition had not agreed to participate, amid some concerns that the United States had failed to promise free elections, which the United States interpreted as a reversion to historic Nicaraguan patterns of forcing the United States to choose sides. President Somoza and President-Elect René Schick, a longtime member of Somoza governments, hoped that the Kennedy administration would take "a more generous view of the developing brand of democracy" in their country. The administration hoped that Schick, whom they considered to be an honest man, could prove to be an independent political actor; U.S. policy was intended to support him in his efforts to do so. The administration in the months ahead held out the carrot of an invitation for a state visit should he succeed in shedding the image abroad that he was "merely a willing puppet" of the Somoza family.[23]

President Schick found his position to be a difficult one. He had shown some independence by ignoring some of the cabinet suggestions proposed by General Somoza. But General Somoza remained in charge of the National Guard, and he used that position to begin what the Nicaraguan president considered "premature politicking" to be his successor. Schick warned him about this, noting that it would hurt his political chances. But Schick at times seemed timid, even indicating that the general would not have to launch a coup; if the general wanted him out of office, he should just tell him and he would go. State Department officials suggested that even as the United States was willing to "bolster his position in case there is trouble," President Schick himself would not try to maintain himself in office. In conversations with the U.S. ambassador, Schick indicated that his own office was bugged by Somoza.[24] There were rumors floating around that he would not even last in power as long as the official Nicaraguan president (Leonardo Argüello Barreto) had in 1947 when he tried to show that he really was in power. U.S. goals in 1963 were to see Schick survive in office so that a constitutional succession process could take hold.[25]

In Honduras, an infant democracy, there was already concern about the direction of the Alliance for Progress. There the Kennedy administration's support for reform in Central America came into conflict with U.S. economic interests in the region, which had been established at the turn of the twentieth century. President Villeda had promised land reform. A land reform bill was drawn up and passed in Congress. Implementation was delayed, however, which gave the, United Fruit Company an opportunity to express its concerns. Vice President and General Counsel Victor G. Folsom warned Secretary of State Rusk in September 1962 that the plan was "more drastic and confiscatory than the one on which Fidel Castro has built a Communist stronghold in the Western hemisphere." But the Honduran Congress claimed that the plan was in keeping with Alliance for Progress guidelines, and U.S. Ambassador Charles Burrows said that he had "been having a lot of difficulty coordinating our belated position on this Honduran law with our far-reaching and long-standing statements with reference to the necessity of land reform and agrarian reform under the Alliance for Progress." Nevertheless, President Villeda promised that changes would be made in the law and that the company's investments would not be threatened. In his White House visit, President Villeda told Kennedy, "As long as a civilized man is head of my country, there is no reason to fear." Kennedy responded that he was pleased, for it was in the interests of both countries for United Fruit to remain in Honduras. By early 1963, however, President Villeda had not yet made clear how he was going to amend the law, leading the banana company to delay its planting program during a time of ongoing ecological crisis. State Department official Edward Rowell told the U.S. ambassador that he was "not a champion of the fruit company," but he wanted "to maintain a situation in which Honduras will receive all the foreign investment it can absorb." He expressed concerns that if United Fruit reduced its interests in Honduras, other companies that might have been interested in investing in the country would not do so.[26]

Political democracy was not to be consolidated in Honduras, however. Honduran politicians on the right, even from the president's own party, did not trust him and had doubts that elections would be held.[27] The president's attempt to create a Civil Guard to replace the rebellious National Police drew opposition from the armed forces. Following the Dominican coup, Undersecretary of State George Ball instructed the U.S. embassy in Tegucigalpa as to "the great concern with which USG would view overthrow of constitutionality in Honduras." The minister of defense, Colonel Oswaldo López Arellano, to whom that message was delivered, ignored advice from the U.S. ambassador and top U.S. military officials and deposed Villeda a little more than a week before his successor would be chosen. The administration had supported the elections, which would have indicated a maturation of the Honduran political system. In early October President Kennedy had written privately to Villeda, "I know that you are doing all in your power to guarantee a peaceful and legitimate transfer of power to your successor, and I wish you to know of my fervent hope for the success of your efforts." Instead, a military man had put himself in power in a bloody coup.[28] The United States had long been concerned that a coup would bring to power a government that would be unsympathetic to reform. State Department officials noted that "The speed with which we have been able to cut off economic assistance to Honduras has been gratifying." Kennedy remarked that U.S. officials had asked for indications of when the Honduran government planned to hold elections. Privately, Colonel López indicated that it would be "useless to have any further talks" with U.S. military officers, "because they wanted definite and immediate commitments from him, particularly with regard to a date for holding presidential elections." (Liberals and communists, he indicated, might "agitate.")[29]

Liberal Democrats were appalled at the coups in Honduras and the Dominican Republic. John R. Roche, the national chairman of the ADA, feared that "stirrings of democracy in that hemisphere will be strangled in their cradle." But they could not discuss these internal political developments without raising the fear of dictatorships "paving the way for a series of takeovers by Castroism."[30] Some later recalled the months during which Bosch was president as a missed opportunity. "For a brief period they [the Dominican people] were exposed to the idea that they were human beings, and then the lights went out again."[31]

State Department officials feared the impact of the two coups on the fate of foreign aid in the U.S. Congress. They also were concerned that the Alliance for Progress needed to demonstrate that it had, in fact, progressed by the 1964 presidential campaign. Moreover, there needed to be some kind of "lasting deterrent" to others who might be interested in launching a coup. The United States wanted to be "very firm about pressing for early elections. Early elections are much easier to hold than later ones." In conversations with Standard Fruit Company officials, they made clear that the United States did not want either liberal governments that allowed "communists to operate so freely" and were "so inefficient themselves, that a country is quickly lost to communist subversion," or a military one, which was "over willing to resort to oppressive tactics." Although the United States "probably would have to accept the dictatorship," the State Department was trying "to modify actions of the coup makers to avoid this Hobson's choice." "The Honduras coup is especially difficult to deal with because it prevented an election." (They had, obviously, not been concerned when this was the case in Guatemala, however.) The State Department hoped that it could convince López to announce that elections would be held in "preferably less than a year's elapsed time."[32] Secretary of State Dean Rusk warned the military leaders in the Dominican Republic and Honduras that the United States viewed them "with the utmost gravity." "Under existing conditions," moreover, "there is no opportunity for effective collaboration by the United States under the Alliance for Progress or for normalization of diplomatic relations."[33]

It is worth noting that Honduras soon disappeared altogether as an issue. U.S. expectations that the military leaders would carry through with their timetable and return to constitutional civilian government were not fulfilled. For Honduras, democracy would not be on the agenda for decades to come.[34] The Dominican Republic, however, where there had been much attention to U.S. efforts and interests for generations, did not disappear, but became one of the major headaches of the Johnson administration in Latin America.

Privately, however, the coups taught a different lesson to Kennedy. He wrote Secretary of Defense McNamara in early October that they suggested the possibility of situations developing "which would require active U.S. military intervention." "I am not sure that we are prepared for this satisfactorily," Kennedy suggested. "This matter deserves the highest priority."[35]

In early October 1963, Assistant Secretary Martin wrote an article for the *New York Herald Tribune* that tried to clarify Kennedy administration policy toward military governments in Latin America. The United States supported civilian governments, the article maintained, and wanted the military to be subordinate to civilian authority. The United States could not necessarily act against governments installed by the military, but it should work to keep their time in power brief and their use of power "to be as considerate of the welfare of the people as possible." Kennedy aide Schlesinger was quite concerned about how this article would be read in Latin America. In a memorandum on what he insisted was not, despite press reports, a "Martin Doctrine," Schlesinger encouraged President Kennedy to clarify U.S. policy at the October 9 press conference and reassure Latin America that the administration continued to rely upon "the forces of progressive democracy," indeed that its "signal contribution" had been to "make an implicit alliance" with those forces. The United States needed to be patient as Latin American conditions made it possible for these kinds of governments to be established and thrive. The Latin American military was not likely to establish such regimes, Schlesinger continued, and the administration should not be on record as praising actually existing military governments. The pragmatic tactical need to work with existing regimes should not be confused with administration policy. Schlesinger suggested reaffirming in a "vivid way our preference for the forces of progressive democracy." A Chilean diplomat told Schlesinger in a sad tone of voice, "we have struggled for years to keep our military out of politics. You are weakening the democratic structure in Chile by inviting them in."[36]

Senator Morse, as well, criticized Martin for paying "lip-service" to the Alliance while undercutting and destroying its "entire premise." He predicted that Martin's statement was a "typical diplomatic smoke-screen of shoulder-shrugging preliminary to recognition and aid to the new dictatorships of the Dominican Republic and Honduras." He predicted that Martin and the "militarists to the south" would kill "the Alliance once and for all," and U.S. policy would return to what it had been in 1957. Military men who seized power needed to be assured that by doing so, they took their countries "out of the Alliance for Progress, as far as U.S. economic and military aid are concerned."[37]

In his October 9 press conference, Kennedy emphasized most of the points Schlesinger had encouraged him to make. He noted that Martin's comments were intended to elucidate why coups take place in Latin America, and that the United States remained "opposed to an interruption of the constitutional system by a military coup." While expressing support for "democratic governments and progress and progressive governments," he also suggested a historical rule that dictatorship leads to communism (a rule based largely, of course, on the Cuban example). The United States and its allies in the Western Hemisphere must use their influence in countries "where coups have taken place to provide for an orderly restoration of constitutional processes."[38]

By the end of 1963, Martin argued, the United States had adopted "a sensible pragmatic, middle of the road course with respect to military coups, one which takes account of Latin American history and attempts to move them forward from where they are, rather than from where one might like them to be." This approach, he suggested, "was under attack in this country and Latin America from both those who respect only power and those who refuse to compromise the principles of democracy. We are far from consensus in a period of tension accompanying needed but disturbing change in which we can expect more upheavals." He later described his approach as trying "to move them forward from where they are, rather than one where one might like them to be."[39] Schlesinger was right that the "Martin Doctrine" was not a doctrine; Kennedy did not live long enough for it to become one. It was, however, an expression of frustration regarding Latin American political realities and U.S. ability to shape them.

Let us turn to the question of military aid, long a concern for liberal Democrats. Certainly, many historians have argued that military aid in the region had negative consequences. Concerns at the time regarding civic action programs were expressed by administration official Morales Carrión. He cited a pamphlet produced by the Guatemalan army about civil action that emphasized the role of the military in economic development and the establishment of closer relations with the people, but that neglected to mention the armed forces' "obligation to defend constitutional principles" or concepts like "freedom," "democracy," and human rights.[40] Claims that the U.S. military educated their Latin American colleagues about subordination to civilian authority have long been questioned. NSC staffer Carl Kaysen warned Edwin Martin and Walt Rostow that General Andrew O'Meara, commander of the Southern Command, had "expressed the view that over the next decade, military governments would be in power in many Latin American countries." That was "probably the best situation we could hope for," he continued, as long as the United States made sure that they were "on our side."[41]

But that was not the Kennedy administration's position, and it is important to look at concrete historical situations to understand them better. We have already seen how the United States had failed to prevent coups in Honduras and the Dominican Republic, but historians have not offered concrete evidence that the United States could have prevented them. The Dominican Republic had failed to become the "showcase for democracy" that it was intended to be, but Bosch had fallen for internal, not external reasons. The Dominican Republic's future was not yet certain. Guatemala, as we have seen, was another matter.

In Peru, the military had established a timetable for elections but still wanted to "minimize APRA influence." The administration had learned its lesson the hard way, but its belief that its pressure had worked in getting the military to establish a timetable would come to naught if the military did not allow elections that were free and fair.[42] The Kennedy administration, for the most part, was convinced that its pressure on Peru in the year before had been successful. It was believed to have possibly influenced the junta toward avoiding "political excesses." Timetables were adhered to, and the election was held. APRA's Haya lost the election, much to the military's relief. The United States wisely had given up its exclusive focus on APRA, and had begun to accept the idea that Popular Action's Fernando Belaunde Terry was both anticommunist and reformist, if still certainly undefined in terms of his political philosophy. (For its part, the Inter-American Association for Democracy and Freedom found hope in APRA's domination of the Peruvian Congress.)[43]

Venezuela, for its part, actually experienced an insurgency inspired, trained, and armed by Cuba. Given the long-standing criticism of Kennedy administration military aid and counterinsurgency training, and its long-term impact on political conditions in Latin America, it is worth noting that a country like Venezuela, which had an active guerrilla movement, was able to consolidate its constitutional system, producing what was, for many decades, considered a model democracy. No current Latin American leader was more admired by Kennedy and members of his administration, and the administration was committed to his political survival and to the holding of the next presidential election to choose his successor. Foreign Service officers in Caracas were focusing a significant amount of effort on making it clear to military officials that the administration would not accept any action by the military against the constitutional government.[44] Betancourt had become the Latin American leader whose counsel was most welcome in the Kennedy administration. Schlesinger expressed "a certain sympathy" with the Venezuelan leader's proposal that no governments that came to power through the use of violence should be recognized. Although Schlesinger said that he "would accept de facto governments," he thought that the United States, "because of its special power and responsibility, must have a special recognition policy within the hemisphere."[45]

Following the conclusion of the Cuban Missile Crisis, Brazil, however, became the major problem area for the United States. Kennedy administration policy toward Brazil was far more complicated than is generally recognized. The arrival of Colonel Vernon A. Walters as army attaché in October 1962 has been seen as a turning point in U.S. attitudes toward a military coup. This is not supported by the evidence we have available. As a young officer, Walters had worked as a translator who helped U.S. forces communicate with the Brazilian military during the Italian campaign at the end of World War II. He developed long-standing friendships with Brazilian officers, who were recognized both as pro-American and as potentially critical political actors. Walters was certainly able to keep the United States informed of attitudes among the military. But his reporting on the political situation in Brazil was consequently the most overwrought. He found the armed forces divided between left and right. He claimed that opponents of the regime were afraid to speak up, which a simple perusal of the daily press would have shown to be not true. Walters feared that unless the government committed unconstitutional acts there would be no real resistance to it. He warned that if the United States did not tie political conditions to aid to Brazil, the United States would be "helping to create another Cuba on an infinitely larger scale," with vast ramifications for the whole South American continent. The United States should only provide aid if the governments removed (unnamed) communists from the government. He predicted that Goulart would establish a "Tito-type state." Walters reinforced the worst aspects of Ambassador Gordon's own thinking. The Kennedy administration, however, as we shall see, continued to be of mixed minds about Goulart and how to handle him.[46]

Certainly, the Kennedy administration had spent significant resources trying to influence the off-year elections in 1962 by providing covert support for anti-Goulart candidates. The results, however, were far from satisfactory. Following what was for at least some officials the sobering victory of a number of leftist leaders in Brazil in October, U.S. policy took, for a time, a somewhat different (and, historically, neglected) turn. The United States did not see an opposition capable of overthrowing the president at the time. If he moved toward a "left-wing dictatorship," the United States needed to have the flexibility to "shift rapidly and effectively" to overthrowing him. The presumed "friendly democratic elements" included "the great majority of the military officer corps." The United States needed to be better informed about the plans of these elements.[47] In the short term, rather than seeking to work with those who sought Goulart's overthrow or attempt to confront him, the Kennedy administration sought to focus on the most important issues and "change the political and economic orientation" of Goulart and his government while influencing his advisers and encouraging "moderate democratic elements in Congress, the Armed Forces and elsewhere." This was due, in part, to a recognition that an "effective military or civilian opposition" was not yet "in a position to act promptly." The Kennedy administration was going to keep its eye on things and be ready to shift to support for his overthrow should events warrant it. A special representative was to be sent to try to influence the Brazilian president. In the event, it would be "brother-protector" Robert. Ambassador Gordon suggested that a visit by President Kennedy could be "indispensable to re-establishing broad popular support" for the United States in Brazil, but concerns about the domestic political impact *in the United States* of a trip to what was increasingly seen as an irresponsible anti-American country helped prevent that from happening. So such a trip by the president was postponed for a third time.[48]

In his conversation with the Brazilian president, Robert Kennedy was not at his most diplomatic. He pressured Brazil to demonstrate that it was interested in cooperating with the United States. He badgered Goulart about removing communists from his cabinet, but he refused to tell Goulart who the United States thought the communists in the cabinet were. Goulart, unsurprisingly, bristled. Historian W. Michael Weis has rightly characterized the encounter as a "disaster." But in the months following Robert Kennedy's visit, Ambassador Gordon noted that, "while not producing miracles," his impact had, "on balance," been "favorable." (He told Secretary of State Rusk that it was "moderately favorable.") The United States was in for a "long siege" in its relations with the Goulart government and would not seek to overthrow it until other alternatives had been tried and/or the forces in opposition to Goulart were stronger. But it was committed to devising a "method of penalties and 'rewards' tied to specific types of GOB actions as method of controlling what generally admitted to be extremely sensitive and dangerous situation in Brazil."[49] Gordon made it clear to Goulart in early 1963 that no request for his removal would be "well-received."[50] But there continued to be tensions between Goulart and Gordon. Goulart told Ambassador Gordon that he "found me personally sympathetic," but he "feared I was getting information too exclusively from his Brazilian enemies."[51]

As Finance Minister San Tiago Dantas told President Kennedy in March 1963, Goulart's strength lay in his ability to "coordinate popular forces and lead them along democratic lines."[52] Gordon thought that Goulart could gain support from the right, although it was not clear how he could do so and support reform (which the United States in other countries ostensibly supported), or even abandon reform and gain the support of the right.[53] In early 1963, the plebiscite in Brazil had finally been held, and Goulart obtained the full executive powers that had been denied him when he became president in August 1961. In the first half of 1963, the influence of the finance minister on the administration was strong, and the administration was fairly happy with attempts to control inflation. President Kennedy himself wrote Goulart, encouraging him to carry out such a program "with the persistence and courageous leadership which only you the president of Brazil can impart," thereby laying the groundwork for "the constructive potentialities of the Alliance for Progress to be fully realized in Brazil." In the short term, his administration seemed to be moving in a direction that Gordon and the Kennedy administration approved. Nevertheless, the intention was to keep Brazil on a "short leash." But the anti-inflation efforts were unpopular with those Goulart considered to be his core supporters. (Schlesinger himself warned that such a policy in the antebellum United States "would probably have retarded American economic growth by a generation.")[54] By the middle of the year Goulart sought to shore up his support in a pluralistic but fragmented left at a time when rural unions were expanding and strikes were proliferating. At the same time the Kennedy administration accelerated aid for state governments in Brazil that were seen as politically friendly.[55]

Soon the anti-inflation program was abandoned, and by the fall many officials were concerned that Brazil "not be taken over by an anti-U.S. Left leadership." Walt Rostow, for his part, believed that President Goulart was "flirting with the idea of a Peronist *coup de main*, which would give him virtually dictatorial powers." But Goulart was seen as trying "to save his political skin" in the wake of the failure of the anti-inflation program. Rostow recommended working with the government to deal with economic stabilization and development issues, while encouraging Goulart to bring more centrists into his government and avoid any hints of a self-coup.[56]

The Kennedy administration and the State Department remained uncertain as to how to interpret the Brazilian president. Assistant Secretary of State for Inter-American Affairs Edwin Martin noted the fundamental differences between how the State Department and how the embassy and the CIA viewed him. The State position was that Goulart was "a small time politician, using a politician's stock in trade of patronage, maneuver, diversion of public funds," and creating confusion and using demagoguery, in order to survive in office. (This is the view that, it seems to me, is more supported by the historical record.) Martin wanted to make clear that, unlike Goulart's domestic critics, President Kennedy was no reactionary. When Kennedy finally visited Brazil, he would be speaking about "peaceful revolutions, agrarian and other basic reforms." "These are the things," Martin insisted, "he believes must take place in Latin America." The United States, moreover, should seek to guarantee that the 1965 presidential elections took place.[57]

Gordon thought that the "major threat to Brazilian democracy at moment [October 1963] comes from Goulart himself." Goulart had asked the Brazilian Congress for a state of siege. Gordon quoted President Kubitschek's remark that the president's state of siege request "was intended as step in coup from top down." (Both seemed to ignore the fact that the president had, after all, gone to Congress for approval, and had done nothing when Congress opposed it.) Congress should impeach Goulart, Gordon argued, but "Brazilian realities might require removal of threat through military action." Such a move would be "pro-constitution and democracy." It "would be tragic" to "sacrifice Senator Morse's own purposes through adherence to formalism."[58]

The evidence from Brazil, however, suggests that, as in many other instances, Kennedy's policies were not settled at the time of his unexpected death. He was concerned enough about Goulart to suggest even direct U.S. action, but at the same time he sent a personal emissary, Averell Harriman, to meet with him. Ambassador Gordon, for his part, remained the one most willing to promote military intervention. And those who want to stress the existence of contingency plans have to recognize that contingency plans are just that, and that, in this case, U.S. action was contingent on Goulart's actions themselves.

In any case, it was important to note that the battle over the interpretation of Goulart was continuing. If, as suggested, Goulart's political goal was survival, some considered it unlikely that he would make any significant and consistent move to the left until he believed that the left was strong enough to allow him to do so. And U.S. officials did not always clearly delineate what a move to the left might entail. Without "clear indications of serious likelihood of a political takeover by elements subservient to and supported by a foreign government, it would be against U.S. policy to intervene directly or indirectly in support of any move to overthrow the Goulart regime."[59] That Goulart himself would establish a government "subservient to and supported by a foreign government" seems ludicrous in retrospect and should have been recognized as such at the time. And while Gordon sought to encourage contingency planning for possible U.S. overt actions in Brazil, such as using the U.S. army to defend the industrial areas in São Paulo while the U.S. navy controlled the coast, it still was based on the assumption that these actions would only take place once Goulart had taken an action which was "clearly unconstitutional."[60]

While Gordon and others expected President Goulart to take such actions, most historians' interpretations of U.S. policy make it seem more consistent and unidirectional, and end up making the 1964 coup inevitable from July 1962 on in a way that the evidence does not support. Kennedy administration debate was robust. Despite Ambassador Gordon's tendency to distort Goulart's policies and practices, the Kennedy administration was hardly of one mind on the subject of Brazil.[61]

At least part of the problem with U.S. strategy at this point had to do with misunderstandings of Goulart himself. That Ambassador Gordon could see the situation as analogous to that of Vargas in 1941, when he converted "from pro-German to pro-Allied stand," dramatically misread the situation. Even had it been true that Vargas has been actually pro-German in 1941, and not just sitting on the fence, waiting either for the best offer or a clear indication which direction would be most advantageous, it could hardly be said that Goulart himself was pro-Soviet or even in that famously uncomfortable position, "on the fence." It was not at all clear how the United States was going to catch him at his most politically vulnerable and therefore malleable, as Gordon hoped. Goulart's fundamental problem was domestic, and few U.S. actions at the time were intended, let alone able, to remedy that.[62]

Even as late as October 1963, the Kennedy administration had cleavages in it, not least of all over the advisability of listening too closely to Governor Lacerda and following his lead. Assistant Secretary of State Martin considered his approach "too far on the right and too fanatically anti-Goulart." Lacerda's tactics, moreover, were "equally irresponsible and unacceptable." The United States needed to demonstrate "more clearly and widely by word, and insofar as possible by action," that the United States favored "social and economic reform just as strongly as we favor financial stability and protection of foreign investment."[63]

Martin, moreover, thought that even Gordon's concerns about Goulart's "demagoguery" were misplaced. He noted that President Roosevelt himself had been accused of being a demagogue. The question was whether Goulart could use his talents to implement reforms. Martin thought that the United States had been treating him as "substantively uneducable" for too long.[64]

Gordon rejected the idea that Goulart was progressive or that there was "active mass support" for his "basic reforms." The government has only "somewhat broadened the circle of Brazilians playing an active part in the nation's political life." Gordon also expressed concerns about the State Department's dismissal of Governor Lacerda as an "irresponsible reactionary," praising what he called his reforms as governor, suggesting that Lacerda was the true progressive. Gordon did not "personally like his tactics," or their "McCarthyist flavor," but Lacerda was "not very far off the mark." He said that Lacerda was the best presidential candidate on the Brazilian political scene. Gordon insisted that Goulart intended to maintain himself in power through a "self-coup" like that of Vargas in 1937, creating a Peronist style of regime. Given his own ineptness, he would soon be pushed aside by the communists. "If God really is Brazilian, Goulart's heart trouble soon will become acute." Barring that, he suggested maybe a visit from President Kennedy would turn things around.[65] At the time of Kennedy's death, the United States still expected that the 1965 presidential elections were going to be held. President Kennedy should use "to the fullest" his "tremendous prestige and influence with the Brazilian people (and his prestige with Goulart)" through frequent statements and correspondence and "formal and informal contacts." But the United States also needed to expand its "contacts and cooperation with the Brazilian military." The fact that the military seized power in early 1964 has led historians to simplify what U.S. policy was in 1963.[66]

By November 1963, however, a plan existed to provide overt support for a successful military action against the Goulart government. But it is important to note that it too was contingent on Goulart actually taking a "clearly unconstitutional or illegal action."[67] Perhaps the most significant thing to come from the plan was an assessment of "fuel oil needs," which was incorporated into Operation Brother Sam in 1964. But, in any case, even at this point, not all of the advice the Kennedy administration was receiving from Brazilians or the analyses proffered by top officials pointed in a unilateral direction. Even Roberto Campos, who had, according to Schlesinger, "given up on President Goulart," did not "share Linc Gordon's conviction that Goulart is aiming to provoke a crisis and install himself as dictator in the tradition of Vargas." Campos considered the Brazilian president "an increasingly desperate fixer and improviser and more and more at the end of his string."[68]

Days before the Kennedy assassination, Goulart met with Kennedy's personal representative, Averell Harriman. It is worth noting that he had been given the State Department memo by Hughes that provided the more sympathetic reading of Goulart's actions. Goulart told Harriman that while Kennedy was "regarded personally with great warmth," the masses were not impressed by the Alliance for Progress and considered Kennedy's government "to be much like previous regime." "Perhaps expectations had been too high." In any case, terms of trade were hurt by "trusts," and supply and demand was not working. But Goulart spoke clearly about his feelings about the U.S. president. "I have picked my candidate for 1964 in the United States but not yet for 1965 in Brazil."[69] Harriman advised the president against going to Brazil in 1964. Although he understood the president's great personal interest in Brazil, Harriman thought that it would hurt his "political position" in the United States to visit a country in which his policies were not supported by the government. Kennedy remained interested in determining whether a better climate of relations between the two countries could be established.[70]

Kennedy never had a chance to visit Brazil, but he did not live to see a military dictatorship established there either. We do not know whether he would have been more engaged with what was going on in Brazil, and therefore more willing to question the interpretation of Goulart's actions proffered by his enemies in the U.S. embassy. His skeptical frame of mind certainly might have tipped the balance against support for a military coup. For that matter, would JFK have been as enthusiastic about the Brazilian military leaders as Lincoln Gordon and President Lyndon Johnson ended up being? Brazil did not have a tradition of military rule, only of military participation in politics, and the Brazilian civilian supporters of the coup in 1964 did not themselves think that long-term military rule would result. If the military had overthrown Goulart, would Kennedy have supported a clear timetable for a return to civilian government, as he did in other places? Would he have been more grudging in his public praise of the new leaders, while privately accepting the necessity of removing the unreliable Goulart in a volatile Cold War context in which the stakes were so high? In any case, no long-standing Latin American dictatorship can be directly and uniquely linked to actions actually taken by the Kennedy administration, as opposed to long-term trends developed under Kennedy. It would be much easier to blame President Johnson in the long run, but liberal Democrats, as we shall see, failed in their own ways during the years following President Kennedy's death.[71]

In any case, it cannot be said that the United States was fully committed to the Brazilian president's removal at the time of Kennedy's assassination. On the 12th of November, Kennedy dictated a memorandum that indicated his frustration with Goulart's "playing a very nationalist game" by "ignoring the Alliance for Progress." But Kennedy had made an effort to understand Third World nationalism and frequently expressed frustration with members of the U.S. Congress who sought to use the Hickenlooper Amendment to punish Latin Americans who were pursuing economic nationalist policies and thereby limit the Kennedy administration's options. And he was conscious of the political restraints the Latin American governments themselves were under with "the radical left to appease at home."[72]

Meanwhile, in Washington, an alliance of conservatives and liberal Democrats was undermining support for foreign aid. The impatience so characteristic of the decade undermined the often limited faith in the oversold ability to transform Latin America. In hearings before the Senate Foreign Relations Committee, Secretary of State Rusk had, in particular, to address the issue of aid for Brazil, which was seen as ungrateful and undisciplined. Liberal Democrats, for their part, focused on the conflict between the reformist and the security aspects of Kennedy administration policy. Senator Morse, in particular, played an important role in blocking foreign aid in the Senate, focusing, as he had since the Eisenhower administration, on his opposition to military aid (though he also thought that foreign aid was bad for the U.S. economy). Church, somewhat disingenuously, wrote (regarding military aid for Latin American and African countries), "We understand that President Kennedy inherited these excesses, and we don't blame him for them. But it is now within his power to come to grips with them." General Lucius Clay, whom Kennedy appointed to head a committee examining foreign aid programs, although willing to cut other foreign aid programs, thought that the Latin American programs should receive the "full amount promised." But this "foreign aid revolt," which historian Robert David Johnson has analyzed so carefully, would not result in a Latin America policy that fulfilled the long-held hopes of liberal Democrats, for, ironically, it was the military assistance programs that were saved at the levels the Kennedy administration wanted.[73]

In the weeks before Kennedy's assassination, the "Latin Americanists" in the administration were feeling isolated. Schlesinger had been asked to write a speech that Kennedy was going to deliver in Miami. "So Dick and I are back in the Latin American picture," he reflected in his journal, "though, as Dick gloomily said, there is no great gain in our writing strong and progressive speeches if Ed Martin remains in control of operations." Morales was resigning. According to Schlesinger, Martin considered him to be Muñoz's man, and the Puerto Rican leader was "running an independent policy for the Caribbean." Morales was "the last Kennedy appointment in ARA." The Foreign Service would now be in control. And there would be no more officials "who [give] the Latin Americans a sense of sympathetic concern with their problems as well as a sense of identification with progressive democracy." Perhaps, in a position with the Brookings Institution, he could "function as an unofficial ambassador to the democratic left" and do more for President Kennedy "outside the government than within."[74]

President Kennedy, for his part, was concerned that Latin America was "simply not receiving enough top-level attention." And yet one is reminded that, once again, he was talking to Schlesinger when he said it, and he knew that was what his aide wanted to hear. If Kennedy wanted his administration to pay the region more attention at the highest levels, he could have done something about it. He was president, after all.[75]

In recent years, it has been suggested that President Kennedy was moving toward an accommodation with Castro through back-channel private negotiations. It is interesting to note that in 1974 Schlesinger (and Dungan, among others) expressed some doubts regarding the significance of such activities. But if Kennedy was somewhat flexible in this regard, it is important to remember that covert actions to remove (or even kill) Castro were continuing even as the secret communications were being initiated. The United States had encouraged its allies to join in the trade embargo. But, despite the U.S. promise not to invade Cuba, U.S. rhetoric regarding Cuba remained strong, and covert actions continued. There was still discussion in 1963 of the possibility of a U.S. invasion "in the event of a general uprising there." Only days before his death, Kennedy asserted that Castro was "still . . . a major danger to the United States." A general shift to isolation and containment rather than removal had largely been made, but it was far from complete. The many fronts of Kennedy's war against Cuba were all in play. Kennedy's death obscures this fact, as it does so much else. He had made no final decisions since he had no reason to make them. He did not think that he was going to die.[76]

In October 1963, President Kennedy continued to see Latin America as posing "the greatest danger." Or, as he put it not long before his death, Latin America was (still) "where the big problems were."[77] Kennedy's policies sought to address an immediate sense of danger by tackling both long-term transformation and short-term strategy. Too much of the literature on Kennedy's policy toward Latin America ignores its unfinished nature. The president continued to be interested in Latin America at the time of his death, if not to the degree that Schlesinger hoped, and was both fearful and understanding of Latin American nationalism. He pursued policies that assumed military rule would only be short-term. He preferred timetables for a return to constitutional government where they could be established. He accepted a military role in civic action, which seemed unwise to its critics at the time and even less prudent later on as it became clear that it deepened the political role of the military. And the emphasis on counterinsurgency, even in countries that lacked insurgencies, may have distorted developments in other places.[78] If he did not see where his policies might lead, he remained opposed to military government as a long-term solution for Latin America's problems, which cannot be said of his successors. Kennedy did not know that he was going to die, and he had not made any definitive decisions about much of anything.

In any case, Kennedy's premature death suggests a finality to his policies or evolution that did not really exist. Kennedy himself may have been sobered by the realities of Latin America that prevented the Alliance of Progress from achieving what had been perhaps overly optimistic goals. A greater realism may have become necessary, though, without sacrificing ideals. Kennedy remained convinced that he could handle the unintended consequences of enhanced military aid. An inattentive president would not necessarily see how military aid and counterinsurgency training might operate on automatic pilot. Liberal Democrats in the years following his death would have to address the consequences of his contradictory policy or create a legacy that could be sold as less problematic. Generally, they preferred the latter route, and the Alliance for Progress became a major component in the president's liberal reputation that overtook the more complicated historical reality. Kennedy's work in Latin America was unfinished, like his life.[79]

At the time of the assassination, both presidential aide Ralph Dungan and Senator Humphrey had been attending a luncheon at the Chilean embassy, emphasizing, for the historian, the critical importance of that country's future.[80] Frances Grant argued that for Latin America "and its people," the death of Kennedy was a "catastrophic blow." Kennedy had "re-expressed the hopes and goals that the democratic leaders had been articulating for three decades of their struggle." But the Inter-American Association for Democracy and Freedom formally expressed that President Johnson, with his knowledge of the Mexican Americans of his home state of Texas, would carry on the commitment to Kennedy's programs in Latin America. Initially, at least, liberal Latin Americanist Democrats would seek to guarantee that this would be so.[81]

Chapter 5

Let Us Continue

Toward the Johnson Alliance

"Let us continue," the new president proposed. In terms of domestic and foreign policy, Lyndon Johnson would build on the Kennedy legacy to a significant degree. He was able to use Kennedy's martyrdom to advance the liberal agenda in areas like civil rights in a way that Kennedy himself, unmartyred, probably could not have done. LBJ did more to promote democracy domestically than any other U.S. president. In terms of foreign policy, the Kennedy legacy was already complex and contradictory, as we have seen. Johnson promised to make the Alliance for Progress a "living memorial" to his predecessor.[1] During the period of his greatest domestic accomplishments, from 1963 to 1965, Johnson began to put his own stamp on regional policy and, to a certain degree, redefined the Alliance for Progress, although he did not simply abandon it as many Kennedy Democrats insisted. Developments in certain countries that had begun under Kennedy came to a head or fruition. Particularly affected during these years were Brazil, Chile, Cuba, and the Dominican Republic.

Johnson had been a liberal New Dealer as a congressman. As a senator representing all of Texas he had moved to the right, and he had generally supported President Eisenhower's foreign policies. In 1955 he had told Stevenson aide Newton Minow that the presidential candidate in 1956 would have to be moderate—"the country's moderate."[2] Johnson was much more conventional than Kennedy had been, and he would take fewer chances internationally. He would worry less about the U.S. image in the Third World generally, and, over time, worry less about its image in Latin America. He was, to some degree, a more traditional liberal Democrat than Kennedy had been. He tended to view international development programs, for example, in terms of New Deal models. Johnson supported development programs in Vietnam's Mekong River Valley, which bore similarities to FDR's Tennessee Valley Authority program. As his own domestic programs developed, he tended to view the Alliance itself as "a collective war on poverty." At his most eloquent, he spoke of the Alliance being embodied "in the aspirations of millions of farmers and workers, of men without education, of men without hope, of poverty-stricken families whose homes are the villages and the cities of an entire continent."[3]

On 26 November 1963, only days following President Kennedy's death, in the East Room of the White House, with Latin American diplomats, as well as Schlesinger and Goodwin, in attendance, President Johnson affirmed his and the nation's continuing commitment to the Alliance for Progress. Johnson invoked Kennedy, even as he made it clear that it was Franklin Roosevelt who had taught him "that nothing is more important to the country I now lead than its association with our good neighbors to the south." By insisting that his interest in Latin America was nothing new and by invoking FDR and the Good Neighbor Policy, Johnson sought to distinguish himself from John Kennedy.[4]

Schlesinger believed that Robert Kennedy should be put in charge of Latin American affairs. "This briefly fascinated [Johnson aide Bill] Moyers," Schlesinger wrote in his journal. Moyers was "sure that Johnson would give Bobby anything he wanted." But later that evening Schlesinger told the grief-stricken younger man that "the appointment would be great for the Alliance and for Latin America but might not be the best thing for his own political future." Kennedy said that he would stay on as attorney general "until the civil rights bill is passed, and thereafter he would be busy in the campaign until November." Kennedy thought that Johnson should be told that, "because of President Kennedy's intense personal concern with Latin America, no appointment should be made to the Latin American post without due consultation with his Latin American executors," including "Kennedy, [Peace Corps Director Sargent] Shriver, Goodwin, and Schlesinger."[5]

Schlesinger was not the only one who thought that the attorney general should play a role in Latin America policy under LBJ, or that Latin America should remain central to U.S. foreign policy. President Kennedy, Richard Goodwin wrote President Johnson, had hoped that a new position in the State Department could be created of "Under Secretary of State for Inter-American Affairs." Goodwin believed that it was essential in the next year to "demonstrate that the Alliance is going ahead full steam—more effectively than before." He anticipated that it would be a "campaign issue we can only deal with effectively if we have really accomplished something—or give the appearance of new accomplishments this year." Besides the domestic considerations, there naturally were international ramifications. Without "an enormous asset in the person of President Kennedy," Latin Americans "now feel rather lost." President Johnson, according to Goodwin, needed to place someone in charge "who will be a symbol of your personal concern and determination—someone who can rally the Latins behind him and impart a new vitality. *This cannot be done by a career officer*" (emphasis in the original). "In fact," he continued, "it can only be done by someone like Sarge Shriver or Robert Kennedy." Goodwin allowed that Johnson might have others in mind. For his part, Goodwin acknowledged that he himself had chosen much of the current leadership, and that had been a mistake. He assured Johnson that he was not interested in a position in administering Latin America policy.[6]

In the weeks following Kennedy's death, the Johnson administration recognized the new government in the Dominican Republic. Senator Morse called this a "sad mistake," placing every democracy "in jeopardy." The United States had "walked out on its responsibility to support and defend democratically elected constitutional governments in Latin America," one of the fundamental promises of the Alliance for Progress. "State Department hypocrisy," he continued, "is no substitute for statesmanship."[7]

Senator Humphrey privately urged President Johnson to give Latin America attention at the highest levels. He encouraged the new president to "give our most active support to the reform-minded non-Communist groups who truly espouse the objectives of the Alliance for Progress." He thought highly of Christian Democratic parties and looked to Eduardo Frei and his fellow party members in Chile, who had a good chance of winning the 1964 presidential election and implementing significant reform. (He exaggerated the importance of Christian Democrats in Brazil.) He warned that "younger progressive groups" should not be led to believe that the United States was turning back to the policies of the Eisenhower years: "the result will be disastrous for the [United States] in Latin America." Publicly, however, he applauded Johnson's attention to the "most critical area in the world today."[8]

As 1963 ended, some of those closest to Kennedy continued to believe that they would have some influence over the makeup of the Johnson administration. "It is clear that what Bobby would like most of all is to be Secretary of State," Schlesinger wrote in his journal, "presumably with Sarge [Shriver] as Vice President."[9] Schlesinger himself was clearly on the way out, as well he knew. He had no private meetings with President Johnson after early December. He had been "studiously not consulted" on the "subjects on which I worked for JFK," including Latin America. On the last Monday in January 1964 (27 January), he submitted his resignation again. This was no formality, and it was accepted immediately. Whether Johnson knew he could not "win him over" or simply did not think that it mattered all that much, he had done nothing to "involve me in the processes of the new administration." Of those in the administration with an interest in Latin America, Schlesinger was the first to leave. While his long-term impact was strongest on the writing of history and the creation of a Kennedy legacy, he continued to seek a role in influencing policy in the present, although largely from behind the scenes and (ultimately, for the most part) to little effect. Schlesinger still thought that Johnson would have to ask Robert Kennedy to be his vice president.[10]

In the aftermath of his brother's assassination, Robert Kennedy certainly had to recover his emotional equilibrium, but he also had to find a new role.

Although as attorney general he had no formal responsibilities in foreign affairs, he had served as his brother's closest adviser on many foreign policy issues. Even if he stayed on as Johnson's attorney general, his duties would now be limited to those of just one, not particularly influential, member of Johnson's cabinet with primarily domestic responsibilities. Over the first half of 1964, he continued to hope that he would be asked to run for vice president in the fall. Goodwin suggested to Schlesinger another possibility as well, including the notion of replacing a possible New York senatorial candidate Adlai Stevenson as U.S. ambassador to the United Nations. The younger Kennedy could engage with international issues, distance himself from the Johnson administration (to some degree), and build a political base in New York politics. Instead, as Johnson finally made it clear that he did not want him on the ticket, the attorney general resigned and ran for the Senate representing the state of New York.[11]

At this point there continued to be conversations about the possibility of creating an undersecretary position for hemispheric affairs. But who would be Johnson's top man? Many Kennedy aides had developed an interest in Latin America that they had not had before. Others had deepened their interests. Johnson wanted Kennedy men to remain with him in order to provide a sense of continuity. Some would leave the Johnson administration as soon as it seemed appropriate to do so. Others would serve for much of the Johnson years, often in new and important capacities. Those who served the Johnson administration and those who left were all involved in a debate over the Kennedy legacy as they sought to influence current Johnson administration policy.[12]

It is often said that Johnson, as a Texan, believed he understood Latin Americans. Yet he was far more committed to one of the traditional verities of postwar U.S. Latin America policy, that trade was better than aid, while his predecessor had been attuned to the region's hunger for social and economic development. Johnson's choice for the top position on Latin America could not have been less popular with many of those who had focused on Latin America in the Kennedy administration. Thomas Mann was seen as a "tough guy" who could consolidate authority over Latin America policy; he mistrusted the very program he was appointed to coordinate. Johnson assured him, "You can count on my intense interest and complete support." Liberal Democrats sought to block his appointment. In a meeting with Bill Moyers, Schlesinger insisted that the choice of Mann would be a "disaster." Schlesinger considered him a "free market ideologist . . . [who] did not really believe in the Alliance for Progress." This would mean a "reversion to the days of John Foster Dulles."[13] Schlesinger thought that Mann's "association has been in the past of Latin America, not in the future." Mann "ably served" "the policies of the Eisenhower administration," Schlesinger argued, but was "not only out of touch with the vital forces in contemporary Latin America—the democratic left, labor, the students, the youth, the intellectuals—but actively unsympathetic to these forces." Schlesinger and other Kennedy men saw his appointment as perhaps "a probe by Johnson and an attack in an area of special interest for the late President." Mann was suspicious of those, whether Kennedy men or "angry young men," who supported "structural change" in Latin America. Mann also quickly removed people who were interested in promoting democracy in Latin America.[14]

Ralph Dungan, who was one of the "very few people in this town for whom the hurting" continued less than a month after Kennedy's assassination, was also thought to be "on the way out" as early as 11 December. Johnson was not turning to him for advice on Latin America. There was concern that the Johnson White House would not even have someone focusing on Latin America. Dungan considered resigning.[15] But in staying on, however, Dungan ended up playing a major role in the administration's Latin America policy, although, as we shall see, he had to leave Washington to do it.

In early March 1964, Senator Morse wrote a letter to Norman Thomas in which he lamented the U.S. recognition of the military governments in Honduras and the Dominican Republic in the months following the assassination. He also noted how sad it was that the Senate Foreign Relations Committee could "be counted upon by a substantial majority vote to support military coups and juntas in Latin America." This was also true, he noted, for the Senate "as a whole." "We just apparently refuse to learn from historical events in Latin America." Too much U.S. foreign policy was "being dictated" by the CIA and the Pentagon. He considered too many of his friends to be "fair weather liberals" given to "expediency and unprincipled accommodation." They owed it to their constituents to follow "where the facts lead." Instead, they are "annoyed by facts."[16]

In mid-March 1964, Assistant Secretary Mann gave a "secret" speech to Foreign Service officers that indicated the administration would not distinguish between military governments and democracies in Latin America. The speech was leaked to New York Times reporter Tad Szulc, who had written widely on Latin America. The speech raised concerns among many like Frances Grant. Grant lamented the "mild denials" of the claims and expressed regret that the "casual makeup" of the U.S. delegation to the inauguration of the first democratically elected Venezuelan president to succeed another one (Raúl Leoni after Betancourt).[17] That one can speak of a Mann Doctrine is due to events in Brazil shortly thereafter; to understand the events of late

March and early April in that country, we have to back up and look at both internal and external forces and the state of play in the months after Johnson became president.

As discussed in the previous chapter, U.S. policy toward Goulart's Brazil was still being vigorously debated at the time of Kennedy's death. Ambassador Gordon had written to Mann in early December that "as you undoubtedly realize, Brazilian problems are going to figure heavily among your concerns of the coming months." "The depth and breadth of the popular anguish at Kennedy's death" demonstrated "how shallow is the anti-Americanism encouraged by some high governmental circles." A report by the Brazilian Strategy Working Group, which was finalized less than a week after JFK's death, argued that Brazilians were psychologically "not entirely geared to mid-twentieth-century demands and leadership responsibilities." The country's social structure and "inchoate party system" and "chaotic economic policies," its "corruption and jobbery," and "the spread of emotional (almost neurotic) nationalism in alliance with communist infiltration," all contributed to a difficult situation. The United States could not have Brazil "as a non-friend or an outright enemy." That "would demonstrably be extremely dangerous and costly to our security and overall interests in Latin America." The United States should have taken into account Brazilian psychological factors. The United States had expected too much in terms of the anti-inflation measures, which were economically necessary but politically impossible. The United States, the study concluded, needed to be more patient.[18]

Ambassador Gordon himself was not patient, and he more than anyone other than military attaché Vernon Walters had a more rigid assessment regarding where Goulart stood. But he told Secretary of State Rusk that given Goulart's psychological state and the pressures on him from the "nationalist-communist alliance," a personal letter from Johnson to Goulart could be a "decisive factor" in preventing him from appointing a "violently anti-American cabinet." Goulart had already written Johnson to express his personal anguish; in death Kennedy, Goulart said, was "fixed in the very act of struggling for generous causes." Johnson told Goulart that "economic development, social justice, and the strengthening of representative democracy are inter-related and that progress in each of those fields can only be made in conjunction with progress in the others." Gordon, however, did not have the relationship with Johnson that he had had with Kennedy. While accustomed to seeing Kennedy during his visits to Washington, Gordon had to wait until March of 1964 to meet Johnson, along with the other ambassadors to Latin American countries who had been "summoned."[19]

The evidence we have suggests that the most significant changes between Kennedy's death and the coup were more internal to Brazil. Civilian politicians and military leaders came together in a conspiracy to oust Goulart. The Brazilian president had not yet committed any unconstitutional acts (and, in fact, never did do so). But those who opposed him were increasingly unwilling to allow him to stay in power until the 1965 election.

On 13 March, his enemies were convinced that Goulart had finally "defined himself" at a rally that included "dangerous elements." His rhetoric always sounded more radical than his actual policy proposals, and he still had not done anything unconstitutional.[20] A week after Goulart's rally, a protest was held in São Paulo in which "almost every middle and upper class family was represented." A U.S. official admitted to finding "worrisome" the fact that much of the lower class was indifferent, perhaps even hostile.[21]

Gordon, recently returned from his visit to Washington, was convinced by late March that Goulart was "now definitely engaged in campaign to seize dictatorial powers, accepting the active collaboration of the Brazilian Communist Party and of other radical left revolutionaries to this end." The Brazilian president was expected to employ "urban street demonstrations, threatened or actual strikes, sporadic rural violence, and abuse of the enormous discretionary financial powers of the federal government." Gordon still thought that if he could be "frightened off this campaign and [served] out his normal term," "[t]his would still be the best outcome for Brazil" and for the United States.[22] Dungan wrote McGeorge Bundy to warn that the United States did not have "a clear appraisal of the current situation." We could "fool ourselves greatly if we posit certain eventualities and crank up even tentative actions in anticipation."[23]

U.S. support for a covert action called Operation Brother Sam was authorized on 20 March 1964. The United States Navy was sending 110 tons of fuel, small arms, and ammunition in anticipation of resistance to a coup. Johnson aide Dungan evidently was out of the loop when he was still speaking on 24 March of the 1965 elections, which they expected to take place. In retrospect, the most legitimate justification the armed forces had for acting was that Goulart had supported lower levels of the military in striking to air their grievances against their superiors. As March ended, the Brazilian military made its move against President Goulart. But many Brazilian civilian elites and the Johnson administration, as well as the military, were ready to see him go. The tanks, ammunition, and fuel the United States sent Brazil's way never reached Brazil, because the ease of Goulart's overthrow had made U.S. aid of that sort unnecessary. On 2 April 1964, Ambassador Gordon spoke of "Brazil's struggle to resist communist domination."[24] "Now the Alliance for Progress should have a real opportunity to successfully carry out its many important objectives."[25] There should be the "[g]reatest possible consideration . . . given to any request for economic emergency assistance . . . to support and strengthen ... the present regime."[26] President Johnson was happy with the result. He congratulated the Brazilians for maintaining constitutional traditions by deposing Goulart even while the president was still in the country. In a conversation with Mann on 3 April, Mann told LBJ, "I hope you're as happy about Brazil as I am." Johnson affirmed that he was. Mann insisted that it was the most important thing to happen in Latin America in three years. The president responded, "I hope they give us *some* credit, instead of hell."[27] Publicly, Johnson expressed his belief "that the transition in Brazil" had been "constitutional." (This was before a military man had yet been chosen to be president by a purged Congress.)[28]

The administration planned to provide aid for the new government from the beginning, although the nature of the government was not at all clear. Assistant Secretary of State Mann questioned Gordon regarding whether interim president Ranieri Mazzilli's successor would be "'above party interest' caliber," given the need "to attack problems on a non-partisan basis."[29] On 3 April, State Department officials completed a statement which indicated that the military had associated itself with "their people's deepest aspirations, as at critical times in the past, shown themselves to be a stabilizing influence and wholly free from ambitions to replace civil by military rule." Even Senator Morse supported Johnson administration policy in Brazil in early April 1964. It would not be clear for many years to come what role the United States had played in the coup itself, and Morse felt confident denying U.S. involvement. And at that point, it must be noted, Mazzilli, president of the lower house of the Brazilian Congress, a civilian, was still the acting president, and it was not yet clear to everyone that he had no real authority. The military had intervened before without taking power.[30] But the military was meeting with congressmen and soon made it clear to them that they had no choice but to elect a military man. A general and World War II veteran named Humberto de Alencar Castello Branco was sworn in as president in less than a fortnight. But even after Castello Branco had become president, it was assumed by many, seemingly including Castello Branco himself, that he would only serve out the remainder of Goulart's term.

Some U.S. officials showed reservations at every twist and turn, although there is no evidence that President Johnson himself had any reservations. The Johnson administration was committed to making the new government work. Following the coup, "AID authorized as many projects as possible in the first three months of the new government's administration."[31] The coup was depicted not only as having saved Brazil, but as having saved the Alliance for Progress.[32]

Although there was little overt resistance to the coup, the military launched a general wave of repression that particularly affected the poorer, northeastern part of the country, in which the political mobilizations of the late 1950s and early 1960s had been particularly shocking to mainstream politicians and military men. Peasant leaders, in particular, were targeted, some "disappeared," many were tortured.

The "Revolution" legitimated itself, which caused Ambassador Gordon some initial misgivings. Although Gordon was surprised by and not initially supportive of the decision of the military to stay in power (he even briefly considered resigning), he quickly came to terms with that decision. He later remarked, "Future historians may well record the Brazilian revolution as the single most decisive victory for freedom in the mid-20th century." He wrote to Dungan, "The new opportunities which this situation opens for us should be evident, and I gather from both correspondence and Hew Ryan's personal visit that this is well appreciated in Washington. I hope that it will continue to be so, because if there is a failure of policy now, the fault will rest with us and we shall have missed an opportunity which is most unlikely to repeat itself."[33]

Gordon was concerned that the mandates of "up to forty left-wing congressmen" would be revoked, "which would be grossly excessive," although he did not doubt that "true subversives" needed to be removed from office. Gordon warned top military men that "our ability to support depends upon domestic congressional and public opinion which is very sensitive to anything which smacks of old-fashioned reactionary Latin American military coup."[34]

But Gordon himself was reassured and sought to assure others like Senator Humphrey that this was not a "military dictatorship," despite Castello Branco's military background. As Gordon told Humphrey and others, he did not accept the idea that a reactionary government had replaced "a truly progressive" reformist one. He said that the "net effect" was "like awakening from a two and a half year nightmare, with an extraordinary opportunity now before us to help restart the course of Brazilian economic and social progress on healthy and durable lines."[35]

Gordon was soon overly committed to the man in charge in the country where he served as ambassador. Gordon admired General Castello Branco and expected him to "use his arbitrary powers with restraint."[36] Castello Branco, for his own part, thought that it was enough that he personally had no long-term interest in personal power. He believed that he was an impartial judge above the political system, in some ways similar to Brazil's second emperor, who dominated Brazilian politics for most of the second half of the nineteenth century.[37] Gordon worried that the United States would miss an opportunity to support the Brazilian government and turn it into a "lasting example" of "accomplishments and leadership" under the Alliance for Progress. He saw the Castello Branco regime early on as "genuinely working in full spirit of

Charter Punta del Este." This was something he had never believed about Goulart. The government needed time and aid to establish its "reformist nature" and gain popular support. He predicted that it would be a "moderate democratic government."[38]

Gordon had encouraged Johnson to send "very warm" congratulations on the occasion of Castello Branco's inauguration. "Our view in the White House," McGeorge Bundy suggested to Johnson, was that he should "be a little careful while this fellow's locking people up." Johnson said that he would be "a little warm," regardless of what the press might say. "I don't give a damn. I think there's some people who need to be locked up here and there too. I haven't got any crusade on 'em but I wish they'd locked up some before they took Cuba."[39]

Few U.S. politicians were that disturbed by the coup. None had admired Goulart. Most were willing to believe the worst about him once he had been definitively removed from power. The Inter-American Association for Democracy and Freedom declared that democracy had been "menaced by both President Goulart and his opponents." The IADF, however, condemned "the indecent haste" with which the U.S. government announced its support for the coup and the support for the government afterward, which certainly was, from its viewpoint, engaged in antidemocratic actions like the arrest of large numbers of citizens and the removal of many elected leaders from their positions.[40] Congressman Donald Fraser, who had served on the House Foreign Relations Committee as a freshman congressman in 1963, was not unhappy to see President Goulart overthrown, and he seemed to have had no concerns about the general who succeeded him. And Robert Kennedy was not any more skeptical of the new military government in Brazil.[41]

Not all liberal Democrats supported the coup. John Rielly, Senator Hubert Humphrey's top aide, called the Johnson administration's "embrace" "hasty, ill-advised." Rielly referred to Gordon, with whom Humphrey was to meet, as the "principal architect of US policy in Brazil" since the coup and a "complete apologist." He advised Humphrey to "express your concern about the trend." Schlesinger was another exception, and, during his travels in Italy in late April, his concerns were exacerbated by the response of the Europeans he talked to. McGeorge Bundy chastised him, noting that "the policy set in the Brazilian case was determined almost entirely by the recommendations of Lincoln Gordon, whose commitment to democratic values and to the policies of President Kennedy himself can hardly be doubted." (Bundy said, "those of us who loved President Kennedy" need "to give our full support to President Johnson.)[42]

At a critical turning point in the history of Latin America's Cold War, liberal Democrats failed to live up to their democratic ideals. Senator Morse was one of the first and one of the few to recognize that the image of the preservation of constitutional government had been an illusion. On 21 April he called for Brazil "to return to framework of constitutionalism quickly." But Morse would be isolated on this point for some time to come. Constitutionalism was not going to return quickly in Brazil.[43]

In the end, no Latin American country received more U.S. aid in the 1960s than Brazil. In the months following the coup, Ambassador Gordon made a push for large amounts of aid for the military regime and criticized forcefully any inadequate proposals that would prevent turning Brazil "into a lasting example" of a "moderate democratic government." This was a "unique moment in course of Latin American affairs. The coming two years are the right time to be in a position to apply resources on a scale sufficient to help consolidate the economic foundations of the enormous political advance made by the Brazilian Revolution last April."[44]

Gordon rarely seemed to recognize the dangers of embracing the "revolutionary" rhetoric of the regime. Mann, for his part, accepted the "desire to eliminate bona fide communist and subversive elements."[45]

Following reports that the U.S. public was concerned about President Johnson's handling of Latin America, National Security Adviser Bundy reassured Senator Humphrey that the problem really was that the administration was simply not doing a good enough job of informing the American people. "[Former General and now President Castello] Branco," he said, "does seem to be turning into quite a fine fellow." By September, as Walt Rostow noted to Assistant Secretary Mann, "We could not conceive of a government in Brazil more mature, more level-headed about relations with the United States, and in its attitudes toward private enterprise."[46]

As noted above, Castello Branco had initially planned to finish Goulart's term and leave office in 1965. This would have been in keeping with the Kennedy timetable policy. But in July he announced that he would not leave office until 1966 in order to achieve his goals. Ambassador Gordon supported Castello Branco extending his time in office in order to better deal with issues that concerned him. The United States "should be reassured in this regard by Castello Branco's obvious determination to help not harm Brazilian democracy."[47]

Johnson, who did so much to deepen democracy in the United States, promised to "encourage democracy" in the hemisphere. Nevertheless, his actions suggest that he lacked a similar missionary impulse in Latin America and that he did not distinguish between democratic and nondemocratic nations, in keeping with the Mann Doctrine.[48] Events in Brazil had hemispheric ramifications that only became clear over time. Most liberal Democrats were blind to them, in large part because they had never supported Goulart. Once he was out of power, their attitudes toward him hardened even more than they had previously toward Juan Bosch. But if civilians in Brazil were surprised that a military man was now in power, there was no reason for anyone to believe in 1964 that the military would stay in power until 1985. This was due to internal Brazilian dynamics, which will be discussed more fully in the following chapter. But the constant references to Brazil as a success story by both the Johnson and Nixon administrations helped shape perceptions of what the region needed.

Senator Hubert Humphrey was among those insisting that Latin America continued to be the priority that President Kennedy had assigned to it "as the most critical area in the world." He argued in a July 1964 *Foreign Affairs* article, in part, that U.S. commitments abroad had gotten out of balance. While he did not argue that Latin America was more important than Europe, he insisted that "the future structure of society and the external policy of Latin nations remains unanswered questions." Moreover, the role of these nations in world affairs was also somewhat up for grabs. The United States needed to act to forge a hemispheric unity that could otherwise slip away. The United States must continue to be committed to the Alliance for Progress, Humphrey argued. The Alliance must continue "to have a mystique all its own, capable of inspiring a following." The Alliance could not turn away from promises for "peaceful revolution." Latin American peoples, he asserted, were no longer marked by the fatalism of previous generations. Humphrey praised the role of Christian Democratic parties in Latin America. He criticized Cuban support for Venezuelan insurgents. He lauded private investment. He also encouraged European involvement in the region. The United States should recommit itself to economic integration, illiteracy eradication, and the other socioeconomic reforms associated with the Alliance. The United States should continue to work most closely with those countries that demonstrated a commitment to the goals of the Alliance, among which he included Castello Branco's Brazil.[49]

In his draft of the foreign affairs plank of the Democratic Party platform in 1964, Ambassador Stevenson affirmed the primacy of relations with Latin America. The United States must have it as its "constant concern to strengthen these relations," both through the Organization of American States and with the individual countries. The United States affirmed its commitment to "rapid economic and social progress and reform to satisfy the legitimate demand for modernization," so that Latin Americans don't "turn in desperation to extremism." Stevenson affirmed that communist subversion was "dangerous only because of this underdevelopment." Nevertheless, he referred to the "Castro regime" as "an alien disease in our midst from which infection may spread." Through the OAS, Cuba would be "quarantined" and "the disease isolated, until the Cuban people regain control of their own affairs and re-store democratic government." Stevenson asserted that the United States must "continue, both bilaterally and through international organizations, to assist generously in the development of emerging nations which are willing and able to use such assistance for the benefit of their people." The United States could not claim to be interested in the welfare of others, and its opposition to the spread of communism could not be realistic if the United States did not "carry out foreign aid programs of the magnitude and scope which modern times require."[50]

Not surprisingly, the final party platform was more modest in its goals, only promising to help developing nations "raise their standard of living and cre-ate conditions in which freedom and independence can flourish." There was to be an "increased priority on private enterprise and development loans." The platform promised support for the Alliance for Progress. There would be further attempts to carry out the OAS resolution to isolate "Castroism and speed the restoration of freedom and responsibility in Cuba." The platform also emphasized the economic benefits the United States received directly from the purchases of "aid-financed commodities." The platform also trum-peted the socioeconomic benefits of Alliance for Progress programs and the ways it had strengthened "the collective will of the nations of the Western Hemisphere to resist the massive efforts of Communist subversion and then headed for the mainland."[51]

The Bolivian military overthrew Paz in November, but even the most crit-ical historian of U.S. policy during this time period is unable to demonstrate that the Johnson administration had backed this coup (unlike the one in Bra-zil). Undoubtedly, Kennedy area policy in support of civic action programs helped establish the popularity of General René Barrientos himself. Paz had hardly been typical of liberal favorites in Latin America, even waiting until 1964 to break diplomatic relations with Cuba. But the Bolivian left was as strongly supportive of the coup as was the right, and the ideological orienta-tion of the new government was hardly clear.[52]

Johnson administration officials believed that they deserved some credit for carrying on the Alliance for Progress. Treasury Secretary Douglas Dillon noted in a speech before of the first Latin American meeting of development financing institutions that there had been more Alliance for Progress loans in the first six months of 1964 than in 1963. Frances Grant wrote Johnson to assure him that the "liberal democratic ranks of Latin America" were hope-ful following the elections. Following the landslide Democratic victory, for-mer Venezuelan President Betancourt wrote Vice President-Elect Hubert Humphrey, encouraging the Johnson administration to help stabilize demo-cratic institutions in the region. Humphrey's frequent trips to Latin America during the Kennedy years and his statements in the months following Kennedy's death added to the confidence that many had that Latin America would be a priority in the coming years.[53]

For Grant, Humphrey, Dungan, and many others, the other most important presidential election in the Western Hemisphere was in Chile. By late 1963, the popularity of the Christian Democrats, in whom they placed great expectations, was increasing. U.S. intelligence analysts saw a continuing "leftward trend in Chile." The "beneficiary of this trend," however, was not the traditional left, but rather the Christian Democratic Party. "This hitherto minor left-center grouping" was "attracting the votes of frustrated reformists who see little hope in the traditional political parties and are antagonized by the communistic tendencies of FRAP." (Presidential candidate Socialist Senator Salvador Allende was again allied with the Communist Party.)[54]

The United States faced an unprecedented challenge in the Western Hemisphere in an election, and the Johnson administration found various ways to try and influence that election; these were largely organized by Ralph Dungan. Alliance for Progress funding had been provided for projects that were supposed to have immediate and, ultimately, political impact, as had been the case in Brazil under Goulart. Deputy Chief of Mission John Jova had to discourage Dungan from arranging a visit by Robert, Edward, or Jacqueline Kennedy during the campaign. This would lead to charges of intervention, Jova said, and "would do us, and Frei, more harm than good." U.S. officials were convinced that they had to make clear that they had a preference even though Allende's coalition was using U.S. support against Frei. But although much was suspected in Chile at the time, few in the United States were aware that the Central Intelligence Agency covertly provided roughly $2.5 million to Christian Democrat Eduardo Frei's presidential campaign.[55]

By late August, McGeorge Bundy assured Humphrey that, besides the good news from Brazil, "If Chile passes its crisis on September 4, as we expect it will, we will have more to crow modestly about." The Johnson administration and its liberal Democratic allies were inspired both by the hope they saw in the Christian Democratic program and the threat they had long seen in the election of a left-wing president.[56]

Since the Chilean electorate for many years had been split in thirds between left, right, and center, it was common for a president to win with only a plurality. Fearful of an Allende victory, the right refused to put forward a serious candidate and voted in general for Frei, and the U.S.-backed candidate won with more than 50 percent of the vote. (Victory, it was recognized immediately, was in part due to the strong support of women for the Christian Democratic candidate.) Frei won with 56 percent of the vote, and he was convinced that he had a mandate for reform.[57]

The ironies of U.S. involvement in the 1964 presidential campaign abound. Covert action of this magnitude certainly violated the promises of nonintervention that had long been commonplace in the United States. The U.S. public was uninformed of U.S. actions in Chile in 1964. It remains unclear how widespread knowledge of this involvement was in official Washington. In Chile itself, U.S. involvement helped polarize the Chilean political system. Frei and Allende had served in the Senate together for years. The rhetoric used in the campaign helped destroy a friendship. But interference in the Chilean campaign had brought to power a man who shared the U.S. vision of reform and development more than any other in the 1960s, even more than Betancourt in Venezuela during the Kennedy years.[58]

Liberal Democrats in the United States were thrilled at the result, which seemed to vindicate U.S. policy. Frei had been a founding member of the Inter-American Association for Democracy and Freedom in 1950. Frei promised a "revolution in liberty." He envisioned his government as a popular one, expressing "the aspirations of the great forgotten masses, which not only want bread, but also dignity, and their fair share of happiness, culture, and responsibility." Over the course of the remainder of the decade, no South American country received more U.S. aid per capita ($1.2 billion in a country of less than ten million people) than did Chile.[59]

Relations between the Johnson administration and Frei got off to a rather rocky start, however. United Nations Ambassador Stevenson, who had been promised a larger role in foreign policy making by the new president, found himself still an errand boy, not least of all when, on the occasion of Frei's inauguration, he was ordered to argue forcefully with the leader regarding his plans to establish diplomatic relations with the Soviet Union. Frei tried to assure Stevenson that his government would be watchful regarding any Soviet misuse of their diplomatic mission. But Stevenson pressed the issue, and Frei and Stevenson ended up arguing heatedly, even in the end speaking over each other.[60]

Despite this rough beginning, and other examples of Johnson administration concerns in the years following regarding the Chilean president's independence on particular political issues, the reformist spirit of the Alliance for Progress stayed alive in Chile during the Johnson years, with land reform and rural unionization programs receiving strong U.S. support.[61]

No one in the Kennedy administration had been more interested in what Frei was trying to accomplish than Dungan, who had continued to be a special assistant to the president after Johnson took office. Dungan was a devout Catholic, with a profound interest in the changes then underway in the Church and, unsurprisingly, an affinity with the kind of progressive Catholic humanism represented by President Frei.[62] As his influence in the White House diminished under Johnson, he had hoped that the president would appoint him either to the ambassadorship in Santiago or to a senior position at the World Bank. As historian Joseph Tulchin notes, Dungan was chosen in part to counteract Thomas Mann's insensitivity regarding the "Chilean need for reforms." Although he neither knew Spanish nor had a business background, both disadvantages according to Bundy, he had "the great advantages of prestige in [LBJ's] Administration, proven sympathy for the progressive anti-Communist effort in Latin America, and a close personal friendship with Frei." Bundy noted that Dungan wanted the job "because it engages all his own convictions." (Politically, it also helped that Dungan was well-regarded in the mainstream liberal press in the United States.) Schlesinger wrote to Johnson to recommend Dungan for the ambassadorship, described the election of Frei as a potential "turning point in the struggle for democratic progress in the Americas." "It is imperative to the future of democracy in Latin America that the new Chilean government succeed." "It is therefore in our interest to give the new Chilean government all the help it can give," he wrote. No one could exert as much influence on Frei's government as Dungan could, and his "practical experience and wisdom in matters of government organization and policy could be of inestimable importance in making sure that the Frei administration gets off on the right foot in its first crucial days." Schlesinger also suggested that to choose a presidential special assistant would send a powerful message of Johnson's "own personal interest and commitment to democratic development in Latin America."[63]

Dungan considered it "unrealistic" "to expect that "the influence of Marxism-Communism can be eliminated as a credible force in Chilean political life." The reformist Christian Democratic Party, however, was committed to increasing the participation of ordinary Chileans in an already vital and dynamic civil society. If the United States could "insure that the Frei Administration [would] have a sufficient degree of success," Dungan predicted, "Marxism-Communism will be a lesser threat at the polls in 1970."[64]

It is instructive to compare the actions of two Kennedy men during the Johnson years, Dungan and Gordon. Both were creative, dynamic, and extremely active diplomats who were attempting to get LBJ's ear and push U.S. policy in Latin America in quite different directions. Both had distinctive visions of what the Alliance for Progress could and should be.[65] By the end of 1964, internal and external dynamics had led to dramatically different directions for two countries that were so critical in determining the success of U.S. policy in the region. Although the U.S. allies in Brazil and Chile in 1964 can be defined superficially as thoughtful men and anti-communist reformers, their political trajectories were mirror opposites. Castello Branco oversaw a shutting down of what had been a dynamic if troubled democracy. Frei's reformist government promised to do something about the country's intractable social problems while enhancing popular participation. Both counted on strong U.S. support during the Johnson years.

Privately, one of National Security Adviser McGeorge Bundy's aides spoke of the "President's public posture on Latin America as of first priority in his thinking" in December of 1964. The Johnson administration was satisfied with how things were going in Latin America. McGeorge Bundy wrote that 1964 had been "a consistently good year in Latin America." "Political freedom" had been "vindicated in Venezuela and Chile. In Brazil and Chile a responsible and progressive new government has begun an important program of economic and social reform—and the threat of a crumbling toward communism has been removed." An editorial in Chile's major newspaper *El Mercurio* after Johnson's inauguration in January 1965 credited him with having provided a "renovating impulse" to the Alliance. Dungan urged Bundy to encourage Johnson to travel to South America, but he was worried that Brazil would be the first country he would visit and encouraged him to visit countries like Peru and Chile, which had elected governments first. Dungan wanted the president to avoid "sterile meetings" like those of the OAS and find a way to convince the "masses of US and Presidential identification with their problems and aspirations."[66]

But 1965 was a turning point in U.S. policy toward Latin America. A major crisis took place in the Dominican Republic. The country had failed to establish a stable government with popular support following the overthrow of Bosch in late September 1963, despite an (admittedly, rather protracted) timetable for elections. In April 1965, an uprising sought to reinstate the deposed president. The Johnson administration quickly dispatched troops based on the claim that "American lives" were in danger. The United States had not invaded a Latin American country since before the establishment of the Good Neighbor Policy under Franklin Roosevelt. U.S. involvement expanded dramatically as President Johnson concluded that "people trained outside the Dominican Republic" were "seeking to gain control."[67]

John Bartlow Martin, whose activities as ambassador to the Dominican Republic were discussed in chapter 4, was called in on a fact-finding mission and to play a role in arranging a cease-fire. He had been worried that the United States might be seen as trying to set up "a new Trujillo" or engage in "a full-scale Marine occupation." In his conversations with the president, Johnson made clear that "another Castro take-over" was likely. Secretary of State Rusk suggested, however, that the last thing they wanted to see was Americans shooting Dominicans. LBJ insisted "sharply" that "the last thing" was a communist takeover. Johnson was less concerned about the prospect of losing support from the other countries in the hemisphere. Bundy suggested that there had to be some way "to use the OAS as a cloak for what we're going to do." Privately, Bundy told Martin that Johnson "really wanted to be able to say that we had sent a good Kennedy liberal down there." To what one imagines was Johnson's satisfaction, Martin himself quickly became convinced that communists were gaining control of the rebellion. But, as we shall see, Martin had little influence over liberal Democrats' varied responses to the invasion. On the island, Martin seems at least to have convinced Bosch that Johnson wanted a "liberal progressive government" established as soon as it was feasible.[68]

Attorney General Kennedy had resigned and made a successful run to represent the state of New York as a senator. He would not serve on the Senate Foreign Relations Committee, and he would still be only a junior senator in a hierarchical and tradition-bound institution, but unlike most in this role, he would not be quiet and wait his turn as it was expected he would. He would speak out frequently on foreign policy issues, and not just on Vietnam. It was expected that he would one day be president, perhaps following the election in 1972. But he had, in the short term, to deal with a Democratic president not named Kennedy. In terms of Latin America, he already had a record, not least of all in Brazil, where he had been highly critical of Goulart and had put pressure on him as his brother's right-hand man. He had been a staunch supporter of counterinsurgency and a friend to Cuban exiles. But while he had learned from mistakes of the Kennedy administration, he tended to gloss over them as he sought to define the Kennedy legacy. As senator, his positions changed, and not always in ways that pleased his former colleagues in the Kennedy administration.[69]

Initially, the New York senator was reluctant to criticize Johnson on a number of issues, "lest it lead to an impression that the Kennedys were breaking with the administration." But an early turning point was the Dominican invasion. Schlesinger, whose influence on the New York senator was stronger than it had been during his brother's presidency, was particularly concerned about the invasion. Schlesinger had been convinced by a conversation he had with Venezuela's former President Betancourt that the policy was wrongheaded. The historian hoped that President Johnson would meet with Betancourt and others who opposed it, and hoped that involving the OAS "would put us back on the right course." (It is striking to note that Schlesinger thought that the Dominican intervention might "weaken acceptance in our own country and throughout the world" of what had to be done in Vietnam.) Betancourt himself did not want to see Bosch back in power. He called him "the best short-story writer and the worst politician in Latin America." He criticized Bosch for not returning to the country, demonstrating "political incompetence and [a] personal lack of *cojones*." Nevertheless, he wanted Bosch's party to form an interim government in anticipation of OAS-sponsored elections and a multilateral peacekeeping force. Schlesinger was present when McGeorge Bundy spoke to Johnson about the possibility of a conversation between the two men. Johnson evidently was not interested in talking to Betancourt; nor were any other members of the administration. Betancourt had convinced Schlesinger that communists were not in control of the rebellion in the Dominican Republic. By the time Johnson agreed to meet with the Venezuelan, he had already publicly declared that they were, and Betancourt seems to have had no effect on Johnson's thinking. Schlesinger suggested that U.S. action without conclusive evidence gave the impression that the United States preferred military dictatorship to "popular democracy." Schlesinger blamed Thomas Mann and his "instinctive anti-liberal views" as well as "fragments of misinformation sent along in good faith, I guess, by the CIA." Furthermore, Schlesinger thought that the United States should have worked together with the Organization of American States, an institution whose importance Mann downplayed (according to Schlesinger).[70]

Schlesinger feared that the United States would support a leader in the Dominican Republic who was a "political primitive" who would "not be able to lead the Dominican Republic along democratic lines." He was certain that the intervention had already given "rise to grave doubts about our judgement and leadership among anti-communist progressive governments in such countries as Venezuela, Chile, and Peru." His son Stephen, who was then studying in England, said people were criticizing what they saw as "a trigger-happy, communist-obsessed, self-serving and unilateral policy in the Dominican Republic." Schlesinger and Burke Marshall convinced Senator Kennedy to give a speech that Schlesinger had drafted (and that Schlesinger called "low-keyed and tactful"). Kennedy spoke of the "tragic events in the last few days in our own hemisphere," but he left out the reference to "a Western Budapest" which had been in a draft of the speech. (Hungary was invaded by the Soviet Union in 1956.) Although this was the first time the New York senator criticized Johnson's policies, it received little attention at the time. The invasion, like most U.S. actions that had strong popular support from the U.S. public, would not be examined closely by Congress.[71]

It has been said by many that Ambassador Stevenson was disillusioned by Johnson's actions in the Dominican Republic, and that the invasion led to further doubts regarding the president's judgment in Vietnam. Journalist Eric Sevareid claimed that Ambassador Stevenson had wondered whether the Johnson administration had acted too quickly, without first garnering Latin American support. Schlesinger also said that Stevenson believed that "the Dominican intervention was hopelessly misconceived and mismanaged." Publicly, of course, Stevenson rejected the idea that Bosch's party itself was communist or extremist, but he insisted that "a small group of well-known communists" had quickly attempted to "seize control." He likewise insisted that the United States did not intend to impose a military junta or, indeed, support any "single man or single group of men" there. But the evidence available regarding his private opinion from this last phase of his life before his sudden death of a heart attack on a London street on 14 July is hardly conclusive. Stevenson had responded positively to Schlesinger's letter regarding the invasion and noted that no issue had caused him so much trouble in the UN since the Bay of Pigs invasion. In a Williams College commencement address in June, he noted that "Since Cuba, we know how irrevocable such a takeover can be, and how little it is thereafter subject to popular control. Yet we know, too, how easy it is to mistake genuine local revolt for Communist subversion." Nevertheless, the man who funded his 1960 trip to Latin America, former Senator William Benton, who was with him shortly before his death, rejected the idea that he had condemned President Johnson's action.[72]

Vice President Humphrey's foreign policy aide John Rielly noted that, given the negative response that the Johnson administration had received from the countries the United States supposedly saw as models for the region (Chile, Costa Rica, and Venezuela), "we could have made a more measured response." He did not reject the premise that it was necessary to prevent another Cuba, but he argued that the United States should have at least consulted the Organization of American States. Privately, Humphrey lamented that he was not consulted on the invasion. Publicly, however, he sought to reassure people that "the support of rightist, reactionary government is not part of U.S. policy." And, publicly as well, he argued that the United States had to act because the OAS and the United Nations failed to do so.[73]

The vice president had owed much of his political advancement in the Senate to former Majority Leader Johnson. Humphrey played a key role in the passage of the civil rights legislation that was presented as a Kennedy legacy but was more a testament to his successor's energies and the long-term impact of a powerful grassroots movement. Humphrey was now Johnson's vice president. Over the course of 1964 he had gone from questioning whether the Kennedy policy of promoting democracy in Latin America had been abandoned to considering the new Brazilian military government one of the main proponents of the Alliance for Progress. As vice president, he had proposed an alternative to Johnson's decision to commit ground troops in Vietnam in early 1965. The resentful president ostracized him for the rest of the year, so Humphrey played no role in the Dominican invasion. In the following year, he became one of the more strident advocates of the Southeast Asian conflict, gradually alienating many of his liberal friends, who came to question both the conduct of the war and the universality of the containment policy, which had been the guiding principle of their Cold War faith since the late 1940s.[74]

Chilean President Frei was primarily concerned about the failure of the United States to address the issue before the Organization of American States prior to sending troops. For him and others, U.S. unilateralism suggested a lack of interest in public opinion in Latin America. Dungan sought to press upon U.S. officials the idea that Chileans were primarily concerned about U.S. interventionism, noting that many felt that if Allende had been elected president, the United States would have invaded Chile.[75]

Ambassador Dungan privately often tried to distance himself from the Johnson administration, not least of all over the invasion. In June of 1965, he wrote Representative Frank Thompson Jr., "those in charge of Latin American policy had better change their views as to the realities of this hemisphere."[76] He was concerned that he had few kindred spirits among U.S. ambassadors to Latin American countries who shared his misgivings about U.S. policies in the region. He hoped for an opportunity to explain to Robert and "Teddy" Kennedy the issues raised by the invasion. Privately, he expressed his opinion that there needed to be an "unhurried seminar" with President Johnson. (Years later, Dungan claimed that this was when U.S. policy toward Latin America went astray.)[77]

Some in the Johnson administration wanted to punish the Frei administration for its refusal to support the U.S. invasion of the Dominican Republic. National Security Adviser McGeorge Bundy complained to Dungan that the United States was supposed to take the Frei government's "sensibilities" into account, but that they did not do the same for the Johnson administration. "We will not continue to make heavy sacrifices to help Chile," Mann wrote Bundy, "unless the Chilean government will cooperate with us on matters of hemispheric security." Continued criticism of U.S. action would have consequences.[78]

Former President Betancourt did not have to take "consequences" into account when he spoke at an Inter-American Association for Democracy and Freedom dinner in his honor in early June. While criticizing Castro's Cuba for its attacks on "Venezuela, the most coveted prize," he criticized "the 'unacceptable' unilateral armed intervention of the United States" for introducing "a new explosive element" in the region and dealing "a harsh blow to the inter-American juridical system." He expressed concerns regarding the possibility of "the installation in the martyred island of a right-wing military dictatorship, and not the reestablishment of constitutionality and democracy." The Organization of American States needed to work to create a way to respond to the threat of more Cubas. If the democratic countries took the leadership on this issue, they would guarantee that this would be an instrument for the Latin American people and not of "small oligarchies." Speaking at the same event, Schlesinger called the invasion an "attempt to deal with a new problem by an old method." The critical question to which no convincing answer had yet been found, according to Schlesinger, was, "How are we to know when a popular uprising becomes a communist revolution?" Neither oligarchs nor foreign investors should decide, and any such judgment should "be made, as far as possible, collectively" and in consultation with democratic leaders who knew communism best "through hard and bitter experience." Abandoning gunboat diplomacy in the early Roosevelt years had helped the United States as World War II began, and he warned that returning to the "Big Stick" approach would not help in the struggle against communism.[79]

The invasion ushered in a new era of aid for the Dominican Republic. U.S. food and emergency relief aid during the occupation helped the anti-Bosch forces in their efforts to marginalize the pro-Bosch forces. As had happened in Brazil and Chile, an emphasis was placed on "impact projects." And while the United States succeeded in stabilizing the situation in the Dominican Republic, they were also creating problematic dynamics that liberal Democrats would not address, as I shall discuss further in the next chapter.[80]

Congressional Democrats with an interest in Latin America, like Minnesota's Donald Fraser, traveled to the island nation in the following months. Fraser expressed some concern that the United States needed to "be sure it's in touch with the full spectrum of political groups in the country." He continued to express support for Johnson's action, but he also hoped that the United States could do a better of job of understanding the "role of communists in this kind of revolution," but he expressed faith in letting people know that they can have an opportunity to "make their choice by ballots instead of through force." Like many other liberals at this time, he expressed a belief in multilateral action. Sacha Volman, a Bosch adviser, continued to try to get Fraser to focus on the domination of the army by people associated with the Trujillo regime.[81]

As early as June 1964, Senator Frank Church had noted that as far as foreign relations went, he was spending "most of the time I have available thinking about Asia and Viet Nam." But Church also noted his agreement with Senator Humphrey that "what happens in Latin America is of primary importance to our country." He developed this idea further in one of his major speeches of the Johnson years, "How Many Dominican Republics and Vietnams Can We Take On?" "Americans are always prepared to fight when their country is threatened," Church asserted in December 1965. "The doubt and the disagreement relate to how deeply we could involve ourselves in civil wars of other countries." People were "wondering" whether the United States was "to be self-appointed firemen scurrying to quench every revolutionary blaze, no matter how repugnant the government that sounds the alarm." Church decried the tendency to "downgrade freedom by equating it with the absence of communism; we upgrade a host of dictatorial regimes by dignifying them with membership in what we like to call the 'Free World.'" The United States offered "a ration of foreign aid, with which we seek to buy a little reform, some small measure of relief, as a substitute for revolution." Those who criticize this policy were accused of being "appeasers," "soft on communism or sold on surrender." But the Senate dissenters were not "isolationists," but "confirmed internationalists." Church himself was opposed at this point to "any unilateral withdrawal of American forces" in Vietnam. He supported the United Nations and "sensible foreign aid programs," the Peace Corps, and NATO. Unrest in the world was due to internal problems, and only "countries enjoying good internal health" could be immune to infection from guerrilla wars, "the germs of which are carried on the winds of change." Church called for "a prudent restraint . . . , a foreign policy more closely tied to a sober assessment of our own national interests." He had been supportive of the Johnson administration's action in the Dominican Republic from the beginning, calling the Caribbean "a region of prime strategic importance to the United States." The Cuban Missile Crisis had shown how much was at stake there. The United States would not "abide" another Castro-style government "so close to our southern shores." He had been certain from the beginning that "Communist elements" had been involved in the Dominican Republic and that Johnson had responded prudently to a "clear and present danger." Months later, he noted, "Although we can debate whether or not Communists had actually seized control of the uprising in Santo Domingo, the President's decision to send in American troops sprang from his most fundamental responsibility as Commander-in-Chief—the defense of the country." This, according to Church, was quite different from Vietnam, "where the security of the United States is not at issue." "Our objective must surely be not to drive the genuine democrats in the Dominican revolution into association with the Communists by blanket characterization and condemnation of their revolution." "Saigon," he noted, "does not stand guard over Seattle." In Vietnam, the United States was fighting "to defend our national reputation." (And, of course, it would prove to be easier to extricate U.S. troops from the Dominican Republic than from Vietnam.) But it was still necessary to avoid converting "the conflict into an American war." ("When we took up the wreckage of empire left behind by the departing French, we ensnared ourselves in a Vietnamese war of secondary importance.") The United States could not impose "an American solution upon every insurgency abroad." Church noted the existing conflict between China and the Soviet Union and the surprising independence of smaller (unnamed) communist countries. "The Communist world is unraveling; it bears no resemblance to a monolithic mass." The United States should "through our diplomacy and our example, guide these currents toward democratic ends."[82]

There was much talk of multilateralism at the time. Could "machinery" in the OAS, Vice President Humphrey wondered in a letter to Lucille Milner, author of *Education of an American Liberal*, be "established to deal with revolutions which raise the possibility of additional Communist governments being established in the hemisphere?"[83] But when a peacekeeping force was established for the Dominican Republic, the most enthusiastic participant was the military government of Brazil.[84]

Dungan at times expressed frustration with what he took to be the attitude of some in the Johnson administration that "countries like Chile should remain compliant lackeys of the United States."[85] Dungan was fighting for his credibility with the Frei government by "preserving the impression in Chile" that he was close to Johnson. But while he met with Vice President Humphrey, he was not able to meet with the president in March of 1965. (Chilean Ambassador Tomic, for his part, had not had his credentials received yet either.)[86]

As far as the post-invasion realities in the Dominican Republic were concerned, Frances Grant wrote Senator William Fulbright regarding her concern that Joaquin Balaguer, whom she referred to as "one of [Trujillo's] most faithful and servile supporters," might end up coming to power. She said that he had done nothing for the Dominican people and had failed to distance himself from his Trujillo connections. She predicted serious "repercussions" if he "should be installed in high office."[87]

Considering what many saw as the overreaction to events in the Dominican Republic, it may seem surprising that Johnson took no dramatic steps against Fidel Castro himself. President Johnson did not have much confidence in the covert action programs conducted during the Kennedy years against Castro, including Cuban exile sabotage operations. These had long been counterproductive, but there was some concern that the Johnson administration would send signals that the United States was willing to live with a Cuba led by Castro. But even Central Intelligence Agency officials by this point recognized that Castro's position was strong. And Johnson was not focused on Cuba as Kennedy had been. As a State Department official responsible for Cuba noted, "I used to get a call . . . every day about something." During Johnson's presidency, "the calls dropped down to probably once a week, then maybe once every two weeks or once a month." As Thomas Mann told Johnson, "As long as that army is loyal to him, he's going to be there until he dies." Most liberal Democrats accommodated themselves to a Western Hemisphere in which Cuba would be isolated and Castro's influence would be increasingly contained. In October 1964 Senator Church assured a constituent that no "new governments friendly to Cuba have come in power since 1961 and several—particularly Brazil—have rid themselves of governments sympathetic to Castro."[88]

The most significant change in U.S. foreign policy during the period covered in this chapter was the expansion of U.S. involvement in Vietnam. Johnson had "chosen war" by sending in ground troops and beginning the bombing of North Vietnam in the spring and continuing to expand U.S. military action in the summer, but he had done so, as LBJ aide Harry McPherson insisted, in part "because he was a liberal himself, and the leader of a liberal party." In one of his few direct comparisons of U.S. policy in Latin America with U.S. policy in Southeast Asia, President Johnson remarked that both represented the "American policy of perseverance in a just cause." The war in Vietnam was much more complicated than the guerrilla struggles in Latin America. Vietnam would occupy liberal Democratic imaginations and swallow up U.S. resources and lives. In contrast, no more major crises developed in Latin America. Stability had been achieved in Brazil and was soon to be achieved in the Dominican Republic, and even the short-term costs of those accomplishments were not widely discussed in the United States. Few seemed to notice that Kennedy's "timetable" policy was no longer being followed. Inevitably, Latin America was going to get less attention and aid. But significant changes took place over the rest of the Johnson years, nonetheless, and liberal Democrats who had engaged with Latin America in the previous decade would have to deal with the consequences of the terms of the Kennedy engagement and the nature of the Johnson disengagement.[89]

Chapter 6

Robert Kennedy, Kennedy Men, the Kennedy Legacy, and the Johnson Alliance

Liberal Democrats, particularly those closely associated with John Kennedy, began to construct a Kennedy legacy for Latin America, even as, in real terms, the Johnson administration and most liberal Democrats had to focus on other parts of the globe. Despite a much-publicized visit by New York Senator Robert Kennedy, Latin America became less of a destination and focus for congressmen during the Johnson years. More still seemed to be at stake in countries like Brazil and Chile. Democracy promotion thrived only in Chile and, to a lesser extent, Venezuela, and was, to a large degree, abandoned in the Dominican Republic, where hopes had been tempered in the Kennedy years but the stakes still had been presumed to be high. Counterinsurgency continued, often almost on automatic pilot as a matter for the military, but with what were considered to be important if largely uncelebrated successes. Liberal Democrats (and liberal ambassadors), even those who had once championed it, were more skeptical regarding its virtues. The costs of containing the left in Brazil, for example, were not clearly evident until the last weeks of the Johnson administration, but the war in Vietnam was making many question the global commitment to containment.

When Robert Kennedy traveled to South America in November 1965, he said that he wanted to let people know that the Alliance for Progress was "still as alive and important as it was under President Kennedy." But he also was somewhat tentatively beginning to criticize Johnson's own policy, if warranted, noting elsewhere that he wanted "to see if the Alliance for Progress is doing as well as it was in President Kennedy's time." Schlesinger saw the senator as arriving "at a critical juncture." Schlesinger certainly hoped that the New York senator would criticize Johnson, since he thought that the administration's "hard-line policies" in Latin America were appealing to the "old oligarchies" and "profoundly dismay[ing] the progressive democrats." When pressed, however, Robert Kennedy was often reluctant to say that the two Democratic presidents had different policies. He rejected the idea that the United States caused "the downfall" of Goulart. He promised Chileans, however, that if a communist was elected president, "there would be no, and there should be no, intervention by the United States." He also promised that the United States did not intend to stay in the Dominican Republic and that there would be free elections there. (Schlesinger encouraged him to sidestep questions about the invasion by making the general point that the communist threat in the Western Hemisphere was "real.")[1]

Ambassador Gordon tried to assure the senator that "the situation" in Brazil was evolving "quite favorably." Journalists and others, however, sought to warn Kennedy against praising the country's military leaders.[2] Anger over the invasion of the Dominican Republic, moreover, Kennedy knew, was widespread throughout the region. On his trip he expressed sympathy for economic nationalism. He visited mines, sugar plantations, and shantytowns.[3] He visited places no one else (since Schlesinger and McGovern) wanted to visit, to really observe Latin American poverty up close. (He was increasingly doing the same in North America.) One Argentine wrote Kennedy to tell him that the poor people living in the shacks were "still wondering why a U.S. Senator paid attention to them." But Kennedy did not seem to note the irony of his visiting a poor neighborhood in Chile that had been named after the deposed Brazilian leader João Goulart.[4]

Kennedy received an enthusiastic response when he went to democratic Peru. There, as in Chile and elsewhere, he spoke with left-wing students who were critical of U.S. policy. His sympathies were fully engaged. In a talk in Brazil he argued that "just being anti-communist" was "self-destructive." In Chile, he noted that, "If I worked in those mines, I would be a Communist too." He warned that "economic progress, without democratic institutions" could not be "very meaningful over a long period of time." The New York senator argued that "the responsibility of our time" was "nothing less than to lead a revolution, a revolution which will be peaceful if we are wise enough; human if we care enough; successful if we are fortunate enough; but a revolution which will come whether we will it or not." "We," he said, not specifying who he was talking about, "can affect its character; we cannot alter its inevitability." He was most impressed with Chilean President Eduardo Frei and his advisers, but was worried that if they did not succeed, a communist government would be able to gain power through electoral means in the next election.[5] He supported reformist elements, "rather than being momentarily safe, and, in the long run, sorry." In the United States, he claimed, "it was the revolution of the New Deal that showed the power of affirmative free government—of government which joins the ideal of social justice to the ideals of liberty."[6]

Over two days in May of the following year, following intensive research by his staff, the New York senator spoke at length and in great detail about the Alliance for Progress, based in part on his trip the year before, but also on conversations he had with people knowledgeable about Latin American affairs. On the first day, he began by making note of President Johnson's trip to Mexico in the previous month, remarking that "even in the midst of crisis in Vietnam and Europe, the President of the United States does not forget that to the south are lands of 230 million people, with whose future we are and must be intimately concerned." He said that Johnson and the United States stood "unequivocally for democracy and social justice." Kennedy sought to emphasize the United States' continuing "commitment to the ideals of the Alliance" and tried to "still the doubts of any, in Latin America and the United States, who question the depth and duration of those ideals." The "greatest danger," he continued, was that the Alliance would be "no more than words," "a precious talisman to be taken from its case and exhibited periodically." The words had to be acted upon. Latin Americans needed to have access to land and a sense of involvement in their societies and political systems. He warned that the United States had too long focused on maintaining "surface calm" there. He spoke of favored Latin American leaders, like Brazil's Kubitschek, Chile's Frei, and Venezuela's Betancourt. And he praised his older brother, who "saw that what was important was not the statistics of economic development, but the human and spiritual reality behind them." There could be "no preservation of the status quo in Latin America." He encouraged a more nuanced view of Latin American politics, and praised "democratic parties speaking for the majority of the people and acting in response to their interests," citing those of Chile, Peru, and Venezuela, in particular. He dwelt on the dreary lives of the poor in urban slums and sugarcane fields, but he also focused on positive economic changes that were taking place. He also included his characterization of the coming revolution, which had been so striking during his South American trip. Moreover, he held out the possibility of that revolution being "guided." He encouraged further U.S. engagement and concrete actions. He spoke at length about the potential and the danger he saw in the role of university students and ways to get them on the side of the United States.[7]

Schlesinger saw RFK in mid-1966 as most interested in foreign policy—"Vietnam, Latin America, Africa." He also had "the burning vision of a world of young people with legitimate and often revolutionary aspirations." The New York senator believed that "American policy will fail unless it recognized these aspirations and seeks the support of the young throughout the world."[8]

Senator Morse praised the speech as the most important that had been given in the Senate since the Alliance had been created five years before. Morse emphasized his understanding that the Alliance for Progress was intended to "be of assistance to the democratic leaders in Latin America, as they are developed, to bring about the necessary social, economic, and political reform that must be achieved in many of those countries if the danger of communism is to be met." He further argued that "at the beginning it was never contemplated that the Alliance for Progress should be a military aid program."[9]

On the following day, Senator Kennedy continued by arguing for enhanced U.S. aid for economic development. He noted that while the United States was much wealthier than it had been in the 1950s, it was providing proportionately less foreign aid than it had been. He rejected the belief that foreign aid was a "giveaway," asserting "that it is both a moral obligation to fellow human beings and a sound and necessary investment in the future." He proposed doubling "capital aid" in the coming years, suggesting that it "might be well to remember that the most we are suggesting is what would be the equivalent for all Latin America of the cost of approximately four weeks of the struggle in Vietnam." He echoed Secretary of State Rusk's proposal that the Alliance for Progress be extended into the 1970s. He also argued for commodity price stabilization efforts. Latin America itself needed to do more to expand its own internal markets through efforts to improve the incomes of the Latin American poor. He viewed with alarm the declining U.S. investment in the region during the Alliance years, but he also offered rhetorical support for Latin American efforts to manage the flow of foreign investment. (Rhode Island Senator Claiborne Pell interjected that "Because of the unpleasant fog of events in far off Vietnam, we have not given the thought and concentration we should give to the problems close at hand—in our own hemisphere.") Senator Kennedy also argued for efforts to slow the growth of Latin America's population (his own sizable progeny notwithstanding).[10]

Furthermore, U.S. policy "must always be directed toward the strengthening of full representative democracy in every country in this continent." And yet he justified the overthrow of Brazilian President Goulart (and distorted the legitimacy of his presidency itself). He said that Brazil "had made considerable steps forward, and considerable steps backward, it seems, on balance, a far better government than the one it replaced; yet it is still far from the constitutional democracy which is its stated objective, which most Brazilians desire, and which I believe is the desire of President Castello Branco." He made clear that he supported U.S. aid of all types to Castello Branco's government. But the United States still needed to speak out on the government's imprisonment of opponents of the regime. The New York senator suggested a return to Kennedy administration policies of making funding to countries in which recent coups have taken place contingent on providing timetables for free elections (which had been a success in Peru, at least).[11]

The communist threat in Latin America continued to be real, Kennedy argued, but it should not be confused with attempts by some to protect their privileges. Moreover, he argued that the intervention in the Dominican Republic had hurt the U.S. image in Latin America, making the need for "vigorous positive action" all the greater. The United States also "must not, by careless or undue aid to the military, hinder Latin Americans in their efforts to eliminate the military's role in their politics." Military aid should be tied to a large extent to the actual existence of an actual threat from an insurgency.[12]

W. Averell Harriman, veteran diplomat and ambassador-at-large for both the Kennedy and Johnson administrations, praised Senator Kennedy for his speech on the Alliance, noting that he had said things "which for a long time had needed emphasis." He said that he had heard that it had gotten a "good reaction among the Latinos." Yet he suggested that he was playing down a subject he knew well and "in which you . . . made a major contribution while you were in the government." Harriman felt that the senator had "downgraded or least gave inadequate attention to the threat of communist insurgency." He suggested that the Tri-Continental Conference (discussed below) had suggested that the greatest threat from Castroite insurgencies was to democratic governments. The international communist support of so-called "'liberation movements' continues to require energetic and detailed attention in the best Robert Kennedy tradition." "Essential as social reforms are they alone cannot suppress the kind of terrorist and guerrilla actions now being mounted with outside support." (After Robert Kennedy was assassinated, Harriman praised him for the "penetrating questions" Kennedy posed during the Special Committee, C.I. [Counterinsurgency] meetings. Furthermore, he said, "I think it is fair to say that many of the countries in Latin America today have Castro's terrorist guerrillas under control due to the foresight and vigor of Robert Kennedy.")[13]

As Edward Kennedy biographer Neal Gabler has written, Robert Kennedy was a liberal senator "by trauma." The New York senator's willingness to throw himself into the poor Latin American neighborhoods echoed his visits to impoverished neighborhoods and Indian reservations in the United States and reflected his deep immersion in the issue of poverty in the years following his brother's death.[14] But otherwise, his discussion of Latin America tended increasingly toward the abstract, and it was, of course, the war in Vietnam and not Latin America policy that propelled him into leadership in opposition to President Johnson.[15] Vietnam was not yet an analogy or a syndrome, but two countries and a war that cost money and lives, and certainly diverted attention from Western Hemisphere affairs. It would also give a bad name to counterinsurgency and nation-building as well for many years to come, but unlike in a few parts of Latin America, democracy promotion had not really been tried there.

The Johnson administration clearly was returning to the emphasis on stability of previous decades. Morse, one of only two senators to vote against the

Tonkin Gulf Resolution, was increasingly disgruntled with Johnson's policies in Latin America. By late 1965, the Castello Branco government had outlawed the existing political parties, replacing them with two parties (one that would support the government and one that would technically be the opposition party) and making elections for president and vice president (and even governors) indirect. Few in Congress other than Senator Morse seemed to recognize the implications of this.[16]

The Johnson administration was more comfortable with military government than the Kennedy administration had been. As Edwin Lieuwen, a prominent University of New Mexico historian, noted in a 1967 report he wrote at the request of Senator Morse for the Subcommittee on American Republics Affairs, which the Oregon senator still chaired, the Johnson administration did not continue the nonrecognition policy which the Kennedy administration had employed somewhat inconsistently. Nor did it require timetables for elections prior to recognition. At the same time, the historian suggested, "The Alliance for Progress may have also contributed to the current wave of military interventions. For it was the view of many Latin American military leaders that the U.S. government's public advocacy and support of crash programs of material development and social change conducted through the medium of authentically democratic regimes was tantamount to encouraging political instability and social disintegration." U.S. military aid remained primarily focused on internal security; Lieuwen considered this threat "distorted and exaggerated." More thought should be given to programs, many of which were, in military terms, irrelevant. But the goal of maintaining the political support of the Latin American military was always implicit. At the same time, the policy of strengthening the military clearly was in conflict with the ostensible goal of supporting democracy in the region. The scholar urged a return to the practice of requiring military governments to plan for elections in the near term. He also demonstrated a confidence that the United States, through its ties with the military, could do more to convince the military to be supportive of civilian authority and democratic government.[17]

Ambassadors Gordon in Brazil and Dungan in Chile continued to promote their visions of the Alliance in their respective countries. Brazil, as noted before, received more U.S. aid than any other Latin American country, and Chile, a much smaller country, received more aid per capita. Their opposing political trajectories reflect the contradictions of liberal Democratic policy during the Johnson years.

Under Castello Branco, a hybrid political system was created, with a Congress purged of those the military considered least desirable and with the extent of its remaining powers left unclear. The military issued a series of "institutional acts" over the next few years that gave shape to the new order.

The military could submit constitutional changes, which the Congress would have thirty days to consider before passing them with a simple majority. The coup had enjoyed considerable civilian support, and civilians did serve in the cabinet as well as in the Congress, but they did not make the most important decisions. Although privately, even as early as June of 1964, Gordon warned of the "danger [of the] militarization of whole political process," Gordon and others in the Johnson administration consistently downplayed the limits of civilian authority in public and always saw President Castello Branco as poised between extremes. (This was only possible if one completely wrote off all civilian Brazilian politician opponents of the regime as extremists.) The Central Intelligence Agency was more skeptical, arguing that despite the president's claims to be "a civilian presiding over a conventional government," "the military are obviously exerting influence on official policies to an unusual degree." In a later report, the CIA noted that "since Castello Branco has been in office, the opposition in Congress has been somewhat timid in its relationship with the executive, partly to avoid antagonizing the watchful military."[18]

Castello Branco and his associates, for their part, believed that only they could enact the reforms necessary to transform Brazil, and that belief made them reluctant to move quickly to restore constitutional democracy. The general had initially intended to simply serve out the rest of Goulart's term and hold elections as scheduled in 1965. In July of 1964, however, the elections were postponed until November 1966, and Gordon applauded the move, which he believed would make important (primarily economic) reforms possible. The United States "should be reassured in this regard by Castello Branco's obvious determination to help not harm Brazilian democracy." Moreover, the general believed that in that time he could teach the Brazilian people how to elect the right kind of politicians. The ambassador, for his part, was more concerned about reporting in the U.S. media that suggested that hard-liners were in control. To congressional critics like Senator William Fulbright, Gordon described the Castello Branco regime as "engaged in a strenuous effort for reform and modernization in addition to the fight against inflation and the reduction of corruption and subversion to tolerable limits." Brazil needed "modernizing reforms (many of a New Deal variety)."[19] Gordon repeatedly sought to shape U.S. opinion regarding Brazil by trying to correct what he saw as mistaken impressions in the media, frequently comparing the regime to that of Roosevelt. He claimed that improvements in the "electoral law" were "strengthening . . . democratic institutions" and that Brazil under Castello Branco was as democratic as "Mexico or France."[20]

And yet Gordon told Secretary of State Rusk that it would "be obvious to department that second institutional act represents severe setback in our own hopes," but tried to assure him that the act fell "well short of outright dictatorship." In private conversation, Gordon told Castello Branco that he was both "shocked at [the] extent of arbitrary powers assumed" and "sorrowful" at the failure to bring about "full constitutional normalization without jeopardizing basic purposes of revolution." Gordon privately expressed surprise that "there seemed to be some indication of desire by armed forces to assume governmental responsibility itself." President Castello Branco, for his part, made it clear that those like former President Kubitschek who thought that he had any intention of returning Brazil to the political situation prior to the coup were mistaken. Given this, he could not really explain how the military could ever accept a return to a truly democratic order. For several weeks, Ambassador Gordon kept the pressure up in private conversations and even urged some kind of public expression of regret by the State Department or President Johnson. Publicly, however, the United States refused to comment on this further move toward arbitrary government, suggesting that it was purely an internal matter. Gordon worried that this made people in the hemisphere believe that the United States either condoned or approved the move. Despite Gordon's concerns that the Castello Branco government was giving in too much to the military hard-liners, the White House worried that to criticize Brazil openly in 1965 might lead to problems with ongoing Brazilian military cooperation in the occupation of the Dominican Republic. By 14 November, Gordon was arguing that "we should have no illusions regarding our ability to influence [the] course of political developments in Brazil." And so, after a brief delay in scheduling loan negotiations, by early December, both McGeorge Bundy and Thomas Mann were arguing that President Johnson should "approve the request for authority to negotiate the $150 million program loan with Brazil," given the country's "outstanding record of self-help" at a time in which the government was "under attack from the left and right-wing extremes." (At that time, the government's only serious domestic critics were centrists and rightists.) Brazil, Mann noted, "is the keystone of our interests on the continent of South America." (There was even some hope in the administration at this point that U.S. aid could be used as leverage to encourage the Brazilians to help out in Vietnam, as well.) Despite the occasional quiet and frank conversation about the country's political direction, Brazil remained the largest recipient of U.S. aid in Latin America.[21]

In any case, despite these political setbacks (which were indicative of more to come), the primary concern of Gordon's interests in Brazil had long been economic. The military government had been welcomed for its embrace of orthodox economic stabilization policies, which stood in stark contrast to the inconsistent and ineffective economic policies of the former civilian administration.[22] The United States also was pleased by the military government's partial turn away from the economic nationalism of the civilian government.

The administration's "lack of fear of unpopularity" was an asset as far as economic reform was concerned. Castello Branco, moreover, spoke in favor of the Alliance for Progress, whereas Goulart had been somewhat skeptical toward it. Gordon used this support for the Alliance in arguing for continued aid as the military assumed more power. It was only through a significant narrowing of the definition of Alliance goals, however, that U.S. aid for the military regime could be justified.[23]

While Gordon's interests were primarily economic, Ralph Dungan's were primarily political. Dungan had the instincts of a politician's aide, and Gordon those of a technocrat. Dungan was even willing to encourage actions by the Frei administration that ran counter to U.S. economic interests, such as the so-called Chileanization of the copper companies, through which the state gradually gained a controlling interest in U.S.-owned companies.[24] Dungan's understanding of development, moreover, was broader. Gordon defined the Alliance as "a sustained and cooperative effort to accelerate economic growth and social progress throughout Latin America, working through democratic institutions based on respect for the individual."[25] Gordon was always good with the details of economic policy and more comfortable talking before economically savvy audiences, though, unfortunately, he was seemingly deaf to the relentless political trend toward increasingly authoritarian government. Gordon later remarked that his "greatest failure as Ambassador" was his "inability in 1965 and 1966 to persuade President Castello Branco to undertake the building of a new kind of political infrastructure, for which he had an unrivaled opportunity."[26] Yet Castello Branco succeeded in creating a totally new, hybrid structure, which, with some modifications, lasted for two decades. Even if one did not expect Gordon as ambassador to criticize publicly the arbitrary policies adopted by the Brazilian government, one could argue that providing so much aid was sending the government the message that the military was free to do whatever it chose.[27]

In the case of Chile, however, substantial economic aid was going to support a government with indisputably reformist credentials. Dungan was hardly alone in thinking that "this government and country probably have as good a potential as any for fulfilling our objectives in the hemisphere." The U.S. Agency for International Development's David Bell noted Chile's disproportionate influence in the region and in Europe, arguing that "the struggle between anti-American Marxism and progressive democracy is nowhere else in Latin America as sharply defined as in Chile."[28] Although the Johnson administration and Ambassador Dungan himself had hoped to stop supporting the Christian Democratic Party directly after the 1964 presidential election, the aid continued, not only to the country and government but to the party itself. Ambassador Dungan, for his part, approved further aid for

Christian Democratic congressional candidates in the March 1965 elections.[29] The Christian Democrats became quite dependent on U.S. aid during the Dungan years, even requesting (and receiving) support during the 1967 municipal elections.[30]

Frei's Chile was a country in which Alliance money was but one component in a vibrant reform process. Although land reform itself affected fewer people than the Chilean president had initially hoped, there were other dynamics at work. Rural unions, in particular, were proliferating in a way that promised to both deepen Chilean democracy while strengthening Christian Democratic influence in the countryside, where the Socialists and Communists were less strong than they were in mining and urban sectors. Literacy campaigns and consciousness-raising programs designed by Brazilian educator Paulo Freire, though not supported by U.S. aid, played an important role in the Revolution in Liberty as well. Nevertheless, government policies also inadvertently, though hardly surprisingly, encouraged efforts by peasants to take matters into their own hands, sometimes leading to violent repression by landowners and even government forces.[31]

Dungan believed that Frei was "determined to awaken the underprivileged and to encourage them to press for a new deal in Chile." He recognized the risks this involved, given that Frei was "playing with forces which cannot always be predicted and controlled," and believed that the United States "should be willing to accept short-term developments in Chile which might seem not to be in its interests."[32] Frei's Chile appealed to those like Minnesota Congressman Donald Fraser and his Republican colleague F. Bradford Morse, who proposed a program known then as Title IX, in which there was "a greater emphasis on involving the people in their own development, in increasing their leverage in the political process."[33]

For his part, Dungan privately felt that the Johnson administration's Latin America policy was "not very creative," but at least not "for the most part" "aggressively negative," and that it followed "at least in form the major lines of the Kennedy policy." "A purely passive policy," however, according to Dungan, was "not good enough when you are trying to nurture something which is new and important." (This relative passivity itself seemed to him to be in direct contradiction to Kennedy's policy.) Dungan worried that Latin Americans were getting the wrong idea about what the United States supported in Latin America.[34] In November 1965, he wrote that "I can't say that I am very pleased with the drift of our LA policy." Nevertheless, he felt obliged to stay on as ambassador even when published reports suggested that he had plans to run for governor of his home state of Pennsylvania.[35]

Dungan was a controversial figure in Chile. Although the U.S. ambassador had generally been a lightning rod for criticism during the Cold War years, given the prominence of the Socialist and Communist parties there, the Frei administration's status as the "number one friend" of Washington in Latin America made Dungan a special target of the left.[36] The left accused him of arriving in Chile at Christmastime like Santa Claus in December 1964 and immediately announcing a $125 million development aid package. Dungan did have a rather grand notion of his responsibilities as ambassador. "Obviously, we are beyond the days when any sane public functionary thinks we can or should try to form the body politique of a foreign society in the image of the United States," but he also believed that it was "possible—and absolutely necessary—to encourage the development of institutions through which not just parties, unions, producers' associations, the majority, especially the masses now effectively outside the national life, can participate in making decisions about how the commonwealth is to be governed." In this sense, he was the perfect ambassador for the Frei administration, because his words so directly echoed the philosophy of Frei himself. Dungan found the early days of the Frei administration to be as exciting as he had found being part of the Kennedy administration in 1961. He told Robert and Ethel Kennedy, though, that there was "no doubt that whatever initial success we have had here is due in large measure to the association that people make between me and the President."[37] Norman Cousins of the *Saturday Review* suggested to Dungan that, given the "almost metaphysical communication-at-a-distance between highly placed figures and the man in the fields" in Latin America, "if the American ambassador is a well-disposed man, the peasant also gets the idea."[38]

Two years later, Vice President Humphrey wrote Ambassador Dungan, "I am sure that you know that I share your belief that the success or failure of the Frei government will have important consequences throughout the hemisphere." The United States needed to do everything it could to help Frei succeed. "If we have to reduce the whole amount because of Vietnam," he continued, "we shouldn't necessarily reduce it by the same percentage in each country."[39]

Throughout his tenure, Dungan remained protective of Frei and of Chilean interests generally, expressing outrage, for example, when a predicted surge in revenues due to increasing copper prices led to proposals to lessen program loans. He frequently complained about bureaucratic issues that prevented aid from flowing and creative ideas being implemented. On the other hand, while he opposed other cuts, he thought that on the "grounds of policy and economy" the United States could "make a substantial cutback on the military side without doing any damage to U.S. interests here in Chile." Before his departure in 1967, he proposed "a phased reduction in the size of the Mil-Group" in Chile. Dungan expressed concerns that while military engagement in civic action programs might be part of a larger attempt to bring about social change, he was not convinced that the United States really wanted the improvement in the military's image that might accompany it. Generally, he told Secretary of State Rusk, the United States needed to "tone down its own military activities in [the] hemisphere."[40]

Dungan's support for the Frei government certainly became an issue toward the end of 1965 and the beginning of 1966 after the agrarian reform (which he considered an "act of humanity") began to be implemented. The Chilean right, in particular, resented the fact that the leader they had voted for was actually carrying through with his promises of reform, and that the United States was backing him. After his comments regarding legislation being considered by the Congress were published in a Chilean periodical, he was criticized for ignoring the rules of proper diplomatic etiquette and interfering in internal Chilean affairs to aid one particular Chilean party (the covert aid to the Christian Democrats itself not yet being known). Rather than rejecting the idea, he embraced it, noting that he "interfered" in order to make it clear to all concerned that he was in sync with the Johnson administration in backing land reform in Chile. Members of the Chilean right also blamed him for the increasing polarization in Chilean society evident during the Frei years.[41]

Dungan actively encouraged liberal Democrats in the United States to take interest in the region as a whole. Following the passage of the Chilean agrarian reform bill, he sent a copy to Frank Church. After expressing admiration for the Idaho senator's speeches regarding the United Nations, he urged him to "look south once in a while." Occasionally, he seems to have lost perspective regarding domestic political realities in the United States, as when, for example, he suggested that a meeting between the Chilean president and Johnson would help the Democrats in the 1966 midterm elections.[42]

As should be evident, Dungan was not in the least risk-averse, and he liked to quote LBJ's advice to Foreign Service officers: "Be restless and discontented with things as they are; always strive and constantly work to change them."[43] He seems to have repeatedly directed the embassy's political section to establish "contact, direct or indirect, with the radical left, especially the Socialists." Political officer Sam Moskowitz reportedly had "been told (by presumably knowledgeable sources) that such attempts would be rebuffed."[44] Dungan himself made numerous efforts to establish contact with Senator Salvador Allende, but Allende rejected his advances.[45]

Publicly, Dungan tried to maintain an optimistic tone regarding the prospects of the Alliance for Progress, even suggesting, at times, that it was stronger under Johnson than it had been under Kennedy. He admonished the members of the Chilean country team that it was "our fault if we have the image or if the United States has the image of being sluggish and not concerned with reform and with revolution."[46] Responding to critics of the Johnson administration, Dungan asserted that "I have been doing nothing more than following current U.S. policy."[47] He wanted to see the Alliance be less bureaucratic and more flexible in responding to difficulties related to the development process. He admitted that "The fact that our policy has not changed is probably not as important as that fact that most Latin American THINK it has" (emphasis in the original). The "mystic" of the Alliance needed to be created or re-created.[48]

Dungan feared that Latin Americans (unfairly, he thought, but perhaps accurately in the case of Ambassador Gordon) believed the United States was only "concerned with increases in the GNP." He continued to press the need to help transform "the structure of Latin American society in a way which will redound to the benefit of all its citizens." Dungan further emphasized the development of "private organizations dedicated to the advancement of the economic, political, and social welfare" of Latin American citizens.[49]

The Alliance had been changing, in ways that were acknowledged and ways that were not. Congressman Fraser of Minnesota accepted the turn away from the Kennedy administration emphasis on promising revolutionary change in Latin America. He recognized that fundamental change was going to take time, noting that the "basic problem" was to "change people." Fraser wanted to see foreign aid changed to emphasize support for small-scale, but nevertheless profound, development of political organization skills and an emphasis on an understanding of development that did not emphasize growth in gross national product. Dungan was one of the few who were sympathetic to this kind of approach, and Chile was one of those countries in which USAID was providing support for "landless and small landholders training and organization." But if Fraser acknowledged that less could be done in the short term, he was no less committed to a total and limitless commitment to his type of foreign aid in Latin America for the next fifty to a hundred years. "Modest progress" was all that could be expected and would be "slow, painful, and exasperating." He recognized that the American people were not necessarily ready to think on that kind of scale.[50]

Dungan had his own ideas about furthering development in Latin America, which he saw as involving "a substantial modernization in thought, methodology, and generally a modification of the framework within which individual citizens make their judgements about all aspects of society." He thought that "more substantial contact with so-called developed or modern societies" would help accelerate the process of "self-generation."[51]

Dungan tried to have an impact in Washington, and not only in Santiago. Dungan directly encouraged President Johnson to send more members of the administration on official visits to Latin America and to generally make himself more visible in the region, including by writing letters to politicians in the region.[52] He advised U.S. politicians and officials to pay particular attention and give precedence to Chile in their dealings with Latin America. He wrote Vice President Humphrey, anxious that he not be seen as trying to push President Johnson (while also seeming to be unaware of how isolated Humphrey was in 1965). He actively encouraged those senators who were critical of U.S. support for military regimes. He had urged Senator Kennedy "to visit Chile before Brazil." "The Chileans," he suggested, "feel that they deserve a pat on the back even more than the Brazilians." Dungan was concerned about the South American leaders President Johnson himself had met. As late as November 1966, President Johnson had only met Bolivian President-Elect (and former General) René Barrientos, and there were plans to meet another military man, Brazil's President-Elect Artur da Costa e Silva. Frei, he lamented, had "been waiting for more than six months for his invitation."[53]

Dungan kept hoping, however. He thought he saw possibilities in Johnson's March 1966 speech in Mexico City, which marked the fifth anniversary of the announcement of the Alliance for Progress. He tried to encourage Johnson as well as other Democratic members of Congress like Kennedy to help regain lost momentum.[54] Others in the administration were following suit. Around the time of the Mexico City speech, Will Bowdler suggested that a visit by Frei to the United States could help President Johnson internationally; a "personal association with Frei [would] enhance the President's image in Latin America." The Chilean administration and its supporters greeted with great enthusiasm the news in late December 1966 that Frei was going to visit the White House in the following year. National Security Adviser Walt Rostow saw potential domestic political benefits in a Frei speech before a joint session of Congress. This would "undercut your critics on the Hill, in the press, and in academic circles that the Alliance has run out of steam and your interest in the area is marginal." (Rostow also hoped that it would distract attention from Vietnam.) As the planning progressed, news reports in the Chilean press noted that the two presidents would toast the occasion with Chilean wine. Dungan, who had been on home leave, was to help Frei and his aides prepare for the trip when he returned.[55]

Salvador Allende, however, had other plans. He had recently become president of the Senate, where the Christian Democrats never constituted a majority during the Frei years. Allende held special meetings of the Foreign Relations Commission regarding the proposed trip. After heated debate, the Chilean Senate, with the support of the right-wing National Party, as well as the Socialist and Communist parties, chose to exercise its constitutional prerogative and deny him permission to go. This was a major disappointment for Ambassador Dungan himself. In the United States, Senate Majority Leader Mike Mansfield pleaded with the Chilean senators to reconsider. For Frei, it seemed less a direct attack on his person than one on his rights as president to direct foreign policy and maintain relations with the most powerful country in the world. Frei did not deny that the Senate was within its legal rights, but he noted that no president had ever been denied the right to travel before. While he briefly considered the possibility of visiting even without Senate approval, in the end, he acceded to constitutional realities.[56]

Frei and Johnson met later that year at a hemispheric meeting of heads of state in Punta del Este, Uruguay, but although the former was clearly flattered by the latter's attention there, it was small and relatively short-lived consolation.[57] In any case, Brazil's president-elect, General Artur da Costa e Silva, not restrained by what was, by this time, a rubber-stamp Congress, already had met President Johnson in late January. Johnson had availed himself of the opportunity to praise Brazil for being "the first to join us in helping the Dominican people resist totalitarian rule" and "making it possible for them to freely choose their own destiny instead of having it imposed upon them." (That Brazilians themselves lacked this right was not remarked upon.)[58]

By late 1966, even Chileans generally supportive of U.S. policy in Latin America agreed that the Alliance "was missing the impetus of its creator."[59] President Frei himself went public with his concerns in an article in *Foreign Affairs* in April 1967, though he only criticized Johnson and the United States fairly obliquely. Noting the Latin American origins of the Alliance, he praised Kennedy for having "injected new life into it." Frei was more critical of Latin American countries and their leaders' lack of commitment to reforms that would aid the popular classes. He criticized the left and right in Latin America who used the nationalism card to help block its implementation (though this was particularly true of Chile itself). More generally, he argued that the Alliance had neither "preserved democracy" (indeed, the number of truly democratic nations in the region had declined) nor "helped to implement substantial changes at the expected rate." He praised the program for the changes that had taken place in education, health care, economic planning, and community organization. But more than half of the countries in Latin America had shown no commitment to land or tax reform and had simply used the Alliance as an excuse to squeeze money out of the United States. "The Alliance in fact became just one more source of assistance instead of a concerted program of mutual cooperation." He criticized the United States for being slow to embrace Latin American economic integration. He tried to push President Johnson to renew his commitment to the Alliance, which seemed to be waning since 1966.[60]

Ambassador Gordon, obviously, would not have agreed with this perception. He left the U.S. embassy in Brazil in February of that year.[61] He continued to believe that the Alliance for Progress, which, Gordon said, had been "the central focus" of his work in Brazil, was making progress. His farewell address is noteworthy for its almost complete lack of reference to political matters, least of all to democracy.[62] He still considered the "Brazilian revolution" to have marked a "profound" shift "in the course of history." By the middle of 1966, however, many of the Brazilian civilian supporters of the military coup two years earlier had turned against the military government.[63]

Gordon seemed not to have recognized how much had already changed in Brazil. While Castello Branco was quite willing to give up his own personal power, he was not ready to hand over power to a civilian. "We must have another military man to consolidate the revolution," he told a supporter. It must be noted in this regard that as early as September of 1965 Gordon had contemplated with equanimity in telegrams to Secretary of State Dean Rusk the possibility that Castello Branco would be succeeded in office by another general. General Costa e Silva ran unopposed for president in the indirect congressional election. This was the pivotal point after which there was no turning back and the reason why military rule lasted in Brazil as long as it did, despite the initial intentions of even many of the military leaders in 1964. Costa e Silva had no timetable for a return to democracy, and the military had no interest in establishing one.[64]

Beginning in 1966, however, Gordon's responsibilities now were not limited to Brazil but concerned much of the rest of the hemisphere as well. He replaced Jack Vaughan as assistant secretary of state for Latin American affairs in March.[65] Church and Robert Kennedy voted in favor of the nomination of Lincoln Gordon as assistant secretary; Massachusetts Senator Edward Kennedy had provided a letter in support of the nomination. Morse opposed his nomination because of Gordon's support for the military government and used the hearings to amplify his criticism of Johnson administration support for military governments generally in Latin America. He said that Kennedy administration policy, which had emphasized economic growth, democracy, and self-help, had "degenerated" under Johnson "into little more than a so-called anti-communist program" and a return to intervention. Gordon still insisted that Brazil's "revolution" had been launched "to preserve and not destroy Brazil's democracy."[66]

In his new position, Gordon was able to put economic development at the forefront of U.S. policy in Latin America. (Journalists Jerome Levinson and Juan de Onís considered 1966 the solid center of the Alliance's "pragmatic phase.") He also had more contact with President Johnson than he had ever had before. Gordon believed that the problem with the Alliance for Progress by this point was more of perception than reality. "[M]any of our Latin American friends have not adequately understood the vigor of President Johnson's commitment to the success of the Alliance and to concrete accomplishments in economic development, social progress, and modernizing reforms under its aegis." He noted the "kinship between domestic programs looking toward the "'Great Society' and the philosophy and practice of the Alliance for Progress."[67] There continued to be a strong feeling among loyal members of the Johnson administration that the president "who has really made the Alliance work" was not getting any credit in this area. And it is certainly true that the new emphases on economic integration and development in the South American interior that Johnson had suggested at the Punta del Este meeting in January 1967 had gotten so little attention that Republican presidential candidate Richard Nixon evidently felt comfortable putting forth similar ideas as his own.[68]

Although Dungan had long indicated a willingness to leave once he no longer felt he could continue supporting Johnson's Latin American policies, it seems to have been largely due to Dungan's wife's health problems that he left Chile in August 1967. In his resignation letter, he praised Johnson's "wise and farsighted policy" and expressed confidence that "under your leadership relations between the United States and Latin America will continue to prosper."[69] In a letter regarding his successor, Dungan noted that "we should be building on our strength in Latin America, that is, Chile."[70] Hearing of the resignation, Frei feared that this would mean a change in U.S. policy and asked U.S. Ambassador to the Organization of American States Sol Linowitz to convey his hopes that the United States would reassert its continuing support when an ambassador was named. Chilean officials praised Dungan for having abandoned the passivity and indifference of his predecessors; his departure would be felt as a loss by those "millions of Latin Americans who are trying to break old molds that keep them from achieving respectable and dignified living standards." Jacques Chonchol, one of the leaders of the Christian Democratic Party's left wing (and later Allende's minister of agriculture), wrote Dungan to express his regret; he called Dungan "a good friend who made serious efforts to understand our problems from within." Ironically, once Dungan had gone, the left-wing newspaper *Punto Final*, which had only recently lambasted him as the "viceroy of Chile," now claimed that he had been pushed out by the Pentagon, which wanted their man, Edward Korry, in as ambassador. Korry, for his part, thought that Dungan and the LBJ administration had been too close to the Christian Democrats and adopted a policy of "public silence, private suasion," and flexibility.[71]

The Brazilian model of military rule spread to neighbor Argentina in 1966. Arturo Illia's willingness to allow the Peronists to campaign openly led to significant victories, which the military did not accept. Kennedy-era Assistant Secretary and U.S. Ambassador in Buenos Aires Edwin Martin saw the coup coming and tried to discourage it. Assistant Secretary Gordon, for his part,

evidently did not see the irony in his opposing the coup, which he characterized as "unwarranted." Robert Kennedy proposed that the Johnson administration follow the example of Kennedy administration policy toward Peru and
establish a timetable for a return to constitutional government. The Johnson
administration, however, was not long in recognizing the new military government, exaggerating the Argentine government's commitment to human
rights and its plans to move to restore democratic government. By the end of
the year, Gordon, in a moment reminiscent of Eisenhower's statements from
the second term, had to assert that he did not like dictatorships. Gordon undercut his own argument by resuming military aid to the regime in early 1967.
In any case, the Johnson administration had not seen itself as exercising significant influence over Argentine internal affairs.[72]

By the summer of 1967, both Dungan and Gordon had chosen to move
out of foreign affairs and to work in educational administration in the
United States. Dungan became chancellor of higher education in New Jersey. Gordon became president of Johns Hopkins University in June, in part
because of President Johnson's increasing "sense of preoccupation with
Vietnam." "I wasn't particularly interested in presiding over a holding operation," he later recalled.[73] By this time, LBJ had virtually no interest in
Latin America.[74] Dungan remarked that it was "very difficult for the United
States to think creatively and operate effectively on more than one international front at a time." As historian Joseph Tulchin notes, after the big crises
in Panama, Brazil, and the Dominican Republic were over, it was hard for
LBJ to focus on the region. The big problem in Latin America as far as the
United States was concerned—Castro himself—was being contained. The
military had become the default option solution for Latin America's problems once again, either through U.S. support for counterinsurgency training or its support for direct military rule, as in Brazil (and soon in most
other South American countries). In Chile itself, of course, the next presidential election was still some years away, and, as things turned out, it
would be the last for quite some time.[75]

The departure of Dungan and the arrival of Edward Korry as U.S. ambassador to Chile marked a shift in U.S. priorities. Korry believed that the
U.S. embassy needed to expand its range of contacts in the Chilean political
scene and lessen its identification with the Frei administration. (The consequences of this shift became clearer later on and will be discussed in the
next chapter.) By 1967 many on the right felt they were being treated as the
"pariahs of society," as one U.S. analyst suggested. While Korry did not necessarily lament the strong identification with Alliance for Progress goals in
Chile, he recognized that this had cost the United States its traditional
friends there.[76]

In the Caribbean, the future and nature of democracy were at stake in the Dominican Republic. Senator Church was hardly alone in hoping for democratic elections as soon as possible following the invasion. But his records indicate little active engagement following the invasion. In a March 1971 letter he noted that he had only been "a sideline spectator in the US Senate" in 1965. But this was part of the problem. A Bosch aide named Sacha Volman, a Democratic Party activist named Allard Lowenstein (who had led the "Dump Johnson" movement), and veteran Socialist Party leader Norman Thomas, all had tried to convince Bosch that the 1966 elections would be free and fair, but liberal Democrats, for their part, had lost what little faith they had had in Bosch himself. During the campaign, Bosch and his allies were harassed. (Thomas himself, to his credit, ended up calling for a congressional inquiry.) The administration mulled over the possibility of a Bosch victory, recognizing that, as much as they might be uncomfortable with it, responding positively to it could help justify the invasion after the fact and prove a continuing commitment to reformist democracy. Far worse, Johnson aide Bill Moyers warned, would be a military coup after a Bosch victory; if it happened while the Johnson administration was "aloof to him, the criticism of LBJ by the liberal community of this hemisphere on top of the anti-Vietnam criticism . . . would become even more onerous." Longtime Trujillo crony Joaquin Balaguer, who had served him as diplomat, minister of education, and puppet president, whom some liberal Democrats, at least, had quite recently disdained, was elected. Almost a year before the election, Secretary of State Rusk had noted that on numerous occasions "Balaguer has in effect signed blank checks for us." President Johnson monitored the election closely. Expectations had been lowered dramatically since 1961, and the Johnson administration was convinced that Balaguer's election was now in U.S. interests. There was no critical attention paid to the conduct and outcome of the elections themselves. Many liberal Democrats were, in the end, relieved when Bosch lost. Humphrey foreign policy aide John Rielly, albeit rather gingerly, had sought to keep Humphrey from attending the inauguration, arguing that there were other more worthy Latin American democracies, but the good soldier went anyway, praising the actions of the OAS and the conduct of the election, and promising U.S. support. In June 1965, Congressman Fraser had predicted that the United States was "going to have to help whatever government is set up in the D.R. for some time to come." President Johnson, for his part, was convinced that the invasion had saved the Dominican Republic from a Castroite takeover, and he was happy with the results of the election. Significant efforts were made to strengthen Balaguer. The Dominican Republic became the fourth-largest recipient of Alliance for Progress aid, indicating that critics of the Alliance were right when they said that it was losing its way. Over the next few years, Volman continued to encourage people like Congressman Fraser to look into the failed promises to incorporate Bosch supporters into the Dominican armed forces. Balaguer employed fraudulent elections and repression of his political enemies to stay in power for many years to come (with a notable exception, as we shall see, during in the Jimmy Carter presidency). Few liberal Democrats paid attention to the longer-term results of the Johnson administration intervention. In the Kennedy era, the Dominican Republic had been expected to be an example of U.S. support for democracy following decades of rule by Rafael Trujillo. In the Johnson years, there had been a return to prioritizing stability.[77]

Although foreign policy discussions naturally focused on Southeast Asia during these years, there continued to be periodic attempts by senators and congressmen to block military aid. Morse continued to decry a military aid program that was "designed to deal with internal security problems." The emphasis on internal security was dangerous because it committed "the United States to support whatever faction holds power." (That, he noted, was "how we got involved in Vietnam.")[78] Senator Church in the fall of 1966 offered an amendment to reduce military aid by $100 million, as historian Robert David Johnson notes, to eliminate such aid to Latin America and Africa. The declining concerns regarding Castro led others as well to question U.S. military assistance programs. Church argued that if the Cuban leader "did not exist, he might have to be invented." While he did not deny that Castro was encouraging guerrilla movements, "both the extent of his intervention and the size of these movements [were] easily susceptible to gross exaggeration." He noted that no Castro-style governments had been established, but many constitutional governments had been overthrown and military dictatorships established. He sought to distinguish between aid for "legitimate defense needs" from that which would "shore up regressive regimes" and "burden poor countries with military establishments they cannot afford." The promise that military aid would promote civilian control, Church argued, was proven wrong in Brazil and Argentina.[79]

Although liberal Democrats like Robert Kennedy were increasingly distancing themselves from overt support for anti-Castro activities, the Cuban leader himself was initiating a new wave of militant action. His longtime right-hand man, Ernesto Guevara, wanted to see a grand Tri-Continental Strategy in which there would be "two, three, many Vietnams."[80]

In places where counterinsurgency seemed the major issue, the Johnson administration saw a number of victories. In Guatemala, where liberal Democratic interest had never been strong, some saw hope in the "remarkable success" of the Julio César Méndez government. Robert Kennedy briefly turned his attention to the country, but Assistant Secretary Gordon dismissed his concerns, saying that it was the Guatemalan communists who were "complaining bitterly about our military mission's effectiveness in counterinsurgency training." Viron Vaky, often the conscience of the State Department in these years, was not alone in seeing the dangers of right-wing "counter-terror," but this issue did not reach significant levels of public attention for some years to come.[81]

In Bolivia, Guevara himself sought to implement part of the Tri-Continental Strategy in an insurgency he led consisting largely of non-Bolivians against a former general, René Barrientos, who had risen to power in the coup that deposed longtime leader Paz Estenssoro in November 1964 and who had legitimated his rule, to some degree, with an election in mid-1966. Che arrived in late 1966, and by March 1967, it had become clear that he was operating there. The Bolivian military sought to use the situation to extract large amounts of military aid from the United States. Guevara himself hoped that the United States would get involved overtly and inflame South American political opinion. Ambassador Dungan as well as U.S. Ambassador to Bolivia Douglas Henderson sought to avoid overestimating the danger and expanding the U.S. presence significantly. The South American revolutionary himself found it difficult to gain support, either from the Bolivian Communist Party or from the local *campesinos*, who informed the Bolivian military of his movements. A U.S. Ranger battalion provided training but kept out of direct involvement in the area where Che's forces operated. By the time the U.S.-trained forces began to operate, Guevara's insurgency was already failing. His easy capture did not detract from the execution that made him a martyr and ensured his continued relevance as a symbolic figure throughout Latin America for decades to come. (Although a Cuban-born CIA agent tried to interrogate him prior to his death, the evidence available suggests that the Bolivian army ordered the execution.)[82]

In Venezuela, as well, guerrillas had been active since the Kennedy years. They had expanded their activities in 1966, and the Johnson administration focused significant resources there. But the Venezuelan armed left was increasingly beset by problems of its own making. Internal divisions by the end of Johnson's term in office had reduced the threat significantly. And in the weeks between Humphrey's defeat and Nixon's inauguration, Venezuela held a third consecutive peaceful election, won for the first time by a candidate not from the Democratic Action Party. The president-elect was a Christian Democrat named Rafael Caldera. Although many of the details regarding the close association between the Johnson administration and the Christian Democrats in Chile were not known at the time, the broad outline of the tie during the Dungan years was clear. This was not unproblematic for the United States elsewhere in South America. The United States had long been associated with Betancourt's Democratic Action Party in Venezuela. The United States was lucky to have two dominant political parties there that were its friends. As Vice President Humphrey's foreign policy aide remarked, the United States could not choose "between two friends in any country." Rafael Caldera assured Humphrey that he did not expect the same kind of preferences from the Johnson administration that Betancourt's party had received from the Kennedy administration. For his part, Humphrey was "happy to cooperate" with the Venezuelan Christian Democrats. Although liberal Democrats had never developed the strong ties with the Venezuelan Christian Democrats that they had with Chile's, the victory has been seen by some historians as a triumph of U.S. policy, in stark contrast to what happened in Brazil during these years. But the Venezuelan example shows that there was not always a direct link between aid for counterinsurgencies and military rule.[83]

By 1968, the Cuban model no longer seemed in danger, from the U.S. perspective, of being replicated anywhere else, and Castro himself had been reduced, for the most part, "to a continuing nuisance," according to National Security Adviser Walt Rostow, "but a nuisance almost irrelevant to the future of Latin America."[84] But there were warning signs, if anyone had the wit to see them and had been listening to the right people. In Nicaragua, President Schick died of a heart attack in 1966. Luis Somoza died in April 1967, but by that point his younger brother had already been chosen as his party's presidential candidate. Anti-Somoza journalist Pedro Joaquin Chamorro warned Robert Kennedy that dishonest elections could lead to "a Dominican Republic type revolt." (Chamorro noted that it was "only natural that Latin America turn its eyes toward another Kennedy.") State violence in early 1967 indicated the unwillingness of the Somozas and the National Guard to countenance any further move toward a democratic political system. The Inter-American Association for Democracy and Freedom kept its eye on the approaching elections. When pressed, Assistant Secretary Gordon sought to assure Frances Grant of U.S. support for "the strengthening of democracy and respect for human rights," but said that U.S. efforts could not "constitute intervention in the internal affairs of other countries." It came as no surprise when Somoza won the election by an unbelievably large margin in an election that provided him with not the slightest degree of political legitimacy. National Security Adviser Rostow informed President Johnson that Somoza was "angling" for an invitation to the president's ranch, but he should "avoid any commitment to see him." Neither the Kennedy administration nor the

Johnson administration had been committed to transforming the Nicaraguan political system, and Nicaragua would languish under the least politically adept of the three Somozas to rule the country. As an already lame-duck president in the summer of 1968, Johnson visited all of the Central American countries, unlike Kennedy, who had made a point of only visiting democratic Costa Rica. Johnson's speeches during this trip were generic. As the first U.S. president to visit Nicaragua while in office, Johnson praised the country's infrastructure growth.[85] Neither Kennedy nor Johnson had been committed to regime change, but there had been hope for a time that there could be a transition away from decades of family dictatorship. That was not to be.

Robert Kennedy endeavored to continue to focus on Latin America, but Vietnam was far too pressing. He did not speak much about Latin America after the middle of 1966 other than briefly in a speech at a dinner for Senator Gaylord Nelson October 1967.[86] But in a revealing moment in August 1967 examined by historian Robert David Johnson, Kennedy sought to increase U.S. economic aid to Latin America from $578 million to $650 million. His fellow New York Senator Jacob Javits described this as a "vote of confidence or no confidence in the future of the Alliance for Progress." Kennedy emphasized what it would do for the children of Latin America, and he expressed fear of "a damaging slowdown in the development of our Alliance for Progress efforts in Latin America." He was challenged by Senators Morse and Ernest Gruening, who joked that Brazil's only contribution to helping the United States in Southeast Asia was providing coffee. On a more serious note, while Morse criticized Latin American countries for failing to adopt self-help measures, he also expressed concern that most of the money would go toward propping up dictatorships. In response, Kennedy used the Cold War rationale that "almost all of the Latin countries have the potential of becoming so unstable that they would accept a Communist government." Kennedy's use of Cold War fears when humanitarian sentiments failed was unsuccessful. Liberals provided the swing votes to defeat his amendment.[87]

The 1968 presidential election certainly did not revolve around Latin American issues. But liberal Democrats nevertheless saw something at stake, as did Latin Americans. Robert Kennedy had addressed Latin American poverty, infant mortality, and life expectancy rates, in a campaign speech he gave at Ball State University on 4 April (shortly before he learned of civil rights leader Martin Luther King Jr.'s death). It was assumed that a President Kennedy in 1969 would make the region more important again as he reasserted U.S. moral leadership. His assassination in June shook up the race and (along with the death of King) caused great concern in Latin America regarding the direction of the United States. Vice President Humphrey, no longer viewed as the liberal hero he had once been, became for many McCarthy and Kennedy supporters the presidential candidate of the bosses. Senator Humphrey had been engaged with Latin America far more than Vice President Humphrey, but for many Latin Americans, Humphrey was remembered more for his activism in the early 1960s and less for his relative invisibility as vice president. He also still had ties with the Chilean Christian Democrats and other reformists. His task force on Latin America included many people associated with the Kennedy Alliance, including Ralph Dungan. The task force policy paper argued that the Latin American military had been "our stickiest wicket." Despite the fears regarding the threat from the left, it was the right that had posed the greatest threat to existing governments. Ben Stephansky and James Theberge suggested that "our voice" had "not been clear, doubtless because our mind has not been clear." Some on the task force thought that it was now time to end aid to Brazil. President Johnson had been "absent-mindedly patronizing." It was important that the next president "re-establish" Kennedy's "attitude of warm respect." His plans as the Democratic presidential candidate for reducing military assistance programs drew praise from the Inter-American Association for Democracy and Freedom. He also promised "to build on the imaginative policies initiated by" President Kennedy and had a perfect foil in this perspective in Kennedy's opponent, Nixon, whose support for "trade, not aid" was rejected by Humphrey and the IADF as a return to Eisenhower policies. Humphrey emphasized continuity in the two Democratic administrations. He praised the victories over insurgents but also emphasized the failure to defeat "poverty, frustration, illiteracy, and hopelessness." He emphasized that democracy was threatened by "gorillas on the right as from guerrillas on the left.""[88]

The Democratic Party platform affirmed both long-standing liberal opposition to Cuba's role as "a source of subversion" and a faith that the "other Latin American states" were "moving ahead under the Alliance for Progress." Despite the deep divisions in the party over the major foreign policy issue, Vietnam, the Alliance for Progress had replaced the Good Neighbor Policy as the organizing principle of Democratic thinking about Latin America; it would remain so to a large degree through the end of the Cold War. But given public antipathy toward foreign aid, it is hardly surprising that the platform cited President Johnson's dictum that "self-help is the lifeblood of economic development."[89]

In the fall of 1968, the Dominican opposition sought to gain support from liberal Democrats regarding political repression by the Balaguer government. Bosch aide Sacha Volman wrote Minnesota Congressman Fraser in the hope that the United States government "would disassociate itself from the close identification it now" had with the Balaguer government. Bosch's party, the Partido Revolucionario Dominicano, "stated that it has the fullest confidence in the liberal orientation of Vice President Humphrey even though the role of the Vice President has enforced upon him public positions which are unpopular in the Dominican Republic and are connected with the 1965 intervention," noting further that he "was not at his best at the inauguration of the present Dominican Government, which he had to attend as President Johnson's representative." Volman noted the importance of "U.S. attitudes" in "domestic Dominican politics in general and in the PRD-communist rivalry in particular." Volman credited the PRD with having "deprived Dominican communists from gaining increased influence by maintaining a strong nationalistic and reformist attitude." Volman wanted to encourage Humphrey "to express again some of his genuine and well-known liberal positions which has created so much enthusiasm in the past in Latin America." This "would contribute toward strengthening both the cause of Dominican democracy" and lay "the foundations for a future improved D.R./U.S. relationship."[90] Other Dominicans were less sanguine. The death of Robert Kennedy stirred "anti-U.S. feelings" in Juan Bosch. He thought that his closest associates were "foolish enough" to "still believe in a possible U.S. democratic foreign policy." Renewed accusations by Balaguer of communist ties had led to "a new green light for police abuses and even assassinations" of PRD members.[91]

In any case, Nixon defeated Humphrey, if only by a slim margin in the popular vote. Senator Wayne Morse, one of the most outspoken liberals in the previous decade, and the chair of the Subcommittee on Western Hemisphere Affairs, was also defeated in a close race. His ideas had never carried the day in the Kennedy and Johnson years; strangely, perhaps, they became more influential after he was no longer in office. Schlesinger, for his part, would never again have the political influence that he had before Robert Kennedy's death.[92]

In Brazil, moreover, 1968 was a turning point. The promulgation of Institutional Act Five (hereafter AI-5) took the mask off military rule. Congress was shut down, and an era of torture and disappearances began. No one could claim after this with any measure of credibility that Brazil was moving in a democratic direction. U.S. support for military rule in Brazil would increasingly have to be justified on the basis of an impressive economic performance.

By the end of the Johnson years, U.S. Latin America policy was ambivalent at best, and generally incoherent. The Alliance had been administered better, but it had long since lost its luster. Its reformist content had declined, outside of Chile. In future years, few liberal Democrats would invoke Johnson's legacies in Latin America. Latin Americans, for their part, once again felt neglected. Liberal Democrats continued to address Kennedy's problematic expansion of military aid, but they generally downplayed it as a defining part of the Kennedy legacy. Johnson's abandonment of timetables was his most significant and lamentable contribution. Invocations of "peaceful and progressive revolution" sounded off-key alongside support for military governments. The perception of intense threat during the Kennedy years had largely disappeared.[93] The United States frequently was relying upon dictators for containment, as it had done under Eisenhower. Following the 1968 election, the liberal Democrats were once again in opposition, but they were slow to conceive of new policies toward Latin America.

The End of the Alliance for Progress and the Origins of the Human Rights Issue in U.S.-Latin American Relations

Liberal Democrats in 1969 were sobered by the loss of the White House to the man who had been John Kennedy's opponent in 1960, former Vice President Richard M. Nixon. Moreover, the war in Vietnam had shown the costs of the containment policy put in place by Harry Truman decades before and had created divisions in the Democratic Party. Latin America was no longer the trouble spot it had been in the Kennedy years. But aside from José Figueres, who returned as Costa Rica's president in 1970, there were almost no Latin American leaders with whom liberal Democrats identified. In the years during which Republicans occupied the White House, liberal Democrats began to craft a new human rights emphasis for Cold War foreign policy, which was to be of particular importance for Latin America. As it was to be in the 1980s, new developments in U.S. Latin American policy were primarily a response to events and trends in a small number of countries, primarily, in this case, Brazil and Chile.

President Nixon claimed early on to be breaking less with the Kennedy/Johnson legacies than it would later seem and to make Latin America "an area of top priority." He prided himself on having traveled to every Latin American country before he was elected. (He tried to make people forget the disastrous 1958 South American trip during which he was spat on and pelted with stones, and nearly lost his life.) But he found it hard to convince Latin Americans and those engaged with Latin America that he shared their concerns. Although he occasionally invoked the Alliance, he primarily returned to Eisenhower's policies, and his Latin America policies were not as liberal as those he had espoused as a candidate in 1960.[1]

On the day following his inauguration, Nixon approached Galo Plaza, the former Ecuadorean president who was the director of the Organization of American States, regarding possible new directions in U.S. policy in Latin America. Nixon wanted to send someone to the region to take stock of Alliance for Progress and Agency for International Development programs, which he viewed skeptically, and not just because they were associated with the Democratic Party and his two predecessors as president. Plaza recommended that Nixon appoint Plaza's old friend and Nixon's recent rival for the presidency, New York Governor Nelson Rockefeller. Although many in the U.S. media and on the Latin American left were critical of the choice of a man whose family name symbolized U.S. capitalism, Latin Americans familiar with his work in the region since the 1930s knew of his unusual fondness for and interest in Latin America.[2]

During his unsuccessful bid for the Republican nomination in 1968, Rockefeller had promised to establish a second Good Neighbor Policy, drawing upon his experience in leading "the way to elimination of Nazi and Fascist influence in South America" during the 1940s. "Close relations with our neighbors," he had argued, "must be the keystone of our foreign policy." Rockefeller had called for a stronger role for the Organization of American States, and economic integration in the Western Hemisphere. He was more than happy to accept Nixon's invitation. He was thrilled at what he saw as an opportunity to help see his decades-old dream of furthering hemispheric unity and economic and social development come to fruition. For his part, OAS Director Plaza "emphasized that the initiative should be with the Latin-Americans and that the United States should be willing to listen and try to understand their point of view." U.S. officials also emphasized that Latin American nations would "take the initiative in solving" their problems. "In the past, the Latin Americans sometimes got the impression that the Americans were there to force programs upon them." Nixon himself insisted that "we have been putting too much emphasis on what we are doing in Latin America and not enough on what we are going to do with our Latin American friends." Nixon stressed the dramatic changes that were taking place in Latin America and what he claimed were the "static" "assumptions and conceptions that guided our policies." An emphasis was placed on listening "to the leaders" and consulting "with them concerning the development of common goals and joint programs of action, which will strengthen Western Hemisphere unity and accelerate the pace of economic and social development." Rockefeller on his own was able to recruit a large number of experts in a wide variety of fields to help prepare for the trips, meeting with Latin American government officials, and writing the final report. If the trips themselves from the U.S. media perspective were largely defined by anti-American incidents of various sorts, they also seemed to indicate a significant degree of interest in the region on the part of the Nixon administration. The report that the mission would produce would be "the central point of reference for the formulation of effective and sensitive policies toward our American neighbors." The concept of the mission itself seemed designed to meet the needs of Nixon and his primary foreign policy adviser, National Security Adviser Henry Kissinger, to make an end run around the State Department, which Nixon considered to have been too powerful in the three previous administrations.[3]

In the end, the trip had more implications regarding U.S. policy toward the Latin American military than it did toward the region per se. In part this reflected Nixon's own predilections, but it also resulted from a number of his-torical accidents. The Chilean Christian Democratic government canceled the trip when it feared that it would enable President Frei's opponents on the left to exploit anti-American feelings and cause more problems for his gov-ernment. Frei told U.S. Ambassador Edward Korry that "Santiago would be turned into an armed camp" if Rockefeller and his aides were to go to Chile. It would serve no useful purpose at this time and do lasting harm to modera-tion and to U.S.-Chilean relations." The cancellation of the trip, however, as well as one to democratic Venezuela, shifted the balance of the mission ever more disproportionately toward the increasingly large number of countries with military governments in the region. Rockefeller himself, while support-ive of efforts in the United States to enhance its own democracy through the civil rights movement, clearly supported many military dictatorships in the region, most notably in Brazil, now in its most repressive period, the so-called *anos de chumbo* or "years of lead."[4]

Rockefeller's advisers saw great potential for collaboration between the United States and Brazil in particular. "There is some substantial evidence that Brazil is beginning to seek a "'special relationship' with the United States." Brazil's size and power, as its well as its accelerating economic growth, com-bined with the pro-U.S. policies of its leaders, made it an important ally and the Rockefeller visit the most important of the mission trips. Brazil was grow-ing "by night," as one author put it, "even while the leaders sleep." At the same time, the current government was "taking increasingly forceful mea-sures to contain student agitation," with the Institutional Act No. 5 having "conferred full dictatorial powers upon the president." More and more mili-tary officers were being appointed to "civilian posts."[5]

Some of those who sought Rockefeller's ear sought to prepare him for what the military leaders of Brazil would tell him about the need to confront sub-version and the failure of civilian politicians "to understand the true spirit of the 1964 revolution." Rockefeller was advised to engage in "useful discussions on the difference between subversion and opposition." He might also discuss human rights violations, which the U.S. public and Congress found hard to understand when those responsible for them were "old friends and allies who say they share our democratic ideals."[6] Brazilian conservatives, such as Eugênio Gudin, for their part, hoped that Rockefeller would convey to U.S. officials the inapplicability of American democracy in their country; "who-ever is able to get into the heads of the Americans, including some of their very capable high government officials, the idea that the 1967 constitution is the most liberal and advanced that our political education can stand will ren-der inestimable service to this country."[7] (Nixon, in his own meeting with Brazilian Ambassador Mario Gibson Barbosa, at this time, emphasized the long-standing ties between the U.S. and Brazil and never touched upon Brazil's repressive domestic policies following the promulgation of Institutional Act No. 5.)[8] Rockefeller was also told to expect an announcement that the Brazilian Congress would be reopened. Supporters of the military government in Congress urged Rockefeller's aides to encourage him to "make some sort of public complimentary reference to the president for this democratic gesture."[9]

During his trip to Brazil, Rockefeller tried to stay clear of public comments regarding Brazilian politics, noting, for example, in response to a question regarding press censorship, that "the purpose of the mission is not [to] express personal opinions." Privately as well, he tried to assure more critical Brazilians that he was trying to encourage the return of Brazilian liberties.[10] In two separate meetings with General-President Costa e Silva, Rockefeller did express concern that "certain actions of his government made it difficult for the United States government to cooperate fully because of press and public reaction in the United States." He later specified the closing of Congress, the suspension of individual rights, the harassment of the press, and "rough tactics . . . used by the police and military without regard to individual liberties." Costa e Silva sought to impress upon Governor Rockefeller his own understanding of recent Brazilian history. He argued that the 1964 coup had been a "revolution of the people." (This was later reflected in Rockefeller's own idiosyncratic view of the military coup, which he claimed had followed "a people's revolt" involving two weeks of protest against the Goulart government.) AI-5 also had been necessary, Costa e Silva assured him, following a young deputy's "violent speech," and because there were "Certain elements in Congress" trying to "nullify" the Revolution. Costa e Silva claimed to be trying to "build a real democracy in Brazil . . . that could function and serve the interests of the people." He promised that following one more "democratic" revision of the constitution, there would be no need for "further intervention by the armed forces." Like his predecessor, he emphasized the idea that his own willingness to leave office indicated how different Brazil's military government was (that his successor would be another general went unspoken). He claimed that Brazil was acting to prevent a communist takeover not only in Brazil but also in neighboring Uruguay. Costa e Silva then made "a prediction that within five years the United States [would] have to do what Brazil did in its 1964 revolution."[11] Rockefeller occasionally expressed personal reservations about Costa e Silva, noting in a telegram to Kissinger following his meetings with the general that "his democratic attitudes [were] limited by his military background."[12] In general, however, in playing the role of listener and reporter, Rockefeller went too far and too faithfully absorbed and transmitted the opinion of the small group of men who were running Brazil.

In the final report, Brazil's challenge was defined as being "whether the military can and will move the nation, with sensitivity and conscious design, toward a transition from military control for a social purpose to a more pluralistic form of government which will enable individual talent and dignity to flourish. Or will they become radicalized, statist, and anti-U.S.?" (That the only real prospect in sight in Brazil and most other Latin American countries at the time was for the continuation of rightist authoritarian government was not even addressed.) Democracy being a "very subtle and difficult problem for most of the other countries in the hemisphere," "for many of these countries, therefore, the question is less one of democracy or a lack of it, than it is simply of orderly ways of getting along." The United States could not worry about "philosophical disagreements it may have with the nature of particular regimes"; it must seek ways of cooperating "to help meet basic needs of the hemisphere." "Diplomatic relations are merely practical conveniences and not measures of moral judgement."[13]

Governor Rockefeller visited many other countries as well and was often greeted by protesters, though he was not personally threatened as Vice President Nixon had been more than a decade before. The "fresh and comprehensive examination" that was promised primarily involved an elimination of any remaining ambivalence regarding military rule and a greater emphasis on improving economic relations in the hemisphere. Nixon's policies, in many ways, marked a return to those when he was Eisenhower's vice president. President Nixon said that the United States "must deal realistically with governments . . . as they are," although, in the Western Hemisphere, this primarily applied to governments of the right and not the left.[14]

In the months following the three mission trips, Rockefeller and his team prepared the final report, while they also sought to influence the larger discussion of U.S.-Latin American relations, which seemed to be spinning out of Nixon administration control. The report noted what Latin Americans considered a deterioration in relations between the United States and the region, which was presumed to have a special relationship with the United States. Rockefeller criticized the media for downplaying promises of movement toward democracy by the Brazilian government. Yet he never indicated an understanding of how powerless the Brazilian Congress had been even before it had been dissolved by AI-5. In any event, Brazil would not become democratic any time soon.[15]

Defining himself against what he considered negative aspects of the Kennedy legacy, Nixon said that there was no need for a "new slogan" for the administration's Latin America policy or for elevated rhetoric. But there was a need for "new policy" and "new approaches." He later recalled that at the time he became president, "the easy assumption of hemispheric community" was "being severely challenged." "The ambitious U.S. undertaking to lead the whole continent to democracy and progress," and the U.S. "directive role in the Alliance for Progress" were no longer appropriate given "accelerating expectations and greater assertion by Latin Americans themselves." Nixon claimed that his Democratic predecessors had not been willing to listen to what Latin Americans themselves actually wanted. The Rockefeller mission was intended to make it possible for the United States and Latin America to embrace "common goals and joint programs of action," strengthening hemispheric unity and speeding up socioeconomic development in the process. The Alliance for Progress had been out of the limelight for long enough that Nixon evidently felt that no one would notice the similarities between his rhetoric and Kennedy's. In any case, he also insisted, the Alliance's "principles still guide us." For all his foreign policy expertise, Latin America would not illustrate the innovative thinking he and his national security adviser, Henry Kissinger, came to personify, like the relaxation of tensions with the Soviet Union known as détente or the opening to China.[16]

The U.S. Congress, increasingly critical of U.S. foreign policy generally by this time (and largely because of the Vietnam War), also had become more skeptical of U.S. policy in the Western Hemisphere. "I heard someone say that for every billion dollars of aid to Latin America, another 100 million people have come under military regimes," Senator Church said. Later in the year Church questioned why the United States was providing more aid for the military government of Brazil than for any country in the world other than India. Rather than be grilled by Senator Church, Rockefeller preferred to testify before Florida Congressman Dante Fascell, his "ardent fan." Rockefeller suggested that the United States should be more humble and less superior in our dealings with Latin American dictatorships: "We still have a lot to do in our country to live up to our concepts of democracy and human dignity."[17]

Even some of those who had accompanied Rockefeller on the mission were sharply critical of Rockefeller's pro-military policy. Privately, Jerome Levinson questioned his companion's assumption "that it is possible to reconcile a desire for an inspirational, moral and idealistic theme with financial and military support for the present government in Brazil." David Bronheim, who had been the deputy U.S. coordinator for the Alliance for Progress from 1965 to 1967, spoke before the Senate Subcommittee on Latin American Affairs in late June and early July. (Rockefeller had asked Bronheim not to appear before the subcommittee.) U.S. training, Bronheim argued, had made Latin American military men "more impatient with the real or imagined managerial deficiencies of civilian rule." Meanwhile, the U.S. emphasis on internal security had promoted "a tendency to see communists everywhere." "Our capacity to influence our good friends in the Brazilian military to move in more truly democratic directions has not been great," Bronheim continued. The Brazilian foreign minister and others were outraged by Bronheim's remarks. Kissinger wrote Rockefeller that "I can understand why the Brazilian government would be unhappy about this kind of public testimony."[18]

Rockefeller himself was unmoved by such talk. (Rockefeller also was concerned about the threat from within, particularly from those in the CIA, AID, and State who opposed military aid.) He emphasized what he called the "forces throughout this hemisphere dedicated to anarchism and the overthrow of all existing institutions." "I do not feel that the United States should deny military assistance to *all* Western Hemisphere countries—including existing democratic governments because *some* countries are temporarily under authoritarian regimes." This was disingenuous. Undoubtedly, there were guerrilla movements that posed a threat to democracy in the region, most notably in Uruguay. Yet Rockefeller wholeheartedly supported military aid for military dictatorships like Brazil, whose guerrilla movements had developed *in response to* military rule. By 1969, the notion that military rule in Brazil was only temporary was purely a matter of faith. Sometimes also the governor made the argument even more narrowly. While visiting Brazil in June, he had written Kissinger to urge the United States to fulfill a promise of $5 million in electronic equipment for the Brazilian navy, claiming that the Brazilian navy was "the strongest force for democracy among military in government." Rockefeller argued that Costa e Silva was ready "to take road to bring Brazil back to democratic regime." If the promise was not fulfilled, he could move "in opposite direction from democracy," ignoring the fact that he already had moved in that direction. More convincingly, Rockefeller argued that U.S. national security interests required a strong military. Latin American democracy was not necessarily in the U.S. national interest.[19]

Rockefeller claimed that the existing military governments represented a new military.[20] "None of the dictators—the military dictators so-called—that I saw are the old-style dictator, the pawn of the oligarch." Latin American leaders were portrayed as being from the people and for the people. "And this goes right across the board," he said, citing examples from Argentina, Brazil, Panama, and Peru. In his testimony before the House Subcommittee on Inter-American Affairs, Rockefeller even prematurely credited Panama with already "going back to a democratic process."[21] In fact, this would not take place until the 1990s.

Not surprisingly, U.S. military officers were themselves making a strong argument in favor of ongoing aid and a strong relationship with their counterparts in the hemisphere. A report written by an anonymous U.S. Southern Command officer emphasized correctly that the Latin American military had been "firm friends of the United States" for decades. Current U.S. policy was now marked by "an increasingly antimilitary bias" and a belief that such aid was anachronistic. The Peruvian military regime's turn toward the left provided his only example of a country that had welcomed the first U.S. military mission and where the military was now "alienated" from the United States. The United States needed the backing of the Latin American military because of military control of political affairs in many countries. The risks attendant on cutting military aid could not be justified at the present time and were unlikely to be reasonable "in the next decade or two." The officer denied that the United States had been able to exercise influence over "domestic political affairs in Latin American countries, large or small." He predicted that "modernization" in these countries would produce increasingly strong revolutionary movements. Latin America's only options would become either extreme right or extreme left. Moreover, it was argued, the military's interests and U.S. interests were "so strongly parallel to our own." The report criticized the delay in providing aid that followed the establishment of AI-5 in Brazil, noting that "the United States is exerting pressure in an effort to force Brazil's military rulers back toward a political system more to U.S. liking. In no other area of the world (except Vietnam) do we presume to do this." Why was it only in Latin America that we were not allowed to "remain on affable terms with dictators and monarchs of all descriptions?" The officer feared a loss of "rapport and mutual trust" between the United States and Brazil in particular. "Brazil would return to constitutional rule without our pressures, perhaps sooner or perhaps later than with them, the trust and rapport will not quickly return." He did not make these recommendations "with an eye to what Congress may or may not tolerate. They are made with the assumption that the Executive will seek to inform and enlighten the Congress as to policies that will or will not work." He also made a plea to respect Latin American sovereignty.[22]

Liberal Democrats came to perceive Brazil's repressive turn fully now that a new U.S. president whose attitude toward the Latin American military was less ambivalent than Johnson's had been. Nixon had long been comfortable with Latin American military men and distrustful of the region's civilian politicians. Toward the end of a South American trip in 1967, he had noted that "United States-style democracy won't work here. I wish it would." Although he was speaking specifically about Argentina, he believed that his words had a more general application. As Nixon privately told Kissinger in October 1969, he favored dictatorships. There would be no crusading idealism or ambivalence for him, no clash between realism and democracy promotion.[23]

Despite Rockefeller's own commitment to the mission, including spending an estimated $750,000 of his own fortune over the course of 1969, and despite the fact that Kissinger had been Rockefeller's protégé, and despite even the time that President Nixon spent discussing the report with the governor, the mission report ended up being largely a dead letter, a kind of a coda to the Alliance for Progress itself. In theory the mission seemed an ambitious idea with partially laudable goals. Instead of moving beyond the Alliance for Progress, the Rockefeller mission served as the last gasp of the Alliance.

Nixon was moving toward the Nixon Doctrine's "policeman" strategy, with a favored nation in each region (the Shah's Iran, for example, in the Middle East). Brazil fit well in this overall approach, and its economic success during these years, the so-called Brazilian miracle, also suggested the irrelevance of political democracy in Latin America as far as the United States was concerned.[24] U.S. support for military government in Latin America became increasingly controversial even as it became less ambivalent.[25] (More generally, Nixon had admired the military leaders of Pakistan; he welcomed Zaire's Mobutu Sese Seko and Indonesia's Sukarno to the White House, both of whom had established themselves in power under Johnson and with the support of Johnson.)[26]

Nixon's enthusiasm for military government did not sit well with liberal Democrats, who had seen military coups proliferate over the previous half decade, most of which, aside from Brazil, they had not supported. Dungan, by this point, was willing to state publicly that U.S. attitudes toward military rule had been unclear since 1963.[27] Church, who had replaced Morse as head of the Subcommittee on Western Hemisphere Affairs, held hearings regarding U.S. military policy in Latin America as a way to address the larger question of what he saw as the "disarray" in U.S. relations with Latin America.[28] Public concern regarding the issue of torture in Brazil was growing. Journalist turned politician and activist Márcio Moreira Alves, the one who had given the "violent" speech Costa e Silva had referred to at the end of 1968, met with Senate Majority Leader Mike Mansfield, hoping they would help in a "campaign to isolate the military regime internationally."[29]

By October 1969 Nixon was seeking to reassure the Inter-American Press Association that the United States still "cared" about Latin America. But the Nixon administration never seems to have had any intention of making Latin America a priority, and most of the administration's ideas for the region involved fairly minor and largely technical programs. But since the Alliance had been intended to be a ten-year commitment when it was announced in 1961, President Nixon continued to refer to it on occasion, and then he quietly stopped talking about it in the last years of his presidency. Nor should we forget National Security Adviser Henry Kissinger's famous statement to Chilean Foreign Minister Gabriel Valdés that "What happens in the South is of no importance." Despite their long-standing relationship, Kissinger and Rockefeller could hardly have thought more differently about the region. Rockefeller had hoped for a large-scale commitment to the region's social and economic development to improve the quality of life, but the primary impact of the mission report was to serve as justification for expanding still further the aid for the region's militaries, whether in power or (increasingly infrequently) subordinate to civilian authority. (Even so, Governor Rockefeller remained an outspoken supporter of Nixon's foreign policy for years to come.) Even Rockefeller's illusions regarding the temporary nature of Latin American military governments would be largely forgotten as the need for stability became ever less assumed. U.S.-Latin American relations continued to deteriorate, not least of all with prodemocratic elements in the region.[30]

Nixon was convinced that the United States had forced reform upon a reluctant Latin America, but this largely reflected his own dislike for the Latin American leaders who had forged strong ties with the Kennedy administration (and, to a lesser extent, the Johnson administration). In March 1969, in a conversation with Ambassador Korry, President Frei acknowledged that "the days when Chile counted for something were gone." By 1971, the ex-president had concluded in a piece he wrote for *Foreign Affairs* that "It appears that with the demise of the Alliance for Progress the policy is, essentially, that there is no policy," leaving the United States "unable to nurture, much less create, a policy that will respond to" a changing Latin America. Nixon was primarily concerned with stability, and, Salvador Allende's Chile aside, he was largely able to devote his energies to other parts of the world.[31]

Senator Church feared that the Alliance for Progress had "done nearly as much harm as good," but still hoped to discover ways to improve U.S. aid policy. He began to push for an end to military aid to Latin America, which had "enhanced the power and prestige of the military establishment in Latin America through the lavish gift of arms, ammunition and equipment. The fruits of this policy are all too evident." He recognized that this was a policy that had only been exacerbated since 1961, despite the hopes of people like him and Morse during the Eisenhower years. While arguing that it was "neither desirable nor possible for one country to impose free political processes on another," the United States could "terminate programs, such as military assistance, which work against democracy by strengthening ruling oligarchies." Church wanted the United States to be less visible in the region. He still had some hope that "a properly designed and conducted program of multilateral economic aid" could "lay the groundwork for free democratic politics in Latin America."[32]

Senator Church had dismissed the Rockefeller mission "as some kind of charade. The age of Marco Polo is long gone." Rockefeller could not "possibly bring back exciting new revelations about the mysterious lands which lie to the south."[33] For a time, however, Senator Church would even see something positive in Nixon's approach. Church praised President Nixon for his refusal to offer "pie-in-the-sky panaceas for Latin America." A request for foreign aid, after all, "would have been an empty gesture." Congress was "in no mood to enlarge foreign aid, nor will it be as long as we remain engaged in the war in Vietnam."[34]

Schlesinger, who had known Henry Kissinger for years, had been happy that he was chosen to be Nixon's national security adviser.[35] But he was soon complaining in the *Atlantic Monthly* about what he called a "visceral indifference to the Latin American ordeal." Schlesinger dismissed Vietnam as "remote and not very germane." And he insisted that Latin America was "far more vital to the national security of the United States." He lamented the abandonment of what he called the "progressive democratic way" of dealing with Latin America, which he saw as exemplified by his former boss, President Kennedy. He claimed that the Alliance for Progress had begun "to change the political consciousness of Latin America." Unfortunately, the Johnson administration had abandoned a "continental commitment to progressive democracy." Economically, the Alliance had become just another U.S. aid program. While he maintained that most of Latin America's problems had to be solved by Latin Americans, the United States could do more to support progressive democrats at a time when the guerrilla dream had been proven to have failed. He briefly seemed to see some hope in populist nationalism of the sort practiced by the left-wing military government in Peru. Nixon was clearly not committed to Latin America, aid had been reduced to Eisenhower administration levels, and ambassadorial choices were embarrassing, Schlesinger maintained. U.S. leaders needed to get back on the side of ordinary Latin Americans, while returning economic interests to their natural position as secondary to strategic interests, and reducing U.S. military aid, which tends to serve the needs of the U.S. "military establishment." The long-term trend, Schlesinger argued, was for a world in which the superpowers would be less dominant. If the United States could respond to Latin American "passion for national independence . . . with intelligence and generosity, there could arise a new sense of hemispheric solidarity stronger and healthier than anything we have yet known in the Americas."[36]

Responding in part to Schlesinger's article, Senator Church suggested that "The more gently we press our hemispheric neighbors, the greater our influence is going to be." "This," he continued, "will not be easy, for self-restraint is the hardest of all lessons for a great power to learn. Too tempting and seductive is the illusion of omnipotence." While he praised the "sincerity" of President Kennedy in creating the Alliance for Progress, he noted that, "Given the magnitude of our effort during the 1960s, we are left to wonder why it produced such disappointing results." "We thought we were seeding the resurgence of democratic governments; instead, we have seen a relentless slide toward militarism." The United States thought it "could remodel Latin America, but the reforms we have prescribed have largely eluded us." Instead of gratitude, "we have seen antagonism grow as our involvement in their problems has deepened." Church also lamented that the United States had "made ourselves a plausible scapegoat for pent-up furies and frustrations for which we bear little or no responsibilities."[37]

Liberals, Church argued, bought into military aid because they believed that it would enable the United States "to exert a tempering influence on the politically ambitious generals, while assuring us of their friendship in case they do take over." Only a small number of democracies remained. "Tempering influence indeed." He cited Ralph Dungan's concerns regarding the perception in Latin America that the Pentagon determined U.S. policy in the region. U.S. military missions should be removed from Latin America.[38]

Church was soon ready to say "farewell to foreign aid" altogether, and to do so as a liberal. Rather than a "decade of development," as had been promised a decade before, "we stand in this year 1971 at the end of one decade of disillusion, with no good reason to believe that we are not now embarked upon another." Experience had shown "that aid programs have little if any relevance either to the deterrence of communism or the encouragement of democracy," although they had "been effective in certain instances in keeping unpopular regimes in power." The United States had achieved stability while focusing on an "anti-Communist obsession which has driven us into league with military dictatorships and oppressive oligarchies all over the world." But it also was an illusion that the United States could transform the countries of the Third World through foreign aid. The United States had neither "the ability to impose reform from outside nor the will to pursue it from within." Leaving behind the "extravagant self-confidence" of the 1960s, the lesson of Vietnam, he concluded, was "that for many countries radical revolution is the only real hope for development."[39]

In a speech the previous year, Congressman Fraser had argued that the United States needed to be more careful in defining what its interests were instead of assuming that the Cold War necessitated an involvement everywhere. He decried the (now publicly known) excessive spending to prevent Allende's election in 1964. He rejected the use of the phrase "Free World" to include Brazil, Greece, and South Africa. Fraser insisted that the United States had "no vital security interests in the Third World." He expressed concerns that U.S. attempts to modernize Third World countries had been destabilizing and that its understanding of development was flawed.[40]

Edward Kennedy had traveled to Brazil and Chile during his brother's presidency as a private citizen to demonstrate the president's interest and to learn about the beginning of administration efforts to help Latin America reform. He met with the presidents of Argentina, Brazil, Colombia, and Venezuela.[41] He won a special election to replace his brother in the Senate in 1962. He became a member of the U.S. Committee for the Inter-American Association for Democracy and Freedom in early 1964.[42] (He had also gone to Chile in 1969 with his wife on a "belated honeymoon.") The Massachusetts senator was the only one of the three Kennedys to embrace life in the Senate, and, as his biographer Neal Gabler has written, he was the most instinctual liberal of the three as well. Following brother Robert's death, Edward Kennedy began expressing an interest in deepening his involvement in Latin American affairs. He was encouraged to do so by President Kennedy's ambassador to the Dominican Republic, John Bartlow Martin. Martin urged him to address Dominican leader Balaguer's repressive practices. Martin's primary concern, however, was that the Massachusetts senator "defend and argue for the continuation of the Alliance for Progress."[43]

In the Mansfield Lecture at the University of Montana in April 1970, Senator Kennedy did indeed call for a renewed commitment to the Alliance for Progress, shorn of its negative associations. The speech was drafted by Mark Schneider, a former reporter and American Political Science Association congressional fellow who had served in the Peace Corps in El Salvador. He acknowledged the "embarrassing reminder" that the Bay of Pigs invasion had provided of "our history of gunboat diplomacy toward the hemisphere" and suggested that the "noble goals" of the Alliance were "perverted by the cold war philosophy symbolized" by that invasion. Kennedy blamed the Pentagon, State Department, and intelligence agencies, however, for U.S. actions in favor of "stability." He argued that the invasion of the Dominican Republic had produced neither "order" nor "democratic rule," "and we have not realized the final cost of that action." He regretted the Alliance's failure "to end the depressing chapter of family dictatorships and military coups" and the continuation of U.S. support for "regimes in Latin America that deny basic human rights," focusing particularly on Brazil. He rejected Nelson Rockefeller's claims of "a new type of military man" in Latin America and joined Church in calling for the withdrawal of all military missions from Latin America, He lamented the lack of public outcry regarding what he saw as the abandonment of the Alliance in general. In a rhetorical flourish, he claimed that the Alliance was, in fact, never tried because the United States "emphasized the need for alliance" and forgot "the need for progress." Unlike Church, he retained a fundamental belief in foreign aid itself, claiming that "we have the capacity, talent, and technology to help bring about the transformation of Latin America without violence and bloody disorder." And while decrying what he considered the excessive repatriation of U.S. company profits, he hoped that private investment in Latin America could be encouraged that would fit with Latin America's own "development goals."[44]

The "test" of hemispheric "political maturity" was going to be the response to events in Chile. After what Senator Edward Kennedy called the "positive and progressive" government of Eduardo Frei, an election had taken place in which a "self-described Marxist" had received the most votes. In a *Saturday Review* article based on the Montana speech, Kennedy praised the "long and distinguished" "history of respect for the political process in Chile." Awaiting a vote by the Chilean Congress, necessary because Allende had not won more than 50 percent of the vote, Kennedy noted, "Regardless of the final outcome, the United States and other nations must respect the right of the Chilean people to choose their own leaders." Former Ambassador Ralph Dungan, recognizing privately that Allende was "going to have a tough time bringing off his vision of a new society," publicly called for a hands-off policy toward Allende's Chile. Dungan privately thought the "initial non-reaction in official circles" encouraging. Edwin Martin, the former Kennedy assistant secretary and U.S. ambassador to Argentina under Johnson, suggested privately that the Socialist leader might not be any worse and that there was a "better than even chance" that he would do "as well for the Chilean people."[45]

To understand the debate over U.S. policy toward Allende's Chile, one has to remember how little U.S. politicians and the U.S. public knew about what that policy was at the time. After all, President Nixon publicly discounted any worries regarding Allende and claimed to respect "the decision of the people of Chile." Nixon said that he told the Chilean ambassador "to tell the new President that as far as the United States was concerned that we recognized the right of any country to have internal policies and an internal government different from what we might approve of." Nixon claimed to be dealing "realistically" with Chile as he did with other countries. The only issue that Nixon would express a concern about was if Chile's foreign policy would act in a way that was "antagonistic" to U.S. interests.[46] Even as late as 1972, Nixon publicly claimed to be dealing "realistically" with Chile as he did with other countries. "Chile's leaders will not be charmed out of their deeply held convictions by gestures on our part." He did note, however, that the Allende government's actions on compensation for the nationalization of the property of U.S. copper companies were "not encouraging."[47] The public neutrality masked a wide variety of covert actions taken from 1970 to 1973, to influence the outcome of the election itself, then to prevent congressional ratification of Allende's victory, and, when that failed, employing a wide variety of means to create a "coup climate" in the country. As often happened during the Cold War, the employment of covert action by a president made public debate over U.S. foreign policy somewhat abstract.[48]

Church himself had been lulled into a sense of complacency regarding the potential for U.S. action in Chile following Allende's inauguration in late 1970. "Five years ago," he suggested, "this town would have been inundated with talk about military intervention; there has been none of this since Allende's election. I consider this a mark of progress, especially when you consider our recent past." Church was no fan of Allende, but he "repeatedly expressed my opposition to United States intervention in Chile and my support for the right of the Chilean people to self-determination."[49] For his part, Senator Kennedy had criticized what he called the "brusque and frigid" response of the Nixon administration to the Allende election. "A wise Administration policy," he told the Chicago Council of Foreign Relations in October 1971, "would have recognized that the Chilean experiment in socialism had been decided by the people of Chile in an election far more democratic than the charade we saw last week in Vietnam."[50]

Angered by the aforementioned editorial by Dungan, his successor Edward Korry noted that Dungan was "regarded universally in this country as the single greatest intervener in the history of our relations with this country." But over the next few months, Korry would covertly at least equal all that Dungan had done (and, as ambassador, at least, Dungan had tended to "intervene" openly).[51]

Meanwhile, the Brazilian government was hoping that the Nixon administration would pay more attention to it and prove that it recognized that Brazil was not a "second-rate nation." Brazil's military dictator Emílio Garrastazu Médici visited the White House in December 1971. Nixon praised Brazil's double-digit economic growth and lamented that Allende's Chile was beset by inflation as a result of policies "guided by political rather than economic motives." The military government thought that Brazil's economic success and strategic importance meant that it should be consulted on regional issues at least.[52]

Church argued in 1972 that the Democratic Party should "acknowledge the obsoleteness of ideological confrontation and with it, of bilateral American military and economic aid programs." Military aid should only be provided to "free governments" (mentioning Israel). The United States had only "a marginal influence . . . in promoting either stability or development." He suggested that the United States only provide "technical assistance grants administered, where feasible, by the Peace Corps."[53]

By 1972 Nixon had stolen liberal Democrats' thunder to some degree, through the opening to China and the easing of tensions with the Soviet Union. The Cold War was becoming increasingly incoherent and would remain so until its end. But Latin America continued to be a place where stricter limits were imposed regarding acceptable behavior of governments that refused to ally themselves with the United States. If Nixon claimed to take governments as he found them, including communist countries like the Soviet Union and Communist China, there were obviously exceptions made for countries in the Western Hemisphere. In response to a question regarding the difference between U.S. policy toward China and Cuba, Nixon said that Cuba remained determined to export revolution. Given that, U.S. policy would not change. Ironically, perhaps, Cuba's devotion to hemispheric revolution had cooled significantly beginning in 1970. And even though National Security Adviser Henry Kissinger was willing to countenance a change in policy toward Cuba, Nixon's response to any such suggestion was quite clear: "I'm not changing the policy toward Castro as long as I'm alive."[54]

Nixon had so many issues he considered of much greater importance in world affairs than Latin America. Yet he frequently had to reassert his interest in Latin America. "We do care. I care," he insisted, yet these assertions rang hollow.[55] Schlesinger, for his part, was concerned about what he saw as "North American indifference to Latin America." Both Dungan and Schlesinger hoped to use the media to keep the United States focused on Latin America.[56] Longtime liberal Democratic favorite José Figueres, recently re-elected to the presidency of Costa Rica, speaking before the Inter-American Association for Democracy and Freedom and introduced by Schlesinger at one of their meetings, said in late 1970, "We are in a new dark age, both in the United States and the rest of the hemisphere. The best we can do now is to emulate the monks of the old dark ages and do our best to keep fires and hopes alive." Privately Figueres lamented the deaths of the Kennedy brothers and the defeats of Stevenson and Humphrey, which he called the "five worst things that have happened to Latin American in the past twenty years.[57]

Looking forward to the 1972 presidential campaign, Frank Mankiewicz thought that a visit to Castro's Cuba or Allende's Chile in 1971 by presidential candidate George McGovern might attract some positive attention. But Latin American issues did not prove to be of primary importance for McGovern in 1972 despite his early criticism of Kennedy administration policy toward Castro almost a decade before. Certainly, the South Dakota senator was seeking to define a new foreign policy in an age of détente. "One of the great limitations of a foreign policy based on anti-communism," he argued, was "that it was a "most undependable way to choose one's enemies or to choose one's friends." He noted that "some of the world's worst scoundrels around the world" were "those who sail under an anti-communist banner." Although some in the campaign feared that the "Come Home America" slogan was being interpreted as a retreat into isolation, it was suggested that another slogan, "Let Us Rejoin the Family of Nations," could help define a new but still internationalist commitment. That slogan was soon forgotten. The campaign was clearly struggling to define a foreign policy agenda for a changing world. The task force that was set up in midyear saw "almost no vote-getting potential" in issues related to Latin America (as Stevenson had remarked almost two decades before), but there were some dangers in even creating such a task force, not least of all the danger that expectations would be raised regarding the campaign's commitment to such issues. Political scientist Abraham Lowenthal suggested to McGovern's foreign policy adviser Abram Chayes that the senator's "posture toward Latin America" could illustrate the "kind of mature, constructive, and modest engagement which would comprise U.S. policy in the post-Vietnam world." McGovern should exemplify the "attractive qualities which are precisely those needed as national attitudes toward Latin America: self-restraint, generosity of spirit, intolerance for brutality, a sense of equity, and impatience with narrow interests." (He further noted that McGovern's position as Kennedy-era director of Food for Peace and vice presidential candidate Sargent Shriver's position with the Peace Corps exemplify "two of the nobler and more attractive aspects of recent foreign policy.") Although the campaign sought to craft a new approach to the region, when McGovern did mention Latin America, he affirmed a sentiment that was by now more than a decade old—that the United States should align itself with those nations "making serious efforts at the fundamental reforms that are necessary to bring about progress for the great numbers of impoverished people." He suggested that the United States could "rededicate" the Alliance for Progress. The goals had been good, he suggested, but there had been "too much fanfare and not enough real commitment." McGovern saw no logic to Nixon's contradictory policies toward China and Cuba. McGovern noted that he hoped to "be able to maintain friendly relations" with Castro's Cuba and Allende's Chile. "What is good for International Telephone and Telegraph or the United Fruit Company isn't necessarily good for this country or for the people of Latin America," he affirmed. Foreign aid should be used for humanitarian purposes and not as "a tool in the Cold War or a way of buying friends." At the same time, he proposed a "demilitarization" of U.S. foreign policy that included a proposal that military aid should only be provided under "exceptional circumstances." The United States had "too often" "pitted itself against the just aspirations of Latin America." He "would hope to reverse that."[58]

The Democratic Party platform in 1972 affirmed the need for "a new foreign policy" "adequate for a rapidly changing world." But it looked back to both the Good Neighbor Policy and the Alliance for Progress, and their "still-living goals—insulation from external political conflicts, mutual non-interference in internal affairs, and support for political liberty, social justice and economic progress." It accused the Nixon administration of having "lost sight of these goals," resulting in "hostility and suspicion" toward the United States "unmatched in generations." It promised to create "an inter-American alliance of equal sovereign nations working cooperatively for development." Military aid would be "sharply" reduced. There would be more exchange of peoples and ideas. Democracies would have "special claims" "on our resources and sympathy." The United States should seek to encourage "nonintervention of military means in domestic affairs of Latin American nations." The platform promised to work toward resolution of conflicts with Cuba "on mutually acceptable terms."[59]

McGovern's proposed Latin America policy combined old and new elements of liberal Democratic thinking. The most innovative thinking reflected McGovern's own long-standing commitment to rethinking U.S. relations with Cuba. But Latin America could hardly be at the forefront of his foreign policy concerns as the Vietnam War continued. His Latin America task force echoed the criticism of Eduardo Frei and others that the Nixon administration still lacked a well-defined policy toward the region after three and a half years in office. Treasury Secretary John Connally was targeted for having said that "economic stability must precede political stability" while visiting Brazil. The Nixon administration policy of "unrelenting hostility toward the elected government of Chile" was also criticized, and the authors noted the failure to "dissuade ITT from [their] illegal and outrageous intervention." The Nixon administration lacked "moral and ethical standards," and its policies had "eroded the stature of the United States created by the Good Neighbor Policy and the Alliance for Progress." The Alliance had drawn "the hemisphere together in an enlightened purpose." But if the report criticized the Nixon administration for relegating the region to the "status of secondary importance," McGovern's priorities themselves were suggested by the fact that the report was only released a little more than a week before the election, in which the Democratic candidate was defeated resoundingly.[60]

In the months following McGovern's defeat, Chile came into focus, and there began to be intimations of a coup. The muckraking journalist Jack Anderson had claimed in March 1972 that International Telephone and Telegraph had sought to block Allende's election in 1970. But Congress delayed an investigation into the subject until after the fall election. Senator Church and the Senate Foreign Relations Committee began to investigate these charges in early 1973. During the hearings Senator Church reaffirmed his belief that the election of Allende had been an example of a people's right to choose its own government, the same right that the United States claimed to be fighting for in South Vietnam. Assistant Secretary of State for Inter-American Affairs Charles A. Meyer maintained that the Nixon administration had promised and held to a policy of "no intervention in the political affairs of

Chile." It was suggested that Ambassador Korry had been told to do anything short of launching a Dominican-style invasion to prevent Allende from taking power in 1970. The hearings were a significant factor in transforming understandings of the U.S. role in the world during this time period. What they revealed was inconclusive to say the least; after contradictory statements by one speaker after another, Church told Assistant Secretary Meyer that "somebody is lying."[61]

In March 1973, at the annual Washington Gridiron Club banquet speech, George McGovern joked that he had wanted to be president so badly that he had "even thought of asking ITT if I could be president of Chile."[62] A few months later, no one was laughing. On 10 September, adopting a far more serious tone, Senator McGovern argued that "the conduct of our foreign policy must be consistent with our professed ideals." A country "conceived in self-determination should not sponsor coups in other countries." "We cannot endure permanently as a free and decent society," he continued, "if we excuse every excess of foreign policy with the easy, irrelevant reply that the Communists are doing it." On the next day, military forces bombed the Chilean equivalent of the White House, La Moneda, and destroyed a long-standing democracy that had been a focus of U.S. interest in Latin America.[63]

Chile provided the concrete issue that liberal Democrats had failed to find in the years since President Kennedy's death. Discussion of human rights had accelerated under Nixon, particularly with hearings held by Church regarding Brazil.[64] But the 11 September 1973 coup in Chile was a major turning point in liberal Democratic thinking about U.S. policy in Latin America. In 1964, when the coup took place in Brazil, liberal Democrats were quick to discount U.S. involvement. But by 1973, the assumption that the United States was involved was immediate and widespread, not least of all because of the hearings held on the actions of multinational corporations earlier that year. Massachusetts Congressman Michael Harrington immediately called for congressional investigations into the role of the United States in undermining the Allende government, part of what he characterized as an "outmoded cold war response." Harrington himself was one of a new breed of congressmen, more skeptical of institutions and willing to take chances. Moreover, from the beginning, many in the U.S. Congress and in the U.S. public saw the coup in Chile as different, because Chile had been understood to be different because of its democratic traditions of long standing (and because the United States had been deeply involved in its internal dynamics since the early 1960s). New York Congressman Ed Koch saw the coup as "a tragedy of the first order, not only for Chile but for the concept of the democratic process." Liberal Democrats generally were not admirers of Allende himself or his government, but they did see something distinctive and valuable in the Chilean political system and feared (correctly, as it turned out) that democracy would not be easily restored. Koch warned that "If democracy is perceived as a mere facade to protect the power and privileges of the oligarchs, to be swept away when the results do not please the elite, then the only other response that can be taken by people who seek social justice is violent revolution, such as Fidel Castro preached." "It would be the greatest tragedy of the coup," he continued, if the coup's final legacy was for democracy "to be characterized as a fraud."[65]

The imprisonment and killing of political enemies by the new military government received an immediate response from the U.S. Congress. Harrington called for the government to respect the "humane treatment of prisoners," respect the right to asylum, and, in general, to adhere to international norms such as the Geneva Convention and the Universal Declaration of Human Rights. With Minnesota Congressman Donald Fraser, Harrington introduced a "sense of the Congress" resolution, calling on President Nixon to ask the military government to respect human rights in Chile.[66]

Senator Kennedy criticized the Nixon administration for not saying anything about "the coup which toppled a democratically elected government, or over the deaths, beating, brutality and repression which have occurred in that land." He supported a resolution that would discourage Nixon from giving economic or military aid to Chile without evidence that Pinochet was "protecting the human rights of all individuals, Chilean or foreign." He introduced an amendment to the foreign aid bill that called on President Nixon to end economic and military assistance to the Chilean government, but the amendment died in conference. Kennedy also asked for the Nixon administration to seek information on the whereabouts of particular Chilean politicians. Human rights had captured his imagination as the creation of refugees had influenced the emergence of his opposition to the Vietnam War. Meanwhile, Nixon provided aid that had not been offered to Chile since Allende's election, including credit for the purchase of wheat.[67]

In a *New York Times* op-ed piece in mid-October, former Ambassador Dungan noted the deep political polarization in Chile in early September. He called Allende's economic policies "pernicious and destructive," while recognizing long-standing and unresolved economic issues. Dungan expressed a "deep affection" for the Chilean people and an admiration for the professional Chilean military officers he had known as U.S. ambassador. While the coup itself was understandable, Dungan believed, the ongoing brutality had come as a surprise to him and was unacceptable. "[A]t a minimum . . . there needed to be "an immediate halt to summary executions, abandonment of mass arrests and detentions, humane treatment of prisoners, freedom of political expression, freedom of the press, a reversal of the moves against the autonomy of the universities, and a speedy return to civilian judicial process." Action needed to be taken to transform Chilean agriculture; "no task" should have "higher priority."[68]

The timing of the coup was important in another respect. At the beginning of August, Congressman Fraser had initiated a series of what would be fifteen hearings on the subject of human rights around the world. Although they paid significant attention to other issues, such as self-determination for Portuguese African colonies and apartheid in South Africa, as well as women's rights and the humanitarian conduct of war, one of the major results was to propose that the United States give greater priority to human rights in foreign policy and seek ways to "discourage governments which are committing serious violations of human rights." Historians have reflected less so far than they might on the multilateral aspects of the recommendations of what was, after all, a report of the subcommittee on international organizations. The United States was not expected to act unilaterally on the issue of human rights, but primarily in conjunction with the United Nations and the Organization of American States, particularly in the latter case by strengthening the Inter-American Commission on Human Rights.[69]

Assistant Secretary of State for Inter-American Affairs Jack Kubisch testified that the embassy was "unable to find any evidence of mass executions" in Chile. Senator Kennedy argued that the United States should "be in no hurry to provide general economic assistance to a regime which has come to power through a violent military coup—especially after years of denying such bilateral assistance and impeding multilateral assistance to a democratically-elected government." On the other hand, the United States must admit Chilean political refugees, he argued.[70]

As early as 20 September, Congressman Fraser sought to begin to change U.S. policy more broadly by calling for the creation of a position in the State Department that would address human rights. Congress would pass legislation requiring reports on countries receiving security aid and calling for an end to aid to countries that demonstrated "a consistent pattern of gross violations of internationally recognized human rights."[71]

As chairman of the Senate Judiciary Subcommittee on Refugees, the Massachusetts senator sent investigators, including former Ambassador Dungan and Kennedy's aide Mark Schneider, to Chile for a week in April 1974, and held hearings on the human rights situation in Chile in July. Prior to their departure, Augusto Pinochet wrote Kennedy, expressing puzzlement, given the "deep and profound memories" that the Kennedy name evoked in Chile of "understanding and friendship," that Kennedy had succumbed to the propaganda campaign that international Marxism had launched against Chile. Kennedy aide Schneider warned his colleagues that the junta saw Allende's followers and even many Christian Democrats as anti-Chile, and that they did not understand why it mattered that there should be "a system of laws" that applied "even to the enemy." Schneider perceived an "*absolute* [emphasis in the original] rejection of the humanity of the opposition" by the junta. Fearing civil war and desiring revenge, they had seen the extreme violence of the first few months following the coup as necessary. Schneider feared that terror had now become "a tactic of governance." Schneider hoped that trust could "be summoned up in a hurry." Ambassador Dungan and his colleagues were able to gain access to people who had been victims of torture. Dungan, who had been hopeful when Allende was elected, now said that there was "no doubt that Allende was a tragedy for Chile." Schneider later recalled that Pinochet assumed that people would recognize that he had saved the country and the Catholic Church. The Chilean leader denied that there had been any torture and that those who claimed to be victims had "scarred themselves." Pinochet later criticized Kennedy for not having come himself and charged that his treatment of Chile represented an "imperialistic mentality." Nevertheless, hundreds of political prisoners were let go as a result of the congressional visit.[72] Dungan testified at the July hearings that actions taken by the military government bore no relation to the security situation inside the country.[73]

Not all liberal Democrats responded in exactly the same way to the coup. Liberal Democrats, after all, had been committed to preventing Allende's election in 1964. Longtime promoter of Latin American democracy Frances Grant, while wanting to protest the military regime, felt compelled to criticize the dead Chilean president for having polarized Chilean society. Congressman Fraser, for his part, responded that he was "reluctant to suggest that the illegal seizure of power by a military group should appear to have justification in actions taken by democratically elected officials." Moreover, he said, "the polarization of the country was exacerbated by right wing groups." (This was a long way from what he had argued at the time of the military coup in Brazil a decade before.)[74]

But it is worth lingering for a moment on how Grant viewed Allende. The Chilean president had participated in the founding meeting of the Inter-American Association for Democracy and Freedom in 1950. Grant and Allende had known each other for a long time, and despite her misgivings, she sent him a congratulatory letter following his inauguration. Even more than Dungan, Grant identified with Frei and followed his lead regarding what was going on in Chile over the next few years. During the Allende years, she repeatedly referred to Frei as "the one hope for the return to democracy" in Chile, and "perhaps the only hope for the restoration of democracy in Chile." And this was when the Chilean Congress was functioning and the media were largely in the hands of the opposition. Following the coup, Grant made telephone calls to Frei and seems to have been assured that while people may have been killed "in battle," there were no executions. She continued adamantly to refuse to believe that the stories about torture, disappearances, and murder were not exaggerated. She accepted Frei's contention that Allende and his followers on the extreme left were armed and ready and preparing for a civil war or to initiate a coup "in the Castro format." Allende had been "unwilling or unable to restrain" extremist elements in his government. Frei himself believed that a coup had been necessary, although he was surprised when the military closed Congress and shut down the universities. He expected that military government could not last. "Chile is not Brazil," he told U.S. Ambassador Nathaniel Davis. Although Frei had initially promised to help with the new government's image abroad, by the end of October he had decided he could not take an "active supportive role" because of human rights violations and would refrain from making comments on Chilean politics over the next year. After traveling to Chile in November, Grant continued to contend that "everyone" in Chile was relieved. Only a year later, when Renán Fuentealba, a member of the Christian Democratic Party, had been expelled, did she become concerned. Ironically, even at the time when human rights was finally becoming an issue, the woman who had fought so hard for so long was now out of step with the people who presumably shared her beliefs. In fact, she complained in 1975 about the "late-comers" who, if they had "helped us in the past, perhaps such tragedies as Chile's might have been averted," and she still maintained that the focus on Chile was unjustified and had been "over-orchestrated."[75]

But Grant was certainly out of step with liberal Democrats on the issue of Chile for much of the 1970s. New political figures arose in the Congress who engaged with Latin America primarily on the issue of human rights. Schlesinger, for his part, criticized President Nixon's alignment "with the colonels in Greece, with the generals in Brazil and Chile (though not in Peru, where the generals lacked suitable reverence for American business), with the dying dictatorships in Portugal as well as with the despots in Moscow and Peking." Schlesinger claimed that "this policy has gone far to sever the bonds that once existed between the United States and the democratic aspirations of ordinary people around the world."[76]

In 1974, Schlesinger wrote Kissinger that "our Latin American policy has been a disaster." "No doubt we will in due course reap the harvest of this pro-authoritarian policy, in Brazil, Chile and elsewhere."[77] But liberal Democrats' commitment to democratic reform in the region had long been compromised. The liberal Democratic drive to make human rights a central component of U.S. foreign policy implied a recognition of the particular human costs of the Cold War consensus in Latin America. In practice the human rights paradigm would seek to minimize that cost. But the earlier liberal Democratic hope of transforming the region had long been abandoned, in part because of the compromises of the Kennedy and Johnson years, but also because of the disillusionment with development. Dungan despaired, privately telling told former Democratic Congressman Charles Porter of "the ability and willingness of the Department of State to become engaged on fundamental matters of human rights." But the belief that something needed to be done was widely shared. The United States was seen as implicated in the kinds of governments that existed in Latin America, and following the end of U.S. military involvement in the Vietnam War, the United States needed to reestablish its moral authority in the global Cold War.[78]

Senator Church argued that U.S. leaders had always maintained that communism could not be freely chosen and that communists had responded that the United States would never accept a communist government established "by peaceful means." President Nixon had confirmed that. In the process, the United States had "grievously impaired the good name and reputation from which we once drew a unique capacity to exercise moral leadership." The United States had become, in Church's words, "a self-appointed sentinel of the status quo."[79]

Certainly, by the end of Nixon's time in office, the Cold War consensus was frayed. The United States had sought to spread the responsibility for containment around, and Brazil was playing an important role in that effort. The withdrawal of U.S. troops from Vietnam suggested a less universal commitment by the United States to containment (which was seen as confirmed by the fall of Saigon in 1975).[80] And while the relaxation of tensions with the Soviet Union hardly meant, as it sometimes seemed, that the Cold War was over or that containment itself had been abandoned, the improvement of relations with China suggested that the ideological justification for the Cold War was increasingly incoherent. Allende had been wrong to think that these developments gave him greater room to maneuver, however. The need to maintain U.S. dominance in the Western Hemisphere had by no means been abandoned. And the threat that Allende and his friend Castro had posed to U.S. hegemony in the Western Hemisphere now had been contained. Liberal Democrats were coming to see the costs containment posed to human rights in the hemisphere. Pushed by activists, as historian James Green and others have shown, few liberal Democrats could afford politically to simply abandon a Cold War understanding of the world, but they would offer a more modest approach to international affairs. But promoting human rights could not succeed without more of a commitment to regime change than they were willing to support. They would seek to influence the behavior of Latin American governments through a reduction in aid. They could not reverse the damage that had already been done, particularly during the Johnson years, by a lack of skepticism toward military governments like those of Brazil, or their failure to engage sufficiently following the invasion of the Dominican Republic. Human rights, first and foremost in Chile under Pinochet, was becoming the liberal Democratic prism through which Latin America would be viewed. Liberal Democrats were once again viewing at least one Latin American country as a real place with real people, and not the abstraction that it had increasingly become following the death of John Kennedy. Liberal Democrats would have a fight on their hands, but they might be able to influence U.S. policy in such a way that Congress could modify the behavior of military governments allied to the United States, if only to a limited degree. To do more than that, they would have to count on public support and a deeper engagement with Latin America than had been seen since the fears of the early 1960s. Without fear to motivate the public or political leaders, only a moralistic and positive commitment to promoting something more than just stability would enable them to go beyond the Cold War consensus.

The new human rights paradigm was neither utopian nor merely an attempt to get Americans to feel good about themselves. It assumed a responsibility of the United States for Latin American affairs. It undoubtedly reflected a scaling back of liberal Democratic aspirations in the region that had been underway for some time. It took the overthrow of a democratically elected government in a country believed to be exceptional for it to coalesce. Liberal Democratic engagement with and neglect of the region during the Johnson years had helped the descent into authoritarianism. Liberal Democrats, long suspicious of Salvador Allende, nevertheless recognized that something significant had changed with his fall. Liberal Democrats were no longer confident about the possibility of U.S. foreign aid to promote democracy or development, and their rhetorical commitment to anti-interventionism would further complicate a broader strategy. But the human rights paradigm at least promised to have an impact on the behavior of governments dependent on the United States for aid. Ending torture, arbitrary imprisonment, and summary executions would be the focus of liberal Democratic policy in Latin America for much of the rest of the decade, and, indeed, of the Cold War.

A new group of liberal Democratic politicians had emerged. The so-called Watergate babies elected in 1974 were much more skeptical of White House actions and pronouncements, and less deferential to tradition and presidents. As a congressional aide, Tom Harkin of Iowa had exposed the conditions in South Vietnam, where inmates were held in small "tiger cages." Harkin entered the House of Representatives with the "Watergate class" of 1974. He focused on human rights issues during his first two terms in office. "That's how I made my mark," he later told journalist and author Adam Clymer. He remained engaged with Latin American issues for the remainder of the Cold War.[81]

Human rights promised an affirmation of U.S. values in a time of distrust. Moral leadership in the world might yet be affirmed. If the United States was not going to transform the world as it had promised to do in the 1970s, it nevertheless promised a way to show leadership internationally. Human rights policy was far from isolationist.[82]

Following Nixon's resignation in August 1974, former Michigan Congressman Gerald Ford became president (he had only been vice president since the preceding December, following Spiro Agnew's resignation in October). A few weeks later President Ford remarked that "when you look at the other areas—Latin America, we are not going to neglect Latin America." Later he mentioned that the Ford administration was "not going to neglect Africa."[83] It was hard not to recognize that both regions were afterthoughts. During the short time that Gerald Ford was in office, there were once again people pressing to move beyond the "inter-American benign neglect" of the Nixon years, in which "the United States had elevated passivity to a diplomatic art," creating a "policy vacuum."[84] Nevertheless, many remained dubious that U.S. policy would change much, given the fact that Henry Kissinger, never one to take Latin America seriously, was now secretary of state and clearly the dominant force in foreign policy. Ford, though an internationalist of long standing, was primarily interested in domestic policy.[85]

President Ford was now plagued by questions regarding U.S. involvement in a Latin American coup to a degree that was unprecedented. He categorically denied that the United States had played a role on 11 September 1973. (He also rejected rather sensibly the idea that a president should ever comment on covert action publicly.) He accepted only U.S. responsibility for seeking to preserve the opposition media and political parties in the face of what he claimed were Allende's antidemocratic tendencies. From a historian's perspective, these tendencies seem minor compared to the actions taken by the leader the Ford administration supported. In any case, the Ford administration did nothing to help preserve opposition media or political parties under Pinochet. When Congress cut off "the modest program of military assistance to Chile," President Ford insisted that he was as interested as Congress in protecting human rights, but that the aid cutoff was not "an effective means to promote that interest."[86]

Secretary of State Henry Kissinger stood firm in the belief that a country's human rights policies should not be a factor in determining the U.S. attitude toward it. (This was true, as far as he was concerned, even for the Soviet Union and its treatment of Jews.) Kissinger was largely in charge of foreign policy.

Congressional pressure mounted to halt aid to countries that were "increasingly indifferent to internationally recognized human rights and [that] deal with their own people in an increasingly oppressive manner." Particular attention was paid to "freedom from torture, arbitrary arrest and detention, and arbitrary curtailment of existing political rights." "Long-term U.S. foreign policy interests" were "not served by maintaining supportive relationship with oppressive governments." Congressman Fraser attempted to meet with Kissinger following reports that former Ambassador to Chile David Popper had been rebuked for his criticism of the Pinochet regime. Unless the executive branch began to provide more than "rhetorical support" for human rights, Congress promised to block foreign aid.[87]

Brazil continued to be of special interest to Secretary Kissinger, and he worked to encourage President Ford to recognize the importance of the relationship with the military regime. The Ford administration sought to revive military aid for Brazil in 1975, arguing not only that it would be good for U.S. national security and aid an ally that was large and increasingly important, but also that Venezuela and Argentina had both bought Sidewinder missiles lately, and the Congress had shown no concerns. Kissinger neglected to mention that both of these countries were still run by constitutional governments at this time. More to the point, Assistant Secretary of State Robert Ingersoll said that "The extent of [human rights] violations and responsibility for them are difficult to determine with precision, but there continues to be reports from a variety of sources indicating that mistreatment of prisoners, including torture still occurs." More persuasively, Ingersoll argued that Brazilian president Ernesto Geisel was "committed to cautious political liberalization," and given resistance to his policies within the military itself, it was not altogether clear that U.S. pressures would not end up being self-defeating. "This is a difficult and delicate process," Ingersoll continued. While military aid would not in itself help improve the human rights, the missiles, at least, could not be used "to carry out repressive internal measures." And it had to be made clear that military aid, Ingersoll affirmed, did not signify support for repression. By undercutting Geisel, Ingersoll noted, the United States would achieve none of its goals. In any case, the president should make the decision based on "the political aspects of national security, rather than the military aspects."[88]

In Chile Pinochet had consolidated his personal power. In July 1974, Decree Law 527 declared him to be the "Supreme Chief of the Nation." In December he was named Chile's president, a title he would not relinquish until January 1990. Institutionally, the creation of a secret police, the National Intelligence Directorate (DINA), in June 1974, answerable only to Pinochet and soon notorious for its brutality, also played a major role in helping keep the population cowed.[89] Kissinger's support for and admiration of the Pinochet regime was unwavering. Its "biggest sin was to have wiped out a leftist government." Equally strong was his disdain for its critics.[90]

Kissinger dismissed human rights privately as "silly." National interests remained key. President Ford publicly was more circumspect, suggesting in December of 1974 that cutting off military aid to the Pinochet regime would not improve human rights in Chile. He asserted elsewhere that "every State has the right to adopt its own system of government and its own economic and social organization" (though it is unlikely that he would have made the same argument in the case of Cuba). Kissinger dismissed Pinochet's critics in the U.S. Congress as being opposed to the military government only because it was pro-America. "Is human rights more severely threatened by this government than Allende?" Kissinger asked one of his aides. To which the man replied, "In terms of freedom of association, Allende didn't close down the opposition party. In terms of freedom of the press, Allende didn't close down the newspapers." Privately, Secretary of State Kissinger repeatedly tried to reassure Chilean leaders that the Ford administration and the State Department "did not intend to harass Chile on this matter." Despite dissent within the State Department, U.S. policy in favor of Pinochet remained constant. In June of 1976, Kissinger went so far as to publicly express U.S. support for human rights in the hemisphere while privately assuring Pinochet that "we are not out to weaken your position."[91]

During the Ford years, the Chilean government received "$160 million in economic aid, $23 million in grants, and $18.5 million in military assistance," not to mention $141 million in loans from the Export-Import Bank and $300 million "in credits" from the Inter-American Development Bank. Private foreign investors, not all of course from the United States, pumped in roughly $3 billion from 1974 to 1978.[92]

Liberal Democrats were particularly concerned that a program that senators like Humphrey and McGovern had been particularly devoted to, the Food for Peace program, was now being used to help Pinochet consolidate his power. According to Senator Kennedy and others, 85 percent of program aid was going to the country, based on the political priorities of the Nixon administration and not on where the need was greatest in the Western Hemisphere. USAID officials insisted that the percentage was no more than 5 percent. In any case, they insisted the food aid was necessary because of the 40 percent decline in agricultural production between 1970 and 1975.[93]

Congressional concern regarding human rights conditions in Chile expanded dramatically in 1974 with the House Armed Services Committee's briefings on U.S. anti-Allende actions, and in 1975 with the Select Committee to Study Government Activities with Respect to Covert Operations, which soon would be known by the name of its head, Senator Church. Numerous attempts were made to block or minimize U.S. aid for the Pinochet government. Besides ignoring congressional intent, the government also sought to deny that human rights abuses were in fact taking place.[94] Congressmen made repeated attempts to ban military aid. "We have made some progress," Fraser insisted, "but not nearly enough—in sensitizing the Department of State to the oppression existing in Chile."[95] In 1975, for example, Congressman Harkin introduced a human rights amendment to the foreign aid bill, which was passed in the House. Senator McGovern's congressional aide John Holum made sure that his name got on the Senate bill. Human rights, Holum wrote McGovern, "should be regarded as a central factor in the development of our post-Vietnam foreign policy," bringing together "a large portion of the constituency you gained though opposition to the war in Vietnam" and "generating the same kind of organizing commitment from peace, academic, and religious activists." The amendment was intended "to have some real impact on human rights conditions." Military aid had made the United States "a direct participant in the internal policies of those governments."[96]

Pinochet in August of 1975 sought support from the Ford administration for an official state visit to Washington. Despite Kissinger's strong support, this was not going to happen. NSC's Low suggested that the administration could expect a good deal of criticism domestically and internationally if Pinochet were to be the first Latin American head of state received by the administration. Yet Low also was reluctant to have it made public that the U.S. had rejected such a visit.[97] In speaking with Brent Scowcroft, Chilean admiral and junta member José Toribio Merino suggested that a "timetable should be established for a return to civilian rule," but he opposed "rapid movement in that direction" and would not accept a role for the Christian Democratic Party in such a process. Scowcroft was expected to praise Chile for improvements in human rights and to let the government know that U.S. "ability to be responsive to the legitimate defense and development needs of your government" would be strengthened by more such improvements.[98] Not all U.S. officials were convinced that the onus was on the United States. Stephen Low criticized the Pinochet government for its "inability to improve its performance on human rights and recognize that truly meaningful changes are necessary to improve its international image."[99]

Even as Congress, Kissinger, and the Ford administration fought over aid to the Pinochet government, the Ford years were a period in which critiques of U.S. foreign policy practices broadened. Although inspired initially by revelations that the Central Intelligence Agency had been engaged in spying inside the United States, contrary to its charter, the wide-ranging hearings chaired by Senator Church inevitably spent some time examining its actions in Chile. Previous generations of lawmakers had preferred to avert their eyes from covert actions taken in the name of national security, in Latin America and elsewhere. The so-called Era of Trust in the intelligence agency (and, to a large degree, the executive branch, as well) had ended, and the Era of Skepticism had been born. Whether the CIA was to be allowed to continue to employ covert action was debated publicly; clearly, fundamental questions regarding postwar foreign policy were being raised. No coup in Latin American history, before or since, received the attention that the Chilean one did. This led people, both politicians and the general public, to believe that they knew more about U.S. involvement in the coup itself than was warranted (as opposed to the overall attempt by the Nixon administration to foment a coup). In testifying before the Church committee concerning prior examples of covert action, Dungan may have been disingenuous regarding what the CIA had been doing during the time he was ambassador. But the most significant activity, in any case, had happened during the presidential campaign itself, when Dungan still served only as an aide to President Johnson, albeit already one deeply concerned with Chilean matters.[100]

As congressional interest in human rights expanded, Latin Americans sought opportunities to testify before Congress on the human rights situation in their country. A particularly important individual was Chilean Orlando Letelier, who had been Allende's ambassador to the United States before heading the ministries of foreign affairs, interior, and defense. He had been imprisoned and tortured before being allowed to go into exile roughly twelve months following the coup, eventually settling in Washington, where he had spent many years and had come to know many U.S. politicians and government officials. He was an outspoken opponent of the Pinochet regime abroad, leading the government to strip him of his Chilean citizenship. On 21 September 1976, Congressmen Fraser and Harkin, as well as George Miller of California, were gathering signatures for a letter in which, citing Article 15 of the United Nations Declaration of Human Rights, they focused on this basic violation of his human rights. They pledged their support for him personally and their own commitment to the restoration of "all human rights in Chile." Before the letter could be sent, Letelier and a U.S. citizen named Ronnie Moffitt were killed by a car bomb that exploded in the streets on Embassy Row in the center of Washington, DC.[101] Senators and congressmen denounced their deaths and attended Letelier's memorial service. Although right-wing Chileans (and DINA) were the "obvious candidates," NSC officials Mary Brownell and Dan Mozeleski argued, "they seem to be *too* obvious [emphasis in the original], and we think they would think twice about creating a martyr for the Chilean left." But evidence soon became clear that the Pinochet regime was responsible, and this consolidated congressional opposition to aid for Chile.[102]

In his failed run for the 1976 Democratic nomination, Senator Church called attention to his support for blocking aid to Latin American governments that came to power through military intervention and called for a reexamination of hemispheric defense and U.S. influence on Latin American governments. He called for nonintervention and major cuts in foreign aid. Jimmy Carter, as we shall see, adopted at least major portions of the liberal Democratic agenda.[103]

By the summer of 1976, the U.S. Congress had moved to cut military and economic aid to the Pinochet regime. President Ford and Secretary of State Kissinger both opposed this move, but they could not stop it. The Nixon-Ford policy toward Chile and the human rights policy that was developing in response to it helped transform thinking about the U.S. role in the world in an age of decreasing Cold War tensions. In an age of cynicism and distrust of government and U.S. foreign policy after Vietnam and Watergate, human rights offered an opportunity to reassert U.S. moral leadership. Following his defeat of Ford in the 1976 election, President Jimmy Carter would have to deal with the consequences. He implemented a human rights policy for which there was no precedent. He would have to deal with a Congress that had taken the lead on the issue and that, to some degree, still believed it owned it, even as the president declared it to be "the soul of our foreign policy."[104]

Chapter 8

Jimmy Carter and Human Rights in South America

Arthur Schlesinger Jr. had hoped that a liberal candidate would emerge in 1976. He wanted Ted Kennedy not to rule himself out in 1975, as he seemed to be doing. He dismissed former Georgia Governor Jimmy Carter as "an intelligent, ambitious opportunist." An unknown on the national stage, Carter was a devout Christian who displayed his beliefs in a way that was unknown among political leaders at the time; he promised a more moralistic approach to foreign policy than that provided in previous years. Generally, Schlesinger was concerned about Carter's anti-government rhetoric in terms of domestic policy and noted, following the 1976 convention, that he assumed that the Massachusetts senator would "serve as the ideological conscience of the Carter administration—and no doubt make Carter a better President than he would be without pressure from the left." Generally, he thought that Carter lacked vision and did not support what Schlesinger called "affirmative national government." As time went on, as he wrote to the new ADA president in mid-1978, "I do not think that Carter is, or is likely to become, either a liberal or even a Democrat."[1]

But despite Schlesinger's own skepticism, Carter became committed to the new liberal Democratic understanding of human rights. Some have argued that his interest in human rights and humanitarian affairs stemmed in part from his failure to engage with the civil rights movement in the 1950s and 1960s. As president, Carter expanded his interest in Latin America. Carter had visited Argentina, Brazil, Colombia, Costa Rica, and Mexico as governor of Georgia. He and his wife "read a chapter in the Bible in Spanish" every night before retiring. In a speech before the Chicago Council on Foreign Relations in March 1976, he had argued that "it must be the responsibility of the President to restore the moral authority of this country in the conduct of foreign policy." In a speech before the Student National Medical Association on the campaign trail in April, he criticized the Republicans for neglecting Latin America and Africa. He criticized Secretary of State Kissinger for suggesting that the United States and military-led Brazil shared the same values, which he called a "gratuitous slap in the face of all those Americans who want a foreign policy that embodies our ideals, not subverts them." Congressman Fraser sought to reassure a wavering leader of the American Civil Liberties Union in Southern California, who was considering not voting for Carter, that Fraser himself was pleased that Carter mentioned "human rights in every one of his foreign policy speeches." The party platform included criticism of "extensive American interference" in Chile and the need to "make clear our revulsion at the systematic violations of basic human rights that have occurred under some Latin American military regimes." In Carter's October debate with Ford, Carter listed the 1973 coup in Chile as one of the primary reasons for "the deep hurt that's come to this country" in terms of its international reputation.[2]

The party platform promised to "restore the Democratic tradition of friendship and support to Third World nations." The United States should work to free political prisoners around the world. The platform affirmed its support for workers' rights around the world, as well as the free movement of peoples. Moreover, the party promised to deliver a greater openness about what U.S. foreign policy actually was. The platform lamented the spread of military rule in Latin America over the previous "eight years." And the platform invoked "the principles of the Good Neighbor Policy and the Alliance for Progress, under which we are committed to working with the nations of the Americas as equals."[3]

The Democrats now had a man in the White House for the first time in almost a decade. In terms of domestic policy, Schlesinger may have been generally right to claim that President Carter was not a liberal. But his adoption of the human rights issue, particularly in Latin America, and his willingness to take risks in the region (explored more fully in the next chapter) would make liberal Democrats hope that their evolving policies would come to fruition. But Carter would find that action on human rights could only sometimes be the priority that he had intended it to be. And what that even meant in practice was often less clear as well.

President Carter was more engaged with more of Latin America than any president since Kennedy. The new president asked for a review of "the major issues of concern to the U.S. and Latin America." It is noteworthy that Carter did not ask for a review of any other regional policy. The study examined whether "current assumptions underlying U.S. policy toward the region as well as the policies themselves" were "appropriate to an effective handling of these issues." The study was to look at not only U.S. interests and how they had changed, but also the "broad psychological climate within the hemisphere." The review was intended to provide options that took "explicit account of the differentiation of Latin America and the Caribbean as between middle range powers and less-developed countries." They should also examine how this fits into the "broader North-South dialogue."[4]

Robert Pastor, a political scientist and the Latin American specialist for the National Security Council, urged the Carter administration to become more involved, not less, in the concerns of what was increasingly becoming known as the Global South. The United States should think of Latin America both as less like one region in itself, because of its internal diversity, and yet as more part of that larger grouping. Latin America should be less dependent on the United States "or any single source," and the United States should "encourage the present trend toward increasingly diversified relations between Latin America, Europe, Japan, and even Eastern Europe." The United States should be more tolerant of regimes of "widely *different political philosophies*, distinguishing only on the basis of their respect for fundamental human rights" (emphasis in the original). The United States also "should pledge its full respect for the sovereignty of each Latin American nation and should commit itself not to undertake unilateral military intervention or covert intervention in their internal affairs." The U.S. "ability to influence events in Latin America appears greatest not when the power equation is most weighted to our advantage, but when we are cognizant and sensitive to the principal norms of the developing world," sovereignty and "social justice." Rather than trying to counter Soviet attempts to spread influence directly and reflexively, the United States needed to focus on issues of greatest concern to Latin America.[5]

The review itself portrayed Latin America and the Caribbean as "more diverse, prosperous, confident, independent and self-aware than any regional grouping in the Third World." They had "an alarming population growth, the dizziest rate of urbanization and the most highly developed systems of military government." Democracy was "weaker today than at any time since the Second World War." The "immediate future" was "not bright." What the United States wanted from Latin America was primarily defined in negative terms: "*not* to aggravate East–West tensions, *not* to deny us access to their energy reserves and other raw materials, *not* to develop nuclear capabilities." The United States wanted "sufficiently stable and healthy economic and political growth *not* to weaken our security, create new global problems, or offend our values." The United States wanted "moderation on North–South issues and support in world councils on matters of importance to us. At our most hopeful we want democratic systems to be revived in this hemisphere."[6]

Carter assured the permanent council of the OAS that "My heart and my interest to a major degree is in Latin America." As Pastor had suggested, Carter frequently referred to his policy as one that recognized the internal diversity of the region. "We don't," he noted, "have a special slogan for Latin America anymore" because "a single United States policy toward Latin America and the Caribbean [made] little sense." He also frequently expressed a commitment to treat each country as distinct. He noted the changes that had taken place in inter-American relations over the previous decade. He promised "a wider and a more flexible approach, worked out in close consultation" with Latin American countries. He praised the role of Latin American nations in "improving North–South negotiations" and, more generally, playing "more independent and important roles in world politics." This portended a "more normal and more balanced and equal relationship between the United States and Latin American countries.[7]

As noted, this was the only region for which President Carter asked the State Department to provide a review of overall policy. In contrast to the Kennedy years, the United States was engaging with Latin America at a time when there were few great threats to its interests there. Pastor hoped that the Carter administration would recognize the increasing economic and political diversity of the region and abandon the idea of a policy of having one policy for a region that did not even exist. ("The idea of Latin America as a *region* is a myth.") Pastor himself was disdainful of the report that the State Department's Bureau of Inter-American Affairs produced. Pastor argued that U.S. influence on Latin America had decreased and Latin Americans were more assertive (as were others in the Third World) on questions of global economic issues. While the "Vietnam trauma" had passed and "reduced insecurity due to détente" had diverted U.S. attention from the developing world, U.S. citizens still thought that a "special relationship" with Latin America existed and demanded "more from Latin America in human rights, restraint on arms transfers, and on other issues, while also promising (though not delivering) more resources to the region." Pastor himself feared a tendency to "adopt a different standard for human rights violations in this hemisphere than for anywhere else." Moreover, he rejected what he called "automatic or fixed formulas." While recognizing that the Organization of American States had been in decline for some time, Pastor argued that human rights was an area in which the OAS had a "comparative advantage," and the United States could achieve more on human rights by working with the Inter-American Commission on Human Rights.[8]

In the report itself, the State Department addressed the issue of how human rights fit into its larger goals and how a human rights policy would affect U.S. relations with Latin America. If the "criticism of repressive governments" put the United States "on the side of change," the United States had "little leverage on how that change comes about." The United States was uncomfortable with the fact that fifteen Latin American governments were "run directly or indirectly by military officers," particularly because some of these governments had consistently violated human rights. Human rights pressures had "raised new fears about U.S. intervention and paternalism." If the United States argued that human rights transcended "national sovereignty," it had to concern itself with the weight of the history of U.S. influence in Latin America. The United States now found it "undesirable" to "prolong" "our historical hegemony and its freight of paternalism." Was it possible to maintain an assumed "special relationship" between the United States and its hemispheric neighbors without them? Could the United States continue to move toward a North–South understanding of the world rather than the East–West understanding that had prompted U.S. actions in the region from Guatemala in 1954 to Chile in 1973? More fundamentally, was the United States willing to renounce all forms of intervention?[9]

Venezuelan President Carlos Andrés Pérez, one of the few Latin American leaders during these years who liberal Democrats considered kindred spirits, praised Carter for having moved beyond "the paternalism of the past" in dealing with Latin America. Like U.S. presidents before him, Carter praised the democratic evolution of the South American country. Flush with oil money, the Venezuela of the Carter years was more inclined to take a leadership role in the Caribbean and Central America. Carter noted approvingly that Venezuela was "the leading country, above all others, including our own, in insisting on the principle of human rights" at the Organization of American States meeting in Grenada. Pérez welcomed the Carter administration human rights policy but warned that it was "illusory to expect the development and implementation of human rights within an international order so deeply anti-democratic as the one in existence." As we shall see, the Venezuelan leader pushed Carter at times, and sometimes took positions that the administration did not appreciate.[10]

By the time of his inaugural address, President Carter could assert that "Our commitment to human rights must be absolute." "Because we are free," he continued, "we can never be indifferent to the fate of freedom elsewhere." Carter further noted that "Our moral sense dictates a clear-cut preference for those societies which share with us an abiding respect for individual human rights."[11] But how this preference would express itself and what this would mean for countries that lacked such a respect remained to be seen. The human rights issue certainly did not simplify foreign policy making, and it was unclear to many, at home and abroad, how it fit in a larger foreign policy framework for the new president. At the same time that Carter was delivering this address, he was also sending a message to the people of the world regarding "how the power and influence of the United States will be exercised." He noted his administration's "desire to shape a world order that is more responsive to human aspirations." The United States would "meet its obligations to help create a stable, just, and peaceful world order." It would "not seek to dominate or dictate to others." The administration claimed to have "a more mature perspective on the problems of the world." The United States recognized its limitations and could not "alone guarantee the basic right of every human being to be free of poverty and hunger and disease and political oppression."

The United States would "cooperate with others in combating these enemies of mankind." The world could "depend on the United States to remain steadfast in its commitment to human rights, freedom and dignity." The United States needed the world's "help" and "active participation." Carter chose to speak to the peoples of the world directly, and not necessarily to their governments, when he noted that the United States would be "sensitive to your own concerns and aspirations." Carter promised that the United States would "do its utmost to resolve differences in a spirit of cooperation."[12]

In a later speech before the United Nations, Carter noted that "All of the signatories of the UN Charter have pledged themselves to observe and to respect basic human rights. Thus, no member of the United Nations can claim that mistreatment of its citizens is solely its own concern." All UN members, furthermore, had the responsibility "to review and to speak when torture or unwarranted deprivation occurs in any part of the world."[13]

It is frequently overlooked that Carter's human rights policy was based not just on religious faith but on a belief in U.S. values, and a belief that the United States could "confidently" continue "to inspire, to persuade, and to lead." "It is a new world, but America should not fear it. It is a new world, and we should help to shape it." Carter had an optimistic faith in democracy and the role that the United States could play in the world. In the bicentennial year, he later recalled, "it was time for us to capture the imagination of the world again."[14]

It was the "inordinate fear of communism" that Carter decried at the University of Notre Dame in May of 1977 that had led to U.S. support for Latin American dictators. As he said before the permanent council of the Organization of America States, the United States was "eager to stand beside those nations which respect human rights and which promote democratic ideals."[15] But was the goal to remove the dictators and promote democracy, which would require significant intervention, or merely to modify their behavior? And if the United States wanted to modify their behavior, was it better to engage with these regimes more or less? Would reducing military aid, as liberal Democrats had been proposing for years, be the answer? And then what?[16]

In his memoirs, Carter argued that his human rights policy was intended to promote human rights within authoritarian countries, thereby enhancing "freedom and democracy" and removing "the reasons for revolutions that often erupt among those who suffer from persecution."[17] He also came to believe that U.S. pressures were part of a larger international community opinion that countries believed that they had to take into account in their internal practices. In the 1979 State of the Union address, Carter noted that "we believe our efforts have contributed to a global awakening."[18]

But it took some time for the Carter administration to communicate effectively on this subject. The U.S. press and, therefore, to a large extent, the

U.S. public had to keep getting reminded that the human rights did not apply solely to the Soviet Union or the Eastern Bloc. The international community was rather confused as well. Illustrative in this regard is a conversation that deputy national security adviser David Aaron had with the Polish minister at its embassy in Washington. Jozef Wiejacz expressed concern that the issue would damage détente. Wiejacz noted that he assumed that the issue was raised in order to undermine relations between the United States and the Eastern Bloc. He made clear that détente had led to an "unprecedented exchange of high-level visitors between the United States and Poland in recent years." Aaron made clear that he believed that the administration "was not afraid to use the word 'détente,' but we wanted greater substance in it, including progress on human rights."[19]

Months passed without the State Department being able to produce a coherent policy statement. Foreign policy skeptics complained to others that there had been no attempt to "relate our human rights policy to our overall foreign policy objectives," leading to a discussion that ignored "the key issues of costs and benefits for the Carter Administration."[20] As late as September 1977, Patricia Derian, head of the Bureau of Human Rights and Humanitarian Affairs, was still insisting that President Carter needed to explain human rights.[21] Throughout the Carter years, the U.S. press remained attentive, perhaps overly so, to the possibility of the Carter administration "backing off" on human rights.[22]

But, as Carter later admitted, he "did not fully grasp all the ramifications of our new policy."[23] Frequently, in both Latin America and the Soviet Union, he demonstrated that he believed that he could criticize governments, meet or correspond with people who opposed those governments, and yet improve relations with those governments (and, in the Soviet Union's case, without harming détente). Moreover, he was convinced that he would be able to change the Soviet and Latin American governments' treatment of their own peoples. Carter's initiatives rarely constituted a consistent policy. As historian Nancy Mitchell has written, Carter "believed in patient diplomacy *and* in the dramatic gesture; he saw beyond the Cold War *and* he was a firm Cold Warrior."[24] His Latin America policies, as the rest of this chapter and the next will demonstrate, were no less inconsistent, sometimes usefully so for strategic purposes, and sometimes with negative consequences.

But it seemed clear to others from the beginning that the human rights policy, if it applied more to the Soviet Union than to China, and less to Asia more generally and the Middle East, it did have a special application for Latin America. Kennedy aide Mark Schneider was asked to serve as deputy to the combative Derian, a former civil rights activist. Latin American governments resented being singled out, while Latin American human rights activists appreciated the attention. Even more particularly, the human rights policy had special implications for South American countries, most notably Argentina, Brazil, and Chile, all of which had acute human rights problems, but which also were at different stages in the consolidation of military rule.[25] The impact of the Carter administration in each case was inevitably not the same either.

Latin American governments, as opposed to many Latin American citizens, were generally not pleased with the new policy. There is no doubt that throughout the Carter years, it put a strain on relations with military governments. Considering how reduced the number of democracies in the region was (limited to Costa Rica, Colombia, and Venezuela at the time of Carter's inauguration), it is hardly surprising that few governments were happy with the possibility of a forceful human rights policy. Carter's rhetorical commitment to human rights did encourage and even embolden activists throughout the region, however, and it did force countries to make some kinds of at least rhetorical commitments, particularly following the June 1977 Organization of American States meeting in Grenada. Historians have long recognized that citizens can employ official language to address their own concrete issues. Given the outsized influence the United States had throughout much of the twentieth century, it made sense that Latin Americans would focus on U.S. policy on this issue. And it is clear that in some countries the human rights policy made some moves toward democratization possible, even if they did not come to fruition, for the most part, during the Carter years.[26]

In any case, how the Carter administration was going to implement the human rights policy was rarely clear, and it is important to note the different options discussed at the time. Venezuelan President Carlos Andrés Pérez proposed a "development fund for those countries which move to democracy or show improvement in their human rights record." But despite Carter's support, the proposal never came to fruition.[27] But if this carrot approach to human rights was not to be, the question of sanctions against countries with poor human rights records also proved more complicated as well. Should the United States oppose loans that "serve basic human need to countries under repressive regimes?" Director of Policy Planning Anthony Lake argued that they should not, "except in response to gross violations of rights of the person." On the other hand, the United States should distance itself "from the security forces of countries which deny freedom of expression."[28]

Lake argued that the administration should only oppose loans for countries that were "gross" violators "of rights to the person," and not just if "legal and institutional instruments of repression remain." Lake contended that the United States should not be seen as "using economic pressure to bring down a particular government." He thought that repressive governments would "be more likely to improve their performance if they believe something short of suicide will bring a lifting of economic sanctions." Lake did not argue in favor of providing such countries with internal security aid. The administration should be working toward the "end to torture and arbitrary arrests worldwide," not to get induce regime change. Lake claimed that the administration's actions against Pinochet differed in "degree" rather than in "kind" from those employed by Nixon against Allende. Nevertheless, he did not argue for "suddenly" resuming "business as usual with Chile" because Chile had become "an emotional issue and our attitude toward it is, rightly or wrongly, a symbol to many of our human rights commitment."[29]

Early discussion of the issue emphasized the global nature of the commitment, if a somewhat vague notion of "how we might inject, in a realistic fashion," as National Security Adviser Zbigniew Brzezinski suggested, "greater concern for human rights into our foreign policy initiatives." "I do not want," he continued, "human rights to become merely a slogan." There was also perhaps a more dim perception that many countries in the world did not provide conditions in which human rights could blossom. For the United States to undertake consistent policies, it needed comparable information on "gross" violations of "internationally recognized human rights." But what if the world did not, after all, agree on what these human rights were? And if there were going to be "special circumstances" that ensured inconsistent policies, there was going to have to be some recognition of what priorities could take precedence over a global and absolute commitment.[30] What was needed was a "refinement of the policy so that day-to-day decisions can be made effectively." Human rights could "never be *the* fundamental part of our foreign policy, which must be firmly rooted in our national security interests."[31]

Congress had taken the lead on human rights, and, as we have seen, had run into significant resistance from the White House during the Nixon/ Ford years. NSC staffer Jessica Tuchman hoped that human rights could provide an opportunity "to radically improve congressional relations." Carter never, however, focused too much an establishing good working relations with Congress (the passage of the Panama Canal treaty, to some degree, discussed in chapter 9, aside). Early on, congressmen who had been involved in forcing the issue onto the national agenda, while pleased with how the administration spoke about the issue, became "restive" about not being consulted on how to put it in practice. In one of those relatively rare occasions on which they were consulted, Congressman Fraser spoke of the need to "institutionalize" human rights so that the "initial momentum" would not be lost and the State Department bureaucracy would "return to its old habits."[32] The political need to take credit often created tension over the issue where there did not need to be.

Although he later considered it one of the few positive achievements of the Carter administration, Schlesinger was one of the few early liberal critics of the human rights emphasis of the administration, arguing that it was a "campaign" more than a foreign policy. While correct in arguing that the policy was applied inconsistently (and would continue to be so), he also feared that the United States had abandoned its role as the "world's policeman in order to become the world's moralizer." Schlesinger expected it to "settle down" and accomplish more "if conducted by quiet pressures than by loud preachments."[33]

More typical in this early period was Ohio Senator Howard Metzenbaum, who gathered signatures in Congress backing Carter's approach to human rights. Carter was concerned about newspaper columnists who criticized the policy, but he was confident that he had "strong support among the American people." At the same time, Carter believed that he could strengthen relations with the very countries whose governments he was criticizing. He contemplated sending former Vice President Nelson Rockefeller on a South American trip to "shore up relations" with countries like Brazil, where his policies had damaged relations. He ended up sending his wife Rosalynn instead, which sent quite a different message.[34] "My hope and expectations," Carter wrote in his diary, "are that her conversations will both convince the people of these countries of our interest and friendship and also provide the leaders with an avenue directly to me for their problems, opportunities, and requests from our government." Few first ladies have taken as active a role in advising their husbands.[35]

The first lady spent three hours a day taking Spanish lessons in 1977. (It would have been too much to expect her to study Portuguese as well.) Her confidence grew over the course of her June trip. She reported that Brazil wanted to prove that it was equal to the United States and would not be dominated, "which suits me fine," Carter wrote in his diary. The Brazilians were concerned about arms agreements with the Soviet Union and about moves toward the normalization of relations with Cuba (which will be discussed in the next chapter). The first lady also accepted materials provided to her by opponents of the military regime and met with people who had been tortured. Some have maintained that this was a turning point in the human rights situation in Brazil. Pastor argued that she "succeeded in walking a very fine line between offending the government and encouraging the opposition."[36]

The administration's commitment to democracy promotion was sometimes later exaggerated. But Peruvian military leader Francisco Morales Bermúdez promised Rosalynn Carter that the country would devise a timetable for returning to democracy. Ironically, when the elections took place in 1980, the victor was Fernando Belaúnde Terry. He had been the candidate who had proved acceptable to the military in the second presidential race during the Kennedy administration (unlike APRA's Haya de la Torre), as well as the president who was overthrown late in the Johnson administration.[37]

At the June 1977 meeting of the OAS in Grenada, Carter administration officials focused on "getting the human rights message across to the Latin Americans," building on his wife's trip and the private meetings that Secretary of State Cyrus Vance had with many Latin American leaders over the previous months. A CIA report raised the question of whether the meeting would be "remembered in the future as the beginning of a new era of understanding between the United States and Latin America or.as the final dissolution of the special relationship most Latin American countries had long assumed they enjoyed with Washington."[38]

Chile remained a test case for human rights. It had particularly symbolic resonance, not least of all, as Robert Pastor noted, "because of the history of U.S. involvement" there. "While other U.S. interests clearly must be considered in evolving policy options for Chile, none can take precedence over our human rights concerns." The United States needed to consider what actions it could realistically take and what "likely internal consequences" would result from "external sources of action."[39] As Pastor suggested to Brzezinski in May 1977, "The policy which we set toward Chile in the months ahead will also have very serious and lasting implications for our policy on human rights. We could draw the line of 'gross violator' around Chile, declare it a pariah, and seek support for such a policy among other democratic countries. If we followed this direction, we could vote against loans . . . , meet with opposition leaders, and essentially keep a distant and cool posture. The expectation would be an alternative to Pinnochet [sic] would emerge." "An alternative policy," he continued, would be "to try to bargain with Pinnochet [sic] seeking specific and concrete signs of moderation and minimal respect for human rights." Pastor noted that either would "have important consequences," and he had not "thought through these issues sufficiently to give you a recommendation." That this was true in May suggests how limited the follow-through had been on the subject of the much-publicized policy.[40]

As was true in the case of Brazil, the worst human rights abuses in Chile had been committed prior to Carter's election. Still, the number of disappearances declined dramatically in his first year in office. The situation was "much improved in certain respects," if still "serious." The State Department said that it would "continue to be of concern until appropriate guarantees of human rights are restored and until Chile is clearly on the path toward constitutional, democratic government." Even Anthony Lake, often skeptical of the application of human rights in particular situations, thought that it was important to keep pressure on Chile, and that it could lead to a "restoration of political freedoms" in a country with strong democratic traditions. Both U.S. history (and public awareness of that history) and congressional concern would make it impossible to change policy "until and unless democracy is restored."[41] The most widely recognized study of human rights during the Pinochet years, the Rettig report, does indicate a significant downturn during the Carter years. One must also take into account several factors. Tens of thousands of Chileans had already gone into exile. The military government had consolidated its control over Chilean society. And the violent actions they had taken against Chilean citizens in the early years were no longer seen as necessary.[42]

The Carter administration, in Latin America as elsewhere, met with opponents of authoritarian governments. One of these, not surprisingly, was the former president of Chile, longtime liberal Democratic favorite Eduardo Frei, who met with Vice President Walter Mondale and Brzezinski. Former President Frei characterized the Chilean situation as "less brutal, but more rigid."[43] Its policy of torture and murder was no longer necessary, but, on the other hand, it was clear that the regime had no intention of opening up its political system. Frei "urged us to continue our strong commitment to human rights and democracy, but he deliberately cautioned against U.S. intervention of any kind" or, interestingly, that the United States should not "be linked to any single party." He urged consistency and expressed his belief that the United States could "create conditions—by words, policies, and meetings" that would have "great influence on developments in Chile." He expressed concerns about military attachés "whose commitment to the 'same values as the White House' was questionable." He noted that a top member of the Pinochet regime, General Gustavo Leigh, had recently said during a trip to Argentina that it did not matter what the president thought because the Pentagon strongly supported the Chilean junta.[44]

Frei argued that Carter's human rights policy might "create problems in the short term but in the long term it [was] the only way." He suggested that the Pinochet government, "based solely on force" and with "no political program of any kind . . . cannot last long." Brzezinski said that the human rights policy was "sincere but also not a crusade." He noted that "by identifying with human rights groups and forces around the world to strengthen the pressures that will have an influence on making democratic government increasingly probable." "We can create a moral framework," the national security adviser continued, "but we cannot determine internal conditions." The Carter administration did not intend to "use direct governmental involvement to influence internal events." Democracy could not be imposed from without, Frei noted. Rather, he was "looking for a broad consensus . . . and he hoped that the armed forces would be incorporated within the consensus." Mondale said that he had been "ashamed to learn of our behavior in Chile" when he had served on the Church committee. Given U.S. involvement in Chilean affairs over the past decade, Mondale argued that the United States had "a special responsibility to deal with the situation in Chile with good sense and respect for our own values as well as Chile's."[45]

Carter met Pinochet, as he did many Latin American leaders, when the Panama Canal treaty was signed. Carter found Pinochet to be a strong and confident leader. Ever the optimist, Carter believed that Pinochet was "beginning to be more worried about outside condemnation on human rights issues."[46] Kennedy aides and other members of nongovernmental associations were concerned with the way the press would portray Carter's meeting with Pinochet. Carter, however, was confident that he had been able to make the administration position clearer to Pinochet in a face-to-face meeting.[47]

On 22 November 1977, Carter wrote Pinochet a letter in which he reiterated his position that "human rights considerations" remained "the major obstacle to restoration of the traditionally close relations between the United States and Chile." But he also spoke more strongly not only of safeguarding and protecting human rights but also of restoring to Chile "the vigorous and open democratic traditions of which all Chileans have justly been proud." This was a much bigger step than anyone in the Chilean government was willing to take.[48] Pinochet felt this letter was "inconsistent with the tone" of their prior meeting.[49] Throughout the Carter years, Pinochet rejected criticisms of his human rights policies. He was "bitter" over what he saw as the "U.S. failure to understand Chile's position and [U.S.] interference in Chilean internal affairs." He rejected "U.S. views" of his administration and claimed "that a majority of the Chilean people support him."[50] U.S. aid for the Chilean government declined dramatically, military aid in particular. (Overall U.S. military aid to Latin America declined from $210 million to $54 million between 1977 to 1979.) Yet the Pinochet regime maintained its popularity with the international banking and business community, undercutting Carter's leverage.[51]

Tensions between Carter and the Brazilian government grew even before his inauguration, based not only on the general thrust of his foreign policy and his public criticism of Brazil but also the interest of Brazil in acquiring nuclear capabilities. The Geisel government broke the long-standing military alliance with the United States, which it had developed during the Second World War and which had been formalized again in 1952. Ironically, perhaps, even as U.S. policy was ever more defined by the human rights policies of Latin American governments, the justification for using it against Brazil itself was waning due to the onset of a limited political opening there.[52] Pastor expressed frustration with "human rights constituencies" in the United States for not recognizing that by 1977 "Brazil is *not* Chile or Argentina."[53]

John Crimmins, U.S. ambassador to Brazil since 1973, for his part, welcomed the new human rights policies.[54] Administration officials met with opponents of Brazil's military government, including members of the official opposition party in Brazil. It was hoped that this would "underscore White House concern for a more open political process and recognition of our interest in dealing with leaders across a wide political spectrum." The Movimento Democrático Brasileiro, Brzezinski told Mondale, "identifies very closely with Democrats and with President Carter." The United States needed to show "future democratic forces" that the United States cared.[55] Pastor was quite concerned that the United States not disillusion democratic forces in Brazil who saw hope in the Carter administration's policy.[56] As he was doing elsewhere in particular parts of the world, President Carter was communicating directly with human rights activists and dissidents in Brazil. Carter had written Cardinal Paulo Evaristo Arns in December 1977 to thank him for the list of people who had disappeared in Brazil since 1971 and expressed his support for habeas corpus and due process in civilian courts. (Carter had been introduced to Cardinal Arns when the two received honorary degrees from the University of Notre Dame in May of 1977.)[57]

Carter visited Brazil in 1978 and received a cool reception from President Geisel, who resented what he saw as the U.S. president's meddling and who expressed a hope at the welcoming ceremony that the visit would help him and his wife "in forming a fair opinion about the Brazilian reality." (For his part, Carter promised frank talk.) Carter met privately with Brazilians active in promoting improvement of the human rights situation, including Raymundo Faoro, head of the Brazilian Bar Association, and with Cardinal Arns. (The State Department, for its part, had advised against meeting with Arns.) But he publicly disavowed any intention of telling Brazilians how to choose their own leaders while he spoke of Brazil's efforts to enhance "the democratic process." Brazilian critics suggested that he was providing "a virtual blessing of the Brazilian regime." In speaking before the Brazilian Congress, however, he spoke of the "right to criticize a government" as one of the most fundamental, but he also recognized the distance Brazil had traveled since his visit as governor in 1972.[58]

But even as President Geisel was easing up on many of the restrictions on political expression, he was not willing to give up real power. The 1978 elections included senators who would be chosen indirectly; the military government reduced the representation of the more populous states in the Electoral College, which would choose future presidents.[59]

Liberal Democratic members of Congress, as well as Congress, sought to influence the behavior of the military government in Argentina, installed in early 1976 following the overthrow of Isabel Perón and which had expanded efforts already begun under Perón to eliminate those seen as "subversive." Senator Church had included the Argentine government among the "morally bankrupt regimes" in a speech in March 1977, and he called for Congress "to join in the new spirit of the Carter administration to encourage the flowering of human rights in nations throughout the world." Although Carter administration officials recognized the threat that had been posed by armed guerrilla movements that had been active in the country for years, they also maintained that the government was using this real threat to act against a wide variety of people who opposed the dictatorship and were not engaged in violent activity.[60]

A Kennedy-Humphrey Amendment cutting off aid to Argentina in September 1977 was not implemented at administration request until September 1978 in order to give the military regime a chance to improve its human rights practices.[61] The human rights situation in Argentina continued to be the worst in South America despite some measures being taken by the summer of 1978 to "curb excesses." Carter administration efforts on behalf of particular individuals, like Jacobo Timerman, had been successful in gaining their release. Patricia Derian herself was not popular in military circles. Her visible support for human rights groups like the Mothers of the Plaza de Mayo, who focused on trying to learn about the fate of their children who had "disappeared," was one of the factors that helped protect them and enabled them to continue to raise these issues without having to leave their country. As the administration perceived some improvements, Pastor informed Brzezinski, "we have switched from voting 'no' on non-basic human needs to loans in the IFI [international financial institutions] to abstaining." The Carter administration hoped that the Argentines would allow a visit by the Inter-American Commission on Human Rights in order that military training and sales of military equipment could take place before the Kennedy-Humphrey Amendment prohibiting more arms transfers took effect on 1 October. For his part, National Security Adviser Brzezinski worried that the policy was no longer effective. President Jorge Videla himself claimed that the war against subversion had been won and that it would be possible to "restore the rule of law." Robert Pastor feared that the United States would be seen as retreating. Argentina had earned a reputation now equal to that of Chile previously. But Pastor was determined that the administration should respond quickly to any positive steps by Videla. "I will work closely with Pete Vaky to try to develop a strategy to make sure that we don't totter over the brink." Henry Kissinger had criticized administration policy toward Argentina, and he attended the

1978 World Cup in Argentina as General Videla's guest of honor. Kissinger's warnings that the ABC countries would join in coalition against the United States had not borne fruit, Pastor asserted, "because these governments distrusted each other more than they despised President Carter."[62]

Pastor also argued that "what Kissinger failed to see is that Jimmy Carter has inspired a younger generation of Latin Americans; no other American President in this century has done that. Even Jack Kennedy, who was loved in Latin America, was suspected in the universities because of his strong anti-Communism and the Bay of Pigs intervention." In contrast, Carter was seen "as a man of great moral stature in Latin America, and that inspires the young and the democratic, and embarrasses, and unfortunately, sometimes infuriates some of the conservatives and the military." Carter's influence had "translated into real influence unlike anything the United States has had since we turned in our gunboats, and at the same time, it has given the United States *a future* [emphasis in the original] in Latin America, which we had almost lost."[63] Derian later complained that Kissinger's criticism reinforced "the belief on the parts of foreign leaders that the U.S. human rights policy will depart the scene with this Administration." That message was "counterproductive in terms of helping real, live human beings today."[64]

Argentina, Pastor wrote, was "still hungry for a return to normalcy in our relations." Previous generations of Argentines had not looked to the United States "to bestow upon them the mantle of legitimacy." Pastor insisted that "it would be a mistake and an injustice if we turned our policy around at this time."[65] In the event, the Inter-American Commission on Human Rights did visit Argentina in September after a period of strong administration criticism and decreased state terrorism. Despite their anger over U.S. pressures, the Argentine military did respond to them and did modify their behavior, in part because of administration actions, but also because General Videla had been correct that the battle against "subversion" had been won, at great cost to the Argentine people.[66]

Over the course of the next few years, the Carter administration saw evidence of its policy's success. In Brazil President Geisel issued an order to the military to prohibit further human rights abuses in July of 1977. Even as stalwart a foe of President Kennedy as João Goulart's brother-in-law Leonel Brizola credited Carter with having saved his life. ("Millions of Brazilians are delighted that Jimmy Carter should come here so that they can publicly express their immense gratitude for everything he did," Brizola remarked in 1984.) Censorship of "written media" was ended in June of 1978. Institutional Act No. 5 was revoked on the first day of 1979. Torture of political prisoners was eliminated by early 1979. And amnesty for many citizens who had gone into exile for political reasons was granted later that year. The Carter administration had high expectations for João Figueiredo, who would be, in the long run, Brazil's last military president.[67]

The Carter administration by mid-1978 thought the human rights policy had been successful, so that they might not need to "continue denying economic and security benefits." But it had been less successful at the *positive promotion of human rights*" (emphasis in the original). Patricia Derian concurred that more should be done with "channeling AID funds to governments with positive records."[68] Carter sought to encourage governments by recognizing improvements that had been made, for example, when political prisoners were released. It was always necessary to assess how real any improvements were (and the failure to do so in Nicaragua, as we shall see, had unfortunate consequences).[69]

But the human rights policy always had its critics, including some in the State Department. The assistant secretary of state for inter-American affairs, Terence A. Todman, gave a speech in February 1978 at the Center for Inter-American Relations. Todman affirmed both the Carter administration's commitment to human rights and to nonintervention, but he also argued against precipitous action before all the facts were in and against unrealistic expectations regarding how quickly governments could change their behavior. The administration should not always make the mistake of giving the political opposition's viewpoints in any particular country undue credence. And the administration needed to make sure that cutting aid did not hurt a nation's poor. Strong statements were to be avoided if they hurt a nation's dignity. Opponents of the human rights policy in Latin America saw this as a welcome sign that the administration was moving toward what they saw as a more balanced approach (and came, as we shall see, at a bad time for the people of Nicaragua). State Department officials scrambled to give assurances that administration policy had not changed in any fundamental way. The U.S. business community, for its part, was largely opposed to the policy, and, over time, had some success in limiting the policy.[70]

Other issues did take precedence in relations with particular countries. The car bombing deaths of Allende administration official Orlando Letelier and U.S. citizen Ronnie Moffitt on the streets of Washington, DC, in September 1976 had complicated U.S. relations with Chile even before Carter had become president. The Pinochet regime's responsibility for their deaths became clear over time, and three men working for the government were indicted in August of 1978 in U.S. court. As Secretary of State Vance noted, the Chilean government had "in effect, condoned this act of international terrorism within the United States." U.S. Ambassador George Landau was recalled three times "to express the concern of the United States government." But the Chilean Supreme Court's October 1979 refusal to extradite officers responsible for their murder exacerbated tensions further. Senators Church and Kennedy pushed for strong action. Defense Secretary Brown and National Security Adviser Brzezinski, however, warned against "aimless punitive actions." Vance recommended reducing the size of the U.S. mission in Santiago, withdrawing the Military Group, and applying further economic sanctions, but was not willing to either recall the ambassador permanently or break diplomatic relations. President Carter settled for a reduction in the mission, "a cool posture," and a strong condemnation of government complicity in the murders themselves. Chile was not allowed to participate in joint naval exercises with the United States and other Latin American nations (including Argentina and Brazil). Pastor and Tom Thornton worried about administration "staying power" on the issue and noted the ramifications for the presidential contest in 1980, in which the incumbent was being challenged by a senator from Massachusetts. "With Mark Schneider running Kennedy's campaign, you can be absolutely certain that a decision to put the 'Letelier phase' behind us and proceed with UNITAS [a joint military exercise] will be noticed. And Kennedy is hungry for issues."[71]

Despite Carter's opposition to his regime, Pinochet's hold on power in Chile was not challenged. He felt confident enough to hold a plebiscite in 1980, which not only ratified the new constitution but also guaranteed that he would remain in power for another eight years at least, institutionalizing the dictatorship. The constitution itself had been drafted under his guidance, and there were to be no popular elections until the end of the decade. Pinochet continued to have the power to deny the right to free assembly, and freedom of the press remained restricted. This represented the longest period of time in Chilean history without some form of representative government (however limited it might have been in practice during the oligarchical era). Given the fact that the country was still under a state of emergency, and limited freedom of expression and assembly already existed, these was no way for the Chilean population to exercise their right to vote in a way that was, in any way, truly free. Pinochet himself warned that those who opposed the constitution wanted to turn back the clock to 10 September 1973. To reinforce this symbolically, he held the obligatory vote on the 11th of September. Anyone who voted no was denigrated as unpatriotic.[72]

With the Soviet invasion of Afghanistan in December 1979, U.S. concerns in South America began to change. (Central America, as we shall see, had its own particular dynamics.) People like Patricia Derian found that they had less influence. U.S. General Andrew Goodpaster visited Argentina in January of 1980. By June, Warren Christopher wrote President Carter, the United States wanted to improve relations with Argentina in order to "foster Argentina's identification with the West and thus to contain Soviet political and economic influence." While the United States continued to want to see improvements in human rights practices, it also needed Argentina to cooperate with U.S. economic measures to punish the Soviets; Argentina could easily undermine U.S. efforts to limit access to grain. More U.S. officials visited Argentina, and, in particular, an emphasis was placed on relations between the U.S. and Argentine armed forces. The Carter administration hoped that the Kennedy-Humphrey Amendment could be modified. But the United States also expected to be able to continue a "dialogue on human rights." The Carter administration assumed that there would be "no new disappearances, including no disappearances of persons alleged to be terrorists." All of those suspected of being engaged in subversive activities should now be subject to due process. President Carter sent a letter to Argentine human rights activist Adolfo Pérez Esquivel, following the announcement that he would be awarded the Nobel Peace Prize. Even Brzezinski acknowledged that "Argentine human rights" had "been a major concern of the Administration." It remained "important that you stress your continuing identification with the issue."[73]

Derian, for her part, came close to resigning in May 1980. At that time she was being dismissed as "an activist if there ever was one." Lincoln Bloomfield complained that the whole team soon acquired quite the opprobrium throughout the button-down elements of the bureaucracy as "the Human Rights Mafia." Derian assistant Schneider did resign to work for Kennedy and had been replaced by someone "much calmer." Nevertheless, Bloomfield did not want to see human rights "get lost in the shuffle," in Argentina or elsewhere. Those who wanted to abandon human rights altogether would "deprive us of one of the central distinctions between the democratic system and the totalitarian system which is the foundation on which those critics think they argue." The human rights community, for its part, may have thought that the policy was a "sham," but, he continued, "they confuse the limits of policy with bad faith regarding the desirable."[74] The Carter administration had never gotten complete control of the issue, and congressmen like Tom Harkin continued to press, in ways that not all in the administration found "constructive." From the other side, Brzezinski and many in the State Department felt that human rights had "ruined" our relations with South American nations.[75]

Patricia Derian complained that while the Carter administration had done more for human rights than any other, it had "done less than we could have or should have." The "mixed message" may have been an improvement over the previous support for "business as usual," but she obviously thought that the message should be consistent in favor of human rights instead. The Carter administration, she complained, was now doing nothing more than drifting along. "I believe that the perception that the President does not support the policy is wrong." The National Security Council frequently was "an obstacle."[76] Looking back at the previous four years, Derian argued that the human rights policy had restored "the world's belief in our commitment to freedom." The United States had arrived at "a new consensus, secure in the foundations of our freedom and our resolve to help the rest of the world achieved the same." Frances Grant praised Derian herself and her department for encouraging liberty throughout the hemisphere.[77]

Taking the long view in the middle of 1979, Thomas Thornton on the National Security Council staff insisted that human rights policy was "probably the main success story of this administration's foreign policy." He advised Lincoln Bloomfield, who took over the position previously held by Jessica Tuchman, that there were "quixotic elements" to the position that he needed to embrace, including accepting the idea that the United States would vote against loans for human rights violators even though they got them in the end anyway. He also recommended that Bloomfield embrace the "adversarial" nature of the position. Your "geographical colleagues will often have good political reasons not to push human rights too hard. Don't let them get away with it." Some people were "as warm-hearted as you." Others were not. They often thought that Carter did not understand "realities (Kissinger lives)." Thornton expressed satisfaction that Derian had been convinced that some human rights violations were more important than others. Thornton advised Bloomfield that when the president happened to be meeting with a leader who had "a human rights problem, insist on getting a shot at the briefing book and talking points. See that they give the President some tough things to say, if he feels so inclined."[78]

Historian Tulio Halperin Donghi later wrote, "A considerable number of Latin Americans probably owe their lives to his efforts, something that cannot be said of any other US President." He was, of course, from Argentina, and his views on this issue were similar to those of Jacobo Timerman, who noted in 1981 that U.S. citizens tend to get "impatient" and "restless" with human rights, wanting to "change a government with a policy." To do that, you need to "send in the Marines. What a human rights policy does is save lives. And Jimmy Carter's policy did. How many? I don't know. Two thousand? Is that enough?" As political scientist Kathryn Sikkink has written, Carter's policies were most effective when they were most "forcefully implemented."[79]

Carter's commitment to human rights could never be as absolute as he promised it would be. There were certainly parts of the world where it was hardly mentioned. And it certainly was less consistently applied even in Latin America, particularly after the middle of 1978, particularly when it conflicted with a disinclination to intervene in other countries' internal affairs, and particularly in Central America, as the next chapter will explain. Carter would later exaggerate the movement toward democracy during his presidency.[80] But in South America, the attempt to modify the behavior of torture states had an effect, encouraging ongoing developments in Brazil, protecting individuals in a horrific time in Argentina, and usefully distancing the United States from a rogue regime in Chile, which, for all the criticism it had received, had consolidated itself. In Central America and the Caribbean, Carter policies were far more inconsistent, and successes there were to be overshadowed by failures, as the following chapter will demonstrate.

Chapter 9

The Carter Administration in Central America and the Caribbean

At its most consistent, Carter administration human rights policy had primarily applied to two South American countries in which military dictatorships had been established during years in which a Republican was in the White House (Chile and Argentina during the administrations of Nixon and Ford) and one in which a Democrat had been president (Brazil under Johnson). These military governments remained in power when Carter left office in early 1981. Human rights abuses had declined in both Brazil and Chile, but this had more to do with internal dynamics and the perceived needs of the military regimes. Human rights abuses rose again in Chile in the early 1980s, but that reinforces the point. But Carter administration policy was not useless, and it did save some lives in Argentina and encourage democratic activism in Brazil, which was undergoing a long, slow transition to civilian rule. Carter administration policy toward Central American and Caribbean countries varied dramatically from one country to another. In some Central American and Caribbean nations, however, the Carter administration largely accepted the status quo. It moved toward a new relationship with a country sometimes seen as a colony (Panama). The administration threatened to break with Cold War assumptions dramatically in another (Cuba). The administration became an important part of a destabilizing dynamic through inconsistent and incompatible policies in yet another country, and then tried to establish a working relationship with the resulting left-wing government (Nicaragua). One could argue that it played a role in Nicaragua that was not all that dissimilar to that of the Eisenhower administration's role in Cuba in the late 1950s. Its policy in El Salvador bore some similarities to Kennedy administration policy. And the Carter administration played a role in restoring democracy in a country in which liberal Democrats had long failed to live up to their ideals (the Dominican Republic).

Carter had inherited a process of negotiations over the fate of the Panama Canal from the Ford administration, but he well knew that it had its political risks. Some of his closest advisers warned him that it was, as biographer Jonathan Alter makes clear, "a classic second-term issue." These negotiations had almost derailed President Ford's hopes for nomination as the Republican presidential candidate in 1976 when he was challenged by Governor Ronald Reagan. Candidate Carter himself had not supported giving up "practical control of the Panama Canal Zone any time in the foreseeable future." But following his election, he was influenced by Cyrus Vance, soon to be secretary of state and a report issued by the Commission on United States-Latin American Relations. By the time the new administration was in place, there was unanimity on moving forward along the lines already established by former Secretary of State Henry Kissinger and his Panamanian counterpart. Carter had come to believe an injustice had to be corrected and that a new treaty could cure "a diplomatic cancer, which was poisoning our relations with Panama."[1] Once he decided to move forward with treaty negotiations, he knew he could count on the support of Ford and Kissinger. Conservative columnist William F. Buckley Jr. had even come to see the logic behind the movement toward a new relationship between the two countries. A terminally ill Hubert Humphrey also supported the treaty but would not live long enough to vote for it.[2]

The Carter administration became far more interested in the treaty's hemispheric and Third World ramifications than in its domestic political consequences. The Panama Canal treaty needs to be understood as part of a larger history, in which the Cold War was less of a factor. Panama's populist leader Omar Torrijos effectively made it into an issue of the long global process of decolonization and generated sympathy and support for his stance in the Third World. At the same time, the United States was forced to include a promise of nonintervention. The treaty had the potential of improving relations with Latin American countries even as human rights was creating tensions.[3]

Torrijos knew little about the U.S. political system and became frustrated with the pace and the process. At the same time, Torrijos had to make an effort to woo U.S. senators. Critics naturally pointed out that Torrijos himself was a military dictator. But Torrijos was not easily defined as either left or right, and many U.S. leaders, from Nelson Rockefeller in 1969 at the beginning of the Panamanian's time as leader to Carter, admired what they perceived as a commitment to the well-being of the poor. Torrijos tried to make it clear to visiting U.S. senators that Panama did not suffer from the same human rights conditions that existed in other countries where a military man was in charge, and that Panama was not a place in which the opposition was repressed. Moreover, Carter believed that he could use the influence he was gaining through the treaty negotiations to move Torrijos toward democracy. In October he began talking about sending a private letter to him concerning the subject. In this handwritten letter, which the president wrote in Spanish, he expressed the "hope that in free elections the Panamanian people might have the chance to vote for him in the near future." But Brzezinski was determined not to have this issue prevent ratification of the treaty. Even after the treaty was ratified, Torrijos resisted making a "firm commitment" to a process of democratization.[4]

Carter was determined to include in the agreement a guarantee that the United States would still have the right after 2000 to act to keep the canal "open and protected" from external threats. Carter thought that the treaty would help the United States in its hemispheric relations, but he knew that he would have to do more to convince the American public. But the discussion of this issue in the Congress and the press frequently employed the language of intervention, which rankled so in Latin America. U.S. politicians, in particular, seemed unable to understand the historical resonances in their poorly worded rhetoric. Senator Church was a rare exception. "Let us make clear to the world that we are not seeking for ourselves the kind of rights the Soviets claimed in Czechoslovakia in 1968." Ultimately, it was the language in the treaty itself that mattered, and the issue was resolved by a promise by both countries to maintain the canal's neutrality together.[5]

Carter would rarely during his presidency work as hard to gain the support of Congress, where the treaty was not popular. As Carter noted in his memoirs, "To reverse oneself from a popular promise to one that is emotionally unpopular requires an exceedingly rare act of courage." He noted in his diary that he hoped that congressmen would read the treaty before denouncing it. This "worked with most of them except for a few nuts like Strom Thurmond [now a South Carolina Republican senator] and Jesse Helms [from North Carolina]."[6]

President Carter began to make more of an effort to sell the treaty to the public and in private meetings with most of the senators he thought could be reasoned with. He emphasized the continuing right to guarantee the neutrality of the canal. He rejected the idea that the United States was retreating from an active role in the Western Hemisphere. And he was not afraid to use the fear of communism to press the public and the Congress to support the treaty, warning that rejecting it would provide "a good opening for outside agitating groups . . . to create dissension," while approving it would "discourage the spread of hostile ideologies in this hemisphere." The treaty would "remove a major source of anti-American feeling." The United States, he noted, would continue to have military bases in the Caribbean to provide defense for the canal.[7]

Democratic Senator Paul Sarbanes of Maryland was now in charge of the Senate Subcommittee on Western Hemisphere Affairs. Frank Church was responsible for shepherding the treaty through the Senate. He had promised that he would only vote for an agreement that protected U.S. "vital interests." He told his constituents that the treaty was "right for the United States, right for Panama, and right for the times in which we live." He and his colleagues recognized the risk they took in supporting it. The victory in the Senate in April 1978 was a victory not only for Carter but for Church and Sarbanes as well, but Carter neglected to acknowledge their contributions. Opponents continued to work against the treaty even after it had been ratified, with consequences for administration policy in Nicaragua, as we shall see. Latin American support for the treaty remained strong. Venezuelan President Pérez called it "the most significant advance in political affairs in the Western Hemisphere in this century."[8]

If Carter had taken a major risk in pushing the Panama Canal treaty through (one that would have negative political consequences in later elections for some of the senators who supported it), he also early on seemed to be willing to take an even greater risk and move toward normalization of relations with Cuba. Secretary of State Vance had announced in January 1977 that there would be no "preconditions on discussions with Cuba." Carter himself was far less willing to give such assurances. Cuban military intervention in Angola in 1975 had heightened tensions between the United States and Cuba after some indications that the Ford administration was willing to make some gestures toward better relations. Certainly, Carter believed, as he asserted in February, that normalization of relations would not take place without the withdrawal of Cuban troops. Nevertheless, discussions could begin. But, as Robert Pastor noted in a memo to his boss Brzezinski, the administration did not yet have a clearly defined policy. Vance could hope to start a process moving, but the United States needed to know what it wanted to achieve and how to keep the process going. The United States certainly wanted to "lessen Cuban dependence on the USSR," and hoped to discourage Cuba from engaging in interventions around the world. The United States also wanted to send a message to the Third World as a whole that the United States could accept a range of political systems. Cuba would have to improve its own human rights practices and provide compensation for property confiscated since Castro came to power. Pastor insisted that the United States could pursue a process that had elements of both a "step-by-step" and a "comprehensive" approach to the problem. It should not "give away easy and friendly gestures" without getting something in return. Pastor, at least, recognized that the compensation issue and the matter of troops in Angola would not be resolved easily "in the next few years, if ever."[9] By mid-March, Carter had concluded "that we should attempt to achieve normalization of our relations with Cuba." In 1977, at least, Brzezinski and others recognized that the United States could not make withdrawal from Angola a precondition for progress on improved relations between the United States and Cuba.[10]

Liberal Democratic senators in 1977 were willing to stick their necks out on relations with Cuba. Frank Church visited Cuba in August of 1977 and returned with assurances from Castro that he understood that normalization would not come easily or quickly. Castro told Church that he also understood that, politically, the Panama Canal treaty had to be the top priority, and that Carter could not move forward on both fronts at the same time. He also told Church that Cuba's involvement in Africa had "no anti-American purpose and that he preferred to send doctors not troops." He noted that he had acted in response to the South African invasion of Angola. Moreover, he asserted, "Cuba was in no way acting as a proxy for the Russians." Castro hoped that the Carter administration would take action against anti-Castro terrorist groups and "explore ways to ease the embargo on trade." Perhaps Carter could meet with Castro at the United Nations General Assembly.[11] In the Ford years, Senator Kennedy had gone to Cuba to meet with Castro and to press for freedom for political prisoners. Around this time, Senator Kennedy proposed ending the trade embargo, which had been established during his brother's presidency. Kennedy suggested that it made little sense given the improvement in relations with the Soviet Union and China.[12]

Senator McGovern, for his part, was willing to go further and faster than the Carter administration was. In an era of arms limitation talks with the Soviet Union and an opening to China, he had long considered the U.S. relationship with Castro's Cuba to be anachronistic. He visited Cuba and met with Castro in 1975. In 1977, the South Dakota senator introduced an amendment that would have "partially" lifted the trade embargo, which had been established in 1962. McGovern believed that the action would allow the United States to "gain some influence on Cuba's international conduct." But it would also "assist, or at least not impede, the Cuban government's genuine effort to foster a better life for a people historically plagued by poverty and illiteracy." Trade between the two countries, McGovern argued further, would lead to "constraints" on the country's actions and diminish the influence of the Soviet Union. McGovern considered lifting the embargo a necessary first step. If Cuba was stronger on socioeconomic rights, it was "obviously weak as regards to the free movement of people and ideas." A "gradual normalization" would "obviously serve to open up Cuban society." If McGovern could convince the Congress to lift the embargo on U.S. exports of food and medicine, it would "explicitly commit Congress to a movement toward normalization." (He assured Carter that any policy "could be reversible.") Carter believed that abandoning the embargo would reduce U.S. leverage over Cuba. Therefore, Carter accepted Brzezinski's argument that the administration "would maintain a position of skeptical [rather than benevolent] neutrality toward McGovern's bill" and that, in any case, "a lifting of the embargo on Cuban goods sold to the United States" would "await negotiations." (McGovern aide John Holum suspected that if some kind of modification in U.S. policy could be passed in Congress, the Carter administration might be willing to move faster toward negotiation with Castro's government.) In any case, Carter was committed to keeping Cuban sugar out of the U.S. market, while Castro rejected the idea of a partial lifting of the trade embargo that created no opportunities for Cuban exports. "One-way trade," Castro had warned McGovern, "did not make sense."[13]

In the early phases, the Carter administration seemed ready to take some risks in the Caribbean. Democracy promotion was not its main concern, despite occasional rhetoric to the contrary. Nevertheless, the Carter administration ended up playing a significant role in a country in which liberal Democrats in the previous decade had made a big mistake. Joaquin Balaguer had dominated Dominican politics for a decade, with and without direct electoral fraud and intimidation of and selective political violence against its enemies, but had received little to no attention from Congress and the White House. As the State Department's Hewson Ryan noted, the U.S. invasion in 1965, perceived as *"one of our great foreign policy blunders,"* had resulted in a *"relationship of paternalism and dependence"* that, if "anachronistic," had *"political and economic benefits for both"* countries. Secretary of State Henry Kissinger had visited in 1976 in order to show, according to Ryan, that *"we do not take good friends for granted"* (emphasis, in all cases, in the original).[14]

President Carter had met with President Balaguer in September 1977, when many hemispheric leaders were in Washington for the signing of the Panama Canal treaty. U.S. Ambassador to the United Nations Andrew Young also had met with the Dominican leader and been assured of Dominican support (and, in the event, co-sponsorship) for the American Convention on Human Rights. Carter told Balaguer that he looked forward to the May 1978 elections and "expressed the hope that they would be conducted with cognizance of everyone's rights." "If Balaguer were to be candidate," however, Carter continued, "he wished him well." Balaguer told Carter that he was not yet certain whether he would be a candidate. But he expressed his belief that there was no one "in his party, nor in the opposition" who could "guarantee peace, progress and unity of the Armed Forces" other than himself. Nevertheless, it would be a sacrifice for him to be president for another term.[15]

Given his advanced age, Balaguer may or not have been playing coy in his remarks. Carter, for his part, did not believe that he had indicated that he preferred Balaguer to win the election. Nevertheless, once Balaguer chose to be a candidate for a fourth term, he was able to use Carter's words and photos of the two presidents together in his campaign literature. Congressman Fraser, who had paid intermittent attention to the Balaguer regime over the years, now took up the issue, and he repeatedly encouraged President Carter to meet with members of the opposition party, the Partido Revolucionario

Dominicano (PRD), to undercut Balaguer's insinuation that the United States hoped that the Dominican people would reelect him. Brzezinski had tried to assure Fraser that "the President's meeting [with Balaguer] did not constitute an endorsement of his candidacy." Carter administration policy was "neutral with respect to particular parties and candidates and positive on the issue of free elections." The national security adviser insisted that the U.S. ambassador would make this point in conversations with President Balaguer. But neither his advisers nor Carter agreed with Fraser's proposal to meet with the opposition and declare that the United States would continue to have "friendly relations" with any honestly elected candidate.[16]

In the weeks prior to the election, Dominican military officers began to talk among themselves about their taking action if an opposition candidate won, leading to attempts by the U.S. embassy to make clear its position that the Carter administration expected the elections to be free and fair. When the elections took place on 16 May 1978, it soon became clear that the opposition candidate, Antonio Guzmán, was winning. The Dominican military stepped in to prevent the votes from being counted. The Carter administration monitored developments closely and kept in touch with democratically elected leaders in Venezuela, Costa Rica, and Colombia, in part out of the conviction, as Carter later expressed it, that "we believe so deeply that democracy must be improved among the Latin American nations on their own initiative." Venezuelan President Pérez, for his part, encouraged Carter to speak out in opposition to the military action, calling it "the most serious crisis in the Caribbean since the Cuban Revolution." (Costa Rica and Colombia also expressed concern, as did West Germany and newly democratic Portugal.) Former U.S. Ambassador John Bartlow Martin, who had hoped to be appointed to an ambassadorship by the administration, weighed in as well, and Brzezinski sought to assure him that there "should be no question in anyone's mind where the United States stands on representative democracy in the Dominican Republic." Balaguer, for his part, "was disappointingly vague and even disingenuous in places" in response to Secretary of State Vance's comments. Meanwhile, within the Dominican Republic, the actions taken by the military received scant support from civil society. Carter and other top officials expressed concern through diplomatic channels initially, including a warning from Secretary of State Vance of the possible consequences for relations between the two countries. Fraser and Kennedy called on Balaguer to force the armed forces to cease intervening in the electoral process. On the 19th, Carter publicly expressed his hope "that the legally constituted electoral authorities in the Dominican Republic will be able to carry out their responsibilities without interference and that the outcome of the elections [would] be respected by all." Following Carter's public statement, and criticism both domestic and foreign, Balaguer and the Dominican military agreed to accept Guzmán's victory. Later that summer, Pastor noted triumphantly in a note to Brzezinski, "Our Latin American policy on democratic elections is beginning to bear fruit." Following his inauguration, President Guzmán released the remaining political prisoners (more than 200, according to the United States). By the following spring, the State Department's Peter Tarnoff could assert that the Dominican Republic had "become one of the best examples in Latin America for individual and political rights."[17]

Brzezinski noted in 1979 in a meeting with Guatemalan Foreign Minister Rafael Castillo that the United States had long had "a predominant influence in Central America." But the United States was now seeking "increased equality and more mature relationships with the governments in Central America."[18] The human rights revolution had sought to clarify decision making in U.S. foreign policy. It did not do so, as more than a decade of conflict in Central America would prove. No country would demonstrate the inconsistency of Carter administration human rights policy more than Nicaragua. Nowhere did the conflict between the ideals of human rights and nonintervention prove to have more tragic consequences.

By the time Carter became president, the last and least of the Somozas, Anastasio Somoza Debayle, had been in power for roughly a decade. President Nixon and Ambassador Turner Shelton had been strong supporters. He had backers in Congress as well, including Democrats like Charlie Wilson of Texas and John Murphy of New York, an old friend from West Point, who played critical roles in the crisis to come. But it was hard to see much chance of change at the beginning of Carter's term. Opposition to Somoza's rule was weak. The Sandinistas, a guerrilla movement formed in the wake of the Cuban Revolution but inspired as well by the man who had fought U.S. occupation in the late 1920s and early 1930s, posed no significant danger to the regime in 1977. Their early efforts in the 1960s had been unsuccessful, and they had fragmented into factions with opposing strategies for achieving their goals. But Somoza provided ample opportunity for opposition to his government to grow, such as the scandals regarding the fraudulent use of emergency aid following the 1972 earthquake, which devastated the capital of Managua. The Carter administration policy was not committed to his removal in 1977, however. It was not even sending clear messages regarding human rights in Nicaragua.

The State Department had delineated the dismal state of human rights in Somoza's Nicaragua in 1976. U.S. Ambassador James Theberge met with Somoza in the first weeks of January 1977 to emphasize the administration's commitment to improvements in human rights. "We did not wish," the ambassador told him, "for there to be any misunderstanding regarding our attachment to human rights and liberty." The Nicaraguan leader rejected the argument that Nicaragua's human rights situation was worse in relative terms and suggested a double standard was being applied internationally. Punitive actions by the administration would merely alienate friendly nations in the Americas, Somoza insisted.[19] Given Carter's stated commitment to human rights, it was assumed that he would cut aid to the dictator. Initially, however, President Carter requested $3.1 million. But when U.S. Under Secretary of State Lucy Benson was asked to justify the request before Congress, she could find no national security concerns that would do so. Assistant Secretary of State for Inter-American Affairs Terence Todman, however, disagreed. And the House of Representatives voted in favor of the administration request. The amount was small, but it did not suggest that the Carter administration was willing to break from status quo thinking on the U.S. relationship with the Somoza dynasty, as some liberals had expected. (Carter's relationship with the Shah of Iran bore many similarities.)[20]

New York Congressman Ed Koch sought to make Nicaragua a test case for the human rights policy. Following Carter's election but before his inauguration, Congressman Koch wrote fellow Congressman Fraser regarding what he saw as "serious gaps in the present law." In many Latin American countries, there was "often no differentiation between the military and the police." He worried about U.S. aid for "internal security." "I don't think we should be in the business of aiding a government to put down a truly indigenous insurgency," he argued. Fraser responded that he thought that there should be not only a distinction between internal and external threats, but also between democratic and nondemocratic governments. He held hearings devoted to Nicaragua for the Foreign Operations Subcommittee. When Somoza learned of the planned hearings, he summoned Ambassador Theberge to his office to complain. He told the ambassador that he did not think the hearings would be balanced. He accused Congressman Koch of "spreading false and defamatory statements," including accusations regarding misuse of USAID funds. While Somoza claimed to admire Carter's human rights policy, he said that he hoped that the United States would understand the threat from "terrorists" in Nicaragua. Moreover, he emphasized how loyal he had been to the United States.[21]

Koch's attempts to cut off aid to Somoza were blocked by Charlie Wilson, who had strong support among conservative Democrats and Republicans. He, Murphy, and Somoza were in close contact. Wilson had gotten a position on the House Appropriations Committee a decade earlier, and he knew how to use his position to get what he wanted. He served on the Foreign Operations Subcommittee, which oversaw foreign economic and military aid. He was quite willing to go to great lengths to protect aid for Somoza. The Carter administration did not place such a high priority on Nicaragua in 1977.[22] Koch, for his part, was elected mayor of New York City in 1977, thus removing him from the fray following his inauguration in January of the following year. But if Republicans and some Democrats criticized President Carter for undermining Somoza through his human rights policies, it was the very inconsistency of his approach (as well as the brutality and intransigence of Somoza himself) that would, in the end, guarantee the victory of an anti-American insurgency for the first time in twenty years.

Somoza himself found a way to ignite a rebellion that never would have happened otherwise. He ordered the assassination of his most prominent and moderate critic, *La Prensa* publisher Pedro Joaquin Chamorro, from an elite family long prominent in the country's political life. Popular revulsion at his death in early January 1978 led to spontaneous uprisings throughout the country.[23]

For the Inter-American Association for Democracy and Freedom, the death of Chamorro was a turning point. They had long sought to get more attention paid to the lack of freedom in Nicaragua, but without effect. Although Frances Grant herself tended to be skeptical regarding the current interest in human rights, the association saw some hope in Carter administration policies. The organization held a memorial service for "the unwavering warrior in the fight for dignity and civil and political liberties of the Nicaraguan people" in March and formed an Ad Hoc Committee for Democracy in Nicaragua. At the service, Grant argued that the death of Chamorro was leading to the unity of opposition forces, as had happened in Cuba against Batista. The IADF called on Somoza to restore democratic rights and asked the Carter administration to press for an investigation into Chamorrro's death. Grant warned that "the shibboleths of human rights will pass into the limit of good intentions, never consummated," like the Good Neighbor Policy and the Alliance for Progress.[24]

The Carter administration did not speak with one voice in 1978. When visiting Venezuela in March, Carter reiterated U.S. commitment to nonintervention "in the internal affairs of other nations," but human rights promotion and anti-interventionism were incompatible. The administration, furthermore, did not make policy in a vacuum, nor could it ignore congressional concerns when other issues got priority. Congressman Wilson used Carter's commitment to the Panama Canal treaty to limit Carter's willingness to act, and loans for Nicaragua were approved in May. In June Venezuela's Pérez urged the administration to pressure Somoza. And then there was the State Department to consider. Assistant Secretary of State Todman's February 1978 speech (discussed in the previous chapter) seemed to suggest a greater skepticism regarding "opposition" movements in Latin America generally, and the

Somoza family newspaper found it easy to portray the speech as favoring the government's policies. In mid-1978, a human rights survey suggested that there was a chance for reform under Somoza, which Assistant Secretary Todman supported. In August, Carter foolishly sent a private message to Somoza expressing his confidence that Somoza would reform. Somoza, not surprisingly, made the letter public. And anti-interventionists on the National Security Council like Lake and Pastor continued to hold sway.[25]

The Carter administration never resolved the tension between the two principles, human rights and nonintervention. By August of 1978, Assistant Secretary of State Vaky (who had replaced Todman) was convinced that Nicaragua would become polarized if left to its own devices. He thought that only the United States could act to remove Somoza. Pastor rejected this idea, arguing that while it might win the administration "some points among certain countries and groups in the hemisphere and in the United States," it would "in the long term . . . compromise the President's moral stature and arouse conservative forces in the United States who already believe we are deserting our close friends." The U.S. role should be that of a "detached goal setter."[26]

Carter had enraged supporters of human rights in Congress when he sent the August letter to Somoza. In the fall of 1978, many liberal groups and activists, from the Americans for Democratic Action, to Frances Grant and the IADF, as well as numerous unions like the United Auto Workers, encouraged the Carter administration to move forcefully against Somoza.[27] The Carter administration continued to struggle with congressional opposition from both sides. Murphy, Wilson, and others wrote to Carter in September 1978 to urge him to show support for "a long and consistent ally of the United States" who was fighting against a group seeking to make "Nicaragua the new Cuba." They sought to shift blame to the State Department, which they claimed was making "misguided application of your policies." Wilson worked hard to fulfill the administration's foreign aid requests in 1978, but only when he knew that there would be continued support for the Somoza regime. President Carter, for his part, supported mediation efforts in which Latin Americans would be involved and the United States would not play the primary role.[28]

The mediation group included representatives from the Dominican Republic and Guatemala. Carter publicly expressed confidence in October that "an enduring, democratic solution" could be found. By November he affirmed that violence was lessening. He continued to express a hope that bloodshed could be controlled, disputes would be minimized, and a government could be formed that would have the support of Nicaraguans. By December Carter expressed confidence that a plebiscite could resolve the conflict. In his 1979 State of the Union address, Carter listed Nicaragua among the countries where the United States was working for a peaceful solution to a dangerous conflict.[29]

At the same time, other neighboring countries were taking clear action as well. Both democratic Venezuela and authoritarian Panama began to supply arms to the opposition. Venezuela had long proposed a more militant position against dictatorship. The high oil prices of the 1970s were now allowing Venezuela to take a more active role itself in the circum-Caribbean region. Visiting Venezuela in December 1978, in order to give his second wife an understanding of why he was "so fond of" the region, Arthur Schlesinger saw events in Nicaragua through a Venezuelan lens. He was convinced that the Somoza regime was finally facing its end. The United States was "dragging its feet," while Carlos Andrés Pérez was actively pushing for his removal.[30]

The human rights people in the State Department felt isolated during the critical stages of the rise of the Sandinistas. Derian complained that in too many situations she and her associates were told that their positions were already "known" and "taken into consideration."[31] Nicaraguan moderates, expecting the Carter administration to act clearly and forcefully, were soon losing out to those willing to take direct and forceful measures. Moreover, the Somoza inclinations to treat all young Nicaraguan men from poor neighborhoods as Sandinistas led them to embrace the label and turn to revolution in self-defense.[32] Frances Grant herself expressed no worries about the Sandinistas, who, she insisted, were only a "fraction" of the larger "democratically oriented" movement. She did warn that the longer the armed struggle continued, the more likely it would be that outside forces would get involved.[33]

Somoza found it easy to deflect pressures from the United States, relying upon both his supporters in Congress and the internal divisions within the administration to guarantee that he would stay in power. The plebiscite that Carter hoped would resolve Nicaragua's internal divisions failed to gain traction. Somoza's actions suggest that he was confident that he would outlast Carter. In early 1979 his congressional allies expressed confidence that their friend would survive. Congressman Murphy wrote a letter to Carter in which he used Carter's praise of Somoza's "attempts to improve human rights." Conversations between Somoza and the U.S. ambassador also confirmed the Nicaraguan president's conviction that he was not in danger of being forced out of office. By the end of January, the mediation efforts had failed, though President Carter seemed not to recognize it.[34]

The Inter-American Association for Democracy and Freedom had accelerated its lobbying efforts. The organization was frustrated that the Carter administration was unwilling to say that Somoza had to go out of fear that a "Castro-like government" would come to power.[35] But the contradictions continued. In early February, Kennedy and other liberal senators were praising "recent actions to dissociate the United States from the Somoza government in Nicaragua" because of his "violation of human rights" and "rejection of mediation efforts." Sanctions were applied, but no other actions were antici-pated. Carter suggested that the United States could "negotiate firmly" with Somoza, but it certainly had not done so yet.[36] By April, Frank Church ex-pressed concern that the longer the United States delayed in making its posi-tion clear in Nicaragua, "the greater the risk of a revolution by the extremists." He claimed that this was what had happened in Cuba. He told a constituent that he did not want to see history repeat itself. But Church's influence on the Carter administration was nonexistent.[37]

In May the Carter administration was being encouraged to vote against International Monetary Fund loans for Nicaragua. But the administration supported them instead. Somoza had detained prominent businessmen. War-ren Christopher spoke with the Nicaraguan ambassador to protest against the detentions. Somoza claimed that the businessmen were going to call for another national strike.[38]

For months following the failure of the mediation efforts, the Carter administration acted as if it had no fixed policy in Nicaragua. The Carter administration's failure to send a clear message continued to undermine the moderate opposition, and the Sandinistas were now united and gaining popular support. By June, the momentum was clearly in the Sandinistas' favor, and the Carter administration sought too late to find an alternative. Congressman Tom Harkin, following a visit in late April, had reported that the National Guard was "everywhere," as were "feelings of fear and repres-sion." When an ABC News reporter named Bill Stewart was executed by a National Guardsman and the film of his death was smuggled out of the country and broadcast internationally on the 20th of June, there was no turn-ing back. Carter characterized this as "an act of barbarism that all civilized people condemn." Liberal members of the House of Representatives like Har-kin and Ted Weiss of New York, as well as the IADF, encouraged the Carter administration to recognize the National Government of Reconstruction, which included moderates like Doña Violeta Barrios de Chamorro, the widow of the Nicaraguan publisher. The congressmen noted that Costa Rica, Panama, Mexico, Venezuela, Colombia, and Ecuador had already done so; they argued that any attempt to "alter the character of the provisional gov-ernment only serves to prolong the civil war and the suffering it has en-tailed." The administration now called for Somoza's resignation. It was too late to prevent a Sandinista victory. They were winning the war. Moderates who might have responded positively to isolating a weak Sandinista move-ment in 1978 could not do so by mid-1979. Although the Carter administra-tion was still somewhat split over what to do in Nicaragua, there was no will to provide new weapons for a National Guard capable of killing a U.S. newsman.[39]

The Carter administration now tried to intervene more forcefully, but it was too little, too late. Somoza left the country, and any efforts to continue "Somocismo without Somoza" were untenable. The Sandinistas entered Managua on 19 July. The makeup of the new government was undetermined, or at least the location of power was. The Junta of National Reconstruction included Doña Violeta. Frances Grant wrote her "dear friend" and said that she trusted that "in her hands, the future of Nicaragua is assured." The Inter-American Association for Democracy and Freedom reveled in the liberation of Nicaragua from decades of leadership by the Somoza family, and took hope in the end to censorship in the country and the promise of democratic pluralism.[40]

The Carter administration was certainly concerned about the Sandinistas' ties to Cuba. Cuban training, aid, and weapons had increased in 1979.[41] But the administration believed that it could avoid what it saw as the errors of the Eisenhower and Kennedy administrations in Cuba and not assume that the government was the enemy of the United States; it did not want to let the Sandinistas portray the United States as an enemy either. Perhaps the Sandinistas could be convinced to act as moderates; perhaps the United States could influence the direction of the revolution. The United States promised aid for reconstruction, and that meant the administration would have to convince the U.S. Congress that the Sandinistas were moderates even if they themselves increasingly did not believe that they were. In a September meeting, Vice President Mondale "noted the junta's desire for an open society that permits diversity of views, and said that the U.S. looks forward to working with them toward that objective." President Carter asserted that the "American people share his feelings of friendship for the new government" and expressed his hope that the government would "truly be non-aligned." The Carter administration aimed "to strengthen the basis for a cooperative relationship between the United States and Nicaragua based on mutual respect." Daniel Ortega and others focused on the country's desperate need for aid. Deputy Secretary of State Warren Christopher emphasized that human rights would be the most significant factor in determining the character of the relationship between the United States and the new government. Human rights had "perhaps [been] the principal engine that brought about the downfall of Somoza." "It could be," Christopher continued, "the principal force that propels the new Nicaragua." Sergio Ramirez responded that it was "precisely the desire for human rights that caused the revolution." In response to Ortega's concerns regarding activities of National Guardsmen, Christopher sought to assure the junta members that the United States would try to "avoid such problems." In November, the administration called for aid for Central American and Caribbean countries in order to "preserve the independence and security of these countries, while expanding democracy and human rights." The United States would seek to help a Nicaraguan economy "crushed by bitter and prolonged strife." In a meeting with junta member Moises Hassan in November, Robert Pastor noted that in a "time of tight budgets and elections, the Administration request was a clear sign for good relations and our interests in a democratic Nicaragua." Even if the economic policies of the new government hardly seemed doctrinaire, the ties to the Cuban government could hardly be denied. But in the short term, at least, even former Somoza supporters like Texas Democrat Jim Wright, a Great Society liberal who had supported the Vietnam War under both Johnson and Nixon, and conservatives like Congressman Henry Hyde were willing to support aid. By the end of 1979, the Sandinistas promised to publicize U.S. support.[42]

Carter called for U.S. assistance on humanitarian grounds, but also justified it as a way to make it possible for the country "to withstand interference from abroad." Carter was committed "to assist in democratic development in Nicaragua" and "to meet the Cuban challenge throughout the Central American region." But he also had emphasized a commitment to "pluralism and democracy" in Nicaragua that few in the administration believed existed as 1980 progressed.[43]

Aid for Nicaragua barely passed by only four votes in February 1980.[44] Carter sent Majority Leader Wright to Nicaragua. Wright reported to his constituents that Nicaragua was "the focal point of a hemispheric struggle between Marxism and freedom." He met with the Sandinistas, as well as with Archbishop Miguel Obando y Bravo and the staff of *La Prensa*. Everyone told him that "with our help," Nicaragua could be "saved for freedom." Obando expressed a wish that the United States not "abandon the field to the Cubans." Wright told Carter that the promise of a $75 million loan had taken on "enormous symbolic importance." All looked to it "as the primary evidence of U.S. friendship."[45] Supporters of aid sought to emphasize the pluralistic nature of the junta and the nationalism inherent in a movement named after Sandino. They also noted that quite a wide variety of countries were providing aid to Nicaragua, including U.S. allies like West Germany. By providing aid, these countries hoped to minimize Cuban influence; the United States should do likewise. To assume that Nicaragua had fallen "irretrievably into the Soviet-Cuban orbit" would be "defeatist." "The die" had "not been cast." (They also sought to put a positive spin on the fact that Nicaragua had abstained rather than voting in favor of the Soviet-Cuban position in the United Nations on Soviet actions in Afghanistan.)[46]

It took some time for the moderates in the junta to realize that they had no power, and there was no way that the Sandinistas were going to let them have any. Fortunately for Carter administration efforts to provide aid, the

Sandinistas were able to find other moderates to replace Violeta Barrios de Chamorro in mid-1980. The departure of Doña Violeta and Alfonso Robelo deeply concerned Frances Grant, but she publicly expressed optimism regarding the new junta members. Speaker of the House Thomas "Tip" O'Neill also expressed approval for the appointment of Arturo Cruz and Rafael Córdova Rivas as substantiating the Nicaraguan government's "commitment to pluralism," which he thought would "improve the climate for passage of legislation." In a letter to the president of the Council of State in Nicaragua, O'Neill noted that these were his "personal views on the prospects of approval by the House of Representatives and were not intended to influence internal matters of the Nicaraguan government." But others, like Majority Leader Wright, were increasingly concerned as the Sandinistas made it clear that elections would be delayed until 1985, despite assurances that they thought they had received in June. He and other congressmen wrote Daniel Ortega to make clear that this news was a "major disappointment" to those who thought that with U.S. "understanding and help" Nicaragua would "move swiftly to a truly democratic society." They recalled Castro's betrayal of promises and noted that "the enemies of Nicaragua in the United States" had predicted such a move. Wright and his colleagues referred to themselves as "friends of Nicaragua," who believed that the Nicaraguan people "can find their own destiny." And they expressed a hope that they would be able to vote sooner rather than later.[47]

The Carter administration was willing to live with a Sandinista government, even if it did not really trust it. But it was not willing to see another left-wing revolutionary government established in Central America. Containment and management of revolutionary change were the new emphases of the administration. A return to Alliance for Progress principles was in the offing as well. Assistant Secretary of State Vaky wrote Vance that the United States had to "prevent the consolidation of extreme left regimes" in Latin America and "contain Cuban/Soviet influence and control." While preventing "armed conflict," the United States would "promote broader political systems and social development and observance of human rights." Vaky believed that the Nicaraguan situation had been unique, and with "stability in Honduras and controlled change in El Salvador and Guatemala," it would remain so. This would require an engagement with Guatemala that had been lacking, and which, in the event, was not forthcoming, in large part because the Carter administration could find no one in Guatemala with whom it was able to work toward "controlled change." Roughly a year later, the Guatemalan government was described as "the strongest and most inhumane in Central America." There would not be "any change in our relationship until Reagan either wins or loses, and [the United States has] a new ambassador in place."[48]

Carter was also concerned about the impact of the revolution on its neighbors. El Salvador was the weakest country, but Carter did not discount the possibility that even Costa Rica, which he and many liberal Democrats over the years had admired for its long-standing constitutional traditions, would prove to be "vulnerable." (Without using the phrase, the domino theory from the Vietnam years clearly was on his mind.)[49]

El Salvador, never much on the radar of the U.S. government, now came to play an extremely significant role and would do so until the end of the administration of George H. W. Bush. The country had a history of military rule following an indigenous and communist rebellion in the early 1930s. A relatively small group of wealthy families seemed, for the most part, to be comfortable with military rule as it long as it did not interfere with their privileges. Land reform had passed El Salvador by during the era of the Alliance for Progress. A limited democratization resulted in the election of a Christian Democrat named José Napoleón Duarte as mayor of the capital of San Salvador. The opening of the political system was reversed definitively in 1972. Most observers believed that Duarte had won the presidential election that year, but the military refused to abide by the results. They brutally beat him and expelled him from the country; he spent many years in exile in Venezuela. In the 1970s, politically active priests and left-wing activists began to work on "consciousness raising" in the countryside. Death squads formed by military men and police officers were created, one of which employed the slogan, "Be a patriot, kill a priest." And a variety of guerrilla movements were established as well, but they remained weak and fragmented.[50]

El Salvador had risen to a level of presidential concern in the first year of the new administration when President Carter became aware of a wave of repression targeting Jesuit priests. Administration officials sought to assure lay Catholics and Catholic clergy in the United States that they were speaking with the Salvadoran government about the need to protect the Jesuits. The administration of General Humberto Romero allowed Patricia Derian in, and the Carter administration judged it to have been a productive visit. When the Salvadoran president visited in September 1977 at the time of the Panama Canal treaty signing, he talked to President Carter about the country's social problems and noted with pride the role of one of his compatriots in drafting the UN Declaration of Human Rights. He claimed to be attempting to engage in dialogue with Church leaders, but affirmed that he had been forced to expel a number of foreign priests. The OAS was allowed to send representatives of the Inter-American Commission on Human Rights.[51]

Toward the end of 1978, the Carter administration began to ponder whether to press the government of El Salvador on socioeconomic and political reform, given the military government's interest in improving relations between the two countries. By January 1979, National Security Adviser Brzezinski was already alerting President Carter to the possibility that the "critical situation in El Salvador" had "the potential for erupting into a full-fledged crisis requiring your attention in the early future." The Salvadoran left was already more popular and unified than it had been.[52] Following the overthrow of Somoza later that year, U.S. concern was inevitably heightened. Visiting members of the Christian Democratic Party told Assistant Secretary of State Vaky that "highly visible, dramatic actions" "were essential to create a credible climate for solution of problems in El Salvador." They urged the United States "to maintain a clear image and a resolute attitude about the road for reform in El Salvador." El Salvador was now being discussed at the highest levels, and the United States began to press the government to undertake reform. (Guatemala was seen as "less urgent.")[53]

"We view the fundamental cause of the instability and polarization in the region as the inability or unwillingness of the governments to address fundamental socioeconomic problems and to widen the base of political participation," Robert Pastor noted in a May 1979 memorandum to Brzezinski.[54] As conditions worsened in Nicaragua, President Carter and his staff began to focus on the larger political ramifications, and how to focus on supporting more open political systems and reducing political violence. The administration was torn between easing up on pressures to improve human rights in El Salvador and encouraging the military government to establish a timetable for elections (congressional ones by 1980 and presidential elections by 1982). In the week following the Sandinista victory, General Romero, for his part, promised to have municipal elections by the following March and told U.S. officials that he had conveyed his support for a civilian successor to military leaders, even as he stepped up repression. In the following months there were discussions regarding the promised elections. Carter administration officials hoped to convince the Christian Democrats to take part in elections, drawing upon Venezuelan influence on Duarte.[55]

A military coup led by reformist military officers established the Junta Revolucionária de Gobierno (Revolutionary Junta Government) in October. This seemed to offer an opportunity for the Carter administration. Brzezinski argued that the coup "may have turned the worst crisis into our best opportunity." Carter promised "to give them every support if they continue to honor human rights and democracy."[56] For the rest of the Carter presidency, there would be a commitment to supporting the government in its attempts to both promote socioeconomic change and survive. The dynamics were similar to those in the Kennedy years, when the U.S. government was paying attention to significant social problems in Latin America in response to the Cuban Revolution. But Carter administration energies were more focused on one particular country than had ever been the case in the early 1960s. Still, the Carter administration faced the same problem that the Kennedy people had. El Salvador's problems were urgent, but they were also of long standing. Government officials demanded "quick impact" programs, but it remained unclear whether the primary goal was to make a difference in the lives of the poor or to simply lessen the appeal of revolution. Once again development (a long-term process) was being subordinated to short-term political goals. But even more immediately, the U.S. military was creating military training teams to address the challenge posed by armed guerrillas.[57]

By early 1980, the three main revolutionary movements were moving toward a united front, but the government junta was seen as "paralyzed in debate and factional struggle." The CIA judged the left as being "determined to seize power in El Salvador during 1980." The junta did not really agree on fundamental questions and found it difficult even to form a cabinet that would last. The army and the Christian Democrats themselves were divided ideologically. CIA officials feared an all-out civil war that could drive the center to the left.[58] But soon the concern shifted to the activities of right-wing death squads who were killing civilians. Robert Pastor feared that the Christian Democrats might leave the junta if the military did not move as decisively against "right-wing terrorists" as it had against the left.[59]

Some in El Salvador argued that the Carter administration's trust in the junta was misplaced. The most prominent critic was Archbishop Oscar Romero (no relation to the former president). He was a priest who had been considered apolitical when he was surprised to be named archbishop in February 1977. The murder of close friends by death squads enraged him. Following a visit in April 1979, Congressman Harkin had praised him as "a kind man, a decent man, a just man." But Carter administration efforts to get him to back the new government, even enlisting the aid of the pope, were unsuccessful. Secretary of State Vance responded to the archbishop's plea to end U.S. aid for the government by noting the common goals the religious leader and President Carter had. Vance expressed confidence in the moderate, reformist character of the government, which he described as the "best prospect for peaceful change." The United States was committed to contributing "to peaceful and progressive solutions" and to providing economic more than military aid, "given the unfortunate role which some elements of the security forces occasionally have played in the past." Military assistance was intended "to defend and carry forward [the junta's] announced program of reform and development." Vance sought to assure the archbishop that the assistance would not be used "in a repressive manner." Vance insisted that U.S. aid for the military would make the armed forces more professional and able to maintain order "with a minimum of lethal force."[60]

Only a little more than two weeks later, Romero was dead, assassinated during Mass by order of Major Roberto D'Aubuisson. The Carter administration called this "a shocking and unconscionable act," but it did not waver in its support of the government and expressed "trust" that the government would move "swiftly and effectively to bring the archbishop's assassins to justice."[61]

An important actor from the United States in El Salvador in 1980 and 1981 was Ambassador Robert White. He had played a role in addressing Chilean human rights issues as deputy ambassador to the OAS and had been proposed by Brzezinski aide David Aaron as the U.S. ambassador to Chile or Peru. He then served in Paraguay instead. By the time he arrived in San Salvador in January 1980, he was recognized as a significant figure in the promotion of human rights. His time in the country would be difficult. By June he claimed that there had been "sufficient signs of improvement in the human rights performance in the Salvadoran military" that he was willing to recommend that the United States loan the military six helicopters. This would enable the United States to maintain influence with the Salvadoran military, which now felt the United States had "abandoned them."[62]

As had happened elsewhere in Latin America in the 1960s, the United States put its faith in reformist Christian Democrats. But the party itself was increasingly split over staying in a government that could not establish control over a military that was implicated in the death of thousands of people in 1980.[63] Duarte, the most prominent civilian member of the junta from March on, promised he would "unequivocally subordinate the military to the junta" in September 1980.[64] The Carter administration was increasingly concerned that Colonel Adolfo Arnoldo Majano, one of the military members of the junta who was most committed to reform and most critical of the military's failure to rein in its own extremists, would be forced out. As the fall wore on, Ambassador White found it necessary to emphasize U.S. support for Majano.[65] Robert Pastor, on the anniversary of the establishment of the government, which he called a "revolution," expressed in no uncertain terms his confidence in the junta. The "revolution" had "brought Salvador rapidly into the 20th century and offered the first hope it has had for social democracy." Carter himself also spoke confidently of "a new and just social order" that was "emerging" in Central America more generally. He expressed a conviction that Central America could find its "way forward, leaving old injustices, without submitting to new tyrannies." On the same day, Duarte "read a new military directive charging the Ministry of Defense with ensuring respect for human rights and the punishment of violators."[66]

But despite the faith that the Carter administration showed in the junta, and even in the military, and its belief that a promise that aid for the military

would only flow when human rights improved, would yield positive results, death squad violence continued. Over the course of the year, 8,000,
including many civilians and moderate politicians, were killed for political
reasons. Patricia Derian was concerned, as she had been in Nicaragua the
year before, that the human rights office was not being included in discussions of U.S. policy toward El Salvador.[67] Out of the repression, however,
unity developed among a diverse group of guerrilla groups and a variety of
civilian groups on the left, including some Christian Democrats who split
from the party.

Carter's defeat in the presidential election on 4 November threatened to
have more impact on El Salvador than any other Latin American country.
White was still confident that the Salvadoran government was moving in the
right direction. It still represented "the best opportunity to defeat the far left
by holding to a steadily moderate course between extremes of right and left.
Reform must continue or the population will lose faith in moderate change."
Although he admitted that "respect for human rights" was "clearly at a low
ebb," he felt that it could be "increased if the government" remained "stable
and its success becomes impossible to deny." A week after the election, White
expressed a hope that someone from the Reagan team needed to send "clear
signals" regarding their policy toward El Salvador. Failing that, Pastor warned,
the moderates would leave the government and the country, and a "bloodbath" would occur. By the end of the month he was calling for a joint statement from Carter and President-Elect Reagan. Specifically, he wanted to see
President Reagan's people reaffirm "the emphasis on human rights."[68]

The tragic rape and murder of four U.S. churchwomen in El Salvador on
December 2nd horrified Ambassador White, who pushed hard to convince
the Carter administration to cut aid for El Salvador. This seemed like a Bill
Stewart moment, and had an impact on U.S. opinion in a way that the death
of thousands of Salvadorans could not.[69] The news made it virtually impossible for the United States to continue providing military support. White argued that withholding aid would demonstrate U.S. sincerity in supporting
"a process of national reconciliation" and opposing "any policy of extermina-
tion." On the 3rd, White met with many top military leaders, who expressed
disappointment in Carter administration backing of the military and what
they considered to be the failure to appreciate the role they had played in supporting reform and the price they were paying in fighting the guerrillas.
White stressed U.S. support for the government, but he also stressed the need
for the Salvadoran government to control the security forces, to "confront the
armed guerrillas with force," not "disappearances, torture and assassination."
The U.S. government, he continued, "had the right and the obligation to accept a standard from the Salvadoran armed forces." Too many officers sup-

ported the killing of Unified Revolutionary Directorate leaders as "a major step toward ridding the country of the leftist menace." They wanted "carte blanche to step up the bloodbath against the left, broadly defined as they define the threat." That direction would lead to "total disaster." He insisted that "indiscriminate killing, as in Nicaragua" would unite "the people against the regime." White and Warren Christopher hoped that this would strengthen the hand of the Christian Democrats in curtailing "indiscriminate violence," improving human rights, consolidating reforms, and moving toward dialogue. White wanted to see the military improve its behavior for at least a month before military aid could be resumed. He was convinced that the guerrillas could not overthrow the government in the coming months. By 23 December, however, Duarte was concerned about the suspension of military aid. He did not feel it provided leverage, because the military had no confidence in the United States. Secretary of State Muskie supported sending economic aid immediately to prove U.S. support for the Christian Democrats. By the end of December, however, Secretary of Defense Harold Brown was emphasizing the need for military aid not only to fight the guerrillas, but also to maintain the support of military officers, who would oppose any attempts to remove civilian leaders from the government (as they had already done twice before). Duarte thought by this point that U.S. threats were not helping because the military expected "a virtual avalanche of US military assistance from the opening of the Reagan administration."[70]

A "final offensive" by the guerrillas, speaking now as one but acting independently, aided by what was judged to be a large supply of arms from Nicaragua, forced the Carter administration's hand by the middle of January. The situation had become "militarily more critical." Despite strong opposition from the secretary of state, Brzezinski argued that it would "be extremely damaging not only to our national interests but to the historical record of this administration to leave office unwilling to take the hard decision to provide lethal assistance to an essentially middle of the road government, beleaguered by revolutionaries almost openly assisted by the Cubans via Nicaragua." This would undermine Carter's Central America policy (from the canal treaty to land reform and democratization) and "play into the hands of our critics, in addition perhaps to permitting in the meantime a very adverse outcome on the ground." Military aid was resumed on 13 January. At the same time, aid for Nicaragua was halted because the Carter administration could no longer deny what it had long suspected, that the Sandinistas were supporting the guerrillas in El Salvador. (Brzezinski warned that the suspension of aid to Nicaragua would lead "to the expulsion of the middle class, the communization of Nicaragua, and could very well precipitate a major international war in Central America.")[71]

In the last weeks of the Carter administration, concerns regarding Sandinista support for the guerrillas in El Salvador were heightened, as were those regarding potential Cuban military intervention in Nicaragua. Covert aid for what were considered "moderate" elements in Nicaragua was provided by the Central Intelligence Agency, though the tendency by some scholars to equate opposition with "Contra" seems unwarranted by the evidence currently available.[72]

Carter's policies in Central America and the Caribbean had pointed in different directions. He had failed to promote human rights in Nicaragua, and his mixed signals undermined the moderates. Somoza's brutality created an opportunity for the Sandinistas. Having achieved power, the Sandinistas found not opposition as they had anticipated, but aid, and hopes that they would prove themselves to be more moderate than their Cuban model. Carter tried to prevent a repetition of the Cuban experience in Nicaragua and of the Sandinista experience in El Salvador, despite the inability of the military to control the human rights abuses that masked the limitations of their counterinsurgency efforts.

But nowhere had Carter administration policies been more incoherent than toward Cuba. Despite early attempts to begin what was expected to be a drawn-out process toward normalization, Cuban activities in Africa continued to be the major roadblock as far as Carter and Brzezinski were concerned. The withdrawal of Cuban troops from Angola had halted in the spring of 1977 because of Angolan government fears of South Africa. Cuban intervention in Ethiopia in response to an invasion by Somalia at the end of 1977, coordinated more directly with the Soviet Union than its actions in Angola had been, made further moves unlikely. (Ethiopia, according to Pastor, "split" Vance and Brzezinski "apart.") New threats in 1978 led to a larger Cuban presence in Angola; as historian Piero Gleijeses argues, the Angolan government never trusted Western powers' willingness or capacity to restrain South Africa. Carter and many of his advisers were increasingly convinced that no improvements in relations between the two countries could occur until Castro abandoned a military presence there, and overheated rhetoric based on inadequate evidence regarding particular Cuban actions exacerbated relations still further. The Cubans, for their part, never accepted the idea that there could not be improvements in relations between the two countries without its withdrawal. In any case, Carter had returned to conventional thinking about Cuba. He at least recognized at times the appeal of a revolutionary model in countries whose conditions were in such need of dramatic transformation. He rejected "Cuba's promise," however, as an "empty one, just as Cuba's claimed independence is a myth." Spurred by the holding of the meeting of nonaligned countries in Havana in 1979, the Carter administration sought to refute Soviet attempts to "stress the independence of Cuban foreign policy." Carter told his team to "stress the truth about the dependence of Cuba on the USSR and the basic identity of their foreign policies." Let me tell "the truth about the Soviet puppet," Carter suggested to Brzezinski.[73]

A tempest in a teapot ended up being more important at the time than it should have been. Strangely enough, a liberal Democrat was largely to blame. Worried about his own reelection chances, Frank Church raised the issue of Soviet troops in Cuba. The Carter administration, for its part, then contributed to the rising sense of hysteria over the issue. It played into a narrative of Soviet actions as taking advantage of détente, which was increasingly viewed as having been discredited. The Carter administration backed itself into a corner even as internally it had to admit that the number of Soviet troops on the island had been roughly the same since 1962. Carter ultimately addressed the "Soviet brigade" issue in a speech to the nation in October of 1979. He had to admit that this was neither "a large force, nor an assault force." It represented "no direct threat" to the United States. Nevertheless, Carter insisted that it contributed a "tension" in the region, as did the increasing Soviet supply of arms to Cuba. Carter promised more surveillance and more military maneuvers in Central America and the Caribbean. But he concluded "that the brigade issue is certainly no reason for a return to the cold war." (And Church's stance on the issue did not save him in his campaign for reelection.)[74]

In his penultimate State of the Union message, Carter claimed that he had forged "a more collaborative relationship" with Latin America, but his primary evidence stemmed from his success in getting the Panama Canal treaty ratified; the direct regional impact of that significant accomplishment was not easy to delineate. It was not clear whether he included Somoza's government among "the world's most repressive regimes," which disappeared in 1979. Carter expressed his concern that Cuba would "thwart the desires of the people of the region for progress within a democratic framework," but also noted his hope that developmental aid was going to have an impact. In some ways, at least in Central America, and particularly in El Salvador, it was as if the clock had been turned back to 1961.[75]

In his last speech to the Organization of American States in late November, President Carter noted that while others gave him credit for putting human rights on the hemispheric agenda, he saw himself as only part of a broader movement (as exemplified by the awarding of the Nobel Peace Prize to Argentine Adolfo Pérez Esquivel). His electoral defeat would not reverse that movement. He spoke of the cause as being "at the service of humanity, rather than at the service of ideological or partisan ends." "Rights" are an important part of the phrase, but the "human" is even more important. "The future of our hemisphere is not to be found in authoritarianism that wears the mask of common consent, nor totalitarianism that wears the mask of justice." Instead, what was needed was "the human face of democracy, the human voice of individual liberty, and the human hand of economic development." He expressed confidence in the future of Latin America.[76]

In his last State of the Union message, he struck a less sanguine tone. He again praised the new partnership with Panama, which could serve as a "model for large and small nations." He mentioned Brazil's ongoing "process of liberalization." But he spoke less confidently of a change in what was going on in Nicaragua. He lamented what he said were increasing restrictions on "the press and political activity, an inordinate Cuban presence in the country and the tragic killing by the security forces of a businessman well-known for his democratic orientation." Carter argued that the United States could not abandon those in Nicaragua who continued to "seek a free society." "As long as those who intend to pursue their pluralistic goals play important roles in Nicaragua, it deserves our continuing support." On the same day, Carter suspended aid to Nicaragua after having received what he saw as conclusive proof that the Sandinistas were providing arms to the Salvadoran guerrillas.[77]

As Carter left office, he had succeeded in helping the Dominican Republic return to democracy. He had resolved a long-standing issue with Panama, to the dismay of many U.S. citizens and politicians, but in a way that would not be challenged by his Republican successors. But he had failed to prevent the victory of leftist revolutionaries in Nicaragua. He had failed to help a reformist government consolidate its control over the military or do anything more than contain a revolution in El Salvador at great cost to its people. Carter ultimately maintained the status quo of abnormal and contentious relations with Cuba. Reform and human rights seemed to be out of the question in Latin America under Ronald Reagan, and liberal Democrats, once again in opposition, would reject much of what the Republican president was trying to achieve in the new Cold War atmosphere that followed the Soviet invasion of Afghanistan. The Carter administration had tried to keep the Cold War out of relations with Nicaragua. President Reagan, however, would see both Nicaragua and El Salvador as important battlefields in the Cold War, at great cost to both.

Chapter 10

Liberal Democratic Resistance and Accommodation in the Reagan/Bush Years

For Republicans, the 1980 election came at a time of a greater perception of threat in Latin America than they had experienced since Fidel Castro came to power. But unlike the early years of the Cuban Revolution, where the sense of danger was more broadly diffused among the general population, the Republican view was not so widely shared. Although a renewed Cold War had begun during the Carter administration with the Soviet invasion of Afghanistan, his policies in the Western Hemisphere remained restrained. The 1980s saw a contest regarding Kennedy's legacies. For Democrats, support for containment was now complicated by their commitment to human rights. President Ronald Reagan's abandonment of human rights, and his efforts in Central America, in particular, were not popular, but he persisted with the latter even in his second term as he began to work toward an end to the Cold War with a new Soviet leader, Mikhail Gorbachev.[1] His successor oversaw the beginning of a new, uncertain era, with U.S. power in the world unchallenged and the triumph of both democracy and pre-Kennedy policies of free trade and foreign investment.

But in the late 1970s, Republicans warned of dangers not seen in Latin America in decades. At the end of 1979, a future member of President Reagan's National Security Council, Roger Fontaine, warned that Carter had "no clear idea what to do" about the radicalization of Central America. Fontaine predicted another guerrilla victory "within a year," as well as the fall of Panama's Omar Torrijos.[2] The Republican Party platform in 1980 argued that the Carter administration was weak and had failed to prevent the "spread" of "Marxist tyrannies," particularly in the case of Nicaragua. Latin America, the platform affirmed, was "an area of primary interest for the United States." Reagan promised that his administration would be strong but not "belligerent."[3]

The new president himself was a former liberal Democrat. He had supported Franklin Roosevelt and the New Deal, and did not vote for a Republican presidential candidate until 1952. In the 1950s he became a spokesman for General Electric and adopted a more classical liberal opposition to taxation and "big government." Although as president he frequently invoked John Kennedy, Reagan changed his party affiliation in 1962. After speaking powerfully in favor of Barry Goldwater at the 1964 convention, he went on to serve as the two-term Republican governor of California.[4] The 1980 elections marked the end of the political careers of liberal Democrats like Senators McGovern and Church. The Republican Party gained control of the Senate, but the Democrats retained control of the House. Reagan thought that he had a mandate, but even with the control of the Senate, his early victories were primarily on domestic issues.[5]

Reagan's understanding of the world was simplistic. He saw the hand of the Soviet Union behind "all the unrest that is going on" in the world. "If they weren't engaged in this game of dominoes, there wouldn't be any hot spots in the world." Other Republicans believed in an extremely active role for the Soviet Union for world domination. In a letter to the president, Wyoming Republican Senator Malcolm Wallop said that a Soviet "military/political offensive" was underway that would "take them to the Rio Grande." As UN Ambassador Jeane Kirkpatrick later said, the Soviets were trying to "incorporate this hemisphere into their global geo-political strategy." Kirkpatrick thought Central America was "the most important place in the world for the United States today."[6]

El Salvador was the country in which the new administration most feared the triumph of a left-wing insurgency, but it was also one where, Secretary of State Al Haig assured President Reagan, "you can win." It became the "first major issue in foreign policy."[7] But El Salvador also was the country around which opposition to administration policy coalesced early. When questioned by Indiana Republican Senator Richard Lugar as to why he was "riled up" over Central America, Edward Kennedy replied that "the issue mattered in Massachusetts." Reagan, for his part, often denied that there was any difference between his policy and that of his predecessor. The administration blamed not only "media disinformation" and the House testimony of former Ambassador Robert White, but also "a worldwide propaganda campaign." Emergency military aid was provided, but Secretary of State Al Haig recommended that food aid "would also help our military package for El Salvador. A number of Congressmen sensitive to pressure by the churches and rights groups— or uncertain about our judgement of the El Salvador situation—will find it easier to support a program with a larger economic component."[8]

Throughout 1981, President Reagan had to address comparisons between El Salvador and Vietnam, even by veteran newscaster Walter Cronkite. As had been true in the Kennedy years in Southeast Asia, the U.S. military presence was limited to "advisers." Congressman Harkin, along with Michigan's John Conyers, New York's Shirley Chisholm, and other liberal Democrats, warned the administration that the presence of military advisers suggested that the administration was emphasizing a "military solution." U.S. casualties could lead to a larger commitment, "forcing the United States into another Vietnam or a humiliating withdrawal, either of which would weaken the United States position in the world." National Security Adviser Richard Allen sought to assure Pennsylvania Republican Congressman William Goodling that the "small number of trainers (not advisers)" would guarantee that there would be no "repetition of the unhappy and ill-conceived Vietnam experience." Despite occasional belligerent rhetoric that Democrats used to their benefit, President Reagan repeatedly found himself insisting that no U.S. troops were "going into combat" in El Salvador or anywhere else in the world, and he would have to continue to do so for years afterward. Allen suggested not even mentioning Vietnam because "even its usage may tend to validate the thesis." Privately, in any case, it was clear that Reagan administration officials saw a connection too—for example, when Fontaine noted that "the war in El Salvador will be won or lost in the United States."[9]

Fontaine urged the administration to employ more positive "historical analogies." "You can't see El Salvador through its Southeast Asia prism." Instead, the U.S. public needed to be informed about the many (and, aside from Nicaragua, unsuccessful) Cuban-inspired and Cuban-backed insurgencies, particularly those during the Kennedy-Johnson years. The most appropriate example of a country in which U.S. aid helped defeat the guerrillas was Venezuela, and "Venezuela today is democratic." But the administration could not use an analogy effectively if the public did not know the history.[10] For Fontaine, the danger in Central America was even greater than it had been in the 1960s when Cuba's support for guerrilla movements lacked the "full backing of the Soviet Union." But the lessons of Vietnam suggested to Fontaine that there should be "no gradualism; no unforeseen escalation; no commitment of U.S. troops to combat operations either directly or in an advisory role.'"[11]

As President Reagan initially focused on taxes, he was unwilling to expend political capital on El Salvador. NSC staffer Fontaine told National Security Adviser Allen that the president "must enter the fray or risk losing El Salvador." He warned of an insurgent victory "at present levels of effort." Guatemala would follow suit and Honduras and Costa Rica would undergo "finlandization." He also suggested that "for all its talk of overcoming the Vietnam syndrome," the United States could not "act decisively closer to home."[12]

Despite rhetoric to the contrary on both sides, the Reagan administration did not break completely from Carter administration policy, not even in El Salvador, and there were often clear echoes of the Kennedy years as well. Candidate Reagan had said that the war had to be won before reform could take place, but, politically, this was not tenable. The new chairman of the Foreign Relations Committee, Senator Jesse Helms, had tried to end support for land reform, but Ambassador Thomas Enders sought to prevent him from continuing to do so. The murder of two American Institute for Free Labor

Development land reform advisers complicated the issue still further. By May Reagan wrote in his diary that he had given the "go ahead to a plan for the Caribbean and Central Am. to help the smaller cos. economically, social reforms, plus military aid to protect against Cuban exported radicals." As early as mid-August, Secretary of State Haig had already recognized that the war was "stalemated." Ambassador Deane Hinton, for his part, recognized the need to try and control the Salvadoran military's behavior.[13]

Despite appearances to the contrary and the impressions of the man himself, the administration would have to rely upon a man and a party that evoked President Kennedy and the 1960s, José Napoleón Duarte and the Christian Democrats. Ironically, the Reagan team, whose attitude toward Duarte "ranged from skeptical to rude," received him coldly in 1981; National Security Adviser Allen seemed to think that he was a Castro admirer. In the long run, Duarte became the Reagan administration's best ally, giving administration policy credibility with people like Edward Kennedy and Tom Harkin. Harkin had met Duarte on a Washington visit when he was in exile. Harkin considered him "a very engaging man fully committed to human rights and democracy, and very sensitive to the needs of his people." But he worried that Duarte had not yet been able to gain control over the military and was perhaps too trusting of the high command. Without Duarte, however, Harkin maintained, "the level of killings would be much higher." As Secretary of State Al Haig privately told Reagan, he was the "best, probably the only hope" (echoes of Chile's Christian Democratic President Eduardo Frei in the 1960s) for a "peaceful, moderate solution." Although he had been "ineffective in confronting the military excesses," Haig noted, "his meeting with you will go far toward strengthening his hand with the military." In early 1982, Reagan claimed, as Carter had before him, to be supporting the center as represented by the Duarte government, "which is between these factions." Duarte gave the Reagan policy credibility in Venezuela, where Duarte had lived; during his meeting with Reagan, President Luis Herrera Campins, a member of the Venezuelan Christian Democratic Party (COPEI), referred to Duarte as "our distinguished friend" and noted the parallels between El Salvador and Venezuela in the 1960s.[14]

Generally, liberal Democrats saw administration policy as leading to greater polarization and radicalization in Central America. Democrats like Congressman Harkin and Connecticut Senator Christopher Dodd, who had served in the Peace Corps in the Dominican Republic, sought to impose human rights conditions on aid to El Salvador, requiring the administration to certify periodically that progress was being made. On the anniversary of the murders of the nuns and lay workers, Harkin called for a political settlement. "Neither side," he insisted, "in the short run can have victory militarily." Kennedy had reached the same conclusion after meeting with Guillermo Ungo, a son of the founder of the Christian Democratic Party who had been Duarte's vice presidential candidate in 1972. Ungo had been a member of the reformist junta until disillusionment over the death squad–led violence in 1980 led him to become a civilian leader of the guerrilla movement. Ungo was calling for a "negotiated peace." Kennedy was unable to convince National Security Adviser Clark to meet with Ungo.[15]

Nicaragua posed a different problem, for both the Reagan administration and for liberal Democrats. The administration primarily criticized the Sandinistas in public for its support for the insurgency in El Salvador. Fontaine even suggested early on that "command control of the insurgency" came "from Managua." But President Reagan was soon committed to his own insurgency, an anti-Sandinista insurgency that was becoming known as the "Contras" (or counter-revolutionaries). For much of the first term, U.S. aid was justified as being used to block the flow of arms to El Salvador, and many Democrats were willing to support this as a legitimate containment strategy. But it became clear to most that this was a task for which the Contras had little appetite. The Contra goal was to overthrow the Sandinista government. And yet Reagan during his first term repeatedly denied that the United States was trying to do that. The administration sought to confer legitimacy upon the Contras by arguing that they had fought against Somoza and had seen their revolution betrayed. But throughout the 1980s, military leadership remained in the hands of former National Guard officers. And Contra brutality severely limited their domestic and international legitimacy. Congressman Harkin complained that aid to the Contras was undermining the "position of those Nicaraguans in the Government and in the opposition who are committed to the democratic and human rights principles of the Nicaraguan revolution." The Contra war helped the government justify repressive measures and a large-scale military build-up. Harkin noted that while opponents of the Sandinistas suffered "restrictions, even imprisonment," they were not killed as they were in El Salvador. Michigan Congressman David Bonior and California Congressman George Miller called administration policy counterproductive since "military pressures" did not improve chances for "political pluralism" to flourish, and "economic pressures" did not slow "overtures . . . to the Soviet Union for aid." Instead, the administration was "producing precisely what it purportedly seeks to avoid."[16]

Liberal Democrats, however, sought to avoid being identified with the Sandinistas. While he was impressed by the Sandinista literacy campaign, Kennedy saw the "authoritarian regime of the left" as marred by its practices of censorship, its "repression of free labor union activity," and its delay of elections. Kennedy sought to encourage negotiations between the Sandinistas and the isolated indigenous peoples on the Caribbean coast and later worked with the administration on providing aid to Brooklyn Rivera, one of their leaders. But the Reagan administration caused problems for itself from the beginning because of its refusal to inform Congress adequately regarding what it was doing in Nicaragua, which never stayed hidden for long. Speaker of the House Tip O'Neill was willing to compromise on El Salvador, but his ideas about Nicaragua and his opposition to the Contras were shaped by his aunt, a Maryknoll nun, and on missionaries' testimony regarding Contra activities and on the benefits that people were receiving from Sandinista programs. O'Neill had broken with Johnson over Vietnam in 1967; he warned of U.S. military involvement in Nicaragua as well. In response to a package of letters from California preschool children who were protesting the death of Nicaraguan children in a twin city day-care center targeted by the Contras, O'Neill told California Congressman Ron Dellums that they would work together "to once and for all put an end to the Administration's ill-considered expedition in Nicaragua."[17]

If Nicaragua was behind revolution in El Salvador, according to the administration, then it was "Cuban adventurism" that was thought to be behind unrest generally in the Caribbean Basin. Previous administrations were not successful at doing more than containing Castro, who now seemed less contained than he had ever been, particularly in Africa, where he was even more of a thorn in Reagan's side, though not the ideological inspiration he had been in Latin America. Secretary of State Haig infamously suggested that the United States had to "go to the source." "You just give me the word, and I'll turn that fucking island into a parking lot." Few in the administration were willing to go that far despite a conviction that Castro was winning in the region. (Following that remark, Deputy Chief of Staff Michael Deaver tried to guarantee that Haig would never be in a room alone again with the president.) The United States needed to foster a multilateral approach as it was doing in Afghanistan, some administration officials argued early on. Bilateral action "would paint the US as an international heavy in the Third World community." The United States, Fontaine maintained, needed to recognize the limits of its power. There was to be no "Reagan Doctrine" in Latin America, beyond "mutual respect," "general respect for democratic process," support for economic development, and opposition to intervention. The United States would provide a "major but fundamentally supportive role" in terms of development and security. The United States was not "going to war in the Caribbean . . . without a proper assessment of Soviet worldwide reaction or the reaction of friends and allies in Western Europe and Latin America," as well as in the U.S. press, the U.S. public, and "above all, the U.S. Congress."[18]

The administration proposed a new emphasis on fighting terrorism, but its emphasis was selective, Congressman Harkin argued, ignoring state terrorism, the "most deadly form of terrorism known to man." The Reagan administration's decision to drop attempts to extradite the killers of Letelier and Moffit suggested that "state terrorism is fine—even if conducted in the streets of Washington, DC." The administration was dismantling the human rights policy of the previous administration and sending an "unequivocal message to our 'friends' abroad: as long as they *profess* to be anti-communist, they can expect no protests from Washington if they torture, assassinate, and imprison without trial in order to install or maintain themselves in power."[19]

Besides the more immediate concerns in Central America, the Reagan administration sought to repair what it saw as the damage done to relations with friendly military governments in South America. "The United States treats its friends with disdain," Otto Reich, a Cuban American who would serve in the administration, had lamented during the campaign.[20] Political scientist Jeane Kirkpatrick, a Democrat herself, provided what became the justification for the Reagan administration by making a distinction between authoritarian regimes, which could change, and totalitarian regimes, which could not. In a meeting shortly before the inauguration, the head of Brazil's national intelligence service told Vice President-Elect George Herbert Walker Bush that the military government "had welcomed the result of the elections in the United States." Bush noted that he thought that Rosalynn Carter's visit had been a mistake, and that Patricia Derian would not be working in Reagan's State Department. Vernon Walters was sent to meet with the military leaders of Brazil he had long been associated with. Although this was intended ostensibly to provide information on administration policy in El Salvador, this was more broadly viewed as a signal of support for the military government. Generally, Walters said, "it is not difficult to see which countries are our friends and which are not."[21]

Administration policy toward the military government of Argentina was also intended to mend fences. (Walters met with them as well.) In a meeting with President Roberto Eduardo Viola, President Reagan and Secretary of State Haig promised "no finger pointing" or "public scolding or lectures" on human rights. Viola responded that he "hoped there would be no private scoldings either." This had the added benefit of creating an alliance on aid for the Contras, which Argentina had already been involved in providing. This worked out well until early 1982, when the military leaders sought to gain popular support from the Argentine population by invading what they called the Malvinas, which the United Kingdom called the Falkland Islands. Although some officials thought that Reagan should back the Argentines, the administration soon chose to aid the British. Many Latin American leaders saw this as a clear violation of the Monroe Doctrine.[22]

The Reagan administration also thought that Pinochet's Chile should be recognized as a friendly country. Secretary of State Haig considered U.S. relations with Chile to be "uniquely encumbered by congressional and executive sanctions." The country's human rights situation had improved under Carter, but Pinochet's lack of cooperation on the Letelier and Moffitt killings ensured that Congress was unlikely to change its policies. Congressman Harkin spoke out in March about the Chilean secret police planning of a "hideous crime with the cooperation and complicity of shadowy elements of the international criminal underworld." The new administration, he said, had promised a war against international terrorism but had "turned its back and walked away from its first challenge." The Reagan administration could do little more than approve an Inter-American Development Bank loan for highway construction. The administration found it difficult to change policy, in part and increasingly because the administration sensed that any improvement in relations with Chile might make it harder to achieve its more immediate goals in El Salvador. Chile's human rights situation worsened during Reagan's first term, as opposition developed in response to difficult economic conditions. As the tenth anniversary of the fall of Allende passed, Senators Kennedy and Cranston, as well as congressmen like Mike Barnes, among others, introduced a resolution calling for an end to dictatorship and a return to democracy.[23]

Some liberal Democrats seem to have been surprised by Reagan's Latin America policy. Schlesinger, who by 1980 was disillusioned completely with Carter, voted for once for a presidential candidate who was not a Democrat, John Anderson, a Republican congressman from Illinois who ran as an independent. Based on Reagan's record in California, Schlesinger did not expect Reagan to be particularly radical. But by March, the former Kennedy aide said that he had been surprised that the "Reagan crowd" was "far more doctrinaire than I expected." He called them "terrible simplifiers," whose Cold War view of the world was dangerous. (He quoted President Kennedy: "Domestic policy can only defeat us. Foreign policy can kill us.") He remained convinced that Carter had not been "a real Democrat and that, human rights and Camp David apart, the Carter years were wasted years."[24]

For its part, in its party platform in 1980, unlike the previous Republican administrations which had emphasized "power," the Democratic Party had made "our values a central factor in shaping American foreign policy."[25] The party had a winning issue in human rights, and it was unlikely to give it up. Congressman Harkin criticized Kirkpatrick's "linguistic gymnastics to make excuses for our favorite dictators." The torture and anti-Semitism, he noted, exhibited by Argentina were no different from those in the Soviet Union. Administration plans to abandon human rights were also rejected by Republicans, as demonstrated by the fate of Ernest Lefever's nomination to succeed Derian. Lefever had been an adviser to Hubert Humphrey on foreign policy in 1968 and had been employed by the liberal Brookings Institution. By this point, however, he had left the Democratic Party and was a prominent critic of Carter's human rights policy. In hearings before the Senate Foreign Relations Committee, Rhode Island's Claiborne Pell noted that this was the most controversial nominee put forward by the administration. Several years before, Lefever had testified before the House of Representatives that all human rights legislation should be abandoned. Pell thought that it was worthwhile to distinguish between authoritarian and totalitarian leaders and that quiet diplomacy could be effective as well. Having recently returned from a trip to Latin America, however, Pell noted that many people had told him "thank God for Carter's human rights policies," because they had an "inhibiting effect on the governments in that part of the world." California's Alan Cranston asserted that human rights had been "one of our most potent weapons in our peaceful competition with communist regimes." Cranston worried that Lefever was unable to see human rights violations by right-wing governments. Jacobo Timerman, an Argentine Jewish journalist who had experienced anti-Semitic abuse and torture under the military government, attended the hearings and was warmly received. The Foreign Relations Committee, controlled after all by Republicans, voted 13–4 to oppose his nomination (only four Republicans voted in favor).[26]

In Lefever's place, the Reagan administration chose Elliott Abrams, a Democrat who had been an aide to New York Senator Daniel Patrick Moynihan. Congressman Harkin hailed the appointment of a person who would carry out "the moral purposes of U.S. foreign policy." Harkin claimed that Abrams was "light years ahead in his understanding." Harkin noted that Carter had failed at times, but Harkin saw Carter as "a model of sobriety and effectiveness in comparison" to Reagan.[27]

Despite his attempts to differentiate himself from previous presidents, Reagan's first trip to the region demonstrated remarkable continuity with the past. He visited Costa Rica and Colombia, both democratic countries President Kennedy had visited, and Brazil, which Kennedy had never ended up visiting. The goal of Reagan's trip was to demonstrate "a sense of priority for neighbors at a time of global recession, post-Falklands uncertainties and continued conflict." Costa Rica and Colombia seemed like safe bets. The Reagan trip was intended "to associate the United States with progress toward democracy." Brazil was still ruled by the military, despite Reagan's reference to it as a democracy "restored." The 1982 congressional elections, however, had been the freest since the establishment of the military government in 1964. The opposition had been extremely successful, particularly in the economically advanced south. Brazil, however, was entering a period of deep economic uncertainty. Reagan thought that the ongoing debt crisis created an opportunity for the rebirth of "free enterprise" and a turn away from the moderate economic nationalism that had marked Brazil for decades. U.S. Ambassador to the United Nations Kirkpatrick argued that "Once we had a special relationship" with Brazil, but "we have systematically humiliated them," leading to "chronic hurt feelings," creating a need to "reassure them."[28]

In a 1982 address to the British Parliament, President Reagan had proclaimed that a "democratic revolution" was "gathering new strength." Little mention was made of Latin America, however. He did refer to "Cuban-backed guerrillas who want power to themselves." And he made the spurious assertion that "Some argue that we should encourage democratic change in right-wing dictatorships, but not in Communist regimes." Some seek to claim that this marked a definitive change in administration policy or claim that it was always the administration's policy. This is hard to reconcile with the earlier embrace of the South American military dictatorships. Nor does it square with President Reagan's comments regarding the most brutal of all Cold War Latin American leaders, proportionately speaking, Efraín Ríos Montt, who, Reagan claimed, was "totally dedicated to democracy in Guatemala." And, for that matter, it does not explain, as we shall see, the failure of the Reagan administration to address the resistible rise of Manuel Noriega.[29]

In a more relevant speech before the Organization of the American States, Reagan quoted John Kennedy. Reagan said that he "caught the essence of our unique mission when he said that it was up to the New World 'to demonstrate that man's unsatisfied aspirations for economic progress and social progress can best be achieved by free men working within a framework of democratic institutions.'" Reagan's limited and rough equivalent to the Alliance for Progress was the Caribbean Basin Initiative, which was intended to provide new trade opportunities for products from Central America and the Caribbean. Reagan compared it to the Good Neighbor Policy, which he grudgingly suggested "did some good," but was "inadequate for today." Majority Leader Jim Wright called on his fellow Democrats to support Reagan's commitment to doing something for "our closest neighbors." Wright lamented the lack of consistency in U.S. policy toward Latin America, remembering the Alliance for Progress as having offered a "modicum of hope," before the United States had "grown weary of, then indifferent" to it. (He recalled Kennedy's policy toward the military government of Peru and Johnson's "securing an electoral system" in the Dominican Republic.) Democrats should "demonstrate that we support our President when he promises constructive measures for Central America." And Wright also invoked the long-standing fear of "another Cuba."[30]

In domestic terms, a new rhetoric on democracy fit with a shift in focus in El Salvador. Although some in the administration initially had thought that a military solution was possible, this increasingly seemed unlikely. Reagan himself was unwilling to address in public the human rights abuses committed by the Salvadoran military, and while claiming to be impartial, he always sought to deflect any such discussion in his reference to "so-called murder squads" and by focusing on acts of violence by the guerrillas. But even Secretary of State Haig had recognized "the need to support credible elections," and the president agreed. In a letter to Haig, Ambassador Hinton argued that elections were "far more likely to lead to peace than negotiations." And that remained Reagan administration policy for the rest of his presidency.[31]

When elections for the constituent assembly were held in March 1982, the observers included Frances Grant, in her last important political activity (she was well into her eighties by this point). "Masses in the cities stood waiting the day long," she reported to the members of the Inter-American Association for Democracy and Freedom, "defying the threats of personal danger." She hoped that this would galvanize "a New Momentum for Democracy in Latin America." President Reagan himself was struck when he heard the story of a woman standing in line to vote who had been hit by "a bullet ricochet" but refused to have it treated until she had voted. He used this story for the rest of his time in office. Guerrilla attempts to disrupt the elections did not play well, although critics noted that those who criticized the left for not participating in the elections ignored the real danger to their lives from the Salvadoran right had they done so.[32]

The elections helped the administration's case in Congress. Even liberal Democrats who had previously opposed military aid were increasingly torn. Former opponents like Clarence "Doc" Long, chairman of the Foreign Aid Subcommittee in the House, were now more willing to support increased military aid. The administration still had to make the case that improvements were being made in controlling the behavior of Salvadoran security forces and in bringing to trial those who were guilty of human rights abuses. Events like the massacre in El Mozote in December 1981, in which hundreds of people were killed by a U.S.-trained military unit, however, kept congressmen like Harkin in opposition and doubting the willingness of the administration to strengthen civilian authority as he believed Carter had done.[33]

In the words of National Security Adviser Clark, Duarte's successor in 1982 as leader of El Salvador, Alvaro Magaña, had been "selected," "not elected," because of his ties to the armed forces. In the eyes of many, he lacked political legitimacy. The guerrillas' control of territory continued to expand in 1983.

Civilian deaths were as high as ever. Duarte worried that the Reagan administration was strengthening the Salvadoran right. U.S. envoy Richard Stone tried to reassure him that the administration was increasingly rejecting support for dictatorships of the right or left. Duarte expressed concern that this was "all a charade." He wrote Reagan to ask him to make a "declaration of support" in favor of "the democratic process in El Salvador.[34] Soon afterward, Vice President Bush went to El Salvador to send a "tough message" on human rights and "democratic process." But El Salvador remained a political problem for the administration.[35]

Reagan enjoyed a surprising foreign policy victory in Grenada, a British Commonwealth island nation with a population the size of a university town. Factional conflict among members of the left-wing New Jewel Movement provided an opportunity to send in troops in late October 1983, ostensibly either to protect the lives of U.S. medical students studying there or to prevent the Soviets from acquiring an air base. The easy military victory was remarkably popular in the United States, giving Reagan a tremendous burst in opinion polls domestically after an approval rating low of 35 percent at the beginning of the year. Although liberal Democrats initially were skeptical, visits by several congressional delegations in early November led them to support the president's actions. The Sandinistas, not surprisingly, were rattled, but the invasion had no long-term impact on U.S. policy in the Western Hemisphere.[36]

Following the advice of Senator Henry Jackson, D-Wash., a bipartisan commission was formed in the summer of 1983 that was to be chaired by Henry Kissinger and that was intended to build a consensus on Central America. This was ironic in numerous ways, since both Jackson and Reagan had been strong critics of Kissinger and détente. Moreover, Kissinger was not generally regarded as someone with an interest in Latin America. And while the commission included people from both parties, liberals were not well represented. (Majority Leader Wright at that time was still seen as someone who backed bipartisanship in foreign policy.)[37]

Some of those who testified before what became known as the Kissinger Commission, however, spoke as if they were back in the early 1960s. The executive vice president of the Pan-American Development Foundation, former State Department official Edward Marasciulo, invoked the "memory left by [nineteenth-century filibuster] William Walker," and he affirmed that "the real war is the war for social development." Schlesinger expressed concern in a letter to Kissinger that the commission had been "set up not to resolve a perplexity but to ratify policy already decided upon and already in place." He was still worried that large-scale and direct U.S. military intervention was likely. Schlesinger testified before the commission that the Alliance had accomplished much less in terms of economic growth than its founders had hoped, in part because their expectations, based on the postwar German and Japanese experience, as well as that of the Marshall Plan, had been excessive. Nevertheless, he thought that it had made a difference, but it had been necessary to have governments that were committed to the "general welfare" of the "dispossessed." He denounced what he called "unilateral U.S. military intervention" and recommended working with other countries in the region that were committed to promoting peace. The United States could provide the "missing component," but only when the "domestic will is democratic, organized, and resolute." Following Schlesinger's testimony, Kissinger told Schlesinger he hoped he would not be surprised if the commission recommended "something like a revival of the Alliance for Progress."[38]

In a war of words in the pages of the *Washington Post*, Congressman Jack Kemp, R-N.Y., claimed that the commission was indeed proposing "a new JFK-style alliance for democratic prosperity." Kemp backed more "security assistance" for El Salvador (and it was hard to imagine that Kennedy would not have been concerned about an insurgency the size of which he himself had never experienced). Kemp said that he accepted that such support would be conditioned on human rights improvements. Edward Kennedy, however, rejected what he considered "a blank check" for the president's "failing policies in Central America." Central America wanted "diplomatic and political alternatives to more guns, more soldiers, and more killing." He argued that the United States was backing repression in El Salvador and expressed concern that the administration had already made clear that it would ignore the report's human rights recommendations. The United States should ease up on the Sandinistas and provide a chance for negotiations to improve the situation there. The United States needed to reverse the tendency to "militarize" Central America.[39]

Reagan's rhetoric now changed somewhat and became more like Kennedy's in emphasizing Central America's pronounced socioeconomic inequities. AFL-CIO leader Lane Kirkland was expected to set his "lobbyists loose on the Hill" in support of the plan. Reporters soon suggested that a deal was in the making. The commission's report, however, had only a limited impact on congressional support for administration policy in Central America, particularly in Nicaragua.[40] Days before the commission's report was issued, it was discovered that the Central Intelligence Agency had been laying mines in Nicaraguan waterways in violation of international law.[41]

Far more important were the results of the 1984 presidential election in El Salvador. The Reagan administration was anxious to see Duarte elected, despite the Salvadoran military's concerns about him, and particularly since his opponent was Roberto D'Aubuisson, who was responsible for the formation of death squads and for ordering the assassination of Oscar Romero. Oliver

North and Constantine Menges recommended denying D'Aubuisson a visa because of the "astounding increase in right-wing death squad activities." To give D'Aubuisson a visa "would send the wrong signal to both the Salvadoran Right and the Congress."[42] When Duarte won the election, Senator Jesse Helms charged that the United States had paid for his victory.[43] Following the "bitter and divisive campaign," it was considered important to invite Duarte to visit the United States "to strengthen his hand" and to help with the "Jackson Plan." Majority Leader Wright, who had been an official elections observer, called for "steady, emphatic commitment to freedom in El Salvador." A guilty verdict in the case of the deaths of the U.S. churchwomen in late May also helped (though it would take years for Salvadoran military men to be found guilty in the death of Salvadoran civilians). A bipartisan consensus had been achieved on El Salvador. Reagan was able to shower the small country with military aid, making it one of the largest recipients of such aid in the 1980s, almost on par with Israel. Ironically, however, hopes for land reform were not fulfilled.[44]

In South America, which was largely neglected, a movement toward civilian government was gaining momentum. This was due not to Reagan administration rhetoric, but to the collapse of their economies. Military leaders, for the most part (excluding Pinochet), were willing to give up power in countries like Brazil because they had no solution to out-of-control inflation and unemployment. Arthur Schlesinger quoted Mexican novelist Carlos Fuentes as saying, "Never do I remember a time when there are so many democratic leaders in Latin America. What an opportunity for the United States. Think what Roosevelt or Kennedy would have done with it! But this administration is wholly oblivious. The grand opportunity slips by like a ship in the night."[45] Reagan administration hopes of improving relations with Chile were complicated by the democratic transition in Argentina that followed military defeat in the Malvinas Islands. U.S. Ambassador James Theberge expressed concern that the United States would expect more from Chile; "progress toward democracy," he insisted, should not be a condition for the end of sanctions. But some in the administration wanted to "follow an activist but gradual approach to influence an orderly and peaceful transition."[46]

Nicaragua remained far more problematic. By the end of 1982, many Democrats had turned against Contra aid as an illegal attempt to overthrow the government. But they remained frustrated by Sandinista behavior. In response to an opposition leader's urging, a number of prominent Democratic congressmen, including Wright, Barnes, and Stephen Solarz, had written Daniel Ortega to put pressure on the Sandinista to hold elections. The content and the context of the letter became obscured by Republicans hoping to make partisan benefit out of the fact that they had addressed him as "Dear Comandante" (which was his title). When elections were finally held in 1985, they pleased no one. The opposition found it hard to decide whether it should participate in the elections, and the Reagan administration was, at best, ambivalent on the matter. Ortega's victory ultimately resolved nothing.[47]

Liberal Democrats were far more concerned with U.S. policy and Contra behavior. They, for the most part, rejected the argument that aid to the Contras served U.S. interests and had any positive impact on Sandinista policies. They saw the Contras as ineffective and unpopular (in Nicaragua and in the United States). Congressman Barnes, chairman of the Subcommittee on Western Hemisphere Affairs, warned that renewed Contra aid would be a "direct slap in the face" of Latin American leaders who were working to achieve peace. Although not effective militarily, they were still attacking nonmilitary targets and killing civilians. Barnes suggested using the money that could be spent on aid for development programs for "our democratic friends and allies in the region." Speaker O'Neill continued to warn that since aid for such a "ragtag group" could only lead to "slaughter and humiliation." Shame and humiliation would lead to U.S. military intervention.[48]

Daniel Patrick Moynihan, who had worked in the Kennedy, Johnson, and Nixon administrations, and had been Ford's ambassador to the United Nations, has been called a neoconservative. He preferred to think of himself as a "liberal dissenter." He had never been all that interested in Latin America, and he certainly was no admirer of the Sandinistas. But by the end of the first term, Moynihan had become frustrated by what he saw as the failure of the Reagan administration to uphold international law. He was outraged regarding the CIA's mining of Nicaraguan harbors, which led to his resignation as vice chairman of the Senate Intelligence Committee (along with Barry Goldwater, R-Ariz.). And he also thought that the administration had missed an opportunity to bring evidence against the Sandinistas for their involvement in El Salvador before the International Court of Justice when the Nicaraguan government sought a judgment against Reagan administration policies. By abandoning the field to the Sandinistas, and then ignoring the court's decision against them, Moynihan argued, the administration was undermining international law, to the detriment of its own policy goals.[49]

The Democratic presidential candidate in 1984 had been an ally as a young man of Hubert Humphrey, and, of course, Carter's vice president. Walter Mondale promised a renewed commitment to human rights as well as to economic aid abroad. In a debate with Reagan, Mondale was strengthened by the recent publicizing of a CIA manual promoting plans for sabotage and murder in Nicaragua. Mondale warned that covert action was strengthening the Sandinistas. He criticized Reagan for selective memory. His "history of Central America is missing some important chapters." Reagan saw "the Soviets and their proxies—as do we all." But he did not see "the centuries of poverty and oppression." Reagan saw "Cuban soldiers—but not Salvadoran death squads." Reagan, Mondale continued, saw "Sandinistas blocking elections—but not generals blocking land reform." Reagan knew what was wrong with "guerrilla sabotage but not with the CIA mining of Nicaraguan waters." Reagan wanted "the approval of world opinion—but not the judgement of the World Court." Reagan accepted his commission's calls for more aid, Mondale suggested, but not for the improvements in human rights that would help the political situation. "Extremism" was stronger and "democratic forces weaker" because of his policies. Mondale praised Duarte and promised a foreign policy that would give him a chance to succeed.[50] The Democratic Party platform promised to address both national security and human rights, to work for peace and democracy internationally and to restore U.S. influence internationally. The platform labeled Reagan's policies in Central America and the Caribbean a failure, and criticized the administration for failing to work with hemispheric allies to achieve peace. The platform promised that a Democratic administration would move beyond paternalism and work with democratic leaders on common problems. The Democrats considered opposition to Reagan administration policy an issue that worked in their favor, but they overestimated the number of people for whom it was an issue that would decide their vote.[51]

In his campaign, Reagan himself reached out to Democrats who had "been loyal to the party of FDR and Harry Truman and JFK." "Were John Kennedy alive today," Reagan proclaimed, "I think he would be appalled by the gullibility of some who invoke his name."[52] Following his overwhelming reelection, due largely to the U.S. economic recovery, Reagan sought to use what seemed an even clearer case for a mandate to press for his policies in Central America. He began to contrast "the two Central American revolutions of 1979, ours [in El Salvador] has succeeded as Nicaragua's has been betrayed." Despite lingering misgivings regarding the situation on the ground, liberal Democrats generally supported the Duarte government. Far more controversial by this point was support for the Contras. Patrick Buchanan encouraged Reagan to go all out in support, calling the Boland Amendment "an American guarantee of the Brezhnev Doctrine in Central America." With his popularity at a new high, Reagan should not "permit the honor of the United States to be stained again by abandoning a fighting ally in the field, nor to permit a second Cuba." Buchanan thought that nothing else would be more important "to the legacy Ronald Reagan wishes to leave to the American people."[53]

Reagan pressured Congress to change its policies, which Reagan thought were a result of a Sandinista disinformation campaign, and established a near-total economic embargo in May of 1985. Sometimes Sandinista policies and actions aided Reagan in making his case, as when Daniel Ortega paid a visit to the Soviet Union immediately following a vote in Congress to defeat Contra aid. In speaking with Julio López, the head of the Bureau of Political Affairs of the Sandinista government, Schlesinger expressed a wish that the Sandinistas would refrain from doing things that "only strengthen the hard-liners in Washington." Anticipating a Democrat-controlled Congress by 1987 (which did, in fact, happen), Schlesinger said that "if they avoided acts of repression in the meantime, the Democrats would be more sympathetic."[54]

Reagan increased the pressure. Republicans stooped to what Democrats saw as "red-baiting" as they questioned the patriotism of congressmen who opposed Contra aid. But, much to their chagrin, liberal opponents of Contra aid finally lost in mid-1985 and continued to face pressure over a series of votes in 1985 and 1986. Democrats were somewhat reluctant at this point to challenge a popular president, even over unpopular policies. For the moment, Reagan finally got what he wanted, or so it seemed.[55]

The situation of the Contras remained problematic, moreover, in ways that the president continually tried to obfuscate. The size of the army expanded, but its effectiveness did not improve. In late October 1986, Reagan wrote of "reform measures to broaden" the Contras' leadership base, the "elimination of human rights abuses," and the "subordination of military forces to civilian leadership," all points that the president had always insisted were not issues or at least had been addressed at some point along the way. But Reagan won in Congress despite the fact that the merits of the case had not changed.[56]

The administration, however, had begun soliciting aid for the Contras covertly from foreign countries, including Saudi Arabia, in early 1984. It sought private aid in the United States as well. And what, in the end, would be most shocking to the American public, he authorized the sale of weapons to Iran in part to raise revenues for them. All of this was in violation of the law. When the Sandinistas shot down a cargo plane in October 1986 that was delivering aid to the Contras, Reagan policy began a long and then rapid unraveling. Revelations over the following months regarding the extent to which the administration had acted against Congress's expressed will helped end the painfully constructed support. By March 1987 Reagan had to admit at least part of what he had done. The president had undermined a cause he had been deeply committed to; the Iran-Contra Affair, as it became known, stripped the administration of its control over the dynamics in Central America.[57] The Democrats, moreover, had regained control of the Senate in 1987. Liberal Democrats had long supported peace plans for Central America that some of the larger neighboring countries promoted.[58]

Far more important for the direction of Central America policy than the off-year elections in the United States was the election of Oscar Arias as president of Costa Rica in 1986. As he promised, the Contras would no longer find shelter in his country. More importantly, he sponsored a peace plan under which foreign support for guerrilla forces of any kind was to end. Arias received the Nobel Peace Prize in 1987, which was certainly premature but which helped him gain further international legitimacy. The Reagan administration sought to penalize him and his country for their independence, even refusing to send Vice President Bush to Arias's inauguration. Liberal Democrats, for their part, had long supported multilateral efforts by Latin American countries. Speaker Wright, for his part, thought that he could make a deal with Reagan, much to the liberals' dismay. Kennedy initially denounced the plan as a "sham," but the Republicans were appalled when the Sandinistas signed on to an agreement reached among the five Central American leaders that would require an end to foreign aid for local insurgencies. Despite being denounced by the Republicans for supporting the agreement, Wright argued that he had never expected that the Central Americans would have to support the Wright-Reagan plan "verbatim," and that, in any case, the fact that all of the Central American countries had agreed made it more likely that they would follow through. In part because of bitter partisan rhetoric that ended any chance of further collaboration, the Reagan administration was increasingly irrelevant. Wright was now allied with Arias, whom he invited to speak before the House of Representatives. More controversially, Wright was meeting with the Sandinistas, as well as with opponents of the regime like Archbishop Miguel Obando and Adolfo Calero. Arias, for his part, was able to get the Sandinistas to compromise in ways that the Reagan administration had never been able to do. Although Ortega remained skeptical that President Reagan would become "a man of peace," he insisted that all of the countries involved, including his own, must abide by the terms of the agreement.[59]

In South America, the Reagan administration had found it difficult to improve ties with the Pinochet government, and not only because of congressional opposition. As Reagan's second term progressed, Chile was increasingly isolated on the continent. In 1986, Senator Kennedy visited Brazil, Uruguay, Argentina, and Peru, all of which had civilian governments. As his aide Nancy Soderberg remarked, it was "a time when democracy was very fragile, and he wanted to align himself with the Democrats [sic]." He met with Rio de Janeiro Mayor Leonel Brizola, an enemy of his brother's administration in the early 1960s, because Brizola "had an identity with the poor." He also visited Chile, where he received an unfriendly response as a protest organized by the Pinochet regime blocked the road into Santiago, and opposition leaders were pelted with eggs by Pinochet supporters. Kennedy denied that he was an enemy of Chile, insisting that he was "an enemy of torture, kidnaping, murder, arbitrary arrest." He held private meetings with the opposition and spoke to people from a park bench, noting that he had come from countries "where the people say 'no' to military juntas. Will Chile be free one day too?" His listeners responded with a call for a "Chile libre." To a crowd of 800 later, he praised the efforts of advocates for human rights and the right of exiles to return. "I have come to a country which has proven anew that the fire of freedom cannot be extinguished—even when the darkness descends, when dictators rule and law is lost, the flame still warms and moves millions of individual indomitable hearts." He continued, "The dictators of the East or the West, from the far left or the far right, offer only the dim security of the slave—or the final security of the grave." He praised U.S. traditions of civilian control over the military.[60]

U.S. Ambassador Theberge was replaced by Harry Barnes, who received strong support from liberal Democrats like Tom Harkin, who had been elected senator in 1984. (It was the Chilean opposition, Harkin affirmed, that represented the "real freedom fighters.") In his statement upon arriving in Chile, Ambassador Barnes spoke "as the official representative of the oldest democracy in our hemisphere to your country which has had such a rich democratic history." He became a visible supporter of the opposition. He attended the funeral of a young man named Ricardo Rojas, who had been set on fire by military officers because of his involvement in protests. Senator Helms claimed Barnes had "planted the flag of the United States in the middle of a communist" action. An administration policy to promote a democratic transition often had moved forward in part to provide cover for policy in El Salvador, but some in the administration, including Elliott Abrams and Secretary of State George Shultz, were ahead of the president himself. In an early 1987 op-ed piece, Senator Kennedy blasted the administration for not pushing Pinochet harder on human and labor rights. Harkin and Kennedy introduced legislation on new sanctions if the government did not move ahead on a wide range of issues. Concern that Pinochet's intransigence would lead to increased internal polarization led to a surprisingly strong statement by Reagan and Shultz on Chilean democracy. In early 1988, a large portion of the Chilean opposition united (the Communist Party itself was excluded). In a plebiscite later that year, which had been called for in the 1980 constitution, the Chilean people voted against extending Pinochet's time in power beyond 1990. The administration by this time was firmly committed to a transition to civilian rule.[61]

Reagan had made himself a political force on the national level by opposing movement toward a new Panama Canal treaty under Ford. Yet as president he made clear that he intended to abide by the terms of the treaty. Following the death of Omar Torrijos in a plane crash in July 1981, the administration hoped that promises to democratize would be fulfilled. Over the next few years, however, despite occasional symbolic efforts to bolster the authority of civilian political leaders, the Reagan administration did little to prevent the consolidation of power by Torrijos's protégé, Manuel Noriega. As head of Panama's intelligence service and for many years before, he had developed ties to the CIA and the U.S. military and had received training at the School of the Americas. As head of the newly named Panama Defense Forces (formerly the National Guard), Noriega cooperated with U.S. efforts in the region, particularly on aid to the Contras, but also with the Drug Enforcement Agency. The administration and the CIA, however, exaggerated his commitment to civilian government and did not seem to have been too troubled when he removed Nicolás Barletta in 1985. This was certainly a moment when the administration could have done more to shore up civilian authority. When Philippine President Ferdinand Marcos was deposed in March 1986, the administration negotiated with Noriega over granting him asylum and ignored the ostensible president. The available documentary evidence cannot yet make clear what, if any, efforts the administration made to influence the evolution of Panama's political system. The evidence we do have suggests that the administration failed to address Noriega's dominance over Panama until he had already become an embarrassment and a danger to the election of a Republican successor.[62]

Although Noriega's support for administration Cold War policies had made him necessary, the Panama crisis as it evolved became the first post–Cold War inter-American crisis. Reporting on his involvement with drug traffickers was published in the *New York Times* in June 1986. In the following February he was indicted by a federal grand jury in Florida. The issue united liberal Democrats like John Kerry and right-wing conservatives like Senator Helms. Helms hoped that the indictment would provide an opportunity to abrogate the canal treaty. But Reagan reaffirmed his commitment to the terms of the treaty. By June 1987 the United States had suspended economic and military aid to Panama.[63] By May 1988, the administration was considering encouraging the dropping of the indictment against Noriega. Vice President Bush wrote to Reagan to plead with him not to do so. He mentioned the concerns of Los Angeles Police Chief Darryl Gates, who said this would be "a severe blow to those who are on the front line fighting these drug traffickers." Bush recognized that decisions like this could not be based "solely on public outcry." But the "political risks" were "severe." "As the party's standard bearer in the fall," Bush warned, "I will be severely damaged."[64]

Noriega became an issue Democrats could use in the 1988 presidential election, but Reagan and Bush tried to make the election a referendum on liberalism. Reagan had frequently been frustrated by opposition to his foreign policies. He had hoped that if the "American people" saw "what the Washington liberals really believe about foreign policy, the naiveté and confusion of mind, I believe that we would shock the American people into repudiating these views once and for all."[65] With communism no longer much of a threat internationally, the danger was internal. And the promise for the U.S. future was found in free trade. The Republicans sought to claim the Kennedy mantle in promising to "pay any price, bear any burden, support any friend, oppose any foe to assure the survival and success of liberty." The Republicans took credit for the progress of democracy in Latin America and saw an enemy in "communist tyranny" in Nicaragua and "military authoritarianism" in Panama. President Reagan referred to himself frequently on the stump as a "former Democrat," contending that that the Democrats had abandoned the principles that had defined them from Roosevelt to Kennedy. "If, like Harry Truman, you want to continue to help those resisting communism," you should vote for Bush. (He associated Kennedy with "lowering tax rates.") The Democratic Party platform (which was surprisingly skimpy) promised the promotion of human rights internationally (including places where it had not been discussed as much in the past like Asia and South Africa), as well as debt relief for Latin America and support for the Arias peace plan (which the Republican platform did not mention). Michael Dukakis did not offer a defense of liberalism for much of the campaign, which, Schlesinger feared, played "into the hands of his foes" and disappointed and discouraged "his friends."[66]

Over the course of the 1980s, the Reagan administration sought to encourage Latin America to accept that attempts to industrialize had failed. They believed that Latin America should abandon economic nationalism, open its markets more completely, and export its way out of its economic difficulties. Pinochet's Chile had already adopted these policies in the 1970s. In the midst of an economic crisis not seen in the region since the Great Depression (when economic nationalism had come to seem so attractive), privatization of state-owned companies and other measures that were being taken out of necessity were now being portrayed as virtues. A return to the "trade, not aid" verity of the Truman/Eisenhower years was in motion. A free-market fundamentalism took hold that rejected a positive role for the state in transforming society that had been so central to the liberal vision. President Bush built on this with his Enterprise for the Americas initiative, an attempt to create a hemispheric free trade zone.[67] In his inaugural address, the victorious Bush proclaimed that "the day of the dictator is over." Nations were "moving toward democracy through the door to freedom," while men and women of the world were moving "toward free markets through the door to prosperity."[68]

The Democrats failed in their hopes for the White House, but they expanded their control over both houses of Congress. Public opinion on liberalism was evidently split. Although the campaign had been strongly partisan, Bush was determined to forge the bipartisan political consensus that his predecessor had been unable to create. In his inaugural address he addressed his friends, "and, yes, I do mean friends—in the loyal opposition, and, yes, I mean loyal."[69] Nowhere was the search for bipartisanship more obvious than in the approach to Central America. Bush thought that Central America had distracted the United States from dealing with more important parts of the world like Europe and Asia, and his longtime friend and Secretary of State James Baker agreed. Bush, Baker, and Wright began to work together. Bush lacked the strong commitment to the Contras that Reagan had, and he knew that congressional support for them was not forthcoming. Bush chose a Democrat, Bernard Aronson, who had worked in the Carter administration, to be assistant secretary of state for inter-American affairs. (Aronson also had supported Contra aid.) "Humanitarian aid" was provided for the Contras to help them "stay alive," while plans for an election moved forward. By March an agreement had been struck. "For the first time in many years," the executive and legislative branches were "speaking with one voice."[70]

Unlike his predecessor, President Bush embraced the Arias peace plan. He quoted the Costa Rican president frequently on the relationship between democracy and peace. Having missed Arias's inauguration, Bush visited the country during its centennial celebration of democracy. "We are back in San José to honor a nation, Costa Rica; a leader, President Arias, and an idea, democracy." He quoted Kennedy from his own visit regarding "the last vestiges of tyranny," which now could be "counted on one hand." Picking up on President Bush's metaphor regarding "the tide of democracy that is sweeping this hemisphere," President Arias remarked that he had told the Nicaraguan leader and candidate Ortega "many, many times" that if the elections "are free and fair," then Ortega would be "swimming along the tide or with the tide."[71]

El Salvador became a public issue once again. President Duarte had been a success in the U.S. Congress, but not at home. The war dragged on and on at great cost to the population. Duarte had failed to establish civilian control over the military. He imposed an austerity program that primarily hurt his own supporters. The Christian Democrats declined dramatically in popularity, and the turnout in the 1988 elections was down by a third from what it had been in 1982. The president also was terminally ill. By June 1989 El Salvador had a new president, Alfredo Cristiani, a civilian member of the right-wing political party (ARENA) who lacked the appeal abroad that Duarte had, despite an expressed willingness to negotiate an end to the war. Liberal Democrats were torn regarding whether to condition aid on progress toward peace. The turning point in the Salvadoran conflict was another "final offensive" by the guerrillas in November that demonstrated their military capacity and the armed forces' weaknesses, but that did not topple the government or inspire a broader uprising. During the offensive, however, the military ordered the killing of six Jesuit priests who taught at the University of Central America and who were prominent supporters of peace negotiations (their housekeeper and her teenage daughter were also killed). After tens of thousands of Salvadoran deaths over the course of the war, these deaths mattered more than any since the four U.S. churchwomen in 1980, reigniting debate in the Congress. By early 1990, it was clear to many that the military was to blame. Senator Dodd introduced legislation that cut military aid in half and would eliminate all aid if the murders were not investigated. The guerrillas were more amenable to negotiation after the defeat of their Sandinista allies in February and faced a restoration of U.S. military aid if they did not take the negotiations seriously. The 50 percent cut in aid caught the Salvadoran right's attention. With UN and Bush administration involvement, a negotiated peace was achieved. The Salvadoran armed forces, which had grown large on U.S. aid, were dramatically reduced, and the guerrillas laid down their arms and transformed themselves into a political party, which (unlike the Contras in Nicaragua) became an important player in a pluralistic political system.[72]

Panama had been a thorn in Bush's side in the presidential campaign, and Noriega's continuation in power remained one of the major foreign policy issues in the first year of the Bush presidency. There was hope that a presidential election in May would resolve the issue, and former President Carter was called on to observe the election. Carter had been involved in a wide variety of domestic and international humanitarian activities since his defeat in 1980, but, politically, he had been isolated. In the weeks after Bush's election, Secretary of State-Designate James Baker reached out to Carter and visited him in Atlanta. Carter's role in the Panama Canal treaty gave him credibility across the political spectrum in Panama. Carter had been close to Torrijos and was a critic of U.S. economic sanctions. Carter joined with former President Ford to cochair the election monitoring team. In late April Carter wrote Noriega a letter denouncing efforts to manipulate the election. Noriega at first rejected the idea of allowing observers from the United States. When he finally agreed to the people Carter named, the Bush administration began to fear that the Noriega regime believed it could trick the former president. When Carter arrived in Panama City, he invoked Torrijos's plans for a transition to democracy. Despite intimidation and violence on the day of the election, it soon became clear that Noriega's candidate had lost. Carter and his aides spent hours trying to convince the dictator to be a statesman and admit defeat. Some of the other members of the team thought Carter was too slow to denounce Noriega. But when Carter finally spoke, his biographer Douglas Brinkley has written, "he exuded deep sorrow, high-minded morality, and unflappable will" as he detailed the attempts by Noriega to steal the election. Noriega declared a state of emergency and "nullified the elections." (Carter, for his part, had clearly returned to the world political stage.) The Panama crisis continued.[73]

The Bush administration refused to recognize the creation of a new government with Noriega's candidate as the head. Economic sanctions remained in place, but the Bush administration was widely perceived as being weak. Military actions were planned to "heighten Noriega's uncertainty, and keep him and his people off guard," while "maintaining maximum flexibility on our side."[74] Over the next few months, the Bush administration was stymied and frequently criticized for failing to act decisively, not least of all when a military coup occurred in October. Finally, following violence and brutality toward U.S. soldiers and a U.S. soldier's wife, the United States invaded Panama. Within a few days U.S. forces had taken Noriega into custody and brought him back to Florida to stand trial. Carter declared that he did not "approve of the military invasion of Panama and other countries just to depose a leader, no matter how disreputable a criminal the person is." The invasion, like that of Grenada in the Reagan years, was politically popular in the United States. Over the next few months, the invasion was justified as an exercise in democracy promotion. Guillermo Endara, the opposition candidate, had been sworn in as president on the U.S. military base. (Several years later, Endara asked Carter to put together another group to observe the next election.)[75]

In Nicaragua, Carter and Arias saw an election as a way to end the violence in the country. The 1990 election, which has been called the most heavily observed election in history, also gave Carter a role as an observer. Carter had developed a personal relationship with Ortega in travels to the country in 1986. The polls said that the Sandinistas would win, and Carter thought that they would as well. But it was important for Ortega that the election be seen as legitimate. Ortega even accepted massive U.S. financial support for his opponent, Violeta Chamorro, the widow of the journalist whose murder had sparked national rebellions back in 1978. President Bush met regularly with her, and she received strong bipartisan support. Liberal Democrats like Senator Harkin demanded that the funding be overt because they thought covert funding, once it became public knowledge, would undermine U.S. allies. The Sandinistas continued to engage in actions that led Arias to criticize the election process. This time around, many thought that Carter was not impartial. But with the United Nations conducting the "quick count" this time around, it was up to Carter to inform Ortega of his surprising defeat. Unlike in Panama, the results were respected. Secretary of State Baker later said that "it was good that Carter was there to help convince Ortega to do the right thing." Early the next day, Ortega announced that he had lost. For Bush, this experience was of a piece with the experience in Eastern Europe over the preceding year. For the Nicaraguan people, it was a vote for peace.[76]

The Cold War was over (though the fighting continued in Guatemala and Colombia). A return to pre-Kennedy policies of "trade, not aid" represented the new consensus, and bilateral trade agreements, as in the 1930s under Roosevelt, represented the new wave in inter-American relations. The Kennedy legacies now were largely irrelevant. But Latin American socioeconomic inequality remained an obstacle to the development of Latin American democracies, forged in a time of economic crisis. Debt-ridden Latin American governments lacked the will and, more importantly, the resources to address these issues. Victorious in the Cold War, the United States saw no reason to address them either.

Conclusion

Cold War Legacies

The Cold War was a distinct phase in the history of U.S. relations with Latin America. U.S. influence had never been greater in the hemisphere as a whole. It was stronger in South America in particular than it had been before, and stronger than it has been since. Beginning during the Eisenhower administration, liberal Democrats with an interest in the area began to argue that the United States could not afford to be associated with military dictators. The United States was seen as having a special responsibility for Latin America. While rhetorically this had been true since the 1820s, that responsibility had a special meaning during the Cold War, when Latin America was supposed to be part of a Free World led by the United States. As former John F. Kennedy aide and Lyndon Johnson Ambassador to Chile Ralph Dungan wrote to *Newsweek* foreign editor Robert Christopher in August 1966, "I would be inclined to put a bit more on the line in an effort to create an atmosphere that the United States was strongly in favor of political and human rights, even if the risk of losing the game was rather large." This was particularly true in Latin America, where "the atmosphere, or rather what the Latins sense we are for or against, is really important."[1]

The Alliance for Progress, which grew out of a critique of Eisenhower administration policy, promised cooperation in a hemispheric project of socioeconomic transformation to meet the ideological challenge of the Cuban Revolution. The Democratic administrations of the 1960s sought allies they could work with in Latin America, but they found relatively few. The Alliance differed based on those leaders and based on administration perception of threat and opportunity in particular countries. At the same time, the Kennedy administration thought that it could provide more military aid and yet not encourage the establishment of military governments. The Kennedy administration seemed genuinely surprised at times when they could not prevent the establishment of military governments. The Kennedy administration was somewhat successful in encouraging military governments that had recently been imposed to establish timetables for a return to constitutional government, most notably in Peru. Military aid, as well as counterinsurgency and police training, all of which expanded under Kennedy, had long-term consequences, though not necessarily in countries where insurgencies modeled on the Cuban Revolution were strongest in the 1960s. Those consequences might have been less dire had his successors been as engaged as Kennedy generally was in Latin American affairs.

Some in the administration, like Arthur Schlesinger, hoped that the administration would do more to promote democracy. While noninterventionist rhetoric could mask an unwillingness to really do something to achieve this end, the temptation of covert action remained strong and gave the lie to claims to adhere to Good Neighbor promises of noninterference, particularly in terms of U.S. involvement in off-year elections in Brazil in 1962 and the presidential election in Chile in 1964. Some in the Kennedy administration thought that a coup would become necessary once the Brazilian president engaged in unconstitutional acts, but others argued forcefully that he would not necessarily do so, and the administration had made no final decisions in November 1963. Anti-Castro actions, on the other hand, led nowhere in Cuba itself, except to a potentially catastrophic crisis in 1962, and Kennedy's successors largely stuck to containment and a trade embargo. The Kennedy administration was impatient, but those who argue for a changed Latin America policy by the end of November 1963 seem to have misunderstood the president himself, and his disinclination to back himself into a corner.

While President Kennedy was alive, many of those who advised him on Latin American matters thought they were being ignored. But after his death, many of them saw a need to influence, or at least criticize, Johnson administration policy by creating an idealized Kennedy legacy in Latin America, an Alliance for Progress as it should have been. The Johnson Alliance was even more complicated, with aid provided in an ever more direct response to perceived political necessity, as Jeffrey Taffet demonstrated and this study confirms. But the Johnson legacy was, in its own way, itself complicated, with the further consolidation of democracy in Venezuela during a counterinsurgency and the deepening of democracy in reformist Chile under another ideal (and idealized) leader. But even more than these two developments, the more powerful example was set in Brazil, with the Johnson administration supporting the end of democracy and failing to impose a timetable for a return to constitutional government before providing massive aid. Over the course of the 1960s and early 1970s, military government in Brazil became associated with economic stabilization and soon, an "economic miracle." This was as much of a turning point in Cold War Latin American history as the Cuban Revolution had been. And certainly the embrace of a leader in the Dominican Republic who had been seen as unacceptable during the Kennedy years suggested how far the Johnson Alliance had gone astray. Whether it would have done so had it not been for a war in Vietnam deserves further study.

Liberal Democratic Latin America policy could be more ambitious and creative, if also more hypocritical and, in retrospect, perhaps more exasperating.

Republicans tended to be more content with the status quo in Latin America, distrustful of reformists, and unabashedly pro-military rule. There were, of course, liberal Republicans in those years, if fewer of them by the end of the 1980s than before. But few liberal Republicans defined themselves in terms of the Kennedy legacy. Nelson Rockefeller had his own legacy, of course, but it was more focused on hemispheric unity and economic development than democracy, and, in any case, Rockefeller was often marginalized in his own party. Richard Nixon was less liberal on Latin America in 1968 than he had been in 1960, and this would have been a different story if Nixon had beaten Kennedy. The Latin American left lost more than it won during the Cold War, and democracy itself was contained throughout the region as well, which kept the region stable if not progressing.

The costs of containment associated with the war in Vietnam helped weaken the consensus on foreign policy, beginning in the Johnson years. This accelerated under President Nixon, who favored military leaders without any of the remaining ambivalence of Johnson. At the same time, the hopes for development and the belief that the United States could help transform Latin America were abandoned as well, even though liberal Democrats frequently found it politically advantageous to invoke Kennedy's Alliance for Progress.

As the Cold War was one of the factors in the success of the civil rights movement in the United States, so too the Cold War in the age of détente created an opportunity for the rise of human rights as an issue in foreign policy, particularly after the death of Chilean democracy on 11 September 1973. Human rights provided a hope for the United States to recapture the moral high ground that had been seen as lost in Southeast Asia. Given the improvement in its own human rights situation with what many believed had been significant change in U.S. race relations, the United States thought it could gain some Cold War victories. The United States was to a large extent implicated in the military dictatorships that dominated in the 1970s; liberal Democrats themselves now found few kindred spirits to support in Latin America. This created an incentive for many to argue even more strongly that the United States needed to try to moderate the countries' behavior, if not necessarily to change their character. Liberal Democrats sought to reclaim the "exceptionalism" that they saw the extremes of Cold War thinking had tarnished. As Robert Kennedy had in 1968, candidate Jimmy Carter spoke of restoring U.S. moral authority in foreign policy in 1976. Human rights was a popular issue, but it also proved a divisive one for people like Ernest Lefever and Jeane Kirkpatrick, both of whom had been Democrats, who saw human rights as unnecessarily weakening traditional U.S. allies. But the divide did not cut in just one way, since Republicans themselves, for the most part, did not support

Lefever when he was nominated to be human rights czar in the Reagan administration.

Implementing a human rights policy was unprecedented and difficult, but it was seen as a powerful weapon in the Cold War. Jimmy Carter, more focused on Latin America than any president since Kennedy, nevertheless found it hard to make human rights work. Military aid certainly was reduced. Carter had some impact on the South American military governments and on South American democracy and human rights activists, but could not see how to effect long-range progress. Moreover, his inability to choose between the ideals of nonintervention and human rights played a role in his failure to contain an insurgency in Nicaragua, the only successful one following the triumph of Fidel Castro two decades before. This led Carter to revive a small-scale Alliance for Progress to prevent a guerrilla victory in El Salvador.

This containment failure weighed heavily on his successor, who sought to restore good relations with military dictatorships in South America and defeat the Sandinistas and an insurgency the Sandinistas backed in El Salvador. Liberal Democrats were uncomfortable with the Sandinista government, but also with the human rights abuses that accompanied the "Contra" insurgency that was so central to Ronald Reagan's policy. But by 1984, they also found a new ally they could join Reagan in supporting. As in Chile under Johnson, the U.S. ally was a Christian Democrat. As we saw, the administration had initially been reluctant to support José Napoleón Duarte. In Duarte's El Salvador, the cost of containment (and the militarization that Edward Kennedy and others warned about) was once again extremely high. In a "lost decade," economically speaking, South American military governments ceded power to civilian ones without significant U.S. help. (And if forced to choose a U.S. citizen as father of contemporary Latin American democracy, I would argue that it was Federal Reserve Chairman Paul Volcker, whose hiking of interest rates in the late Carter years produced the debt crisis that made this possible.[2]) Another liberal Democratic favorite, Oscar Arias of Costa Rica, helped construct a path for an end to Cold War struggles in Central America that Democrats embraced.

Since the end of the Cold War, Latin America has not been a central concern of the United States. The United States has primarily sought to fight a war on drugs and enhance economic cooperation. U.S. neglect created opportunities for other extra-hemispheric powers, most notably China. Liberal Democratic leaders (and others too) only occasionally saw a security threat in elected left-wing governments (including the return of Sandinista Daniel Ortega, this time without the support of the poets and the priests). Free-market fundamentalism has not delivered on its promises, and socioeconomic inequality remains a major issue in no danger of resolution any time soon.

In recent years, political corruption has been a significant issue in Latin America, though one that has never been addressed in any consistent fashion. One can see the corruption issue developing even as the Cold War ended, when developments during the Bush administration forecast future problems in the region. Leaders favored by the United States would not fare well. The United States had long viewed Venezuela as a model democracy. But over the course of the 1980s, the South American country was hit hard by a precipitous drop in oil prices. Carlos Andrés Pérez, Jimmy Carter's old friend, elected on an anti-austerity platform, had immediately reversed himself following his election, leading to an uprising in the capital city that was crushed with great force. Not recognizing the dangerous new dynamics in the country, Bush praised "the changes your nation is making in its economic orientation," "Venezuela's version of what I have heard described as 'Perezstroika.'" In Brazil, Bush praised economic liberalization that accelerated following its first presidential elections since 1960. Fernando Collor de Mello, from a wealthy landowning family long prominent in politics in the poor northeastern state of Alagoas, was photogenic and actively promoted the kind of privatization programs that the Bush administration supported. Reagan's first ambassador to Brazil, Langhorne Motley, told Bush that Collor had "reacted with the predictable resentment of a Brazilian patriot" when "the Carter administration instructed Brazil on nuclear policy and human rights." Motley told Bush that Collor needed no lectures" and was hoping for "*personal rapport* [emphasis in the original] for future dealings." Bush saw him as the future of Latin America, and perhaps he was, because he would resign on corruption charges in the last weeks of the Bush presidency to avoid being impeached. Pérez suffered a similar fate only a few months later.[3]

Economic crisis in Venezuela in an era of falling gas prices had undercut the model democracy, leading to the rise of a democratically elected left-wing leader, Hugo Chávez, who prospered for a time as oil prices rose, and in recent years, his chosen successor, Nicolás Maduro, neither of whom has been popular among U.S. leaders. By 2019, the country's historic socioeconomic crisis and the questioning of the legitimacy of Maduro's reelection by a wide variety of countries led many to question what the U.S. role should be in Latin America. Many Democratic presidential candidates in 2020 believed that Maduro should resign. But the means of convincing him to do so were controversial. Presidential candidate and Senator Cory Booker, D-N.J., noted that "we cannot simply anoint a new Venezuelan government—that would be repeating the mistakes of our dark history in the region." Most candidates supported some kind of sanctions that would have an impact on top officials (a policy also embraced by President Donald Trump). Candidates almost universally opposed intervention in Venezuela's internal affairs. But only an outlier like Marianne Williamson criticized U.S. actions meant to undermine the Venezuelan government over the previous seventeen years.[4]

As people choose to vote with their feet and not make revolution in their own country, the "threat" to U.S. interests in Latin America has changed. The 2020s may see a new liberal Democratic approach for the Western Hemisphere, but there does not seem to be a need for one "Latin America" policy anymore, as the Carter administration had discovered back in the 1970s. So far, the hemispheric goals of the new administration of President Joseph Biden are limited, as promises of $4 billion in aid to resolve internal matters in Central America are intended to discourage migration. But migration flows are a result of both long-term and shorter-term factors, and the Alliance for Progress should definitely have proven how difficult it is to address short-term concerns that have such deep-rooted causes. Generally, it is not clear that the United States still aspires to hemispheric, let alone global, leadership. Few U.S. leaders and pundits still evoke the notion of a "Free World." And even more rarely does one hear reference to the possibility of the United States being a "good neighbor to the world."[5]

Historians generally prefer a more nuanced portrayal of the U.S. role in the world, and certainly the faith in exceptionalism that often undergirded U.S. claims to leadership rarely has proponents in the academic community. The triumphalism that accompanied the end of the Cold War encouraged little critical thinking about that period of history. But the Cold War may have other lessons worth attending to.

In his foundational work on Kennedy administration Latin America policies, Stephen Rabe lamented, like many a historian, that critical treatments of President Kennedy have not made a dent in his popular reputation, or in his image in Latin America. His signature program, the Alliance for Progress, remained a touchstone for the Democratic Party during the Cold War, as I have shown, despite a general recognition by many that it had been a failure. Like Kennedy's Peace Corps, the Alliance projected an image of U.S. idealism abroad. (The Peace Corps itself, of course, has shown remarkable staying power.) Human rights, for its part, also became associated with a Kennedy for many Latin Americans. In 2008, the president of Chile, Michelle Bachelet, presented the last remaining Kennedy brother, "one of the great and true friends of Chile," with the Order to the Merit of Chile in Hyannis Port, Massachusetts. President Bachelet, a victim of torture herself following the overthrow of the Allende government in 1973, told the terminally ill Massachusetts senator, "You were there for us when human rights were massively and systematically abused. You not only understood, you acted accordingly. In you, we see the United States we love and esteem."[6] Brother Robert would have been pleased.

Notes

Introduction

1. Robert F. Kennedy, "Announcement of Candidacy for President," 16 March 1968, in Guthman and Allen, eds., *RFK: Collected Speeches*, pp. 320–22; see also Palermo, *Robert F. Kennedy and the Death of American Liberalism*, pp. 114 and 131; Gabler, *Catching the Wind*, p. 366. Regarding the impact of the Vietnam War, see, for example, McCrisken, *American Exceptionalism and the Legacy of Vietnam*, pp. 27–33.

2. John F. Kennedy, "Inaugural Address," 20 January 1961, *Public Papers [PPPUS]: Kennedy, 1961*, p. 1.

3. Samuel Moyn, "Imperial Graveyard: Review of *Our Man: Richard Holbrooke and the End of the American Century* by George Packer," *London Review of Books*, 6 February 2020, p. 23; see also Craig and Logevall, *America's Cold War*, pp. 225 and 294.

4. Dwight David Eisenhower, "Special Message to the Congress on the Situation in the Middle East," 5 January 1957, *PPPUS: Eisenhower, 1957*, pp. 6–16; Westad, *Global Cold War*, pp. 66–72, 110–11, and 124–26, Taubman, *Khrushchev*, pp. 348, 354, 359–60, 532–33, 748, and 786–87.

5. Parker, *Hearts, Minds, Voices*, particularly pp. 1–5, 8, and 116–39; Harmer, "The 'Cuban Question' and the Cold War in Latin America, 1959–1964," pp. 127–28 and 149; Muehlenbeck, *Betting on the Africans*, pp. xi–xviii, 34–57, and 223–36.

6. Cobbs Hoffman, *The Peace Corps and the Spirit of the 1960s*, particularly pp. 1–12, 23–35, 183–86, and 251–59.

7. Taffet, *Foreign Aid as Foreign Policy*; Keys, *Reclaiming American Virtue*, particularly pp. 1–10.

8. Brands, *What America Owes the World*, p. vii. At times, U.S. leaders focus more on the conflict between domestic political ideals and practices. At other times, they address the tensions between what they perceive as the success of U.S. democracy at home and the failure of (often exaggerated) attempts at democracy promotion abroad. See, for example, Obama, *A Promised Land*, pp. xv–xvi and 308–10.

9. Smith, *Why Wilson Matters*, pp. 8–9, 12, 13–16, and 19; Manela, *Wilsonian Moment*, pp. xi, 3, 6, 10, and 21; Woodrow Wilson, "Presidential Inaugural Address," in DiNunzio, ed., *Woodrow Wilson: Essential Writings and Speeches*, pp. 366–69.

10. Brands, *What America Owes the World*, pp. 22 and 47–49, Even the best work on Wilson largely ignores Latin America. Mexico aside, Latin America receives four scant pages in Cooper, *Woodrow Wilson*, pp. 245–49. Cooper at least recognizes that for Wilson perceived security considerations were more important than idealistic ones, and that he did not yet see Latin America as ready for democracy. See p. 59. For other examples of the treatment of Latin America by Wilson specialists, see also Ambrosius, *Woodrow Wilson and American Nationalism*, pp. 35–36 and 218–19; Knock, *To End All Wars*, pp. 25–30, 43, and

84. Scholars often rely upon "An Address on Latin American Policy," 27 October 1913, Di-Nunzio, ed., *Woodrow Wilson: Essential Writings*, pp. 380–83. Regarding the limits of knowledge about U.S. activities in the Western Hemisphere, see, for example, Manela, *Wilsonian Moment*, p. 88. Regarding actual U.S. policies, see, for example, Tillman, *Dollar Diplomacy by Force*, pp. 59–91, 102, 122, and 131; Schmidt, *United States Occupation of Haiti*, pp. 8–10, 15, 46–47, 53–56, 58–59, 67, 70–71, and 114–15; Eisenhower, *Intervention!*, particularly pp. xvi, 101–6, 230–34, and 299–308; Rosenberg, "World War I, Wilsonianism, and Challenges to U.S. Empire," pp. 852–63; Wright, "Unilateral Pan-Americanism," pp. 46–64. Regarding Roosevelt's role in the expansion of U.S. responsibilities, see, for example, Thompson, *Great Power Rising*, pp. 2, 5, 79, and 82–92. For Secretary of State Robert Lansing's attempts to rein Wilson in, see LaFeber, *Inevitable Revolutions*, p. 55. Note the Democratic Party's expression of commitment to respect for the sovereignty of "small states" in "1916 Democratic Party Platform," 14 June 1916, pp. 6–7, *American Presidency Project*, www.presidency.ucsb .edu.

11. "Republican Party Platform of 1912," 18 June 1912, p. 5, and "Republican Party Platform of 1924," pp. 2 and 7, 10 June 1924, *American Presidency Project*, www.presidency.ucsb.edu.

12. "1920 Democratic Party Platform," 28 June 1920, p. 5, "1924 Democratic Party Platform," 24 June 1924, pp. 19 and 23, "1928 Democratic Party Platform," 26 June 1928, pp. 10–11, *American Presidency Project*, www.presidency.ucsb.edu.

13. Brandes, *Herbert Hoover and Economic Diplomacy*, pp. 49, 197, and 199; Herbert Hoover, "Annual Message to the Congress on the State of the Union," 3 December 1929, *PPPUS: Hoover, 1929*, p. 406; McPherson, "Herbert Hoover, Occupation Withdrawal, and the Good Neighbor Policy," pp. 623–39; McPherson, *The Invaded*, pp. 211–12; Gellman, *Good Neighbor Diplomacy*, particularly pp. 29–39, 44–48, 58, 117–41, 211, and 226–28. It should be noted that Herbert Hoover rejected what he called a "false liberalism" in favor of his own classical liberal beliefs. See "Addresses during the Campaign: New York City, 22 October 1928," *PPPUS: Hoover, 1929*, p. 583. Regarding his postelection trip, see "Addresses during a Trip to Central and South America," pp. 615–58. On his first stop in Honduras, he began by announcing, "I come to pay a call of friendship. . . . I would wish to symbolize the friendly visit of one good neighbor to another." Regarding liberalism as understood during the Cold War, see, for example, Hamby, *Liberalism and Its Challengers*, pp. 3–5.

14. "Draft by Sumner Welles of a Statement on Pan-American Policy," roughly 21 February 1933, and "From the Inaugural Address of March 4, 1933," in Nixon, ed., *Franklin D. Roosevelt and Foreign Affairs*, vol. 1, pp. 18–20; Pike, *FDR's Good Neighbor Policy*, pp. 128–32, 164–76, and 208; Schmidt, *United States Occupation of Haiti*, 106–7. Regarding Roosevelt's understanding of Wilson, see "Speech by Roosevelt at the Woodrow Wilson Foundation Dinner, Mayflower Hotel, Washington, December 28, 1933," in Nixon, ed., *Franklin Roosevelt and Foreign Affairs*, vol. 1, particularly pp. 558–60: in the speech he makes clear his opposition to armed intervention; the 1932 Democratic Party platform promised "reciprocal tariff agreements." See the Cordell Hull quotation in Lochery, *Brazil: The Fortunes of War*, p. 2; Zeiler, *Free Trade, Free World*, pp. 3–4 and 7–13; see "1932 Democratic Party Platform," 27 June 1932, pp. 2, 3, and 5, and "Republican Party Platform of 1932," p. 11, in *American Presidency Project*, www.presidency.ucsb.edu.

15. Pike, *FDR's Good Neighbor Policy*, pp. 137–47 and 221–23; Freidel, *Franklin D. Roosevelt*, pp. 216–17; "1936 Democratic Party Platform," 23 June 1936, p. 9, *American Presidency Project*, www.americanpresidency.ucsb.edu.

16. Roorda, *The Dictator Next Door*, pp. 27 and 38–39; Gobat, *Confronting the American Dream*, pp. 205–20. Ironically, Gobat argues, the power of the National Guard derived from U.S. efforts to promote free and fair elections. Rural strongmen were replaced by one single patron, the National Guard.

17. "1940 Democratic Party Platform," 15 July 1940, p. 3, and "Republican Party Platform of 1940," 24 June 1940, pp. 4 and 5, *American Presidency Project*, www.americanpresidency .ucsb.edu.

18. Reich, *Life of Nelson A. Rockefeller*, pp. 166–69, 172, 208, and 216–17; Rivas, *Missionary Capitalist*, pp. 2–6, 51–52, and 58–63; Cobbs, *Rich Neighbor Policy*, pp. 38–45; Richard Norton Smith notes that Roosevelt was Rockefeller's "lifelong hero." See *On His Own Terms*, pp. xvi, 121, 142, 164, 193, and 211. By 1944, the Republicans were claiming that they could provide "a genuine Good Neighbor Policy, commanding their respect, and not one based on the reckless squandering of American funds by overlapping agencies." See "Republican Party Platform of 1944," 2 June 1944, p. 3, *American Presidency Project*, www.american presidency.ucsb.edu.

19. Langley, *America and the Americas*, pp. 156–66; Truman, "Special Message to the Congress Transmitting Bill for Inter-American Military Cooperation," 6 May 1946, *PPPUS: Truman, 1946*, pp. 233–35; McCann, *Brazilian-American Alliance*, particularly 147, 149–50, 187–88, and 197–459; Freidel, *Franklin D. Roosevelt*, pp. 367, 386, and 458. The Latin American Training Center—Ground Division, based in the Panama Canal Zone, was created in 1946. It became the U.S. Army School of the Americas in 1963. See Nelson-Pallmeyer, *School of Assassins*, p. 2.

20. Smith, *Democracy in Latin America*, pp. 37–38, 315, 319, and 346–51; Drake, *Between Tyranny and Anarchy*, pp. ix, x–xii, 1–3, 6–7, 133–62, and 165–66; Bethell and Roxborough, "Latin America between the Second World War and the Cold War," pp. 167–89; Spruille Braden Papers, Columbia University, Archival Collections, Box 36; Roorda, *Dictator Next Door*, pp. 186 and 203–14; Ellis O. Briggs to Secretary of State, 5 July 1944, Rockefeller Archive Center, Record Group 4, Nelson Aldrich Rockefeller, Personal, Department of State, Assistant Secretary of State, Box 18, Folder 125; Schwartzberg, *Democracy and U.S. Policy in Latin America during the Truman Years*, pp. 1–7 and 45–90.

21. Adolf Berle Jr. Diary, 3 September 1945, Adolf Berle Papers, Franklin D. Roosevelt Presidential Library, Box 217, August 1945–1951 Diary, August–October 1945 folder. For an early expression of his interest in Latin America, see Arthur M. Schlesinger Jr., "Good Fences Make Good Neighbors: Bradenism Is Bankrupt and the U.S. Is Trying Again, but a Hemispheric Army Alone Cannot Counter *Peronismo* and Communism," *Fortune*, August 1946, pp. 131–35, 161, 163–64, 167–68, and 170–71.

22. Leffler, *Preponderance of Power*, p. 7. Leffler is, of course, not really focused on Latin America.

23. Leffler, *Preponderance of Power*, pp. 11, 54, 172–73, and 449. Regarding "Latin Americanist" concerns regarding the region's place in overall U.S. policy, see, for example, Rockefeller to Hull, 4 April 1944, RAC, RG 4, NAR, Personal, CIAA, Box 6, Folder 45; Rockefeller to Roosevelt, "Memorandum for the President: Suggested U.S. Policy toward Latin America," 3 January 1945, RG 4, NAR, Personal, Department of State, Assistant Secretary, Box 20, Folder 144; Truman, "Message to the Congress on the State of the Union and on the Budget for 1947," 21 January 1946, *PPPUS: Truman, 1946*, p. 43; Truman's fullest statement on the Good Neighbor Policy is "Address before the Governing Board of the Pan American Union," 15 April 1946, *PPPUS: Truman, 1946*, pp. 200–202; Truman exaggerated the

commitment of his administration and the nations of Latin America to democracy; Truman, "Special Message to the Congress on Greece and Turkey," 12 March 1947, *PPPUS: Truman, 1947*, pp. 176–80; Leffler, *Preponderance of Power*, pp. 59–60; Smith, *Last Years of the Monroe Doctrine*, pp. 41–63.

24. Leffler, *Preponderance of Power*, pp. 12–13.

25. Zeiler, *Free Trade, Free World*, pp. 4–5, 14, 19, 75–88, 138–40, 145–46, 150, 164–65, 167–71, and 191–94.

26. Nasaw, *Remarkable Life and Turbulent Times of Joseph P. Kennedy*, p. 637.

27. Offner, *Hubert Humphrey*, p. 5; "Progressive Party Platform," in Johnson, ed., *National Party Platforms*, particularly pp. 436–41; "Platform of the States' Rights Party," 14 August 1948, "Republican Party Platform of 1948," 21 June 1948," pp. 2, 11, and 12, *The American Presidency Project*, www.presidency.ucsb.edu.

28. "1948 Democratic Party Platform," 12 July 1948, pp. 1–7 and 16, *The American Presidency Project*, www.presidency.ucsb.edu. Henry Wallace had demonstrated great interest in Latin America during his vice presidency. See Culver and Hyde, *American Dreamer*, particularly pp. 296–300.

29. Bethell and Roxborough, "Latin America between the Second World War and the Cold War," pp. 168–69, 177–80, and 182–85; Schwartzberg, *Democracy and U.S. Policy*, pp. 165–67; French, *Brazilian Workers' ABC*, pp. 181–84; Pavilack, *Mining for the Nation*, pp. 245–48; Lockhart, *Chile, the CIA and the Cold War*, pp. 91–92 and 114–17; Field, "Transnationalism Meets Empire," pp. 305–34. Others have examined the impact of liberal anticommunism on political dynamics in the United States. See, for example, Offner, *Humphrey*, pp. 43–48.

30. Longley, *The Sparrow and the Hawk*, particularly pp. 21–22, 28–30, 42, 47, 52, 56–57, 63–91, and 100–101; Moulton, "The Dictators' Domino Theory," pp. 945–61; Ameringer, *Democratic Left in Exile*.

31. Schlesinger, *Vital Center*, pp. 8, 13–14, 16, 24, 98, 102, 145, 166–68, 199, 208, 218, and 219–29.

32. Beisner, *Dean Acheson*, pp. 270–72; Reich, *Life of Nelson Rockefeller*, pp. 430–32 and 447–67; Rivas, *Missionary Capitalist*, pp. 173–206; Cobbs, *Rich Neighbor Policy*, pp. 59–74; the quotation is from Smith, *On His Own Terms*, p. 212; Westad, *Global Cold War*, p. 51. Cobbs writes, "Ironically . . . American leaders virtually did away with foreign aid as a policy or practice where it was first developed." See p. 3. See also Truman, "Annual Budget Message to the Congress 1953," 21 January 1952, *PPPUS: Truman, 1952–1953*, p. 73.

33. See documents in Frances Grant Papers, Minutes, Box 27, Planning Committee, 1949–1950 folder; Grant to Mario Monteforte Toledo, 1 June 1949, IADF, General Files, Box 55, Guatemala, 1949–1950 and 1981 folder; Grant, "Remarks at a Meeting of the Pan American Women's Association, Reporting on the Havana Conference for Democracy and Freedom," Grant Papers, Rutgers University, Pan-American Women's Association, Box 19, General Files, 1950–59, Havana Conference Report, 1950. Regarding those who participated in the event and those who gave it moral support, see "Inter-American Association for Democracy and Freedom: Report of the Havana Conference, Havana, Cuba—May 12–15, 1950," Grant Papers, IADF Publications, Box 63, Havana Conference Report. See also former Oregon Congressman Porter and Alexander, *The Struggle for Democracy in Latin America*, which is dedicated to Grant, "who for three decades has aided the struggle for democracy in Latin America." See also Ameringer, *Democratic Left in Exile*, pp. 222–34; Longley, *Sparrow and the Hawk*, pp. 121–22; Figueres Ferrer, "Mensaje de José Figueres Ferrer a la Con-

ferencia Interamericana Pro Democracia y Libertad," 12 May 1950, *Escritos de José Figueres Ferrer*, pp. 369–14.

34. Beisner, *Acheson*, pp. 12, 13–14, 15, 117, 266–80, 469, and 579–84; Immerman, *CIA in Guatemala*, pp. 128–33; Gleijeses, *Shattered Hope*, pp. 238–42; Cullather, *Secret History*, p. 31; Longley, *The Sparrow and the Hack*, particularly p. 123. As Immerman shows, liberal favorite Figueres was also strongly opposed to the Guatemalan leader but did not want to see any plan implemented that required a significant role for Somoza. Gleijeses suggests, "There was no liberal way to overthrow Árbenz—the road to Guatemala City passed through Managua, not through San José." See Gleijeses, *Shattered Hope*, pp. 240–41. In the end, there was no proof that the Soviet Union and Guatemala under Árbenz were working together. See Immerman, *CIA in Guatemala*, p. 185.

35. Schwartzberg, *Democracy and U.S. Policy*, 204–15; Pérez, *On Becoming Cuban*, p. 448.

36. "1952 Democratic Party Platform," 21 July 1952, pp. 1–2, 5, 7, 10, and 11, *The American Presidency Project*, www.presidency.ucsb.edu.

37. Leffler, *Preponderance of Power*, pp. 271–72.

38. "Republican Party Platform of 1952," pp. 2, 4, 5, 7, and 8, *The American Presidency Project*, www.presidency.ucsb.edu; Cobbs, *Rich Neighbor Policy*, pp. 196–97.

39. See, for example, "Roosevelt to the Congress," 2 March 1934, in Nixon, ed., *Franklin D. Roosevelt and Foreign Affairs*, vol. 2, pp. 1–3; "Roosevelt to the Congress," 3 January 1936, "State Department Draft of a Foreign Policy Statement for the Democratic Platform," 17 June 1936, and "From the 1936 Democratic Party Platform," in Nixon, ed., *Franklin Roosevelt and Foreign Affairs*, vol. 3, pp. 152–53, 327–29, and 336–37; Wood, *Making of the Good Neighbor Policy*, pp. 7, 52, 59, 118–40, 148–52, 155, 285–87, and 360–61; Gellman, *Good Neighbor Diplomacy*, pp. 29–39, 44–48, 58, 117–41, 211, and 226–28. Gellman asserts, "The ascension of Harry Truman to the White House ended the Good Neighbor era."

40. See "Democratic Party Platform of 1952," "Democratic Party Platform 1956," and "Republican Platform 1956," in Johnson and Porter, eds., *National Party Platforms, 1840–1972*, pp. 476, 527–28, and 556.

41. See Wood, *Dismantling of the Good Neighbor Policy*, pp. x and 152–90.

42. Immerman, *CIA in Guatemala*, pp. 4–5; Hitchcock, *Age of Eisenhower*, pp. xvi, xvii, 51–52, 57, 87–88, 99, and 108; Mackenzie and Weisbrot, *Liberal Hour*; Johnson, *Congress and the Cold War*, p. 115; Leffler, *For the Soul of Mankind*, pp. 8–9, 57–58, and 79–83. Regarding Guatemala, see Eisenhower, "Address at the Illinois State Fair at Springfield," 19 August 1954, and "Address at the Hollywood Bowl, Los Angeles, California," 23 September 1954, *PPPUS: Eisenhower, 1954*, pp. 731 and 870; Eisenhower also admired the reciprocal trade agreements achieved under Roosevelt. See Eisenhower, "Annual Message to the Congress on the State of the Union," 3 February 1953, *PPPUS: Eisenhower, 1953*, p. 15.

43. Eisenhower, "Letter to the President of the Senate and the Speaker of the House of Representatives Recommending Establishment of a Commission on Foreign Economic Policy," 2 May 1953, *PPPUS: Eisenhower, 1953*, pp. 252–54; Eisenhower, "Annual Budget Message to the Congress, Fiscal Year 1956," 17 January 1955, *PPPUS: Eisenhower, 1955*, p. 129.

44. Berle, 16 October 1958 diary entry, FDR Library, Berle Papers, Diary, Box 219, 1956–60, 1958 folder.

45. See, for example, Kruse, *Fault Lines*, pp. 7, 14–15, 17, and 34; Kalman, *Right Star Rising*, pp. 38–39, 60–61, and 77–90; Borstelmann, *The 1970s*, pp. 25, 27–29, 30–33, 45, 202–7, and 272.

Chapter 1

1. Arthur M Schlesinger Jr. to William McCormick Jr., 15 February 1955, in Schlesinger and Schlesinger, eds., *Letters of Arthur Schlesinger*, p. 104. Schlesinger "helped draw up the principles" for the Inter-American Association for Democracy and Freedom. See Frances Grant to *Newsweek*, 4 August 1965, Frances Grant Papers, Alexander Library, Special Collections, Correspondence, Box 30, Arthur Schlesinger Jr. folder. In a 6 January 1955 letter to José Figueres, Schlesinger lamented that the "definition for a possible Latin America policy for the United States is lacking." See Arthur M. Schlesinger Jr. to Figueres, Private Files, John F. Kennedy Library, Incoming Correspondence Files, Box B-13, José Figueres (1953–1961) folder. The evolution of Schlesinger's thinking on Latin America and the Alliance for Progress is discussed in Schlesinger, *A Thousand Days*, pp. 170–75 and 186–205. Regarding the Dwight David Eisenhower administration's support for dictatorship, see, for example, R. P. Crenshaw to Staats, 15 April 1957; "De-Briefing of U.S. Ambassador to Venezuela, Dempster McIntosh," 15 April 1957, Dwight David Eisenhower Presidential Library, White House Office Files, National Security F Staff, Operations Coordinating Board Central Files, Box 76, OCB Latin America Files 10 (4) folder. At least some in the State Department thought that "the decoration" of the Venezuelan president "was a mistake." See Ambassador John Casper Dreier, "Statement on the United States and the Promotion of Political Democracy in Latin America," 15 July 1957, Record Group 59, National Archives II, Assistant Secretary for Inter-American Affairs (Rubottom) 1957–1959, Box 3, OAS folder; "Progress Report on U.S. Policy toward Latin America," NSC 5613/1, White House Files, NSC Staff, OCB Central Files, Box 77, OCB 901.4, Latin America File #11 (7) folder. In this latter document it was argued that "continued U.S. adherence to the policy of nonintervention in the internal affairs of Latin America countries including dictatorships has strengthened the view of liberal circles in Latin America and in the United States that this government favors dictatorships."

2. Eisenhower, "The President's News Conference of March 19, 1953," *PPPUS: Eisenhower, 1953*, p. 31; Eisenhower, "Annual Message to the Congress on the State of the Union," 7 January 1954, *PPPUS: Eisenhower, 1954*, p. 9.

3. See José Figueres to Schlesinger, 24 October 1954, Adlai Stevenson Papers, Princeton University Library, Seeley G. Mudd Manuscript Library, Box 73, Folder 9, Arthur Schlesinger 1954 folder. Note that Figueres noted that "with all their advantages, modern republics have made Plato's philosopher-king impossible." See also Kyle Longley, *The Sparrow and the Hawk*, pp. 1–4, 7–10, 25–27, 45–85, and 121–24. Costa Rica's democracy evolved over a long period of time, which could be said of few Latin American countries other than Chile and Uruguay. The major biography of Schlesinger ignores, for the most part, his lifelong interest in Latin America: Aldous, *Schlesinger*. See also Schlesinger, "Good Fences Make Good Neighbors," *Fortune*, August 1946, pp. 131–35, 161, 163, 167–68, and 170–71; and Schlesinger, *A Life in the Twentieth Century*, pp. 391–93. For a discussion of liberal anti-communism and realism in foreign policy, see Freedman, *Kennedy's Wars*, pp. 13–17.

4. Martin, *Adlai Stevenson and the World*, pp. 110–12, 162, and 276. Regarding his plans to visit Latin America, see p. 457. The Organization of American States and the United States had supported Figueres when his government was attacked by forces aided by Nicaraguan dictator Anastasio Somoza. See 18 January 1955 speech, Adlai Stevenson Papers (MC #124), Box 150, Folder 7, Series 2: Speeches, 2 January 1955–22 March 1955 folder. Schlesinger praised

the statement for its impact on Latin America even if it "caused no excitement on La Salle Street" in Chicago. See Schlesinger to Stevenson, 25 January 1955, Adlai Stevenson Papers (MC #124), Box 73, Folder 10, Arthur M. Schlesinger, 1955. Schlesinger noted the "immense sense of neglect" in Latin America. Regarding the events themselves, see Longley, *The Sparrow and the Hawk*, pp. 142–49. Regarding the complacency as far as Latin America was concerned, see Harry S. Truman, "Annual Budget Message to the Congress: Fiscal Year 1953," 21 January 1952, *PPPUS: Truman, 1952–1953*, p. 73. See the issues Stevenson's study groups were examining in 1955 in Martin, *Stevenson and the World*, p. 205.

5. Robert J. Alexander to Adlai Stevenson, 24 January 1955, 24 November 1955, 26 December 1955, and 16 January 1956, and Stevenson to Alexander, 13 December 1955 and 25 June 1956, Adlai Stevenson Papers (MC #124), Box 2, Folder 11, Robert J. Alexander folder. See also the undated letters from Stevenson's aides regarding Alexander's offer. Regarding the authorship of the lines in the Tampa and Pensacola speeches, see Schlesinger to Newt Minow, 28 April 1956, Box 73, Folder 11, Arthur M. Schlesinger 1956 folder, and "Banquet at Pensacola, Florida, 14 April 1956, in Box 155, Folder 1, Series 2: Speeches, April 10, 1956–April 17, 1956. Alexander encouraged Stevenson to recognize the potential of Brazil. See Alexander to Stevenson, "Report on Brazil," 13 May 1956, Adlai Stevenson Papers (MC #124), Box 2, Folder 11, Robert J. Alexander folder.

6. Figueres to Schlesinger, 22 December 1955, Adlai Stevenson Papers (MC #124), Box 73, Folder 10, Arthur Schlesinger Jr. 1955.

7. H. A. Hoyt, ARA, "Some Thoughts on the Evaluation of the Nixon Trip," 14 May 1958, and Rubottom for Nixon, 15 May 1958, RG 59, NARA II, Assistant Secretary for Inter-American Affairs (Rubottom) 1957–59, Box 7, 1958 Nixon Trip folder; "Exchange of Letters between the President and President Kubitschek of Brazil," 10 June 1958, *PPPUS: Eisenhower, 1958*, pp. 463–65; Kubitschek to Eisenhower, 19 July 1960, White House Office Files, Office of the Staff Secretary, Eisenhower Library, International Series, Box 2, Brazil (3), March–December 1960 (note that Kubitschek still felt that he did not have Eisenhower's attention even at this late date); Dulles to Kubitschek, 7 August 1958, John Foster Dulles Papers, Eisenhower Library, JFD Chronological Files, Box 16, August 1958 (2) folder (Dulles wrote that he "was deeply impressed by the fact that your own personality embodies this dynamic concept" of development); regarding the Nixon trip and the plans for a trip by President Eisenhower's brother Milton, see, for example, Allen W. Dulles, "Memorandum for the Secretary of State: The Likelihood of Anti-U.S. Demonstrations during Dr. Eisenhower's Central American Tour," 27 May 1958, Eisenhower Library, John Foster Dulles Papers, White House Memoranda, Box 8, Series: Conv. with Dulles, Allen W. (All Intelligence Material) (3) folder; "Telephone Call to Allen Dulles," 19 June 1958, Eisenhower Library, John Foster Dulles Papers, Telephone Call Series, Box 8, June 2, 1958–July 31, 1958 (5) folder; Taffet, *Foreign Aid as Foreign Policy*, pp. 13–19; Alexander, *Juscelino Kubitschek and the Development of Brazil*, particularly pp. 160–253 and 279–96; Darnton, "Asymmetry and Agenda-Setting in U.S.-Latin American Relations," pp. 55–92.

8. Eisenhower, "Toast by the President at a Dinner Given in His Honor by President Alessandri," 29 February 1960, *PPPUS: Eisenhower, 1960–1961*, p. 251; McPherson, *Yankee No!*, pp. 9–11 and 20–37.

9. Eisenhower, "Special Message to the Congress on the Establishment of the Inter-American Development Bank," 11 May 1959, *PPPUS: Eisenhower, 1959*, p. 373; Rabe, *Eisenhower and Latin America*, pp. 101–16.

10. See Eisenhower's response to the assassination of Guatemalan dictator Carlos Castillo Armas, "Statement by the President on the Death of President Armas of Guatemala," 27 July 1957, and "The President's News Conference of July 31, 1957," *PPPUS: Eisenhower, 1957*, pp. 570 and 573. Eisenhower called the Guatemalan leader "a champion of freedom and a strong anti-Communist." Eisenhower also praised his secretary of state, John Foster Dulles, as "a foe only to tyranny." See "Statement by the President on the Death of John Foster Dulles," 24 May 1959, *PPPUS: Eisenhower, 1959*, p. 419; Dreier to Rubottom, "Attitude of United States and OAS toward Dictatorial Government," in NARA II, RG 59, Assistant Secretary of State for Inter-American Affairs (Rubottom), 1957–59, Box 12, 1959 Dictatorships folder; Rubottom to Cabot, Box 15, 1959 Policy Folder; NSC 5902, "Statement of U.S. Policy toward Latin America," NSC 4902/1, 16 February 1959, Eisenhower Library, White House Office Files, OSA, NSA, NSC Series, Policy Papers Subseries, Box 26, NSC 5902—Latin America (1) folder; Rubottom to Acting Secretary (Herter), NARA, RG 59, ASSIAA (Rubottom), 1957–1959, Box 16, 1959—Visits—Latin America. See, for example, "Memorandum of a Conversation between the President and the Acting Secretary of State, White House, Washington, December 23, 1959," in *Foreign Relations of the United States [FRUS], President Eisenhower's Trip in 1960*, p. 270. Note that NSDC 5902 in February 1959 specifically discounted the possibility of an "overt Communist aggression or takeover" in any Latin American country. See also Taffet, *Foreign Aid as Foreign Policy*, p. 19. Regarding Betancourt's ties to the IADF, for example, see his "Address at Farewell Dinner," 5 February 1958, Grant Papers, Latin American Country Files, Box 48, Venezuela: Personalities, Rómulo Betancourt, Dinner, 1958 folder. See also "Second Inter-American Conference for Democracy and Freedom," Maracay, April 22–27, 1960, Report of U.S. Delegation," IADF General Files, Maracay Conference, 1956–1961 folder.

11. Rubottom also suggested that the fault lay more with Latin America than with the United States. See Rubottom to Cabot, 2 February 1959, in RG 59, Assistant Secretary of State for Inter-American Affairs (Rubottom), 1957–59, Box 15, 1959 Policy folder.

12. See Smith, *Tiger in the Senate*, pp. 25–27; 117–20, 146–59, 179–87, 209–11, 261–68, 313–19, 327–28, 394, 400–406, and 417–19. Regarding Wayne Morse's long-standing internationalism, see, for example, Divine, *Foreign Policy and U.S. Presidential Elections, 1940/1948*, p. 163; Wayne Morse, "A Changing World Calls for a Changing Foreign Policy," 20 October 1959 Speech at Oregon's International Relations Club, pp. 6–7, Wayne Morse Papers, University of Oregon Library, Special Collections, General Correspondence, Series A, Box 49, Foreign Policy 1958–1960 folder. In Szulc, *Twilight of the Tyrants*, the veteran correspondent suggested that "indications are that democracy, so late in coming and still taking its first shaky and tentative steps forward, is here to stay in Latin America." See p. 4. For the larger domestic context, see, for example, Johnson, *Congress and the Cold War*, particularly pp. 14–34. See also Leffler, *For the Soul of Mankind*, pp. 9, 57–58, and 83.

13. Wayne Morse, "How Many Foreign Policy Mistakes Can We Afford?" Speech Delivered before the Illinois Independent Voters, 22 April 1958, Chicago, Illinois, Wayne Morse Papers, General Correspondence, Series A, Box 44, Foreign Policy 1958–1960 folder; Morse, "Shall Our Foreign Policy Be Guided by the Experts or the Politicians," pp. 13, 15–16, and 18–19, Excerpts from Senator Morse's Remarks, Colgate Foreign Policy Conference, 5 July 1958, in Morse Papers, General Correspondence, Series A, Box 44, Foreign Policy 1958–1960 folder. Regarding Eisenhower administration military aid programs, see, for example, Eisenhower, "Annual Budget Message to the Congress: Fiscal Year 1955," 21 Janu-

ary 1954, *PPPUS: Eisenhower*, 1954, p. 136; See the discussion of military aid in Johnson, *Congress and the Cold War*, pp. 77–78, and Francis, "Military Aid to Latin America in the U.S. Congress." pp. 389–404.

14. See Frank Church, "An Inter-American Police Force: Would It Work?" pp. 1–3, 4, and 6, undated but from 1959, Senator Frank Church Collection, Boise State University Library Special Collections, Series 2.2, Foreign Relations, Box 44, Latin America 1957–60 folder. For a lengthy if incomplete treatment of Church's thinking on Latin America, see Tremayne, unpublished doctoral dissertation, "Delusions and Reality." See also Grant to Secretary of State John Foster Dulles, 27 March 1958, Grant Papers, Latin American Country Files, Box 41, Cuba before 1959 folder.

15. See Carl Marcy to Frank Church, 21 March 1957, Senator Frank Church Collection, Series 2.2, Foreign Relations, Box 47, Latin America—Dominican Republic folder; note that Church was already opposed to what he considered excessive government secrecy (including the Mutual Security Act), which "had no relation whatever to the real needs of our national security." See his 26 February 1960 letter to Drew Pearson, in Box 44, Latin America 1957–1960 folder.

16. See the materials in Lincoln Gordon Papers, Harvard Business School, Box 7, Conferences and Meetings, Box 7, John F. Kennedy Library. See also Gordon, "A Proposal for a Program of Research and Experimenting in Initiating New Joint U.S. and Foreign Enterprises Abroad," March 1956, Gordon Papers, Harvard Business School, Box 56, Subject Files, Brazil Research Project, Proposals 1956 folder. (Gordon was interested in more investment in Brazil by smaller U.S. companies, and he was pleased that the Kubitschek administration was supportive of further private investment.) Gordon to Joseph E. Slater, Assistant Managing Director, Development Loan Fund, 25 November 1960, Gordon Papers, Harvard Business School, Box 65, Subject Files, Foreign Aid Policy, 1961 (1 of 4) folder. See also Roy R. Rubottom Jr., "Address: Latin American Development and U.S. Industry," in Box 9, as well as "Exploratory Mission to Latin America—1959," Box 54, Subject Files: Exploratory Mission to Latin America July–August 1959 (1 of 2) folder; Alfred Wolf, Lincoln Gordon, and Reynold Carlson, "Ford Foundation Mission to Brazil," July–August 1959, Subject Files, Box 64, Ford Foundation Mission to Brazil, Background Material and Notes, 1959–1960 (1 of 4) folder. See also Gordon, "A Long-Range Approach to Foreign Aid," p. 5, Lincoln Gordon Papers, Ambassador to Brazil, Box 114. See also Smith, *Lincoln Gordon*, pp. 59, 63–64, 118–61, and 213–16. Frank Church's interest in Latin America was partially sparked by a conference on inter-American economic relations in Buenos Aires in 1957. See Tremayne, "Delusions and Reality," pp. 37–43.

17. For a surprisingly brief discussion of the liberal Democratic response to the Cuban Revolution, see Welch, *Response to Revolution*, pp. 112–15. Regarding Grant and the IADF, see, for example, "Batista Routed by Rebels," "Cuba Begins Renaissance," and "Weathervane," *Hemispherica*, January 1959, February 1959, and September 1959, respectively; see also Grant to Roberto Agromonte (former ambassador and Ortodoxo politician and member of the new government), 23 January 1959, Grant Papers, Latin American Country Files, Box 41, Cuba: Before 1959 folder; See Church's 9 February 1969 letter to Mr. and Mrs. Norbert Brinkman of Idaho Falls, the 24 February 1960 letter to Zenda Rose (a high school student in Weston, Idaho), the 4 May 1960 letter to James H. Bradley of Pocatello, the 25 June 1960 letter to Archie Kennedy of Blackfoot, and the 12 August letter to Mr. and Mr. T. D. Cowan of Boise, in Senator Frank Church Collection, Series 2.2, Foreign Relations,

Box 46, Cuba 1959–60 folder. For a general overview of congressional opinion regarding Cuba, see McKercher, "Steamed Up," pp. 599–627. The crowds Michelle Chase describes in her article on Cuban outrage regarding the denunciation of the trials by Morse and others presumably did not know or may not have cared that Morse had been a staunch critic of Batista. See her "The Trials," in Grandin and Joseph, eds., *A Century of Revolution*, particularly pp. 165–72 and 179–86.

18. See, among others, Schlesinger to William Blair, 16 November 1959, and Blair to Schlesinger, 24 November 1959, Adlai Stevenson Papers (MC #124), Box 74, Folder 1, Arthur Schlesinger, 1959–1960 folder; see also Figueres to Stevenson, "Memorandum," 9 November 1959, and 22 January 1960, and Stevenson to Figueres, 4 February 1960, Box 449, Folder 3, Series 9, Travel Materials, Costa Rica: 1960 folder.

19. Johnson, ed., *Papers of Adlai E. Stevenson*, vol. 7, pp. 402–45; Stevenson to Figueres, 14 April 1960, Stevenson Papers, Princeton University, Box 449, Folder 3, Series 9, Travel Materials: Costa Rica 1960; Benton to William Blair, 30 November 1959; Benton, "Call upon the Governor by Augusto Frederico Schmidt," pp. 7–8, Box 452, Series 9, Travel Materials, William Benton, Excerpts 1960 folder, and Benton to Stevenson, 25 April 1969, Stevenson Papers (MC #124), Box 11, Folder 1, William Benton, November 1959–April 1960 folder; "Governor Stevenson's Press Conference: Santiago, Chile: March 7, 1960," pp. 5–6, Box 448, Folder 2, Series 9, Travel Materials, Chile—Correspondence: 1960 folder; See also Galbraith to Stevenson, 4 December 1959, Box 36, Folder 2, John Kenneth Galbraith; Schlesinger and Schlesinger, eds., *Letters of Schlesinger*, p. 104; Martin, *Stevenson and the World*, pp. 478–91. See also Benton, *Voice of Latin America*.

20. U.S. Congress, Senate, *Report of Senator Wayne Morse on a Study Mission to the Committee on Foreign Relations*, 20 February 1960, pp. 2, 3, 19, 21, 27, and 33. The countries he visited were Argentina, Bolivia, Brazil, Chile, Colombia, and Venezuela; see also Johnson, *Congress and the Cold War*, pp. 84–85.

21. U.S. Congress, Senate, *Report of Senators Wayne Morse and Bourke R. Hickenlooper to the Committee on Foreign Relations*, 27 February 1961.

22. Frank Church, 19 August 1960 Press Release, Senator Frank Church Collection, Series 2.2, Foreign Relations, Box 44, Latin America 1957–1960 folder.

23. Schlesinger, *Thousand Days*, p. 21; Wayne Morse to *Washington Star*, 4 November 1959, in Wayne Morse Papers, General Correspondence, Series A, Box 70. Morse was also critical of Senator Hubert Humphrey, D-Minn., primarily for his support of military aid for dictators, but considered him "many times preferable to Kennedy." See his 7 June 1960 letter to Loyd M. Key of Milton-Freewater, Oregon, in the same box, John Kennedy folder. See Ashby and Gramer, *Fighting the Odds*, p. 175, and Schlesinger, *Thousand Days*, pp. 9–14. Regarding Morse and Kennedy, see p. 21. Schlesinger was aware that Kennedy often tried to appear more liberal in his conversations with him. See p. 119.

24. Ashby and Gramer, *Fighting the Odds*, pp. 125–26 and 129–35.

25. Schlesinger and Schlesinger, eds., *Letters of Arthur Schlesinger*, p. 17.

26. Schlesinger to Stevenson, 16 May 1960, in Schlesinger and Schlesinger, eds., *Letters of Schlesinger*, p. 198. Schlesinger feared that if Kennedy thought he and economist John Kenneth Galbraith might "cause the slightest trouble when he starts appealing to Republicans, he will drop us without a second thought." See 15 July 1960 entry in Schlesinger and Schlesinger, eds., *Journals, 1952–2000*, pp. 78–79.

27. Galbraith to Stevenson, 12 August 1960, Stevenson Papers (MC #124), Box 36, Folder 2, John Kenneth Galbraith.

28. Schlesinger and Schlesinger, *Journals, 1952–2000*, p. 78.

29. Logevall, *JFK: Coming of Age in the American Century*, pp. xix, 448–51, 486–87, and 554–56; Stephanson, "Senator John F. Kennedy: Anti-Imperialism and Utopian Deficit," pp. 1–24; Schlesinger, *Robert Kennedy and His Times*, pp. 100–101; Freedman, *Kennedy's Wars*, pp. 32–41. The major work on Kennedy's Latin America policies is Rabe, *The Most Dangerous Area in the World*. Regarding Benton, see Jason C. Parker, *Hearts, Minds, Voices*, pp. 18 and 20. Benton had also advised Nelson Rockefeller when he headed the Office of Inter-American Affairs.

30. See Preble, *John F. Kennedy and the Missile Gap*; Dean, "Masculinity as Ideology," pp. 29–62. Regarding the 1958 election, see, for example, Martin, *Stevenson and the World*, pp. 442–43. Kennedy's definition of liberal comes from "Speech of Senator John Kennedy, Commodore Hotel, New York, New York: Acceptance of Liberal Party Nomination, September 14, 1960," in Senate Subcommittee on Communications, *Freedom of Communications: Final Report*, p. 239.

31. John F. Kennedy, "Remarks of Senator John F. Kennedy Speaking at Democratic Dinner, San Juan, Puerto Rico," 15 December 1958, in FDR Library, Berle papers, Subject Files, 1946–71, Box 94, Latin American Task Force folder.

32. "Excerpts from Address of Senator John F. Kennedy, Stanford University, Palo Alto, California," 12 February 1960, Pre-Presidential Papers, John F. Kennedy Library, 1960 Campaign Files, Speeches, Statements, and Sections, Foreign Affairs: New Approach to Latin America folder.

33. Adolf Berle, 24 January 1958, 31 January 1958, 26 March 1958, and 2 April 1958 diary entries, FDR Library, Berle Papers, Diary, Box 219, 1956–60, 1958 folder. See also the 7 April 1958 letter to Figueres in the same folder. Regarding Berle's role in favor of Eisenhower administration policy toward Guatemala, see Longley, *Sparrow and the Hawk*, pp. 122–23. Regarding the State Department, see 12 May 1958 letter from Figueres to Berle. See Berle to Villeda Morales, 9 July 1958. For more on Castro, see Berle to Schlesinger, 16 April 1958, Schlesinger, John F. Kennedy Library, Private Files, Incoming Correspondence File, 1945–1960, Box No. P-9, Adolf Berle (1947–1960) folder. The reference to "our mutual friend, Don Pepe" is in Berle to Schlesinger, Schlesinger, Private Files, John F. Kennedy Library, Incoming Correspondence File, 1945–1960, Box No. P-9, Adolf Berle (1947–1960) folder. In the previous year, Schlesinger made a "rewarding and exciting trip to Costa Rica," the "beacon of democratic hope throughout the hemisphere." See Schlesinger to Figueres, 14 September 1954, Box P-13, José Figueres (1953–1960) folder.

34. Berle, 16 October 1958 diary entry, FDR Library, Berle Papers, Diary, Box 219, 1956–60, 1958 folder. President Eisenhower "said it was strange that he used to think of Betancourt as a leftist and now was beginning to look like a rightist in relation to the pro-Castro, pro-Communist attacks against him." See "Memorandum of a Meeting with the President, White House, Washington, November 29, 1960, 11:00 a.m.," *FRUS, 1958–1960*, vol. 6: *Cuba*, p. 1127.

35. Berle, 9 December 1958 entry, FDR Library, Berle Papers, Diary, Box 219, 1956–60, 1958 folder.

36. Berle, 29 December 1958 and 28 December 1959 diary entries, FDR Library, Berle Papers, Diary, Box 219, 1956–60, 1958 and 1958 Diary folders.

37. See Berle to Frances R. Grant, 15 October 1958, Secretary General, Inter-American Association for Democracy and Freedom, FDR Library, Berle Papers, Diary, Box 219, 1956–60, 1958 folder.

38. Berle, 25 March 1959 diary entry, FDR Library, Berle Papers, Diary, Box 219, 1956–60, Diary 1959 Folder.

39. Berle, 25 March 1959, 17 April 1959, 20 April 1959, 1 May 1959, 20 May 1959, and 8 June 1959 diary entries, FDR Library, Berle Papers, Diary, Box 219, 1956–60, Diary 1959 folder; see the discussion of this time period in Brown, *Cuba's Revolutionary World*, pp. 47–68.

40. Berle, 28 June 1960 diary, FDR Library, Berle Papers, Box 219, Diary, 1956–1960, Diary 1960 folder.

41. Berle, 14 July 1960 and 19 July 1960 diary entries, FDR Library, Berle Papers, Box 219, Diary, 1956–1960, Diary 1960 folder.

42. Berle, 21 July 1960 entry, FDR Library, Berle Papers, Box 219, Diary, 1956–1960, Diary 1960 folder.

43. Berle, 14 October 1960 and 26 October 1960 diary entries, FDR Library, Berle Papers, Box 219, Diary, 1956–1960, Diary 1960 folder.

44. See Adolf Berle speaking for Senator John Kennedy, 6 October 1960, pp. 3–4, and Liberal Party Broadcast, 25 October 1960, in FDR Library, Berle Papers, Box 151, Speeches 1960, Speeches May–December 1960 folder.

45. "Democratic Platform 1960" and "Republican Platform 1960," in Johnson and Porter, eds., *National Party Platforms*, pp. 578–79 and 605. See also Divine, *Foreign Policy and U.S. Presidential Elections, 1952/1960*, p. 216.

46. See, for example, Chester Bowles to Dean Rusk, "Considerations Regarding the Selection of Top Policy Makers," 18 December 1960, in JFK Library, Papers of Arthur Schlesinger, White House Files, Subject File, 1961–1964, Box WH3A. Regarding Eisenhower, see, for example, John Foster Dulles, Memorandum for the President, 3 September 1953, Eisenhower Library, John Foster Dulles Papers, JFD Chronological Series, Box 5, Dulles Chronological Sept 1953 folder. Regarding the Kennedy-Roosevelt connection, see Leuchtenburg, *In the Shadow of FDR*, p. 106. For Kennedy speeches, see, among others, "Advance Release Text: Speech of Senator John F. Kennedy, VFW Convention, Detroit, Michigan, August 26, 1960," "Text of Telephone Address by Senator John F. Kennedy, AMVET Convention, Miami Beach, Florida, August 26, 1960," "Speech of Senator John F. Kennedy, High School Auditorium, Pocatello, Idaho, September 6, 1960," "Speech of Senator John F. Kennedy, Civic Auditorium, Portland, Oregon, September 7, 1960," "Remarks of Senator John F. Kennedy, Cortez Hotel Plaza, El Paso, Texas, September 12, 1960," and "Remarks of Senator John F. Kennedy, Liberty Mall, Cook Memorial Library, Libertyville, Illinois, October 25, 1960," Senate Subcommittee on Communications, *Freedom of Communications: Final Report*, pp. 51–52, 55, 128–29, 159, 199, and 745. Regarding the Good Neighbor Policy and democracy promotion, see, for example, Robert J. Alexander to Stevenson, "Report on Brazil," 13 May 1956, Adlai Stevenson Papers (MC #124), Box 2, Folder 11, Robert J. Alexander folder. For a provocative discussion of how Latin America did (or did not) become part of the Third World, see Parker, *Hearts, Minds, Voices*, particularly pp. 116–39.

47. Schlesinger, 6 August 1960 journal entry, in Schlesinger and Schlesinger, eds., *Journals*, p. 81.

48. "Speech by Senator John F. Kennedy, Democratic Rally, George Washington High School Stadium, Alexandria, Virginia, August 24, 1960," "Press Conference of Senator John F. Kennedy, Portland, Maine, WGAN-TV, September 2, 1960," "Remarks of Senator John F. Kennedy, The Alamo, San Antonio, Texas, September 12, 1960," and "Speech by Senator John F. Kennedy at a Democratic Fund-Raising Dinner in Syracuse, New York, September 29, 1960," Senate Subcommittee on Communications, *Freedom of Communications: Final Report*, part 1: *Kennedy Speeches*, pp. 43–44, 87–88, 202–3, and 411. His longest treatment of Cuba is "Speech of Senator John F. Kennedy, Cincinnati, Ohio, Democratic Dinner, Thursday, October 6, 1960," pp. 510–16.

49. Inter-American Association for Democracy and Freedom Press Release, 26 October 1960, Grant Papers, IADF General Files, Box 55, Cuba—B Press Releases 1959–60 folder.

50. "Following Are Excerpts of Remarks by Senator John F. Kennedy, Johnstown, PA, October 15, 1950," "Text of a Telegram to Vice President Richard M. Nixon from Senator John F. Kennedy on Fifth Debate, Dated October 23, 1960," in *Freedom of Communications: Final Report*, part 1: *Kennedy Speeches*, pp. 607–8 and 725–26, as well as "Partial Transcript of the Speech of the Vice President at Muhlenberg College Gymnasium, Allentown, PA (October 22, 1960)," "Remarks of the Vice President, Market Square, Harrisburg, PA, October 24, 1960," and "Remarks of the Vice President at Downtown Rally, Fresno, CA, November 4, 1960," Senate Subcommittee, *Freedom of Communications: Final Report*, part 2: *Nixon Speeches*, pp. 710–11, 719, and 1025. In earlier public statements, Nixon had rejected calls for a Big Stick approach toward Cuba. See "Speech by Vice President Richard M. Nixon, VFW Convention, Detroit, Michigan, August 24, 1960," and "Press Conference of Vice President Richard M. Nixon, Hotel Sheraton, Detroit, Michigan, August 24, 1960," Senate Subcommittee, *Freedom of Communications, Final Report*, part 2: *Nixon Speeches*, pp. 31 and 33. He noted that "getting rid of Castro" would not "solve the problem of Communist appeal in Latin America, as well as in Cuba." He promised that Cubans, having learned what communism was under Castro, would get rid of him, "just as the Guatemalans got rid of their communists." See "Remarks of Vice President Nixon, Television Program, Channel 4, New York, NY, October 20, 1960," p. 695. In the Muhlenberg speech, he suggested that only a "quarantine" policy had been necessary to remove the government of Jacobo Árbenz. See p. 712. Regarding the violation of treaties, see Nixon's comments on *Face to Face*, "Nixon-Kennedy, Fourth Joint Television-Radio Broadcast, Friday, October 21, 1960," Senate Subcommittee, *Freedom of Communications: Final Report*, part 3: *Joint Appearances*, p. 265. Schlesinger claimed that Kennedy had not even seen the statement on Cuba, blaming Richard Goodwin (with the approval of Sorensen and Pierre Salinger). Schlesinger emphasized Kennedy's interest in "collective action." "In all probability, Kennedy would have approved the text, although he told me later he would have changed the phrase "fighters for freedom" to "forces of freedom."" He suggested Schlesinger call James Reston and Walter Lippmann and say that Kennedy was offering "moral and psychological, not military, support." Schlesinger denied that Cuba was a "central theme" of the campaign. See Schlesinger, *Thousand Days*, pp. 72–73; Divine, *Foreign Policy and U.S. Presidential Elections, 1952/1960*, pp. 268–70.

51. "Remarks of the Vice President at Fordham University, Bronx Gym, Bronx, NY, October 5, 1960," "Partial Transcript of Speech by the Vice President, Public Hall, Cleveland, Ohio, October 6, 1960," "Remarks of Vice President Nixon, Television Program, Channel

4, New York, NY, October 20, 1960," and "Press Conference of Vice President Richard M. Nixon, Honolulu, Hawaii, August 3, 1960," Senate Subcommittee, *Freedom of Communications: Final Report*, part 2: *Nixon Speeches*, pp. 444, 479, 695, and 1167.

52. Berle, 28 November 1960, 8 December 1960, and 9 December 1960 diary entries, FDR Library, Berle Papers, Box 219, Diary, 1956–1960, Diary 1960 folder. Sorensen on behalf of President-Elect Kennedy to Berle, 6 December 1960, FDR Library, Berle Papers, Box 94, Subject Files, 1946–71, Latin American Task Force folder; Martin, *Stevenson and the World*, pp. 552–54. See also Smith, *Lincoln Gordon*, pp. 219–23, and Schlesinger, *Thousand Days*, p. 157.

53. Berle to Sorensen, 18 December 1960, FDR Library, Berle Papers, Box 219, Diary, 1956–1960, Diary 1960 folder.

54. See "Task Force on Immediate Latin American Problems," 4 January 1961, Pre-Presidential Papers, John F. Kennedy Library, Transition Files, Task Force Reports, Box 1074, Latin America folder. See John F. Kennedy, "Letter to Adolf Berle on Receiving Final Report of the President's Task Force on Latin America." 8 July 1961, in *PPPUS: Kennedy, 1961*, p. 497. More revealing, naturally, are the entries in Berle's 1961 diary, available in the FDR Library, Berle Papers, Box 220, Diary 1961–1965, January–May 1961 folder. See, particularly, 5 January, pp. 2–3; 8 January, pp. 1–2; 27 February, p. 11; 3 May, pp. 1–2; 20 June, p. 4; 29 June, p. 1; and 7 July, pp. 2–4. Regarding the possibility of losing of the Cold War in Latin America, see Berle to Moscoso, 10 January 1961, in FDR Library, Berle Papers, Box 94, Subject Files, 1946–1971, Latin American Task Force, Jan–Feb 1961 folder.

55. "Latin America: Draft Resolution, Americans for Democratic Action, 13th Annual Convention," Grant Papers, Box 53, Americans for Democratic Action, January 6, 1958–November 20, 1958 folder.

56. See, for example, Chester Bowles to Dean Rusk, "Considerations Regarding the Selection of Top Policy Makers," 18 December 1960, in JFK Library, Papers of Arthur Schlesinger, White House Files, Subject File, 1961–1964, Box WH3A.

57. See, for example, Chester Bowles to Dean Rusk, "Considerations Regarding the Selection of Top Policy Makers," 18 December 1960, in JFK Library, Papers of Arthur M. Schlesinger Jr., White House Files, Subject File 1961–1964, Box WH3A, Chester Bowles 12/18/60–4/18/61 folder.

58. See, for example, Muehlenbeck, *Betting on the Africans*, particularly pp. 37, 47, and 122–40.

59. Field, *From Development to Dictatorship*; Gobat, *Confronting the American Dream*.

60. "Report to Honorable John F. Kennedy from Adlai Stevenson," November 1960, Pre-Presidential Papers, John F. Kennedy Library, Transition Files, Box 1074, Adlai Stevenson Report folder; Stevenson to Sorensen, 30 December 1960, Stevenson Papers (MC #124), Box 47, Folder 4, John F. Kennedy.

61. Lincoln Gordon, "Latin American Economic and Social Development," and "Essential Points for Inclusion in Early Comprehensive Statement on Economic and Social Policy toward Latin America," both 15 December 1960, Gordon Papers, Harvard Business School: Subject Files, Box 78, Latin American Aid and Development folder. In a 13 February 1961 personal letter to Kennedy Holland, president, Institute of International Education, Gordon noted that his "own connection with the task force" was "concerned with the implementation of the Bogotá program."

62. Schlesinger, 6 February 1961 journal entry, Schlesinger and Schlesinger, eds., *Journals*, p. 103. Note here his early thoughts on the "middle class revolution."

63. Frances R. Grant, "Whither, U.S. Policy?" *Hemispherica*, December 1960, p. 1. She worried that "democratic sectors" could not "resist a new disillusionment." "If we fail again to understand their problems, the future will hold U.S. responsible for their failure; as we must hold ourselves responsible."

Chapter 2

1. Kennedy, "Inaugural Address," 20 January 1961, *PPPUS: Kennedy, 1961*, p. 1–3; Martin, *Stevenson and the World*, p. 568.

2. "The President's News Conference of January 25, 1961," *PPPUS: Kennedy, 1961*, p. 10–11 and 23. For the "peaceful revolution of hope," see also "Annual Message to the Congress on the State of the Union," 30 January 1961, p. 23.

3. Schlesinger, "Journals: 14 February 1961," pp. 93–94, Arthur M. Schlesinger Jr. Papers, New York Public Library, Journals, Box 311, March 1961 folder.

4. Knock, *Rise of a Prairie Statesman*, particularly pp. 101–2, 123, 158–59, 161–64, 180–86, 215–20, 224–25, 256–57, and 259–61. For a further explication of his thinking on "agricultural surpluses as a constructive instrument of American foreign policy," see George S. McGovern, "Food for Peace Resolution," 28 January 1959, George McGovern Papers, Box 470, Congress, 1957–1960 Food for Peace folder, Mudd Manuscript Library, Princeton University; McGovern, *War against Want*. For his opinions on Henry Wallace, see his *Grassroots*, pp. 43–45. Regarding the background of the Food for Peace program, see Ahlberg, *Transplanting the Great Society*, pp. 11–41 and 45–58.

5. Schlesinger, "Journals: 14 February 1961," pp. 10–13 and 18, Arthur M. Schlesinger Jr. Papers, New York Public Library, Journals, Box 311, 1961 February folder; Knock, *Rise of a Prairie Statesman*, pp. 261–64.

6. Schlesinger, "Journals: 14 February 1961," pp. 43, 45, Arthur M. Schlesinger Jr. Papers. Manuscript and Archives Division, Astor, Lenox, and Tilden Foundations, Journals, Box 311, 1961 February folder; George McGovern, "Food for Peace Mission: Argentina and Brazil, February 14–20, 1961," McGovern Papers, Box 474, "Latin American Food for Peace Mission" folder, and McGovern to Kennedy, "Resume of Country Reports of the Food for Peace Mission Technical Study Mission to South America, February 13–March 13, 1961," 30 March 1961, Mudd Manuscript Library, Princeton University.

7. Schlesinger, "Journals: 14 February 1961," pp. 46, 49, and 53, Arthur M. Schlesinger Jr. Papers, New York Public Library, Journals, Box 311, 1961 February folder.

8. Schlesinger, "Journals: 14 February 1961," pp. 23–24, Arthur M. Schlesinger Jr. Papers, New York Public Library, Journals, Box 311, 1961 February folder.

9. Anson, *McGovern*, p. 109; "McGovern, "Resume of Country Reports of the Food for Peace Technical Study Mission to South America, February 13–March 13, 1961," and McGovern to Kennedy, 18 July 1962, McGovern Papers, Box 472 Reports: Re Food for Peace, 1961 folder.

10. George C. McGhee to Berle, "Implementation of the Act of Bogotá," 3 March 1961, Richard Goodwin Papers, John Kennedy Library, Subject Files, Box 1, Act of Bogotá Implementation folder. One immediate response was the creation of a pilot project to provide "surplus feed grains to increase the production of protein-rich poultry and livestock." See

"Statement by the President on the Progress of the Food for Peace Programs in Latin America," 29 March 1961, *PPPUS: Kennedy, 1961*, p. 245.

11. Kennedy, "Address at a White House Reception for Members of Congress and for the Diplomatic Corps of the Latin American Republics." 13 March 1961, *PPPUS: Kennedy, 1961*, pp. 171–72 and 174.

12. Taffet, *Foreign Aid as Foreign Policy*, pp. 20–23, 26–27, and 29–35.

13. Kennedy, "Address at a White House Reception for Members of Congress and for the Diplomatic Corps of the Latin American Republics," 13 March 1961, *PPPUS: Kennedy, 1961*, p. 175. See U.S. Ambassador to Chile Charles Cole's remarks regarding President Kennedy's praise for the Bolivian revolution, which, as the ambassador characterized it, armed the workers, confiscated land without compensation, and took over mines and the property of other foreign companies. See Cole to Edwin Martin, 29 October 1963, JFK Library, Edwin Martin Papers, Box 21, Travel—Bolivia folder.

14. Gordon, "United States Relations with Latin America, Especially Brazil," August 1961, JFK Library, Gordon Papers, Series 3: Ambassador to Brazil, Articles and Publications, Box 115, United States Relations folder.

15. "Declaration of Latin American Democratic Parties, March 18, 1961: On President Kennedy's Speech of March 13, 1961," Stevenson Papers (MC #124), Box 32, Folder 9, José Figueres, Mudd Manuscript Library, Princeton University.

16. See Schlesinger to Kennedy, 10 March 1961, and Accompanying "Report to the President on Latin American Mission, February 12–March 3, 1961," in *FRUS, 1961–1963*, vol. 12, pp. 10–18.

17. Kennedy, "Message to President Kubitschek of Brazil," 29 January 1961, and "Address at a White House Reception for Members of Congress and for the Diplomatic Corps of the Latin American Republics," 13 March 1961 in *PPPUS: Kennedy, 1961*, pp. 28, 171, and 174. On the background of the Alliance for Progress, see *FRUS, 1961–1963*, vol. 12, particularly pp. 1–10. The best work so far on the Alliance for Progress by a historian is Taffet, *Foreign Aid as Foreign Policy*. His primary focus is on the four countries (Brazil, Chile, Colombia, and the Dominican Republic) that received 60 percent of the Alliance aid, and on the Johnson years. Taffet argues convincingly that the Alliance was "a political program designed to create certain types of political outcomes." See p. 10. The Alliance needs to be understood both in the Latin American context and in the larger drive for "modernization" and "development." See Kirkendall, *Paulo Freire and the Cold War Politics of Literacy*, and Cullather, "Development? It's History," pp. 641–53. The creation of the Agency for International Development, like the Peace Corps, was one of the long-lasting institutional achievements of the Kennedy administration.

18. See, for example, Latham, *Modernization as Ideology*, particularly pp. 3–8, 23–31, 44–46, 55–68, and 69–108; see also Andrew David and Michael Holm, "The Kennedy Administration and the Battle over Foreign Aid: The Untold Story of the Clay Committee," pp. 65–67.

19. "Memorandum for the President" and "Report to the President on Latin American Mission, Feb 12–March 3, 1961," particularly pp. 1, 4, 8, and 16, in JFK Library, Arthur Schlesinger Jr. Papers, White House Files, Subject files, Box WH-14, Latin America—report—3/10/61 folder.

20. Grant to Berle, 7 February 1961 and 21 February 1961, Grant Papers, Correspondence, Box 29, Adolf Berle folder. See "Statement by the AFL-CIO Executive Council on Political Relationship with Latin America, February 18, 1961, Miami Beach, Fla.," in JFK Library,

Arthur Schlesinger Jr. Papers, White House Files Subject Files, Box WH-13, Latin America 1/7/61–2/28/61 folder.

21. "ADA 14th Convention: Latin American Resolution," 14 May 1961, in Schlesinger Papers, White House Files, Subject File 1961–1964, Box WH-3, Americans for Democratic Action 5/31/61–5/14/61 folder.

22. James Loeb to Schlesinger, White House Files, John Kennedy Library, Classified Subject Files, Box WH-43 Peru 5/61–8/62 folder.

23. Schlesinger, "Journals: 25 June 1961," p. 219, Arthur M. Schlesinger Jr. Papers, New York Public Library, Journals, Box 311, June 1961 folder. See Schlesinger to Arthur and Elizabeth Schlesinger (undated, mid-June 1961), Schlesinger and Schlesinger, eds., *Letters of Schlesinger*, pp. 245–46; Schlesinger to JFK, "Memorandum for the President: Bureau of Inter-American Affairs, Department of State," 27 June 1961, JFK, Arthur Schlesinger Jr. Papers, White House Files, Subject Files, 1961–1964, Box WH-2, Alliance for Progress, 6/27/61–3/15/62 folder.

24. As the group struggled in mid-1962, an "alternative would be to make Bobby chairman, but I can hear State scream." See RFK to Bundy, 23 July 1962, Kennedy Library, NSF, Meetings and Memoranda, Box 319, Special Group (CI) Meetings 6/8/61–11/2/62 folder. Francis, "Military Aid to Latin America in the U.S. Congress," pp. 402–4. The administration also supported the dramatic expansion of police training programs. Although these have their roots in the constabulary training programs of the early twentieth century, they did not during the Cold War result in the coming to power of police, unlike military, officers in Latin America. See Kuzmarov, "Modernizing Repression," pp. 191–208 and 220–21.

25. Kennedy to Fowler Hamilton, Agency for International Development, 19 February 1962, JFK, NSF, Meetings and Memoranda, Box 335, NSAM folder; L. D. Battle to Bundy, 5 February 1962 and 28 February 1962, in Box 333, NSAM 118: State/Def Report folder. In Box 332, NSAM 114 folder, see Bundy to Rusk, 2 November 1961, "Training for Friendly Police and Armed Forces in Counter-Insurgency, Counter-Subversion, Riot Control and Related Matters." Robert Kennedy had suggested a team from the FBI and the military survey the security situation in an 11 September 1961 memo to the president. See Box 331, NSAM 88 folder. Military aid and modernization programs were often inextricably linked; see Latham's discussion of Vietnam in *Modernization as Ideology*, pp. 151–207.

26. See Kennedy to McNamara, "Training of Latin American Armed Forces," 5 September 1961, in *FRUS, 1961–1963*, vol. 12: *American Republics*, p. 180; for an extended discussion of these issues with the Joint Chiefs of Staff, see "Memorandum of Conference with President Kennedy," 23 February 1961, in *FRUS, 1961–1963*, vol. 8, pp. 48–54. See also "Memorandum from the Executive Secretary of the Department of State (Battle) to the President's Special Assistant for National Security Affairs (Bundy)," p. 221, and "U.S. Policy for the Security of Latin America in the Sixties," 19 May 1961, in *FRUS, 1961–1963*, vol. 12, pp. 173–76; Rusk, "Circular Telegram from the Department of State to All Posts in the American Republics," 18 April 1962, p. 226. Regarding the relationship between military aid and the Alliance, see "Memorandum from the Joint Chiefs of Staff to President Kennedy," 30 November 1961, pp. 197, 199, and 201, from the same volume. For the argument that the United States preferred to support military-led modernization, see also Thomas C. Field Jr., "Ideology as Strategy: Military-Led Modernization and the Origins of the Alliance for Progress in Bolivia," pp. 147–83. See also the discussion in Gambone, *Capturing the Revolution*, pp. 47–55.

27. William H. Brubeck, "Memorandum from the Executive Secretary of the Department of State (Battle) to the President's Assistant for National Security Affairs (Bundy)," 5 February 1962, in *FRUS, 1961–1963*, vol. 12: *American Republics*, pp. 214–15.

28. "Memorandum from Acting Secretary of State Chester Bowles to the Deputy Assistant Secretary of State for Politico-Military Affairs (Kitchen): Military Aid to Central American Countries," 29 September 1961, in *FRUS, 1961–1963*, vol. 12: *American Republics*, pp. 190–91.

29. Schlesinger, "Journals: 14 February 1961," pp. 19–20, Arthur M. Schlesinger Jr. Papers, New York Public Library, Journals, Box 311, 1961 February folder.

30. See Rusk to Morse, 15 September 1962 in *FRUS, 1961–1963*, vol. 12: *American Republics*. See the discussion of congressional concerns in "Memorandum from the Deputy Coordinator for Foreign Assistance (Bell) to Secretary of State Rusk," 25 June 1961, in *FRUS, 1961–1963*, vol. 12: *American Republics*, p. 176.

31. Schlesinger, "Journals: 3 May 1961: Memorandum for the President: Reactions to Cuba in Western Europe," Arthur M. Schlesinger Jr. Papers, New York Public Library, Box 311, May 1961 folder. Schlesinger expressed concern that Rostow had "convinced himself that guerrilla subversion has now become the essential Communist weapon." See pp. 533–34 in Box 312, January 1962 folder. Schlesinger praised Rusk's speech's emphasis on "social and economic content" on page 552. See also p. 558.

32. MemCon, "Inter-American Defense College." 11 April 1962, in *FRUS, 1961–1963*, vol. 12: *American Republics*, pp. 224–25.

33. Schlesinger, *Thousand Days*, p. 183; Schlesinger, "Memorandum for the President: The Crisis in Bolivia," Schlesinger Papers, JFK Library, White House Files, Subject Files 1961–1964, Box WH-3, Bolivia folder. Schlesinger, 24 February 1961 journal entry, Schlesinger and Schlesinger, eds., *Journals*, p. 105; Field, *From Development to Dictatorship*, particularly pp. 3, 6, 8, 10, 11, 56, and 105; for a more balanced approach, see Siekmeier, *The Bolivian Revolution and the United States*, particularly pp. 4–10, 50–55, and 79–98. Regarding Kennedy and the nonaligned countries, see, for example, Muehlenbeck, *Betting on the Africans*.

34. Joint Chiefs of Staff, "Memorandum for the Secretary of Defense: US Plan of Action in Cuba," 27 January 1961, JFK, NSF Countries, Box 61A, Cuba—Subjects: Paramilitary Study Group Taylor Report, Part III: Annex 7 folder.

35. Schlesinger, 19 March 1961 and 23 March 1961 journal entries, Schlesinger and Schlesinger, eds., *Journals*, p. 107.

36. Schlesinger, 5 April 1961 journal entry, Schlesinger and Schlesinger, eds., *Journals*, p. 108. Schlesinger, "Journals, March 1961," p. 98, Arthur M. Schlesinger Jr. Papers, New York Public Library, Journals, Box 311, March 1961 folder; Schlesinger to Berle, Mann, Bundy, and Tracy Barnes, undated, and Murrow to Schlesinger, undated, JFK Library, Schlesinger Papers, White House Files, Subject Files, 1961–1964, Box WH-6, Cuba White Paper—undated folder.

37. Memorandum of a Meeting with the President, White House, Washington, November 29, 1960, 11:00 A.M.," *FRUS, 1958–1960*, vol. 6: *Cuba*, p. 1128; Schlesinger, 5 April 1961 journal entry, Schlesinger and Schlesinger, eds., *Journals*, pp. 108–9.

38. Schlesinger and Schlesinger, eds., *Journals*, pp. 109–11; Schlesinger to Kennedy, 15 March 1961," *FRUS, 1961–1963*, vol. 10: *Cuba: January 1961–September 1962*; see also "The Inspector General's Survey of the Cuban Operation, October 1961," in Kornbluh, ed., *The Bay of Pigs Declassified*, pp. 24, 37, and 52. Historian Robert Dallek notes that Schlesinger

proposed a covert operation that would have forced Castro to respond in a way that made it possible for Kennedy to take more aggressive action. (Dallek believes that this made Kennedy less trusting of Schlesinger from that time on, though he does not provide evidence for this.) Dallek, *Camelot's Court*, pp. 136–37.

39. Schlesinger, "Journals: 18 April 1961," p. 142, Arthur M. Schlesinger Jr. Papers, New York Public Library, Journals, Box 311, April 1961 folder; "Statement by José Figueres," 27 April 1961, Grant Papers, Latin American Country Files, Box 41, Costa Rica: Personalities, 1960–1962 folder.

40. Regarding the Senate Foreign Relations Committee's briefing by the CIA, see Morse to Ray Prichard of Central Point, Ore., 31 January 1961, Wayne Morse Papers, University of Oregon Library Special Collections, Foreign Relations, Box 43, Foreign Relations 1-1 Correspondence folder. See also the 17 April 1961 press release in the same box, Foreign Relations—Cuba 1961 folder. Regarding his frustration with the administration regarding the failure to inform him, see the undated telegram to Rusk in the same folder.

41. Martin, *Stevenson and the World*, p. 581.

42. Schlesinger, "Journals: 23 May 1961," pp. 187–88, Arthur M. Schlesinger Jr. Papers, New York Public Library, Journals, Box 311, May 1961 folder.

43. Johnson, ed., *Papers of Adlai E. Stevenson*, vol. 8, p. 53; "Statements by Ambassador Adlai Stevenson, United States Representative in Committee One, On the Cuba Complaint," Stevenson Papers (MC #124), Box 345, Folder 8, Series 5, Subseries 4: U.S. Ambassador, Cuba: 1960–October 1961 folder; Schoultz, *That Infernal Little Cuban Republic*, pp. pp. 167–68.

44. Adlai Stevenson, "Lessons from Cuba," 23 April 1961, Stevenson Papers (MC #124), Box 345, Folder 8, Series 5: Subseries 4: U.S. Ambassador—Cuba 1960–October 1961 folder; Martin, *Stevenson and the World*, pp. 585–90.

45. "Statement by the United States Committee of the Inter-American Association for Democracy and Freedom," undated, Grant Papers, IADF General Files, Cuba—Miscellaneous 1958–62 folder.

46. Arthur M. Schlesinger, "Journals: 10 May 1961," p. 185, Arthur M. Schlesinger Jr. Papers, New York Public Library, Journals, Box 311, May 1961 folder. (At the time Kennedy was focused on Laos.)

47. Freedman, *Kennedy's Wars*, p. 397.

48. Schlesinger, 22 April 1961 journal entry, Schlesinger and Schlesinger, eds., *Journals*, p. 120.

49. See Church to Glen Richards of Nampa, Idaho, 26 May 1961, Senator Frank Church Collection, Boise State University Library Special Collections, Series 2.2 Foreign Relations, Box 44, Latin America 1961 folder.

50. See, for example, the 4 May 1961 letter to Ray Tuttle of Nampa and the 8 May 1961 letter to Milton Small of the Boise Committee on Foreign Relations in Senator Frank Church Collection, Boise State University Library, Special Collections Series 2.2 Foreign Relations, Box 46, Cuba 1961 Folder. See also "Church Feels Castro Has Backing of Majority of Cuban Residents," *Lewiston Morning Tribune*, 24 April 1961.

51. See Morse to John S. Lawson of the American Jewish Committee, 12 May 1961, Wayne L. Morse Papers, University of Oregon Library, Special Collections, Foreign Relations, Box 43, Foreign Relations—Latin America—Correspondence folder. See Wayne Morse, "The Situation in Cuba," *Congressional Record*, 24 April 1961, pp. 6179–80 and 6185–86.

52. Robert Kennedy's comment to Taylor is quoted in Thomas, *Robert Kennedy*, pp. 125; James Symington to Robert Kennedy, 10 July 1962, Robert Kennedy, Attorney General Papers, Attorney General's Confidential Files, Special Group (Augmented) Operation Mongoose, Box 211, Mongoose—General 7/62–12/62; "Guidelines for Operation Mongoose," 5 March 1962, and Lansdale, "The Cuba Project," 20 February 1962, JFK Library, NSF, Meetings and Memoranda, Box 319, Special Group (Augmented) General 1/62–6/62 folder. Lansdale's "Review of Operation Mongoose," 25 July 1962, claimed that they had "numerically the largest US intelligence effort inside a Communist state." This is the Special Group (Augmented) 7/62 folder; Robert Hurwitch, 7 August 1962, also in Box 319, Special Group (Augmented) General 8/62 folder; see also Schoultz, *That Infernal Little Cuban Republic*, pp. 176–79; Lansdale assumed that the administration would eventually employ U.S. forces in Cuba. See Gleijeses, *Conflicting Missions*, p. 19.

53. Thomas, *Robert Kennedy*, pp. 175–79; regarding Robert Kennedy's hopes for the exiles, see also Brown, *Cuba's Revolutionary World*, p. 129.

54. Schlesinger, 21 August 1961 journal entry, Schlesinger and Schlesinger, eds., *Journals*, p. 129.

55. Schlesinger, "Journals: 23 May 1961," p. 189, Arthur M. Schlesinger Jr. Papers, New York Public Library, Journals, Box 311, May 1961 folder.

56. Schlesinger, 18 June 1961 journal entry, Schlesinger and Schlesinger, eds., *Journals*, p. 121.

57. Rusk to All American Diplomatic Posts in the Other American Republics, 5 May 1961, JFK Library, NSF, Trips and Conferences, Box 250A, Ambassador Adlai Stevenson's Trip to Latin America 6/61, 5/1/61–6/9/61 folder; Schlesinger, "Memorandum for the President: Assistant Secretary of State for Inter-American Affairs," 18 April 1961, Schlesinger Papers, JFK Library, White House Files, Subject File, 1961–1964, Box WH-3, Latin America 3/8/61–4/20/61 folder.

58. Stevenson knew why he was going. See, for example, his letter to the U.S. ambassador to the United Kingdom, David K. E. Bruce, 27 May 1961, and "Report to the President on South American Mission, June 4–22, 1961," in Johnson, ed., *Papers of Adlai E. Stevenson*, vol. 8, pp. 69 and 75–83; Stevenson to Gerald W. Johnson, 6 July 1961, p. 90. See also Stevenson, "Inter-American Press Association Luncheon, Waldorf Astoria, New York," 16 October 1961, Stevenson Papers (MC #124), Series 2: Speeches: Box 176, Folder 2. Sacha Volman was appalled that Stevenson was to visit Paraguay. See his 3 June 1961 letter to Norman Thomas, Stevenson Papers (MC #124), Box 453, Folder 2, Series 9, Travel Materials, Latin America—Correspondence 1961. Stevenson insisted that he had discussed the ways in which "protection of civil rights, free elections, and democratic procedures would greatly enhance international respect for Paraguay." See the 13 June 1961 letter in Folder 10 in the same box. See also Martin, *Stevenson and the World*, pp. 642–43.

59. Solberg, *Hubert Humphrey*, pp. 11–20, 94–98, 113–23, 157–59, and 218–19; Offner, *Hubert Humphrey*, pp. 103–4, 115, 146, 161–62, and 168–69; Johns, *The Price of Loyalty*, pp. 11 and 23; Latham, *Modernization as Ideology*, p. 113; Hubert Humphrey Papers, Minnesota Historical Society, Senate Legislative Files, 150.B.15.10 (F), Box 297, Colombia folder, and Humphrey to John E. Ogilvie of Valley Stream, New York, 24 March 1962, Alliance for Progress—Latin America folder, Minnesota Historical Society.

60. Arthur M. Schlesinger, "Journals: 7 June 1961," pp. 199–200, Arthur M. Schlesinger Jr. Papers, New York Public Library, Journals, Box 311, May 1961 folder.

61. Schlesinger, "Journals: Memorandum for the President: Personnel Problems," 10 June 1961, Arthur M. Schlesinger Jr. Papers, New York Public Library, Journals, Box 311, June 1961 folder.

62. See, for example, Gleijeses, *Dominican Crisis*, pp. 20–29 and 303–7. We are still lacking definitive evidence regarding U.S. involvement in the assassination. All we can say for certain is that the administration was able to maintain an appearance, at least, of plausible deniability.

63. Schlesinger, "Journals 30 August 1961," pp. 312–15, Arthur M. Schlesinger Jr. Papers, New York Public Library, Box 311, August 1961 folder.

64. Boomhower, *John Bartlow Martin*, pp. 49 and 205–7. Regarding Kennedy's concerns about the possibility of a "communist-oriented regime" replacing Trujillo, see Dean Rusk to JFK, "Memorandum for the President: The Dominican Republic," 15 February 1961, NSF Countries, Box 66, Dominican Republic: General 1/61–6/61 folder; "Martin Report on the Dominican Republic," pp. 25, 27, 84, 89, and 102–3, Robert Kennedy Papers, John Kennedy Library, Attorney General Papers, Attorney General's Classified Files, Box 206, Dominican Republic (2 of 3) folder.

65. Richard Goodwin, "Memorandum for the President," 3 October 1961, NSF, John Kennedy Library, Box 66, Countries, Subjects—Murphy Trip 8/61–5/63 folder.

66. See, for example, "Department of State Guidelines for Policy and Operations," March 1962, JFK Library, NSF, Ralph Dungan Papers, Box 393, Dominican Republic 1/62–5/62 folder; see also Gleijeses, *Dominican Crisis*, pp. 47–50.

Chapter 3

1. Regarding threat perception in Central America, see "Memorandum from Acting Secretary of State Bowles to President Kennedy," 29 September 1961 in *FRUS, 1961–1963*, vol. 12: *American Republics*, p. 188.

2. "Memorandum from Acting Secretary of State Bowles to President Kennedy," 29 September 1961, *FRUS, 1961–1963*, vol. 12: *American Republics*, pp. 188–90.

3. See Berle to Kennedy, 21 November 1960, in FDR Library, Berle Papers, Box 219, Diary, 1956–1960, Diary 1960 folder. See "Remarks of Welcome at the White House to President Villeda of Honduras," 30 November 1962, pp. 847–48, and "The President's News Conference of December 12, 1962," *PPPUS: Kennedy, 1962*, p. 872; Morris, *Honduras: Caudillo Politics and Military Rulers*, pp. 11–12 and 35–38.

4. Katherine Bracken to Charles R. Burrows, 13 July 1961, in Record Group 59, Bureau of Inter-American Affairs, Office of Central American Affairs, Records Relating to Honduras, 1957–74, Box 3, Political—Local/General—1961 folder.

5. Inter-American Association for Democracy and Freedom, "Memorandum on United States-Latin American Relations," undated but from 1962, Grant Papers, IADF General Files, US-Latin America Policy 1962 folder; Wimberly Coerr to U.S. Embassy, Managua, Nicaragua, 17 September 1961, John F. Kennedy, NSF, Countries, Box 143A, Nicaragua, General 1961–1962 folder; William T. Jentzer Jr., "Conversation with Fernando Agüero," JFK, NSF, Dungan Papers, Box 395, Nicaragua 6/62 folder.

6. Kennedy to Betancourt, 5 July 1961, in JFK Library, NSF Countries, Box 192, Venezuela General 1/61–6/61 folder; John Calvin Hill, "Outline Internal Defense Plan," in JFK Library, Schlesinger Papers, White House Files, Classified Subject Files, Venezuela 12/61–

11/63 folder. Stewart to SecState, 1 July 1962, in JFK Library, NSF Countries, Box 192, Venezuela, General 7/1/62–8/19/62 folder; Schlesinger to Dungan, 17 April 1962, JFK Library, Schlesinger Papers, White House Files, Classified Subject File, Box WH-49, Venezuela 12/61–11/63 folder (in this message, Schlesinger suggested that Kennedy ask Betancourt for advice regarding the coup in Peru); "Demands on President Romulo Betancourt by Moderate Military Personnel to Crush Leftist Conspiracies," 7 June 1962, p. 2, in JFK Library, NSF Countries, Box 192, Venezuela, General 6/5/62–6/30/62 folder. Kennedy to Betancourt, 11 August 1961, in JFK Library, NSF Countries, Box 192, Venezuela 7/61–9/61 folder. Schlesinger emphasizes the appropriateness of President Kennedy's decision to visit Betancourt and Alberto Lleras Camargo on his trip to South America in 1961. See *Thousand Days*, p. 767–69; for a liberal Democratic view of what was going on, see two books by Alexander, *The Venezuelan Revolution*, particularly pp. 5–9, 76–84, 105–17, 126–30, and 297–319, and *Rómulo Betancourt and the Transformation of Venezuela*, particularly pp. 180–84, 224–48, 252–53, 465–97, 502–22, and 552–58; see also Miller, *Precarious Paths to Freedom*, particularly pp. 66–101. Regarding the urban poor and Betancourt, see Velasco, *Barrio Rising*, pp. 100–110.

7. Randall, *Colombia and the United States*, pp. 216, 222–26, 231–37, and 248–51; Darnton, "Asymmetry and Agenda-Setting in U.S.-Latin American Relations: Rethinking the Origins of the Alliance for Progress," pp. 55–92. Taffet, *Foreign Aid as Foreign Policy*, pp. 149–74; Karl, *Forgotten Peace*, pp. 2–4, 16–37, and 123–29; Offner, *Sorting Out the Mixed Economy*, pp. 50–67 and 78.

8. Schlesinger to Bundy, 10 August 1961, JFK Library, Richard Goodwin Papers, Subjects, Box 11, Schlesinger, Arthur M., Jr. Folder.

9. Fulton Freeman to SecState, 3 November 1961, JFK, NSF Countries, Box 26A, Colombia General 1961 folder. I am not discussing his trip to Mexico earlier in the year because Mexico did not have a "substantial and broad-range assistance program." See David Bell's testimony in *Hearings before the Committee on Foreign Relations, United States Senate, Foreign Assistance Act of 1963*, p. 630.

10. Regarding the Eisenhower administration's enthusiasm for Alessandri, see Dulles to Eisenhower, 29 October 1958, Eisenhower Library, White House Office Files, Office of the Staff Secretary, International Series, Box 2, Chile (1), October 1958–March 1960 folder. The Eisenhower administration had long lamented the Chilean public's lack of concern about the communists, which they saw as "just another national political group." See "Recommended Plan of Operations Pursuant to NSC 1290d," 14 July 1955, Eisenhower Library, White House Office, NSC Staff Papers, OCB Central Staff Files, Box 26, OCB 091, Chile (3) folder. See "Conversation between the President and the Chilean University Study Team at the White House," 2 March 1961, in JFK Library, NSF Countries, Box 20A, 1/61–9/61. On President Alessandri's resentment of what he considered "excessive and unrealistic insistence by the United States that Chile make rapid progress in such fields as tax and agrarian reform," see L. D. Battle, "Appointment with the President for Charles W. Cole, Ambassador to Chile," 8 March 1962, in JFK Library, NSF Countries, Box 20A, Chile, General 1/62–6/62 folder. See also Brubeck to Dungan, "Arguments for and against Inviting President Alessandri to the United States and State/AID Conclusion," August 1962, in Box 20A, Chile 7/62–10/62 folder; Hollis B. Chenery to Hamilton, Coffin, Moscoso, and Goodwin, "U.S. Aid Strategy under the Alliance for Progress," in JFK Library, NSF, Ralph Dungan Papers, Box 391, Chile 1/62–4/62 folder; Mansfield to Kennedy, "Proposed Visit of the President of

Chile to the United States," 28 July 1962, in JFK Library, NSF, Ralph Dungan Papers, Box 391A, Chile General 6/1/62–8/14/62 folder.

11. "Chile Department of State Guidelines Policy and Operations," March 1962, particularly pp. 2, 4, 7, 10, and 15, in JFK Library, NSF, Ralph Dungan Papers, Box 391, Chile General 5/1/62–5/21/62 folder; "Alessandri Briefing Book 12/11/62–12/15/62," in JFK Library, NSF Countries, Box 21A, Briefing Book folder.

12. See Tomic to Humphrey, 10 April 1962, Frei to Humphrey, 17 April 1962, and Humphrey to Frei, 3 May 1962 in Humphrey Papers, 150. B.15.10 (F), Box 297, Chile folder. On the development of the party, see Fleet, *Rise and Fall of Chilean Christian Democracy*, particularly pp. 43–79. Note that U.S. attitudes toward Frei had been positive since the mid-1950s at least. See, for example, E. S. Staples, "Notes for Mr. Holland," 31 July 1956, RG 59, NARA II, Records of the Office of South American Affairs, Box 1, 1956, Communism folder. Staples mentioned that Frei had joined in the anti-American chorus "two years ago" (at the time of the overthrow of Jacobo Árbenz of Guatemala).

13. For information on U.S. long-term policy toward Chile beginning in the Kennedy administration, see the 15 October 1962 memo from Otto H. Kerican, USAID economic adviser in Chile, to Dungan in JFK Library—National Security Files, Ralph A. Dungan—Chile General, 10/6/62–11/30/62 folder; Fleet, *Rise and Fall of Chilean Christian Democracy*.

14. Note that Field, in "Ideology as Strategy," primarily makes comparisons to non–Latin American examples, and does not always stick to the Kennedy era either. See pp. 151, 153, and 183.

15. John Rielly, "Venezuela," undated, Hubert Humphrey Papers, Minnesota Historical Society, Humphrey Senatorial 150.B.15.12 (F), Latin America: Venezuela folder.

16. Arthur M. Schlesinger Jr., "Journals: 31 March 1962," pp. 669 and 671, Arthur M. Schlesinger Jr. Papers, New York Public Library, Journals, Box 312, March 1962 folder.

17. See Rusk to U.S. Embassy, Argentina, 10 February 1962, JFK, NSF Countries, Box 6, Argentina 1/62–2/62 folder; "Memorandum from the Assistant Secretary of State for Inter-American Affairs (Martin) to Secretary of State Rusk," 13 6 April 1962, in *FRUS, 1961–1963*, vol. 12: *American Republics*, particularly pp. 376–78. Regarding Betancourt's response, see A. E. Breisky, "Memorandum from the Executive Secretary of the Department of State (Battle) to the President's Special Assistant for National Security Affairs (Bundy)," 14 April 1962, pp. 379–80; "Memorandum from the Director the Bureau of Intelligence and Research (Hillsman) to Secretary of State Rusk," 27 April 1962, pp. 383–84; Schlesinger, 31 March 1962 journal entry, p. 669, Schlesinger Papers, New York Public Library, Journals, Box 312, March 1962 folder.

18. Humphrey Papers, Senate Legislative Files, 150.B.15.10 (F), Box 297, Argentina folder; Schlesinger, "Memorandum for the President," 30 March 1962, JFK Library, NSF, Ralph Dungan papers, Box 389, Argentina 3/62–11/62 folder; Fowler Hamilton, "Memorandum for the President: Effects of the Alliance for Progress on Argentine Election Results," 6 April 1962, JFK Library, NSF, Meetings and Memoranda, Box 335, NSAM 141 folder; Schlesinger, 31 March 1962 journal entry, p. 669, Schlesinger Papers, New York Public Library, Journals, Box 312, March 1962 folder.

19. Schlesinger to Sacha Volman (then with the Institution of Political Education in Costa Rica), 15 November 1961, JFK Library, Richard Goodwin Papers, Subjects, Box 10, Peru folder; James Loeb to Arthur Schlesinger, 19 October 1961, Loeb to State, "Political Situation: Peru," 28 December 1961, Schlesinger Papers, John F. Kennedy Library, White House

Files, Classified Subject Files, Box WH-43, Peru 5/61–8/62 folder. Depending on the audience, the administration gave mixed messages regarding whether it preferred APRA, but most thoughtful observers recognized the overall tilt. See Martin to McGhee, "Peruvian Elections: Action Recommendations in Relation to Peruvian Elections and Possible Military Intervention," 6 June 1962, JFK Library, NSF, Ralph Dungan Papers, Box 396A, Peru 5/62–12/62 folder. Senator Humphrey had supported Loeb's nomination, noting his knowledge of Spanish and the labor movement. He called him "a sophisticated anti-communist." See Humphrey to Chester Bowles, 9 February 1961, Grant Papers, Correspondence, Box 29, Hubert Humphrey folder.

20. Schlesinger, "Journals: 1 August 1962," pp. 770–71, Arthur M. Schlesinger Jr. Papers, New York Public Library, Journals, Box 312, August 1962 folder. (Prior to this, Kennedy had specifically mentioned that it should not necessarily be the president who should have made the statement. See 30 July 1962, pp. 768–69, July 1962 folder.) See also Grant to Kennedy, 20 July 1962, Grant Papers, Correspondence, Box 29, Mr. and Mrs. John F. Kennedy folder.

21. Ball to Loeb, "Telegram from the Department of State to the Embassy in Peru," 24 March 1962, p. 858; "Memorandum from the Undersecretary of State (Ball) to President Kennedy," 27 July 1962, pp. 865–66; and Martin to Ball, "Military Assistance to Peru," pp. 877–78, in *FRUS, 1961–1963*, vol. 12: *American Republics*. See also USIS, "Untitled," 17 August 1962, Douglas Henderson Papers, Ambassadorial Correspondence, Box 1, 1962 folder. Schlesinger, "Peru," JFK Library, NSF, Ralph Dungan Papers, Box 396A, Peru 5/62–12/62 folder. See also Schlesinger, 30 July 1962 journal entry, pp. 768–70, Schlesinger Papers, New York Public Library Journals, Box 312, July 1962 folder. Loeb himself ended up feeling dismissed by Kennedy "as a standard Americans for Democratic Action liberal who allowed his personal preferences to interfere with the handling of the situation." The president had "no great passion to give him another assignment." Goodwin had to write the president and assure him that he was not a "knee-jerk liberal." See Schlesinger, 12 August 1962 journal entry, p. 784, also in Box 312, August 1962 folder.

22. See, particularly, Stewart to SecState, 11 August 1962 and 14 August 1962 in JFK Library, NSF Countries, Box 192, Venezuela, General 7/1/62–8/19/62 folder; MemCon, "Venezuela Defense Requirements," undated, in the same box, 9/1/62–9/20/62 folder. See also Brown, *Cuba's Revolutionary World*, pp. 259–60.

23. Schlesinger, "Memorandum for the President," 31 March 1962. JFK Library, President's Office Files, Countries, Box 112A, Brazil—Security Briefing Book 1962.

24. Belk to Bundy, 1/26/61, in JFK Library, National Security Files, Country Files, Box 12, Brazil General 1/26/61–2/24/61 folder.

25. Arthur M. Schlesinger Jr., "Journals: 27 August 1961," p. 309, Arthur M. Schlesinger Jr. Papers, New York Public Library, Journals, Box 311, August 1961 folder; Smith, *Lincoln Gordon*, p. 238.

26. Goulart had also been Kubitschek's vice president. U.S. distrust of him had been of long standing. See "Visit of Vice President Goulart of Brail," 26 April 1956, RG 59, NA II, ASSIAffairs (Holland), 1953–56, Box 3, Brazil 1956 folder. Holland said that Goulart saw himself as a "national patriot" and a "leftist." "In fact he is probably neither." Those who did not exaggerate his ties to Brazilian communists tended, like Holland, to exaggerate his ties to the deposed Argentine leader, Juan Perón. See also OCB, "Status Report Items," Eisenhower Library, White House Office, NSF Staff, OCB, Central File Series, Box 73, OCB 091.4 Latin America File #4 (6) folder. In the same folder, see R. P. Crenshaw Jr., OCB Staff Rep-

resentative, "Items Submitted by State for Next Status Report"; for Schlesinger's opinions regarding the political situation, see Schlesinger, "Journals: 27 August 1961," p. 309, Schlesinger Papers, New York Public Library, Journals, Box 311, August 1961 folder.

27. CIA, Office of the Director, "Memorandum on Quadros' Resignation," in JFK Library, Arthur M. Schlesinger Jr. Papers, White House Files, Classified Subject Files, Box WH-26, Brazil 4/61–3/62 folder.

28. U.S. Embassy to White House, 1 September 1961, in JFK Library, NSC Countries, Box 12, Brazil General 8/61–9/61 folder.

29. U.S. Embassy to SecState, 6 September 1961, in JFK Library, NSC Countries, Box 12, Brazil General 8/61–9/61 folder.

30. Bond to SecState, 6 September 1961, in JFK Library, NSC Countries, Box 12, Brazil General 8/61–9/61 folder.

31. Bond to SecState, 6 September 1961, in JFK Library, NSC Countries, Box 12, Brazil General 8/61–9/61 folder.

32. See National Intelligence Estimate 93-2-61, "Short-Term Prospects for Brazil under Goulart," 7 December 1961, available in the Lyndon Baines Johnson Library.

33. Teodoro Moscoso to Gordon, 11 November 1961, Teodoro Moscoso Papers, John F. Kennedy Library, Correspondence File, Box 4, 11/9/61–11/30/61 folder; Gordon to Robert Woodward, Ambassador to Spain, 2 June 1962, Gordon Papers, JFK Library, Series 3: Ambassador to Brazil, Box 115, Chron Files Jan–June 1962 folder; Smith, *Lincoln Gordon*, pp. 226–27, 241–42, 243, and 247.

34. MemCon, Kennedy and Kubitschek, 15 September 1961, pp. 2, 4, 5, and 6, in JFK Library, NSF Countries, Box 12, Brazil General 10/61–11/61 folder.

35. See "Minutes of Conversation between President João Goulart and Attorney General Robert Kennedy," 19 December 1962, pp. 9–10, in JFK Library, NSF Countries, Box 13A, Brazil, General 12/21/62–12/31/62.

36. Walter J. Stoessel Jr., Director, Executive Secretariat, 17 February 1961, JFK Library, NSF Countries, Box 12, Brazil General 1/26/61–2/24/61 folder; L. D. Battle, "Request for Appointment with the President for Governor Carlos Lacerda, of the State of Guanabara (Brazil)," in the same box folder, Brazil General 10/61–11/61 folder; Stevenson, 28 March 1962, JFK Library, NSF Countries, Box 12A, Brazil General 3/16/62–3/21/62 folder.

37. Gordon to SecState, 22 October 1961, in JFK Library, NSF Countries, Box 12, Brazil General 10/61–11/61 folder; Bond to SecState, 25 November 1961, in JFK Library, NSF Countries, Box 12, Brazil General 10/61–11/61 folder.

38. Gordon to SecState, 27 March 1962, in JFK Library, Arthur Schlesinger Papers, White House Files, Classified Subject Files, 4/61–3/62 folder; Gordon to Edward S. Mason, 4 January 1962, Gordon Papers, Series 3: Ambassador to Brazil, Box 115, Chron File: Jan–June 1962. It is noteworthy that he uses this phrase in a private letter to a former colleague at Harvard. See Leacock, *Requiem for Revolution*, p. 103.

39. Niles W. Bond, Deputy Chief of Mission, 19 July 1962 Airgram, in JFK Library, NSF Countries, Box 13, Brazil—General—7/62 folder.

40. See "Toasts of the President and President Goulart," 3 April 1962, in *PPPUS: Kennedy, 1962*, pp. 287–89.

41. Schlesinger, "Memorandum for the President," 31 March 1964, and Gordon to SecState, 27 March 1962, NSF Countries, Box 112A, Brazil—Security: Briefing Book, Goulart Visit: 4/62 folder.

42. Salinger to Kennedy, 27 July 1962, JFK, NSF, Ralph Dungan Papers, Box 390, Brazil Trip 10/61–12/62 folder.

43. Ralph Dungan, "Memorandum for the President," 17 July 1962, JFK Library, NSF, Ralph Dungan, Box 390, Brazil Trip folder.

44. Schlesinger, "Journals: 5 April 1962," p. 682, Arthur M. Schlesinger Jr. Papers, New York Public Library, Journals, Box 312, April 1962 Folder.

45. "Meeting on Brazil," 30 July 1962, pp. 9–10, 12, 17, and 18, and "Meeting on Peruvian Recognition," pp. 37–38 in Naftali, ed., *Presidential Recordings: John F. Kennedy, The Great Crises*, vol. 1, whitehousetapes.net/transcript/kennedy.

46. Schlesinger, "Journals: 30 July 1962," p. 770, Arthur M. Schlesinger Jr. Papers, New York Public Library, Journals, Box 312, July 1962 folder.

47. Gordon to SecState, 24 July 1962, and Niles Bond, "Brazilian Crisis," 19 July 1962, JFK Library, NSF Countries, Box 13, Brazil—General 7/62 folder.

48. Schlesinger and Schlesinger, eds., *Journals*, p. 146.

49. Arthur M. Schlesinger Jr., "Journals: 31 March 1962," pp. 646–48, Arthur M. Schlesinger Jr. Papers, New York Public Library, Journals, Box 312, March 1962 folder.

50. Schlesinger, "Journals: 14 May 1962," pp. 710–11, Arthur M. Schlesinger Jr. Papers, New York Public Library, Journals, Box 312, May 1962 folder.

51. See Schlesinger, 13 July 1962 entry, Schlesinger and Schlesinger, eds., *Journals*, p. 160.

52. See Schlesinger, 13 July 1962, Schlesinger and Schlesinger, eds., *Journals*, pp. 160–61.

53. See Schlesinger, 19 August 1962 entry, Schlesinger and Schlesinger, eds., *Journals*, p. 164.

54. See Schlesinger, 25 December 1962 journal entry, Schlesinger and Schlesinger, eds., *Journals*, p. 182.

55. Wofford, *Of Kennedys and Kings*, p. 95; Stossel, *Sarge*, p. 176; Schlesinger, *A Thousand Days*, p. 147. Arthur M. Schlesinger Jr., "Journals: 31 March 1961," pp. 652–53, Arthur M. Schlesinger Jr. Papers, New York Public Library, Journals, Box 312, March 1962 folder. Schlesinger had recently returned from a trip to West Germany and Paris. For the more general comment, see Schlesinger and Schlesinger, eds., *Journals*, p. 161; Woods, *LBJ: Architect of American Ambition*, p. 494.

56. Schlesinger, "Journals: 12 November 1961," pp. 452–54 and 456–57, Arthur M. Schlesinger Jr. Papers, New York Public Library, Journals, Box 311, Nov–Dec 1961 folder.

57. Schlesinger, "Journals: 15 October 1962," p. 855, Arthur M. Schlesinger Jr. Papers, New York Public Library, Journals, Box 312, October 1962 folder. He even had the support of Roberto Campos at this point, the Brazilian economist later to be derided as "Bobby Fields" for his perceived pro-American neoliberal economic policies under the Brazilian military government.

58. Schlesinger, "Journals: 4 September 1962," pp. 817–19, Arthur M. Schlesinger Jr. Papers, New York Public Library, Journals, Box 312, September 1962 folder. Dungan later commented on their lack of involvement in a mid-September statement on Cuba. "Well, it certainly makes you feel a vital member of the Latin American team, doesn't it!" See 16 September 1962, p. 824. (Schlesinger had to admit that "it was an excellent statement.")

59. Ray Cline, Deputy Director (Intelligence) for Acting Director of Central Intelligence, 6 September 1962, Kennedy Library, NSF, Meetings and Memoranda, Box 319, Special Group (Augmented) General 9/62 folder. Regarding the Soviet buildup in Cuba, see, for example, Roger Hillsman to Rusk, "Meaning of Increased Soviet Aid to Cuba," 1 September 1962,

Kennedy Library, NSF, Meetings and Memoranda, Box 338, NSAM 181 folder. The best source on the administration experience of the crisis remains Stern, *Averting "The Final Failure,"* particularly pp. 78, 81, 100–101, 108–9, 122, 127, 140, 147, 150–51, 156, 168–69, 190–91, 206–7, 224, 236, 268–69, 285–86, 295–96, 302, 306, 308–9, 336, and 387. Robert Alexander to Schlesinger, 3 December 1962, JFK, NSF, Meetings and Memoranda, Box 327, Staff Memoranda, Arthur Schlesinger, 7/62–6/63 folder; Schoultz, *That Infernal Little Cuban Republic,* p. 186. See also "Letter from Chairman Khrushchev to President Kennedy," 18 April 1961, in White, ed., *The Kennedys and Cuba,* p. 32. On the Soviet decision, see Fursenko and Naftali, *"One Hell of a Gamble,"* pp. 170–84. Tanya Harmer emphasizes the convergence of interests among Latin American governments from 1959 to 1964 in "The 'Cuban Question,'" pp. 115–51; for a rich hemispheric treatment, see Renata Keller, "The Latin American Missile Crisis," pp. 195–222; regarding San Román, see Thomas, *Robert Kennedy,* p. 234. Regarding the unlikelihood of Castro government's surviving five more years, see "Remarks and Questions and Answer Period before the American Society of Newspaper Editors," 19 April 1963, *PPPUS: Kennedy, 1963,* p. 330.

60. Arthur M. Schlesinger Jr., "Journals: 28 October 1962," pp. 859, 870, and 872, Arthur M. Schlesinger Jr. Papers, New York Public Library, Journals, Box 312, October 1962 folder.

61. Johnson, ed., *Papers of Stevenson,* vol. 8, pp. 349–52; Martin, *Stevenson and the World,* pp. 741–48.

62. See letters from Fraser to constituents and others from 1963 in Donald Fraser Papers, 145.C.2.3 (B), Cuba Correspondence 1963–1965 folder. Solberg, *Humphrey,* pp. 117–18. See remarks on meeting with Venezuelan representative Sosa Rodriguez in Stevenson to Rusk, 30 November 1962, JFK Library, NSF Countries, Box 43, Cuba Cables 11/30/62–12/31/62 (1 of 4) folder.

63. Schoultz, *That Infernal Little Cuban Republic,* pp. 186 and 192; Thomas, *Robert Kennedy,* pp. 235–39; Coleman, *The Fourteenth Day,* p. 149.

64. Kennedy, "Radio and Television Report to the American People on the Soviet Arms Buildup in Cuba," 22 October 1962, *PPPUS: Kennedy, 1962,* pp. 806–9.

Chapter 4

1. The speech was reproduced in George McGovern, *A Time of War, A Time of Peace,* pp. 96–102; Knock, *Rise of a Prairie Statesman,* pp. 287–89.

2. Humphrey, "Minnesota Radio Tape of March 19, 1963 for Broadcast Week Beginning March 24," Minnesota Historical Society website, accessed May 2016.

3. MemCon, 25 January 1963, "Farewell Call of Ambassador Jones before Departing for Peru," in *FRUS, 1961–1963,* vol. 12: *American Republics,* p. 880.

4. Arthur M. Schlesinger Jr., "The Alliance for Progress: Prospects, Perils and Potentialities," 11 May 1963, in JFK Library, Schlesinger Papers, White House Files—Subject Files, Box WH-2, Alliance for Progress 4/6/63–5/11/63 folder.

5. "Remarks of Senator Wayne L. Morse," 25 June 1963, pp. 1–3, in Morse Papers, University of Oregon Library Special Collections, F.

6. Pearson, "Strong Impression That U.S. Government Supporting Christian Democratic Party," 3 July 1962, in JFK Library, Schlesinger Papers, White House Files, Classified Subject Files, Box WH-28, Chile 1/62–9/63 folder; Frei to Dungan, 17 April 1962, JFK Library,

NSF Countries, Box 20A, Chile, General 1/62–6/62. See the *Topaze* cartoon in JFK Library, NSF, Ralph Dungan Papers, Box 391, Chile General 5/1/62–5/28/62 folder.

7. See Otto H. Kerican, Economic Advisor, USAID/Chile, to Ralph Dungan, Special Assistant to the President, 15 October 1962, and accompanying document, "The Need for a Change in Our Chilean Program," in JFK Library, NSF, Ralph A. Dungan Papers, Box 391A, Chile—General, 10/6/62–11/30/62 folder. In Box 392, Chile, General 1/63, see Belcher to Martin, "LAPC Meeting," 8 January 1963. In the same box, see "Chile—Review of United States Policy Regarding 1964 President Election, and Proposed Task Force on Problems of American Copper Companies." See also Sigmund, *The Overthrow of Allende and the Politics of Chile, 1964–1976*, pp. 27–28.

8. Pearson, "A Program of Political Action in Chile," 17 October 1962, and Charles W. Cole, "Summary of Political Situation in Chile," JFK Library, NSF, Ralph A. Dungan Papers, Box 392, Chile General 1/63 folder.

9. "Chile Department of State Guidelines Policy and Operations," March 1962, particularly pp. 16 and 19, in JFK Library, NSF, Ralph Dungan Papers, Box 391, Chile General 5/1/62–5/21/62 folder.

10. Regarding Martin's interest in the ambassadorship, see, for example, Martin to Schlesinger, 15 May 1961 and 1 June 1961, John Bartlow Martin Papers, Library of Congress, Correspondence, Box 44, March 1961–January 1962 folder; In the same box, see Martin, "Political Reconstruction of the Dominican Republic," and entries for 29 November and 22 December 1962, Ambassador's Journal, Jan–Dec 1962 folder; Martin, "The Task Ahead," 1 August 1962, National Education Association dinner speech, Box 50, NEA folder; see also Martin to Stevenson, 22 December 1962, Stevenson Papers (MC #124), Box 55, Folder 9, John Bartlow Martin, 1958–1964 folder; see "Progress Report on NSAM-153," JFK Library, NSF, Dungan Papers, Box 393, Dominican Republic, 10/62–12/62 folder; regarding attempts to discourage Balaguer from being a candidate, see the authorless, untitled document, 12 November 1962, JFK Library, NSF Countries, Box 66, Dominican Republic, 4/62–12/62 folder. MemCon, "Views of Dominican President-Elect Juan Bosch," 4 January 1963, and MemCon, "Conversation between the President and Dr. Juan Bosch, President-Elect of the Dominican Republic," 10 January 1963, JFK Library, NSF, Dungan Papers, Dominican Republic 1/63–5/63 folder. Regarding a "stag dinner" Schlesinger held for Bosch, see Arthur M. Schlesinger Jr., "Journals: January 6, 1963," pp. 943–44, Arthur Schlesinger Jr. Papers, New York Public Library, Journals, Box 312, Jan–Feb 1963 folder. Regarding other liberal Democratic attitudes toward Bosch, see also John Rielly, "Background on Juan Bosch," 4 January 1963, Humphrey papers, Senate Legislative Files, 150.B.15.11 (B), Box 298, Dominican Republic folder. Martin to Brzezinski, 28 May 1978, Carter Library, White House Central Files, Countries, CO-23, CO-42, 1/20/77–1/20/81 folder. See also Dungan, "Memorandum for the President," 10 January 1963, JFK Library, NSF, Ralph Dungan Papers, Box 393, Dominican Republic 1/63–5/63 folder; Schlesinger to Martin, 5 February 1963, and Martin to Schlesinger, 11 February 1963, JFK Library, Schlesinger Papers, White House Files, Classified Subject Files, Box WH-32A, Dominican Republic 6/61–2/64 folder. Gleijeses, *Dominican Crisis*, pp. 50–64. See also Martin, *Overtaken by Events*, p. 83.

11. William H. Brubeck to McGeorge Bundy, "President Juan Bosch of the Dominican Republic," JFK Library, NSF, Ralph Dungan Papers, Box 393, Dominican Republic, 6/63–9/63 and undated; John Bartlow Martin, "Urgent Joint Embassy/AID/ Recommendations for $17 Million Loan now to Help Save the Bosch Government," 6 August 1963, and "Six Months

in a Quandary," particularly pp. 2, 13, 15, and 16, in same folder; Martin to State Department, 22 September 1963, JFK Library, NSF Countries, Box 67A, Dominican Republic, Cables 9/21/63–9/24/63 folder; for a rather different interpretation, see Chester, *Rag-Tags, Scum, Riff-Raff, and Commies*, pp. 18 and 32–41; Gleijeses, *Dominican Crisis*, pp. 88–99 and 106; see "Talking Paper for Dungan for Bosch," 16 October 1963, in Box 393A, Dominican Republic 10/16/63–16/31/63 folder; see "Things That Should Be Said," *Hemispherica*, October 1963. See also Martin, *Overtaken by Events*, pp. 308–11, 319–20, 323–28, 343–71, 450–53, 479–80, 521–23, and 547–90.

12. Arthur M. Schlesinger Jr., "Journals: October 1963," pp. 1151, Arthur M. Schlesinger Jr. Papers, New York Public Library, Journals, Box 313, October 1963 folder. Schlesinger said that Humphrey was "very eloquent and impassioned (and right)." See Johnson, "Progressive Dissent," p. 67.

13. Tillman to Morse, 30 September 1963, in Morse Papers, University of Oregon Library Special Collections, Subject Files, Foreign Relations, Box 46, Foreign Relations 1-1, Latin America 1963 folder.

14. Schlesinger, "Journals: October 1963," pp. 1147–50, Arthur M. Schlesinger Jr. Papers, New York Public Library, Journals, Box 313, October 1963 folder.

15. See the folders in Box 393A, Ralph Dungan Papers, Kennedy Library, NSF, Box 393A. In that box, see Schlesinger, "Memorandum for the President," 11 December 1963; Martin, *Overtaken by Events*, pp. 595–614.

16. Schlesinger mentions unnamed "Costa Rican leaders" who were skeptical, while Morales and Moscoso preferred the return of Bosch to power. Schlesinger, "Journals: October 1963," p. 1151, Arthur M. Schlesinger Jr. Papers, New York Public Library, Journals, Box 313, October 1963 folder.

17. Dungan to Luis Muñoz Marín, 16 November 1963, and King to Rusk, 22 November 1963, JFK Library, NSF Countries, Box 68, Dominican Republic, Cables 11/16/63–11/22/63 folder.

18. "Address at the Teatro Nacional in San José upon Opening the Presidents' Conference," 18 March 1963, p. 264; "Remarks at El Bosque Housing Project Near San José," p. 269; and "Remarks at the Ambassador's Residence, in Response to a Welcoming Declaration by Christian Democratic Youth," 20 March 1963, *PPPUS: Kennedy, 1963*, p. 270.

19. See "Toast of the President at a Dinner at the Casa Presidencial in San José," 18 March 1963, *PPPUS: Kennedy, 1963*, p. 267.

20. Figueres to Stevenson, 16 March 1963, Stevenson Papers, Box 32, Folder 9.

21. Kennedy, "Special Message to the Congress on Free World Defense and Assistance Programs," 2 April 1963, *PPPUS: Kennedy, 1963*, pp. 300–302.

22. The best book on the ten "years of spring in the land of eternal tyranny" remains Gleijeses, *Shattered Hope*; my treatment of Kennedy administration policy is based on Friedman, *Rethinking Anti-Americanism*, pp. 151–55.

23. Katherine Bracken to Aaron Brown, 29 June 1961, in RG 59, Bureau of Inter-American Affairs, Office of Central American Affairs, Records Pertaining to Nicaragua, 1958–1962, Box 2, Ambassador Aaron S. Brown (Correspondence) 1961 folder; Aaron Brown to John McIntyre, 4 February 1963, RG 59, Bureau of Inter-American Affairs, Office of Central American and Panamanian Affairs, Political Affairs and Relations folder; Martin to Robert Kennedy, 25 June 1963, in RG 59, Bureau of Inter-American Affairs, Office of Central American and Panamanian Affairs, Box 1, Political Affairs, Visits, Meetings 1963 folder. See also W. L. S. Williams, "Nicaragua—Plan of Action from January 6, 1964 to December 1964,"

RG 59, Bureau of Inter-American Affairs, Office of Central American Affairs, Records Relating to Nicaragua, 1963–75, Box 1, LAPC 1963; Ball to U.S. Embassy, Managua, 23 August 1963, JFK Library, NSF Countries, Box 143A, Nicaragua, General 1963 folder.

24. Department of State, "Guidelines for Policy and Operations: Nicaragua," pp. 1–2, 16
October 1962, JFK Library, Schlesinger, White House Files, Classified Subject Files,
Box WH-42, Nicaragua 6/62–12/62 folder.

25. MemCon, René Schick and Ambassador Brown, 23 July 1963; V. Lansing Collins to
Martin, 24 July 1963; and Collins to Brown, 26 July 1963, in NARA II, RG 59, Bureau of Inter-
American Affairs, Office of Central American and Panamanian Affairs, Box 1, Political
Affairs and Relations—General Policy, Background folder. See Gambone's treatment of
these issues in *Capturing the Revolution*, pp. 110–12.

26. Victor G. Folsom to Secretary of State Rusk, 11 September 1962; Charles Burrows to
Edward Rowell, 17 September 1962; and MemCon, "Honduran Agrarian Reform and the
United Fruit Company," RG 59, Bureau of Inter-American Affairs, Office of Central American Affairs, Records Relating to Honduras, 1957–74, Box 3, Agrarian Reform—Honduras,
1962 folder; Burrows to Edwin Martin, 6 February 1963, and Rowell to Burrows, 8 February 1963, in Box 5, Economic Affairs—Agrarian Reform—Honduras, 1963 folder. Folsom
also wrote letters to Senators like Hubert Humphrey. See Humphrey Papers, Senate Legislative Files, 150.B.15.10 (F), Box 297, Business Leaders Meeting—Alliance for Progress folder.

27. See, for example, "Views of Prominent Nationalists Concerning Elections in 1962 and
1963," 27 September 1961, and "Views of Right-Wing Liberals Concerning Present Conditions in Honduras and 1963 Elections," 14 December 1961, in RG 59, Bureau of Inter-
American Affairs, Office of Central American Affairs, Records Relating to Honduras,
1957–74, Box 3, Political—Local/General—Honduras 1961 folder.

28. Morris, *Honduras: Caudillo Politics*, p. 38; "Honduras—Plan of Action from Present
to December 27, 1963," Ball to Embassy, Tegucigalpa, 25 September 1963, JFK Library, NSF
Countries, Box 105, Honduras: General 12/62–9/63 folder; JFK Library, Schlesinger Papers,
White House Files, Classified Subject Files, Box WH-37, Honduras folder; Kennedy to
Villeda, 1 October 1963, JFK Library, NSF Countries, Box 105, Honduras 10/1/63–10/5/63
folder; "Honduras: Situation Report," 4 October 1963, JFK Library, NSF, Dungan Papers,
Box 394, Honduras 11/62–5/64 folder.

29. Edward Burrows, "Comments on Guidelines," 4 May 1962, p. 3, in RG 59, Bureau of
Inter-American Affairs, Office of Central American Affairs, Records Relating to Hondu-
ras, 1957–1974, Box 3, Guidelines—Honduras 1962 folder; in same box, see Collins to Cot-
trell, 16 October 1963, in POLI—Post-Coup Honduras, 1963 folder; MemCon, "Situation in
Honduras," 30 September 1963, in Box 5, MemCon Honduras 1963 folder; "The President's
News Conference of October 9, 1963," p. 770, and "The President's News Conference of
November 14, 1963," p. 851, in *PPPUS: Kennedy, 1963*; "Comments of Col. Oswaldo López
Arellano, Head of the Military Government, Regarding Honduran Relations with the
United States," 11 November 1963, JFK Library, NSF Countries, Box 105, Honduras, Gen-
eral 11/63 folder. The general stayed in power for eight more years. See Rusk to U.S.
Embassy, Tegucigalpa, 18, November 1963, JFK Library, NSF Countries in same box,
Honduras—General 11/63 folder.

30. John Roche, ADA Press Release, "ADA Asks President Withdraw Military Aid Latin
America—Cut Off Aid Honduras," 3 October 1963, Humphrey Papers, MHS, Senatorial
Files, 150.C.10.2 (F), Dominican Coup folder.

31. Dale MacIver to Donald Fraser, 26 May 1965, "Nick Kotz and the Dominican Republic," quoting Leroy Collins at an American Bar Association meeting in Puerto Rico, Donald Fraser Papers, 145.C..2.3 (B), Dominican Republic 1965 folder. Collins also noted that a literacy program was canceled following Bosch's fall.

32. Rowell to Clinton Knox, Chargé d'Affaires, 31 October 1963, in RG 59, Bureau of Inter-American Affairs, Office of Inter-American Affairs, Records Relating to Honduras, 1957–1974, Box 5, POLI—Post-Coup Honduras 1963 folder; MemCon, "Honduras—General Situation," 28 October 1963.

33. See "Statement by Secretary Rusk," 5 October 1963, in Senator Frank Church Collection, Boise State University Library Special Collections, Series 2.2 Foreign Relations, Box 47, Latin America—Dominican Republic folder.

34. Note that the "Honduras: Plan of Action from February to December 1964" has as its objective the promised transition. See Dungan Papers, Kennedy Library, NSF, Box 394, Honduras 11/62–5/64 folder. López stayed in power until 1971 and returned to power for an additional three years later in the 1970s.

35. Kennedy to McNamara, 4 October 1963, NSF, Ralph Dungan Papers, Box 394, Honduras 11/62–5/64 folder.

36. The text of the article can be found attached to "Interview with Edwin McCammon Martin," 7 April 1988, Foreign Affairs Oral History Collection of the Association for Diplomatic Studies and Training, Library of Congress, pp. 53–54. See "Editorial Note" and "Memorandum from the President's Special Assistant (Schlesinger) to President Kennedy," 8 October 1963, FRUS, 1961–1963, vol. 12: American Republics, pp. 149–52.

37. "Remarks of Senator Wayne Morse," 7 October 1963, pp. 1–4, in Morse Papers, University of Oregon Library Special Collections, Subject Files, Foreign Relations, Box 46, Foreign Relations 1-1, Latin America 1963 folder.

38. See "The President's News Conference," 9 October 1963, in PPPUS: Kennedy, 1963, pp. 770–71.

39. Edwin M. Martin to Ambassador Mann, "Legacy of Unsolved Problems," 31 December 1963, p. 2, in JFK Library, Ralph Dungan Papers, Box 20, Ambassador to Chile, Files, ARA folder.

40. A. Morales Carrión to Ed Martin, 16 April 1963, Schlesinger Papers, JFK Library, White House Files, WH-11, Subject File, 1961–1964, Guatemala folder.

41. Carl Kaysen, Deputy Special Assistant to the President for National Security Affairs, to Ed Martin and Walt Rostow, undated, JFK Library, White House Files, Classified Subject Files, Box WH-38, Inter-American Defense College folder. He had visited the Fort Gulick school for Latin American officers in the Panama Canal Zone. Schlesinger argued that there needed to be more instruction "in the ethos of democracy and the requirements of democratic society." Schlesinger to Dungan, "Inter-American Defense College," 7 November 1962 in same folder.

42. Douglas Henderson to SecState, 17 October 1962, JFK Library, NSF Countries, Box 151A, Peru General 8/15/62–12/21/62 folder.

43. A March State Department report suggested that "a Belaunde victory would now appear preferable." See Department of State, "Peru: Guidelines for Policy and Operations," pp. 20, 21, 24, and 44, March 1963, JFK Library, NSF, Ralph Dungan Papers, Box 396A, Peru 1/63–6/63 folder. Note the way Edwin Martin and Belaunde's personal assistant were speaking at cross purposes when he tried to assure him that Belaunde, who had accepted the

support of communists in the past, might even be right of center. If so, Martin responded, that was "something to be feared, since it seemed" to him "that major changes were required in Peru which would take a stronger impetus than might come from someone who was substantially right of center." See Edwin Martin, MemCon, "Dinner Conversation with President Belaunde's Personal Secretary," 31 July 1963, JFK Library, NSF, Ralph Dungan Papers, Box 396A, Peru 7/63–4/64 folder. See also "Belaunde Begins Regime," *Hemispherica*, September 1963.

44. "You represent all that we admire in a political leader," Kennedy told Betancourt as he welcomed him to the White House in February 1963. He cited his "liberal leadership" and noted that he was "the great enemy of the Communists in this hemisphere." See "Remarks of Welcome at the White House to President Betancourt of Venezuela," 19 February 1963, *PPPUS: Kennedy, 1963*, p. 184; Michael Tarver with Alfredo Angulo Rivas, Rathnam Indurthy, and Luis Loaiza Rincón, *Venezuelan Insurgency, 1960–1968*. See, particularly, Stewart to SecState, 11 August 1962, and 14 August 1962 in JFK Library, NSF Countries, Box 192, Venezuela, General 7/1/62–8/19/62 folder; MemCon, "Venezuela Defense Requirements," undated, in the same box, 9/1/62–9/20/62 folder; Edwin Martin to Special Group (Counterinsurgency), "Internal Defense Plan for Venezuela: Second Progress Report—April–August 1963," undated, JFK Library, Schlesinger Papers, White House Files, Classified Subject Files, Box WH-49, Venezuela 12/61–11/63 folder. Martin suggested that cutting back on oil imports might be the only effective form of leverage that the administration would have in the event of a coup. See p. 8.

45. Arthur M. Schlesinger Jr., "Journals: 21 May 1963," p. 1030, Arthur M. Schlesinger Jr. Papers, New York Public Library, Box 312, May 1963 folder. Schlesinger noted that "with 20 more Betancourts, Latin American would be ok."

46. See Green, *We Cannot Remain Silent*, pp. 33–34; Weis, *Cold Warriors and Coups d'Etat*, pp. 156–57; Leacock, *Requiem for Revolution*, p. 128; Vernon A. Walters, Colonel, Army Attaché, to Major General Alva R. Fitch, Assistant Chief of Staff for Intelligence, Department of the Army, 6 March 1963, JFK Library, NSF, Ralph Dungan papers, Box 390A, Brazil 1/63–6/63 folder.

47. "U.S. Short Term Policy in Brazil," particularly pp. 1, 4, and 5, in JFK Library, NSF Countries, Box 13, 12/1–12/16/62 folder; William H. Draper Jr. et al., "Report to the President by the Interdepartmental Study Group on Brazil," 3 November 1962, in JFK Library, Schlesinger Papers, White House Files, Classified Subject Files, Box WH-26, Brazil 9/62–2/63 folder.

48. McGeorge Bundy, "NSC Executive Committee Meeting," and "Memorandum for the National Security Council Executive Committee Meeting of 11 December 1962," JFK Library, NSF, Ralph Dungan Papers, Box 390, 11/62–12/62 folder; Gordon to SecState, 18 December 1962 (2 of 2), JFK Library, NSF Countries, Box 13A, Brazil: General 12/16/62–12/31/62 folder. See also Hilty, *Robert Kennedy, Brother Protector*.

49. Gordon to SecState, 18 December 1962, and "Minutes of Conversation," 19 December 1962, and Gordon to SecState, 4 January 1963, JFK Library, NSF Countries, Box 13A, Brazil 12/16/62–12/31/62 folder; Weis, *Cold Warriors and Coups d'Etat*, p. 158: Leacock, *Requiem for Revolution*, pp. 136–38.

50. Gordon to SecState, 17 January 1963, in JFK Library, NSF Countries, Box 13, Brazil, General 1/63 folder.

51. Gordon, 7 January 1963, JFK Library, NSF Countries, Box 13A, Brazil, General 1/63 folder.

52. MemCon, "Conversation between President and FinMin Dantas," 11 March 1963, in JFK Library, NSF Countries, Box 13A, Brazil, General 3/12/63–3/21/63 folder.

53. Gordon to SecState, undated, but early April 1963, JFK Library, NSF Countries, Box 14, Brazil, General 4/63 folder.

54. Gordon to Dean George Baker, Harvard Business School, 9 January 1963, Gordon Papers, JFK Library, Series 3: Ambassador to Brazil, Box 116, Chron: Jan–Feb. 1963 folder; Kennedy to Goulart, 20 May 1963, in the same box, in the March–May 1963 folder; Rusk to U.S. Embassy, Rio, 15 March 1963, JFK Library, NSF Countries, Box 43A, Cuba Cables 3/15/63–4/19/63 (1 of 4) folder; Schlesinger to Bundy, "The Press Conference and Brazil," 13 December 1962, in Box 13, Brazil, General 12/1/62–12/15/62 folder; Gordon to Kennedy, "Brazilian Political Developments and US Assistance," 7 March 1963. Gordon also noted, somewhat wistfully, that there was no "adequate leadership, organization, or strength to carry out such a coup successfully."

55. Weis, *Cold Warriors and Coups d'Etat*, pp. 161–62.

56. W. W. Rostow, "Brazil," 2 October 1963, in JFK Library, NSF, Ralph A. Dungan, Box 390A, Brazil 7/63–10/63 folder.

57. Edwin Martin to Lincoln Gordon, 23 August 1963, JFK Library, NSF, Ralph A. Dungan, Box 390A, Brazil 7/63–10/63 folder. For a more forceful enunciation of his concerns regarding U.S. support for Lacerda, see his 16 August 1963 letter to Gordon in JFK Library, NSF, Box 14, Brazil, General 8/21/63–8/31/63 folder. For an example of the CIA viewpoint he is, in part, responding to, see Central Intelligence Agency, National Intelligence Estimate No. 93-2-63, "Situation and Prospects in Brazil," 10 July 1963, LBJ Library, NSF, National Intelligence Estimates, Box 9. For the Bureau of Intelligence and Research (INR) analysis, see Thomas L. Hughes to Martin, 21 August 1963, JFK Library, NSF, Ralph A. Dungan papers, Box 390A, Brazil 7/63–10/63 folder. Hughes insisted that the United States was committed to reform in Brazil and should not assume that Goulart's own reformism "is only a part of a sinister design." Although historians tend to focus on pro-Lacerda opinions in the Kennedy years, for an example of anti-Lacerda opinion, see also L. D. Battle, "Memorandum for Kenneth O'Donnell," 18 October 1961, JFK Library, NSF Countries, Box 12, Brazil, General 10/61–11/61 folder. If Ambassador Gordon was "disturbed by the Department's assessment of Lacerda as an irresponsible reactionary," I would argue that while no reactionary, he was, frequently, irresponsible. See Gordon to Martin, "Political Trends and Contingencies in Brazil," 21 August 1963, JFK Library, Arthur Schlesinger Papers, White House Files, Classified Subject Files, Box WH-26, 6/63–9/63 folder.

58. See Gordon to Martin, 18 October 1963, in RG 59, Central Foreign Policy Files, 1963, Box 3312, AID 2/1/63 Brazil folder.

59. See "Approved Short Term Policy for Brazil," 11 October 1963, JFK Library, NSF, Meetings and Memoranda, Box 315, Standing Group Meeting, Meeting of 10/1/63 folder.

60. See Gordon, "Contingency Planning Brazil," 4 November 1963, JFK Library, NSF Countries, Box 14A, Brazil, General 11/1–11/15/63 folder.

61. See Rabe, *Most Dangerous Area in the World*, pp. 68–71 and 179; Weis, *Cold Warriors and Coups d'Etat*, pp. 162–69; See also, for example, "A Contingency Plan for Brazil," 6 January 1964, JFK Library, NSF, Ralph A. Dungan Papers, Box 391, Brazil 12/63–9/64 folder.

62. Gordon to SecState, 19 November 1962, JFK Library, NSF Countries, Box 13, Brazil, General 11/14/62–11/30/62 folder. Recent research in Soviet records suggests that President Goulart was making a significant effort to improve relations. That was in keeping with his "independent" stance. See Hershberg, "Soviet-Brazilian Relations and the Cuban Missile Crisis." particularly pp. 178–208.

63. Martin to Gordon, 16 August 1963, in JFK Library, NSF Countries, Box 14, Brazil, General 8/21/63–8/31/63 folder.

64. Martin to Gordon, JFK Library, NSF Countries, Box 14, Brazil, General 8/21/63–8/31/63 folder.

65. Gordon to Martin, "Political Trends and Contingencies in Brazil," 21 August 1963, JFK Library, Arthur Schlesinger Papers, White House Files, Classified Subject Files, Box WH-26, 6/63–9/63 folder; Gordon to SecState, JFK Library, NSF Countries, Box 14, Brazil, General 21/Aug–31/Aug/1963 folder.

66. "Proposed Short-Term Policy—Brazil," October 1963, JFK Library, NSF Countries, Box 14A, Brazil, General 10/1/63–10/15/63 folder.

67. Gordon, "Contingency Planning Brazil," 4 November 1963, in JFK Library, NSF Countries, Box 14A, Brazil, General 11/1/63–11/15/63 folder.

68. Lincoln Gordon, "Contingency Planning—Brazil," 4 November 1963, JFK Library, NSF Countries, Box 14A, Brazil 11/1/63–11/15/63 folder; Arthur M. Schlesinger Jr., "Journals: October 1963," pp. 1160–61, Arthur M. Schlesinger Jr. Papers, New York Public Library, Journals, Box 313, October 1963 folder.

69. Gordon to SecState, 20 November 1963, JFK Library, NSF Countries, Box 14A, Brazil, General 11/16/63–11/22/73 folder.

70. See Harriman to SecState and Dungan, "Presidential Visit to Brazil," and Dungan's response, in JFK Library, NSF Countries, Box 14A, Brazil, General 11/16–11/22/63 folder.

71. Kennedy was famously skeptical of the military frame of mind due to his experience in World War II. See "Meeting on Europe and General Diplomatic Matters," in Naftali, *Presidential Recordings: Kennedy, Great Crises*, vol. 1, p. 47. Kennedy's special counsel, Theodore C. Sorensen, claims that the president admired the competence and appreciated the pro-Americanism of the Latin American military. See his *Kennedy*, pp. 535–36. I have found no confirmation of this in the documents except for the 30 July 1962 conversations cited above. Assistant Secretary Martin later wrote that he personally "would not have given even quiet support" to the 1964 coup, "even if it had not resulted, as it did, in military rule in Brazil for 21 years." (His counterpart in the Johnson administration was Thomas Mann.) See Martin, *Kennedy and Latin America*, p. 311. Kennedy did support a coup in Vietnam, of course, but seemed generally, if foolishly, surprised by how it played out. See, for example, Freedman, *Kennedy's Wars*, pp. 367–97. Historians too often ignore the insights of Stepan, *The Military in Politics*.

72. Ted Widmer, ed., *Listening In*, pp. 248 and 285–86. The transcript is incorrect, as even a casual listening to the recording itself will confirm.

73. *Hearings before the Committee on Foreign Relations, Foreign Assistance Act of 1963*, pp. 12–13, 28–29, and 31; Johnson, *Congress and the Cold War*, pp. 92–104, 128, 169, 175, 194, 203–8, 592–95, 642, 649, 665, and 669; David and Holm, "Kennedy Administration and Battle over Foreign Aid," pp. 67–68 and 83–84; the Church quotation is from Ashby and Gramer, *Fighting the Odds*, p. 172.

74. Schlesinger, "Journals: 27 October 1963," pp. 1180–81, Arthur M. Schlesinger Jr. Papers, New York Public Library, Journals, Box 313, October 1963 folder.

75. Schlesinger, "Journals: 6 November 1963," pp. 1182, Arthur M. Schlesinger Jr. Papers, New York Public Library, Journals, Box 313, November 1963 folder.

76. Stern, Averting "The Final Failure," p. 412; Arthur M. Schlesinger Jr., "Journals: 9 September 1974," pp. 2434–35, Arthur M. Schlesinger Jr. Papers, New York Public Library, Journals, Box 315, September 1974 folder; Schoultz, That Infernal Little Cuban Republic, pp. 200–208 and 212. See also "Memorandum for the Record Drafted by Chairman of the JCS Taylor," 28 February 1963, in White, The Kennedys and Cuba, p. 308; "Address and Question and Answer Period in Tampa before the Florida Chamber of Commerce," 18 November 1963, PPPUS: Kennedy, 1963, p. 867.

77. Attwood, The Reds and the Blacks, p. 134. Attwood, a former Look reporter, had been Kennedy's ambassador to Guinea. Rabe, Most Dangerous Area in the World, p. 19.

78. See D'Haeseleer, Salvadoran Crucible, pp. 39–47.

79. Robert Dallek credits his wife Geraldine Dallek with providing the title for his biography. See Dallek, An Unfinished Life, p. 715; see also Gabler, Catching the Wind, pp. 212–14 and 246–47.

80. Solberg, Humphrey, p. 239.

81. "Americas Mourn President Kennedy," Hemispherica, December 1963.

Chapter 5

1. Lyndon Johnson, "Address before a Joint Session of Congress," 27 November 1963, PPPUS: Johnson, 1963–1964, p. 9; "Remarks on the Alliance for Progress to Representatives of the Continent of Latin America," PPPUS: Johnson, 1963–1964, p. 7.

2. Martin, Stevenson and the World, pp. 210–11.

3. Rakove, Kennedy, Johnson, and the Nonaligned World, pp. xxv and 187; See Small, At the Water's Edge, p. 37. Johnson, "Remarks in Los Angeles at a Mexican Fiesta Given in His Honor by President López Mateos," 22 February 1964, and "Remarks on the Third Anniversary of the Alliance for Progress," 16 March 1964, PPPUS: Johnson, 1963–1964, pp. 309 and 384.

4. See Schlesinger, 26 November 1963 journal entry, Schlesinger and Schlesinger, eds., Journals, p. 208. See Johnson, "Remarks on Alliance for Progress to Representatives of the Countries of Latin America," 26 November 1963, PPPUS: Johnson, 1963–1964, book 1, pp. 6–7. See the 16 December 1964 memo from Robert M. Sayre to McGeorge Bundy, "Invitation to President Johnson to Visit Brazil," in the LBJ Library, NSF Countries, Latin America— Brazil, Box 10, "Memos 9/64–11/64" folder. See also "Una Nueva Era para los Presidentes de Estados Unidos," El Mercurio 21 January 1965, p. 3. Gordon noted in the 1964 interview that Johnson had been "rather skeptical at the start," but later "endorsed the program with a kind of vigor which was not present in his first pronouncements." See p. 82. See also Leuchtenburg, Shadow of FDR, p. 134.

5. See Schlesinger, 5 December 1963 journal entry, Schlesinger and Schlesinger, eds., Journals, p. 213. For a more nuanced, if still not entirely balanced, perspective on Mann, see Thomas Tunstall Allcock, "Becoming 'Mr. Latin America,'" pp. 1017–45, and Thomas C. Mann, pp. 63–89. See also Shannon, Heir Apparent, pp. 98–99.

6. Richard Goodwin, "Memorandum for the President," 27 November 1963, Library of Congress, W. Averell Harriman Papers, Box 502, Arthur Schlesinger Jr. 1963 folder.

7. Morse, "Press Release: Untitled, 14 December 1963," in Morse Papers, University of Oregon Library Special Collections, Subject Files, Foreign Relations, Box 46, Foreign Relations—Latin America—1964 folder. Deposed leader Bosch sent a letter to Morse in which he praised him for his support of constitutional government in the Dominican Republic. See Juan Bosch to Morse, 2 February 1964, in Morse Papers, University of Oregon Library Special Collections, Subject Files Foreign Relations, Box 46, Foreign Relations—Latin America—1964 folder.

8. Humphrey to Johnson, 14 December 1963, Humphrey Senatorial Files, MHS, 150.D.14.4 (4), and "Humphrey Lauds President's Steps on Latin American Affairs," Press Release, 16 December 1963, Foreign Policy: Alliance for Progress: Thomas Mann folder.

9. See Schlesinger, 23 December 1963 journal entry, Schlesinger and Schlesinger, eds., *Journals*, p. 217.

10. Arthur M. Schlesinger Jr., "Journals: 11 March 1274," p. 1281, Arthur M. Schlesinger Jr. Papers, New York Public Library, Journals, Box 313, Jan–May 1964 folder. Months later, LBJ complained to Galbraith that Schlesinger had not "come in to discuss with me his objections to our LA policy." See "Journals: 23 July 1964," p. 1291 in the same box. See Schlesinger, 30 December 1963, 18 January, and 31 January 1964 journal entries, Schlesinger and Schlesinger, eds., *Journals*, pp. 218–19 and 223–24. See also 11 March 1964, p. 1274, Schlesinger Papers, NYPL, Journals, Box 313, Jan–May 1964 folder.

11. Schlesinger, 18 June 1964 journal entry, p. 1288, Arthur M. Schlesinger Jr. Papers, New York Public Library, Journals, Box 313, Jan–May 1964 folder. Schlesinger also suggested that serving as ambassador to the UN "would help kill the public impression of him as the ruthless prosecutor."

12. See Caro, *Passage of Power*, particularly pp. 344–45, 351, 409, and 410–12.

13. See Schlesinger, 5 December 1963 journal entry, Schlesinger and Schlesinger, eds., *Journals*, p. 213.

14. See the 15 December 1963 letter from President Johnson to Mann, Lyndon Baines Johnson Presidential Library, NSF Countries, Latin America, Box 3, 6/67–9/67 folder. Schlesinger, "Memorandum for the President," 14 December 1963, in JFK Library, Schlesinger Papers, White House Files, Subject Files, Alliance for Progress, 10/16/62–12/31/63 folder. Regarding liberal Democrats' concerns about Mann, see also the drafts of a letter for Humphrey to Johnson that was written by John Rielly, 13 December 1963, Humphrey Senatorial Files, 150.D.14.4, Foreign Policy: Latin America: Thomas Mann folder; Caro, *Passage of Power*, pp. 581–82. Robert Dallek argues that Johnson administration policies demonstrated continuities in particular with Kennedy's intentions at the time of his death. See his *Flawed Giant*, pp. 92 and 96. Edwin McCammon Martin, *Kennedy and Latin America*, p. 465. Martin (Mann's predecessor) argues that the problem was that Johnson preferred stability to change and "did not share Kennedy's interest in Latin America." See p. 460. "As a result the AFP continued in name but its political spirit was dead." Regarding the Mann appointment, see "Letter to Thomas C. Mann upon His Assuming New Responsibilities for Latin American Affairs," December 15, 1963," in *PPPUS: Johnson, 1963–1964*, vol. 1, p. 56. On Mann's opinions, see also Woods, *LBJ: Architect of American Ambition*, p. 495, although he misrepresents Schlesinger's position. Schlesinger's claim that LBJ's Latin America policy was pro-corporate and insufficiently prodemocratic is not without foundation. Schlesinger considered the ap-

pointment of Mann "a declaration of independence, even perhaps a declaration of aggression, against the Kennedys." See his *Robert Kennedy and His Times*, pp. 680–81, 748–49, and 756. Regarding Mann's official position on the Alliance for Progress, see the speech he gave before the Washington Institute of Foreign Affairs in May 1964, "The Alliance for Progress," State Department: Bureau of Public Affairs, June 1964, no. 7. His primary concerns expressed here were economic and not social or political, and in this way he was similar to Ambassador Gordon. Regarding Mann's pro-military inclinations in Central America in the previous decade, see Holden, *Armies without Nations*, pp. 159 and 169. The so-called Mann Doctrine is discussed in *FRUS, 1964–1968*, vol. 31: *South and Central America; Mexico*, pp. 28–29. See also Rabe, *Most Dangerous Area in the World*, pp. 176–79; Leacock, *Requiem for Revolution*, pp. 198–99; Tulchin, "The Promise of Progress: U.S. Relations with Latin America during the Administration of Lyndon B. Johnson," pp. 219–21 and 231–33.

15. Bill Wirtz listed the two Kennedy brothers, of course, and himself, as well as Dungan and Schlesinger. See 15 December 1963 entry, Schlesinger and Schlesinger, eds., *Journals*, p. 216. Rielly to Humphrey, "Latin American Policy at the White House," 11 December 1963, Humphrey Senatorial Files, MHS, 150.D.14.4 (4), Foreign Policy: Latin America: Thomas Mann folder.

16. Morse to Norman Thomas, 3 March 1964, Morse Papers, University of Oregon Library Special Collections, Subject Files, Foreign Relations, Box 46, Foreign Relations—Latin America—1964 folder.

17. Gordon Chase to Bundy, "Deterrence of Latin Dictators—Tad Szulc Article," 19 March 1964, LBJ Library, NSF Countries, Latin America, Box 1, 11/63–6/64 folder. Frances Grant to *New York Times*, 25 March 1964, Frances Grant Papers, Latin American Country Files, Box 47, Venezuela—Letters to the New York Times folder.

18. Gordon to Mann, 7 December 1963, and Gordon to Barry Bingham, 20 November 1963, Gordon Papers, Series 3: Ambassador to Brazil, Chron Files, Box 116, Oct–Dec 1963 folder; Ellsworth Bunker and Edward P. Maffitt, Chief of Staff, Brazilian Strategy Working Group, Department of State, "National Policy Series, Brazil, Final Draft," 27 November 1963, NSF, Ralph Dungan Papers, Box 391, Draft Brazil 12/9/63 folder.

19. "Exchange of Letters with President Goulart of Brazil," 23 December 1963 and 13 December 1963, *PPPUS: Johnson, 1963–1964*, pp. 81–82. Regarding the Johnson letter, see Gordon to Rusk, 19 December 1963, NSF, Ralph Dungan Papers, Box 391, Brazil 12/63–9/64 folder; Johnson to Goulart, 19 December 1963, in JFK Library, NSF, Ralph A. Dungan Papers, Box 391, Brazil 12/63–9/64 folder; see also Leacock, *Requiem for Revolution*, pp. 85 and 198. No visit with President Johnson was scheduled in January when Gordon met with State Department officials. In the 10 July 1969 interview for the LBJ Library (hereafter Gordon interview, LBJ Library 1969) with Paige E. Mulhollan, he notes how disappointed and even "disturbed" he had been that he had not met with Johnson then. See pp. 12–13. See Gordon to Dungan, 22 January 1964, NSF, Ralph Dungan Papers, JFK Library, Box 391 12/63–9/64 folder. He seems to have been responding to a 1 November 1963 letter.

20. Mein for Gordon, 18 March 1964, LBJ Library, NSF Countries, Brazil, Box 9, 11/63–2/64 folder.

21. Telegram, 24 March 1964, in LBJ Library, NSF Countries, Brazil, 11/63–3/64 folder.

22. Gordon to Rusk, 27 March 1964, LBJ Library, NSF Countries, Brazil, Box 9, 3/64 folder.

23. Dungan to Bundy, 24 March 1964, NSF, Ralph Dungan Papers, Box 391, 12/63–9/64 folder.

24. Gordon to Rusk, 2 April 1964, LBJ Library, NSF Countries, Brazil, Box 10, LA—Brazil, Cables folder.

25. Gordon to Rusk, 2 April 1964, LBJ Library, NSF Countries, Brazil, Box 10, LA—Brazil, Cables folder.

26. Gordon to Rusk, 2 April 1964, LBJ Library, NSF Countries, Brazil, Box 10, LA—Brazil, Cables folder.

27. Beschloss, ed., *Taking Charge*, p. 306.

28. "The President's News Conference of April 4, 1964." *PPPUS: Johnson, 1963–1964*, p. 437.

29. See Mann to Gordon, 2 April 1964, and "Draft Departmental Statement," 3 April 1964, in LBJ Library, NSF Countries, Box 10, Latin America—Brazil, Cables 4/64 folder.

30. See Stepan, *The Military in Politics*, pp. 85–121.

31. See "Background Paper: Policy Framework Governing A.I.D. Lending to Brazil, 1961–1964," p. 4, in LBJ Library, NSF Countries, Brazil, Box 12, Brazil, 10/67–11/68 folder.

32. See "Background Paper: Policy Framework Governing A.I.D. Lending to Brazil, 1961–1964," p. 5, in LBJ Library, NSF Countries, Brazil, Box 12, Brazil, 10/67–11/68 folder.

33. Leacock, *Requiem for Revolution*, p. 224.

34. Gordon to Rusk, 7 April 1964, in LBJ Library, NSF Countries, Box 10, Latin America—Brazil, Box 10, Cables folder.

35. For a sympathetic portrayal of his presidency, see Dulles, *President Castello Branco*. Regarding Gordon's immediate reaction to the establishment of a government, see p. 17. Regarding the suspension of political rights, see pp. 30–31 and 42–43. Gordon minimized the importance of Kubitschek's loss of rights in a 4 June 1964 cable to Secretary of State Dean Rusk, and only later (10 June 1964) asked Castello Branco "how he would explain it in my place." See LBJ Library, NSF Countries, Latin America—Brazil, Box 10, Cables 4/64–8/64 folder. In a personal letter, Gordon said that the "deprivation of political rights" was "not a very meaningful action," although he did not explain why. See Gordon to John Perry Miller of Yale University, 2 June 1964, Gordon Papers, Series 3: Ambassador to Brazil, Box 116, May–August 1964 folder. Journalist Elio Gaspari, in the first book in a multivolume history of military rule, refers to the Castello Branco regime as a "temporary" and also as an "embarrassed" dictatorship. See *A Ditadura Envergonhada*, p. 129. For a balanced appraisal, see Skidmore, *Politics of Military Rule in Brazil*, particularly pp. 16–65. Regarding torture, see pp. 24–25. See also Leacock, *Requiem for Revolution*, pp. 216–17. Gaspari argues that the government's failure to punish the torturers in September 1964 represented a critical moment in the development of the dictatorship. See *A Ditadura Envergonhada*, particularly pp. 141–51. In a letter to *Commonweal* in 1970, Gordon remarked that "no cases of torture were brought to my attention," a rather odd statement given that they were covered in the not yet censored press. See "An Exchange of Views: Torture in Brazil," *Commonweal*, 7 August 1970, pp. 378–79 and 398. Gordon remained in denial on this subject. See his *Brazil's Second Chance*, pp. 60–75. Regarding the suspension of political rights and Johnson's opinions regarding developments in Brazil, see the transcript of a telephone conversation between Johnson and Mann in *FRUS, 1964 to 1968*, vol. 31, pp. 42–43, 45, and 468–69. Regarding Gordon's initial misgivings, see pp. 461–63, and Levinson and de Onís, *Alliance That Lost Its Way*, pp. 90–91. See also Gordon to Hubert Humphrey, 17 April 1964, and Gordon to Colgate University President Vincent M. Barnett, Jr., 13 April 1964, Gordon Papers, Series 3: Ambassador to Brazil, Series 3: Ambassador to Brazil, Chron File: Jan–April 1964 folder. Regarding the general U.S. response to the establishment of the military govern-

ment, see Green, "Clerics, Exiles, and Academics," pp. 87 and 90–91. It should be clear even from the title that relatively few in the United States were concerned about the political direction in Brazil during the Johnson years. Few knew about Operation Brother Sam until a decade later with the publication of Parker, *Brazil and the Quiet Intervention.* Note that Gordon refers to having "taken certain contingency precautions, but it was fortunate that they proved to be unneeded." He wrote this in a 17 April 1964 letter to General Lauris Norstad, President, Owens-Corning, in the Jan–April 1964 folder listed above.

36. See Dulles, *Castello Branco,* p. 17. Regarding the admiration he felt for Castello Branco and the vast improvement he perceived in the quality of leadership in comparison to former President Goulart, see pp. 1–3 of the 20 April 1964 telegram in which Gordon reports on his "first private talk with Castello Branco" in LBJ Library, NSF Countries, Latin America—Brazil, Box 10, Cables 4/64–8/64 folder. Regarding Assistant Secretary Mann's concerns about the government's use of "procedures which do not afford accused the opportunity to know the precise charges against him and to make his defense," see 9 June 1964 letter from Mann to Gordon in the same folder.

37. Dulles, *Castello Branco,* p. 76; Leacock, *Requiem for Revolution,* pp. 226–28 and 230. See the excellent biography of the Brazilian emperor by Barman, *Citizen Emperor.*

38. See Gordon to Rusk, 9 June 1964, NSF, Ralph Dungan Papers, JFK Library, Box 391, Brazil 12/63–9/64 folder. See also LBJ's letter to the Brazilian president, "Exchange of Messages with the President of Brazil, September 5, 1965," in *PPPUS: Johnson, 1963–1964,* vol. 2, pp. 1047–49.

39. Beschloss, ed., *Taking Charge,* p. 318.

40. See, for example, the coverage in "Brazilian Pot Boils Over," *Hemispherica,* April 1964.

41. Fraser agreed with the characterization of the Goulart government as a "clique of Communist profiteers and real gangsters . . . with [the] help of the labor unions [and] professional agitators." See his 19 June 1964 letter to V. N. Burkhart of E. J. Longyear Company, Donald Fraser Papers, 145.3.2.3 (B), Brazil Correspondence, 1964–1965 folder. Even as late as June 1966, Robert Kennedy remained convinced that the Castello Branco government was better "than the one it replaced." See Robert Kennedy to Donald I. Shultz, Formulários Nacional Ltda., São Paulo, JFK Library, Senate Papers, Box 41, Correspondence: Subject File 1966, Foreign Affairs 7/21/66–7/31/1966 folder.

42. Rielly to Humphrey, 19 June 1964, Humphrey Papers, MHS, Humphrey Senatorial Files, 150.B.16.5 (B), Brazil 1964 folder; Schlesinger, "Notes on the Italian Situation," 23 April 1964, and Bundy to Schlesinger, 12 May 1964, LBJ Library, NSF, Memos to the President, Box 1, 5/1–27/64 folder. European leaders were worried that the Johnson administration had abandoned what had been perceived as a Kennedy policy of supporting democracy and returning to the "Eisenhower-Dulles policy of backing military regimes of the right." Schlesinger said that he could have defended administration policy better "if I understood the reasons for the new policy myself."

43. See, for example, Wayne Morse, "The New President of Brazil," *Congressional Record,* 3 April 1964, pp. 6851–52. See his comments on 21 April 1964, p. 8611.

44. See Gordon's 8 June 1964 telegram in JFK Library, NSF, Ralph A. Dungan Papers, Box 391, Brazil 12/63–9/64 folder, as well as his 14 November 1964 telegram in RG 59, Central Foreign Policy Files, 1964–1966, Box 537, untitled folder.

45. Taffet, *Foreign Aid as Foreign Policy,* p. 95; See Mann to Gordon, 9 June 1964, in LBJ Library, NSF Countries, Brazil, Box 10, Cables 4/64–8/84 folder.

46. Regarding U.S. support for the coup, see Parker, *Brazil and the Quiet Intervention*, pp. 68–70 and 72–87. Regarding loans and other economic aid, see pp. 87–100. as well as Levinson and de Onís, *The Alliance That Lost Its Way*, pp. 15, 88, 101–2, 117–20. Regarding the increasing number of U.S. officials in Brazil, see Leacock, *Requiem for Revolution*, p. 226. See 31 August 1964 letter from McGeorge Bundy to Senator Humphrey, LBJ Library, NSF Countries, Latin America, Box 2, 6/64–8/64 folder. See also 7 September 1964 memo from W. W. Rostow to Thomas Mann, "Reflections and Recommendations on Brazil," p. 9 in LBJ Library, NSF Countries, Latin America—Brazil, Box 10, Cables 9/64–11/65 folder.

47. Gordon to State, 23 July 1964, LBJ Library, NSF Countries, Brazil, Box 10, Cables 4/64–8/84 folder.

48. See, for example, the study by journalist and author Kotz, *Judgement Days*. See Johnson, "Remarks to the Ambassadors of Nations Participating in the Alliance for Progress, May 11, 1964," in *PPPUS: Johnson, 1963–1964*, vol. 1, p. 679.

49. Hubert Humphrey, "U.S. Policy in Latin America," *Foreign Affairs* 42, no. 4 (July 1964): 585–601.

50. Adlai Stevenson, "First Draft of Foreign Affairs Plank for Democratic Platform," 5 August 1964, in Johnson, ed., *Papers of Stevenson*, vol. 7, pp. 599–601.

51. "Democratic Platform 1964," in Johnson and Porter, *National Party Platforms*, pp. 643 and 652–53. The Republicans, for their part, promised "liberation" for communist countries, including Cuba. See "Republican Platform 1964," pp. 688–89.

52. Field, *From Development to Dictatorship*, pp. 80–84, 140, 162–64, and 189–96.

53. Remarks by the Honorable Douglas Dillon, Secretary of the Treasury, before the first Latin American meeting of Development Financing Institutions, 30 November 1964, p. 8, Library of Congress, W. Averell Harriman Papers, Box 430, Alliance for Progress folder; Grant to Johnson, 5 November 1964, Frances Grant Papers, Correspondence, Box 29, Lyndon Johnson folder; Betancourt to Humphrey, 6 November 1964, Humphrey Papers, Minnesota Historical Society, Senatorial Files, 150.B.16/5 (B), JER Reading File folder.

54. See National Intelligence Estimate No. 94-63, "The Chilean Situation and Prospects," in LBJ Library, particularly pp. 1–2, 6, and 19–20; Humphrey's aide, John Rielly, argued that the Christian Democrats looked to him for leadership. See Rielly to Humphrey, "Visit of Chilean Delegation," 13 October 1964, Humphrey Papers, MHS, Humphrey Senatorial Files, 150.B.16.5 (B), Chilean Elections 1964 folder.

55. For information on U.S. long-term policy toward Chile beginning in the Kennedy administration, see the 15 October 1962 memo from Otto H. Kerican, USAID economic adviser in Chile, to Dungan in JFK Library, NSF, Ralph A. Dungan Papers, Chile General, 10/6/62–11/30/62 folder. See also Taffet, *Foreign Aid as Foreign Policy*, pp. 76–77; Lockhart, *Chile, The CIA and the Cold War*, pp. 139–40. The best account we have of U.S. relations with Chile during this time period is Hurtado-Torres, *Gathering Storm*. Regarding the election of Frei and his proposed program, see Gazmuri, Arancibia, and Góngora, *Frei y su Época*, vol. 2, particularly pp. 559–65. See Mann's gleeful comment in conversation with Johnson, "We're going to win this election in Chile; things look good, we've done a hell of a lot of work on that." Johnson, for his part, seems to have been singularly uninformed about what was going on; see *FRUS, 1964–1968*, vol. 31, pp. 45–46. See also pp. 545–46, 557, 575–76, 582–83, and 592. See also Sigmund, *United States and Democracy in Chile*, pp. 22–25, and Kornbluh, ed., *Pinochet File*, pp. 3–6. Ralph Dungan was not forthright in his testimony in the *Intelligence Activities Senate Resolution 21: Hearings before the Select Committee to Study*

Government Operations with Respect to Intelligence Activities of the United States Senate, Ninety-Fourth Congress, First Session, vol. 7: *Covert Action, December 4 and 5, 1975*, pp. 23–26. See also the "Chart Covering Covert Action Expenditures in Chile by Technique, 1963–1973," p. 95. Regarding his support for Frei and the Christian Democrats, see his 1 June 1965 letter to Bernard Norwitch, Senator's Joseph Clark's administrative assistant, in JFK Library, Papers of Ralph A. Dungan, Ambassador to Chile Files, Box 17, Correspondence—Pennsylvania. A different understanding of U.S.-Chilean relations can be found in Sater, *Chile and the United States*, pp. 142–43 and 158. Sater exaggerates, from my perspective, Frei's "independence," as does, to some degree, Taffet. Regarding the 1958 election and its impact on U.S. policy, see pp. 69–78, 86, 91–92, and 143–48. See Jova to Dungan, 14 May 1964, Kennedy Library, NSF, Ralph Dungan Papers, Box 392, Chile 1/64–10/64 folder. For Allende's use of U.S. support for Frei, see Cole, 29 July 1964, RG 59, Central Foreign Policy Files, 1964–1966, Box 2029, POL 14, 6/1/64.

56. See Bundy to Senator Hubert Humphrey, 31 August 1964, LBJ Library, NSF Countries, Latin America, Box 2, 6/64–8/64 folder.

57. Robert A. Stevenson, Counselor of Embassy for Political Affairs, "Observations on Senator Eduardo Frei's Election as President of Chile," 20 October 1964, in RG 59, Central Foreign Policy Files, 1964–1966, Box 2028, POL 15-1, 10/1/64.

58. See Hurtado-Torres, *Gathering Storm*, particularly 4–6, 12, and 46.

59. "Remarks by President Frei at a Dinner for the Special Delegations Attending His Inauguration—La Moneda, November 4, 1961," Stevenson Papers, Box 454, Folder 12, Series 9, Travel Materials, Chile and Panama: 1964; "Chile Hands Victory to Frei," *Hemispherica*, September 1964; Dorothy M. Jester, "Semi-Annual Politico-Economic Assessment—Chile," in RG 59, Central Foreign Policy Files, 1964–1966, Box 2025, POL 2-1, Joint Weekas folder. See Taffet, *Foreign Aid as Foreign Policy*, pp. 7 and 67–93. Taffet calculates that Chile received 11.8 percent of Alliance for Progress money, making Chile the third largest recipient (and, by far, the least populous country of the three). A more comprehensive analysis of U.S. aid to Chile during this time period can be found in his unpublished doctoral dissertation, "Alliance for What?" Note that Ralph Dungan argued that Kennedy and Dungan himself had "bet on the gang" beginning in 1962. See Dungan to Bernard Norwitch, Administrative Assistant to Senator Joseph Clark (D-Penn.), 1 June 1965, Ralph Dungan Papers, JFK Library, Ambassador to Chile Files, Box 21, Chronological File, June 1965 folder.

60. Martin, *Stevenson and the World*, pp. 781–84, 806–7, and 817–19.

61. Humphrey to Dungan, 26 December 1964, JFK Library, Papers of Ralph Dungan, Box 15, Ambassador to Chile Files, Correspondence H folder.

62. Schlesinger, *A Thousand Days*, p. 603.

63. See Schlesinger Papers, NYPL, Journals, Box 312, pp. 652–53, March 1962 folder. Note that Dungan refers to President Frei as "Eduardo" in a 23 December 1964 letter to *Look* senior editor Leonard Gross in JFK Library, Personal Papers of Ralph A. Dungan, Ambassador to Chile files—Correspondence C. See Tulchin, "Promise of Progress," pp. 221–22 and 226. The memo itself is reproduced on pp. 595–96 of *FRUS, 1964–1968*, vol. 31. See also McGeorge Bundy's 16 June 1964 memo to Johnson in pp. 51–52. Regarding Dungan's interest in Chilean affairs, see his 18 January 1964 memo to Bundy on p. 549, as well as the editorial note on p. 551. The unsolicited letter of recommendation Schlesinger sent on 15 September 1964 to President Johnson regarding Dungan's qualifications for the position is available in Lyndon Baines Johnson Presidential Library, Box 81, Ralph Dungan folder. Johnson

replied that he agreed "with your reasoning and your views," but he also expressed concern about losing Dungan's valuable contributions in Washington. Humphrey's top aide was also focused on getting Dungan appointed ambassador, primarily because of his strong ties to the Christian Democratic Party, as well as his personal tie to President Kennedy and his experience working with the Alliance, but also because of Dungan's frustrations with Mann. See Rielly to Humphrey, 3 February 1964 and 7 May 1964, Humphrey Papers, Humphrey Senatorial Files, 150.B.16.5, Chile 1964 folder. In a 27 July 1964 letter, Rielly suggests that this was going to be the most important ambassadorial appointment in the next year and a half, presuming that Gordon stayed on as ambassador to Brazil. See Humphrey Senatorial Files, 150.B.16.5, New York Times Interview Sept 64 folder. While describing a "progressive" candidate with qualities similar to Dungan's, Gordon Chase recommended that Milton Eisenhower or David Rockefeller be offered the position. See the 18 September 1964 "Ambassador to Chile" memo from Chase to Bundy, LBJ Library, NSF Countries, Latin America—Chile, Box 13, Memos 9/64–11/64 folder. Allcock also notes the conflict between Mann and Dungan in "Becoming 'Mr. Latin America,'" pp. 1041–42.

64. A good introduction to President Eduardo Frei's thought in English is his article "The Aims of Christian Democracy," *Commonweal*, 9 October 1964, pp. 63–66. Regarding Frei's attempt to deepen Chilean democracy, see Kirkendall, "Paulo Freire, Eduardo Frei, Literacy Training and the Politics of Consciousness Raising in Chile," pp. 687–717. For an argument that the United States helped undermine a constitutional government in the early 1960s, which was also engaged in a similar project, see Kirkendall, "Entering History," pp. 168–89. Regarding the support of Chile for the Alliance for Progress, see, for example, Frei's inaugural address in *Obras Escogidos*, pp. 299–305. See also the editorials "Chile Frente a Una Nueva Politica Social y Económica," *El Mercurio*, 17 January 1965, p. 19, and "Estados Unidos Frente a Nuestro Desarrollo," *El Mercurio*, 15 April 1965, p. 3. See also Taffet, *Foreign Aid as Foreign Policy*, pp. 78–80. Regarding the changing political system in the late 1950s and early 1960s, see, for example, Sater, *Chile and the United States*, p. 130. Dungan's hopes are expressed in the 12 February 1965 preliminary draft for a "National Policy Paper on Chile," available in National Archives II, RG 59, Central Foreign Policy Files, 1964–1966, Box 2030, POL 1, Gen. Policy Background.

65. See Lincoln Gordon, Oral History Interview with John E. Rielly, 30 May 1964, John F. Kennedy Library (hereafter Gordon interview 1964), pp. 3–7.

66. See McGeorge Bundy, "U.S. Foreign Policy since November 1963," 12 January 1965, LBJ Library, NSF, Memos to the President, Box 1/1–2/28/65 folder. See the 16 December 1964 memo from Robert M. Sayre to McGeorge Bundy, "Invitation to President Johnson to Visit Brazil," in the LBJ Library, NSF Countries, Latin America—Brazil, Box 10, Memos 9/64–11/64 folder. See also "Una Nueva Era para los Presidentes de Estados Unidos," *El Mercurio*, 21 January 1965, p. 3; Dungan to Bundy, 3 February 1965, Dungan Papers, JFK Library, Ambassador to Chile Files, Box 13, Correspondence: Bundy, McGeorge folder; Dungan to Rusk, 12 February 1965, Box 21, Chronological File, February 1965 folder.

67. "Statement by the President upon Ordering Troops into the Dominican Republic," 28 April 1965, and "Statement by the President on the Situation in the Dominican Republic," 30 April 1965, *PPPUS: Johnson, 1965*, pp. 461 and 465; Beschloss, ed., *Reaching for Glory*, pp. 284–91, 297–305, 311–12, 330–35, and 338. See also Woods, "Conflicted Hegemon," pp. 753–66. See also Martin, *Overtaken by Events*, p. 629.

68. John Bartlow Martin, undated report, particularly pp. 14–16 and 20, John Bartlow Martin Papers, Library of Congress, Box 50, Reports and Other Writings folder; Martin later wrote to Schlesinger to encourage Robert Kennedy to suggest to the pope that Emmanuel Clarizio should be nominated for his role in arranging the cease-fire. (He also suggested that it would be "all right with me if he nominates us jointly.") See Martin to Schlesinger, 25 September 1965, Correspondence, Box 34, Schlesinger, Arthur M., Jr. folder; Gleijeses, *Dominican Crisis*, pp. 77 and 259. Gleijeses maintains that Martin relied solely on the U.S. embassy and "his old friend Tony Imbert Barrera," though this seems out of character for the veteran journalist. See also Martin, *Overtaken by Events*, pp. 640–80 and 704–28.

69. Regarding Robert Kennedy and Cuban exiles during the early 1960s, see Evan Thomas, *Robert Kennedy*, pp. 174–79 and 235–39. Regarding his ideas about counterinsurgency, see Schlesinger, *Robert Kennedy and His Times*, pp. 498–503. Schlesinger focuses on its political aspects and wants to distinguish it from counterrevolution.

70. See Schlesinger "to the children," 9 May 1965, Schlesinger and Schlesinger, eds., *Letters of Schlesinger*, p. 294.

71. See Schlesinger "to the children," 9 May 1965, Schlesinger and Schlesinger, eds., *Letters of Schlesinger*, p. 295–96; Schlesinger, 2 May 1965, Robert Kennedy Papers, JFK Library, Senate Correspondence, Personal File, 1964–1965, Box 11, Schlesinger, Arthur 5/1965–8/1965 folder. Joseph Dolan to Robert Kennedy, 27 May 1965, Joseph Dolan Papers, Box 1, Memoranda 5/11/65–5/27/65 folder. Regarding other Democrats who were opposed to Johnson policy in the Dominican Republic, see Woods, *Fulbright*, pp. 383–85. Fulbright's speech in opposition "destroyed his relationship with Lyndon Johnson." See Palermo, *In His Own Right*, pp. 12–13.

72. Eric Sevareid, "The Final Troubled Hours of Adlai Stevenson," Johnson, ed., *Papers of Adlai Stevenson*, vol. 8, pp. 438–39. The Williams College commencement address quotation is on p. 773; the "single man" quotation from a speech before the UN Security Council is on p. 760. See also Schlesinger to Stevenson, 10 May 1965, and Stevenson to Schlesinger, 14 May 1965, Stevenson Papers (MC #124), Box 74, Folder 2, Arthur Schlesinger Jr. 1961–1965 folder; "Statement by Ambassador," 3 May 1965; Stevenson Papers (MC #124), Box 348, Folder 6, Series 5, Subseries 4: U.S. Ambassador, Dominican Republic 1965 folder; see Schlesinger to Richard Goodwin and Bill Moyers, 10 May 1965, Schlesinger and Schlesinger, eds., *Letters of Schlesinger*, pp. 297–98; Martin, *Stevenson and the World*, pp. 844–47 and 861–63; Schlesinger, 16 July 1965 journal, Arthur Schlesinger Jr. Papers, New York Public Library, Journals, Box 313, July 1965 folder; William Benton, "Sen. Benton Reports on Stevenson's Last Hours," *Sunday Herald*, 18 July 1965, p. 3.

73. John Rielly to Humphrey, 30 April 1965, Humphrey Papers, Minnesota Historical Society, Vice President: Foreign Affairs, 150.E.13.9 (B), Box 922, Correspondence: DR May 1965 folder; see also, for example, Humphrey to David S. Richie of Moorestown, NJ, 4 June 1965, Humphrey Papers, Vice President: Foreign Affairs, 150.E.12.6 (F), Box 909, Latin American: DR: June–September 1965 folder; Offner, *Hubert Humphrey*, p 231.

74. Regarding civil rights legislation, see, for example, Zelizer, *Fierce Urgency of Now*, pp. 7–10 and 85–130, Solberg, *Humphrey*, pp. 161–64, 170–71, 222–27, 240–56, and 265–98; Offner, *Hubert Humphrey*, pp. 230–32, 244, 246–47, 263, and 266; Johns, *Price of Loyalty*, pp. 27–37, 39, and 43. A SUNY-Fredonia student, Richard A. Caulk, criticized Humphrey for his failure to speak out on the invasion. See Caulk to Humphrey, 10 May 1965,

Humphrey Papers, MHS, Humphrey Vice Presidential Files, 150.E.17.8 (F) South America [*sic*]—Dominican Republic folder.

75. Dungan to Bundy, 30 April 1965, Ralph Dungan Papers, JFK Library, Ambassador to Chile Files, Box 21, Chronological File, April 1965 folder; Dungan to Harriman, 5 May 1965, in same box, May 1965 folder.

76. See 23 June 1965 letter to Representative Frank Thompson Jr., in JFK Library, Ralph Dungan, Ambassador to Chile Files, Box 21, Chronological, June 1965. Regarding other Democrats' concerns about the invasion, see also Woods, *LBJ*, pp. 625 and 630–31. Assistant Secretary of State Mann would not have been amused. See his 10 November 1965 memo to Bundy in LBJ Library, NSF Countries, Latin America—Chile, Box 13, Memos 10/65–7/67 folder.

77. See Dungan's 1 June 1965 letter to Robert Kennedy in JFK Library, Papers of Ralph Dungan, Ambassador to Chile Files, Box 16, Correspondence Files—K; Dungan to William Dentzer, 18 May 1965, Director, Office of Bolivian-Chilean Affairs, Box 21, Chronological Files, May 1965 folder. In the June folder, see the Dungan to "Teddy" Kennedy 1 June 1965 letter. Dungan also worried about the impact of the invasion on other, less stable countries in the hemisphere. See Ralph A. Dungan, "Rockefeller Failure in Latin America Traced to Ambiguous, Weak U.S. Policy," *Los Angeles Times*, 7 July 1969.

78. Mann, "Memorandum for Mr. McGeorge Bundy," 10 November 1965 in LBJ Library, NSF Countries, Chile, Box 13, Memos 10/65–7/67 folder; William Dentzer Jr., Director, Bolivian-Chilean Affairs, State Department, to Dungan, 11 May 1965, Ralph Dungan Papers, JFK Library, Ambassador to Chile Files, Box 14, Correspondence, Dentzer, William folder; Bundy to Dungan, 21 June 1965, Dungan Papers, JFK Library, Ambassador to Chile Files, Box 13, Correspondence: Bundy, McGeorge folder.

79. "Address of Rómulo Betancourt, Former President of Venezuela, at the Dinner Given in His Honor by the Inter-American Association for Democracy and Freedom, at the Hotel Roosevelt, June 3, 1965, on the Fifteenth Anniversary of the Founding of the Association," Frances Grant Papers, Latin American Country Files, Box 48, Venezuela—Personalities—Betancourt Dinner, 1965 (2 of 4) folder; Arthur Schlesinger Jr., "Remarks at IADF Dinner in Honor of Rómulo Betancourt," 3 June 1965, in the same folder.

80. See Taffet, *Foreign Aid as Foreign Policy*, pp. 123 and 138–41.

81. See the letters from Fraser to Lyndon Johnson 19 May 1965; Abraham Lowenthal, 14 December 1965; C. I. Saltzman of Minneapolis, 1 October 1965; Dennis James of Morton Grove, IL, 2 July 1965; and Sacha Volman, 2 December 1965, all in Donald Fraser Papers, Minnesota Historical Society, 145.C.2.3 (B), Dominican Republic 1965 folder.

82. See Church to Hubert Humphrey, 16 June 1964, in Senator Frank Church Collection, Boise State University Library Special Collections, Series 2.2 Foreign Relations, Box 44, Latin America 1963/1964 folder. Regarding his initial response to the invasion of the Dominican Republic, see Church, Untitled Press Release, 4 May 1965, in Box 47, Latin America—Dominican Republic folder. See also Church, "How Many Dominican Republics and Vietnams Can We Take On?" Case Western Reserve University speech, 11 December 1965, in Senator Frank Church Collection, Boise State University Library Special Collections, 10.6 Special Files, Box 2, Foreign Policy 1968–1969 folder.

83. Humphrey to Lucille Milner, 7 May 1965, Humphrey Papers, Minnesota Historical Society, 150.E.12.6, Vice President: Foreign Affairs, Box 909; Dungan to Bundy, 30 April 1965, Ralph Dungan Papers, JFK Library, Ambassador to Chile Files, Box 21, Chronological File,

April 1965 folder. Dungan suggested "anything that can be done to give multilateral cover even at this point would go long way toward ameliorating grave concern GOC and adverse political effects." See also Dungan to Johnson and Rusk, 7 May 1965, in May 1965 folder, which notes that Frei affirmed his "deep friendship with U.S." and "desire to work cooperatively," but that the Chilean Congress was not likely to approve troops.

84. Gleijeses, *Dominican Crisis*, pp. 260–63.

85. John Rielly to Humphrey, 10 August, 1965, Humphrey Papers, Minnesota Historical Society, Vice President: Foreign Affairs, 150.3.13.5 (B), Box 918, President Frei's Trip to Europe folder.

86. "Vice-President's Meeting with Ambassador Dungan," 25 March 1965, Humphrey Papers, Minnesota Historical Society, 150.3.13.5 (B), Box 918.

87. Grant to William Fulbright, 18 June 1965, Frances Grant Papers, Rutgers University, Alexander Library, Box 59, IADF General Files, U.S. Senate 1958–65 folder.

88. Regarding Johnson's (and Rusk's and McNamara's) skepticism regarding sabotage operations, see "Memorandum for the Record," *FRUS, 1964–1968*, vol. 32: *Dominican Republic; Cuba: Haiti; Guyana*, pp. 548–49; For further discussions, see "Paper Prepared in the U.S. Government," undated, p. 557, and Desmond Fitzgerald, "Memorandum for the Record 7 April 1964," p. 629; "Central Intelligence Agency Memorandum," 2 July 1964; Church to Robin Colwin of Post Falls, Idaho, 2 October 1964, in Senator Frank Church Collection, Boise State University Library Special Collections, Series 2.2 Foreign Relations, Box 47, Cuba 1964–1969 folder. Regarding Johnson's Latin America policy, see, for example, Tulchin, "The Promise of Progress," pp. 230–31; see also LeoGrande and Kornbluh, *Back Channel to Cuba*, pp. 114–15 and 118; Brown, *Cuba's Revolutionary World*, pp. 163–95; Bohning, *Castro Obsession*, p. 197; Schoultz, *That Infernal Little Cuban Republic*, p. 5.

89. Logevall, *Choosing War*; McPherson, *A Political Education*, p. 383. "Remarks at a Ceremony in Observance of the Sixth Anniversary of the Alliance for Progress," 17 August 1967, *PPPUS: Johnson, 1967*. The best attempt I have seen to address directly the impact of the Vietnam War on U.S.-Latin America policy is Taffet, *Foreign Aid as Foreign Policy*, pp. 176–87.

Chapter 6

1. Schlesinger, *Robert Kennedy and His Times*, p. 754; Shannon, *Heir Apparent*, pp. 124 and 287; "Visit of Senator to São Paulo: Discussion between Senator Kennedy and Students," 20 November 1965, Senate Papers, Trips, Box 12, 11/1965: Latin America Transcript Discussion with Students: São Paulo, Brazil folder; "Senator Robert F. Kennedy with University Students: Estadio National: 15 November 1965," also in Box 12: 11/1965 Students National Stadium, Santiago, Chile folder; Schlesinger to Robert Kennedy, 29 October 1976, Senate Correspondence, Personal Files, 1964–1968, Box 11, Schlesinger 9/65–3/66 folder. For a fuller Schlesingerian view of the trip, see Shesol, *Mutual Contempt*, pp. 277–83. Shesol suggests that Kennedy hoped that the visit would "unleash democratic forces he had no official responsibility—or ability—to contain." The best book on the transformation of the New York senator during these years remains Palermo, *In His Own Right*. His treatment of Latin America, however, is limited. See pp. 12–13.

2. Gordon to Robert Kennedy, 9 September 1965, JFK Library, Robert F. Kennedy—Senate Papers, Trips, 1965 Latin American Correspondence folder.

3. Vanden Heuvel and Gwirtzman, *On His Own*, pp. 164–77: Nathan Miller (*Baltimore Sun*) to Polly, 29 September 1965, Robert Kennedy, Senate Papers, JFK Library, Trips, 11/65: Latin America: Correspondence: Brazil 9/65 folder.

4. José Bechinol to Morse, December 1965, Wayne Morse Papers, University of Oregon Library Special Collections, Box 47, Foreign Relations, Foreign Relations 1-1, Alliance for Progress 1965 folder; regarding his increasing experience of poverty in the United States, see Schmitt, *President of the Other America*, particularly pp. 177–82 and 195–98.

5. Shannon, *Heir Apparent*, p. 128; "Visit of Senator to São Paulo: Discussion between Senator Kennedy and Students," 20 November 1965, Senate Papers, Trips, Box 12, 11/1965: Latin America Transcript: Discussion with Students: São Paulo, Brazil folder; see also "Senator Robert F. Kennedy's Visit to Recife," in same folder; "Draft: 10 November 1965: University Students: Lima, Peru," Senate Papers, Speeches, Box 9, 11: 65 Latin America folder.

6. Quoted in Ross, *Robert F. Kennedy*, pp. 432–33.

7. Robert Kennedy, "The Alliance for Progress: Symbol and Substance," 9 May 1966, *Congressional Record—Senate*, p. 10090–104. See also Vanden Heuvel and Gwirtzman, *On His Own*, pp. 173–77. Schlesinger argued that Kennedy wanted to "recall the Alliance to its original purposes." See Schlesinger, *Robert Kennedy and His Times*, p. 755. John Bartlow Martin had been among the people Kennedy looked to for advice prior to and after the speech. See Martin to Angie (presumably Novello), 11 April 1966, and Martin to Kennedy, 27 May 1966, John Bartlow Martin papers, Library of Congress, Box 35, Correspondence, 1966 Robert Kennedy folder.

8. Arthur M. Schlesinger Jr., "Journals: 28 July 1966," p. 1395, Arthur M. Schlesinger Jr. Papers, New York Public Library, Journals, Box 313, July 1966 folder; Schlesinger to Robert Kennedy, 16 April 1965, Box 77, Robert Kennedy folder.

9. Robert Kennedy, "The Alliance for Progress: Symbol and Substance," 9 May 1966, *Congressional Record—Senate*, pp. 10102 and 10104.

10. Robert Kennedy, "The Alliance for Progress: Symbol and Substance," 10 May 1966, *Congressional Record—Senate*, pp. 10187–91.

11. Robert Kennedy, "The Alliance for Progress: Symbol and Substance," 10 May 1966, *Congressional Record—Senate*, pp. 10191–94.

12. Robert Kennedy, "The Alliance for Progress: Symbol and Substance," 10 May 1966, *Congressional Record—Senate*, pp. 10194–96.

13. See W. Averell Harriman to Robert Kennedy, 24 May 1966, and "Notes on Senator Robert F. Kennedy," 3 October 1968, Library of Congress, W. Averell Harriman Papers, Box 480, Robert F. Kennedy, 1968–1969 folder.

14. Gabler, *Catching the Wind*, p. 266; Schmitt, *President of the Other America*.

15. See, for example, Palermo, *In His Own Right*.

16. Small, *At the Water's Edge*, pp. 30–32, 42, and 45; the "greatest test" quotation is from Ashby and Gramer, *Fighting the Odds*, p. 162; see also Green, *We Cannot Remain Silent*, pp. 55 and 73.

17. Lieuwen, *Survey of the Alliance for Progress: The Latin American Military*.

18. Regarding Gordon's analysis that "much of army officer corps . . . represent modernizing elements of middle class which is in revolt against remnants of Vargas tradition," see 8 June 1964 cable from Gordon to Rusk in LBJ Library, NSF Countries, Latin America—Brazil, Box 10, Cables 4/64–8/64 folder. Regarding "militarization," see p. 4 of the 10 June 1964 memo in the same folder. Regarding the extension of his mandate, see Gordon's

23 July 1964 memo. The CIA's 26 March 1965 evaluation of the Castello Branco presidency can be found in a special report, "The Role of the Military in the Brazilian Government," in the Memos 9/64–11/65 folder in the same box. See particularly pp. 1, 3, 6, and 7. See also the 17 June 1966 CIA Current Intelligence Weekly Special Report, "Brazil's New Two-Party System," in LBJ Library, NSF Countries, Latin America—Brazil, Memos 12/65–3/67 folder.

19. See Gordon's 4 October 1965 letter to Arkansas Senator J. William Fulbright in JFK Library, Papers of Ralph Dungan, Ambassador to Chile Files—Correspondence—Lincoln Gordon.

20. See Gordon's 7 September 1965 letter to the editorial page editor of the *New York Times* in JFK Library, Robert F. Kennedy, Senate Papers—Trips—11/65—Box 1—Latin America Correspondence.

21. See the discussion in Dulles, *Castello Branco*, pp. 197–98 and 239–45; Leacock, *Requiem for Revolution*, pp. 236–37, as well as Skidmore, *Politics of Military Rule*, pp. 45–49 and 64–65, and Taffet, *Foreign Aid as Foreign Policy*, pp. 95 and 115–21. See Gordon's 3 November 1965 letter in which he reports on his conversation with the Brazilian president in *FRUS, 1964–1968*, vol. 31, pp. 488–93, as well as the response from Secretary of State Dean Rusk on pp. 493–94, and Gordon's 14 November 1965 telegram on pp. 495–98. Other useful information can be found in LBJ Library, NSF Countries, Latin America, Brazil, Box 10, Cables 9/64–11/65 folder, particularly Gordon's cables from 27 October 1965 and 3, 4, and 14 November 1965. Thomas Mann's 8 December 1965 letter to Johnson can be found in the Cables 12/65–3/67 folder in Box 11. Bundy's 7 December 1965 letter, "AID Program Loan to Brazil," can be found in the Memos 12/65–3/67 folder; Gordon to John Tuthill, 27 October 1966, LBJ Library, NSF Name File, Bowdler Memos (1 of 2) folder; regarding Vietnam, see the 11 December 1965 letter from Averell Harriman to Gordon in the Memos 12/65–3/67 folder.

22. Dulles, *Castello Branco*, p. 18.

23. See Dulles, *Castello Branco*, pp. 18 and 63–67; Skidmore, *Politics of Military Rule*, pp. 29–39 and 55–56; Levinson and Onís, *Alliance That Lost Its Way*, pp. 194–204 and 209–10; Leacock, *Requiem for Revolution*, pp. 225 and 237–38. See Gordon's 10 June 1964 conversation with Castello Branco in *FRUS, 1964–1968*, vol. 31, pp. 467–70, and his 10 August 1964 letter to Mann, particularly pp. 471–78. See also Gordon to Rusk, 27 October 1965, in LBJ Library, NSF Countries, Latin America, Brazil, Box 10, Cables 9/64–11/65 folder. See also the enthusiastic 3 December 1965 memo from Rusk to Johnson, pp. 499–503 See also Gordon's 7 September 1965 letter to the editorial page editor of the *New York Times* in JFK Library, Robert F. Kennedy, Senate Papers—Trips—11/65—Box 1—Latin America Correspondence. Regarding U.S. perceptions of the difference between Goulart's and the military's interest in the Alliance, see, for example, the 18 January 1967 "Background Paper" for President-Elect Costa e Silva's visit in LBJ Library, NSF Countries, Latin America—Brazil, Box 9, Pres-Elect Costa e Silva Visit 1/67 (2 of 2) Folder.

24. See Dungan's 13 November 1965 telegram to McGeorge Bundy in *FRUS, 1964–1968*, vol. 31, pp. 618–20, and the responses on pp. 620–38. Regarding Chileanization, see Sater, *Chile and the United States*, pp. 144–46, and Hurtado-Torres, *Gathering Storm*, pp. 97–117. Regarding other Chilean policies that Dungan supported even when they hurt the United States, see Taffet, "Alliance for What?" pp. 238–40.

25. See his 31 October 1961 speech to the American Society and American Chamber of Commerce, reproduced in Gordon, *A New Deal for Latin America*, pp. 9–17.

26. See "An Exchange of Views: Torture in Brazil," *Commonweal*, 7 August 1970, p. 379. Regarding the tendency to define Brazil's problems as primarily economic, see the 26 March 1966 discussion regarding Gordon's successor in Thomas C. Mann, "Memorandum for the President," pp. 1–2, in LBJ Library, NSF Countries, Latin America—Brazil, Box 11, Memos 12/65–3/67 folder. William D. Rogers, involved as special counsel to the U.S. coordinator to the Alliance for Progress in 1962 and as deputy U.S. coordinator beginning in 1963, notes that "events in Brazil tended to blur the political aspirations of the Alliance." See his *Twilight Struggle*, p. 136.

27. Taffet suggests that the Brazilian "case demonstrates how the Alliance for Progress lost its reformist goals and moral compass." See *Foreign Aid as Foreign Policy*, p. 8. See also the table on p. 96 and 115–21.

28. See 28 June 1965 letter to Jack Funari of the Agency for International Development in JFK Library, Personal Papers of Ralph Dungan, Ambassador to Chile Files, Box 15, Correspondence F; 6 November 1965, David E. Bell, "Memorandum for the President," in LBJ, NSF Countries, Latin America—Chile, Box 13, Memos 10/65–7/67 folder. An extremely positive appraisal of the Frei administration by a veteran North American correspondent can be found in Gross, *The Last Best Hope*.

29. "Editorial Note," "Memorandum for the 303 Committee, 25 January 1965," in *FRUS, 1964–1968*, vol. 31, pp. 598–99 and 606–8.

30. See "Editorial Note," in *FRUS, 1964–1968*, vol. 31, p. 641.

31. See Tinsman, *Partners in Conflict*, pp. 92–127; Kirkendall, *Paulo Freire and the Cold War Politics of Literacy*, pp. 61–89; Harmer, *Beatriz Allende*, pp. 84–85, 95–98, and 135–36.

32. 12 February 1965 preliminary draft for a "National Policy Paper on Chile," available in National Archives II, RG 59, Central Foreign Policy Files, 1964–1966, Box 2030, POL 1, Gen. Policy Background.

33. See F. Bradford Morse to Dungan, 20 April 1967, Ralph Dungan Papers, JFK Library, Ambassador to Chile Files, Box 17, Correspondence Morse, Congressman Brad folder; Dungan, "Transcript of Remarks Made by Ambassador Dungan to Country Team on November 15, 1966," in Box 20, Speech Material 1966 folder. See also U.S. Congress, House, *Report of the Special Study Mission to Chile, Peru, and the Dominican Republic*.

34. See 1 June 1965 letter to Bernard Norwitch, Box 17, Correspondence—Pennsylvania; Dungan to Robert Christopher, foreign editor, *Newsweek*, 23 August 1966, Ambassador to Chile Files, Box 14, Correspondence—Christopher, Robert folder.

35. See 23 November 1965 letter to Bernard Norwitch, Senator Joseph Clark's administrative assistant, in JFK Library, Papers of Ralph Dungan, Ambassador to Chile Files, Box 17, Correspondence—Pennsylvania folder.

36. *El Mercurio* lamented what it suggested must have been a "bitter experience" for one who had tried to aid Chile's social and economic development. See the editorial "La Embajada de EE.UU. y la Guerra Fria," *El Mercurio*, 20 June 1967, p. 3. For a critique from the left, see, for example, "La CIA sin antifaz" and "Dungan, el de la CIA," *Punto Final*, February 1967, pp. 20–21.

37. JFK Library, Papers of Ralph Dungan, Ambassador to Chile Files, Box 20, The Ambassador as Foreign Affairs Manager undated folder; Dungan to Hugh Sidey (*Time* magazine), 23 December 1964, in Box 18; Dungan to Honorable and Mrs. Robert Kennedy, 4 January 1965 in Box 21.

38. See the 25 February 1966 letter of Norman Cousins to Dungan in JFK Library, Personal Papers of Ralph Dungan, Ambassador to Chile Files, Box 14, Correspondence—Cousins, Norman.

39. Humphrey to Dungan, 10 November 1966, JFK Library—Papers of Ralph Dungan—Box 15, Ambassador to Chile Files, Correspondence H folder; see also a series of letters from John Rielly to Humphrey beginning 19 October 1966, Hubert Humphrey Vice Presidential Files, 1965–1966, 150.E.14.3 (B).

40. See Dungan to Gordon, 7 April 1966 and 18 April 1966, Ralph Dungan Papers, JFK Library, Ambassador to Chile Files, Box 22, Chronological File, April 1966 folder; Dungan to Bronheim, Deputy Assistant Administrator for Latin America, AID, 10 May 1966, in May 1966 folder; Humphrey aide John Rielly supported Dungan on the political advantage of maintaining high levels of support for the kind of government Frei represented. See a series of letters including from Rielly to Humphrey, 19 October 1966, and Humphrey to Rostow, 23 November 1966, Humphrey Papers, MHS, Vice Presidential Files, 1965–1966, 150.E.14.3 (B); Dungan to Gordon, 28 April 1964, Box 15, Correspondence, Gordon, Lincoln folder; Dungan to Alvin Friedman, Special Assistant to the Assistant Secretary of International Security Affairs, 29 January 1965, Ralph Dungan, JFK Library, Ambassador to Chile Files, Box 21, Chronological File: January 1965 folder; Dungan to Rusk, "Summit—Arms Limitation," 28 July 1966, in Box 22, Chronological Files: July 1966 folder; Dungan to Katzenbach, Acting Secretary of State, 24 February 1967, Ralph Dungan Papers, JFK Library, Ambassador to Chile Files, Box 23, Chronological Files: February 1967 folder. Dungan insisted that the ambassador was the only one who could judge what was necessary to achieve U.S. national objectives.

41. Norbury, "Arrest and Acquittal of National Party's Leaders: Background and Consequences," 16 September 1967, in RG 59, Central Foreign Policy Files, 1967–1969, Box 1977, POL 12, Chile. See Gazmuri, Ancibia, and Góngora, *Frei y su Época*, vol. 2, p. 576; Sigmund, *United States and Democracy in Chile*, pp. 27–28; Levinson and Onís, *Alliance That Lost Its Way*, p. 238; 28 January 1966 letter from Dungan to James Loeb Jr. of Adirondack Publishing in JFK Library, Papers of Ralph Dungan, Ambassador to Chile Files, Box 16, Correspondence L; *El Mercurio* partially backed Dungan in the controversy. See the editorial "Declaraciones del Embajador de Estados Unidos," 8 January 1966, which argues that his comments generally were in keeping with U.S. policy since the Punta del Este conference in 1961. Given the intensity of the political debate over the issue and the complexity of specific components of the reform yet to be resolved, the newspaper suggested it might have been better for him not to comment on it. (The newspaper had serious reservations about certain aspects of the Frei administration proposal.) Dungan's "interference" was revisited again in a speech on the Senate floor by National Party Senator Pedro Ibañez Ojeda, reprinted in *El Mercurio*, 13 December 1967, p. 35, under the title "La CIA, la Embajada Norteamericana y el Diario 'Clarín.'" For the critique from the left, see, for example, "Ralph Dungan, Virrey de Chile," *Punto Final*, June 1967, p. 2. Those on the Chilean right, such as former President Alessandri, could not understand why the United States was supporting Frei's reforms. See Joseph John Jova, "Memorandum of Conversation: President Alessandri's Views on Current, Political/Economic Situation," 21 January 1965 in RG 59, Central Foreign Policy Files, 1964–66, Box 2025, POL 2-1, Joint Weekas Chile folder.

42. See undated letter from Dungan to Church, Senator Frank Church Collection, Boise State University Library Special Collections, Series 2.2 Foreign Relations, Box 46, Latin

America—Chile #1 folder; McGeorge Bundy to Johnson, "Staff Assistance in Latin America," 16 June 1964, LBJ Library, NSF, Memos to the President, Box 2, 6/1–30/64 folder. In the same box, 7/1–9/30 folder, see Bundy to Johnson, "Ralph Dungan and Chile." Dungan to Gordon, 6 June 1966, Dungan Papers, JFK Library, Ambassador to Chile Files, Box 22, Chronological Files: June 1966 folder.

43. See 7 June 1966 memo from Dungan to embassy staff in JFK Library, Ambassador to Chile Files, Box 22, Chronological—June 1966 folder.

44. 30 March 1966 Memo to Sam Moskowitz, JFK Library, Papers of Ralph Dungan, Ambassador to Chile Files, Chronological Files, Box 22, March 1966.

45. See Dungan's 7 May 1965 letter to Allende in JFK Library, Papers of Ralph Dungan, Ambassador to Chile Files, Chronological File: May 1965.

46. See "Remarks Made by Ambassador Dungan to Country Team on Nov. 15, 1966," in JFK Library, Papers of Ralph Dungan, Ambassador to Chile Files, Box 20, Speech Material 1966.

47. See 24 October 1965 letter from Dungan to John Goshko in JFK Library, Ambassador to Chile Files, Correspondence, Box 15—John Goshko.

48. See, for example, JFK Library, Papers of Ralph Dungan, Ambassador to Chile files, Box 20, Speech Material 1966, "Transcript of Remarks Made by Ambassador Dungan to Country Team on 15 November 1966," The Ambassador as Foreign Affairs Manager undated folder.

49. See Dungan's 21 September 1965 letter to Senator Edward M. Kennedy in JFK Library, Ambassador to Chile Files, Box 16, Correspondence—K.

50. See, for example, Fraser to John Masica of Minneapolis, 30 November 1965, Fraser Papers, Minnesota Historical Society, 145.C.2.4 (F), Foreign Aid—Political Developments folder, and Fraser to Gerald Heaney of Duluth, MN, 11 March 1965, in Foreign Policy General folder in same box; Fraser to Dungan, 7 February 1966, 145.C.3.1 (B), Chile 1966 folder; Fraser to Editor, *Challenge*, 15 February 1967, 145.C.3.2 (F), Foreign Aid 67 folder. In a 1968 letter to Benjamin Rosenthal, D-N.Y., he wrote, "What we are really fighting for is the capacity, and the sensitivity, to see a society in the totality, to understand the interplay of people, institutions, ideology, and so forth." He lamented the dominance of economists in foreign aid offices. See 151.I.11.2 (F), Foreign Aid—Political Developments—1968 folder. He later emphasized the need to concentrate "on groups and individuals closer to the people," emphasizing bottom-up approaches. See Fraser to Tom Veblen of Minneapolis, 2 February 1969, 151.I.11.6 (F), Foreign Aid—Political Development 1969 folder; Fraser to Sidney Weintraub, Director, USAID/Santiago, Chile, 2 February 1968, 151.I.11.2 (F), Chile 1968 folder.

51. See Dungan to Schlesinger, 9 May 1966, Arthur M. Schlesinger Jr. Papers, New York Public Library, Correspondence, Box 38, Ralph Dungan folder. In his 19 July 1966 letter to Schlesinger, Dungan expressed his concerns that "very little material regularly reaches the Latin American middle and upper classes which contributes to the broadening and modernization of their outlook on social, economic and cultural subjects outside their own region or country."

52. See Dungan's 21 September 1965 letter to Senator Edward M. Kennedy in JFK Library, Ambassador to Chile Files, Box 16, Correspondence—K. See Dungan's 18 May 1966 letter to Robert Kennedy, also in Box 16, Correspondence Files—K, as well as his 20 April 1966 letter to Johnson in Box 16, Files—Correspondence—J. See Dungan's 1 September 1965 letter to President Johnson in Ambassador to Chile files—Correspondence—J.

53. See the 3 February 1965 letter to McGeorge Bundy in JFK Library, Papers of Ralph Dungan, Ambassador to Chile Files, Chronological, Box 21, February 1965; 31 August 1965 letter from Dungan to Robert Kennedy in JFK Library, Robert F. Kennedy—Senate Papers—Trips—Latin American, Box 1; see also 29 November 1966 letter in JFK Library, Ambassador to Chile Files, Correspondence—Lincoln Gordon. The possibility of Johnson visiting South America was of great interest to the Chilean newspaper *El Mercurio*, which made it the subject of its lead editorial on 19 February 1965, p. 3. In early March, however, it was announced that he would not be visiting.

54. See Dungan's 20 April 1966 letter to President Johnson and the 18 May 1966 letter to Senator Robert Kennedy in JFK Library, Papers of Ralph Dungan, Ambassador to Chile Files, Box 16, Correspondence—J and Correspondence—K, respectively. Dungan was clearly quite pessimistic about U.S.-Latin American relations by the time he wrote to Kennedy. For the speech itself, see LBJ, "Statement by the President on the Fifth Anniversary of the Alliance for Progress, March 14, 1966," in *PPPUS: Johnson, 1966*, vol. 1, pp. 317–19. Johnson's speech was not particularly inspired and focused on topics such as road-building, electrification, coffee pricing, sugar tariffs, etc.

55. See William G. Bowdler to Bob Komer, "Frei Visit," 3 March 1966, in LBJ Library, NSF Countries, Latin America—Chile, Box 13, Cables 10/65–7/67 folder. Note that he also suggested that it could help Johnson in Congress and with the "liberal press." See "Statement by the President on the Forthcoming Visit of President Frei of Chile, December 20, 1966," in *PPPUS: Johnson, 1966*, vol. 2, p. 1446. See the lead editorial, "El Viaje del President Frei a EE.UU.," *El Mercurio*, 22 December 1966, p. 3, as well as the news story on the front page of the 7 January 1967 issue of the same newspaper.

56. Regarding planning for the trip, see "Statement by the President on the Forthcoming Visit of President Frei of Chile," 20 December 1966, *PPPUS: Johnson, 1966*, p. 1446; 29 December 1966 memo from Walt Rostow to President Johnson, "Program for Frei Visit," LBJ Library, NSF Countries, Chile, Box 12, President Frei Visit folder. See also the news stories, "Debate el Viaje de Frei," *El Mercurio*, 10 January 1967, p. 1; "Senado Rechazó Permiso a S.E.," *El Mercurio*, 18 January 1967, p. 1, as well as the lead editorials "Lamentable Decisión del Senado," *El Mercurio*, 18 January 1967, p. 3; "Se Duda de Nuestra Democracia," *El Mercurio*, 21 January 1967, p. 3. For Frei's response, see "Discurso al negar el Senado el permiso constitucional para su viaje a Estados Unidos," in *Obras Escogidos*, pp. 327–34. For his private communications regarding the possibility of making the trip in spite of the Senate decision, see, for example, 19 January 1967 cable from Dean in LBJ Library, NSF Countries, Brazil/Chile, Box 12, President Frei Visit folder; 20 January 1967, Bowdler to Rostow, Box 13, Memos 10/65–7/67 folder.

57. See the lead news story, "Presidents Johnson y Frei se Reunirán Hoy," *El Mercurio*, 13 April 1967, p. 1.

58. See "Toasts of the President and President-Elect Costa e Silva of Brazil, January 26, 1967," in *PPPUS: Johnson, 1967*, vol. 1, pp. 89–91.

59. See the lead editorials, "Roosevelt y Kennedy en la Política de EE.UU," 22 November 1966, p. 3, and "La Alianza que Perdió el Camino," *El Mercurio*, 18 March 1967, p. 3.

60. Eduardo Frei Montalva, "Urgencies in Latin America: The Alliance That Lost Its Way," *Foreign Affairs* 45, no. 3 (April 1967): 437–48.

61. See Gordon's "Farewell Talk to American Society and American Chamber of Commerce in Rio," p. 3, in JFK Library, Papers of Ralph Dungan, Ambassador to Chile Files, Box 20—Speech Material 1966.

62. See Gordon's "Farewell Talk to American Society and American Chamber of Commerce in Rio," p. 5, in JFK Library, Papers of Ralph Dungan, Ambassador to Chile Files, Box 20—Speech Material 1966.

63. Dulles, *Castello Branco*, pp. 178 and 322–28.

64. Quoted in Dulles, *Castello Branco*, p. 181. See the discussion in Skidmore, *Politics of Military Rule*, pp. 51–53. The 22 September 1965 cable from Gordon to Rusk can be found in the LBJ Library, NSF Countries, Latin America—Brazil, Cables 9/64–11/65 folder.

65. See Vanden Heuvel and Gwirtzman, *On His Own*, p. 174.

66. See Green, *We Cannot Remain Silent*, p. 74; "Senators Scrutinize US Policy," *Hemispherica*, February 1966; U.S. Congress, Senate, *Nomination of Lincoln Gordon to Be Assistant Secretary of State for Inter-American Affairs*, particularly pp. 3–12.

67. See Lincoln Gordon's 21 March 1966 letter to Dungan in JFK Library, Ambassador to Chile Files, Box 15, Correspondence—Lincoln Gordon, as well as the Gordon interview, LBJ Library, 1969, pp. 17 and 26. Gordon had been considered for the job in 1964, but Brazil was seen as "so important" that he "could not be spared." See Mann to Gordon, 23 March 1964, Gordon Papers, JFK Library, Series 3: Ambassador to Brazil, Box 116, Jan–April 1965 folder. In this letter, Mann had suggested that the previous year had been a good one for the United States in the Western Hemisphere.

68. See, for example, Jack Valenti's 15 March 1966 Memorandum for the President in LBJ Library, White House Central Files, Box 204, Lincoln Gordon folder; 27 February 1968, Dick Moose to Walt Rostow, LBJ Library, NSF Countries, Latin America, Box 4; 7 February 1968, Rostow to LBJ, "Response to Nixon's Statement on Latin America," both in 1/68–5/68 folder; U.S. Congress, Senate, *Hearings before the Committee on Foreign Relations, United States Senate: Latin American Summit Conference*. See also Taffet, *Foreign Aid as Foreign Policy*, pp. 181–94.

69. See the 14 June 1967 resignation letter Dungan sent to President Johnson in LBJ Library, Office Files of John Macy, Dungan, Ralph A., D-Penn. folder. See the 26 June 1967 letter from President Johnson to Dungan in response in JFK Library, Papers of Ralph Dungan, Ambassador to Chile Files, Box 20, Resignation (Acceptance of by LBJ). His wife had suffered from an "encapsulated TB," according to Dungan's 24 February 1967 letter to Juan de Onís of the *New York Times*, in Ambassador to Chile Files, Box 14, Correspondence—Juan de Onís.

70. 19 June 1967 letter to Nicholas Katzenbach in LBJ Library, Office Files of John Macy, Dungan, Ralph A. folder.

71. Korry had long been interested in Chile. See his 9 November 1964 letter from his position as U.S. ambassador to Ethiopia in JFK Library, Papers of Ralph Dungan, Box 20, Ambassador to Chile Files, Congratulations, 11/64–12/64 folder; Sol M. Linowitz, 19 June 1967, "Conversation with President Frei of Chile," in LBJ Library, NSF Countries, Latin America—Chile, Box 13, Memos 10/65–7/67 folder. See the 13 July 1967 letter from Guillermo Videla Vial to Dungan in JFK Library, Personal Papers of Dungan, Ambassador to Chile Files, Box 19, Correspondence V. See "Ralph Dungan, Virrey de Chile," *Punto Final*, June 1967, p. 1967. See also the editorial, "La Embajada de EE.UU. y la Guerra Fría," *El Mercurio*, 20 June 1967, p. 3. See also Sigmund, *United States and Democracy in Chile*, pp. 34–35. See "Frei no ha Perdido el Favor de la Casa Blanca," *Punto Final*, July 1967, pp. 8 and 9, and "Edward Korry, Hombre del Pentágono," *Punto Final*, November 1967, p. 27. For Korry's own description of his approach, see the 11 May 1968 airgram, "Dialogue: Tomic—

The Ambassador, #1," pp. 2 and 3, in LBJ Library, NSF Countries, Latin America—Chile, Box 14, Cables 8/67–11/68 folder. See Taffet's comparison of Dungan and Korry in "Alliance for What?" p. 348, and Hurtado-Torres, *Gathering Storm*, pp. 12, 77–79, and 81.

72. Edwin Martin to Dungan, 23 August 1966, Ralph Dungan Papers, JFK Library, Ambassador to Chile Files, Box 17, Correspondence: Martin, Edwin folder. Martin noted that the conspirators were happy that he was so openly opposed to the coup, because it helped them demonstrate that the coup "was strictly national movement and not . . . Pentagon inspired." In meeting with Ambassador Edwin Martin, Vice President Humphrey was to stress his appreciation for Martin's support for "freely elected constitutional regimes." See John Rielly to Humphrey, "Your Meeting with Ambassador Ed Martin," 27 June 1966, Humphrey Papers, Minnesota Historical Society, Vice President: Foreign Affairs, 150.E.13.6 (F), Box 919. Robert Kennedy to *New York Times*, 8 July 1966, Robert Kennedy Papers, Senate Papers, Box 41, Correspondence: Subject File, 1966, Foreign Affairs 6/21/66–7/11/1966 folder; Gordon to Dungan, 28 June 1966, Gordon Papers, JFK Library, Assistant Secretary of State, Box 141, Correspondence 1966–1967 B–I folder. Regarding the U.S. decision to recognize the new government, see Rusk, "Recognition of Argentine Government: Ongania's July 9th Speech," 12 July 1966, Humphrey: Vice President: Foreign Affairs, 150.3.13.3 (B), Box 916, Argentina 1965–1966 folder. In a speech to the Overseas Press Club a couple of weeks before, Gordon had noted that there had been no new coups in two years. See 16 June 1966, Gordon Papers, JFK Library, Box 143, Series 4: Assistant Secretary of State File, Speech Files: Overseas Press Club folder. In Box 144, Edwin Martin, "Telegram from the Embassy in Argentina to the Department of State," 30 June 1966, *FRUS, 1964–1968*, vol. 31: *South and Central America: Mexico*, pp. 315–16; See "Transcript of Background Press and Radio News Briefing," 28 December 1966, Speech File: Transcript folder; Dungan to Katzenbach, Acting Secretary of State, 24 February 1967, Ralph Dungan Papers, JFK Library, Ambassador to Chile Files, Box 23, Chronological Files: February 1967 folder. Fraser expressed concern regarding the decline of agricultural cooperatives under the new military government. See Fraser to David Bronheim, Deputy U.S. Coordinator, AID, 21 February 1967, Fraser Papers, 145.C.3.2 (F), Alliance for Progress 67 folder.

73. See Gordon Oral History Interview, LBJ Library, 1969, p. 42.

74. See Tulchin, "The Promise of Progress," p. 225. A telling example of this general lack of interest in foreign policy unrelated to Southeast Asia is provided by the experience of the U.S. ambassador-designate to Portugal, Admiral George W. Anderson, which is described in Rodrigues, *Salazar-Kennedy*, pp. 305–6. In their one meeting, Admiral Anderson had his picture taken with President Johnson, but there was no "consultation," despite the story released to the press. See also Rabe, *Most Dangerous Area in the World*, pp. 181–83.

75. Dungan clearly would not have supported this emphasis on the military. See the 21 September 1966 letter to Ben Bradlee of the *Washington Post* in JFK Library, Papers of Ralph Dungan, Ambassador to Chile Files, Box 13, Correspondence, and the 18 July 1966 letter to Senator Fulbright in Box 15, Correspondence Senator J. W. Fulbright. See also Dungan's 17 February 1966 letter to Norman Cousins of the *Saturday Review* in Box 14, Correspondence— Cousins, Norman. See the lead editorial, "Roosevelt y Kennedy en la Politica de EE.UU.," *El Mercurio*, 22 November 1966, p. 3. See Tulchin, "Promise of Progress," pp. 234 and 242–43. Regarding the containment of Castro's revolutionary aspirations in the region, see "National Intelligence Estimate 80/90-68, March 20, 1968," in *FRUS, 1964–1968*, vol. 31, pp. 170–72 and Gleijeses, *Conflicting Missions*, pp. 220–22. On counterinsurgency in Bolivia, see Ryan,

Fall of Che, particularly pp. 58–62, 82–102, and 125–46. See also Taffet, "Alliance for What?" pp. 214–16.

76. See Edward Korry, "MemCon: Alessandri's Views of Actual Political-Economic Situation in Chile," 19 December 1969, in RG 59, Central Foreign Policy Files, 1967–69, Box 1976, POL 6 Chile. See also Norbury, "Arrest and Acquittal of National Party Leaders: Background and Consequences," 16 September 1967, RG 59, Central Foreign Policy Files, 1967–1969, Box 1977, POL 12 Chile. See also Korry, "Fitting the President for Pants," 3 January 1968, RG 59, Central Foreign Policy Files, 1967–1969, Box 1981, Pol. Affairs.

77. See Church to George Washington University student Nancy Cleveland, 18 March 1971, in Senator Frank Church Collection, Boise State University Library, Series 2.2 Foreign Relations, Box 47, Latin America—Dominican Republic folder; Rusk, 22 May 1965, NSF Countries, Box 51, Dominican Republic—Davidson (2 of 2) folder; "Contingency Paper," undated, and Bill Moyers to William Bowdler, 16 May 1966; for close monitoring, see Rostow to Johnson, 10 May 1911 7:45 P.M. and 11 May 1966 2:35 P.M. in the same folder, LBJ Library, NSF, Intelligence File, Box 10, Dominican Republic Elections folder; Rielly to Humphrey, 27 May 1966, Humphrey Papers, Vice President: Foreign Affairs, 150.e.13.4 (F), Box 917; Misc. Countries 1965–1966 folder; see "Statement by Vice President Humphrey on the Occasion of His Departure for the Dominican Republic," 30 June 1966, and others available on the Minnesota Historical Society website, www.mhs.org; Fraser, "Memorandum: Norman Thomas Called," 28 February 1966, Fraser Papers, Minnesota Historical Society, 145.C.3.1 (B), Dominican Republic 1966 folder; Fraser to Roger Joseph of Minneapolis, 1 June 1965, Donald Fraser Papers, Minnesota Historical Society, 145.C.2.3 (B), Dominican Republic 1965 folder; "Memorandum of Conversation," 11 April 1967, and "Information Memorandum for the President's Special Assistant (Rostow) to President Johnson," 16 January 1968, *FRUS, 1964–1968*, vol. 32: *Dominican Republic: Cuba: Haiti: Guyana*, pp. 455 and 509; For private and public expressions of liberal Democratic relief, see Alexander to Grant, 27 July 1966, Grant Papers, Rutgers University, Alexander Library, Special Collections, Box 28, Correspondence Files, Robert Alexander 1961–1969 folder; Frances R. Grant, "Reappraising the Dominican Elections," *Hemispherica*, July–August 1966. In his remarks during his trip for the inauguration, Humphrey promised Alliance aid "to advance the social and economic well-being of the Dominican People"; see "Statement by Vice President Humphrey on the Occasion of His Arrival in the Dominican Republic," 30 June 1966, on the Minnesota Historical Society website listed above; See also Humphrey to Johnson, 5 July 1966, LFJ Library, NSF, Name File, Humphrey Vol. 2 (2 of 2) folder; Volman to Fraser, 26 May 1967, Fraser papers, 145.C.3.2 (F), Latin America 1967 folder; Taffet, *Foreign Aid as Foreign Policy*, pp. 123 and 138–47; Chester, *Rag-Tags, Scum, Riff-Raff, and Commies*, pp. 10, 231–51, and 283–89; Chafe, *Never Stop Running*, pp. 256–75.

78. See Morse to Robert Shenk of St. John's University (Minnesota), 16 April 1965, in Morse Papers, University of Oregon Library Special Collections, Box 46, Subject Files, Foreign Relations, Box 46, Foreign Relations—Latin America—1965 folder. See also his 6 July 1965 and 7 June 1965 letters to historians E. Bradford Burns (in the same folder) and John L. Phelan in Box 47, Foreign Relations 1-1, 1965 folder.

79. See Johnson, *Congress and the Cold War*, pp. 126–28. "The Military Assistance and Sales Act of 1966," 27 July 1966, *Congressional Record*, pp. 17338–40 and 17346–47; see Church, "The Case for Cutting Military Assistance," 1966, Senator Frank Church Collection, Boise State University Library Special Collections, 7.9 Issue Books, Box 7, Foreign Aid 1966–1971

folder; Dungan to Church, 12 August 1964, and Church to Dungan, 22 August 1966, Ralph Dungan Papers, JFK Library, Ambassador to Chile Files, Box 14, Ambassador to Chile Files, Box 14, Correspondence: Church, Frank folder; George McGovern told Church, "You have broken the first teat off the sacred cow."

80. See Dosal, *Comandante Che*, particularly pp. 193–218; Brown, *Cuba's Revolutionary World*, pp. 200–221.

81. See the series of reports by Robert L. Alexander in *Hemispherica*, September and October 1967; "Memorandum from Viron P. Vaky of the Policy Planning Council to the Assistant Secretary of State for Inter-American Affairs (Oliver)," 29 March 1968; Gordon to Robert Kennedy, 7 December 1966, JFK Library, Adam Walinsky Papers, Senate Subject File, 1965–1968, Box 12, Foreign Policy Guatemala folder; *FRUS, 1964–1968*, vol. 31: *South and Central America: Mexico*, pp. 237–41.

82. Ryan, *Fall of Che*; Dosal, *Comandante Che*, pp. 219–45; Harmer, *Beatriz Allende*, pp. 109–10. See also Dungan to Rusk, 31 March 1967, Ralph Dungan Papers, JFK Library, Ambassador to Chile Files, Box 23, Chronological Files: February 1967 folder; "Memorandum from the President's Special Assistant (Rostow) to President Johnson," 1 July 1966, and "Memorandum for Director of Central Intelligence Helms," 13 October 1967, *FRUS, 1964–1968*, vol. 31: *South and Central America: Mexico*, pp. 363–64 and 381–82.

83. Rielly to Humphrey, "Your Meeting with Dr. Rafael Caldera," 4 February 1965, and "MemCon: Caldera Visit," 5 February 1965, Humphrey Papers, Vice President: Foreign Affairs, 150.E.13.5 (B), Box 918; "Telegram from the President's Special Assistant (Rostow) to President Johnson in Texas," 24 June 1967, and "Telegram from the Embassy in Venezuela to the Department of State," 15 March 1967; "Memorandum of Conversation," 11 April 1967, *FRUS, 1964–1968*, vol. 31: *South and Central America: Mexico*, pp. 143–45, 1119–20, and 1126–28; Brown, *Cuba's Revolutionary World*, pp. 268–79; Miller, *Precarious Paths to Freedom*, pp. 145–211. For a rather more complex view of Venezuelan politics during this time period, see Alejandro Velasco, *Barrio Rising*, pp. 111–30.

84. Brown, *Cuba's Revolutionary World*, pp. 221–22; W. W. Rostow, "The United States and the Changing World: Problems and Opportunities Arising from the Diffusion of Power," Remarks at the National War College, 8 May 1968, LBJ Library, NSF, Name File, Box 7 Rostow Memos (1 of 2) folder.

85. Gordon to Grant, 8 February 1967, Frances Grant Papers, Rutgers University, Alexander Library, Special Collections, Box 45, Nicaragua: Situation in Nicaragua folder; see Gambone, *Capturing the Revolution*, pp. 113–16, 118, and 185–90; Pedro Joaquin Chamorro to Robert Kennedy 15 December 1966, Robert Kennedy Papers, Senate Papers, Correspondence: Subject Files, 1966. Evidence does not suggest that the Johnson administration or the State Department were particularly enthusiastic about Somoza's election. See, for example, Rostow to Johnson, 27 February 1967, LBJ, NSF Countries, Box 63, Nicaragua, Volume I (2 of 2) folder; "Information Memorandum from the Director of the Office of Central American Affairs (Burrows) to the Assistant Secretary of State for Inter-American Affairs (Gordon)," 10 January, 1967 *FRUS, 1964–1968*, vol. 31: *South and Central America: Mexico*, pp. 212–13; "Remarks upon Arrival at Managua, Nicaragua," 8 July 1968, *PPPUS: Johnson, 1968–1969*, p. 797.

86. See his comments regarding returning his attention to the region following the 1966 off-year election in Robert Kennedy to Santiago Polanco Abreu, Resident Commissioner of the Commonwealth of Puerto Rico, 14 November 1966, Robert Kennedy, JFK Library,

Senate Papers, Box 43, Correspondence: Subject Files 1966, Foreign Affairs 11/14/66 #1 folder; the remarks from the Nelson speech are in Ross, *Robert F. Kennedy*, p. 444.

87. Johnson, *Ernest Gruening and the American Dissenting Tradition*, pp. 280–87; see *Congressional Record*, 17 August 1967, pp. 22950–72.

88. "RFK Positions on the Issues: Foreign Aid," Abram Chayes Papers, JFK Library, Box 3, RFK 1968 Campaign: RFK Positions on the Issues folder no. 1; Solberg, *Humphrey*, particularly pp. 328, 332–38, and 355–71; Ben Stephansky and James Theberg, "Policy Paper by the Latin American Task Force," pp. 2, 6–9, and 25, Humphrey Papers, MHS, 148.B.14.4 (F), 1968 Campaign Task Force Files, Foreign Policy Task Force: Latin America 1968 folder. Robert F. Kennedy, Ball State University, 4 April 1968, Ball State University Libraries, accessed via YouTube, 29 June 2018; Inter-American Association for Democracy and Freedom press release, 1 November 1968, Frances Grant Papers, Rutgers University, Alexander Library, Special Collections, Box 27, Minutes, US Committee, 1964–1968 folder"; "Statement on Latin America," 20 October 1968, Humphrey Papers, MHS, Humphrey 1968 Campaign Files, 150.F.19.8 (F) Rielly: Foreign Policy: Latin America folder. In "L.A. Speech Notes" from earlier in the year, there is a reference to "not high priority." Virginia Prewett suggests that the main point was to inspire the American people to support it. See Prewett to Humphrey, 14 July 1968.

89. "Democratic Platform 1968," in Johnson, ed., *National Party Platforms*, pp. 723 and 726–27. The Republicans, for their part, claimed that the Democrats had abandoned the Monroe Doctrine. See "Republican Platform 1968," p. 760. The Alliance was not invoked, but the Republicans still committed themselves to attack on the region's "chronic problems of poverty, inadequate economic growth and consequent poor education throughout the hemisphere." "Economic integration" was also to be pursued. Regarding the debate over Vietnam, see, for example, Longley, *LBJ's 1968*, pp. 3, 8, 56–83, and 205–31; Johns, *Price of Loyalty*, pp. 75–104 and 111–21; Offner, *Humphrey*, pp. 260 and 293–305.

90. Sacha Volman to Donald Fraser, 12 June 1968, Arthur M. Schlesinger Jr. Papers, New York Public Library, Box 139, Sacha Volman folder.

91. Sacha Volman to Schlesinger, 19 June 1968, Arthur M. Schlesinger Jr. Papers, New York Public Library, Correspondence, Box 139, Sacha Volman folder. See also the 9 June 1968 letter from Juan Bosch to Volman.

92. Johnson, *Congress and the Cold War*, pp. 149–50; see Schlesinger's 11 March 1976 journal entry in Schlesinger and Schlesinger, eds., *Journals*, p. 408: "I have been totally out of things since RFK died, and never more so than this year. I am frank to say that I miss it. Politics is the best of all spectator sports."

93. See Johnson, "Latin American Summit Conference," Senate, *Hearings: Latin American Summit Conference*, p. 1; Regarding the Latin American feelings of neglect, see Wayne Morse and Dean Rusk on p. 95. W. W. Rostow, "The United States and the Changing World: Problems and Opportunities Arising from the Diffusion of Power," Remarks at the National War College, 8 May 1968, LBJ Library, NSF, Name File, Box 7, Rostow Memos (1 of 2) folder.

Chapter 7

1. See, for example, Nelson Aidukaitis to Robert Haldeman, 11 November 1968, Richard M. Nixon Library, White House Central Files, Box 13, Brazil, 1969–1970 folder. The UPI pressman was trying to arrange a meeting between the president-elect and a Brazilian sen-

ator who "thought Mr. Nixon had not approached the problems of Latin America, and of Brazil, in his campaign for the Presidency."

2. Regarding Rockefeller's background in Latin America, see Reich, *Life of Nelson A. Rockefeller*, pp. 166–70. See also Darlene Rivas, *Missionary Capitalist*, particularly pp. 2–6, 21–67, and 209–24. See the letter from Chilean President Eduardo Frei to Rockefeller, 12 March 1969, Nixon Library, WHCF, Subject Categories, Box 7, South America folder.

3. See Rockefeller's campaign promises in "Rockefeller for President" press release, 2 July 1968, in Rockefeller Archive Center (hereafter RAC), RG 15, Nelson Aldrich Rockefeller (hereafter NAR), Gubernatorial, James Cannon Files, Box 12, Folder 101. Regarding his selection and the mission's mission, see "Telephone Conversation with Galo Plaza," 22 January 1969, RAC, RG 15, NAR, Gubernatorial, James Cannon Files, Box 12, Folder 101. See "The President's News Conference of February 6, 1969," and "Statement Announcing Governor Nelson A. Rockefeller's Mission to Latin America, February 17, 1969," in *PPPUS: Nixon, 1969*, pp. 70 and 106. See also Nixon's undated letters to Rockefeller in RAC, RG 4, NAR, Personal, Box 148, Folder 1201. Regarding Latin American "self-help," see "Advisory for Background Briefing to be used by Ron Ziegler, White House Press Secretary, the State Department Press Office, and the Governor's Office" in the James Cannon Files, Box 16, Folder 137. Regarding Nixon's attitude toward the State Department, see, for example, Bundy, *Tangled Web*, pp. 52–55. See also Persico, *Imperial Rockefeller*, pp. 99–109.

4. Regarding his support for civil rights, see, for example, Gervasi, *Real Rockefeller*, p. 12; Arsenault, *Freedom Riders*, p. 336. Regarding the cancellation of the Chilean trip, see Korry's 3 June 1969 telegram in RG 59, Central Foreign Policy Files, 1967–1969, Box 1977, POL 7, 1/1/68; "GOC Cancels Rockefeller Visit," 4 June 1969, in Box 1979, POL 15-1, Chile. See also "Transcript of Remarks of Governor Nelson A. Rockefeller at the National Conference of UPI editors and publishers," 7 October 1969, p. 5. Regarding Frei's fears concerning the trip, see Korry, "Frei, Comments on Politics," 29 May 1969, in Box 1976, POL 2.

5. See Rodney Campbell, "Briefing Background Material Brazil for Governor Nelson A. Rockefeller," pp. 7–9 and 66–68 in RAC, RG 4, Box 100, Folder 785. The best currently available treatment of this particular period in the history of military rule is Gaspari, *A Ditadura Escancarada*.

6. See the 21 April 1969 letter from Chargé d'Affaires William Benton to Rockefeller, RAC, RG 4, NAR, Personal, Washington DC Files, Box 151, Folder 1222.

7. See Eugenio Godin's letter in RAC, RG 4, NAR, Personal, Box 151, Folder 1223.

8. See Berent Friele to Nelson Rockefeller, 24 February 1969, RAC, RG 4, NAR, Personal, Box 151, Folder 1220.

9. See Joseph Persico to Hugh Morrow, 2 June 1969, RAC, RG 4, NAR, Personal, Box 172, Folder 1401.

10. See materials in the press office folder in RAC, RG 15, NAR, Gubernatorial, Box 60, Folder 1286, as well as the 29 July 1969 letter to Homero da Mota Paiva in RAC, RG 4, NAR, Personal, Box 151, Folder 1224.

11. See NAR Notes, pp. 64–78. See the Nixon/Rockefeller White House news conference in RAC, RG 15, NAR, Gubernatorial, Press Office, PR Files, Latin American Mission.

12. See Rockefeller to Kissinger telegram, 18 June 1969, in RAC, RG 4, NAR, Personal, Box 148, Folder 1201.

13. "Country Report: Brazil," pp. 64–65, in RAC, RG 4, NAR, Personal, Box 100, Folder 787.

14. See "Letter to Governor Rockefeller on Receiving His Report on His Latin American Mission," 2 September 1969, *PPPUS: Nixon, 1969*, p. 704; "Remarks to the Annual Meeting of the Inter-American Press Association," 31 October 1969, p. 900; "Remarks to the Assembly of the Organization of American States," 14 April 1969, p. 282.

15. See materials in the press office folder in RAC, RG 15, NAR, Gubernatorial, Press Office, PR Files. See also *Quality of Life in the Americas*, p. 5.

16. "Remarks to the Assembly of the Organization of American States," 14 April 1969, p. 281, *PPPUS: Nixon, 1969*, p. 281; see also his "Statement on the 10th Anniversary of the Alliance for Progress," 17 August 1971, pp. 891–92, *PPPUS: Nixon, 1971*, and "Message to the Congress Transmitting Third Annual Report on United States Foreign Policy," p. 259, *PPPUS: Nixon, 1972*; see "Statement Announcing Governor Nelson A. Rockefeller's Mission to Latin America." 17 February 1959, *PPPUS: Nixon, 1969*, pp. 106–7; "The President's News Conference of February 6, 1969," p. 70; "Remarks to the Annual Meeting of the Inter-American Press Association," 31 October 1969, pp. 894–96 and 900. The best available overview of Kissinger's policies is Rabe, *Kissinger and Latin America*.

17. See Schmitz, *United States and Right-Wing Dictatorships*, pp. 6–7, 37, and 59–61; Ashby and Gramer, *Fighting the Odds*, pp. 290–92. See "Senator Frank Church on US Aid to Latin America," *Congressional Record*, 11 November 1969; See Cannon to Rockefeller, "Congressional Comment on the Presidential Mission," 30 March 1969, RAC, RG 15, NAR, Gubernatorial, Box 12, Folder 102. See also p. 9 of his 20 November 1969 testimony before the Senate Subcommittee on Western Hemisphere affairs in RAC, RG 15, NAR, Gubernatorial, Press Offices, PR Files, Latin American Mission, Box 61, Folder 1300. James Cannon refers to Dante Fascell as Rockefeller's fan in Cannon to Rockefeller, "Meeting with Representative Dante Fascell," 29 September 1969, RAC, RG 15, NAR, Gubernatorial, Box 12, Folder 102. "As you know, Church is trying to stop all military assistance to Latin America."

18. See Jerome Levinson to Rockefeller and Cannon, RAC, RG 15, NAR, Gubernatorial, James Cannon Files, Box 14, Folder 117. See Rockefeller to Kissinger, 19 September 1969, RAC, RG 4, NAR, Personal, Box 148, Folder 1201. He had testified on 24 June and 8 July. Kissinger responded on 4 October. Regarding Rockefeller's two-hour meeting with Nixon on the 3rd of September in San Clemente, California, see RAC, RG 15, NAR, Gubernatorial, James Cannon Files, Box 17, Folder 148.

19. See Rockefeller to Kissinger, 1 December 1969, RAC, RG 4, NAR, Personal, Box 1408, Folder 1201; Rockefeller to Nixon, "Executive Action to Restore Western Hemisphere Military Aid," 3 December 1969, in RAC, RG 4, NAR, Personal, Box 148, Folder 1201. Regarding aid for the Brazilian navy, see Rockefeller to Kissinger, 19 June 1969, RAC, RG 4, NAR, Personal, Box 148, Folder 1201; *Quality of Life*, pp. 20–21.

20. This was first argued by Latin Americanist and historian John J. Johnson in *Role of the Military in Underdeveloped Countries*.

21. See Rockefeller's 21 July 1969 address delivered at the Center for Inter-American Affairs in New York, particularly p. 19, in RAC, RG 15, NAR, Gubernatorial, Press Office—PR Files, Latin American Mission, Box 60, Folder 1293. His House testimony is in the same box, Folder 1297. See particularly pp. 89 and 88–89. See also Schmitz, *United States and Right-Wing Dictatorships*, particularly pp. 87–93.

22. "U.S. Arms Policies in Latin America and their influence on U.S. objectives," particularly pp. 1, 2, 4, 23–25, RAC, RG 15, NAR, Gubernatorial, James Cannon Files, Box 13, Folder 111. See also *Quality of Life in the Americas*, p. 53.

23. Dallek, *Nixon and Kissinger*, p. 227; for the private conversation between Nixon and Kissinger, see also Lawrence, "History from Below," pp. 273–74; Schmitz, *United States and Military Dictatorships, 1965–1989*, p. 87. Nixon privately expressed his skepticism regarding Latin American democracy. When the *Washington Post* suggested that military-run Argentina was said to be "badly tarnished" by riots experienced during the Rockefeller mission trip, he asked Kissinger, "Henry, were the governments in 'democratic' Chile, Venezuela, and Colombia tarnished by similar riots?" See Alexander Butterfield to Kissinger, 2 June 1969, Nixon Library, WHCF, Box 9, Argentina, 1969–1970 folder.

24. See Westad, *Global Cold War*, p. 201. For the limitations of the Nixon Doctrine in Brazil, see Spektor, *Kissinger e o Brasil*, particularly pp. 13–16, 22–41, 49–153, and 184–86.

25. See Schmitz, *United States and Right-Wing Dictatorships*, pp. 7 and 105–11.

26. Bundy, *Tangled Web*, p. 105.

27. Ralph A. Dungan, "Rockefeller in Latin America Traced to Ambiguous, Weak US Policy," *Los Angeles Times*, 7 July 1969.

28. U.S. Congress, Senate, *United States Military Policies and Programs in Latin America: Hearings before the Subcommittee on Western Hemisphere Affairs of the Committee on Foreign Relations*.

29. Regarding liberal Democrats' concerns over Brazil, see, for example, Frances Grant to Adolf Berle, 21 May 1969, Frances Grant Papers, Rutgers University, Alexander Library, Special Collections, Correspondence, Box 29, Correspondence: Adolf Berle folder. See also the letters regarding torture in Brazil in the fall of 1970 in the Walter Mondale Papers, MHS, 153.K.5.6F, Foreign Relations—Latin America folder; see Green, *We Cannot Remain Silent*, p. 147.

30. Regarding the relationship between Rockefeller and Kissinger, see Persico, *Imperial Rockefeller*, pp. 82–83 and 243, and Dallek, *Nixon and Kissinger*, pp. 49–50. Regarding his relationship with Nixon, see Persico, pp. 240–43 and 246. Regarding Kissinger, see also Reich, *Life of Nelson A. Rockefeller*, pp. 614–15, 626, and 658–63. See Kissinger's reassuring words regarding the report in his letters to Rockefeller, 29 September 1969 and 9 October 1969, RAC, RG 4, NAR, Personal, Box 148, Folder 1201. As the year neared its end, Rockefeller proposed that the Nixon administration create a "small Western Hemisphere Advisory Committee of three to five people," which "could follow with and for you some of the hot situations, which with the pressure of events elsewhere sometime cannot get the full attention they deserve." See Rockefeller to Kissinger, 4 November 1969, RAC, RG 4, NAR, Personal, Box 148, Folder 1201. See also Persico, *Imperial Rockefeller*, p. 107; *Quality of Life in the Americas*, p. 56. Regarding Rockefeller's later claim that Nixon had "the most successful four-year foreign policy of this century," see his 31 October 1972 talk before the National Press Club in Washington, DC, in RAC, RG 15, NAR, Gubernatorial, James Cannon Files, Box 16, Folder 136. The only references to Latin America in the speech he actually delivered are to strong economic performances in Brazil and Mexico. Drafts suggest that he had hoped to talk more about Latin America. The importance historians have granted the mission is suggested by the fact that Robert Dallek ignores the mission entirely (as he does the kidnapping of U.S. Ambassador to Brazil Charles Burke Elbrick in September.) See *Nixon and Kissinger*, particularly pp. 227–30. Regarding the relationship between the Rockefeller Mission and the Alliance for Progress, see Taffet, *Foreign Aid as Foreign Policy*, pp. 185–94.

31. See Garthoff, *Détente and Confrontation*; Westad, *Global Cold War*, p. 194; Bundy, *Tangled Web*, pp. 199–200; Dallek, *Nixon and Kissinger*, pp. 228–29; Lawrence, "History from

Below," pp. 269–88; "Telegram from the Embassy in Chile to the Department of State," 25 March 1969, *FRUS, Chile, 1969–1973*, pp. 10–13; Eduardo Frei Montalva, "The Second Latin American Revolution," *Foreign Affairs* 50, no. 1 (October 1971): 94–95; Ashby and Gramer, *Fighting the Odds*, pp. 255–57 and 290–91. Regarding Church's "farewell to foreign aid" speech, see pp. 364–66. See also Green, *We Cannot Remain Silent*, particularly pp. 234–54. More needs to be done on the impact of détente on the Third World. See Harmer, *Allende's Chile*, particularly pp. 3–5, 149–52, and 257–65.

32. Church to Oren Campbell (unidentified), 22 September 1969, Senator Frank Church Collection, Boise State University Library, Series 2.2 Foreign Relations, Box 47, Latin America—El Salvador-Ecuador folder; draft of letter to constituents, 16 April 1969, Box 44, Latin America 1969 folder. See also Church to James R. Green of Manufacturers Hanover in New York, 24 October 1969, in Box 44, Latin America 1969 folder.

33. Quoted in Tremayne, "Delusions and Reality," p. 164. Note that Church cited Mârcio Moreira Alves; see p. 165.

34. Church, 31 October 1969 press release, Senator Frank Church Collection, Boise State University Special Collections, Series 2.2 Foreign Relations, Box 44, Latin America 1969 folder.

35. Schlesinger and Schlesinger, eds., *Journals*, p. 302. "Henry said ruefully, 'All I can say is I hope you will feel equally glad about it a year from now.'"

36. Schlesinger, "The Lowering Hemisphere," *Atlantic Monthly*, January 1970, pp. 79–87.

37. Church, 10 April 1970 press release, Senator Frank Church Collection, Boise State University Library Special Collections, Series 2.2 Foreign Relations, Box 45, Latin America 1970 folder. The complete text is available in Church, "Toward a New Policy for Latin America," *Congressional Record—Senate*, 10 April 1971, pp. 11211–17.

38. Church, "Toward a New Policy for Latin America," p. 11213.

39. Church, "Farewell to Foreign Aid—A Liberal Takes Leave," *Congressional Record—Senate*, 29 October 1971, pp. 38252–58. See Keys on liberal Democrat Donald Fraser in *Reclaiming American Virtue*, pp. 81–84. Regarding Chile specifically, although primarily in 1974, see pp. 168–73.

40. Donald Fraser, "The Non-Economic Side of Development," Speech before the Minnesota Foreign Policy Association, 27 February 1970, Donald Fraser Papers, Congressional Office Files, Minnesota Historical Society, 151.H.4.1 (B), Congress and Foreign Policy folder.

41. See the correspondence in John Kennedy Library, NSF, Trips and Conferences, Box 252, Edward Kennedy's Trip to Latin America, 7/8/61–7/31/61 folder.

42. Grant to John Plank, 7 February 1964, Frances Grant Papers, Box 30, Correspondence, John Plank folder, Alexander Library, Special Collections.

43. Gabler, *Catching the Wind*, pp. 194–95, 256–57, and 266; John Bartlow Martin to Edward Kennedy, 26 April 1969 and 2 June 1969, John Bartlow Martin Papers, Library of Congress, Box 97, Kennedy, Edward folder. Martin said that he should "kiss off the Rockefeller fiasco with a paragraph more in sorrow than in anger." See also Inter-American Association for Democracy and Freedom, "Minutes of the Meeting of November 20, 1968," Overseas Press Club, Frances Grant Papers, Rutgers University, Alexander Library, Special Collections, Box 27, Minutes, United States Committee, 1964–1968 folder.

44. This appeared as "Beginning Anew in Latin America," *Saturday Review*, 17 October 1970, pp. 18–21. See Brazilianist James Green's discussion of the impact of the speech in *We Cannot Remain Silent*, pp. 237–38. See also "Interview with Mark Schneider (2/2/2009) (1)," pp. 3–5 and 9–13, millercenter.org/oralhistory/interview/mark_schneider (accessed

1 October 2015). Schneider stayed with Kennedy following the end of the fellowship until 1977. Schneider had spoken with Frank Mankiewicz, Richard Goodwin, Ben Stephansky, and others. See John Bartlow Martin to Edward Kennedy, 26 April 1969, John Bartlow Martin Papers, Library of Congress, Box 97, Kennedy, Edward folder. Martin had called for a major Senate speech in which he would "defend and argue for the continuation of the Alliance for Progress."

45. Kennedy, "Beginning Anew in Latin America," p. 20; Dungan to Reverend Charles Curry of Santiago, 14 July 1971; Dungan to C. Richard Pogue, 28 September 1970; and Edwin Martin to Dungan, 2 November 1970, Dungan Papers, JFK Library, Chancellor of Higher Education Files, Box 27, Chile—Correspondence (5 of 6) folder.

46. "Third Annual Report to the Congress on United States Foreign Policy," 9 February 1972, *PPPUS: Nixon, 1972*, pp. 261–64; "'A Conversation with the President': Interview with Four Representatives of the Television Networks," 4 January 1971, *PPPUS: Nixon, 1971*, p. 12. Harmer makes clear that Allende himself was confused about Nixon's intentions and thought that troubles in Southeast Asia would prevent the administration from being so actively involved in South America. See *Allende's Chile*, pp. 86–88, 91, and 103.

47. "'A Conversation with the President': Interview with Four Representatives of the Television Networks," 4 January 1971, *PPPUS: Nixon, 1971*, p. 12; "Third Annual Report to the Congress on United States Foreign Policy," 9 February 1972, *PPPUS: Nixon, 1972*, pp. 261–64.

48. Bundy, *Tangled Web*, pp. 200–203. (His accounts of Chile policy on pp. 421–23 are less reliable.) See also Kornbluh, *Pinochet File*, pp. 80–82. Regarding its covert actions, see pp. 82–96. These built on attempts prior to the inauguration but after the election to create a "coup climate." See pp. 16–35. Note Henry Kissinger's comment that "one can agree that overt hostility might hamper covert action." See "Minutes of a Meeting of the Senior Review Group," 17 October 1970, *FRUS, Chile, 1969–1973*, p. 392.

49. Church to Bruce Vandervort and Al Gedicke of Community Action on Latin America, Madison, Wisconsin, 25 May 1972, Senator Frank Church Collection, Boise, State University Library Special Collections, Series 2.2 Foreign Relations, Box 46, Chile #2 folder. Church encouraged his group to make its views "known to Senators who might be inclined to support intervention." Regarding his complacency regarding U.S. policy, see his 4 December 1970 letter to professors from the Land Tenure Center at the University of Wisconsin. Regarding the Nixon administration's interest in appearing neutral following Allende's inauguration, see, for example, Kornbluh, *Pinochet File*, pp. 80–82. Regarding its covert actions, see pp. 82–96. These built on previous attempts prior to the inauguration but after the election to create a "coup climate." See pp. 16–35.

50. Edward Kennedy, quoting himself, in "Tragedy in Chile," *Congressional Record*, 17 September 1973, p. 29862.

51. See Ambassador Edward Korry's comments at a Country Team meeting in "Editorial Note," *FRUS, 1969–1976*, vol. 21: *Chile, 1969–1973*, pp. 3–4. See his complaints regarding Dungan's op-ed in "Backchannel Message from the Ambassador of Chile (Korry) to the Undersecretary for Political Affairs (Johnson) and the President's Assistant for National Security Affairs (Kissinger)," in *FRUS, Chile, 1969–1973*, p. 305; Lockhart, *Chile, The CIA, and the Cold War*, pp. 139–40.

52. Berent Friele to Kissinger, 28 September 1970, and accompanying MemCon, Nixon Library, WHCF, Box 13, Brazil, 1969–1970 folder; "Fourth Annual Report to the Congress on United States Foreign Policy," 3 May 1973, *PPPUS: Nixon, 1973*, p. 438.

53. See Church, "Before the Platform Committee of the Democratic Party," 22 June 1972, Senator Frank Church Collection, Boise State University Library Special Collections, 7.9 Issue Books, Box 7, Foreign Relations—General-2 folder.

54. "'A Conversation with the President': Interview with Dan Rather of the Columbia Broadcasting System," 2 January 1972, pp. 10–11; Tanya Harmer, "Two, Three, Many Revolutions?" pp. 65–89; LeoGrande and Kornbluh, *Back Channel to Cuba*, p. 123.

55. See "First Annual Report to the Congress on United States Foreign Policy for the 1970s," 18 February 1970, *PPPUS: Nixon, 1970*, p. 133.

56. See Schlesinger to Dungan, 26 January 1970, Arthur M. Schlesinger Jr. Papers, New York Public Library, Correspondence, Box 38, Ralph Dungan folder.

57. Arthur M. Schlesinger Jr., "Journals: 18 October 1970", Arthur M. Schlesinger Jr. Papers, New York Public Library, Journals, Box 314, 1970 folder.

58. Frank Mankiewicz to Gary (Hart?), 23 July 1971, Frank Mankiewicz Papers, John F. Kennedy Library, McGovern 1972 Campaign, Box 20, Subject File: Latin America folder; George McGovern, "McGovern on the Issues," McGovern Papers, Mudd Manuscript Library, Princeton University, Box 107, Issues: Various folder; McGovern to Agencia Latinoamericana de Información, 20 June 1972, McGovern Papers, Box 99, Latin America 1972 folder. See also the 16 June 1972 letter to Fausto P. Ponte, Associate Executive Editor, *Excelsior*, in the same folder; see also the 10 June 1972 translation of an interview, McGovern Papers, Box 92, Cuba 1972 folder. See also "Proposed McGovern Campaign Position on the Relationship of the US with the Developing Third World Countries and Why McGovern Should Give Emphasis to the Subject," pp. 2 and 12, Abram Chayes Papers, John F. Kennedy Library, McGovern 1972 Campaign, Box 5, Developing Countries (2) folder; "Testimony of Hon. Abram Chayes before the Panel on Foreign Policy of the Democratic Platform Committee," Box 4, McGovern 1972 Campaign, Chayes Speeches, 6/22/72 folder. Note the comment from the discussions of the 28 August 1972 meeting of the "Latin America Panel" that "it was clear from the discussion that the Latin American panel was working without any over-all guidelines for basic foreign policy." This is in the Latin America (4) folder. Human rights activist Brady Tyson was then a member of the panel. See also the discussion in letters from July in the Latin America (3) folder. See Ad Hoc Latin America Taskforce to Ted van Dyk, "Priorities for Background Papers," 7 July 1972, in Latin America (1) folder; Abraham Lowenthal to Abram Chayes, "Some Ideas on the McGovern Statement on Latin America," 13 August 1972, in Latin America (2) folder.

59. "Democratic Platform 1972," Johnson, ed., *National Party Platforms*, pp. 814 and 816. The Republicans, for their part, committed to Nixon's détente and peace, promised "a special importance" for the Western Hemisphere, including "a more mature partnership" between the countries and a "firm commitment to the common pursuit of economic progress and social justice." The Republican discussion of Cuba, however, was untouched by the relaxation of tensions between the United States and the larger communist nations. See "Republican Platform 1972," pp. 847–51 and 853. See also the "Africa and Latin America" section in Abram Chayes Papers, John F. Kennedy Library, McGovern 1972 Campaign, Box 8, Platform Committee 3 folder. The draft singled out U.S. ambassadors John Bartlow Martin (Dominican Republic) and James Loeb (Peru) from the Kennedy years and Lincoln Gordon (Brazil) for praise. Chayes was the campaign's top foreign policy adviser.

60. Ben S. Stephansky and Thomas J. Liggett, "Latin America Task Force for McGovern," pp. 4, 5, 10, 13, 20, and 35–36. Stephansky had been Kennedy's ambassador to Bolivia.

Liggett served on the Board of Missions of the Christian Church. Stephansky hints at the difficulties the task force had in achieving unanimity in his 9 October 1972 letter to Abram Chayes, in Abram Chayes Papers, John F. Kennedy Library, McGovern 1972 Campaign, Box 6, Latin America (4) folder.

61. See U.S. Congress, Senate, *Multi-National Corporations and United States Foreign Policy: Hearings before the Subcommittee on Multinational Corporations of the Committee on Foreign Relations, United States Senate, Ninety-Third Congress, on the International Telephone and Telegraph Company, 1970–1971*, 20–22, 27–29 March, and 2 April 1973, Parts I and II. See particularly pp. 1, 85, 122, 191, 402, and 427 in Part I; Ashby and Gramer, *Fighting the Odds*, pp. 416–33; Johnson, *Congress and the Cold War*, pp. 197–98. The historian most convinced that U.S. economic interests prompted U.S. support for the coup is Qureshi. See her *Nixon, Kissinger, and Allende*, pp. xii–xiii, 50–51, 67–71, and 86–88; her evidence is hardly conclusive. Note that Kissinger said that compensation, for example, was "not the important issue." See "Minutes of a Meeting of the Senior Review Group," 17 October 1970, *FRUS, Chile, 1969–1973*, p. 395. Regarding the comparison to the 1965 invasion of the Dominican Republic, see President Nixon's complaint that Ambassador Korry had been instructed to take such an action: "he just failed, the son of a bitch, that is his main problem. He should have kept Allende from getting in." See "Editorial Note," regarding 23 March 1972 comments, on p. 785.

62. George McGovern, "Gridiron Club Banquet Speech, 10 March 1973," in Arthur M. Schlesinger Jr. Papers, New York Public Library, perhaps Box 93, George McGovern folder no. 2.

63. McGovern, "Military Globalism vs. The Good Society," 10 September 1973, McGovern Papers, Mudd Manuscript Library, Box 556, McGovern Legislation (1) folder.

64. The best general history of human rights policy as it relates to Latin America so far is Sikkink, *Mixed Signals*. See pp. 5–6, 20–21, and 48–76. Sikkink argues that the "human rights issue provided a vehicle for Congress to attack the executive and assert greater control over foreign policy." See p. 52. See also the discussion in Moyn, *Last Utopia*, pp. 140–41, and Kelly, "The 1973 Chilean Coup and the Origins of Transnational Rights Activism," pp. 165–86, and also Kelly, *Sovereign Emergencies*, particularly 61–207; see also Fraser to Rita Hauser, 14 August 1973, regarding plans to hold hearings on the international protection of human rights. He cited the countries of Brazil, the Soviet Union, Ireland, Greece, Burundi, and Uganda. This letter is in Fraser Papers, Minnesota Historical Society, 149.G.12.5 (B), Foreign Affairs—Human Rights Hearings folder.

65. See, for example, Jonathan B. Bingham, "Coup in Chile," *Congressional Record*, 13 September 1973, p. 29800, which reproduces an editorial from the same day in the *Washington Post*; Michael Harrington, "On United States Policy toward Chile," *Congressional Record*, 12 September 1973, p. 29390; Benjamin S. Rosenthal, "Human Rights in Chile," *Congressional Record*, 2 October 1973, p. 32617; Joe Moakley, "Investigation of Chilean Coup," *Congressional Record*, 12 September 1973, p. 29530; Mike Mansfield, "Events in Chile," *Congressional Record*, 21 September 1973, p. 30808. See also Edward Koch, "The Death of a Democracy: The Fall of Allende," *Congressional Record*, 17 September 1973, p. 29962; Edward Kennedy, "Tragedy in Chile," *Congressional Record*, 17 September 1973, p.29862; Johnson, *Congress and the Cold War*, pp. 196–99. Harrington and Koch are discussed in Johnson, *Congress and the Cold War*, pp. 181, 217–18, and 229. Regarding the hearings on International Telephone and Telegraph's involvement in Chilean politics and collaboration

with the Central Intelligence Agency, see Ashby and Gramer, *Fighting the Odds*, pp. 426–33; see also John R. Bawden, "Cutting Off the Dictator," pp. 513–43.

66. Michael Harrington, "Respect for Human Rights in Chile," *Congressional Record*, 20 September 1973, p. 30785.

67. Quoted in Robert Dallek, *Nixon and Kissinger*, p. 513. Edward Kennedy, "Chile," *Congressional Record*, 9 October 1973, pp. 33271–72. See also the 2 October discussion on pp. 32570; Gabler, *Catching the Wind*, pp. 312–13. Keys seems to both recognize and not recognize the importance of Latin America in the rise of the human rights issue. See *Reclaiming American Virtue*, p. 150.

68. Dungan, "The Junta's Challenge in Chile," 13 October 1973, *New York Times*, p. 35.

69. U.S. Congress, House, *Human Rights in the World Community: A Call for U.S. Leadership, Report of the Subcommittee on International Organizations and Movements of the Committee on Foreign Affairs, U.S. House of Representatives*, 1974, pp. xi, 1–3, 8, 17, 41, and 47–48. It should be noted that human rights was not supposed to take precedence over national security concerns.

70. Quoted in Clymer, *Edward M. Kennedy*, pp. 196–97. See also "Questions of Developments in Chile Submitted to the Department of State by Senator Edward M. Kennedy," *Congressional Record*, 2 November 1973, pp. 35770–71; Edward Kennedy to Attorney General William B. Saxbe, 3 November 1974, Adam Clymer Papers, Research Materials, Box 12, 1974—General (1 of 2) folder. In this letter, Senator Kennedy noted that thousands went to other countries while the United States only aided nineteen people.

71. See also Kennedy's discussion of this issue in the *Congressional Record*, 2 October 1973, p. 32573. See also Sikkink, *Mixed Signals*, pp. 69–70.

72. Mark Schneider, "Untitled," 15 April 1974, and Augusto Pinochet to Edward Kennedy, 27 March 1974, Dungan Papers, JFK Library, Chancellor of Higher Education Files, Box 26, Chile 1974 folder; see also Schneider, "Chronology of Senate Subcommittee: Chile Investigation, April 1974," and Pinochet to Kennedy, 5 May 1974, in the same box, Chile Correspondence (2 of 6) folder; "Interview with Mark Schneider (1)," pp. 31–33; Dungan to Tom Sullivan (*Herald-News*, Passaic, New Jersey), 27 February 1974, Dungan Papers, JFK Library, Chancellor of Higher Education Files, Box 26, Chile folder.

73. See Kennedy, "Human Rights Violations in Chile," *Congressional Record*, 23 July 1974, p. 24731; "American Policy toward Chile," *Congressional Record*, 5 February 1974, p. 2149. He had used his position on this subcommittee to address issues related to the Vietnam War during the Johnson years. See Palermo, *In His Own Right*, p. 19.

74. Fraser to Frances Grant, 25 February 1974, Fraser Papers, Minnesota Historical Society, 149.G.13.8 (F), Chile 1974 folder.

75. See Grant to Salvador Allende, 2 November 1970, Box 40, Chile, Correspondence, Political folder. Regarding Frei's thoughts regarding the coup, see the October letters from Nathaniel Davis to Kissinger, in Nixon Library, NSC, Box 778, Chile 1 January 1973–31 March 1974 folder; regarding the attempts to reach Frei by phone following the coup, see the 23 September 1973, 24 September 1973, and 20 October 1973 entries in Grant Papers, Box 4, Diaries, Diary Record, 1973 (3 of 3) folder. See the undated "Statement on Chile" by the Inter-American Association for Democracy and Freedom, which was signed by Schlesinger, Loeb, and others, in Box 40, Chile—Statement on Chile folder. See the correspondence in Box 40, including Grant to Shelby Appleton, 4 October 1971, and Sol Greene, 14 October 1971 (both of the International Ladies Garment Workers Union), and "The Situation in Chile,"

24 September 1973, Frances Grant Papers, Rutgers University Alexander Library, Special Collections, Latin American Country Files, Box 40, Chile—Personalities—Eduardo Frei 1971 folder, and Chile—Ms. Grant's Trip 1973 folder. In the same box, see Frei to Grant, 16 December 1974, and Grant to Frei, 23 December 1974, Chile Personalities Eduardo Frei 1974–1980 folder. See her coverage in the October 1973 and November 1973 issues of *Hemispherica*. Many were unhappy with Grant at the time. See also her responses in Box 34, Foreign Letters 1974 (1 or 2) folder, and the ones in the Domestic Letters 1975 folder. See the 2 April 1975 letter to Gertrude Rosenblum, a member of an Amnesty International chapter in Stamford, CT. Grant often believed the regime's claims regarding those on the left. Her resentment is clear in her 7 July 1975 letter to Lilian Montecino of Washington, DC. See also the 4 February 1976 letter to Staunton Calvert in the Domestic Letters 1976 folder.

76. See Schlesinger to Kissinger, 5 November 1974, Schlesinger and Schlesinger, eds., *Letters of Schlesinger*, p. 434.

77. Schlesinger to Kissinger, 5 November 1974, Arthur M. Schlesinger, Jr. Papers, New York Public Library, Journals, Box 315, October 1974 folder.

78. Dungan to Charles Porter, 16 August 1974, Dungan Papers, JFK Library, Chancellor of Higher Education Files, Box 26, Chile Correspondence (2 of 6) folder. See also Dungan to Kissinger in the same box, Chile Correspondence (1 of 6) folder.

79. Frank Church, "Covert Action: Swampland of American Foreign Policy," pp. 5 and 7; 4 December 1975, Pacem in Terris IV Conference, Senator Frank Church Collection, 7.9 Issue Books, Foreign Relations II, 1972–1977, Boise State University Library, Special Collections.

80. Edward Kennedy wrote in 1975 that "The lesson [of Vietnam] is that we must throw off the cumbersome mantle of world policeman and limit our readiness to intervene in areas where our interests are truly endangered." Quoted in Holsti and Rosenau, *American Leadership in World Affairs*, p. 67.

81. Lawrence, *Class of '74*, pp. ix, 3, 4, 6, 28, and 53–55; Kornbluh, *Pinochet File*, pp. 222–25; Ashby and Gramer, *Fighting the Odds*, p. 449; Johnson, *Congress and the Cold War*, pp. 215–16; See Adam Clymer, "Interview with Senator Tom Harkin, Washington, DC, 8 June 1995," in Adam Clymer Papers, John F. Kennedy Library, Interviews, Box 3, H (Haar–Hyman) folder. Ford referred to them as "a new generation of wildass Democrats." MemCon, 3 December 1974, Ford Presidential Library, NSA Memorandum of Conversations, 1973–77, Box 7, MemCons.

82. See, for example, Hamby, *Liberalism and Its Challengers*, p. 6.

83. "Remarks at a Luncheon for Members of the Republican National Committee and the Republican National Finance Committee," 16 September 1974, *PPPUS: Ford, 1974*, p. 145.

84. "Significance of Santiago," 30 June 1976, in Gerald Ford Presidential Library, National Security Adviser, Presidential Country Files for Latin America, 1974–1977, Box 3, Chile (3) folder; Scowcroft to Kissinger, "Untitled," 10 June 1976, in Ford Library, Project File on Pinochet/Chile, Box 1, Latin America—HAK Messages to President folder. Nixon, it was claimed, at least had been trying to move beyond the "paternalism" of the Alliance for Progress years.

85. Mieczkowski, *Gerald Ford and the Challenges of the 1970s*, pp. 274–75 and 280–82.

86. "The President's News Conference of September 16, 1974." *PPPUS: Ford, 1974*, pp. 150–51; "Statement on Signing the Foreign Assistance Act of 1974," *PPPUS: Ford, 1974*, p. 780;

"Question-and-Answer Session with Students at the Stanford University School of Law," 21 September 1975, *PPPUS: Ford, 1975*, pp. 1482–83.

87. Letter to Kissinger, 18 September 1974 and 11 November 1974, Fraser Papers, 151.H.3.3 (B), Dear Colleagues/Kissinger folder; see also Hubert Humphrey, "Opening Statement: Human Rights Hearings," 7 March 1978, McGovern Papers, Mudd Manuscript Library, Princeton University, Box 930, Human Rights 1977 folder; Keys, "Congress, Kissinger, and the Origins of Human Rights Diplomacy," pp. 823–51.

88. Kissinger to Ford, "Presidential Determination for Sale of the Sidewinder Missile to Brazil," 20 May 1975, in Ford Library, NSA, NSC, Latin American Affairs Staff: Files, 1974–1977, Box 1, Brazil—Political, Military (2) folder. See also Robert Ingersoll, Deputy Secretary of State, "Presidential Determination: Sidewinder Missile Sales to Brazil," 16 April 1975, and undated "Justification for Presidential Decision Regarding Sale of the Sidewinder Missile to Brazil" in the same folder.

89. For U.S. documents indicating Pinochet's direct control over DINA, see Kornbluh, *Pinochet File*, pp. 164–66, and the following document section, which is not paginated.

90. MemCon 14 June 1976, in Ford Library, NSA, Memoranda of Conversations, 1973–1977, Box 19, MemCon June 14, 1976 folder.

91. Kornbluh, *Pinochet File*, pp. 226–33; "Statement on Signing the Foreign Assistance Act of 1974," 30 December 1974, in *PPPUS: Ford, 1974*, p. 780; "Remarks at a Reception for Chiefs of Delegation to the General Assembly of the Organization of American States," 10 May 1975, in *PPPUS: Ford, 1975*, p. 662.

92. See Sater, *Chile and the United States*, pp. 190–92.

93. Jean P. Lewis, USAID Acting Assistant Administrator for Legislative Affairs, to Edward Kennedy, 24 October 1975, McGovern Papers, Mudd Manuscript Library, Princeton University, Box 529, Chile and PL 480 1975 folder; see also the Senate discussion in *Congressional Record*, 3 November 1975, 34741, 34751–54, and 34760–61. See also Harmer, *Allende's Chile*, p. 249.

94. Kornbluh, *Pinochet File*, pp. 222–25.

95. Fraser to Anne Winston of Washington, DC, 22 October 1974, Fraser Papers, Minnesota Historical Society, 149.G.9.7 (B), Chile 1975 folder.

96. John Holum to McGovern, 30 October 1975 and 11 December 1975, McGovern Papers, Mudd Manuscript Library, Princeton Library, Box 556, Human Rights (2) folder.

97. See Low to Scowcroft, "Chilean President's Visit to the US," 8 August 1975, in Ford Library, NSA, Presidential Country Files for Latin America, 1974–1977, Box 3, Chile (3) folder.

98. See Mary Brownell to Brent Scrowcroft, "Your Meeting with Admiral José Toribio Merino," 9 July 1976, pp. 1 and 4, in Ford Library, NSA, Presidential Country Files for Latin America, Box 3, Chile (3) folder.

99. Low to Scowcroft, "Meeting with Chilean Ambassador Trucco," 26 February 1976, in Ford Library, NSA, Presidential Country Files for Latin America, 1974–1977, Box 3, Chile (3) folder.

100. Johnson, *Season of Inquiry Revisited*, particularly pp. xiii, 1–3, 7, 145–50, and 264–71; see U.S. Congress, Senate, *Intelligence Activities Senate Resolution 21: Hearings before the Select Committee to Study Governmental Operations with Respect to Intelligence Activities*, pp. 1, 18, 24, and passim.

101. See, for example, Jacobo Timerman to Fraser, 30 September 1976, Fraser Papers, Minnesota Historical Society, 149.G.9.8 (F), Argentina 1976 folder. Draft of letter by Fraser,

Tom Harkin, and George Miller, Fraser Papers, Minnesota Historical Society, 149.G.9.8 (F), Chile 1976 folder. Ronnie Moffitt worked with Letelier at the Institute for Policy Studies, a left-wing think tank, in Washington. Her husband, who was also in the car, was injured but survived the explosion. Mark Schneider recalled that Letelier had been scheduled to meet with Senator Kennedy on the day of his death. See "Interview with Mark Schneider (1)," pp. 39–40.

102. Mary Brownell and Dan Mozeleski, "Bombing of Former Chilean Ambassador's Car," 21 September 1976, in Ford Library, NSC, Latin American Affairs Staff: Files, 1974–1977, Box 1, Chile—Political, Military (3) folder; "Tribute to Orlando Letelier," *Congressional Record*, 27 September 1973, pp. 32407–8 and 32424; McPherson, "Letelier Diplomacy," pp. 445–57, and *Ghosts of Sheridan Circle*, particularly pp. 2–5, 8, 44–46, 57–60, and 95–97.

103. See "Frank Church's Record on the Issues," pp. 6 and 7; "Script for the Captioned ABC Evenings News," 30 March 1976; "Transcript of Announcement Speech in Idaho City," p. 6, Senator Frank Church Collection, 5.5 Campaign, Box 6, Boise State University Library, Special Collections. Church primarily argued for continuing aid to Western Europe and Israel, "where our stakes are large."

104. See, for example, Johnson, *Season of Inquiry Revisited*, pp. 100–101; McCrisken, *American Exceptionalism and the Legacy of Vietnam*, pp. 36–39. The conflict between these two ideals would have unintended consequences in Nicaragua. See LeoGrande, *Our Own Backyard*, pp. 16–21.

Chapter 8

1. Schlesinger and Schlesinger, eds., *Journals*, pp. 293, 406, 415–16, and 437; Schlesinger to Patsy Mink, 11 July 1978, in Schlesinger and Schlesinger, eds., *Letters of Schlesinger*, p. 456; Schlesinger to Ray Jenkins (an aide and press officer in the Carter administration), 20 December 1982, in Schlesinger and Schlesinger, eds., *Letters of Schlesinger*, p. 470. Regarding Carter's ideological complexity, see Alter, *His Very Best*, pp. 196–97, 239, 248, and 286–87. As the governor of Georgia in 1972, Carter hoped to block George McGovern's candidacy. Schlesinger's attitude toward Carter was similar to that of other northeastern liberals. He told a friend that he could not vote for someone who prayed three times a day. See Alter, p. 241.

2. I obviously reject the notion that Carter had not focused on human rights during the presidential campaign until after it had been included in the Democratic Party platform that year. See the discussion in Moyn, *The Last Utopia*, pp. 153–61; Keys, *Reclaiming American Virtue*, pp. 215 and 232–41. Carter clearly rejected this idea, as in a speech as early as December 1974 in which he expressed a hope that "this country [would] set a standard within the community of nations of courage, compassion, integrity, and dedication to basic human rights and freedoms." See Carter, *Keeping Faith*, p. 143. See also "Remarks by Jimmy Carter," 15 March 1976, *FRUS, 1977–1980*, vol. 1: *Foundations of Foreign Policy*, pp. 15–26; Carter, Student National Medical Association Speech, 16 April 1976, and Fraser to Stanley K. Sheinbaum of Los Angeles, 30 September 1976, Fraser Papers, Minnesota Historical Society, 152.K.10.5 (B); Lieuwen, *Survey of the Alliance for Progress*, p. 67; "Presidential Campaign Debate of October 6, 1976," *PPPUS: Ford, 1976*, pp. 2413 and 2435, Jimmy Carter folder; Carter, *White House Diary*, p. 15. See also Alter, *His Very Best*, pp. 104–16, 190–91, 355–56, and 629. I would argue that human rights was not just a Cold War weapon, but it

clearly was one. See also Schmitz and Walker, "Jimmy Carter and the Foreign Policy of Human Rights," pp. 113–43. See also Gates, *From the Shadows*, pp. 89–96, 536–37, and 572.

3. "Democratic Party Platform," 12 July 1976, pp. 54–57 and 74–75, *The American Presidency Project*.

4. Zbigniew Brzezinski, "Presidential Review Memorandum NSC-17: Review of U.S. Policy toward Latin America," Carter Library, NLC-12-37-9-63; Pastor to Brzezinski, "PRC Meeting on Latin America," 14 March 1977, Carter Library, NLC-24-61-4-7-7.

5. Pastor to Brzezinski, "PRC Meeting on Latin America," 14 March 1977, Carter Library, NLC-24-61-4-7-7.

6. "Presidential Review Memorandum NSC 17: Review of U.S. Policy toward Latin America," Carter Library, NLC-17-25-1-1-3.

7. See also Carter, "Organization of the American States. Address before the Permanent Council," 14 April 1977, in *PPPUS: Carter, 1977*, vol. 1, pp. 612 and 615.

8. Pastor to Brzezinski, "PRC Meeting on Latin America," 14 March 1977, Carter Library, NLC-24-61-4-7-7.

9. "Presidential Review Memorandum NSC 17: Review of U.S. Policy toward Latin America," Carter Library, NLC-17-25-1-1-3.

10. "Visit of President Pérez of Venezuela. Toasts of the President at a Dinner Party Honoring the Venezuelan President. June 28, 1977." *PPPUS: Carter, 1977*, vol. 2, pp. 1183–85.

11. See "Inaugural Address of President Jimmy Carter," 20 January 1977, *PPPUS: Carter*, book 1, pp. 2 and 3.

12. Carter, "Remarks to People of Other Nations on Assuming Office," 20 January 1977, *PPPUS: Carter*, book 1, pp. 4–5.

13. Carter, "United Nations, Address before the General Assembly," 17 March 1977, *PPPUS: Carter, 1977*, vol. 1, p. 449.

14. Carter, "University of Notre Dame, Address at Commencement Exercises at the University," 22 May 1977, *PPPUS: Carter, 1977*, vol. 1, pp. 956–57; Carter, *Keeping Faith*, p. 144; McCrisken, *American Exceptionalism and the Legacy of Vietnam*, pp. 57–72.

15. Carter, "University of Notre Dame, Address at Commencement Exercises at the University," 22 May 1977, *PPPUS: Carter, 1977*, vol. 1, p. 956; Carter, "Organization of the American States, Address before the Permanent Council," 14 April 1977, in *PPPUS: Carter, 1977*, vol. 1, p. 612.

16. Keys is right to note the improvisational nature of much of Carter foreign policy. See her *Reclaiming American Virtue*, pp. 250–56 and 259–64.

17. Carter, *Keeping Faith*, p. 143.

18. Carter, "State of the Union." 19 January 1978, in *PPPUS: Carter, 1978*, vol. 1, p. 95. See also the enhanced written version of the 1979 State of the Union address from 25 January 1979 in *PPPUS: Carter, 1979*, vol. 1, p. 162.

19. David Aaron, MemCon, "Minister Josef Wiejacz, Embassy of the Polish People's Republic," 16 February 1977, Carter Library, National Security Adviser, Brzezinski Materials, Subject File, Box 33, MemCons, David Aaron, 2/77–12/78 folder. Regarding the presumed emphasis on the Soviet Union, see, for example, the 23 February 1977 news conference on p. 220 of *PPPUS: Carter, 1977*, book 1. Carter noted, "I have never had an inclination to single out the Soviet Union as the only place where human rights are abridged." See also the 9 March 1977 news conference, p. 341, and the 30 April 1977 news conference, p. 765.

20. Lake to Christopher, 30 June 1977, *FRUS, 1977–1980,* vol. 2: *Human Rights and Humanitarian Affairs,* pp. 205–6.

21. Derian to Lake and Christopher, 15 September 1977, *FRUS, 1977–1980,* vol. 2: *Human Rights and Humanitarian Affairs,* pp. 254–55.

22. Tuchman to Brzezinski, 23 November 1977, *FRUS, 1977–1980,* vol. 2: *Human Rights and Humanitarian Affairs,* pp. 300–301.

23. Carter, *Keeping Faith,* p. 144.

24. Carter, *Keeping Faith,* p 146; Mitchell, "The Cold War and Jimmy Carter," p. 69. See also Peterson, "Carter Administration and Promotion of Human Rights in the Soviet Union," pp. 628–656.

25. See CIA, "Human Rights," 21 March 1977, *FRUS, 1977–1980,* vol. 2: *Human Rights and Humanitarian Affairs,* pp. 67–68. Neoconservative Joshua Muravchik credited Schneider with shaping Carter administration policy. See his "Kennedy's Foreign Policy: What the Record Shows," *Commentary* 68, no. 6 (December 1979): 32.

26. Tuchman to Brzezinski, 23 November 1977, *FRUS, 1977–1980,* vol. 2: *Human Rights and Humanitarian Affairs,* pp. 300–301.

27. MemCon, "President Carter's Second Meeting with the President of Venezuela during his State Visit," 29 June 1977, Carter Library, NSA Brzezinski Materials, Subject Files, Box 35, MemCons President 6/77 folder; Carter, "Organization of the American States, Address before the Permanent Council," 14 April 1977, in *PPPUS: Carter, 1977,* vol. 1, p. 612.

28. Anthony Lake, "Human Rights "Sanctions,'" Carter Library, NLC-24-56-1-8-4.

29. Lake to Christopher, 10 August 1978, *FRUS, 1977–1980,* vol. 2: *Human Rights and Humanitarian Affairs,* pp. 507–9.

30. Brzezinski to Jessica Tuchman of the National Security Staff, 17 January 1977; State Department, "Guidelines on U.S. Foreign Policy for Human Rights," undated, *FRUS, 1977–1980,* vol. 2: *Human Rights and Humanitarian Affairs,* pp. 2–5.

31. Nimetz to Christopher, 15 July 1977, *FRUS, 1977–1980,* vol. 2: *Human Rights and Humanitarian Affairs,* p. 213.

32. Tuchman to Brzezinski, 24 January 1977, p. 9, and Jenkins to Vance, 10 February 1977, *FRUS, 1977–1980,* vol. 2: *Human Rights and Humanitarian Affairs.* Lucy Wilson Benson, Under Secretary of State for International Security Affairs, pp. 37–38. Regret regarding the lack of "regular contact" with Congress was still being expressed months later. See Douglas Bennet (Congressional Relations) to Christopher, pp. 200–201. Correspondence often suggested that both sides believed that they "owned" the issue. See the letters in Donald Fraser Papers, 151.H.4.2 (F), Human Rights, 1974–1978 folder.

33. Schlesinger to *London Daily Express,* after 100 days, Arthur Schlesinger Jr. Papers, New York Public Library, Journals, Box 317, May–August 1977 folder.

34. Carter, 25 March 1977 entry and 25 March 1977, *White House Diary,* p. 37. The other countries which refused military aid on the same grounds were Argentina, El Salvador, Guatemala, and Uruguay.

35. Carter, 30 May 1977 entry, *White House Diary,* p. 59; "Rosalynn Carter's Trip to the Caribbean and Latin America, Remarks of the President and Mrs. Carter on Her Return. June 12, 1977," *PPPUS: Carter, 1977,* vol. 1, p. 1098; "Rosalynn Carter's Trip to the Caribbean and Latin America, Remarks of the President and Mrs. Carter Prior to Her Departure from Brunswick, Georgia," 30 May 1977," *PPPUS: Carter, 1977,* vol. 1, p. 1041.

36. Carter, 7 June 1977 entry, *White House Diary*, p. 61; Green, *We Cannot Remain Silent*, pp. 336–37.

37. Alter, *His Very Best*, p. 311; "Letter from President Carter to Peruvian President Morales Bermudez," 24 June 1977; MemCon, 6 September 1977, "Intelligence Assessment Prepared in the Central Intelligence Agency," May 1980, *FRUS, 1977–1980*, vol. 24: *South America: Latin America Region*, pp. 859–61 and 884–89; Halperín Donghi, *Contemporary History of Latin America*, pp. 385–86.

38. CIA, Directorate of Intelligence, "The OAS General Assembly and the Human Rights Issue," 28 June 1977, Carter Library, NLC-24-60-5-1-3.

39. Pastor to State, "Policy Review on Chile," 26 May 1977, Carter Library, NSA Brzezinski Materials, Country Files, Box 7, Chile 1/77–1/81 folder.

40. Pastor to Brzezinski, "Proposed Visit of President Frei," 13 May 1977, Carter Library, White House Central Files, Country Files, Box CO-15, CO-33, 1/20/77–1/20/81 folder.

41. Peter Tarnoff to Brzezinski and the White House, "Status Report on Progress in Human Rights in Latin America," 7 April 1979, Carter Library, NSA Brzezinski Materials, Subject Files, Box 29, Human Rights, 4/79–4/80 folder. See also Anthony Lake, "Human Rights 'Sanctions,'" Carter Library, NLC-24-56-1-8-4. Lake noted that Nixon had been more successful in blocking Allende's access to loans than the United States had been "in cutting off Pinochet's financial sources."

42. Sikkink, *Mixed Signals*, p. 125.

43. Pastor to Brzezinski, "Proposed Visit of President Frei," 13 May 1977, Carter Library, White House Central Files, Country Files, Box CO-15, CO-33, 1/20/77–1/20/81 folder. In the same folder, see also Brzezinski to Carter, "The Vice President's Meeting with Eduardo Frei," 25 May 1977.

44. Pastor to Brzezinski, "Proposed Visit of President Frei," 13 May 1977, Carter Library, White House Central Files, Country Files, Box CO-15, CO-33, 1/20/77–1/20/81 folder. In the same folder, see also Brzezinski to Carter, "The Vice–President's Meeting with Eduardo Frei," 25 May 1977.

45. See Pastor to Brzezinski, "Proposed Visit of President Frei," 13 May 1977 in Carter Library, White House Central File, Subject File, Countries, Box CO-15, CO-33, 1/20/77–1/20/81 folder. In the same folder see Brzezinski to Carter, "The Vice President's Meeting with Eduardo Frei," 1 June 1977, and the 25 May 1977 MemCon. See also Peter Tarnoff to Brzezinski, "Possible Talking Points for Ex-President Frei's Call on the Vice President, May 25, 1977 at 11:30 A.M.," 24 May 1977, in Carter Library, White House Central Files, Subject File, Countries, Box CO-13, CO-32, 1/20/77–1/20/81 folder.

46. Carter, 6 September 1977 entry, *White House Diary*, p. 91.

47. Thornton to Brzezinski, 31 August 1977 evening report, Carter Library, NLC-10-4-7-22-5; "Meeting with President Augusto Pinochet Ugarte of Chile: Remarks to Reporters Following the Meeting," 6 September 1977, *PPPUS: Carter, 1977*, pp. 1538–39.

48. See Carter's 22 November 1977 letter to Pinochet in Carter Library, White House Central Files, Subject Files, Countries, Box CO-15, CO-33, 1/20/77–1/20/81 folder.

49. Memorandum for Dr. Brzezinski, "Noon Notes," 14 December 1977, p. 2, in Carter Presidential Library, RAC Machine, NLC-1-4-7-25-2.

50. Memorandum for Brzezinski, "Chilean President Pinochet's January 30, 1978 Letter to President Carter," 3 March 1978, Carter Library, NLC-14-19-3-14-8.

51. Brinkley, *Unfinished Presidency*, p. 19; see Sater, *Chile and the United States*, pp. 192–95.

52. Gaspari, *Ditadura Encurralada*, pp. 373, 378–80, and 383–98.

53. See Pastor to Brzezinski, "Your Request for Comments on the Brazil Memo," 4 November 1977, in Carter Library, White House Central File, Subject File, Countries, Box CO-13, CO-22, 9/1/77–12/31/77 folder.

54. See Gaspari, *Ditadura Encurralada*, pp. 374–75.

55. Christine Dodson, National Security Council Staff Secretary, to Peter Tarnoff, Executive Secretary, Department of State, "Possible Meeting with Brazilian Opposition Party Members," 13 July 1977, in Carter Presidential Library, White House Central Files, Countries CO-13, CO-22, 1/20/77–1/20/81 folder.

56. Pastor to Jody Power and Jerry Schecter, 18 October 1977, Carter Library, White House Central Files, Subject File, Countries, Box CO-13, CO-22, 9/1/77–12/31/77 folder.

57. See Carter to Arns, 28 December 1977 in Carter Library, White House Central Files, Subject Files, Countries, CO-13, CO-22, 1/1/78–4/30/78 folder.

58. Brinkley, *Unfinished Presidency*, p. 134. See "Remarks of President Carter and President Ernesto Geisel at the Welcoming Ceremony, 29 March 1978," "Remarks before the Brazilian Congress, 30 March 1978," "Joint Communique Issued Following Meetings between President Carter and President Geisel," and "The President's Trip to Africa: Remarks during a Briefing for Reporters on Board Air Force One En Route to Monrovia, 3 April 1978," in *PPPUS: Carter, 1978*, pp. 626–27, 632–38, and 670. Regarding the honorary degrees for Arns and Carter from Notre Dame, see Carter, "Address at Commencement Exercises at the University." 22 May 1977, in *PPPUS: Carter, 1977*, pp. 954–55.

59. Gaspari, *Ditadura Encurralada*, pp. 365–67.

60. Frank Church, "Argentina: State of Siege," *Congressional Record*, 10 March 1977, p. 3959; "Briefing Memorandum from Richard Feinberg of the Policy Planning Staff to Secretary of State Vance," 19 November 1977, *FRUS, Carter Administration, 1977–1980*, vol. 24: *South America: Latin America Region*, p. 239.

61. Schmidli, *Fate of Freedom Elsewhere*, p. 81.

62. Pastor to Brzezinski and Aaron, "Argentina: Your Questions," 9 August 1978," Carter Library, NLC-24-77-8-4-8.

63. Pastor to Brzezinski and Aaron, "Argentina: Your Questions," 9 August 1978," Carter Library, NLC-24-77-8-4-8.

64. Derian to Vance, 16 July 1979, *FRUS, 1977–1980*, vol. 2: *Human Rights and Humanitarian Affairs*, p. 591.

65. Pastor to Brzezinski and Aaron, "Argentina: Your Questions," 9 August 1978," Carter Library, NLC-24-77-8-4-8.

66. Schmidli, *Fate of Freedom Elsewhere*, pp. 81–82 and 142–55; Sikkink, *Mixed Signals*, pp. 135–37.

67. Gaspari, *Ditadura Encurralada*, pp. 365–67; Peter Tarnoff to Brzezinski and the White House, "Status Report on Progress in Human Rights in Latin America," 7 April 1979, Carter Library, NSA Brzezinski Materials, Subject Files, Box 29, Human Rights, 4/79–4/80 folder. The State Department recognized that, public perception to the contrary, human rights in Brazil were already improving in early 1977. See Michael Hornblow, "Presidential Review Memorandum, NSC-17: Review of United States Policy toward Latin America," Carter Library,

NLC-17-26-1-1-3. Regarding the Carter administration's hopes for Brazil under Figueiredo, see "Brazil," Carter Library, NLC-7-4-3-1-6; see also Brinkley, *Unfinished Presidency*, p. 134.

68. Anthony Lake, "Human Rights 'Sanctions,'" Carter Library, NLC-24-56-1-8-4.

69. See Brzezinski to Vance on Argentina's actions, 9 July 1977, *FRUS, 1977–1980*, vol. 2: *Human Rights and Humanitarian Affairs*, p. 210.

70. "Address by the Assistant Secretary of State for Inter-American Affairs (Todman)," 14 February 1978, *FRUS, Carter Administration, 1977–1980*, vol. 24: *South America: Latin America Region, 1977–1980*, particularly 106–7, and the following "Editorial Note," p. 111; see Schmidli, *Fate of Freedom Elsewhere*, pp. 95–98, 106–19, and 161–73.

71. Robert Gates to Pastor, "Vance-Brown-Brzezinski Luncheon," 12 October 1979, Carter Library, NLC-24-84-6-8-8; Brzezinski to Vance, "Letelier/Moffitt Case," undated but clearly written in response to Vance to Carter, "Letelier/Moffitt Case," 19 October 1979, Carter Library, NLC-24-85-1-1-9; Pastor to Brzezinski, "Comments on Thornton's Memo on Chile," 20 February 1980, Carter Library, NLC-24-57-6-8-8; Christine Dobson to Denis Clift, 23 October 1980, Carter Library, White House Central Files, Countries, Box CO-15, CO-33, Confidential, 1/20/77–1/20/81 folder. See also Church and Kennedy to Carter, 14 May 1979, in the same folder; McPherson, "Letelier Diplomacy," pp. 460–62; McPherson, *Ghosts of Sheridan Circle*, p. 219.

72. Frei, "Discurso con Motivo del Plebiscito de 1980," in Gazmuri, Aranciba, and Góngora, *Eduardo Frei Montalva (1911–1982)*, pp. 502–9 and 519–20.

73. Warren Christopher to Carter, "Steps to Improve US-Argentine Relations," Carter Library, NLC-24-98-8-3-7. Note that Brzezinski pushed improved U.S.-Argentine relations even though he did not expect any cooperation on a grain embargo. See Brzezinski to Carter, "Memorandum for the President: U.S. Policy toward Argentina," Carter Library, NSA Brzezinski Materials, Country Files, Box 5, Argentina 2/80–1/81 folder. Brzezinski particularly thought military channels would be most effective. Secretary of State Edmund Muskie was less supportive, but thought the United States could "maintain private dialogue and avoid public confrontation that would make this dialogue difficult." See Muskie to Carter, 8 October 1980; Brzezinski to Carter, "Letter to Argentine Nobel Prize Winner," October 1980. Thomas Thornton, in his 17 October 1980 letter to Brzezinski, noted that the United States was "apparently, the only country to be sending a letter at this time. But we should be." (All of these messages are in the same folder.) Regarding Derian's isolation, see Schmidli, *Fate of Freedom Elsewhere*, pp. 177–81.

74. Lincoln Bloomfield, "Paper Prepared in the National Security Council," undated but mid-1980, *FRUS, 1977–1980*, vol. 2: *Human Rights and Humanitarian Affairs*, pp. 628–32.

75. "Paper Prepared by the Global Issues Cluster of the National Security Council Staff," undated, *FRUS, 1977–1980*, vol. 2: *Human Rights and Humanitarian Affairs*, p. 519.

76. Derian to Vance, 22 October 1979, *FRUS, 1977–1980*, vol. 2: *Human Rights and Humanitarian Affairs*, pp. 605–6.

77. "Human Rights: A U.S. Asset," *Hemispherica*, October–November 1980.

78. Thornton to Bloomfield," undated, but mid-1979, *FRUS, 1977–1980*, vol. 2: *Human Rights and Humanitarian Affairs*, pp. 588–90.

79. Halperín Donghi, *Contemporary History of Latin America*, p. 342. Sikkink quotes a *Washington Post* article from 22 May 1981 in *Mixed Signals*, p. xx. See also p. 144. See also Brinkley, *Unfinished Presidency*, pp. 134–36.

80. Sikkink, *Mixed Signals*, p. 123.

Chapter 9

1. Carter, *Keeping Faith*, p. 155; Jorden, *Panama Odyssey*, pp. 341–44. It should be noted that Robert Pastor played the major role in organizing the commission study.

2. Jorden, *Panama Odyssey*, pp. 347–48 and 458; Alter, *His Very Best*, p. 373. "'Suppose there is no second term?' he told Rosalynn." It would be an exaggeration to state that President Johnson had initiated a long-term process toward negotiating a new treaty, although he made some effort toward this end. See Mark Atwood Lawrence, "Exception to the Rule?" pp. 20–21 and 46.

3. Hamilton Jordan and Pastor to Carter, "Meeting with General Torrijos," 14 October 1977, Carter Library, NSA Brzezinski Materials, Country Files, Box 60, Panama 1–10/77 folder. See also Tom Long, "Putting the Canal on the Map," pp. 431–55; Jorden, *Panama Odyssey*, pp. 19–20.

4. Carter, 27 October 1977 entry, 23–27 November 1977 entry, and 17 June 1978 entry, *White House Diary*, pp. 124 and 141; Hamilton Jordan and Pastor to Carter, "Meeting with General Torrijos," 14 October 1977, Carter Library, NSA Brzezinski Materials, Country Files, Box 60, Panama 1–10/77 folder; Brzezinski to Carter, "Senator Byrd's Trip—An Assessment," Carter Library, NSA Brzezinski Materials, Country Files, Box 60, 11/77–3/78 folder.

5. Carter, 2 March 1977 entry and 29 July 1977 entry, *White House Diary*, pp. 29 and 73; Jorden, *Panama Odyssey*, pp. 358–59, 385, 474–75, 581–82, and 602. Ambassador Jorden did his part to make senators like Joseph Biden aware of the historical framework in which Panamanians (and Latin Americans) understood these issues.

6. Carter, 9 August 1977 entry, *White House Diary*, p. 80; Carter, *Keeping Faith*, pp. 159–78. Regarding public attitudes toward the treaty, see the correspondence in Senator Frank Church Collection, Boise State University Library, Special Collections, Series 2.2 Foreign Relations, Box 48, Panama Canal 1975 folder, and Box 49, Panama Canal April 1978 folder.

7. See, for example, "Panama Canal Treaties. Question-and-Answer Session by Telephone with Participants in a Town Hall Meeting on the Treaties in Hattiesburg, Mississippi," 16 January 1978, p. 84; Carter to Richard Stone, 27 January 1978, p. 228; Carter, "State of the Union," 19 January 1978, p. 95; Carter, "Panama Canal Treaties. Address to the Nation," *PPPUS: Carter, 1978*, vol. 1, pp. 258–63.

8. Jorden, *Panama Odyssey*, pp. 465, 504–5, 516–17, 522, 603, and 620; Ashby and Gramer, *Fighting the Odds*, p. 550; Carter, *Keeping the Faith*, pp. 181–85. Church got little credit in Carter's memoirs as well. Jorden notes that seven of the senators who supported the treaty were defeated later that year. An additional eleven lost in 1980. See *Panama Odyssey*, pp. 682. See, for example, Church to Grove and Ellen Koger of Meridian, Idaho, Senator Frank Church Collection, Series 2.2 Foreign Relations, Box 49, Panama Canal April 1978 folder, and Church to Lee Bybee, Boise, Idaho, Box 48, Panama Canal 1978 folder. In Box 45, Latin America 1977–1980 folder, see Church to James L. Wood of Fruitland, Idaho, 13 September 1977.

9. William D. Rogers to McGovern, 18 December 1975, McGovern Papers, Mudd Manuscript Library, Princeton University, Cuba (3) folder. Rogers wrote that the idea of sending baseball players to Cuba "was imminent at one time but it is not imminent now." See Ford, "Remarks and a Question-and-Answer Session at the University of New Hampshire in Durham," 8 February 1976, *PPPUS: Ford, 1976*, p. 225. Pastor to Brzezinski, "Cuba Policy—PRC Meeting," 8 March 1977, Carter Library; NSA Brzezinski Materials, Country Files, Box 13;

Cuba 1–4/77 folder; Cuban withdrawal had briefly seemed possible, but Castro always insisted that the troops would not depart until the Angolan government decided that they should do so. See Gleijeses, *Visions of Freedom*, pp. 34–35 and 44.

10. Presidential Directive NSC-6 from 15 March 1977 is on p. 155 of LeoGrande and Kornbluh, *Back Channel to Cuba*. Pastor to Brzezinski, "Your Lunch with Senator Church: Cuba," 1 August 1977, Carter Library, NLC-17-28-7-3-3. Regarding conflicts over Cuba and Angola, see Mitchell's discussion in *Jimmy Carter in Africa*, pp. 485–86.

11. Church to Castro, "Visit to Cuba," 12 August 1977, Carter Library, NSA Brzezinski Materials, Country Files, Box 13, Cuba 5–10/77 folder. Church's trip to Cuba cost him politically. See the correspondence in Senator Frank Church Collection, Boise State University Library Special Collections, Box 47, Cuba 1977 folder. He had to assure constituents that the trip did not imply approval of Castro's regime.

12. Edward Kennedy to colleagues, 4 March 1975, Senator Frank Church Collection, Series 2.2 Foreign Relations, Box 47, Cuba 1970–1975 Folder, Boise State University Library, Special Collections.

13. Regarding McGovern's thinking about and visit to Cuba, see McGovern, *Grassroots*, pp. 276–86; John Holum to McGovern, "Cuba Embargo Amendment—Administration Agreement," 20 April 1977, McGovern Papers, Mudd Manuscript Library, Princeton University, Box 556, Cuba (3) folder; Pastor to Brzezinski, 2 May 1977, Brzezinski to Carter, 27 April 1977, and McGovern to Carter, "Merits and Tactics of Partially Lifting the Cuban Embargo," 19 April 1977, Carter Library, NSA Brzezinski Materials, Country Files, Box 13, Cuba 5–10/77 folder; LeoGrande and Kornbluh, *Back Channel to Cuba*, p. 165.

14. Hewson A. Ryan to Kissinger, "Objectives of Your Visit to the Dominican Republic," 28 May 1976, Carter Library, NLC-24-57-3-12-6. The Inter-American Association for Democracy and Freedom gave the country some attention, but the issue had gained no traction in the years since 1966. See, for example, *Hemispherica*, May 1970.

15. MemCon, "President Carter/President Balaguer Bilateral," 8 September 1977, Carter Library, NLC-24-19-5-1-8.

16. See, for example, Fraser's 2 March 1973 letter regarding the treatment of opposition political leaders in Fraser Papers, 149.G.12.5 (B), Dominican Republic 1973 folder; Pastor to Brzezinski, "Letter to Donald Fraser," 21 December 1977, Brzezinski to Fraser, 27 December 1977, Brzezinski to Vance, "Elections in Latin America and the Caribbean," undated, 5 December 1977, and Fraser to Carter, 11 November 1977, Carter Library, White House Central Files, Countries, Box CO-23, CO-42, Executive, 1/20/77–1/20/81 folder. Rick Underfurth expressed frustration that there continued to be a need to explain why Carter had met with Latin American leaders during the treaty signing. In an undated letter, Brzezinski noted how "sobering" it was "to know how a few remarks in the United States can have such an enormous impact in a small country." See also the correspondence in Carter Library, White House Central Files, Countries, Box CO-23, CO-42, 1/20/77–1/20/81 folder. The Carter administration removed a pro-Balaguer ambassador. See also House of Representatives, Committee on International Relations, Subcommittee on International Organizations, "Review of the Elections in the Dominican Republic: The 1978 Presidential Elections," 23 May 1976, particularly pp. 1, 6, 9–11, 16, and 21–26; Atkins and Wilson, *Dominican Republic and the United States*, pp. 171–82; Hartlyn, *Struggle for Democratic Politics in the Dominican Republic*, p. 122.

17. Regarding his ambitions, see John Bartlow Martin to Anthony Lake, 15 October 1976, Martin to Brezenski (*sic*), 27 October 1976, and other letters in John Bartlow

Martin Papers, Library of Congress, Box 97, Politicians: Carter, Jimmy folder. See also Zbigniew Brzezinski to Martin, 4 November 1976, in which the soon-to-be National Security Adviser notes that he certainly could stand to learn something about the Caribbean, though he expressed doubts that he would be "that directly involved." Martin's later letters (11 May 1977 and 2 June 1977 to Senator Adlai Stevenson III) make clear that he hoped for an appointment as ambassador to "Venezuela, Bolivia, Portugal, and, above all, Spain." "Telegram from the Embassy in the Dominican Republic to the Department of State," 11 April 1978, and "Telegram from the Department of State to the Embassy in the Dominican Republic," 15 April 1978, *FRUS, 1977–1980*, vol. 23: *Mexico, Cuba, and the Caribbean*, pp. 531–32; See the Situation Room to Brzezinski, 17 May 1978, Carter Library, NLC-1-6-3-22-77; Situation Room to Deputy Assistant to the President for National Security Affairs David Aaron, 19 May 1978, Carter Library, NLC-1-6-3-31-7; AmEmbassy Caracas to SecState, "President Perez Letter to President Carter on the Dominican Republic," 17 May 1978, Martin to Carter, 28 May 1978, Brzezinski to Martin, 19 June 1978, Carter Library, White House Central Files, Countries, Box CO-23, CO-42, 1/20/77–1/20/81 folder; "Morning Reading Item," 18 May 1978, Carter Library, NLC-133-215-7-8-0. Vance to Carter, 19 May 1978, Carter Library, NLC-128-13-8-13-3; Carter, "Presidential Election in the Dominican Republic," 19 May 1979, *PPPUS: Carter, 1978*, vol. 1, pp. 931–32; Pastor to Brzezinski, 19 July 1978, Carter Library, White House Central Files, Countries, Box CO-23, CO-42, 1/29/77–1/20/81 folder; Peter Tarnoff to Brzezinski, "Status Report on Progress of Human Rights in Latin America," 7 April 1979, Carter Library, NSA Brzezinski Materials, Subject Files, Box 29, Human Rights 4/79–4/80 folder.

18. MemCon, "Meeting with Foreign Minister Rafael Castilo Valdez," 11 May 1979, Carter Library, NSA Brzezinski Materials, Subject Files, Box 33, MemCons Brzezinski 3–6/79 folder.

19. "Telegram from the Embassy in Nicaragua to the Department of State," 25 January 1977, *FRUS, 1977–1980*, vol. 15: *Central America, 1977–1980*, p. 170.

20. Kagan, *Twilight Struggle*, p. 30.

21. Ed Koch to Fraser, 16 December 1976, and Fraser to Koch, 23 December 1976, Fraser Papers, 149.G.9.8 (F), Foreign Policy—1976 folder; see State Department to Koch, 29 July 1977, Carter Library, White House Central Files, Countries, Box CO-47, CO-114, General, 1/20/77–1/20/81 folder; Theberge to Vance, "President Somoza's Message to Secretary and President Regarding April 5 Congressional Hearing on Human Rights," 2 April 1977, Carter Library, NSA Brzezinski Materials, Subject Files, Box 28, Human Rights 2–4/77 folder.

22. Although more than a bit breathless and not always completely reliable, the best source on Congressman Wilson remains Crile, *Charlie Wilson's War*, pp. 33–39 and 77–78.

23. Grant and Chamorro had been corresponding since the late 1950s at least. See Pedro Joaquin Chamorro, 5 June 1957, and Grant to Pedro Joaquin Chamorro, 19 February 1958, Frances Grant Papers, Latin American Files, Box 45, Nicaragua: Personalities: PJ Chamorro folder. In a 10 February 1972 letter, Grant asked Chamorro, "Who, beside yourself, is expressing opposition to . . . Somoza?" In a 24 February 1972 letter, she asked, "Is there a true opposition?" President Somoza had complained to the U.S. Ambassador in March of 1977 that Chamorro was aiding the Cubans, the FSLN, and the communists internationally in trying to discredit his regime with the accusations of human rights abuses. See "Telegram from the Embassy in Nicaragua to the Secretary of State," 3 March 1977, *FRUS, 1977–1980*, vol. 15: *Central America, 1977–1980*, p. 173.

24. "Defy Somoza," *Hemispherica*, January 1975; "Honor Pedro Chamorro as Martyr," *Hemispherica*, March 1978; "We Focus on Nicaragua," *Hemispherica*, June–July 1978; IADF Press Release, "Position Paper Sent to Carter Administration," March 1977, Frances Grant Papers, Rutgers University, Alexander Library, Special Collections, Box 30, Correspondence, Terence Todman folder; "Proposed Statement for President Somoza," "Proposed Statement for President Somoza," and IADF News Release regarding Chamorro Memorial, Box 45, Latin American Country Files, Nicaragua: Chamorro Memorial Meeting folder.

25. "Address by the Assistant Secretary of State for Inter-American Affairs (Todman)," 14 February 1978, *FRUS, Carter Administration, 1977–1980*, vol. 24: *South America: Latin America Region, 1977–1980*, pp. 107, and the following "Editorial Note," p. 111; Kagan, *Twilight Struggle*, pp. 52–53 and 61–62; "Caracas, Venezuela. Informal Exchange Following Meetings between President Carter and President Pérez," 28 March 1978, *PPPUS: Carter, 1978*, vol. 1, p. 617.

26. Pastor to Brzezinski, "Nicaragua," 29 August 1978, Carter Library, NLC-17-12-11-1-7. Note that Brzezinski wrote Carter that he believed that "the success of your new approach to Latin America has been that we avoided telling the Latin Americans how to organize their own governments, but rather have stated in very general terms that we have an obvious *preference* for these countries which share our democratic values." See Brzezinski to Carter, "Senator Byrd's Trip—An Assessment," undated, Carter Library, NSA Brzezinski Materials, Country Files, Box 60, Panama 11/77–3/78 folder.

27. See the letters in Carter Library, White House Central Files, Countries, Box CO-47, CO-114, General, 1/20/77–1/20/81 folder.

28. Murphy, Wilson, Larry McDonald, and others to Carter, 22 September 1978, Carter Library, White House Central Files, Countries, Box CO-46, CO-114, 1/1/78–12/31/78 folder; "Memorandum from the President's Deputy Assistant for National Security Affairs (Aaron) to President Carter," 15 September 1978, *FRUS, 1977–1980*, vol. 15: *Central America, 1977–1980*, p. 270; "Additional Talking Points on Nicaragua Provided by Henry Owen," undated but early 1979, Carter Library, Walter Mondale Papers, Box 2, Talking Points Foreign Policy Breakfast 1/79–6/79 folder.

29. "International Mediation Group for Nicaragua," 2 October 1978, p. 1694; "The President's News Conference of November 9, 1978," p. 1993, both in *PPPUS: Carter, 1978*, vol. 2. Carter, "State of the Union," 23 January 1979, *PPPUS: Carter, 1979*, vol. 1, p. 107. See also the enhanced written version from 25 January 1979 on p. 160.

30. Kagan, *Twilight Struggle*, pp. 80–82; Gerardo Sánchez Nateras, "The Sandinista Revolution and the Limits of the Cold War in Latin America: The Dilemma of Non-Intervention during the Nicaraguan Crisis, 1977–1978," *Cold War History* 18, no. 2 (2018): 111–29; Arthur Schlesinger Jr., 28 December 1978, p. 2870, Schlesinger Papers, New York Public Library, Journals, Box 315, Sept–December 78 folder.

31. Derian to Vance, 22 October 1979, *FRUS, 1977–1980*, vol. 2: *Human Rights and Humanitarian Affairs*, p. 603.

32. Zimmermann, *Sandinista*, pp. 211–20.

33. Grant to Jon Lewine of West Steelbridge, MA, 13 November 1978, Frances Grant Papers, Rutgers University, Alexander Library, Special Collections, Box 35, Domestic Letters 1978 folder.

34. Murphy to Carter, 22 January 1979, Carter Library, White House Central Files, Countries, Box CO-46, CO-114, 1/1/79–6/30/79 folder. Vance suggested that a plebiscite could

still resolve the crisis. See Vance to Murphy, 10 February 1979 letter in same folder. See also "Telegram from the Embassy in Nicaragua to the Department of State," 13 January 1979, *FRUS, 1977–1980*, vol. 15: *Central America, 1977–1980*, pp. 488–89. Regarding Carter's failure to understand what had happened, see "Memorandum from Robert Pastor of the National Security Council Staff to the President's Assistant for National Security Affairs (Brzezinski)," 31 January 1979, in the same volume of *FRUS*, p. 514.

35. Ad Hoc Committee for Nicaraguan Democracy, "Report on the Visit of Our Delegation to Washington," 10 January 1979, Frances Grant Papers, Alexander Library, Special Collections, Box 45, Latin American Country Files, Nicaragua: U.S. State Department Washington Trip folder.

36. Kennedy, Javits, Cranston, Hatfield, and Sarbanes to Carter, 9 February 1979, Carter Library, White House Central Files, Countries, Box CO-46, CO-114, 1/1/79–6/30/79 folder. See also "Memorandum from Robert Pastor of the National Security Council Staff to the President's Assistant for National Security Affairs (Brzezinski)," 7 March 1979, *FRUS, 1977–1980*, vol. 15: *Central America, 1977–1980*, p. 524.

37. Church to Mr. and Mrs. Marion Ley of Fayette, Idaho, 30 April 1979, Senator Frank Church Collection, Series 2.2 Foreign Relations, Box 47, Latin America—Nicaragua—1978/1979 folder.

38. LeoGrande, *Our Own Backyard*, p. 23; Pastor to Brzezinski, "Evening Report," 11 May 1979, Carter Library, NLC-10-20-6-5-7.

39. Kagan, *Twilight Struggle*, pp. 95–100; Tom Harkin, "Prepared Statement on Central American Trip," 26 April 1979, Frances Grant Papers, Rutgers University, Alexander Library, Special Collections, Box 33, Correspondence, U.S. Congress 1979 folder. Tom Harkin, Ted Weiss, and others to White House, 21 June 1979, Carter Library, White House Central Files, Countries, Box CO-47, Executive, CO-114, 8/1/79–1/29/81 folder; IADF, 26 June 1979, Frances Grant Papers, Rutgers University, Alexander Library, Special Collections, Box 45, Latin American Country Files, U.S. State Department Washington Trip folder; Carter, "Bill Stewart," 21 June 1979, *PPPUS: Carter, 1979*, vol. 1, p. 1113.

40. Grant to Violeta Barrios de Chamorro, 31 January 1969, Frances Grant Papers, Alexander Library, Special Collections, Box 45, Latin American Country Files, Personalities: Violeta Chamorro folder. In the same box, see S. Fanny Simon, coordinator, Ad Hoc Committee for Nicaraguan Democracy, and Frances Grant letter to IADF supporters, 14 August 1979, in the Nicaragua: U.S. State Department Washington Trip folder; Grant to Miguel D'Escoto, 1 September 1979, in Box 34, Foreign Letters 1978/1979 folder. See the coverage in "New Era Begins in Nicaragua," *Hemispherica*, August–September 1979, and Frances R. Grant, "Nicaragua Seeks Its National Identity," *Hemispherica*, May 1980.

41. Pastor to Brzezinski, "Cuba and Nicaragua," 21 June 1979, Carter Library, NSA Brzezinski Materials, Country Files, Box 14, Cuba 6/79 folder.

42. Kagan, *Twilight Struggle*, pp. 123–27; Pastor to Brzezinski, "Evening Report," 16 November 1978, Carter Library, NLC-10-25-3-10-9; MemCon, "Summary of the President's Meeting with Members of the Nicaraguan Junta," Carter Library, NLC-7-37-6-2-6; "Meeting with Members of the Nicaraguan Junta," 24 September 1977, *PPPUS: Carter, 1979*, vol. 2, p. 1722; "United States Assistance to Central America and the Caribbean. Message to the Congress Transmitting Proposed Legislation," *PPPUS: Carter, 1979*, vol. 2, p. 2103; Pastor to Brzezinski, "Evening Report," 5 December 1979, Carter Library, NLC-10-25-6-19-7; Brzezinski to Carter, "Central American Supplemental," 11 June 1980, Carter Library, NSA

Brzezinski Materials, Country Files, Box 46, Latin America 6/80–1/81 folder. Wright hoped to find some non-earmarked funds, but the State Department insisted that there were none available. Regarding the Inter-American Association for Democracy and Freedom's support for aid, see Frances Grant to Penn Kemble, 4 September 1979, Frances Grant Papers, Rutgers University, Alexander Library, Special Collections, Box 58, Nicaragua Letter Campaign 1978–1980 folder. She promised that "should the government go totalitarian, the IADF will of course denounce it. You need not have any worry on that score." Grant worried about creating a "self-fulfilling prophecy." See the 25 October 1979 letter to IADF encouraging support for U.S. aid; see also Wright, *Worth It All*, pp. 43–44; see also Flippen, *Speaker Jim Wright*, pp. 162–64, 180–82, 216–17, and 272.

43. Carter, "Special Central American Assistance Act of 1979," 31 May 1980, *PPPUS: Carter, 1980–1981*, vol. 2, p. 1017; J. Brian Atwood, Assistant Secretary for Congressional Relations, Department of State, to Church, 4 October 1979 and 20 December 1979, Senator Frank Church Collection, Boise State University, Special Collections, Series 2.2 Foreign Relations, Box 47, Latin America—Nicaragua folder. Frances Grant was beginning to have her doubts by the fall of 1980, but still expressed confidence in Arturo Cruz. See the 16 September 1980 letter to John Richardson, President, Youth for Understanding, and compare it to the 2 October 1980 letter to Arturo Cruz, Box 51, Nicaragua: Correspondence, 1979–1982 folder. See also an undated later letter to Violeta Barrios de Chamorro in the same folder.

44. Dick McCall to Church, "Re: Nicaragua Aid Package," 29 February 1980, Senator Frank Church Collection, Boise State University Library, Special Collections, 10.6 Special Files Box 2, Foreign Relations Committee—Misc. 1980 folder.

45. *The Wright Slant: A Report from Jim*, 30 June 1980, Jim Wright Papers, Special Collections, Mary Couts Burnett Library, Texas Christian University, Box 890, Wright Slant/ Nic. and Central America folder; Wright to Carter, 10 June 1980, Jim Wright Papers, Special Collections, Mary Couts Burnett Library, Texas Christian University, Box 726, Letters to the President folder.

46. Lee Hamilton, Dante Fascell, David Obey, et al. to colleagues, 21 February 1980, Jim Wright Papers, Box 1133, Iran, Nic., Panama folder.

47. O'Neill to Bayardo Arce, 4 June 1980, Tip O'Neill Papers, Kirk O'Donnell Files, Box 20/39, 20/1 Nicaragua—Nicaraguan Embassy and President Ortega folder; Grant to Alfonso Robeo, 14 August 1980, and Grant to Violetta Barrios de Chamorro, 27 August 1980 and 2 October 1980, Frances Grant Papers, Rutgers University, Alexander library, Special Collections, Box 34, Foreign Letters, 1980 folder; Frances R. Grant, "Nicaragua Seeks Its National Identity," *Hemispherica*, May 1980. Grant was hopeful in part because there was no single figure comparable to Fidel Castro who was dominating the political scene. See also Wright, *Worth It All*, pp. 47–48; Wright et al. to Daniel Ortega, 4 September 1980, Jim Wright Papers, Special Collections, Mary Couts Burnett Library, Texas Christian University, Box 739, Dear Comandante Letters folder.

48. Vaky to Vance, "Goals for Latin America," 13 August 1979, Carter Library, NLC-133-149-5-2-2. Note that at the time of the Panama Canal treaty signing, President Carter's conversation with President Kjell Langerud was almost solely concerned with Guatemala's territorial claims on Belize. See Carter Library, NSA Brzezinski Materials, Subject Files, Box 35, MemCons President 9/1–18/77 folder. See also MemCon, "Meeting with Foreign Minister Rafael Castillo Valdez," 11 May 1979, Carter Library, NSA Brzezinski Materials, Subject Files, Box 33, MemCons Brzezinski 3–6/79 folder. Pastor to Aaron and Brzezinski,

"Central America: The View from Our Chiefs of Mission," 11 August 1980, Carter Library, NLC-24-89-2-8-8. In a conversation with Pastor, Guatemalan leader Lucas "said, in effect, that we have different views of how to deal with the subversive problem in Guatemala, and that there was no way in his mind to bridge that difference." Lucas had "clearly opted for the 'Argentine strategy.'" Lucas expected support following a victory by Reagan, which he anticipated would happen. See Pastor to Brzezinski and Aaron, "U.S. Policy to Guatemala—SCC (I): Recommendations and Next Steps," 20 August 1980, Carter Library, NLC-024-89-7-1-0.

49. Carter, 20 July 1979 entry, *White House Diary*, p. 346.

50. LeoGrande, *Our Own Backyard*, pp. 33–34 and 38. Work on this period is becoming increasingly sophisticated; see, for example, Chávez, *Poets and Prophets of the Resistance*, pp. 3–19 and 220–40; Ching, *Stories of Civil War in El Salvador*, pp. 35–40; Wood, *Insurgent Collective Action and Civil War in El Salvador*.

51. "Paper Prepared in the Department of State," undated, *FRUS, 1977–1980*, vol. 15: *El Salvador, 1977–1980*, pp. 899–902; Christine Dobson, Staff Secretary, National Security Council, to Peter Tarnoff, Executive Secretary, Department of State, undated, Carter Library, NSA Brzezinski Materials, Country Files, Box 20, El Salvador 1/77–1/80 folder. See also the letters in Carter Library, White House Central Files, Countries, Box CO-24, CO-46, 1/20/77–1/20/81 folder. See also the MemCon, "President Carter/El Salvador President Romero Bilateral," 8 September 1977, Carter Library, NSA Brzezinski Materials, Subject Files, Box 35, MemCons President 9/1–18/77 folder.

52. "Action Memorandum from Assistant Secretary of State for Inter-American Affairs (Vaky) to Acting Secretary of State Christopher," 21 December 1978, *FRUS, 1977–1980*, vol. 15: *El Salvador, 1977–1980*, pp. 911–12; Brzezinski to Carter, 24 January 1978, Carter Library, NLC-1-13-9-8-9.

53. Memorandum for Brzezinski, 3 August 1979, Carter Library, NLC-1-1107-9-2. The Policy Planning Committee meeting involved Secretary of State Vance, Secretary of Defense Harold Brown, and others.

54. "Memorandum of Robert Pastor of the National Security Council Staff to the President's Assistant for National Security Affairs (Brzezinski," 10 May 1979, *FRUS, 1977–1980*, vol. 15: *Central America, 1977–1980*, p. 89.

55. "Minutes of a Policy Review Committee Meeting," 11 June 1979, *FRUS, 1977–1980*, vol. 15: *Central America, 1977–1980*, pp. 1212–13; "Telegram from the Embassy in Honduras to the Department of State," 26 July 1979, *FRUS, 1977–1980*, vol. 15: *El Salvador, 1977–1980*, pp. 938–41. See also "Telegram from the Department of State to the Embassy in El Salvador," pp. 961–64.

56. "Memorandum from the President's Assistant for National Security Affairs (Brzezinski) to President Carter," undated, p. 1268, and Marginal Note by President Carter, "Paper Prepared in the Department of State," undated, though probably 16 October 1979, *FRUS, 1977–1980*, vol. 15: *El Salvador, 1977–1980*, p. 975.

57. Thornton to Brzezinski, "Evening Report," 26 December 1979, Carter Library, NLC-10-26-2-7-3; "United Assistance to Central America and the Caribbean: Message to the Congress Transmitting Proposed Legislation." *PPPUS: Carter, 1979*, vol. 2, p. 2103; Schuhrke, "Agrarian Reform and the AFL-CIO's Cold War in El Salvador," pp. 543–49; I remain unconvinced that the Carter administration supported an "Indonesian" solution to the situation in El Salvador. See Chávez, *Poets and Prophets of the Resistance*, p. 200.

58. William E. Odom to Brzezinski, "Weekly Report," 16 January 1980, Carter Library, NLC-10-26-5-20-5; Director of Central Intelligence to National Intelligence Officers, "Alert Memorandum: El Salvador," 24 January 1980, Carter Library, NLC-12-20-11-5-9.

59. Pastor to David Aaron, "Evening Report," 1 February 1980, Carter Library, NLC-10-27-1-2-8.

60. "Memorandum from the President's Assistant for National Security Affairs (Brzezinski) to President Carter," 16 February 1980, FRUS, 1977–1980, vol. 15: El Salvador, 1977–1980, pp. 1046–47; Thomas C. Kelly, United States Catholic Conference to Clarence D. Long, House of Representatives, 17 February 1980, and Vance to Archbishop Romero, 11 March 1980, Carter Library, NSA Brzezinski Materials, Country Files, Box 20, El Salvador 3/80 folder; Tom Harking, "Prepared Statement on Central American Trip," 26 April 1979, Frances Grant Papers, Rutgers University, Alexander Library, Special Collections, Box 33, U.S. Congress 1979 folder.

61. Carter, "Archbishop Oscar Arnulfo Romero." 25 March 1980, PPPUS: Carter, 1980–1981, vol. 1, p. 534.

62. David Aaron to Mondale, 5 April 1977, Carter Library, NLC-133-186-22-1-3.; Brzezinski to Carter, "Memorandum for the President," 17 June 1980, Carter Library, NLC-1-15-7-18-8.

63. See S. Fanny Simon, "El Salvador Poised for Civil War," Hemispherica, February 1980.

64. Pastor to Brzezinski, "Evening Report," 5 September 1980, NLC-24-55-2-16-6.

65. See the correspondence from August to November in Carter Library, NSA Brzezinski Materials, Country Files, Box 21, 8–11/80 folder.

66. Pastor to Brzezinski, "Evening Report," 15 October 1980, Carter Library, NLC-10-32-5-2-8. Pastor to Brzezinski, "Evening Report," 17 October 1980, Carter Library, NLC-10-32-5-9-1; Carter, "Foreign Policy: Radio Address to the Nation," 19 October 1980, PPPUS: Carter, 1980–1981, vol. 3, p. 2339.

67. Derian to Christopher, 30 April 1980, FRUS, 1977–1980, vol. 2: Human Rights and Humanitarian Affairs, p. 621.

68. White to SecState, 11 November 1980, White to SecState, 28 November 1980, and White to SecState, 30 November 1980, Carter Library, NSA Brzezinski Materials, Country Files, Box 21, 8–11/80 folder. See also "Memorandum of Robert Pastor of the National Security Council Staff to the President's Assistant for National Security Affairs (Brzezinski)," 6 November 1980, FRUS, 1977–1980, vol. 15: Central America, 1977–1980, p. 1131.

69. LeoGrande, Our Own Backyard, p. 64.

70. White to SecState, 3 December 1980, Carter Library, NSA Brzezinski Materials, Country Files, Box 21, 12/80–1/81 folder; White to SecState, 12 December 1980, Christopher to White, 13 December 1980, Aaron to Brzezinski, 15 December 1980, White to SecState, 15 December 1980, Carter Library, NSA Brzezinski Materials, Country Files, Box 21, El Salvador 12/80–1/81 folder; Dion to SecState, 23 December 1980, and Dion to SecState 30 December 1980, Carter Library, NSA Brzezinski Materials, Country Files, Box 21, El Salvador 12/80–1/81 folder; Harold Brown to Carter, "Security Assistant to El Salvador," 30 December 1980, Carter Library, Papers of Walter Mondale, Box 1, Foreign Policy Breakfasts (1/80–6/80) folder.

71. Muskie to Carter, undated, Carter Library, NSA Brzezinski Materials, Country Files, Box 21, El Salvador 12/80–1/81 folder; Brzezinski to Carter, "Military Assistance to El Sal-

vador," 14 January 1981, Carter Library, NSA Brzezinski Materials, Country Files, Box 21, El Salvador 12/80–1/81 folder. Also involved was a perception that there had been progress in the investigation of the murder of the churchwomen. See FBI Director William Webster, "Memorandum to the President," 5 January 1981, Carter Library, NLC-128-11-9-3-6 folder. Brzezinski expressed confidence as well in the junta's imminent actions on land reform. See also "Memorandum from the President's Assistant for National Security Affairs (Brzezinski) to President Carter," undated, *FRUS, 1977–1980*, vol. 15: *Central America, 1977–1980*, p. 1310. See also Arnson, *Crossroads*, p. 51; Ching, *Stories of Civil War*, pp. 40–42.

72. "Memorandum of Notification Prepared in the Central Intelligence Agency for the Special Coordination Committee," 5 December 1980, *FRUS, 1977–1980*, vol. 15: *Central America, 1977–1980*, pp. 791–95.

73. Regarding the short-term withdrawal of 12,000 Cuban troops from Angola and Castro's decision to suspend further removal of troops, see Gleijeses, *Visions of Freedom*, pp. 43–44; regarding Cuban aid to Ethiopia, see p. 45. Gleijeses is convinced that the Carter administration began supporting Jonas Savimbi in Angola fairly early on. See pp. 52–53. Regarding Cuban reinforcements in Angola, see p. 97. As early as the University of Notre Dame speech, it should be noted, Carter characterized Cuba's actions as an attempt by the Soviet Union to impose its kind of society on another. Carter, "University of Notre Dame. Address at Commencement Exercises at the University," 22 May 1977, *PPPUS: Carter, 1977*, vol. 1, p. 959. Note, however, Guy Erb's and Tom Thornton's concern, as early as November 1977, that a speech by President Carter on Cubans in Africa would "run counter to the type of North–South political climate which we have tried, with some success to create." See Tom Thornton and Guy F. Erb to Brzezinski, "Proposed Presidential Speech on Cuba in Africa," 21 November 1977, Carter Library, NSA Brzezinski Materials, Country Files, Box 13, Cuba 11/77–2/78 folder. Regarding McGovern's push to recognize the Angolan government and the Angolan distrust of the West vis-à-vis South Africa, see pp. 103 and 112. See Brzezinski to SecState, Director CIA/Director, International Communication Agency, "Publicizing the Cuban-Soviet Relationship," 12 July 1979, Carter Library, NSA Brzezinski Materials, Country Files, Box 14, Cuba 7-8/79 folder. See also the handwritten note by Carter on Brzezinski to Carter, "Daily Report," 12 July 1979, in the same box. See Vaky to Newsom, "Further Responses to Second Demarche on Cuba to Selected Latin American Countries," 4 October 1979, Carter Library, NLC-SAFE 4 a-14-31-4-6. See also Peter Tarnoff, "Lining Up Latin Americans against Cuba," Carter Library, NLC-SAFE 4 a-14-31-4-6. Pastor spoke of inducing "Thermidor in Cuba." He thought that it was possible. See Pastor to Brzezinski, "Cuba," 17 January 1980, Carter Library, NLC-128-1-18-6-3. Although this document suggests a greater willingness to continue progress in relations between the two countries than was evident elsewhere, Castro made it clear that he thought "normalization of relations between the U.S. and Cuba could only occur in a period of detente between the U.S. and USSR, not in a period like the present, of rising tensions." See also Carter's comments before the group Caribbean and Central American Action, 9 April 1980, *PPPUS: Carter, 1980–1981*, vol. 1, p. 625. See also LeoGrande and Kornbluh, *Back Channel to Cuba*, pp. 166, 168–75, 191, 193, 200–201, and 223.

74. See the discussion in Gleijeses, *Visions of Freedom*, pp. 126–33, and LeoGrande and Kornbluh, *Back Channel to Cuba*, pp. 207–10; Carter, "Peace and National Security," 1 October 1979, *PPPUS: Carter, 1979*, vol. 2, pp. 1803–5. See also Ashby and Gramer, *Fighting the Odds*, pp. 591–99; Coleman, *Fourteenth Day*, p. 207.

75. Carter, "State of the Union," 21 January 1980, *PPPUS: Carter, 1980–1981*, vol. 1, pp. 173 and 177.

76. Carter, "Organization of American States: Remarks at the 10th Regular Session of the General Assembly," 19 November 1980, *PPPUS: Carter, 1980–1981*, vol. 3, pp. 2734–36.

77. Carter, "State of the Union." 16 January 1981, *PPPUS: Carter, 1980–1981*, vol. 3, pp. 2988–90; LeoGrande, *Our Own Backyard*, p. 69.

Chapter 10

1. Regarding the unpopularity of Reagan's policies, see Gates, *From the Shadows*, p. 293.

2. Roger W. Fontaine, "Caribbean and Central America Update," 27 December 1979, Ronald Reagan 1980 Campaign Papers, Ronald Reagan Library, Box 458, Foreign Policy, Fact Book folder.

3. "Republican Party Platform of 1980," 15 July 1980, pp. 39–41, *The American Presidency Project*. See also "Foreign Policy," Policy Statement, E. 3, 31 January 1980, Reagan Library, Ronald Reagan 1980 Campaign Papers, Box 371, Field Ops—Issues—Foreign Policy.

4. Rossinow, *Reagan Era*, p. 11; Cannon, *President Reagan*, pp. 66–74; "Address to the Nation on Policy in Central America," 9 May 1984, *PPPUS: Reagan, 1984*, p. 663.

5. Rossinow, *Reagan Era*, pp. 28–29.

6. Karen Elliot House, "Reagan's World," *Wall Street Journal*, 3 June 1980; Malcolm Wallop to Reagan, 5 May 1983, Executive Secretariat, NSC, Box 31, Latin America General 5/4/83–5/17/83 folder; Dave Gergen to Judge Clark, Aram Bakeshian, and Fred Ikle, 9 March 1983, Executive Secretariat, NSC, Country Files, Reagan Library, Box 30, El Salvador 1/1/83–10/31/83 folder. See also Rossinow, *Reagan Era*, p. 78.

7. LeoGrande, *Our Own Backyard*, p. 81; Adam Clymer, "Greg Craig Interview, 27 September 1998," JFK Library, Clymer Papers, Interviews, Box 3, C (Cadell-Cuomo) folder; "The President's News Conference," 6 March 1981, *PPPUS: Reagan, 1981*, p. 208. On Carter representing "America's will" by providing arms against the "final offensive," see "Address before a Joint Session of the Congress on Central America," 27 April 1983, *PPPUS: Reagan, 1983*, p. 602.

8. See, for example, Robert Schweitzer to Richard V. Allen, 10 March 1981, Roger Fontaine Papers, Reagan Library, Box 4, Congressional (Feb–Mar 1981). Schweitzer characterizes administration policy as thoughtful and "extremely modest." See also Haig to Reagan, "Additional Assistance for El Salvador," Executive Secretariat, NSC, Country Files, Box 30, El Salvador, 1/20/81–5/31/81 folder; "Excerpt from an Interview with Walter Cronkite of CBS News," 3 March 1981, *PPPUS, Reagan, 1981*, p. 209; Reagan, "Wednesday, February 11," Brinkley, ed., *Reagan Diaries*, p. 4; LeoGrande, *Our Own Backyard*, p. 89; Smith, *Resisting Reagan*, pp. 86 and 89–92.

9. "The President's News Conference," 6 March 1981, *PPPUS: Reagan, 1981*, pp. 206–7. When a reporter said that he wanted to return to the subject of El Salvador, Reagan replied, "Must you?" See also "Excerpts from an Interview with Walter Cronkite of CBS News," 3 March 1981, pp. 192–93; Roger Fontaine to Richard Allen, "Talking Points for Your Meeting with Dean [*sic*] Hinton, Ambassador-Designate to El Salvador, Today at 5:00 P.M.," 22 April 1981, Executive Secretariat, NSC, Box 30, El Salvador, 1/20/81–5/31/81 folder; Allen to Edwin Meese and James Baker, "Why El Salvador Isn't Vietnam," 25 February 1981, in the same folder; Mailgram from Harkin, Conyers, Chisholm, et al., March 1981, Roger Fontaine Papers, Reagan Library, Box 4, Congressional 10–21 April 1981 folder. Richard

Allen to William Goodling, undated but late February 1981, Fontaine Papers, Box 4, Congressional (February–March 1981) folder. Rossinow, *Reagan Era*, p. 24; For an example of Reagan feeling compelled to insist that he was not planning to send "American combat troops into action anywhere in the world," see "The President's News Conference," 18 February 1982, *PPPUS: Reagan 1982*, p. 182; Cannon, *Reagan*, pp. 289–90 and 298; LeoGrande, *Our Own Backyard*, pp. 5–9; Smith, *Resisting Reagan*, pp. 93–97.

10. Fontaine to Allen, "Why El Salvador Isn't Vietnam," 27 February 1981; Allen to Meese and James Baker, "Why El Salvador Isn't Vietnam," 25 February 1981, Executive Secretariat, NSC, Reagan Library, Country Files, Box 30, El Salvador, 1/20/81–5/31/81 folder.

11. Fontaine to James W. Nance, "U.S. Objectives and Policies Regarding Central America," 29 December 1981, Executive Secretariat, NSC, Box 31, Latin America—General 9/18/81–12/29/81 folder.

12. Cannon, *Reagan*, pp. 162–63; Fontaine and Schweitzer, "El Salvador: Biting the Bullet," 12 September 1981, Executive Secretariat, NSC, Country Files, Box 30, El Salvador, 6/1/81–12/31/81 folder. In the same folder, see Haig to Reagan, 11 August 1981, and Hinton to SecState, 18 November 1981.

13. Roger Fontaine to Richard Allen, Executive Secretariat, National Security Council, Reagan Library, Box 31, LA General, 2/24/81–7/16/81 folder. Regarding Helms and El Salvador, see Link, *Righteous Warrior*, p. 246; Schuhrke, "Agrarian Reform and the AFL-CIO's Cold War in El Salvador," pp. 527 and 549–50; Reagan, "Thursday May 18," Brinkley, ed., *Reagan Diaries*, p. 21; LeoGrande, *Our Own Backyard*, pp. 90 and 94–97.

14. José Napoleón Duarte, *My Life*, p. 159. Note that Secretary of State Al Haig told President Reagan that the public did not understand administration policy, "particularly our support of Duarte." See 6 July 1981, 11 August 1981, and 21 September 1981 memos, Executive Secretariat, NSC, Reagan Library, Box 30, 6/1/81–12/31/81 folder. Regarding an unscheduled meeting between Duarte and Kennedy, see Haig, "Secretary's Meeting with Duarte, Waldorf Astoria, September 29, 1981," 12 October 1981, Executive Secretariat, NSC, Country Files, Box 30, El Salvador, 6/1/81–12/31/81 folder; Tom Harkin, "Testimony on El Salvador, Statement before the Subcommittee on Inter-American Affairs of the Committee on Foreign Affairs," 2 March 1982, Political Papers Collections, Thomas R. Harkin Collection, Drake University, Cowles Library, Archives and Special Collections, Box S-10, Testimony on El Salvador folder; "Exchange with Reporters on the Situation in El Salvador and Budget Issues," 12 February 1982, *PPPUS: Reagan, 1982*, pp. 174–75; "Toasts of the President and President Luis Herrera Campins of Venezuela at the State Dinner," 17 November 1981, *PPPUS: Reagan, 1981*, pp. 1054 and 1061.

15. Arnson, *Crossroads*, pp. 69–74; Tom Harkin, "Anniversary of Death of U.S. Nuns in El Salvador," 4 December 1981, Political Papers Collections, Thomas R. Harkin Collection, Box S-10, "Anniversary" folder; Edward Kennedy to Clark, 26 May 1982, Executive Secretariat, NSC, 1/1/82–12/31/82 folder; LeoGrande, *Our Own Backyard*, pp. 131–34. See "A Democratic Alternative for Central America," *Congressional Record*, 9 December 1982, pp. 29629–30.

16. Fontaine to Janet Colson, "Nicaraguan Aid to Salvadoran Insurgency," 24 March 1981, Executive Secretariat, NSC, Country Files, Reagan Library, Box 30, El Salvador 1/20/81–5/31/81 folder; Tom Harkin, "Human Rights Outline" and "An Agenda for Elliott Abrams," 10 December 1981, Political Papers Collection, Thomas R. Harkin Collection, Drake University Archives and Special Collections, Cowles Library, Box S-10, "Human Rights 1981" folder, and Box L-22, Human Rights—Harkin Address to UN Association, respectively;

"Remarks and a Question-and-Answer Session with Reporters on Domestic and Foreign Policy Issues," 14 April 1983, David Bonior and George Miller, "Report to the Speaker," Tip O'Neill Papers, O'Donnell Files, Box 19/38, 19/4 Nicaragua CoDel Visits folder; *PPPUS: Reagan, 1983*, p. 540; "Telephone Interview with Forrest Sawyer of WAGA-TV in Atlanta, GA," 27 July 1984, *PPPUS: Reagan, 1984*, p. 1116. Regarding the continuing concerns over the human rights ramifications of the Contra war, see George Miller, D-Calif., to colleagues, 18 April 1985, Jim Wright Papers, Box 739, Nicaragua folder. See Jon Alterman, "A Narrative of Your Position on Contra Aid," 3 February 1988, Daniel Patrick Moynihan Papers, Library of Congress, Legislative File, Subject Files, Box 1541, Central America—Countries—Nicaragua—Correspondence folder.

17. Peace, *A Call to Conscience*, pp. 46–47; Kagan, *Twilight Struggle*, p. 198; LeoGrande, *Our Own Backyard*, pp. 299–305, and 454–75; Edward Kennedy, "Private Sector Assistance for Nicaragua," *Congressional Record*, 20 October 1981, p. 24489; Jenkins, "The Indian Wing," pp. 182 and 187; Adam Clymer, "Interview with Greg Craig," 27 February 1995," Adam Clymer Papers, JFK Library, Interviews, Box 3, C (Cadell-Cuomo) folder; Keeley, "Reagan's Real Catholics vs. Tip O'Neill's Maryknoll Nuns," pp. 536–42; Farrell, *Tip O'Neill and the Democratic Century*, pp. 611–14; O'Neill to Ron Dellums, 11 February 1985, Tip O'Neill Papers, Boston College, Kirk O'Donnell Files, Box 19:38, 19/3, Nicaraguan Background and Briefing Reports 1985 folder.

18. LeoGrande, *Our Own Backyard*, pp. 81–82; Roger Fontaine and Robert L. Schweitzer, "Policy Toward Cuba, Central America, and the Caribbean: Status Report," 17 April 1981, and Fontaine to Schweitzer, 26 October 1981, Fontaine Papers, Box 9, Latin America, U.S. Policy toward (October 1981) folder. See also Fontaine to Allen, "Important Problems for the US in Latin America," 25 June 1981, Executive Secretariat, NSC, Country Files, Box 31, Latin America General 2/24/81–7/16/81 folder. Regarding Cuba, presumably Allen wrote in the margins, "I thought Haig had a plan!!" The Cuban military mission, in any case, expanded in Nicaragua in the early Reagan years, but the Sandinistas thought it would help politically to reduce its size in Reagan's second term. See Gleijeses, *Visions of Freedom*, pp. 218 and 320–21.

19. Tom Harkin, "Human Rights Outline," Political Papers Collection, Harkin Collection, Drake University Archives and Special Collections, Cowles Library, Box S-10, "Human Rights 1981" folder. In Box S-17, see "Reagan Administration Blind to State Terrorism," 5 February 1981, in the folder with the same name.

20. Otto Reich, "Thoughts on the Current State of White House Security and Relations," undated, RR 1980 Campaign Papers, Reagan Library, Box 458, Foreign Policy, Fact Book folder. The 1980 party platform also criticized the Carter administration's "economic and diplomatic sanctions linked to its undifferentiated charges of human rights violations." See "Republican Party Platform of 1980," 15 July 1980, p. 40, *The American Presidency Project*.

21. Jeane Kirkpatrick, "Dictatorships and Double Standards," *Commentary* 68, no. 5 (November 1979): 34–45; MemCon, 13 January 1981, Meeting between Bush and General Luis Araripe, 13 January 1981, Executive Secretariat, Country Files, Reagan Library, Box 26, Brazil 2/4/81–9/3/81 folder. Regarding Walters, see Sayre to SecState, 18 February 1981 in the same folder; see also "Haig's Emissary in Guatemala Discounts Charges of Rights Abuse," *Washington Post*, 14 May 1981.

22. Walters to SecState, 26 February 1981, and MemCon, 17 March 1981, Roger Fontaine Papers, Box 1B, 17 March 1981—President Viola folder; Leopoldo Galtieri to Reagan,

26 May 1982, Roger Fontaine Files, Box 1, Argentina May 1982 folder. The best source on Argentina and the Contras remains Armony, *Argentina, the United States, and the Anti-Communist Crusade in Central America*, particularly, for our purposes, pp. 58–71.

23. See, for example, Haig to Reagan, "Our Policy toward Chile," 16 February 1981, Executive Secretariat, NSC, Reagan Library, Box 29, Chile 1/20/81–7/31/84 folder (4); "Statement of Rep. Tom Harkin, House Subcommittee on Inter-American Affairs," 9 March 1981, Political Papers Collections—Thomas R. Harkin Collection, Drake University, Archives and Special Collections, Cowles Library, Box S-10, Subcommittee on Inter-American Affairs folder. James Theberge, who had been a U.S. ambassador to Somoza's Nicaragua and would soon be Reagan's ambassador to Chile, complained that when he spoke before the House in favor of ending the Kennedy-Humphrey sanctions, the State Department had not sent a representative. See Allen to Theberge, 20 April 1981, Roger Fontaine Collection, RAC, Box 4, Chile, May 1981 folder. Kennedy and Cranston's resolution can be found in *Congressional Record*, 15 September 1983, pp. 24464 and 24465. The earliest linkage I have found between Reagan policy toward Chile and Reagan policy toward El Salvador is Fontaine, "Certification of Chile," 8 July 1982, NSC, Executive Secretariat, Country Files, Chile 1/20/81–7/31/84 (4) folder; Morley and McGillion, *Reagan and Pinochet*, pp. 32–45 and 54–67.

24. See, for example, Schlesinger to John Kenneth Gailbraith, 30 October 1980, Schlesinger to George Kennan, 9 March 1981, and Schlesinger to Ray Jenkins, 20 December 1982, Schlesinger and Schlesinger, eds., *Letters of Arthur Schlesinger Jr.*, pp. 462–65, 466, and 470–71; Arthur Schlesinger Jr., "The Soviet Conspiracy and World Unrest," *Wall Street Journal*, 23 February 1981,

25. "1980 Democratic Party Platform," 11 August 1980, p. 40, *The American Presidency Project*. The platform also stressed support for "human rights and political liberalization" in Argentina, Chile, El Salvador, and Guatemala, among other countries. See p. 50.

26. Tom Harkin, "Human Rights Outline," Political Papers Collection, Harkin Collection, Drake University and Special Collections, Cowles Library, Box S-10, "Human Rights 1981" folder, and Box S-15, Democratic National Committee, Human Rights Award dinner; 22 October 1981; "Nomination of Ernest Lefever, Senate Committee on Foreign Relation," 18 May 1981, pp. 7–9, Counsel for the President, Box 6, Nomination folder; Sikkink, *Mixed Signals*, pp. 155–56.

27. Harkin, "An Agenda for Elliott Abrams," 10 December 1981, Box L-22, Human Rights—Harkin Address to UN Association, Political Papers Collections, Thomas R. Harkin, Drake University, Cowles Library, Archives and Special Collections; Sikkink, *Mixed Signals*, pp. 156–58.

28. "Issues and Objectives for President's Visit to Brazil, Colombia, and Costa Rica," 23 November 1982, and NSC Meeting, "Issues and Objectives," undated, Executive Secretariat, Meetings Files, Reagan Library, Box 7, President's Trip to Latin America folder; "Response to Questions Submitted by Latin American Newspapers," 30 November 1982, *PPPUS: Reagan, 1982*, p. 1529.

29. Ronald Reagan, "Address to Members of the British Parliament," *PPPUS: Reagan, 1982*, pp. 742–45; "Question-and-Answer Session with Reporters on the President's Trip to Latin America," 4 December 1982 *PPPUS: Reagan, 1982*, pp. 1563 and 1565. "We have been looking for a way to strengthen Rios Montt's position," Alfonso Sapia-Bosch wrote National Security Adviser Clark, "but it would be a mistake for President Reagan to receive Rios Montt

at this time." Senator Roger Jepsen, R-Iowa, had been hoping a meeting could be arranged. See Sapia-Bosch to Clark, 17 September 1982, Roger Fontaine Collection, RAC, Box 8.

30. "Remarks on the Caribbean Basin Initiative to the Permanent Council of the Organization of American States," 24 February 1982, and "Remarks on the Caribbean Basin Initiative at a White House Briefing for Chief Executive Officers of United States Corporations," 28 April 1982, *PPPUS: Reagan, 1982*, pp. 210, 215, and 527; Jim Wright, "Promises to Keep," *Los Angeles Times*, 1 June 1983, p. 6; Jim Wright, "Let's Close Ranks on Central America," 27 December 1982, Wright Papers, Box 709, Latin America folder. Although Reagan was "the most partisan President I have ever served with," the Democrats should not embarrass him.

31. Allen, "Elections or Negotiations in El Salvador," and Allen to Haig, "The President's Views on Election in El Salvador," 18 March 1981, Executive Secretariat, NSC, Country Files, Box 30, El Salvador, 1/20/81–5/31/81 folder; Hinton to Haig, 16 July 1981, Executive Secretariat, NSC, Country Files, Box 30, El Salvador 6/1/81–12/31/81 folder; "Remarks and a Question-and-Answer Session with Elected Republican Woman Officials," 13 January 1984, *PPPUS: Reagan, 1984*, p. 36. Reagan's strongest criticism of the Salvadoran right came in an "Interview with Robert L. Bartley and Albert R. Hunt of the *Wall Street Journal* on Foreign and Domestic Issues," 2 February 1984, p. 163.

32. "Interview in New York City with Members of the Editorial Board of the *New York Post*," 23 March 1982, *PPPUS: Reagan, 1982*, p. 367; "The President's News Conference," 31 March 1982, *PPPUS: Reagan, 1982*, p. 402; Frances Grant to IADF, undated, Frances Grant Papers, IADF General Files, Correspondence 1980–1981, and undated, Rutgers University, Alexander Library, Special Collections.

33. William P. Clark and Kenneth Duberstein, "Meeting on El Salvador with Selected Bipartisan House and Senate Members," 26 February 1983, Executive Secretariat, NSC, Country Files, Box 30, El Salvador, 1/1/83–10/31/83 folder. See also the reference to disagreements in the office of Bill Bradley, D-N.J., in memos and letters from mid-June 1983 in the 6/6/83–7/6/83 folder (some close to Dodd, some close to the administration). Regarding administration assurances on "progress," however "disturbingly slow," see Shultz to O'Neill in the same box, El Salvador 1/1/83–10/31/83 folder. Tom Harkin, "U.S. Policy in El Salvador," Los Angeles, 16 May 1982, and "Testimony on El Salvador, Statement before the Subcommittee on Inter-American Affairs, Committee on Foreign Affairs," 2 March 1982, Political Papers Collections, Thomas R. Harkin Collection, Box S-10, Drake University, Cowles Library, Archives and Special Collections.

34. Roger Fontaine, handwritten notes, 3 June 1983, Roger Fontaine Papers, Reagan Library, Box 20, Meetings Notebooks, pp. 19 and 20. See Clark, "Visit of President Magaña," 16 June 1983, and Lawrence Eagleberger, Acting Secretary, "Visit of Alvaro Magaña, President of El Salvador, June 16–18," Executive Secretariat, NSC, Country Files, Box 30, El Salvador 1/1/83–10/31/83 folder. Note that Clark refers straightforwardly and with a critical distance to "right-wing death squads." In the same folder, see Duarte to Reagan, 29 November 1983. See also Wood, *Insurgent Collective Action and Civil War in El Salvador*, p. 28.

35. Constantine Menges and Oliver North, 28 November 1983, and McFarlane to Reagan, "Vice-Presidential Stop in El Salvador," 30 November 1983, Executive Secretariat, NSC, Reagan Library, Box 30, El Salvador 11/1/83–3/31/84 folder.

36. "Remarks of the President and Prime Minister Eugenia Charles of Dominica Announcing the Deployment of United States Forces in Grenada," 25 October 1983, and "Address to the Nation on Events in Lebanon and Grenada," 27 October 1983, *PPPUS: Reagan,*

1982, pp. 1506 and 1520; Kane, *Selling Reagan's Foreign Policy*, pp. 193–94, 203–4, 208–9, and 217; Cannon, *Reagan*, p. 234.

37. "Remarks to Reporters on Receiving the Report of the National Bipartisan Commission on Central America," 11 January 1984, *PPPUS: Reagan, 1984*, p. 26; LeoGrande, *Our Own Backyard*, pp. 237–40; Kissinger to Wright, 28 January 1984, Jim Wright Papers, Box 1176, Correspondence to Jim Wright from Prominent Individuals folder.

38. "Talking Points: Meeting with National Bipartisan Commission on Central America," undated, "Session on Social Development, Day 1, September 7, 1983," and "Session on Economic Development," September 13, 1983, Executive Secretariat, NSC, Country Files, Box 27, Central American Commission folder; Schlesinger to Kissinger, 25 July 1983, Schlesinger and Schlesinger, eds., *Letters of Schlesinger*, p. 477. For a lunchtime discussion of the commission with Kissinger, see Schlesinger, 19 August 1983, and 17 September 1983, Schlesinger and Schlesinger, eds., *Journals*, pp. 553–56.

39. Jack Kemp, "The Kissinger Commission Report: 'Sí,' and 'No,'" *Washington Post*, 15 January 1984.

40. "Informal Exchanges with Representatives of *Le Figaro*, Together with Written Responses to Questions Submitted by the Newspaper," 22 December 1983, and "Radio Address to the Nation on Recommendations of the National Bipartisan Commission on Central America," 18 January 1984, *PPPUS: Reagan, 1984*, pp. 16 and 38–39; Tom C. Korologos, "The Kissinger Report," 16 January 1984, Executive Secretariat, NSC, Box 27, Central American Commission; Arnson, *Crossroads*, p. 148.

41. Cannon, *Reagan*, pp. 330–31; "Statement by Principal Deputy Press Secretary Speakes on United States Policy in Central America," 10 April 1984, *PPPUS: Reagan, 1984*, p. 503.

42. North and Menges, "Visa Requests of Tomás Borge and Robert D'Aubuisson," 23 November 1983, Executive Secretariat, NSC, Country Files, Box 30, El Salvador 1/23/83–3/19/84 folder.

43. "Remarks and a Question-and-Answer Session with Reporters on Foreign and Domestic Issues," 14 May 1984, *PPPUS: Reagan, 1984*, p. 695.

44. Director of Central Intelligence, Special National Intelligence Estimate, "El Salvador: Election Outlook," 6 March 1984, Executive Secretariat, NSC, Country Files, Box 30, El Salvador, 11/1/83–3/31/84 folder; "Shultz to Reagan, Visit of May 12–23, 1984," and "Talking Points for Meeting with President-Elect Duarte," undated, in the same box, 4/1/84–5/31/84 folder; Wright, "El Salvador," 26 March 1984, and Duarte to Wright, 27 August 1984, Jim Wright Papers, Box 739, El Salvador folder; see Wright, *Congressional Record*, 10 May 1984, pp. 11871–72; Regarding Helms's opinions on Duarte and D'Aubuisson, see Link, *Righteous Warrior*, pp. 246–51; LeoGrande, *Our Own Backyard*, pp. 5 and 243–82; Brian D'Haeseleer, *The Salvadoran Crucible*, pp. 7 and 13; Stephen G. Rabe, *The Killing Zone*, p. 171; regarding the failure of land reform, see Kowalchuck, "Salvadoran Land Struggle," pp. 187–89; Schuhrke, "Agrarian Reform and the AFL-CIO's Cold War in El Salvador," pp. 550–53.

45. See Halperin Donghi, *Contemporary History of Latin America*, pp. 364–68 and 378–79; Schlesinger, 12 November 1984, p. 3685, 6 November 1985, p. 3847, and Arthur M. Schlesinger Jr. Papers, New York Public Library, Journals, Box 317, November–December 1985 folder.

46. Shultz to Reagan, "Visit to ASEAN Countries and to Chile by Ambassador-at-Large Vernon A. Walters," undated, Executive Secretariat, NSC, Country Files, Box 29 Chile 1/20/81–7/31/84 (3) folder. Pinochet still considered Reagan the best U.S. president as far as Chile's interests were concerned. Theberge to "Elliott," 10 January 1984, same box,

1/20/81–7/31/84 (1) folder. See also Constantine Menges, Raymond Burghardt, Jacqueline Tillman, and Oliver North to Robert C. McFarlane, "Latin America—Urgent Issues Requiring Discussion," 27 November 1984, Executive Secretariat, NSC, Box 28, Latin America General 10/12/84–11/29/84 folder; Tony Motley, "U.S. Policy toward Chile," 12 December 1984, Executive Secretariat, NSC, Box 29, Chile 11/19/84–12/24/84 folder.

47. Wright, Barnes, Solarz, Obey, et al. to Ortega, 20 March 1984, Jim Wright Papers, Box 739, Dear Comandante Letters, Wright to Duwood McAlister, *Atlanta Journal*, 25 April 1984, in same box, Nicaragua folder.

48. See, for example, Democratic Study Group, "Aid to the Contras: Round II," 4 June 1985, Jim Wright Papers, Box 788, Nicaragua folder; DSG, "More Aid to the Contras—Response to Reagan Rhetoric," 11 March 1984, Jim Wright Papers, Box 924, Nicaragua—Aid to the Contras folder; Barnes to Reagan, 22 January 1986, Jim Wright Papers, Box 1058, Contra Aid folder; "Statement of Speaker Thomas O'Neill," 21 February 1986, Jim Wright Papers, Box 1058, Contra Aid folder.

49. Troy, *Moynihan's Moment*, p. 92; Arnson, *Crossroads*, pp. 168–72; Jon Alterman, "A Narrative of Your Position on Contra Aid," 3 February 1988," Daniel Patrick Moynihan Papers, Library of Congress, Legislative File, Box 1541, Central America—Countries—Nicaragua—Correspondence folder; Tom Melia, "Memorandum for Senator Moynihan," 8 October 1985, Moynihan Papers, Legislative and Subject Files, Central America 1985–1986 folder; Moynihan, "The International Court of Justice," *Congressional Record*, 10 May 1984; Moynihan to Shultz, 30 November 1984, Box 1543, Central America Countries 1984 folder.

50. Mondale, "Presidential Announcement Speech," 21 February 1984, John Bartlow Martin Papers, Library of Congress, Campaigns, 1984 Presidential Primary Campaign (Walter Mondale) folder; Mondale, "Speech before American Society of Newspaper Editors," 10 May 1984, Mondale Papers, Minnesota Historical Society, 153.J.1.10 Foreign Policy Pack folder, and "Press Release 12 January 1984," Nicaragua folder in same box; "Debate between the President and Former Vice President Walter F. Mondale in Kansas City, Missouri," 21 October 1984, *PPPUS: Reagan, 1984*, pp. 1590–91. McGovern thought that Mondale was too close to Lane Kirkland on Central America. See McGovern to Schlesinger, 19 April 1984, Schlesinger Papers, NYPL, Correspondence, MssCol 17775, Box 90, George McGovern, folder 1. Congressman Wright, however, had feared that Mondale was following the "destructive" "McGovern line" on El Salvador. Mondale assured that him that they were in agreement. See Wright to Mondale, 21 June 1983, and Mondale to Wright, 15 August 1983, Jim Wright Papers, Box 713, Walter Mondale folder.

51. "1984 Democratic Party Platform," 18 July 1984, pp. 33, 35, and 42–44, *The American Presidency Project*.

52. "Remarks at a Reagan-Bush Rally in Grand Rapids, Mich.," 20 September 1984, and "Address to the Nation on United States Policy on Central America," 9 May 1984, *PPPUS: Reagan, 1984*, pp. 1341 and 663.

53. "Remarks Following Discussions with President José Napoleón Duarte of El Salvador," 16 May 1985, *PPPUS: Reagan, 1985*, p. 620; Patrick Buchanan to Reagan, "Central America," 22 February 1985, Patrick Buchanan Files, Box 1, Nicaragua folder; LeoGrande, *Our Own Backyard*, pp 312–14 and 320–46.

54. Reagan, "Tuesday, February 18," Brinkley, ed., *Reagan Diaries*, p. 391; see, for example, Arthur Schlesinger, 27 March 1986 journal entry, pp. 3906–7, Box 317, February 1986 folder; LeoGrande, *Our Own Backyard*, pp. 426–28.

55. Cannon, *Reagan*, pp. 335–38 and 521–25; LeoGrande, *Our Own Backyard*, pp. 387–408, 436–38, 446–60, and 477–504; "Speaker's Press Conference," 19 March 1985, Tip O'Neill Papers, Eleanor Kelley Files, Burns Library, Boston College, Box 51, 6/14 Nicaragua 1986 folder; see the debate in *Congressional Record*, 20 March 1986, including statements, for example, by Georgia Republican Congressman Newt Gingrich, pp. 5814–15; Eldon Kenworthy, "United States Policy in Central America," *Current History*, December 1987, pp. 401–4.

56. Reagan to Shultz, "Assistance to the Nicaraguan Democratic Resistance," 22 October 1986, David S. Addington File, Box 11, Nicaragua Background Material (6) folder; LeoGrande, *Our Own Backyard*, pp. 434–36; Arnson, *Crossroads*, pp. 181–217.

57. The best full-length treatment is Byrne, *Iran-Contra*; Cannon, *Reagan*, pp. 581 and 586–662; Colin Powell and Howard Baker to White House and National Security Council Staff, "Private Aid to the Nicaraguan Democratic Resistance," 10 February 1988, Howard Baker, Chief of Staff, Box 4, Nicaraguan Peace Plan folder. Reagan referred to the Contras as "the people of Nicaragua" in "Remarks and a Question-and-Answer Session with Member of the City Club of Cleveland, Ohio," 11 January 1988, *PPPUS: Reagan, 1988*, p. 21; Eldon Kenworthy, "United States Policy in Central America," *Current History*, December 1987, pp. 401–4.

58. LeoGrande, *Our Own Backyard*, pp. 87, 349–63, and 528–36.

59. Rossinow, *Reagan Era*, p. 265; LeoGrande, *Our Own Backyard*, pp. 510–49; Arnson, *Crossroads*, pp. 221–27; Longley, "An Obsession," pp. 226–31; Flippen, *Speaker Jim Wright*, pp. 364–70; Wright, *Worth It All*, particularly pp. 89–41; Democratic Study Group, "Nicaragua Peace Talks," 19 November 1987, Jim Wright Papers, Box 824, Central America Trip; Wright, "Give the Peace Plan a Chance," 23 September 1987, Jim Wright Papers, Box 702, Nicaragua folder; "Statement to the Press by President Ortega Regarding the Recent Vote in the US House of Representatives on Contra Aid," 4 February 1988, Jim Wright Papers, Box 702, Nicaragua folder.

60. Adam Clymer, "Nancy Solderberg, 31 March 1997," Clymer Papers, JFK Library, Interviews, Box 5, S (Saris-Sweeney) folder; Clymer, *Edward M. Kennedy*, pp. 387–89; Adam Clymer, "Greg Craig, 27 February 1995," Box 3, C (Cadell-Cuomo) folder; see also "Mark Schneider (1)," Box 5.

61. Shultz to Reagan, March 1985, Presidential Personnel, Office of Records, Box 9, Harry G. Barnes folder; "Ambassador's Arrival Statement," 28 October 1985, Speeches and Statements 1978–86 folder; "Interview with Mike Wallace," 28 October 1986, Speeches and Statements, 1978–1986 folder; As a good ambassador should, he also spoke with Pinochet supporters. See Barnes, "Summary Notes: Lunch with the 'Si,'" 27 May 1988, Harry G. Barnes Papers, Library of Congress, Correspondence 1988. Edward M. Kennedy, "America Sides with Pinochet's Atrocities," *Los Angeles Times*, 2 January 1987; Harkin, "The Search for Justice in Chile," 11 September 1987, Political Papers Collections, Thomas R. Harkin Collection, Drake University, Cowles Library, Archives and Special Collections. Box S-11, WOLA folder; Barnes to Ruth Adams, Director, Program on Peace and International Cooperation, John D. and Catherine T. MacArthur Foundation, 8 August 1988, Harry Barnes Papers, Correspondence 1988 folder; see also Reagan, "Tuesday, November 18 [1986]," Brinkley, ed., *Reagan Diaries*, p. 451; Morley and McGillion, *Reagan and Pinochet*, pp. 96–97, 105–6, 112–24, 136–46, 201–14, 225–26, 251–52, and 265–80; regarding Harkin, see Johnson, *Congress and the Cold War*, p. 279.

62. L. Paul Bremer III, Executive Secretary to Richard Allen, 5 September 1981, Executive Secretariat, NSC, Country Files, Box 33, Panama 8/19/81–11/20/81 folder; Kenneth Dam

to Reagan, "Visit of Ricardo de la Espriella, President of Panama, October 1, 1982," 27 September 1982, in same box, Panama 9/29/82 folder; "DCI, Special National Intelligence Estimate, Panama: Prospects for the Election," 5 April 1984 in same box, Panama 2/16/84–4/27/84 folder; Oliver North to McFarlane, "Your Meeting with David Rockefeller, Regarding Panama," 25 October 1984, in the same box, Panama 5/22/84–10/25/84; Cannon, *Reagan*, pp. 296–97. Sosa, *In Defiance*, p. 17; Dinges, *Our Man in Panama*, pp. 137–54, 160–64, and 219–43. Many of the claims in the Dinges book are not yet backed by available documents.

63. "Remarks and a Question-and-Answer Session with Students and Faculty at Oakton High School in Vienna, Virginia," *PPPUS: Reagan, 1988*, p. 380; Link, *Righteous Warrior*, pp. 323–28.

64. Bush to Reagan, "Noriega," 13 May and 18 May 1988, Howard Baker, Chief of Staff Files, Box 4, Panama folder.

65. "Remarks at the Annual Dinner of the Conservative Political Action Conference," 30 January 1986, *PPPUS: Reagan, 1986*, p. 108.

66. See. for example, "Remarks at a Republican Party Rally in Cape Girardeau, Missouri," 14 September 1988, and "Remarks at a Campaign Rally for Senator Chic Hecht in Reno, Nevada," 1 November 1988, *PPPUS: Reagan, 1989*, pp. 1166 and 1429; "Republican Party Platform of 1988," 16 August 1988, pp. 9–10 and 35–37, *The American Presidency Project*; "1988 Democratic Party Platform," 18 July 1988, p. 5, *The American Presidency Project*; Schlesinger, 18 October 1988, Schlesinger and Schlesinger, eds., *Journals*, p. 661.

67. See J. William Middendorf, U.S. Ambassador to the OAS, 23 June 1981, Roger Fontaine Papers, Box 11, OAS 6/23/81–6/30/81 folder; "Remarks to a White House Briefing for Members of the Council of the Americas," 12 May 1987, *PPPUS: Reagan, 1987*, p. 502. One of Reagan's most complete statements on his economic philosophy as it related to Latin America is "Remarks at a White House Briefing for Members of the Council of the Americas," 12 May 1987, *PPPUS: Reagan, 1987*, pp. 501–3; Morley and McGillion, *Reagan and Pinochet*, p. 46.

68. "Inaugural Address," 20 January 1989, *PPPUS: Bush, 1989*, p. 1.

69. "Inaugural Address," 20 January 1988, *PPPUS: Bush, 1989*, p. 1.

70. "The President's News Conference of January 17, 1989," "Nomination of Bernard Aronson," 28 February 1989, "The President's News Conference of March 7, 1989," "Bipartisan Accord on Central America," and "Statement on the Bipartisan Accord on Central America," 24 March 1989," *PPPUS: Bush, 1989*, pp. 24, 157–58, 183, and 307–9; Brinkley, *Unfinished Presidency*, pp. 270–71; LeoGrande, *Our Own Backyard*, pp. 553–55; Arnson, *Crossroads*, pp. 228–29 and 231–35.

71. "Statement on the Bipartisan Accord on Central America," 24 March 1989, "Advance Text of Remarks upon Departure for the Centennial Celebration of Costa Rican Democracy in San José," 27 October 1989, "Remarks at the Welcoming Ceremony in San José, Costa Rica," 27 October 1989, and "Exchange with Reporters in San José, Costa Rica, on the Situation in Nicaragua," 27 October 1989, *PPPUS: Bush, 1989*, pp. 310 and 1404–6. See also Arias to Wright, 6 June 1989, Congressional Research Service translation, Jim Wright Papers, Box 1176, Correspondence to Jim Wright from Prominent Individual folders.

72. LeoGrande, *Our Own Backyard*, pp. 564–78; Arnson, *Crossroads*, pp. 242–64; D'Haeseleer, *Salvadoran Crucible*, p. 101–2; "Statement by Press Secretary Fitzwater on the

Murders at the University of Central America," 16 November 1989, *PPPUS: Bush, 1989*, p. 1531; Sebastian Rene Arandia, "Burden of the Cold War: The George H. W. Bush Administration and El Salvador," particularly pp. 62–114.

73. Brinkley, *Unfinished Presidency*, particularly pp. xv, xviii, xix, 56–57, 76–92, 176–98, and 268–95.

74. "U.S. Actions in Panama," 22 July 1989, NSC, NSD Files, Bush Library, Box 1, NSD-17-July 22, 1989, U.S. Actions in Panama folder; "National Security Directive 21: U.S. Policy toward Panama under Noriega after September 1, 1989."

75. Brinkley, *Unfinished Presidency*, pp. 201–3; Matthews, *Colin Powell*, pp. 111–17. Check "Exchange with Reporters Prior to Discussion with President Violeta Chamorro of Nicaragua," 9 April 1992, *PPPUS: Bush, 1992*, p. 574.

76. "Exchange with Reporters Prior to Discussion with President Violeta Chamorro of Nicaragua," 9 April 1992, *PPPUS: Bush, 1992*, p. 574. Letters to Republican and Democratic Party Leaders on Support for the Nicaraguan National Opposition Union," 24 January 1990, *PPPUS: Bush, 1990*, pp. 89–90; "Remarks at the Welcoming Ceremony for President Violeta Chamorro of Nicaragua," 17 April 1991, *PPPUS: Bush, 1991*, p. 385; Brinkley, *Unfinished Presidency*, pp. 298–311; LeoGrande, *Our Own Backyard*, pp. 560–64; Arnson, *Crossroads*, pp. 234–38. It later became clear that covert aid had continued.

Conclusion

1. Ralph Dungan to Robert Christopher, 23 August 1966, Ambassador to Chile Files, JFK Library, Box 14, Correspondence—Christopher, Robert folder.

2. Alter, *His Very Best*, pp. 478–81; Halperín Donghi, *Contemporary History of Latin America*, pp. 338–42, 350, 353, and 365–67.

3. "Remarks at the Welcoming Ceremony for President Carlos Andrés Pérez of Venezuela," 26 April 1990, *PPPUS: Bush, 1990*, p. 569; Langhorne Motley to Bush, 25 January 1990, Bush Library, WHORM, Subject Files CF, Box No. 1, Brazil folder.

4. "The Democratic Candidates on Venezuela," 30 July 2019, https://www.cfr.org/article /presidential-candidates-venezuela, accessed 14 August 2019; see also Gill, ed., *Future of U.S. Empire in the America*, particularly pp. 12, 13, 37–51, and 341–42.

5. Natalie Kitroeff and Michael D. Shear, "Billions in Aid, but the Migrants Keep Coming," *New York Times*, 6 June 2021, pp. 1 and 12; Gates, *Exercise of Power*, pp. 4, 8–9, 11, 17, 47, 186–87, and 387–415; Gideon Rose, "The Insiders' Insider: Review of *Exercise of Power: American Failures, Successes, and a New Path Forward in the Post-Cold War World*," *New York Times Book Review*, 21 June 2020, p. 10; McMaster, *Battlegrounds*. McMaster's book exemplifies the lack of concern in recent decades regarding developments in Latin America. Venezuela is only mentioned briefly on p. 114 in reference to China, and attention elsewhere in this book by one of President Donald Trump's national security advisers is severely limited. See p. 423. The Trump administration, to some degree, revived the unilateralism and the racism of early twentieth-century foreign policy. See Gill, *Future of U.S. Empire*, pp. 6–8, 88–92, and 97–102.

6. Rabe, *Most Dangerous Area in the World*, pp. 1–7; "Chilean President Honors Sen. Kennedy," United Press International, 24 September 2008; Stephen G. Rabe, *Kissinger and Latin America*, pp. 142 and 250.

Bibliography

Primary Sources

Manuscripts

Simi Valley, California
  Ronald Reagan Presidential Library
    1980 Campaign Papers
    Howard Baker Papers
    Patrick Buchanan Papers
    Roger Fontaine Papers
    National Security Files
Yorba Linda, California
  Richard M. Nixon Presidential Library
    White House Central Files
Atlanta, Georgia
  Jimmy Carter Presidential Library
    National Security Files
    Remote Archives Capture
    Walter Mondale Papers
    White House Central Files
Boise, Idaho
  Boise State University Library
    Frank Church Papers
Des Moines, Iowa
  Drake University
    Tom Harkin Papers
Abilene, Kansas
  Dwight David Eisenhower Presidential Library
    John Foster Dulles Papers
    White House Office Files
College Park, Maryland
  National Archives II
    Record Group 59
Boston, Massachusetts
  Boston College
    Tip O'Neill Papers
  John F. Kennedy Library
    Abram Chayes Papers
    Adam Clymer Papers

Ralph Dungan Papers
Richard Goodwin Papers
Lincoln Gordon Papers
John F. Kennedy Pre-Presidential Papers
Robert Kennedy Papers
Frank Mankiewicz Papers
Edwin Martin Papers
Teodoro Moscoso Papers
National Security Files
Oral History Interviews
Arthur M. Schlesinger Jr. Papers
White House Files
Ann Arbor, Michigan
  Gerald Ford Presidential Library
National Security Files
St. Paul, Minnesota
  Minnesota Historical Society
    Donald Fraser Papers
    Hubert Humphrey Papers
    Walter Mondale Papers
New Brunswick, New Jersey
  Rutgers University
    Frances Grant Papers
Princeton, New Jersey
  Princeton University Library
    George McGovern Papers
    Adlai Stevenson Papers
Hyde Park, New York
  Franklin D. Roosevelt Presidential Library
    Adolf Berle Papers
New York, New York
  Columbia University
    Spruille Braden Papers
  New York Public Library
    Arthur M. Schlesinger Jr. Papers
Sleepy Hollow, New York
  Rockefeller Archive Papers
    Nelson Aldrich Rockefeller Papers
Eugene, Oregon
  University of Oregon Library
    Wayne Morse Papers
Austin, Texas
  Lyndon Baines Johnson Presidential Library
    National Security Files
    Oral History Collection
    White House Office Files

College Station, Texas
　George Herbert Walker Bush Library
　　National Security Files
　　WHORM
Fort Worth, Texas
　Texas Christian University
　　Jim Wright Papers
Washington, DC
　Library of Congress
　　Harry G. Barnes Jr. Papers
　　W. Averell Harriman Papers
　　John Bartlow Martin Papers
　　Daniel Patrick Moynihan Papers

Government Publications

Congressional Record
Foreign Relations of the United States
Lieuwen, Edwin. *Survey of the Alliance for Progress: The Latin American Military.*
　Washington, DC: Democratic Platform Committee, 1976.
Public Papers of the Presidents of the United States. Washington, DC: United States
　Government Printing Office.
Quality of Life in the Americas: Report of a U.S. Presidential Mission for the Western
　Hemisphere. n.p., 1969.
U.S. Congress. House of Representatives. *Human Rights in the World Community: A Call*
　for U.S. Leadership, Report of the Subcommittee on International Organizations and
　Movements of the Committee on Foreign Affairs. Washington: Government Printing
　Office, 1974.
U.S. Congress. House of Representatives. Edward R. Roybal, Donald M. Fraser, and
　F. Bradford Morse. *Report of the Special Study Mission to Chile, Peru, and the*
　Dominican Republic, November 6–19, 1965. 89th Congress. House of Representatives.
　Committee on Foreign Affairs.
U.S. Congress. Senate. Committee on Commerce. Subcommittee on Communications.
　Freedom of Communications: Final Report of the Committee on Commerce,
　Subcommittee of the Subcommittee on Communications. Washington, DC:
　Government Printing Office, 1961.
U.S. Congress. Senate. *Hearings before the Committee on Foreign Relations, Foreign*
　Assistance Act of 1963.
U.S. Congress. Senate. *Hearings before the Committee on Foreign Relations, Latin*
　American Summit Conference, 17 and 21 March 1967.
U.S. Congress. Senate. *Intelligence Activities Senate Resolution 21: Hearings before the*
　Select Committee to Study Government Operations with Respect to Intelligence
　Activities of the United States Senate, Ninety-Fourth Congress, First Session, vol. 7:
　Covert Action, December 4 and 5, 1975.
U.S. Congress. Senate. *Multi-National Corporations and United States Foreign Policy:*
　Hearings before the Subcommittee on Multinational Corporations of the Committee on

Foreign Relations, United States Senate, Ninety-Third Congress on the International Telephone and Telegraph Company, 1970–1971.

U.S. Congress. Senate. *Nomination of Lincoln Gordon to be Assistant Secretary of State for Inter-American Affairs: Hearings before the Committee on Foreign Relations, U.S. Senate, 89th Congress, Second Session, 7 February 1966.*

U.S. Congress. Senate. *Prepared at the Request of the Subcommittee on American Republics Affairs of the Committee on Foreign Relations, United States Senate.* 9 October 1967.

U.S. Congress. Senate. *Report of Senators Wayne Morse and Bourke R. Hickenlooper to the Committee on Foreign Relations, United States Senate, 27 February 1961.*

U.S. Congress. Senate. *Report of Senator Wayne Morse on a Study Mission to the Committee on Foreign Relations, United States Senate, 20 February 1960.*

U.S. Congress. Senate. *United States Military Policies and Programs in Latin America: Hearings before the Subcommittee on Western Hemisphere Affairs of the Committee on Foreign Relations, United States Senate, Ninety-First Congress, 24 June and 8 July 1969.*

Periodicals

Atlantic Monthly	Los Angeles Times
Commentary	El Mercurio
Commonweal	New York Times
Current History	New York Times Book Review
Foreign Affairs	Punto Final
Fortune	Saturday Review
Hemispherica	Wall Street Journal
London Review of Books	Washington Post

Published Primary Sources

Beschloss, Michael R., ed. *Reaching for Glory: Lyndon Johnson's Secret White House Tapes, 1964–1965.* New York: Simon & Schuster, 2001.

———. *Taking Charge: The Johnson White House Tapes, 1963–1964.* New York: Simon & Schuster, 1997.

Brinkley, Douglas, ed. *The Reagan Diaries.* New York: Harper Perennial, 2007.

Carter, Jimmy. *White House Diary.* New York: Farrar, Straus and Giroux, 2010.

DiNunzio, Mario R., ed. *Woodrow Wilson: Essential Writings and Speeches of the Scholar-President.* New York: New York University Press, 2006.

Figueres Ferrer, José. *Escritos de José Figueres Ferrer: Política, Economía y Relaciones Internacionales.* San José, Costa Rica: EUNED; Fundación pro Centro Cultural y Histórico José Figueres Ferrer, 2000.

Frei Montalva, Eduardo. *Obras Escogidos (Período 1931–1982).* Santiago, Chile: Centro de Estudios Políticos Latinoamericanos Simón Bolívar and Fundación Eduardo Frei Montalva, 1993.

Guthman, Edwin O., and C. Richard Allen, eds. *RFK: Collected Speeches.* New York: Viking, 1993.

Johnson, Donald Bruce, ed. *National Party Platforms*. Urbana: University of Illinois Press, 1978.

Johnson, Walter, ed. *The Papers of Adlai E. Stevenson*, vol. 7: *Continuing Education and the Unfinished Business of American Society, 1957–1961*. Boston: Little, Brown, 1977.

———. *The Papers of Adlai E. Stevenson*, vol. 8: *Ambassador to the United Nations, 1961–1965*. Boston: Little, Brown, 1979.

Kornbluh, Peter, ed. *The Bay of Pigs Declassified*. New York: New Press, 1998.

———. ed. *The Pinochet File: A Declassified Dossier on Atrocity and Accountability*. New York: New Press, 2003.

Naftali, Timothy, ed. *The Presidential Recordings: John F. Kennedy, The Great Crises*, vol. 1: *July 30–August 1962*. New York: W. W. Norton, 2001.

Nixon, Edgar B., ed. *Franklin D. Roosevelt and Foreign Affairs*, vol. 1: *January 1933–February 1934*. Cambridge, MA: Harvard University Press, 1969.

Schlesinger, Andrew, and Stephen Schlesinger, eds. *Journals, 1952–2000: Arthur M. Schlesinger Jr.* New York: Penguin Press, 2007.

———, eds. *The Letters of Arthur Schlesinger Jr.* New York: Random House, 2013.

White, Mark J., ed., *The Kennedys and Cuba: The Declassified Documentary History*. Chicago: Ivan Dee, 1999.

Widmer, Ted, ed. *Listening In: The Secret White House Recordings of John F. Kennedy*. New York: Hyperion, 2012.

Secondary Sources

Ahlberg, Kristin L. *Transplanting the Great Society: Lyndon Johnson and Food for Peace*. Columbia: University of Missouri Press, 2008.

Aldous, Richard. *Schlesinger: The Imperial Historian*. New York: W. W. Norton, 2017.

Alexander, Robert J. *Juscelino Kubitschek and the Development of Brazil*. Athens: Ohio University Monographs in International Studies, 1991.

———. *Rómulo Betancourt and the Transformation of Venezuela*. New Brunswick, NJ: Transaction Publishers, 1982.

———. *The Venezuelan Revolution: A Profile of the Regime of Rómulo Betancourt*. New Brunswick, NJ: Rutgers University Press, 1964.

Allcock, Thomas Tunstall. "Becoming 'Mr. Latin America': Thomas C. Mann Reconsidered." *Diplomatic History* 38, no. 5 (November 2014): 1017–45.

———. *Thomas C. Mann: President Johnson, the Cold War, and the Restructuring of Latin American Foreign Policy*. Lexington: University Press of Kentucky, 2018.

Alter, Jonathan. *His Very Best: Jimmy Carter, A Life*. New York: Simon & Schuster, 2020.

Ambrosius, Lloyd E. *Woodrow Wilson and American Nationalism*. New York: Cambridge University Press, 2017.

Ameringer, Charles D. *The Democratic Left in Exile: The Antidictatorial Struggle in the Caribbean, 1945–1959*. Coral Gables: University of Miami Press, 1974.

Anson, Robert Sam. *McGovern: A Biography*. New York: Holt, Rinehart and Winston, 1972.

Armony, Ariel C. *Argentina, the United States, and the Anti-Communist Crusade in Central America, 1977–1984*. Athens: Ohio University Center for International Studies, 1997.

Arnson, Cynthia J. *Crossroads: Congress, the President, and Central America, 1976–1993*, 2nd ed. University Park: Penn State University Press, 1983.

Arsenault, Raymond. *Freedom Riders: 1961 and the Struggle for Racial Justice*. New York: Oxford University Press, 2006.

Ashby, LeRoy, and Rod Gramer. *Fighting the Odds: The Life of Senator Frank Church*, 2nd ed. Carlton, OR: Ridenbaugh Press, 2014.

Atkins, G. Pope, and Larman C. Wilson. *The Dominican Republic and the United States: From Imperialism to Transnationalism*. Athens: University of Georgia Press, 1998.

Attwood, William. *The Reds and the Blacks: A Personal Adventure*. New York: Harper & Row, 1967.

Barman, Roderick J. *Citizen Emperor: Pedro II and the Making of Brazil, 1825–91*. Stanford: Stanford University Press, 1999.

Bawden, John R. "Cutting Off the Dictator: The United States Arms Embargo of the Pinochet Regime, 1974–1988." *Journal of Latin American Studies* 45, no. 3 (August 2013): 513–43.

Beisner, Robert L. *Dean Acheson: A Life in the Cold War*. New York: Oxford University Press, 2006.

Benton, William. *The Voice of Latin America*. New York: Harper Brothers, 1961.

Bethell, Leslie, and Ian Roxborough, "Latin America between the Second World War and the Cold War: Some Reflections on the 1945–1948 Conjuncture." *Journal of Latin American Studies* 20, no. 1 (May 1988): 167–89.

Bohning, Donald. *The Castro Obsession: U.S. Covert Operations Against Cuba, 1959–1965*. Dulles, VA: Potomac Books, 2005.

Boomhower, Ray E. *John Bartlow Martin: A Voice for the Underdog*. Bloomington: Indiana University Press, 2015.

Borstelmann, Thomas. *The 1970s: A New Global History from Civil Rights to Economic Inequality*. Princeton, NJ: Princeton University Press, 2012.

Brandes, Joseph. *Herbert Hoover and Economic Diplomacy: Department of Commerce Policy, 1921–1928*. Pittsburgh: University of Pittsburgh Press, 1962.

Brands, H. W. *What America Owes the World: The Struggle for the Soul of Foreign Policy*. New York: Cambridge University Press, 1998.

Brinkley, Douglas. *The Unfinished Presidency: Jimmy Carter's Journey beyond the White House*. New York: Penguin Books, 1999.

Brown, Jonathan C. *Cuba's Revolutionary World*. Cambridge, MA: Harvard University Press, 2017.

Bundy, William. *A Tangled Web: The Making of Foreign Policy in the Nixon Presidency*. New York: Hill and Wang, 1998.

Byrne, Malcolm. *Iran-Contra: Reagan's Scandal and the Unchecked Abuse of Presidential Power*. Lawrence: University Press of Kansas, 2014.

Cannon, Lou. *President Reagan: The Role of a Lifetime*. New York: Public Affairs, 2000.

Caro, Robert A. *The Years of Lyndon Johnson: The Passage of Power*. New York: Vintage Books, 2012.

Carter, Jimmy. *Keeping Faith: Memoirs of a President*. New York: Bantam Books, 1982.

Chafe, William H. *Never Stop Running: Allard Lowenstein and the Struggle to Save American Liberalism*. New York: Basic Books, 1993.

Chase, Michelle. "The Trials: Violence and Justice in the Aftermath of the Cuban Revolution." In *A Century of Revolution: Insurgent and Counterinsurgent Violence during Latin America's Long Cold War,* edited by Greg Grandin and Gilbert M. Joseph. Durham, NC: Duke University Press, 2010.

Chávez, Joaquín M. *Poets and Prophets of the Resistance: Intellectuals and the Origins of El Salvador's Civil War.* New York: Oxford University Press, 2017.

Chester, Eric Thomas. *Rag-Tags, Scum, Riff-Raff, and Commies: The U. S. Intervention in the Dominican Republic, 1965–1966.* New York: Monthly Review Press, 2001.

Ching, Erik. *Stories of Civil War in El Salvador: A Battle over Memory.* Chapel Hill: University of North Carolina Press, 2016.

Clymer, Adam. *Edward M. Kennedy: A Biography.* New York: William Morrow, 1999.

Cobbs, Elizabeth A. *The Rich Neighbor Policy: Rockefeller and Kaiser in Brazil.* New Haven, CT: Yale University Press, 1992.

Cobbs Hoffman, Elizabeth. *The Peace Corps and the Spirit of the 1960s.* Cambridge, MA: Harvard University Press, 1998.

Coleman, David G. *The Fourteenth Day: JFK and the Afterman of the Cuban Missile Crisis.* New York: W. W. Norton, 2014.

Cooper, John Milton, Jr. *Woodrow Wilson: A Biography.* New York: Alfred A. Knopf, 2009.

Craig, Campbell, and Fredrik Logevall. *America's Cold War: The Politics of Insecurity.* Cambridge, MA: Harvard University Press, 2009.

Crile, George. *Charlie Wilson's War: The Extraordinary Story of the Largest Covert Operation in History.* New York: Atlantic Monthly Press, 2003.

Cullather, Nick. "Development? It's History." *Diplomatic History* 24, no. 4 (Fall 2000): 641–53.

———. *Secret History: The CIA's Classified Account of Its Operations in Guatemala, 1952–1954.* Stanford, CA: Stanford University Press, 1999.

Culver, John C., and John Hyde, *American Dream: A Life of Henry A. Wallace.* New York: W. W. Norton, 2000.

Dallek, Robert. *Camelot's Court: Inside the Kennedy White House.* New York: HarperCollins, 2013.

———. *Flawed Giant: Lyndon Johnson and His Times, 1961–1973.* New York: Oxford University Press, 1998.

———. *Nixon and Kissinger: Partners in Power.* New York: HarperCollins, 2007.

———. *An Unfinished Life. John F. Kennedy, 1917–1963.* New York: Oxford University Press, 2003.

Darnton, Christopher. "Asymmetry and Agenda-Setting in U.S.-Latin American Relations: Rethinking the Origins of the Alliance for Progress." *Journal of Cold War Studies* 14, no. 4 (Fall 2012): 55–92.

David, Andrew, and Michael Holm, "The Kennedy Administration and the Battle over Foreign Aid: The Untold Story of the Clay Committee." *Diplomacy & Statecraft* 27, no. 1 (March 2016): 65–92.

Dean, Robert D. "Masculinity as Ideology: John F. Kennedy and the Domestic Politics of Foreign Policy." *Diplomatic History* 22, no. 1 (January 1998): 29–62.

D'Haeseleer, Brian. *The Salvadoran Crucible: The Failure of U. S. Counterinsurgency in El Salvador, 1979–1992.* Lawrence: University Press of Kansas, 2017.

Dinges, John. *Our Man in Panama.* New York: Random House, 1990.

Divine, Robert A. *Foreign Policy and U.S. Presidential Elections, 1940/1948*. New York: New Viewpoints, 1974.

———. *Foreign Policy and U.S. Presidential Elections, 1952/1960*. New York: New Viewpoints, 1974.

Dosal, Paul J. *Comandante Che: Guerrilla Soldier, Commander, and Strategist*. University Park: Penn State University Press, 2003.

Drake, Paul W. *Between Tyranny and Anarchy: A History of Democracy in Latin America, 1800–2006*. Stanford, CA: Stanford University Press, 2009.

Duarte, José Napoleón. *My Life*. New York: Putnam, 1986.

Dulles, John W. F. *President Castello Branco: Brazilian Reformer*. College Station: Texas A&M University Press, 1980.

Eisenhower, John S. D. *Intervention! The United States and the Mexican Revolution, 1913–1917*. New York: W. W. Norton, 1993.

Farrell, John Aloysius. *Tip O'Neill and the Democratic Century*. Boston: Little, Brown, 2001.

Field, Thomas C., Jr. *From Development to Dictatorship: Bolivia and the Alliance for Progress in the Kennedy Era*. Ithaca, NY: Cornell University Press, 2014.

———. "Ideology as Strategy: Military-Led Modernization and the Origins of the Alliance for Progress in Bolivia." *Diplomatic History* 36, no. 1 (January 2012): 147–83.

———. "Transnationalism Meets Empire: The AFL-CIO, Development, and the Private Origins of Kennedy's Latin American Labor Program." *Diplomatic History* 42, no. 2 (April 2018): 305–34.

Fleet, Michael. *The Rise and Fall of Chilean Christian Democracy*. Princeton, NJ: Princeton University Press.

Flippen, J. Brooks. *Speaker Jim Wright: Power, Scandal, and the Birth of Modern Politics*. Austin: University of Texas Press, 2018.

Francis, Michael J. "Military Aid to Latin America in the U.S. Congress." *Journal of Inter-American Studies* 6, no. 3 (July 1964): 389–404.

Freedman, Lawrence. *Kennedy's Wars: Berlin, Cuba, Laos, and Vietnam*. New York: Oxford University Press, 2000.

Freidel, Frank. *Franklin D. Roosevelt: A Rendezvous with Destiny*. New York: Little, Brown, 1990.

French, John D. *The Brazilian Workers' ABC: Class Conflict and Alliances in Modern São Paulo*. Chapel Hill: University of North Carolina Press, 1992.

Friedman, Max Paul. *Rethinking Anti-Americanism: The History of an Exceptional Concept in American Foreign Relations*. Cambridge: Cambridge University Press, 2012.

Fursenko, Aleksandr, and Timothy Naftali, *"One Hell of a Gamble": Khrushchev, Castro, and Kennedy, 1958–1964*. New York: W. W. Norton, 1997.

Gabler, Neal. *Catching the Wind: Edward Kennedy and the Liberal Hour, 1932–1975*. New York: Random House, 2020.

Gambone, Michael D. *Capturing the Revolution: The United States, Central America, and Nicaragua, 1961–1972*. Westport, CT: Praeger, 2001.

Garthoff, Raymond L. *Détente and Confrontation: American-Soviet Relations from Nixon to Reagan*. Washington, DC: Brookings Institution, 1985.

Gaspari, Elio. *A Ditadura Encurralada*. São Paulo: Companhia das Letras, 2004.

———. *A Ditadura Envergonhada*. São Paulo: Companhia das Letras, 2002.

———. *A Ditadura Escancarada*. São Paulo: Companhia das Letras, 2002.

Gates, Robert M. *Exercise of Power: American Failures, Successes, and a New Path Forward in the Post-Cold War World*. New York: Alfred A. Knopf, 2020.

———. *From the Shadows: The Ultimate Insider's Story of Five Presidents and How They Won the Cold War*. New York: Simon & Schuster, 1996.

Gazmuri, Cristián, Patricia Arancibia, and Álvaro Góngora. *Eduardo Frei y su Época*, Santiago: Aguilar Chilena de Ediciones, 2000.

Gellman, Irwin F. *Good Neighbor Diplomacy: United States Policies in Latin America, 1933–1945*. Baltimore: Johns Hopkins University Press, 1979.

Gervasi, Frank. *The Real Rockefeller: The Story of the Rise, Decline and Resurgence of the Presidential Aspirations of Nelson Rockefeller*. New York: Atheneum, 1964.

Gill, Timothy, ed. *The Future of U.S. Empire in the America: The Trump Administration and Beyond*. New York: Routledge, 2020.

Gleijeses, Piero. *Conflicting Missions: Havana, Washington, and Africa, 1959–1976*. Chapel Hill: University of North Carolina Press, 2002.

———. *The Dominican Crisis: The 1965 Constitutionalist Revolt and American Intervention*. Translated by Lawrence Lipson. Baltimore: Johns Hopkins University Press, 1978.

———. *Shattered Hope: The Guatemalan Revolution and the United States, 1944–1954*. Princeton, NJ: Princeton University Press, 1991.

———. *Visions of Freedom: Havana, Washington, Pretoria, and the Struggle for Southern Africa, 1976–1991*. Chapel Hill: University of North Carolina Press, 2013.

Gobat, Michel. *Confronting the American Dream: Nicaragua under U.S. Imperial Rule*. Durham, NC: Duke University Press, 2005.

Gordon, Lincoln. *Brazil's Second Chance: En Route toward the First World*. Washington, DC: Brookings Institution Press, 2001.

———. *A New Deal for Latin America: The Alliance for Progress*. Cambridge, MA: Harvard University Press, 1963.

Green, James N. "Clerics, Exiles, and Academics: Opposition to the Military Dictatorship in the United States, 1969–1976." *Latin American Politics and Society* 45, no. 1 (Spring 2003): 87–117.

———. *We Cannot Remain Silent: Opposition to the Brazilian Military Dictatorship in the United States*. Durham, NC: Duke University Press, 2010.

Gross, Leonard. *The Last Best Hope: Eduardo Frei and Chilean Democracy*. New York: Random House, 1967.

Halperín Donghi, Tulio. *The Contemporary History of Latin America*. Edited and Translated by John Charles Chasteen. Durham, NC: Duke University Press, 1993.

Hamby, Alonzo L. *Liberalism and Its Challengers: F.D.R. to Reagan*. New York: Oxford University Press, 1984.

Harmer, Tanya. *Allende's Chile and the Inter-American Cold War*. Chapel Hill: University of North Carolina Press, 2011.

———. *Beatriz Allende: A Revolutionary Life in Cold War Latin America*. Chapel Hill: University of North Carolina Press, 2020.

———. "The 'Cuban Question' and the Cold War in Latin America, 1959–1964." *Journal of Cold War Studies* 21, no. 3 (Summer 2019): 114–51.

———. "Two, Three, Many Revolutions? Cuba and the Prospects for Revolutionary Change in Latin America, 1967–1975." *Journal of Latin American Studies* 45, no. 1 (February 2013): 65–89.

Hartlyn, Jonathan. *The Struggle for Democratic Politics in the Dominican Republic.* Chapel Hill: University of North Carolina Press, 1998.

Hershberg, James G. "Soviet-Brazilian Relations and the Cuban Missile Crisis." *Journal of Cold War Studies* 22, no. 1 (Winter 2020): 175–209.

Hilty, James W. *Robert Kennedy, Brother Protector.* Philadelphia: Temple University Press, 1997.

Hitchcock, William I. *The Age of Eisenhower: America and the World in the 1950s.* New York: Simon & Schuster, 2018.

Holden, Robert H. *Armies without Nations: Public Violence and State Formation in Central America, 1821–1960.* New York: Oxford University Press, 2004.

Holsti, Ole, and James N. Rosenau. *American Leadership in World Affairs: Vietnam and the Breakdown of Consensus.* Boston: Allen & Unwin, 1984.

Hurtado-Torres, Sebastián. *The Gathering Storm: Eduardo Frei's Revolution in Liberty and Chile's Cold War.* Ithaca, NY: Cornell University Press, 2020.

Immerman, Richard H. *The CIA in Guatemala.* Austin: University of Texas Press, 1982.

Jenkins, James. "The Indian Wing; Nicaraguan Indians, Native American Activists, and US Foreign Policy, 1979–1990." In *Beyond the Eagle's Shadow: New Histories of Latin America's Cold War,* edited by Virginia Garrard-Burnett, Mark Atwood Lawrence, and Julio E. Moreno. Albuquerque: University of New Mexico Press, 2013.

Johns, Andrew L. *The Price of Loyalty: Hubert Humphrey's Vietnam Conflict.* Lanham, MD: Rowman & Littlefield, 2020.

Johnson, John J. *The Role of the Military in Underdeveloped Countries.* Princeton, NJ: Princeton University Press, 1962.

Johnson, Loch K. *A Season of Inquiry Revisited: The Church Committee Confronts America's Spy Agencies,* 2nd ed. Lawrence: University Press of Kansas, 2015.

Johnson, Robert David. *Congress and the Cold War.* New York: Cambridge University Press, 2006.

———. *Ernest Gruening and the American Dissenting Tradition.* Cambridge, MA: Harvard University Press, 1998.

———. "The Progressive Dissent: Ernest Gruening and Vietnam." In *Vietnam and the American Political Tradition: The Politics of Dissent,* edited by Randall B. Woods. Cambridge: Cambridge University Press, 2003.

Jorden, William J. *Panama Odyssey.* Austin: University of Texas Press, 1984.

Kagan, Robert A. *A Twilight Struggle: American Power and Nicaragua, 1977–1990.* New York: Free Press, 1996.

Kalman, Laura. *Right Star Rising: A New Politics, 1974–1980.* New York: W. W. Norton, 2010.

Kane, N. Stephen. *Selling Reagan's Foreign Policy: Going Public vs. Executive Bargaining.* Lanham, MD: Lexington Books, 2018.

Karl, Robert A. *Forgotten Peace: Reform, Violence, and the Making of Contemporary Colombia.* Berkeley: University of California Press, 2017.

Keeley, Theresa. "Reagan's Real Catholics vs. Tip O'Neill's Maryknoll Nuns: Gender, Intra-Catholic Conflict, and the Contras." *Diplomatic History* 40, no. 3 (June 2016): 530–58.

Keller, Renata. "The Latin American Missile Crisis." *Diplomatic History* 39, no. 2 (April 2015): 195–222.

Kelly, Patrick William. "The 1973 Chilean Coup and the Origins of Transnational Rights Activism." *Journal of Global History* 8, no. 1 (March 2013): 165–86.

———. *Sovereign Emergencies: Latin America and the Making of Global Human Rights Politics*. New York: Cambridge University Press, 2018.

Keys, Barbara J. "Congress, Kissinger, and the Origins of Human Rights Diplomacy." *Diplomatic History* 34, no. 5 (November 2010): 823–51.

———. *Reclaiming American Virtue: The Human Rights Revolution of the 1970s*. Cambridge, MA: Harvard University Press, 2014.

Kirkendall, Andrew J. "Entering History: Paulo Freire and the Politics of the Brazilian Northeast, 1958–1964." *Luso-Brazilian Review* 41, no. 1 (Summer 2004): 168–89.

———. "Kennedy Men and the Fate of the Alliance for Progress in LBJ Era Brazil and Chile." *Diplomacy & Statecraft* 18, no. 4 (December 2007): 745–72.

———. *Paulo Freire and the Cold War Politics of Literacy*. Chapel Hill: University of North Carolina Press, 2010.

———. "Paulo Freire, Eduardo Frei, Literacy Training and the Politics of Consciousness Raising in Chile, 1964 to 1970." *Journal of Latin American Studies* 36, no. 4 (November 2004): 687–717.

Knock, Thomas J. *The Rise of a Prairie Statesman: The Life and Times of George McGovern*. Princeton, NJ: Princeton University Press, 2016.

———. *To End All Wars: Woodrow Wilson and the Quest for a New World Order*. New York: Oxford University Press, 1992.

Kotz, Nick. *Judgement Days: Lyndon Baines Johnson, Martin Luther King Jr., and the Laws That Changed America*. Boston: Houghton Mifflin, 2005.

Kowalchuck, Lisa. "The Salvadoran Land Struggle in the 1990s." In *Landscapes of Struggle: Politics, Society, and Community in El Salvador*, edited by Aldo Lauria-Santiago and Leigh Binford. Pittsburgh: University of Pittsburgh Press, 2004

Kruse, Kevin M. *Fault Lines: A History of the United States since 1974*. New York: W. W. Norton, 2019.

Kuzmarov, Jeremy. "Modernizing Repression: Police Training, Political Violence, and Nation-Building in the 'American Century.'" *Diplomatic History* 33, no. 2 (April 2009): 191–221.

LaFeber, Walter. *Inevitable Revolutions: The United States in Central America*, 2nd ed. New York: W. W. Norton, 1993.

Langley, Lester D. *America and the Americas: The United States in the Western Hemisphere*, 2nd ed. Athens: University of Georgia Press, 2010.

Latham, Michael E. *Modernization as Ideology: American Social Science and "Nation Building" in the Kennedy Era*. Chapel Hill: University of North Carolina Press, 2000.

Lawrence, John A. *The Class of '74: Congress after Watergate and the Roots of Partisanship*. Baltimore: Johns Hopkins University Press, 2018.

Lawrence, Mark Atwood. "An Exception to the Rule? The Johnson Administration and the Panama Canal." In *Looking Back at LBJ: White House Politics in a New Light*, edited by Mitchell Lerner. Lawrence: University Press of Kansas, 2005.

———. "History from Below: The United States and Latin America in the Nixon Years." In *Nixon in the World: American Foreign Relations, 1969–1977*, edited by Fredrik Logevall and Andrew Preston. New York: Oxford University Press, 2008.

Leacock, Ruth. *Requiem for Revolution: The United States and Brazil, 1961–1969*. Kent, OH: Kent State University Press, 1990.

Leffler, Melvin P. *For the Soul of Mankind: The United States, the Soviet Union, and the Cold War*. New York: Hill and Wang, 2007.

———. *A Preponderance of Power: National Security, the Truman Administration, and the Cold War*. Stanford, CA: Stanford University Press, 1992.

LeoGrande, William M. *Our Own Backyard: The United States in Central America, 1977–1992*. Chapel Hill: University of North Carolina Press, 1998.

LeoGrande, William M., and Peter Kornbluh, *Back Channel to Cuba: The Hidden History of Negotiations between Washington and Havana*. Chapel Hill: University of North Carolina Press, 2014.

Leuchtenburg, William E. *In the Shadow of FDR: From Harry Truman to Ronald Reagan*, rev. ed. Ithaca, NY: Cornell University Press, 1983.

Levinson, Jerome, and Juan de Onís. *The Alliance That Lost Its Way: A Critical Report on the Alliance for Progress*. Chicago: Quadrangle Books, 1970.

Link, William A. *Righteous Warrior: Jesse Helms and the Rise of Modern Conservatism*. New York: St. Martin's Press, 2008.

Lochery, Neill. *Brazil: The Fortunes of War: World War II and the Making of Modern Brazil*. New York: Basic Books, 2014.

Lockhart, James. *Chile, The CIA, and the Cold War: A Transatlantic Perspective*. Edinburgh: Edinburgh University Press, 2019.

Logevall, Fredrik. *Choosing War: The Lost Chance for Peace and the Escalation of War in Vietnam*. Berkeley: University of California Press, 1999.

———. *JFK: Coming of Age in the American Century*. New York: Random House, 2020.

Long, Tom. "Putting the Canal on the Map: Panamanian Agenda-Setting and the 1973 Security Council Meetings." *Diplomatic History* 38, no. 2 (April 2014): 431–55.

Longley, Kyle. *LBJ's 1968: Power, Politics, and the Presidency in America's Year of Upheaval*. New York: Cambridge University Press, 2018.

———. "An Obsession: The Central American Policy of the Reagan Administration." In *Reagan and the World: Leadership and National Security, 1981–1989*, edited by Bradley Lynn Coleman and Kyle Longley. Lexington: University Press of Kentucky, 2017.

———. *The Sparrow and the Hawk: Costa Rica and the United States during the Rise of Figueres*. Tuscaloosa: University of Alabama Press, 1997.

Mackenzie, G. Calvin, and Robert Weisbrot. *The Liberal Hour*. New York: Penguin Books, 2008.

Manela, Erez. *The Wilsonian Moment: Self-Determination and the International Origins of Anticolonial Nationalism*. New York: Oxford University Press, 2007.

Martin, Edwin McCammon. *Kennedy and Latin America*. Lanham, MD: University Press of America, 1994.

Martin, John Bartlow. *Adlai Stevenson and the World*. Garden City, NY: Doubleday, 1977.

———. *Overtaken by Events: The Dominican Crisis from the Fall of Trujillo to the Civil War*. Garden City, NY: Doubleday, 1966.

Matthews, Jeffrey J. *Colin Powell: Imperfect Patriot*. Notre Dame, IN: University of Notre Dame Press, 2019.

McCann, Frank D., Jr. *The Brazilian-American Alliance, 1937–1945*. Princeton, NJ: Princeton University Press, 1973.

McCrisken, Trevor B. *American Exceptionalism and the Legacy of Vietnam: U.S. Foreign Policy since 1974*. New York: Palgrave Macmillan, 2003.

McGovern, George S. *Grassroots: The Autobiography of George McGovern*. New York: Random House, 1977.

——. *A Time of War, A Time of Peace*. New York: Random House, 1968.

——. *War against Want: America's Food for Peace Program*. New York: Walker Company, 1964.

McKercher, Asa. "Steamed Up: Domestic Politics, Congress, and Cuba, 1959–1963." *Diplomatic History* 38, no. 3 (June 2014): 599–627.

McMaster, H. R. *Battlegrounds: The Fight to Defend the Free World*. New York: HarperCollins, 2020.

McPherson, Alan. *Ghosts of Sheridan Circle: How a Washington Assassination Brought Pinochet's Terror State to Justice*. Chapel Hill: University of North Carolina Press, 2019.

——. "Herbert Hoover, Occupation Withdrawal, and the Good Neighbor Policy." *Presidential Studies Quarterly* 44, no. 4 (December 2014): 623–39.

——. *The Invaded: How Latin Americans and Their Allies Fought and Ended U.S. Occupations*. New York: Oxford University Press, 2014.

——. "Letelier Diplomacy: Non-State Actors and US-Chilean Relations." *Diplomatic History* 43, no. 3 (June 2019): 445–68.

——. *Yankee No! Anti-Americanism in U.S.-Latin American Relations*. Cambridge, MA: Harvard University Press, 2003.

McPherson, Harry. *A Political Education*. Boston: Little, Brown, 1972.

Mieczkowski, Yanek. *Gerald Ford and the Challenge of the 1970s*. Lexington: University Press of Kentucky, 2005.

Miller, Aragorn Storm. *Precarious Paths to Freedom: The United States, Venezuela, and the Latin American Cold War*. Albuquerque: University of New Mexico Press, 2016.

Mitchell, Nancy. "The Cold War and Jimmy Carter." In *The Cambridge History of the Cold War*, vol. 3: *Endings*, edited by Melvyn P. Leffler and Odd Arne Westad. Cambridge: Cambridge University Press, 2010.

——. *Jimmy Carter in Africa: Race and the Cold War*. Washington, DC: Woodrow Wilson Center Press, 2016.

Morley, Morris, and Chris McGillion. *Reagan and Pinochet: The Struggle over U.S. Policy toward Chile*. New York: Cambridge University Press, 2015.

Morris, James A. *Honduras: Caudillo Politics and Military Rulers*. Boulder, CO: Westview Press, 1984.

Moulton, Aaron Coy. "The Dictators' Domino Theory: A Caribbean Basin Anti-Communist Network, 1947–1952." *Intelligence and National Security* 34, no. 7 (2019): 945–61.

Moyn, Samuel. *The Last Utopia: Human Rights in History*. Cambridge, MA: Harvard University Press, 2010.

Muehlenbeck, Philip E. *Betting on the Africans: John F. Kennedy's Courting of African Nationalist Leaders*. New York: Oxford University Press, 2012.

Nasaw, David. *The Remarkable Life and Turbulent Times of Joseph P. Kennedy*. New York: Penguin Books, 2012.

Nelson-Pallmeyer, Jack. *School of Assassins*. Maryknoll, NY: Orbis Books, 1997.

Obama, Barack. *A Promised Land*. New York: Crown, 2020.

Offner, Amy C. *Sorting Out the Mixed Economy: The Rise and Fall of Welfare and Developmental States in the Americas*. Princeton, NJ: Princeton University Press, 2019.

Offner, Arnold A. *Hubert Humphrey: The Conscience of the Country*. New Haven, CT: Yale University Press, 2018.

Palermo, Joseph A. *In His Own Right: The Political Odyssey of Senator Robert F. Kennedy*. New York: Columbia University Press, 2001.

———. *Robert F. Kennedy and the Death of American Liberalism*. New York: Pearson Longman, 2008.

Parker, Jason C. *Hearts, Minds, Voices: U.S. Cold War Public Diplomacy and the Formation of the Third World*. New York: Oxford University Press, 2016.

Parker, Phyllis. *Brazil and the Quiet Intervention, 1964*. Austin: University of Texas Press, 1979.

Pavilack, Jody. *Mining for the Nation: The Politics of Chile's Coal Communities from the Popular Front to the Cold War*. University Park: Penn State University Press, 2010.

Peace, Roger. *A Call to Conscience: The Anti-Contra War Campaign*. Amherst: University of Massachusetts Press, 2012.

Pérez, Louis A., Jr. *On Becoming Cuban: Identity, Nationality and Culture*. New York: HarperCollins, 1999.

Persico, Joseph E. *The Imperial Rockefeller: A Biography of Nelson A. Rockefeller*. New York: Simon & Schuster, 1982.

Peterson, Christian Philip. "The Carter Administration and the Promotion of Human Rights in the Soviet Union, 1977–1981." *Diplomatic History* 38, no. 3 (June 2014): 628–56.

Pike, Fredrick B. *FDR's Good Neighbor Policy: Sixty Years of Generally Gentle Chaos*. Austin: University of Texas Press, 1995.

Porter, Charles O., and Robert J. Alexander. *The Struggle for Democracy in Latin America*. New York: Macmillan Company, 1961.

Preble, Christopher A. *John F. Kennedy and the Missile Gap*. DeKalb: Northern Illinois University Press, 2004.

Qureshi, Lubna Z. *Nixon, Kissinger, and Allende: U.S. Involvement in the 1973 Coup in Chile*. Lanham, MD: Lexington Books, 2009.

Rabe, Stephen G. *Eisenhower and Latin America: The Foreign Policy of Anti-Communism*. Chapel Hill: University of North Carolina Press, 1988.

———. *The Killing Zone: The United States Wages War in Latin America*. New York: Oxford University Press, 2012.

———. *Kissinger and Latin America: Intervention, Human Rights, and Diplomacy*. Ithaca, NY: Cornell University Press, 2020.

———. *The Most Dangerous Area in the World: John F. Kennedy Confronts Communist Revolution in Latin America*. Chapel Hill: University of North Carolina Press, 1999.

Rakove, Robert R. *Kennedy, Johnson, and the Nonaligned World*. New York: Cambridge University Press, 2013.

Randall, Stephen J. *Colombia and the United States: Hegemony and Interdependence*. Athens: University of Georgia Press, 1992.

Reich, Cary. *The Life of Nelson A. Rockefeller: Worlds to Conquer, 1908–1958*. New York: Doubleday, 1996.

Rivas, Darlene. *Missionary Capitalist: Nelson Rockefeller in Venezuela*. Chapel Hill: University of North Carolina Press, 2002.

Rodrigues, Luís Nuno. *Salazar-Kennedy: A Crise de Uma Aliança*. Lisbon: Editorial Notícias, 2002.

Rogers, William D. *The Twilight Struggle: The Alliance for Progress and the Politics of Development in Latin America*. New York: Random House, 1967.

Roorda, Eric Paul. *The Dictator Next Door: The Good Neighbor Policy and the Trujillo Regime in the Dominican Republic, 1930–1945*. Durham, NC: Duke University Press, 1998.

Rosenberg, Emily S. "World War I, Wilsonianism, and Challenges to U.S. Empire." *Diplomatic History* 38, no. 4 (September 2014): 852–63.

Ross, Douglas. *Robert F. Kennedy: Apostle of Change*. New York: Trident Press, 1968.

Rossinow, Doug. *The Reagan Era: A History of the 1980s*. New York: Columbia University Press, 2015.

Ryan, Henry Butterfield. *The Fall of Che Guevara: A Story of Soldiers, Spies, and Diplomats*. New York: Oxford University Press, 1998.

Sánchez Nateras, Gerardo. "The Sandinista Revolution and the Limits of the Cold War in Latin America: The Dilemma of Non-Intervention during the Nicaraguan Crisis." *Cold War History* 18, no. 2 (2018): 111–29.

Sater, William F. *Chile and the United States: Empires in Conflict*. Athens: University of Georgia Press, 1990.

Schlesinger, Arthur M., Jr. *A Life in the Twentieth Century: Innocent Beginnings, 1917–1950*. Boston: Houghton Mifflin, 2000.

———. *Robert Kennedy and His Times*. New York: Ballantine Books, 1978.

———. *A Thousand Days: John F. Kennedy in the White House*. Boston: Houghton Mifflin, 1965.

———. *The Vital Center: The Politics of Freedom*. New Brunswick, NJ: Transaction Publishers, 2009.

Schmidli, William Michael. *The Fate of Freedom Elsewhere: Human Rights and U.S. Cold War Policy toward Argentina*. Ithaca, NY: Cornell University Press, 2013.

Schmidt, Hans. *The United States Occupation of Haiti, 1915–1934*. New Brunswick, NJ: Rutgers University Press, 1995.

Schmitt, Edward R. *President of the Other America: Robert Kennedy and the Politics of Poverty*. Amherst: University of Massachusetts Press, 2010.

Schmitz, David F. *The United States and Right-Wing Dictatorships, 1965–1989*. Cambridge: Cambridge University Press, 2006.

Schmitz, David F., and Vanessa Walker, "Jimmy Carter and the Foreign Policy of Human Rights: The Development of a Post-Cold War Foreign Policy." *Diplomatic History* 28, no. 1 (January 2004): 113–43.

Schoultz, Lars. *That Infernal Little Cuban Republic: The United States and the Cuban Revolution*. Chapel Hill: University of North Carolina Press, 2009.

Schuhrke, Jeff. "Agrarian Reform and the AFL-CIO's Cold War in El Salvador." *Diplomatic History* 44, no. 4 (September 2020): 527–53.

Schwartzberg, Steven. *Democracy and U.S. Policy in Latin America during the Truman Years*. Gainesville: University Press of Florida, 2003.

Shannon, William V. *The Heir Apparent: Robert Kennedy and the Struggle for Power*. New York: Macmillan, 1967.

Shesol, Jeff. *Mutual Contempt: Lyndon Johnson, Robert Kennedy, and the Feud That Defined a Decade*. New York: W. W. Norton, 1997.

Siekmeier, James F. *The Bolivian Revolution and the United States, 1952 to the Present*. University Park: Penn State University Press, 2011.

Sigmund, Paul E. *The Overthrow of Allende and the Politics of Chile, 1964–1976*. Pittsburgh: University of Pittsburgh Press, 1977.

———. *The United States and Democracy in Chile*. Baltimore: Johns Hopkins University Press, 1993.

Sikkink, Kathryn. *Mixed Signals: U.S. Human Rights Policy and Latin America*. Ithaca, NY: Cornell University Press, 2004.

Skidmore, Thomas E. *The Politics of Military Rule in Brazil, 1964–85*. New York: Oxford University Press, 1988.

Small, Melvin. *At the Water's Edge: American Politics and the Vietnam War*. Chicago: Ivan Dee, 2005.

Smith, A. Robert. *Tiger in the Senate: The Biography of Wayne Morse*. Garden City, NY: Doubleday, 1962.

Smith, Bruce L. R. *Lincoln Gordon: Architect of Cold War Foreign Policy*. Lexington: University Press of Kentucky, 2015.

Smith, Christian. *Resisting Reagan: The U.S. Central American Peace Movement*. Chicago: University of Chicago Press, 1996.

Smith, Gaddis. *The Last Years of the Monroe Doctrine, 1945–1993*. New York: Hill and Wang, 1994.

Smith, Peter H. *Democracy in Latin America: Political Change in Comparative Perspective*, 2nd ed. New York: Oxford University Press, 2012.

Smith, Richard Norton. *On His Own Terms: A Life of Nelson Rockefeller*. New York: Random House, 2014.

Smith, Tony. *Why Wilson Matters: The Origins of American Liberal Internationalism and Its Crisis Today*. Princeton, NJ: Princeton University Press, 2017.

Solberg, Carl. *Hubert Humphrey: A Biography*. New York: W. W. Norton, 1984.

Sorensen, Ted. *Kennedy*. Old Saybrook, CT: Konecky & Konecky, 1965.

Sosa, Juan B. *In Defiance: The Battle against General Noriega Fought from Panama's Embassy in Washington*. Washington, DC: Francis Press, 1999.

Spektor, Matias. *Kissinger e o Brasil*. Rio de Janeiro: Jorge Lahar Editor, 2009.

Stepan, Alfred. *The Military in Politics: Changing Patterns in Brazil*. Princeton, NJ: Princeton University Press, 1971.

Stephanson, Anders. "Senator John F. Kennedy: Anti-Imperialism and Utopian Deficit." *Journal of American Studies* 48, no. 1 (2014): 1–24.

Stern, Sheldon M. *Averting "The Final Failure": John F. Kennedy and the Secret Cuban Missile Crisis Meetings*. Stanford, CA: Stanford University Press, 2003.

Stossel, Scott. *Sarge: The Life and Times of Sargent Shriver*. Washington, DC: Smithsonian Books, 2004.

Szulc, Tad. *Twilight of the Tyrants*. New York: Henry Holt and Company, 1959.

Taffet, Jeffrey F. *Foreign Aid as Foreign Policy: The Alliance for Progress in Latin America*. New York: Routledge, 2007.

Tarver, Michael, Alfredo Angulo Rivas, Rathnam Indurthy, and Luis Loaiza Rincón. *Venezuelan Insurgency, 1960–1968: A Successful Failure*. Bloomington, IN: Xlibris, 2001.

Taubman, William. *Khrushchev and His Era*. New York: W. W. Norton, 2003.

Thomas, Evan. *Robert Kennedy: His Life*. New York: Simon & Schuster, 2000.

Thompson, John M. *Great Power Rising: Theodore Roosevelt and the Politics of U.S. Foreign Policy*. New York: Oxford University Press, 2019.

Tillman, Ellen D. *Dollar Diplomacy by Force: Nation-Building and Resistance in the Dominican Republic*. Chapel Hill: University of North Carolina Press, 2016.

Tinsman, Heidi. *Partners in Conflict: The Politics of Gender, Sexuality, and Labor in the Chilean Agrarian Reform, 1950–1973*. Durham, NC: Duke University Press, 2002.

Troy, Gil. *Moynihan's Moment: America's Fight against Zionism as Racism*. New York: Oxford University Press, 2013.

Tulchin, Joseph S. "The Promise of Progress: U.S. Relations with Latin America during the Administration of Lyndon B. Johnson." In *Lyndon Johnson Confronts the World: American Foreign Policy, 1963–1968*, edited by Warren I. Cohen and Nancy Bernkopf Tucker. Cambridge: Cambridge University Press, 1994.

Vanden Heuvel, William, and Milton Gwirtzman. *On His Own: Robert F. Kennedy, 1964–1968*. New York: Doubleday, 1970.

Velasco, Alejandro. *Barrio Rising: Urban Popular Politics and the Making of Modern Venezuela*. Berkeley: University of California Press, 2015.

Weis, W. Michael. *Cold Warriors and Coups d'Etat: Brazilian-American Relations, 1945–1964*. Albuquerque: University of New Mexico Press, 1993.

Welch, Richard E., Jr. *Response to Revolution: The United States and the Cuban Revolution, 1959–1961*. Chapel Hill: University of North Carolina Press, 1985.

Westad, Odd Arne. *The Global Cold War*. New York: Cambridge University Press, 2007.

Wofford, Harris. *Of Kennedys and Kings: Making Sense of the Sixties*. New York: Farrar, Straus and Giroux, 1980.

Wood, Bryce. *The Dismantling of the Good Neighbor Policy*. Austin: University of Texas Press, 1985.

———. *The Making of the Good Neighbor Policy*. New York: Columbia University Press, 1961.

Wood, Elisabeth Jean. *Insurgent Collective Action and Civil War in El Salvador*. Cambridge: Cambridge University Press, 2003.

Woods, Randall B. "Conflicted Hegemon: LBJ and the Dominican Republic." *Diplomatic History* 32, no. 5 (November 2008): 753–66.

———. *Fulbright: A Biography*. Cambridge: Cambridge University Press, 1995.

———. *LBJ: Architect of American Ambition*. New York: Free Press, 2006.

Wright, Jim. *Worth It All: My War for Peace*. Washington, DC: Brassey's, 1993.

Wright, Micah. "Unilateral Pan-Americanism: Wilsonianism and the American Occupation of Chiriquí, 191–1920." *Diplomacy & Statecraft* 26, no. 1 (Spring 2015): 46–64.

Zeiler, Thomas W. *Free Trade, Free World: The Advent of GATT*. Chapel Hill: University of North Carolina Press, 1999.

Zelizer, Julian E. *The Fierce Urgency of Now: Lyndon Johnson, Congress, and the Battle for the Great Society*. New York: Penguin Books, 2015.

Zimmermann, Matilde. *Sandinista: Carlos Fonseca and the Nicaraguan Revolution*. Durham, NC: Duke University Press, 2000.

Unpublished Doctoral Dissertations and Master's Theses

Arandia, Sebastian Rene. "Burden of the Cold War: The George H. W. Bush Administration and El Salvador." Unpublished master's thesis, Texas A&M University, 2010.

Taffet, Jeffrey. "Alliance for What? United States Development Assistance in Chile during the 1960s." Unpublished doctoral dissertation, Georgetown University, 2001.

Tomlin, David Brennan. "The Cold War and U.S.-Guatemalan Relations during the 1960s." Unpublished master's thesis, Texas A&M University, 2011.

Tremayne, Russell Mark. "Delusions and Reality: The Evolution of Frank Church's Ideas on U.S.-Latin American Policy, 1956–1980." Unpublished doctoral dissertation, University of Washington, 1990.

Index

Belaúnde Terry, Fernando: elected
president, 90, 192–93
Belk, Samuel, 67
Benton, William: Latin America trip with
Stevenson, 27–28; on Stevenson's opinion
of U.S. invasion of the Dominican
Republic, 120
Berle, Adolf, Jr., 8, 12, 21, 23, 26; advising
John Kennedy, 31, 32, 33, 34, 37–38; and
Árbenz, 32; and Betancourt, 32; as bridge
between Good Neighbor Policy and
Alliance for Progress, 31–32; and Castro,
32, 33, 34; on departure of Rockefeller, 8;
and Figueres, 32; isolation and departure,
57; and Villeda Morales, 32; on what
nonintervention did not mean, 12, 37
Betancourt, Rómulo, 11, 32, 38, 62; and
Berle, 23, 32; on Juan Bosch, 118; and
Cuban Missile Crisis, 75; and Grant, 23;
and Kennedy, 62–63; on 1964 election,
113; praised by Morse as "one of the great
liberals of our time," 28; and Stevenson,
27; on U.S. invasion of the Dominican
Republic, 118, 119, 121–22
Biden, Joseph, 259
Bloomfield, Lincoln, 202
Bolivia, 43, 113; Kennedy administration
and, 49–50
Bolívar, Simón: invoked in announcement
of Alliance for Progress, 43
Bonior, David, 233
Booker, Cory, 258
Bosch, Juan, 11, 44, 112, 117, 118; impact of
death of Robert Kennedy on, 150; as
president-elect and president, 81–83
Bowles, Chester, 32, 48, 57
Braden, Spruille, 7–8
Brazil, 10, 15, 16, 25–26, 28, 29, 42–43, 91–98,
101, 106–11, 126, 131–34, 150, 154–56,
157–58, 183, 195–96, 200, 203, 204, 228,
251, 255; democracy in, 22–23; desire for
"special relationship" with United States,
154; and the Dominican Republic, 124;
improvements in human rights situation
in, 196, 198–99; as Nixon's favorite, 166;
onset of "years of lead" in, 150; threat

perception, 67; U.S. aid for government
following military coup, 107, 108, 111;
U.S. ally during World War II, 7;
U.S. contingency planning, 96
Briggs, Ellis, 7, 56
Brizola, Leonel, 198, 246
Brown, Harold, 200; and military aid to
El Salvador, 225
Brzezinski, Zbigniew, 193, 194, 200, 207, 221,
225; on Carter and Balaguer, 210; on
dangers of ending aid to Nicaragua, 225;
on effect of pressures on Argentina, 197;
on human rights, 191; and Panama Canal
Treaty, 205; warning against "aimless
punitive actions" in response to Letelier
case, 200
Buchanan, Patrick, 244
Buckley, William, Jr., 205
Bundy, McGeorge, 67, 107, 111, 114, 119; on
Castello Branco, 111; on continuity in
Kennedy and Johnson policies in Brazil,
110; on Frei criticism of U.S. invasion of the
Dominican Republic, 121; on U.S. invasion
of the Dominican Republic, 117, 118
Bush, George Herbert Walker, 222, 258;
assurances to military governments as
vice-president-elect, 235; and Central
America, 250; and Costa Rica, 250;
liberalism as issue in 1988 presidential
election, 248–49; and Manuel Noriega,
248–49; partisan candidate, bi-partisan
president, 250; pressures on El Salvador
as vice-president, 240

Caldera, Rafael, 146–47
Campos, Roberto, 26
Carter, Jimmy, 2, 17–18, 182; and Balaguer,
209–11; and Brazil, 183, 195–96; and
Central America, 226; on coup in Chile,
184; and Cuba, 207–9, 226–27; and
Anastasio Somoza Debayle, 214, 216; as
elections observer in Nicaragua, 252–53;
as elections observer in Panama, 251–52;
no fixed policy in Nicaragua, 216; and
human rights, 182, 183–84, 186–204,
227–28, 256, 257; impact of reelection

Cranston, Alan: and Augusto Pinochet, 236; and human rights, 237

Cristiani, Alfredo, 250

Cuba, 1, 3, 5, 6, 7, 12, 14, 15, 17, 18, 50–51, 101, 112, 113, 204, 207–9; hostility in, 15; Kennedy administration policy following Cuban Missile Crisis, 76; in 1960 presidential campaign, 33, 35–36; Nixon administration and, 167; threat perception, 112, 234; threat perception ebbing, 16, 124–25, 147; troops in Africa, 207–8, 226, 234

Cuban Missile Crisis, 15, 74–76, 76, 123

Cuban Revolution, 1, 13, 43; exporting, 112; John Kennedy's understanding of appeal of, 55

D'Aubuisson, Roberto, 223, 241

Democracy, 3, 6, 10, 14, 18, 19, 22–23, 31, 58, 86–87, 129, 131, 238, 242, 253, 255; Alliance for Progress and, 45, 129; and Carter administration, 192–93, 209–11; and economic crisis, 242, 257; human rights and, 188; and intervention in elections in Brazil, 92, 114; and intervention in elections in Chile, 114–15; and Latin America task force recommendations, 38; and nonintervention, 10, 147; and U.S. involvement in election in Nicaragua, 252; and U.S. military missions, 67; and World War II, 7–8

Derian, Patricia, 189, 199, 200; and Argentina, 197, 198; on Carter administration human rights record, 201–2; and El Salvador, 220, 224; on National Security Council as obstacle, 202; and Nicaragua, 215, 224; and Ronald Reagan administration, 235

Détente, 17, 166; and human rights, 256; and limitations regarding Latin America, 166–67

Development, 14, 22, 141–42; in Brazil, 28, 29; Kennedy administration and, 38, 39; New Deal models under Johnson, 101

Dodd, Christopher, 232

Dominican Republic, 3, 7, 11, 14, 15, 16, 17, 25, 43, 90, 101, 103; after death of Rafael Trujillo, 57–59; elections in, 80–81, 144; repression in, 149–50; restoration of democracy in, 204, 209–11; "showcase of democracy," 15, 17, 117; U.S. aid following invasion of, 122, 144–45; U.S. invasion of, 117–22

Duarte, José Napoleón, 18, 220, 221, 239, 240, 250, 251, 257; as "best and probably the only hope," 232; bipartisan consensus following election of, 241–42; and initial treatment by Reagan administration, 232; and liberal Democrats, 232, 244

Dukakis, Michael, 249

Dulles, Allen, 22

Dulles, John Foster, 22, 104

Dungan, Ralph, 15, 62, 71, 254; and Allende, 165; and caution regarding military aid for Bolivia, 146; and Christian Democrats (Chile), 79–80; compared to Lincoln Gordon, 116–17, 134; on coup in Chile, 171–72; and Cuban Missile Crisis, 75; and election in Chile (1964), 114; and early elections in the Dominican Republic, 83; and human rights, 175; on Humphrey Latin America task force, 149; interest in Latin America, 73; and Johnson administration, 105, 124, 135; as Latin Americanist, 73; leaving Chile, 142; and military coup in Chile, 171–72; and nomination as U.S. ambassador to Chile, 115–16; on possibility of coup in Brazil, 107; and possibility of reducing military aid to Chile, 136–37; and Revolution in Liberty, 115, 116, 135; testimony before Frank Church committee, 181; trip to Chile (1974), 172–73; as U.S. ambassador to Chile, 135–40, 142; on U.S. invasion of the Dominican Republic, 121; on U.S. policy toward military governments, 139, 160

Eisenhower, Dwight David, 1, 13–15, 22–23, 101, 103, 105, 151, 204; and democracy, 19, 22–23; and Latin America, 19, 22; and military governments, 19, 22, 23; and Paraguay, 23; South America trip (1960), 22–23

El Salvador, 17, 18, 204, 220–226, 228; and Chile, 236; as early foreign policy challenge to Reagan administration, 230–33; elections in, 239; "final offensive" (1980), 225, "final offensive" (1989), 250–51; land reform, 231–32, 242; murder of Jesuit priests in, 251; peace in, 250–51; rape and murder of U.S. churchwomen in, 224; resumption of U.S. military aid, 225; unification of left in, 222; Vietnam analogy, 230–31

Figueiredo, João: and Carter administration hopes, 198–99
Figueres, José, 10, 20, 38, 152; on Bay of Pigs invasion, 51, 84; and Berle, 32; hopes for modern Good Neighbor Policy, 27; hopes for U.S. support for democracy, 10; and President Kennedy's trip to Costa Rica, 83–84; on Richard Nixon Latin America policy, 167; quoted by John Kennedy in announcement of Alliance for Progress, 43–44; and Stevenson, 20, 21, 26–27; and support for Alliance for Progress, 44–45; on U.S. toleration of dictatorship, 11
Fontaine, Roger: on Carter response to radicalization of Central America, 229; domino theory in Central America, 231; on Reagan administration policy in Latin America, 234; on Venezuela, 231; on Vietnam analogy in El Salvador, 231
Food for Peace, 41–43, 179
Ford, Gerald, 17, 177–78, 179, 180, 182; and human rights, 177; and the military coup in Chile, 177; and Panama Canal Treaty, 204–5
Foreign Aid Revolt, 98
Fraser, Donald, 178, 191; and Carter's support for human rights, 183–84; on coup in Brazil, 110; on coup in Chile, 173; and Cuban Missile Crisis, 76; in the Dominican Republic, 122, 144; on the Dominican Republic, 209–210; and flawed development policies, 163; and foreign aid and fundamental change, 138; and human rights, 171, 172, 191, 212;

Orlando Letelier and, 181; and Nicaragua, 212; and Revolution in Liberty in Chile, 135
Frei, Eduardo, 11, 14, 64, 79–80, 114–17; and Carter administration, 194–95; influence on Frances Grant, 173–74; on Johnson Alliance for Progress, 140; on U.S. invasion of the Dominican Republic, 121; U.S. visit thwarted by Allende, 139–40
Frondizi, Arturo, 42, 64–65
Fuentes, Carlos, 242

Gailbraith, John Kenneth, 27
Geisel, Ernesto, 178, 195–96, 198
Good Neighbor Policy, 4–6, 17, 20, 27, 32, 34, 102, 117, 153, 169; beyond, 14; continuation of, in 1948 Democratic party platform, 9; continuation of, in 1952 Democratic party platform, 12; and democracy, 6, 35; hopes for modern version of, 27; "inadequate for today," 238; invoked in 1972 Democratic party platforms, 168; invoked in 1976 Democratic party platform, 184; in 1956 Republican party platform, 13; restoration of, in 1956 Democratic party platform, 13; restoration of, in 1960 Democratic party platform, 34
Goodpaster, Andrew: visits Argentina, 200
Goodwin, Richard, 15, 55, 58–59, 104; and Kennedy legacy, 102–3; interest in Latin America, 56, 72–73
Gorbachev, Mikhail, 229
Gordon, Lincoln, 36, 39, 44, 56, 69; and Castello Branco, 109; on differences between Marshall Plan and Alliance for Progress, 44; on establishment of military government in Argentina, 142; on Goulart, 70–71, 72, 92–93, 94, 95, 96, 106, 107, 108, 110; interest in Latin America, 25–26; as member of President-Elect Kennedy's Latin America task force, as assistant secretary of State, 141–42; on nonintervention, 147; and Quadros, 67–68; as U.S. ambassador to Brazil, 69, 72, 91–98, 106–12, 132–34, 140–41

administration and, 15, 45, 88–89; Nixon administration and, 16, 17, 153–60, 170–71; Reagan administration and, 17, 235–36; timetables and, 66, 90–91, 131, 254

Miller, George, 233

Mondale, Walter, 217; meeting with Frei, 194–95; as presidential candidate, 243–44; and Sandinistas, 217

Monroe Doctrine, 3, 4, 6, 43, 235–36

Morales Carrión, Arturo, 47, 83; on democratic forces in the Dominican Republic, 58; and lack of support for Alliance for Progress in the State Department, 47

Morse, Wayne, 94; abortive presidential campaign, 29; and Alliance for Progress, 79; and Batista, 24; and Bay of Pigs invasion, 52; and Castro, 26; criticism of Robert Kennedy, 148; defeat in 1968 re-election campaign, 150; and democracy in Latin America, 103; distrust of John Kennedy, 29; early recognition of dangers of military rule in Brazil, 16, 110–11; on Eisenhower foreign policy, 24; hopes for social transformation of Latin America, 23, 24; initial reaction to military coup in Brazil, 108; and Johnson administration, 103, 105, 130–31; on Johnson Alliance for Progress, 103, 128–29, 130–31; Latin America trip, 28–29; liberalism, 23–24; and Martin statement on military coups, 89; and military aid, 14, 24, 128–29, 145; opposition to Gordon appointment as assistant secretary of State, 141; praise for Robert Kennedy, 128–29; on recognition of government of Dominican Republic, 103

Moscoso, Teodoro, 69, 83; as member of President-Elect Kennedy's Latin America task force, 36

Mothers of the Plaza de Mayo, 197

Movimento Democrático Brasileiro (Brazilian Democratic Movement), 196

Moyers, Bill, 103–4, 144

Moynihan, Daniel Patrick, 237; and Nicaragua, 243

Muñoz Marín, Luis, 19, 26, 32, 83; "good neighbors" and "and alliance for progress," 37

Murphy, John: as enabler of Anastasio Somoza Debayle, 211, 215

Muskie, Ed: and need to demonstrate support for Christian Democrats in El Salvador, 225

Nicaragua, 3, 4, 5–6, 17, 33, 60, 61, 85–86, 147–48, 199, 204, 207, 225, 228, 233–34, 252–53

Nixon, Richard, 16–17, 22, 27, 36, 256; and Allende, 165; and Alliance for Progress, 142, 152, 157; assurances that still "cared" about Latin America, 160, 167; and Brazil, 166; and Somoza Debayle, 211; and Latin America in 1968 presidential campaign, 149; and Latin American military, 159; and Latin American reformists, 161; liberalism in 1960 presidential campaign, 36; and military government in Chile, 171; and presidential campaign (1960), 36; Rockefeller Mission, 152–60; South American trip (1958), 22

Nixon Doctrine, 160

Nonintervention, 5–6, 12, 13, 33, 34, 115, 182, 187, 206, 213; and democracy, 10, 255; and dictatorship, 25; and human rights, 17, 199; and Nicaragua, 214

Noriega, Manuel, 247–48, 251–52; and ostensible civilian authority in Panama, 248; Vice-President Bush and, 248

North, Oliver: on visa for D'Aubuisson, 241–42

Obando y Bravo, Miguel, 218

O'Neill, Tip, 219; and Nicaragua, 234

Operation Mongoose, 54–55, 76

Operation Pan-America, 22; Latin America's enthusiasm for, 28

Organization of American States, 8, 112–13, 118, 120, 121, 124, 152, 172, 185, 186, 188, 190, 193, 238; anti-Trujillo sanctions, 57

Ortega, Daniel, 217, 242–43, 245, 250, 252, 257

Panama, 3, 5, 17, 204, 228, 247–48, 251; involvement in Nicaragua, 215; U.S. invasion of, 252; U.S. sanctions toward, 248, 252

Panama Canal Treaty, 191, 204–7, 208, 228

Paraguay, 23

Pastor, Robert, 193–94, 195–96, 197, 200, 207, 211, 218, 223, 224; and Argentina, 198; on Rosalynn Carter's Latin America trip, 192; comparing Jimmy Carter with John Kennedy, 198; and removal of Somoza Debayle, 214; on diversity of Latin America, 186; encouraging greater U.S. engagement with Global South, 184–85; on human rights, 185, 186; on "Latin America policy on democratic elections," 211; on roots of Central American crisis in closed political systems and lack of reform, 221; on United States as "detached goal setter," 214; on U.S. policy toward Chile, 193; working with Vaky on Argentina, 197

Peace Corps, 2, 259

Pell, Claiborne, 237

Pérez, Carlos Andrés, 187, 190, 207, 258; and election in Dominican Republic, 210; and human rights, 187, 190; and Nicaragua, 213, 215; on Panama Canal Treaty, 207

Pérez Jiménez, Marcos, 19, 22, 32

Perón, Juan, 8, 65

Peronists, 65

Peru, 15, 43, 192–93, 238; coup in, 66; promise to restore democracy in, 192; success of Kennedy timetable policy in, 90; timetables for elections set in, 66

Pinochet, Augusto, 18, 178–79, 180, 191, 193–95, 200; letter to Edward Kennedy, 172; Reagan administration and, 236, 247

Plaza, Galo, 152–53

Point Four, 11

Puerto Rico, 31

Quadros, Jânio, 42; brief presidency of, 67–68; Gordon and, 67–68

Ramírez, Sergio, 217

Reagan, Ronald, 17–18, 224, 228; adherence to Panama Canal Treaty, 247; Caribbean Basin Initiative, 238; changes party affiliation, 229; continuity with Carter policies, 231; and contras, 244–45; and democracy, 238, 239; and El Salvador, 230, 231–32, 239; impact of 1980 victory on El Salvador, 224; and John Kennedy, 229, 238, 244, 249; Latin American trip, 237–38; liberalism as issue in 1988 presidential election, 248–49; and neo-liberalism, 249; opposition to Panama Canal Treaty, 204, 247; and Franklin Roosevelt, 229, 244, 249; and Truman, 244, 249; on not sending U.S. troops into combat, 231

Reich, Otto, 235

Rielly, John: on coup in Brazil, 110; on U.S. invasion of the Dominican Republic, 120

Rockefeller, Nelson, 6, 8, 10, 160–61, 205, 192, 256; promises second Good Neighbor Policy in failed presidential bid, 153; support for Trujillo, 7

Rockefeller Mission, 152–60

Rojas, Ricardo, 247

Romero, Humberto, 220, 221

Romero, Óscar, 241; criticism of Jimmy Carter administration support for government of El Salvador, 222; death of, 223

Roosevelt, Franklin Delano, 4–7, 9, 10, 12, 21, 23, 31, 59, 60, 102

Roosevelt, Theodore, 3

Rostow, Walter: on Castello Branco, 111; on Goulart, 93; on Johnson Alliance for Progress, 139

Rusk, Dean, 48, 64, 132, 137; and Cuban Missile Crisis, 75; on election timetables, 88

Sandinistas, 61, 217–19, 225, 226, 228, 240, 242–43; Carter administration and, 217–19, 225; elections in, 243; liberal Democrats and, 233–34

Sandino, Augusto César, 61

Sarbanes, Paul: and Panama Canal Treaty, 206–7

Schick, René, 85–86, 147

Schlesinger, Arthur M., Jr., 10–11, 14, 16, 21, 26, 29, 38, 39–40; and Africa, 73; and "appeasement of business," 73; on Bay of Pigs invasion, 51, 53; and Betancourt, 45–46, 79; on Carter, 183, 236; concerns, 72–73, 74, 79, 98; on coup in Brazil, 110; and Cuba, 50; and Cuban Missile Crisis, 75; decline in political influence following death of Robert Kennedy, 150; and democracy in Latin America, 15, 45–46, 88–89, 238, 242, 255; dismissal of human rights as a campaign not a policy, 192; and failure of New Frontier, 74; and Goulart, 68; initial impressions of John Kennedy, 29–30; interest in Latin America, 20; isolation of "Latin Americanists," 72–73, 74, 75–76, 77, 98; and Johnson administration, 102, 103; on Edward Kennedy's presidential prospects, 183; and Kennedy legacy, 102, 103; and Kissinger, 162, 174; and Kissinger Commission, 240–41; and Mann, 104–5, 119; "middle class revolution," 45; and military, 48; and military coup in Brazil, 110; missing human rights, 236; on Nicaragua, 215; on Nixon Latin America policy, 162, 174; "North American indifference to Latin America," 167; recommending Ralph Dungan as U.S. ambassador to Chile, 116; and responsibility for Latin America in Kennedy administration, 39–40; and State Department, 46–47; South American trip, 41–43; and Stevenson, 19, 20; support for presidential candidate John Kennedy, 30; surprised by Reagan's policies, 236; on U.S. invasion of the Dominican Republic, 118–19, 122; "Vital Center" liberalism, 11–12

Schneider, Mark, 164; as deputy to Patricia Derian, 189; and Edward Kennedy

presidential campaign, 200; visit to Chile (1974), 172–73

Shriver, Sargent, 102, 168

Shultz, George, and Chile, 247

Somoza, Luis, 61, 84, 85, 147; and isolation during Kennedy years, 84

Somoza Debayle, Anastasio, 85, 211–17; on hope for invitation to visit Johnson, 147; promises democratic elections in 1963, 61

Somoza García, Anastasio, 5–6, 27, 29, 33; death of, 58; opposition to spread of democracy, 10

Sorensen, Ted, 36, 39

Stephansky, Ben, 49; on Humphrey Latin America task force, 149

Stevenson, Adlai, 12, 20–21, 26–28, 41; and Bay of Pigs invasion, 52–53; and Costa Rican democracy, 20; and Cuban Missile Crisis, 75–76; develops interest in Latin America, 26–28; disinterest in Latin America, 19, 20; draft of 1964 Democratic Party foreign policy platform, 112–13; and Frei, 115; and Johnson administration, 104, 115; Latin America trip (1960), 26–28; Latin America trip following Bay of Pigs invasion (1961), 56; on "recognition of a special responsibility for Latin America," 39; and U.S. invasion of the Dominican Republic, 119–20

Stewart, Bill, 216

Taft, William Howard, 3

Theberge, James: as member of Humphrey Latin America task force, 149; as U.S. ambassador to Chile, 242, 247; as U.S. ambassador to Nicaragua, 211–12

Thomas, Norman, 105; and the Dominican Republic, 144

Thornton, Thomas: concerns about "staying power" on human rights, 200; human rights as "probably the main success story" in Carter foreign policy, 202; "quixotic elements" of human rights policy, 202

Timerman, Jacobo, 197, 202, 237, 212, 213–14

Todman, Terence: and Nicaragua, 212, 213; human rights and nonintervention, 199; impact of speech on Nicaragua, 213–14

Torrijos, Omar, 205–6, 229; death of, 247

Trade, 3, 4, 5, 6, 9, 12, 13, 18, 22, 25, 238, 249, 253

Trujillo, Rafael, 5, 7, 16, 25, 27; hemispheric isolation and death, 57; opposing spread of democracy, 10

Truman, Harry, 8–12, 13, 31

Truman Doctrine, 8, 9, 30

Trump, Donald, 258

Tuchman, Jessica: Congress and human rights, 191

Ungo, Guillermo, 233

Vaky, Viron, 146, 197, 214, 219, 221; earlier recognition of danger of state terror, 146; fear of "consolidation of extreme left regimes," 219; hopes for broader support for reforms, 219; and removal of Somoza Debayle, 214

Vance, Cyrus, 193, 199, 207, 219, 222; on election in the Dominican Republic, 210; influence on president-elect Carter on Panama Canal treaty, 205; meetings with Latin American leaders, 193; recommendations regarding Letelier case, 200; response to criticism of Jimmy Carter administration policy in El Salvador by Óscar Romero, 222; warnings regarding possible crisis in El Salvador, 221

Vargas, Getúlio, 7, 67

Venezuela, 7, 11, 19, 22, 32, 37, 62, 67, 105, 112, 126, 146–47, 187; democracy in, 23, 117, 126, 255; and Duarte, 220, 232; "hinge to the situation," 37; importance of, 62, 79, 82; involvement in Nicaragua, 215; no Rockefeller Mission trip to, 154

Videla, Jorge, 197

Vietnam War, 1–2, 16, 120, 125, 126, 129, 130, 152, 169, 186; and El Salvador, 230–31; as liberal cause, 125; compared to U.S. invasion of the Dominican Republic, 122–24; impact on U.S.-Latin American relations, 125

Villeda Morales, Ramón, 32, 61; and Adolf Berle Jr., 61; criticism of land reform policy in, 86; fall of, 86–87

Viola, Roberto Eduardo, 235

Volcker, Paul, 257

Volman, Sacha, 122, 144, 145; on hopes for Humphrey presidency, 149–50

Wallace, Henry, 9, 42

Wallop, Malcolm, 230

Walters, Vernon, 106, 235; arrival as military attaché in Rio de Janeiro, 91; friendships formed with Brazilian military during World War II, 91

White, Robert, 223, 224–25, 230; blamed by Ronald Reagan administration for public opinion regarding El Salvador, 230

Williamson, Marianne, 259

Wilson, Charlie: enabler of Anastasio Somoza Debayle, 211, 212, 213

Wilson, Woodrow, 2–4

World War I, 3

World War II, 6–8

Wright, Jim, 218, 219; and Alliance for Progress, 238; and George Herbert Walker Bush's bi-partisan foreign policy, 250; and Caribbean Basin Initiative, 238–39; and Nicaragua, 218, 219; and support for Central American peace plan, 246, 250; and support for deal with Reagan on Central American peace plan, 246; "Dear Comandante" letter, 242–43; election observer in El Salvador, 242; Great Society liberal and supporter of Vietnam War, 218

CPSIA information can be obtained
at www.ICGtesting.com
Printed in the USA
LVHW042023260522
719869LV00004B/652